DEMOSTHENES

ON THE CROWN

TO

HENRY JACKSON

IN TOKEN OF
A FRIENDSHIP OF MORE THAN THIRTY YEARS

DEMOSTHENES DE CORONA

Edited by
W. W. Goodwin

Published by Bristol Classical Press
General Editor: John H. Betts

(by arrangement with the Syndicate of the Cambridge
University Press)

Cover illustration: Demosthenes from Roman copies of a full-length statue by Polyeuktos of Athens, ca. 280 B.C., Vatican Museums, Rome and Ny Carlsberg Glyptotek, Copenhagen [drawing by Jean Bees].

This impression 2002

This edition reprinted 1982, 1990 by
Bristol Classical Press
an imprint of
Gerald Duckworth & Co. Ltd.
61 Frith Street, London W1D 3JL
Tel: 020 7434 4242
Fax: 020 7434 4420
inquiries@duckworth-publishers.co.uk
www.ducknet.co.uk

First published by Cambridge University Press 1904
and reprinted up to 1970

A catalogue record for this book is available
from the British Library

ISBN 0 86292 022 1

Printed in Great Britain by
Antony Rowe Ltd, Eastbourne

PREFACE.

THIS volume is chiefly an abridgment of the large edition of Demosthenes on the Crown which was prepared by me for the Syndics of the University Press and published in 1901. The critical notes are omitted, and such remarks on the text as seemed necessary are introduced in the explanatory notes. The notes, the Historic Sketch, and especially the Essays, have been abridged, while some more elementary matter has been added in the notes. I have attempted to give what I deem most essential to an understanding of this masterpiece of oratory. No mere commentary can make a speech like this intelligible to those who have not an accurate knowledge of the events which are discussed, and of their relation to other events. No adequate treatment of historical points is possible in scattered notes, and references to a general history (even to Grote or Curtius) are not sufficient. The student of Demosthenes needs a connected narrative of the events which especially concern him, with references to the authorities, without being distracted by other details in which he has no immediate interest. To meet this want, I have given an "Historical Sketch" of the period from the accession of Philip to the battle of Chaeronea, in which I have enlarged disproportionately on the events and questions discussed in the orations of Demosthenes and Aeschines on the Crown, and have alluded slightly (or perhaps not at all) to many important matters which are not essential to the study of these speeches. This would be unpardonable in a history: but this sketch assumes a general knowledge of the history of the period which it covers, and makes no pretence to being such a history in itself. With this view, I have given what may seem undue prominence to the negotiations which led to the Peace of Philocrates; for a minute knowledge of these is absolutely necessary to a correct understanding of the brief but cogent argument of Demosthenes in Cor. §§ 17—52, and to a fair judgment of the whole political course of both Demosthenes and Aeschines at this decisive crisis in the history of Athens. Much new light has been thrown upon the period which I have treated from inscriptions recently discovered by the French explorers at Delphi and from the *Corpus Inscriptionum Atticarum*. In preparing this sketch I have made constant use of Grote and of Schaefer's *Demosthenes und Seine Zeit*.

In revising the text I have in most cases followed the authority of the Codex Σ, especially when it is supported by its companion L¹. See Essay VII. In preparing the commentary I have been constantly aided by the long line of editors, whose names are too familiar to need mention. I must, however, express my great obligation to Westermann and Blass, especially for references to parallel passages and for other illustrations. I have found it impossible to give credit for every remark and reference which may be borrowed from these or other recent editors: many of these are found in the notes of Dissen and the older editors, and many have long been in my own collection of notes. Nothing is harder to trace than old references, and most of those relating to Demosthenes on the Crown may now be assumed to be common property.

I take great pleasure in expressing (not for the first time) my deep indebtedness to Dr Henry Jackson of Trinity College, Cambridge, who did me the inestimable service of reading and revising the proofs of the large edition. There are few pages in that volume which have not had the benefit of his criticism.

For the picture of the Scythian bowman in page 280 I am indebted to the kindness of my former pupil, Miss Florence A. Gragg, who photographed the figure in the Museum at Athens.

I have avoided many discussions of grammatical points in the notes by references to my *Syntax of the Greek Moods and*

Tenses (M. T.), and I have occasionally referred to my *Greek Grammar* (G.). The references to Grote IX.—XII. are made to the first edition; those to earlier volumes to the second edition. I have made no attempt to be neutral on the question of the patriotism and the statesmanship of Demosthenes in his policy of uncompromising resistance to Philip. It seems to me that the time for such neutrality is past. I cannot conceive how any one who knows and respects the traditions of Athens, and all that she represents in the long contest of free institutions against tyranny, can read the final attack of Aeschines and the reply of Demosthenes without feeling that Demosthenes always stands forth as a true patriot and statesman, who has the best interests of his country at heart and upholds her noblest traditions, while Aeschines appears first as a trimmer and later as an intentional (if not a corrupt) ally of Philip in his contest with Athens. That the policy of resistance to Philip's aggressions failed at last is no discredit to the patriotism or the statesmanship of Demosthenes. Can any one, even at this day, read the pathetic and eloquent appeal of Demosthenes to posterity in Cor. §§ 199—208, and not feel that Athens would have been unworthy of her glorious past if she had submitted to Philip without a struggle for liberty, even if Chaeronea and all its consequences had been seen by her in advance? Her course was plain : that of Demosthenes was even plainer.

W. W. GOODWIN.

HARVARD UNIVERSITY,
CAMBRIDGE, MASS.,
November 6, 1903.

CONTENTS.

ΔΗΜΟΣΘΕΝΟΥΣ

ΠΕΡΙ ΤΟΥ ΣΤΕΦΑΝΟΥ

ΠΡΩΤΟΝ μὲν, ὦ ἄνδρες 'Αθηναῖοι, τοῖς θεοῖς
εὔχομαι πᾶσι καὶ πάσαις, ὅσην εὔνοιαν ἔχων ἐγὼ
διατελῶ τῇ τε πόλει καὶ πᾶσιν ὑμῖν, τοσαύτην ὑπάρξαι μοι παρ' ὑμῶν εἰς τουτονὶ τὸν ἀγῶνα, ἔπειθ'

PROOEMIUM : §§ 1—8. The solemn
earnestness with which Demosthenes
undertook this vindication of his whole
political life is shown by the unusual
and impressive prayer with which he
begins, and still more by its repetition.
He shows the same spirit in the appeal to the Gods in § 141, with which
he introduces his account of the fatal
events which led to Chaeronea, and
in his peroration (§ 324).

§ 1. 1. τοῖς θεοῖς πᾶσι καὶ πάσαις,
to all the Gods and Goddesses. Θεός is
Goddess as well as God, θεά being
poetic ; thus ἡ θεός is the common
title of Athena. A slight extension of
the solemn formula πᾶσι καὶ πάσαις
becomes absurdly comic in Ar. Av.
866 εὔχεσθε ὄρνισιν 'Ολυμπίοις καὶ
'Ολυμπίῃσι πᾶσι καὶ πάσῃσιν.

2. εὔνοιαν : εὔνοια may mean *devotion* based on any superiority or
merit, including *loyalty* of a subject
to a prince or of a servant to his
master (even of a dog to his mistress),
devotion to a benefactor, and even
enthusiasm for the success of a con-
testant in the games (though felt by
a stranger). Here it means a good
citizen's loyal *devotion* to the state.

See Jackson's note on εὔνοια in
Trans. of Cambr. Philol. Soc. II. p.
115, where he explains the word in
Arist. Pol. I. 6 (1255ᵃ, 17) as "loyalty,
i.e. the willing obedience which an
inferior renders to a kind and considerate superior." He refers especially to Arist. Eth. IX. 5, §§ 3, 4
(1167ᵃ, 18), ὅλως δ' εὔνοια δι' ἀρετὴν
καὶ ἐπιείκειάν τινα γίνεται, ὅταν τῳ
φανῇ καλός τις ἢ ἀνδρεῖος ἤ τι τοιοῦτον.
—ἔχων διατελῶ : ἀντὶ τοῦ ἀεὶ ἔχω,
'Αττικῶς. Schol. (See M.T. 879.)
The words ἔχων διατελεῖ with εὔνοια
probably occurred in Ctesiphon's decree. Aeschines (III. 49) quotes from
the decree ὅτι διατελεῖ καὶ λέγων καὶ
πράττων : see the spurious indictment
(below) § 54¹⁰, and § 57²⁻³.

3. ὑπάρξαι μοι, *be granted me* (*be
made available to me*). The fundamental idea of ὑπάρχω in this sense is
best seen in τὰ ὑπάρχοντα, *the resources* or *the existing conditions,* i.e.
*what is available, what one has to
depend on* : see note on ὑπάρχειν § 95⁵,
and βέλτιστον ὑπάρχει, IX. 5.

4. ἀγῶνα : see note on ἀγωνίζομαι,
§ 3³.—ἔπειθ', *secondly* : simple ἔπειτα
(without δέ) is the regular rhetorical

ὅπερ ἐστὶ μάλισθ' ὑπὲρ ὑμῶν καὶ τῆς ὑμετέρας 5
εὐσεβείας τε καὶ δόξης, τοῦτο παραστῆσαι τοὺς
θεοὺς ὑμῖν, μὴ τὸν ἀντίδικον σύμβουλον ποιήσασθαι
περὶ τοῦ πῶς ἀκούειν ὑμᾶς ἐμοῦ δεῖ (σχέτλιον γὰρ
ἂν εἴη τοῦτό γε), ἀλλὰ τοὺς νόμους καὶ τὸν ὅρκον, ἐν 2
ᾧ πρὸς ἅπασι τοῖς ἄλλοις δικαίοις καὶ τοῦτο γέγραπται, τὸ ὁμοίως ἀμφοῖν ἀκροάσασθαι. τοῦτο δ' ἐστὶν
οὐ μόνον τὸ μὴ προκατεγνωκέναι μηδὲν οὐδὲ τὸ τὴν
εὔνοιαν ἴσην ἀποδοῦναι, ἀλλὰ τὸ καὶ τῇ τάξει καὶ τῇ 5
ἀπολογίᾳ, ὡς βεβούληται καὶ προῄρηται τῶν ἀγωνιζομένων ἕκαστος, οὕτως ἐᾶσαι χρήσασθαι.

formula after πρῶτον μέν (see §§ 8, 18, 177, 235, 248 : cf. 267). Thucydides generally has this, but often ἔπειτα δέ.

5. ὅπερ ἐστὶ : sc. εὔχομαι, referring to the whole sentence ὅπερ... ἀκροάσασθαι. The relation of ὅπερ to τοῦτο here is clearly that of ὅ τι (§ 8⁶) to the following τοῦτο.—ἐστὶ μάλισθ' ὑπὲρ ὑμῶν, concerns you especially (more than myself).

6. εὐσεβείας : referring to the oath (§ 2). Greek εὐσέβεια reached a lower level than our *piety*, including negative abstinence from impiety, so that one who does not break his oath is so far εὐσεβής. —τοῦτο παραστῆσαι ὑμῖν, *may put this into your hearts* : τοῦτο refers back emphatically to the omitted antecedent of ὅπερ, as οὕτως (§ 2⁷) to that of ὡς, and is explained by μὴ τὸν ἀντίδικον κ.τ.λ.

8. τοῦ πῶς...δεῖ : explained by τὸ καὶ...χρήσασθαι (end of § 2) : cf. περὶ τοῦ ὅντινα τρόπον χρὴ ζῆν, Plat. Rep. 352 D.

§ 2. 1. τὸν ὅρκον : the Heliastic oath, which each judge had sworn. The document in XXIV. 149—151 purporting to be this famous oath (hardly authentic) has this clause : καὶ ἀκροάσομαι τοῦ κατηγόρου καὶ τοῦ ἀπολογουμένου ὁμοίως ἀμφοῖν. For the

connection of the laws with the oath, see note on § 6⁵.

2. δικαίοις, *just provisions*.

3. ἀκροάσασθαι : this (Σ) or ἀκροᾶσθαι (L) is far preferable to the emendation ἀκροάσεσθαι, the fut. infin. being exceptional with τό. The infin. with τό here denotes simply *the provision for hearing both sides impartially* and is not in oratio obliqua (M.T. 96, 111).

4. τὸ μὴ προκατεγνωκέναι : *not having decided against* (κατά) *either party in advance*, the perf. expressing completion (M.T. 109) : τὸ μὴ προκαταγνῶναι would be timeless, like τὸ ἀκροάσασθαι (above) and τὸ ἀποδοῦναι and τὸ ἐᾶσαι (below). — οὐδὲ (sc. μόνον), *nor only* (cf. § 93¹'²).

5. ἴσην (pred.), *in equal measure.* —καὶ τῇ τάξει...χρήσασθαι, i.e. *to allow everyone to adopt not only* (καί) *that order of argument but also* (καί) *that general plan of defence which* etc.

6. ἀπολογίᾳ refers strictly to the defence, which alone remained.—ὡς... ἕκαστος : ἕκαστος is made subject of the relative clause, as this precedes ; we reverse the order, and translate it with χρήσασθαι. —τῶν ἀγωνιζομένων ἕκαστος (not ἑκάτερος), acc. to Weil, is "tout homme qui plaide sa

Πολλὰ μὲν οὖν ἔγωγ᾽ ἐλαττοῦμαι κατὰ τουτονὶ 3
τὸν ἀγῶνα Αἰσχίνου, δύο δ᾽, ὦ ἄνδρες Ἀθηναῖοι, καὶ
μεγάλα, ἐν μὲν ὅτι οὐ περὶ τῶν ἴσων ἀγωνίζομαι· οὐ
γάρ ἐστιν ἴσον νῦν ἐμοὶ τῆς παρ᾽ ὑμῶν εὐνοίας διαμαρτεῖν καὶ τούτῳ μὴ ἑλεῖν τὴν γραφήν, ἀλλ᾽ ἐμοὶ 5
μὲν—οὐ βούλομαι δυσχερὲς εἰπεῖν οὐδὲν ἀρχόμενος
τοῦ λόγου, οὗτος δ᾽ ἐκ περιουσίας μου κατηγορεῖ.
ἕτερον δ᾽, ὃ φύσει πᾶσιν ἀνθρώποις ὑπάρχει, τῶν μὲν
λοιδοριῶν καὶ τῶν κατηγοριῶν ἀκούειν ἡδέως, τοῖς
ἐπαινοῦσι δ᾽ αὐτοὺς ἄχθεσθαι· τούτων τοίνυν ὃ μέν 4
ἐστι πρὸς ἡδονὴν τούτῳ δέδοται, ὃ δὲ πᾶσιν ὡς ἔπος
εἰπεῖν ἐνοχλεῖ λοιπὸν ἐμοί. κἂν μὲν εὐλαβούμενος

cause," a general expression. He remarks that ἀγωνίζομαι applies especially to the defendant.

This is a dignified appeal against
the offensive demand of Aeschines
(III. 202), that the court should
either refuse to hear Demosthenes
or (at least) compel him to follow
his adversary's order of argument.
Both parties could not be heard impartially if one were compelled *by
the court itself* to present his case
in the most damaging order at his
opponent's dictation.

§ 8. 1. πολλά: sc. ἐλαττώματα.

2. καὶ μεγάλα, *even serious.*

3. ἀγωνίζομαι, like ἀγών, used
of contests of all kinds, here of a
lawsuit. See the pun on the two
meanings of ἀγωνίσασθαι περὶ θανάτου in IV. 47.

4. διαμαρτεῖν, *to forfeit*: cf. ἀποστερεῖσθαι, § 5⁴, and the following
words.

5. μὴ ἑλεῖν τὴν γραφήν, *not to
gain his case*: cf. Ὀλύμπια νικᾶν,
Thuc. I. 126; ψήφισμα νικᾷ, Aesch.
III. 68; πολλὰς...γραφὰς διώξας οὐδεμίαν εἷλεν, Ant. 2, Aᵃ, 5. A victorious defendant is said γραφὴν (δίκην)
ἀποφυγεῖν, a defeated defendant γρα-

φὴν (δίκην) ὀφλεῖν.—ἀλλ᾽ ἐμοὶ μὲν: a
familiar ἀποσιώπησις, often quoted by
the rhetoricians. What is plainly
meant would sound unpleasant (δυσχερές) and suggest disaster in the
opening of his speech. See Quint.
IX. 2, 54, who quotes "quos ego—
sed motos praestat componere fluctus,"
Aen. I. 135.

7. ἐκ περιουσίας, *at an advantage,*
lit. *from an abundance*, like a rich
man who stakes little compared with
his wealth. In Luke xxi. 4, the rich
cast into the treasury "of their abundance" or "superfluity," ἐκ τοῦ περισ-
σεύοντος αὐτοῖς.

8. ἕτερον δ᾽ (sc. ἐλάττωμα) corresponds to ἐν μὲν in 3, and keeps up
the construction of πολλὰ ἐλαττοῦμαι
in 1.—δ...ὑπάρχει, *which is a natural
disposition of the whole human race*:
πᾶσιν ἀνθρώποις suggests the subject
of ἀκούειν and ἄχθεσθαι, which explain
ἕτερον.

§ 4. 2. ἐστι πρὸς ἡδονήν, *makes
for pleasure* (ἐστὶν ἡδύ, Schol.): cf.
Aeschyl. Pr. 494, ἂν εἴη δαίμοσιν πρὸς
ἡδονήν.—ὡς ἔπος εἰπεῖν modifies πᾶσιν.
Aeschines (III. 241) had warned the
court against the self-glorification of
Demosthenes.

τοῦτο μὴ λέγω τὰ πεπραγμέν᾽ ἐμαυτῷ, οὐκ ἔχειν
ἀπολύσασθαι τὰ κατηγορημένα δόξω οὐδ᾽ ἐφ᾽ οἷς 5
ἀξιῶ τιμᾶσθαι δεικνύναι· ἐὰν δ᾽ ἐφ᾽ ἃ καὶ πεποίηκα
καὶ πεπολίτευμαι βαδίζω, πολλάκις λέγειν ἀναγκα-
227 σθήσομαι περὶ ἐμαυτοῦ. πειράσομαι μὲν οὖν ὡς
μετριώτατα τοῦτο ποιεῖν· ὅ τι δ᾽ ἂν τὸ πρᾶγμ᾽ αὐτὸ
ἀναγκάζῃ, τούτου τὴν αἰτίαν οὗτός ἐστι δίκαιος ἔχειν 10
ὁ τοιοῦτον ἀγῶν᾽ ἐνστησάμενος.

Οἶμαι δ᾽ ὑμᾶς πάντας, ὦ ἄνδρες Ἀθηναῖοι, ἂν 5
ὁμολογῆσαι κοινὸν εἶναι τουτονὶ τὸν ἀγῶν᾽ ἐμοὶ καὶ
Κτησιφῶντι καὶ οὐδὲν ἐλάττονος ἄξιον σπουδῆς ἐμοί·
πάντων μὲν γὰρ ἀποστερεῖσθαι λυπηρόν ἐστι καὶ
χαλεπόν, ἄλλως τε κἂν ὑπ᾽ ἐχθροῦ τῳ τοῦτο συμ- 5
βαίνῃ, μάλιστα δὲ τῆς παρ᾽ ὑμῶν εὐνοίας καὶ φιλανθρωπίας, ὅσῳπερ καὶ τὸ τυχεῖν τούτων μέγιστόν

5. **ἀπολύσασθαι**: see § 50[6].

6. **καὶ πεποίηκα καὶ πεπολίτευμαι**: a familiar form of rhetorical amplification (opposed to modern ideas
of style), for which ordinary speech
would use πεπολίτευμαι alone. Other
instances are βεβούληται καὶ προῄρηται
(§ 2[6]), πεπραγμένων καὶ πεπολιτευμένων
and κατεψεύδου καὶ διέβαλλες (§ 11[3-7]),
ἐτραγῴδει καὶ διεξῄει (§ 13[6]), διέβαλλε
καὶ διεξῄει (§ 14[2]), ἐδίδαξας καὶ διεξῆλθες (§ 22[10]), πολεμεῖν καὶ διαφέρεσθαι (§ 31[4]). In these cases one
verb is generic and the other specific;
but sometimes two verbs of nearly or
quite the same meaning are used together for a similar rhetorical effect,
as πράττειν καὶ ποιεῖν (§ 62[4]), ζώντων
καὶ ὄντων (§ 72[3]).

7. **βαδίζω**, *proceed*, more formal
than *come* or *go*.

8. **ὡς μετριώτατα** : cf. the full form
ὡς ἂν δύνωμαι μετριώτατα, § 256[9].

9. **ὅ τι...ἀναγκάζῃ**, *whatever the
case itself may require of me* (lit. *compel me*): with ἀναγκάζω without an

infin. cf. Quint. XI. 1, 22, qui *hoc* se
coegisset.

10. **δίκαιος ἔχειν**: the common
personal construction (M. T. 762).
The apodosis is future in sense, after
the future ὅ τι ἂν ἀναγκάζῃ.

11. **τοιοῦτον ἀγῶν᾽**, *a suit like
this*, i.e. in which Ctesiphon is indicted and Demosthenes accused: cf.
§§ 12—16.

§ 5. 1. **ἂν ὁμολογῆσαι** (so Σ
and L): ἂν after a comma is allowed
when words belonging to the same
clause precede, as here ὑμᾶς πάντας
(M.T. 222).

3. **οὐδὲν ἐλάττονος**, *quite as great*.

4. **πάντων ἀποστερεῖσθαι**, *to be
deprived of anything*; cf. πανταχοῦ,
anywhere, § 81[6].

7. **ὅσῳπερ**, (by so much) *as*: the
implied τοσούτῳ is felt as limiting
μάλιστα (sc. λυπηρὸν καὶ χαλεπόν).—
καὶ before τὸ τυχεῖν expresses the
parallelism (so to speak) between
losing and *gaining* the privileges:
see ἃ καὶ διεκωλύθη, § 60[4], and note.

ἐστιν. περὶ τούτων δ' ὄντος τουτουὶ τοῦ ἀγῶνος, 6
ἀξιῶ καὶ δέομαι πάντων ὁμοίως ὑμῶν ἀκοῦσαί μου
περὶ τῶν κατηγορημένων ἀπολογουμένου δικαίως,
ὥσπερ οἱ νόμοι κελεύουσιν, οὓς ὁ τιθεὶς ἐξ ἀρχῆς
Σόλων, εὔνους ὢν ὑμῖν καὶ δημοτικός, οὐ μόνον τῷ 5
γράψαι κυρίους ᾤετο δεῖν εἶναι ἀλλὰ καὶ τῷ τοὺς
δικάζοντας ὀμωμοκέναι, οὐκ ἀπιστῶν ὑμῖν, ὥς γ' ἐμοὶ 7
φαίνεται, ἀλλ' ὁρῶν ὅτι τὰς αἰτίας καὶ τὰς διαβολάς,
αἷς ἐκ τοῦ πρότερος λέγειν ὁ διώκων ἰσχύει, οὐκ ἔνι
τῷ φεύγοντι παρελθεῖν, εἰ μὴ τῶν δικαζόντων ἕκαστος
ὑμῶν τὴν πρὸς τοὺς θεοὺς εὐσέβειαν φυλάττων καὶ 5
τὰ τοῦ λέγοντος ὑστέρου δίκαι' εὐνοϊκῶς προσδέξεται,

Such a καί can seldom be expressed in English, except by emphasis.

§ 6. 2. ἀξιῶ καὶ δέομαι: see note on § 4⁶.

3. δικαίως belongs to ἀκοῦσαι, from which it is separated partly for emphasis, and partly to bring it directly before ὥσπερ. It cannot be taken with ἀπολογουμένου, as the laws (§ 2³) have no reference to ἀπολογία, but require the judges to hear both sides impartially.

4. ὁ τιθεὶς ἐξ ἀρχῆς, i.e. *the original maker*: ὁ νόμον τιθείς is used like νομοθέτης, for the *lawgiver*, whose title is perpetual.

5. δημοτικός, *a friend of the people* or *of popular government*: see Ar. Nub. 1187, ὁ Σόλων ὁ παλαιὸς ἦν φιλόδημος τὴν φύσιν. —**οὐ μόνον...ὀμω-μοκέναι**: i.e. Solon thought that these provisions for an impartial hearing should have not merely the ordinary sanction which all laws have by enactment (τῷ γράψαι), but the further security which they gained by the judges swearing to uphold them. This double sanction was secured by enacting that these provisions of law should be a part of the Heliastic oath. γράφω, besides mean-

ing *to propose a law* or *decree*, often refers to *the enactment* as a whole, as here.

§ 7. 2. τὰς αἰτίας καὶ τὰς δια-βολὰς, here used like λοιδορία τε καὶ αἰτία in XXII. 21, 22. There αἰτία is thus defined, as opposed to ἔλεγχος: αἰτία μὲν γάρ ἐστιν ὅταν τις ψιλῷ χρη-σάμενος λόγῳ μὴ παράσχηται πίστιν ὧν λέγει, ἔλεγχος δὲ ὅταν ὧν ἂν εἴπῃ τις καὶ τἀληθὲς ὁμοῦ δείξῃ. Commonly, αἰτία refers to an accusation, whether true or false: cf. § 12⁷ (εἴπερ ἦσαν ἀληθεῖς). See Shilleto on Thuc. I. 23 and 69.

3. τοῦ πρότερος λέγειν: in public suits (γραφαί) in the Heliastic courts, each side spoke once (though the time might be divided among several speakers), the plaintiff first; in private suits (δίκαι), and in the Areopagus, each side was allowed a second argument.

4. παρελθεῖν, *to escape (get by)*: ὡς ἐπὶ δρομέων. Schol.

6. τοῦ λέγοντος ὑστέρου, *the second (later) speaker*, i.e. the defendant (τοῦ φεύγοντος): see Ar. Vesp. 15, σὺ λέξον πρότερος, Dem. I. 16, τοὺς ὑστάτους... εἰπόντας.—**δίκαι'**, *pleadings*, the statement of his *rights*: cf. § 9⁸ (see West.).

καὶ παρασχὼν ἑαυτὸν ἴσον καὶ κοινὸν ἀμφοτέροις
ἀκροατὴν οὕτω τὴν διάγνωσιν ποιήσεται περὶ ἁπάντων.

Μέλλων δὲ τοῦ τε ἰδίου βίου παντός, ὡς ἔοικε, **8**
λόγον διδόναι τήμερον καὶ τῶν κοινῇ πεπολιτευμένων,
βούλομαι πάλιν τοὺς θεοὺς παρακαλέσαι, καὶ ἐναντίον ὑμῶν εὔχομαι πρῶτον μὲν, ὅσην εὔνοιαν ἔχων
228 ἐγὼ διατελῶ τῇ πόλει καὶ πᾶσιν ὑμῖν, τοσαύτην **5**
ὑπάρξαι μοι εἰς τουτονὶ τὸν ἀγῶνα, ἔπειθ' ὅ τι
μέλλει συνοίσειν καὶ πρὸς εὐδοξίαν κοινῇ καὶ πρὸς
εὐσέβειαν ἑκάστῳ, τοῦτο παραστῆσαι πᾶσιν ὑμῖν
περὶ ταυτησὶ τῆς γραφῆς γνῶναι.

- Εἰ μὲν οὖν περὶ ὧν ἐδίωκε μόνον κατηγόρησεν **9**
Αἰσχίνης, κἀγὼ περὶ αὐτοῦ τοῦ προβουλεύματος
εὐθὺς ἂν ἀπελογούμην· ἐπειδὴ δ' οὐκ ἐλάττω λόγον

—προσδ(ξεται, shall receive kindly,
take under his protection.
7. **κοινόν**: impartial.
8. **οὕτω** repeats with emphasis the
idea of παρασχὼν...ἀκροατήν.— **διάγνωσιν,** decision (between two sides).
§ **8.** 2. **λόγον διδόναι,** to render
an account, used often of the formal
accounts which all officers of state

rendered at the εὔθυναι: see Aesch.
III. 11, 12, and cf. § 62⁵ (below), λόγον...λαβεῖν.
6. **ὅ τι...ἑκάστῳ**: see note on ὅπερ
...δόξης, § 1⁵.
8. **παραστῆσαι**: sc. τοὺς θεούς
(subj.), as in § 1⁶.—**τοῦτο γνῶναι,** to
give that judgment.

In §§ **9—52** the orator replies to
charges which are foreign to the indictment (ἔξω τῆς γραφῆς). We have
(1) an introduction in § 9; then (2) he
speaks of his private life in §§ 10,
11; then (3) of his public policy in
§§ 12—52.
Under (3) we have an introduction (§§ 12—16), and the defence of
his policy concerning the Peace of
Philocrates (§§ 17—52). The last
contains an introduction (§ 17), the
narration (§§ 18--49), and the conclusion (§§ 50—52).
§ **9.** 1. **εἰ...κατηγόρησεν,** i.e. if

he had confined his accusation (in his
speech) to the charges in his indictment (γραφή): see the same distinction between κατηγορεῖ and κρίνει in
§ 15⁵,⁶.
2. **προβουλεύματος**: the strict name
of a bill which had passed only the
Senate, though the less exact ψήφισμα
was often applied to it: see § 56¹.
3. **εὐθὺς ἂν ἀπελογούμην,** I should
at once proceed (lit. be now proceeding)
to my defence, etc. Cf. § 34⁴.—**οὐκ
ἐλάττω,** quite as much (as in his proper
accusation).

τἄλλα διεξιὼν ἀνήλωκε καὶ τὰ πλεῖστα κατεψεύσατό
μου, ἀναγκαῖον εἶναι νομίζω καὶ δίκαιον ἅμα βραχέα, 5
ὦ ἄνδρες Ἀθηναῖοι, περὶ τούτων εἰπεῖν πρῶτον, ἵνα
μηδεὶς ὑμῶν τοῖς ἔξωθεν λόγοις ἠγμένος ἀλλοτριώτερον τῶν ὑπὲρ τῆς γραφῆς δικαίων ἀκούῃ μου.
Περὶ μὲν δὴ τῶν ἰδίων ὅσα λοιδορούμενος βεβλα- 10
σφήμηκε περὶ ἐμοῦ, θεάσασθε ὡς ἁπλᾶ καὶ δίκαια
λέγω. εἰ μὲν ἴστε με τοιοῦτον οἷον οὗτος ᾐτιᾶτο (οὐ
γὰρ ἄλλοθί που βεβίωκα ἢ παρ᾽ ὑμῖν), μηδὲ φωνὴν
ἀνάσχησθε, μηδ᾽ εἰ πάντα τὰ κοινὰ ὑπέρευ πεπολί- 5
τευμαι, ἀλλ᾽ ἀναστάντες καταψηφίσασθ᾽ ἤδη. εἰ δὲ
πολλῷ βελτίω τούτου καὶ ἐκ βελτιόνων, καὶ μηδενὸς

4. **τἄλλα διεξιὼν** belongs to both
ἀνήλωκε and κατεψεύσατο.—ἀνήλωκε:
often of lavish expense.—**τὰ πλεῖστα**:
the antithesis to the comp. οὐκ ἐλάττω
seems to show that the superl. is to
be taken literally. The statements
repudiated by Demosthenes about his
private life and the Peace of Philocrates
can well be said to *outnumber* all the
others.

7. **ἀλλοτριώτερον**, *less kindly* (*with
greater alienation*).

8. **τῶν...δικαίων**: like δίκαια, § 7⁶.
Two genitives with ἀκούω are rare.—
ὑπὲρ: in the same sense as περί, as
often in the orators, who, however,
often observe the common distinction.
Cf. § 1⁵ and § 11³ᵃⁿᵈ ⁶, and XXIII. 19,
τοὺς περὶ τῶν νόμων λόγους ἀκούσῃ μου.

The reply in §§ **10**, **11** to the
charges against his private life and
character amounts merely to a scorn-
ful refusal to discuss them, and an
appeal to the judges to decide against
him at once if they believe them.

§ **10**. 1. **περὶ τῶν ἰδίων**: with
ὅσα βεβλασφήμηκε (not with λέγω),
the omitted antec. of the cognate ὅσα
being understood as limiting θεάσασθε

...λέγω, as regards all the calumnies
which he has abusively uttered about
my private life. The whole sentence
περὶ μὲν...λέγω is parallel to ὑπὲρ μὲν
...ἐξετάσω in § 11⁶. (West., Bl.)—
λοιδορούμενος βεβλασφήμηκε: for the
relation of λοιδορία and βλασφημία to
κατηγορία see § 123². βλασφημία is
slander, a special form of λοιδορία,
abuse in general. Our word *blasphemy*
(like many others) never goes beyond
the special meaning which it derives
from the ecclesiastical Greek: cf. *angel,
apostle, hypocrite, liturgy, litany*, etc.

3. **τοιοῦτον**: sc. ὄντα (M.T. 911).
So βελτίω (7) and χείρονα (8).

4. **μηδὲ φωνὴν ἀνάσχησθε** = μηδὲ
φθεγγόμενόν με ἀνάσχησθε, i.e. *stop
my speech at once*.

5. **πάντα τὰ κοινά**: i.e. settle the
case without reference to my public
acts.

7. **βελτίω καὶ ἐκ βελτιόνων**, *better
and better born*: cf. τίς ὢν καὶ τίνων,
§ 126⁵ (below). See Terent. Ph. i. 2,
65, bonam bonis prognatam.—**μηδενὸς
τῶν μετρίων χείρονα**, i.e. *quite as
good as any of our respectable citizens*
(cf. § 126⁷): this moderate expression
is made more effective by ἵνα...λέγω.

τῶν μετρίων, ἵνα μηδὲν ἐπαχθὲς λέγω, χείρονα καὶ
ἐμὲ καὶ τοὺς ἐμοὺς ὑπειλήφατε καὶ γιγνώσκετε, τούτῳ
μὲν μηδ' ὑπὲρ τῶν ἄλλων πιστεύετε (δῆλον γὰρ ὡς 10
ὁμοίως ἅπαντ' ἐπλάττετο), ἐμοὶ δ', ἣν παρὰ πάντα
τὸν χρόνον εὔνοιαν ἐνδέδειχθ' ἐπὶ πολλῶν ἀγώνων
τῶν πρότερον, καὶ νυνὶ παράσχεσθε. κακοήθης δ' 11
ὤν, Αἰσχίνη, τοῦτο παντελῶς εὔηθες ᾠήθης, τοὺς
περὶ τῶν πεπραγμένων καὶ πεπολιτευμένων λόγους
ἀφέντα με πρὸς τὰς λοιδορίας τὰς παρὰ σοῦ
229 τρέψεσθαι. οὐ δὴ ποιήσω τοῦτο· οὐχ οὕτω τετύ- 5
φωμαι· ἀλλ' ὑπὲρ μὲν τῶν πεπολιτευμένων ἃ
κατεψεύδου καὶ διέβαλλες ἐξετάσω, τῆς δὲ πομπείας
ταύτης τῆς ἀνέδην γεγενημένης ὕστερον, ἂν βουλο-
μένοις ἀκούειν ᾖ τουτοισί, μνησθήσομαι.

12. **ἐπὶ πολλῶν ἀγώνων**: see §§ 249,
250, where he speaks of being brought
to trial "daily" after the battle of
Chaeronea.

§ **11. 1. κακοήθης...εὔηθες ᾠήθης**:
an untranslatable παρονομασία, the sarcastic effect of which, as pronounced by
Demosthenes, can easily be imagined.
κακοήθης, *ill-natured, malicious*, is in
antithesis to εὔηθες, *good-natured* (in
the double sense of our *simple*). The
idea (imperfectly expressed) is: *malicious (ill-natured) fellow though you
are, you conceived this perfectly simple
(silly) notion*.

3. **πεπραγμένων καὶ πεπολιτευμένων**: see note on § 4⁶.

5. **τετύφωμαι**: cf. τετυφῶσθαι, IX.
20. If τυφῶ is connected with Τυφῶν
or Τυφώς, τετύφωμαι must mean *I am
distracted* or *crazed*, like ἐμβρόντητος
(§ 243⁷). If it is derived from τῦφος,
mist or *smoke* (see Lidd. & Sc.), τετύφωμαι means *I am stupefied, befogged*
or *wrapt in smoke*.

7. **πομπείας**, *ribaldry* (*procession-
talk*). See Harpocr.: πομπείας καὶ
πομπεύειν ἀντὶ τοῦ λοιδορίας καὶ

λοιδορεῖν. The Scholia have: πομπείας, λοιδορίας, ὕβρεως· ἐν ταῖς πομ-
παῖς προσωπεῖά τινες φοροῦντες ἀπ-
έσκωπτον τοὺς ἄλλους, ὡς ἐν ἑορτῇ
παίζοντες, ἐπὶ ἁμαξῶν φερόμενοι. See
ἐξ ἁμάξης, § 122⁷, and πομπεύειν,
§ 124².

8. **ἀνέδην**, *loosely, without check*:
cf. ἀνίημι and ἄνεσις.—**ἂν...τουτοισί**:
if these (judges) *shall wish to hear it*.
See Thuc. VI. 46, τῷ Νικίᾳ προσδεχο-
μένῳ ἦν, and other examples in M.T.
900. Whiston compares Liv. XXI. 50,
quibusdam volentibus novas res fore.

§§ **12—16.** After thus dismissing
the private charges as unworthy of a
reply, he comes to the charges against
his conduct with regard to the Peace
of Philocrates in 346 B.C. In this
introduction he dwells on the outrage
of bringing such grave charges against
a statesman in a way which neither
allows the accused a fair opportunity
to defend himself, nor gives the state
any adequate remedy against him if
he is guilty, while it may entail grave
consequences on an innocent person.

Τὰ μὲν οὖν κατηγορημένα πολλά, καὶ περὶ ὧν 12
ἐνίων μεγάλας καὶ τὰς ἐσχάτας οἱ νόμοι διδόασι
τιμωρίας· τοῦ δὲ παρόντος ἀγῶνος ἡ προαίρεσις
αὕτη· ἐχθροῦ μὲν ἐπήρειαν ἔχει καὶ ὕβριν καὶ λοιδορίαν καὶ προπηλακισμὸν ὁμοῦ καὶ πάντα τὰ τοιαῦτα· 5
τῶν μέντοι κατηγοριῶν καὶ τῶν αἰτιῶν τῶν εἰρημένων,
εἴπερ ἦσαν ἀληθεῖς, οὐκ ἔνι τῇ πόλει δίκην ἀξίαν
λαβεῖν, οὐδ' ἐγγύς. οὐ γὰρ ἀφαιρεῖσθαι τὸ προσελ- 13

§ 12. 1. **περὶ ὧν ἐνίων**, about
which in some cases : ἐνίων qualifies
ὧν (West.). Cf. XXVII. 23, καὶ ὅσα
ἕνια.

3. **ἡ προαίρεσις αὕτη· αὕτη·** (so Σ)
is much more expressive than αὐτή
(with no stop), pointing vividly to the
following statement of the true purpose of Aeschines. It also gives τῶν
μέντοι κατηγοριῶν κ.τ.λ. (6) its proper
relation to ἐχθροῦ μέν. The Schol.
charges this passage with ἀσάφεια
πολλή. The thought is as follows:—
The charges include some of the
gravest known to the law, which
provides the severest penalties for
the offences; but this suit was never
brought to punish anybody for these.
I will tell you what its object is
(αὕτη): it is to give a personal enemy
an opportunity to vent his spite and
malice, while it gives the state no means
of properly punishing my crimes if I
am guilty. The first clause, τὰ μέν...
τιμωρίας (1—3), states the gravity of
the actual charges, and is opposed to
the following τοῦ δὲ...αὕτη. The latter
introduces the double construction,
(a) ἐχθροῦ μέν...τοιαῦτα and (b) τῶν
μέντοι...οὐδ' ἐγγύς, in which the motive of Aeschines and the inadequacy
of this suit to deal with the alleged
crimes are declared. The last two
clauses are confirmed, (a) by οὐ γάρ...
δίκαιόν ἐστιν (§ 13^{1-4}), (b) by ἀλλ' ἐφ'
οἷς...γραφόμενον (§ 13^{5-11}). Finally,
οὐ γὰρ δήπου...ἐγράψατο (§ 13^{11-13})

shows that Aeschines, by his present
action, virtually admits that the course
just pointed out (ἐφ' οἷς...γραφόμενον)
is the only consistent one.

4. **ἐπήρειαν**, malice (cf. § 13²): see
ἐπηρεάζω, maliciously insult, §§ 138⁴,
320⁶.—**ἔχει**, involves, contains.

7. **εἴπερ ἦσαν ἀληθεῖς**, si verae
erant (not essent), a simple supposition, with nothing implied as to its
truth : there is no need of reading οὐκ
ἐνῆν in the apodosis.—**οὐκ ἔνι**, it is
not possible, i.e. by this suit.

8. **οὐδ' ἐγγύς** (sc. ἀξίαν), nor anything like it.

§ 13. Here the orator gives the
most striking proof of his adversary's
malicious purpose (ἐπήρειαν), viz. his
bringing a form of suit by which he
hoped to deprive Demosth. of the
power to defend himself (λόγου τυχεῖν). It must be remembered that
Aesch. had not merely prosecuted
Ctesiphon instead of Demosth., but
had also (III. 200—202) besought the
judges most earnestly not to allow
Demosth. to speak as Ctesiphon's
advocate.

1. **οὐ γὰρ ἀφαιρεῖσθαι κ.τ.λ.** : in
Σ δεῖ is crowded into the line by a
later hand after ἀφαιρεῖσθαι. If we
omit δεῖ, ἀφαιρεῖσθαι and τοῦτο ποιεῖν
with their adjuncts are subjects of
οὔτε...ἔχον οὔτε πολιτικὸν οὔτε δίκαιόν
ἐστιν, the negation of οὐ and οὐδ'
being thrice repeated in οὔτε. As we
naturally omit οὐ in translation (that

10 ΔΗΜΟΣΘΕΝΟΥΣ

θεῖν τῷ δήμῳ καὶ λόγου τυχεῖν—οὐδ' ἐν ἐπηρείας
τάξει καὶ φθόνου τοῦτο ποιεῖν—οὔτε μὰ τοὺς θεοὺς
ὀρθῶς ἔχον οὔτε πολιτικὸν οὔτε δίκαιόν ἐστιν, ὦ
ἄνδρες Ἀθηναῖοι· ἀλλ' ἐφ' οἷς ἀδικοῦντά μ' ἑώρα 5
τὴν πόλιν, οὖσί γε τηλικούτοις ἡλίκα νῦν ἐτραγῴδει
καὶ διεξῄει, ταῖς ἐκ τῶν νόμων τιμωρίαις παρ' αὐτὰ
τἀδικήματα χρῆσθαι, εἰ μὲν εἰσαγγελίας ἄξια πράτ-
τονθ' ἑώρα, εἰσαγγέλλοντα καὶ τοῦτον τὸν τρόπον εἰς
κρίσιν καθιστάντα παρ' ὑμῖν, εἰ δὲ γράφοντα παρά- 10
νομα, παρανόμων γραφόμενον· οὐ γὰρ δήπου Κτησι-

we may translate οὔτε), we can give
the emphatic οὐδ' (2) the force of *still
more* (*dazu*, Bl.), and translate, *for
to try to take away my right to come
before the people and be heard—still
more to do this by way of malice and
spite—is neither right nor patriotic*
(see note on 4) *nor just*. ἀφαιρεῖσθαι
is conative (cf. § 207⁵). For ἀφαιρεῖσθαι as subject (where we might
expect τὸ ἀφαιρεῖσθαι, were it not
for the following τὸ προσελθεῖν), see
Thuc. III. 38, ἀμύνασθαι δὲ, τῷ
παθεῖν ὅτι ἐγγυτάτω κείμενον, ἀντίπαλον ὂν μάλιστα τὴν τιμωρίαν ἀνα-
λαμβάνει.—τὸ προσελθεῖν...τυχεῖν
here is the right of every accused
citizen to be heard before the popular
court, which is here called δῆμος, as
it is often addressed ἄνδρες Ἀθηναῖοι.

2. ἐν ἐπηρείας τάξει, *by way of*
(venting) *malice*: cf. § 63³, ἐν τῇ...
τάξει, and XX. 81, ἐν ἐχθροῦ μέρει.
So III. 31.

3. οὔτε...οὔτε...οὔτε after οὐ: see
Eur. frag. 322 (N.), οὐκ ἔστιν οὔτε
τεῖχος οὔτε χρήματα οὔτ' ἄλλο δυσφύ-
λακτον οὐδὲν ὡς γυνή.

4. ὀρθῶς ἔχον: stronger than
ὀρθόν.—πολιτικὸν, properly *belonging
to the state* (see § 246⁷), here *due to
the state* from a citizen: cf. X. 74, οὐκ
ἴσως οὐδὲ πολιτικῶς. Such conduct,
it is meant, is *not fair to the state*.

In IX. 48, πολιτικῶς refers to the
simple old-fashioned Spartan style of
warfare.

5. ἐφ' οἷς...ἑώρα : a condensed
form for ἐπὶ τοῖς ἀδικήμασιν ἃ ἀδικοῦντά με ἑώρα.

6. οὖσι τηλικούτοις (= εἰ ἦν τηλι-
καῦτα), supposing them to have been
so great. ἐτραγῴδει καὶ διεξῄει (see
note on § 4⁶), set forth in his tragic
style (i.e. pompously), referring to the
theatrical days of Aeschines, like ὑποκρίνεται, § 15⁵. Cf. XIX. 189, ταῦτα
τραγῳδεῖ.

8. χρῆσθαι (sc. δίκαιον ἦν, supplied
from δίκαιόν ἐστιν in l. 4), *he ought to
have employed*.

9. εἰσαγγέλλοντα and γραφόμενον (11) express the manner of
χρῆσθαι, and with it make the apodoses to the conditions εἰ...ἑώρα and
εἰ...παράνομα (sc. ἑώρα). εἰσαγγέλλω
is *to indict* by εἰσαγγελία (a state
prosecution), as γράφομαι is (properly)
to indict by ordinary γραφή. Notice
the distinction between γράφοντα παράνομα, *proposing illegal measures*, and
παρανόμων γραφόμενον, *indicting for
illegal proposals*. For the double
meaning of the passive of γράφω see
note on § 56⁴.

11. οὐ γὰρ...ἐγράψατο : οὐ γὰρ
δήπου belongs to both clauses, Κτησ.
μὲν and ἐμὲ δ' κ.τ.λ. : *for it surely*

φῶντα μὲν δύναται διώκειν δι' ἐμέ, ἐμὲ δ', εἴπερ ἐξελέγ-
ξειν ἐνόμιζεν, αὐτὸν οὐκ ἂν ἐγράψατο. καὶ μὴν εἴ τι 14
τῶν ἄλλων ὧν νυνὶ διέβαλλε καὶ διεξήει ἢ καὶ ἄλλ'
ὁτιοῦν ἀδικοῦντά με ὑμᾶς ἑώρα, εἰσὶ νόμοι περὶ
πάντων καὶ τιμωρίαι, καὶ ἀγῶνες καὶ κρίσεις πικρὰ
καὶ μεγάλ' ἔχουσαι τἀπιτίμια, καὶ τούτοις ἐξῆν 5
230 ἅπασιν χρῆσθαι· καὶ ὁπηνίκ' ἐφαίνετο ταῦτα πεποιηκὼς καὶ τοῦτον τὸν τρόπον κεχρημένος τοῖς πρός με,
ὡμολογεῖτ' ἂν ἡ κατηγορία τοῖς ἔργοις αὐτοῦ.
νῦν δ' 15
ἐκστὰς τῆς ὀρθῆς καὶ δικαίας ὁδοῦ καὶ φυγὼν τοὺς
παρ' αὐτὰ τὰ πράγματα ἐλέγχους, τοσούτοις ὕστερον
χρόνοις αἰτίας καὶ σκώμματα καὶ λοιδορίας συμ-
φορήσας ὑποκρίνεται· εἶτα κατηγορεῖ μὲν ἐμοῦ, 5
κρίνει δὲ τουτονί, καὶ τοῦ μὲν ἀγῶνος ὅλου τὴν

cannot be that he is prosecuting Ctesiphon on my account, and yet would
not have indicted me myself if etc. See
note on § 179³.

12. **δι' ἐμέ, ἐμὲ δ'** : emphatic repetition.

§ 14. 1—3. **εἴ τι...ἑώρα** : if he ever
saw me etc., a simple supposition, to
which **εἰσὶ νόμοι** and **ἐξῆν** are a natural
apodosis; **ἐξῆν**, he might, implies no
unreal condition. Cf. **ἐφ' οἷς ἑώρα**,
§ 13⁵.—**ὧν...διέβαλλε καὶ διεξήει**, i.e.
which he slanderously related : cf. § 13⁶.

3—5. **νόμοι...τἀπιτίμια** : there is
no tautology here. He first mentions
laws and their prescribed penalties
(τιμωρίαι), which would be used in
ἀγῶνες ἀτίμητοι, in which the law
fixed the penalties; then processes and
(special) suits, in which heavy penalties could be inflicted by vote of the
court (ἀγῶνες τιμητοί). ἐπιτίμια, like
τιμήματα, are especially penalties
which the judges assess (τιμῶσι).

6. **ὁπηνίκ' ἐφαίνετο** is so nearly
equivalent to εἰ ποτε ἐφαίνετο (M.T.
528), that if he had ever been seen best
translates it. It is often impossible to

express an unreal condition in English
by a relative sentence : here whenever
he had been seen would not be clear.

7. **κεχρημένος τοῖς πρός με**, to
have dealt with me (managed his
relations to me).

8. **ὡμολογεῖτ' ἄν**, would have been
consistent, the impf. referring to the
various occasions of κεχρημένος. If
he had brought the proper suits
(ἀγῶνες καὶ κρίσεις) against me personally at the time of each offence,
his style of accusation (κατηγορία)
before the court would have been
consistent with his conduct ; whereas now κατηγορεῖ μὲν ἐμοῦ, κρίνει
δὲ τουτονί (§ 15⁵), this being his present
ἔργον.

§ 15. 3. **τοσούτοις ὕστερον χρόνοις** : the Peace of Philocrates was
sixteen years old at the time of the
trial.

5. **ὑποκρίνεται**, he plays his part:
cf. ἐτραγῴδει in § 13⁶. The word
implies not only pomposity but dis-
simulation.—**κατηγορεῖ...κρίνει** : see
note on § 14⁸.

6. **τοῦ ἀγῶνος ὅλου προΐσταται**,

πρὸς ἔμ' ἔχθραν προΐσταται, οὐδαμοῦ δ' ἐπὶ ταύτην
ἀπηντηκὼς ἐμοὶ τὴν ἑτέρου ζητῶν ἐπιτιμίαν ἀφελέσθαι φαίνεται. καίτοι πρὸς ἅπασιν, ὦ ἄνδρες 16
Ἀθηναῖοι, τοῖς ἄλλοις οἷς ἂν εἰπεῖν τις ὑπὲρ Κτησιφῶντος ἔχοι, καὶ τοῦτ' ἔμοιγε δοκεῖ καὶ μάλ'
εἰκότως ἂν λέγειν, ὅτι τῆς ἡμετέρας ἔχθρας ἡμᾶς
ἐφ' ἡμῶν αὐτῶν δίκαιον ἦν τὸν ἐξετασμὸν ποιεῖσθαι, 5
οὐ τὸ μὲν πρὸς ἀλλήλους ἀγωνίζεσθαι παραλείπειν,
ἑτέρῳ δ' ὅτῳ κακόν τι δώσομεν ζητεῖν· ὑπερβολὴ γὰρ
ἀδικίας τοῦτό γε.

Πάντα μὲν τοίνυν τὰ κατηγορημέν' ὁμοίως ἐκ 17
τούτων ἄν τις ἴδοι οὔτε δικαίως οὔτ' ἐπ' ἀληθείας
οὐδεμιᾶς εἰρημένα· βούλομαι δὲ καὶ καθ' ἓν ἕκαστον
αὐτῶν ἐξετάσαι, καὶ μάλισθ' ὅσα ὑπὲρ τῆς εἰρήνης
καὶ τῆς πρεσβείας κατεψεύσατό μου, τὰ πεπραγ- 5
μέν' ἑαυτῷ μετὰ Φιλοκράτους ἀνατιθεὶς ἐμοί. ἔστι

he puts foremost in (at the head of)
his whole suit.
7. **οὐδαμοῦ**, nowhere, i.e. never :
cf. οὖ in § 125[1] with following ἐνταῦθα.—**ἐπὶ ταύτην**, upon this ground
(that of our enmity), keeping the
figure of ἀπηντηκὼς ἐμοί, having met
me—or with a view to this, i.e. to
fight it out (West., Weil, Bl.) : cf.
ἐνταῦθ' ἀπήντηκας; § 125[5].
8. **ἐπιτιμίαν ἀφελέσθαι**, i.e. to
inflict ἀτιμία, which Ctesiphon would
incur as a public debtor if he were
unable to pay his fine if convicted.
§ 16. 3. **δοκεῖ**, personal, sc. τις
(from 2): we translate it seems that
one might say, because we must use a
finite verb to express ἂν λέγειν (M.T.
754).
5. **δίκαιον ἦν**, we ought (M. T.
416): here of present time.—**τὸν ἐξετασμὸν ποιεῖσθαι**, to settle up.
7. **ἑτέρῳ ὅτῳ...ζητεῖν**, to seek what
other man we can harm, ἑτέρῳ
standing emphatically before the in-

direct interrogative ὅτῳ: the direct
question would be ἑτέρῳ τίνι...
δώσομεν ;

For the argument of §§ 17—52
on the Peace of Philocrates, with its
three divisions, see note before § 9.
§ 17. 1. **ὁμοίως** with πάντα, all
alike.
2. **ἐπ' ἀληθείας οὐδεμιᾶς**, with no
regard to truth.
3. **εἰρημένα** : or. obl. with ἴδοι
ἄν.—**καθ' ἕν, singly**.—**ἕκαστον**: obj. of
ἐξετάσαι (West.) : cf. καθ' ἕνα ἕκαστον
ἡμῶν ἀποστερεῖν, XXI. 142.
4. **ὑπὲρ** (like περί) : see note on
§ 9[8].
6. **ἀνατιθεὶς ἐμοί**, putting upon me.
Originally Aeschines prided himself
on his close connection with Philocrates in making the peace : see 1.
174, τὴν εἰρήνην τὴν δι' ἐμοῦ καὶ Φιλοκράτους γεγενημένην. (See § 21[8], and
note ; and Hist. § 23.)

δ' ἀναγκαῖον, ὦ ἄνδρες 'Αθηναῖοι, καὶ προσῆκον
ἴσως, ὡς κατ' ἐκείνους τοὺς χρόνους εἶχε τὰ πράγματ'
ἀναμνῆσαι, ἵνα πρὸς τὸν ὑπάρχοντα καιρὸν ἕκαστα
θεωρῆτε. / 10
Τοῦ γὰρ Φωκικοῦ συστάντος πολέμου, οὐ δι' ἐμὲ 18
(οὐ γὰρ ἔγωγε ἐπολιτευόμην πω τότε), πρῶτον μὲν
ὑμεῖς οὕτω διέκεισθε ὥστε Φωκέας μὲν βούλεσθαι
231 σωθῆναι, καίπερ οὐ δίκαια ποιοῦντας ὁρῶντες, Θηβαίοις δ' ὁτιοῦν ἂν ἐφησθῆναι παθοῦσιν, οὐκ ἀλόγως 5
οὐδ' ἀδίκως αὐτοῖς ὀργιζόμενοι· οἷς γὰρ εὐτυχήκεσαν
ἐν Λεύκτροις οὐ μετρίως ἐκέχρηντο· ἔπειθ' ἡ Πελο-

7. καὶ προσῆκον ἴσως, and becoming as well (as necessary).
9. ἀναμνῆσαι : sc. ὑμᾶς, which is
added in most MSS. Cf. XX. 76,
ταῦθ' ὑπομνῆσαι πειράσομαι.—πρὸς...
καιρὸν, with reference to its special
occasion (that which belonged to it).
§ 18. 1. Φωκικοῦ πολέμου: the
Sacred or Phocian War began in 356
—355 and ended in 346 B.C. Demosthenes made his first speech in the
Assembly (on the Symmories) in 354
B.C. (Hist. §§ 4, 8.)
2. ἐπολιτευόμην: cf. § 60¹.
3. οὕτω διέκεισθε: when we compare this judicious account of the
feelings of the Athenians towards
the Phocians and Thebans in 346 B.C.
and earlier with the impassioned language of the speech on the Embassy
and of the Second and Third Philip-
pics, we see the sobering effect of
time and of recent events. When
the Thebans were exulting in the
devastation of Phocis by Philip, and
the political interests of Athens demanded that the Phocians should be
protected as allies, Demosthenes
seemed to overlook their sacrilegious
plundering of Delphi, which he now
acknowledges. Again, the intimate
alliance of Thebes and Athens in
339 B.C., and still more the destruc-

tion of Thebes by Alexander in 335,
had changed the Athenians' bitter
hatred to the deepest sympathy.
Still the orator cannot deny the old
hostility against Thebes, nor the chief
ground for it.
5. (ὥστε) ὁτιοῦν ἂν ἐφησθῆναι
παθοῦσιν: see M. T. 592 and 211.
It is often hard to express in English
the distinction between the infin. and
the finite moods with ὥστε, especially
when the infin. has ἂν and must therefore be translated by a finite verb.
The thought is, you were (so) disposed (as) to wish...and to feel that
you would be pleased etc. (M.T. 584).
ἐφησθῆναι ἂν has its protasis implied
in παθοῦσιν. The position of Φωκέας
μὲν (3) and Θηβαίοις δ' shows their
strong antithesis.
6. οἷς εὐτυχήκεσαν, their successes :
sc. τοῖς εὐτυχήμασιν (obj. of ἐκέχρηντο).
Cf. περὶ ὧν ἠγνωμονήκεσαν, § 94².
7. ἐν Λεύκτροις: for the battle of
Leuctra in 371 B.C. see Grote X. ch.
78. See XX. 109, showing the feeling of Demosth. himself in 355 :
μεῖζον Θηβαῖοι φρονοῦσιν ἐπ' ὠμότητι
καὶ πονηρίᾳ ἢ ὑμεῖς ἐπὶ φιλανθρωπίᾳ
καὶ τῷ τὰ δίκαια βούλεσθαι. See note
on § 98⁴.—ἔπειθ', after πρῶτον μὲν :
see note on § 1⁴.

πόννησος ἅπασα διειστήκει, καὶ οὔθ' οἱ μισοῦντες
Λακεδαιμονίους οὕτως ἴσχυον ὥστε ἀνελεῖν αὐτούς,
οὔθ' οἱ πρότερον δι' ἐκείνων ἄρχοντες κύριοι τῶν 10
πόλεων ἦσαν, ἀλλά τις ἦν ἄκριτος καὶ παρὰ τούτοις καὶ παρὰ τοῖς ἄλλοις ἅπασιν ἔρις καὶ ταραχή.
ταῦτα δ' ὁρῶν ὁ Φίλιππος (οὐ γὰρ ἦν ἀφανῆ) τοῖς 19
παρ' ἑκάστοις προδόταις χρήματα ἀναλίσκων πάντας
συνέκρουε καὶ πρὸς αὐτοὺς ἐτάραττεν· εἶτ' ἐν οἷς
ἡμάρτανον ἄλλοι καὶ κακῶς ἐφρόνουν, αὐτὸς παρε-
σκευάζετο καὶ κατὰ πάντων ἐφύετο. ὡς δὲ ταλαι- 5
πωρούμενοι τῷ μήκει τοῦ πολέμου οἱ τότε μὲν βαρεῖς
νῦν δ' ἀτυχεῖς Θηβαῖοι φανεροὶ πᾶσιν ἦσαν ἀναγκασθησόμενοι καταφεύγειν ἐφ' ὑμᾶς, Φίλιππος, ἵνα μὴ
τοῦτο γένοιτο μηδὲ συνέλθοιεν αἱ πόλεις, ὑμῖν μὲν
εἰρήνην ἐκείνοις δὲ βοήθειαν ἐπηγγείλατο. τί οὖν 20
συνηγωνίσατ' αὐτῷ πρὸς τὸ λαβεῖν ὀλίγου δεῖν ὑμᾶς
ἑκόντας ἐξαπατωμένους; ἡ τῶν ἄλλων Ἑλλήνων,

8. **διειστήκει**, *was in dissension
(distracted)*.—οἱ μισοῦντες : these were
especially the Messenians and Arcadians, with their new cities Messene
and Megalopolis, established by
Epaminondas, and the Argives.
10. οἱ πρότερον ἄρχοντες are oli-
garchies which were maintained by
Sparta in Peloponnesus before Leuctra,
and were overthrown by the later
revolutions.
11. ἄκριτος ἔρις καὶ ταραχή,
hopeless strife and confusion. ἄκριτος
is *not admitting of settlement* (κρίσις).
§ 19. 2. προδόταις : for the names
of some of these see § 48; a longer
black list is given in § 295.
3. συνέκρουε, *brought into collision
(knocked together)* : cf. συνέκρουον, 163[5],
and ξυγκρούειν, Thuc. I. 44.—ἐν οἷς
ἡμάρτανον ἄλλοι, *in others' blunders*,
cf. οἷς εὐτυχήκεσαν, § 18[6], ἐν οἷς
ἐπιστεύθητε in § 100[6], ἐν οἷς εἰσηγ-

γελλόμην in § 250[1], ἐν οἷς σεμνύνομαι
in § 258[4], ἐν οἷς ἔπταισεν in § 286[6],
ἐν οἷς εὐτύχησεν in § 323[9], ἐν αὐτοῖς
οἷς χαρίζονται in IX. 63.
5. κατὰ πάντων ἐφύετο, *he was
growing above all their heads*, i.e. so
as to threaten them all.
6. τῷ μήκει : cf. δεκέτης γεγονώς,
Aesch. III. 148.—βαρεῖς, *overbearing,
offensive.*
7. νῦν δ' ἀτυχεῖς : after 335 B.C.
See Schol., and notes on §§ 18[3] and
35[10].—ἀναγκασθησόμενοι : in *or. obl.*
with the personal φανεροὶ ἦσαν.
8. καταφεύγειν ἐφ' ὑμᾶς : no such
possibility is suggested by the language
of Demosthenes at the time of the
peace; but times had changed.
§ 20. 2. ὀλίγου δεῖν, full form of
ὀλίγου (M. T. 779), qualifies ἑκόντας
ἐξαπατ., *almost willing dupes*: cf.
μικροῦ, § 151[3].
3. ἡ Ἑλλήνων : the actual subject

εἴτε χρὴ κακίαν εἴτ' ἄγνοιαν εἴτε καὶ ἀμφότερα ταῦτ'
εἰπεῖν, οἳ πόλεμον συνεχῆ καὶ μακρὸν πολεμούντων 5
ὑμῶν, καὶ τοῦτον ὑπὲρ τῶν πᾶσι συμφερόντων, ὡς
ἔργῳ φανερὸν γέγονεν, οὔτε χρήμασιν οὔτε σώμασιν
οὔτ' ἄλλῳ οὐδενὶ τῶν ἁπάντων συνελάμβανον ὑμῖν·
οἷς καὶ δικαίως καὶ προσηκόντως ὀργιζόμενοι ἑτοίμως
232 ὑπηκούσατε τῷ Φιλίππῳ. ἡ μὲν οὖν τότε συγχωρη- 10
θεῖσα εἰρήνη διὰ ταῦτ', οὐ δι' ἐμέ, ὡς οὗτος διέβαλλεν,
ἐπράχθη· τὰ δὲ τούτων ἀδικήματα καὶ δωροδοκήματ'
ἐν αὐτῇ τῶν νυνὶ παρόντων πραγμάτων, ἄν τις ἐξε-
τάζῃ δικαίως, αἴτι' εὑρήσει. καὶ ταυτὶ πάνθ' ὑπὲρ 21
τῆς ἀληθείας ἀκριβολογοῦμαι καὶ διεξέρχομαι. εἰ
γὰρ εἶναί τι δοκοίη τὰ μάλιστ' ἐν τούτοις ἀδίκημα,
οὐδέν ἐστι δήπου πρὸς ἐμέ· ἀλλ' ὁ μὲν πρῶτος εἰπὼν
καὶ μνησθεὶς ὑπὲρ τῆς εἰρήνης Ἀριστόδημος ἦν ὁ 5
ὑποκριτής, ὁ δ' ἐκδεξάμενος καὶ γράψας καὶ ἑαυτὸν

appears in the alternative εἴτε...εἴτε.
See § 270[7], and XXIII. 156: ἡ ὑμε-
τέρα, ὦ ἄνδρ. Ἀθ., εἴτε χρὴ φιλαν-
θρωπίαν λέγειν εἴθ' ὅ τι δήποτε.
4. **κακίαν**, *baseness*, here in the
sense of *worthlessness*.
5. **πόλεμον μακρόν**: the so-called
Amphipolitan War with Philip (357
—346 B.C.), which ended with the
Sacred War. See Hist. § 3.
7. **σώμασιν**, *lives*: cf. § 66[9].
10. **συγχωρηθεῖσα**, *conceded, acquiesced in*: Athens showed no alacrity
in making the peace, though she was
deceived as to the main point.
11. **διέβαλλεν**, *slanderously declared*: see Aesch. III. 57 (end), 60.
13. **τῶν νυνὶ...εὑρήσει** (sc. τις): the
firm foothold in Greece which Philip
secured by the peace, especially his
influence in the Amphictyonic Council,
it is implied, made him at last the
victor of Chaeronea.
§ 21. 1. **ὑπὲρ τῆς ἀληθείας**, *from
regard for (in the interest of) truth*.

2. **ἀκριβολογοῦμαι καὶ διεξέρχομαι**: see note on § 4[5].
3. **τὰ μάλιστ'**, *even most clearly*,
with δοκοίη: cf. § 95[6].
4. **οὐδέν...πρὸς ἐμέ**, *it is no concern of mine*: cf. §§ 44[8], 60[3]. This
may be an emphatic present apodosis,
referring to the present condition
implied in εἰ...δοκοίη, *if it should
appear that there is* (εἶναι) *any fault*;
or it may be an emphatic future expression, as in Pind. Isth. IV. (V.) 14,
πάντ' ἔχεις, εἴ σε τούτων μοῖρ' ἐφίκοιτο
καλῶν, *you have the whole, should a
share of these glories fall to you*.
5. **Ἀριστόδημος**: a tragic actor
of good repute, one of the company
in which Aeschines once served (XIX.
246). For his informal mission to
Philip in 348—347 B.C. see Hist. § 13.
6. **ὁ ἐκδεξάμενος**, *his successor* (he
who *took* the business *from him*).—
γράψας: i.e. *moved* the peace, which
was named from this motion of Philocrates.

μετὰ τούτου μισθώσας ἐπὶ ταῦτα Φιλοκράτης ὁ
Ἁγνούσιος, ὁ σός, Αἰσχίνη, κοινωνός, οὐχ ὁ ἐμός,
οὐδ' ἂν σὺ διαρραγῇς ψευδόμενος, οἱ δὲ συνειπόντες
ὅτου δήποτε ἕνεκα (ἐῶ γὰρ τοῦτό γ' ἐν τῷ παρόντι) 10
Εὔβουλος καὶ Κηφισοφῶν· ἐγὼ δ' οὐδὲν οὐδαμοῦ.

ἀλλ' ὅμως, τούτων τοιούτων ὄντων καὶ ἐπ' αὐτῆς τῆς 22
ἀληθείας οὕτω δεικνυμένων, εἰς τοῦθ' ἧκεν ἀναιδείας
ὥστ' ἐτόλμα λέγειν ὡς ἄρ' ἐγὼ πρὸς τῷ τῆς εἰρήνης
αἴτιος γεγενῆσθαι καὶ κεκωλυκὼς εἴην τὴν πόλιν
μετὰ κοινοῦ συνεδρίου τῶν Ἑλλήνων ταύτην ποιή- 5
σασθαι. εἶτ' ὦ—τί ἂν εἰπών σέ τις ὀρθῶς προσ-
είποι; ἔστιν ὅπου σὺ παρών, τηλικαύτην πρᾶξιν
καὶ συμμαχίαν ἡλίκην νυνὶ διεξῄεις ὁρῶν ἀφαιρού-
μενόν με τῆς πόλεως, ἠγανάκτησας, ἢ παρελθὼν
ταῦτα ἃ νῦν κατηγορεῖς ἐδίδαξας καὶ διεξῆλθες; 10
καὶ μὴν εἰ τὸ κωλῦσαι τὴν τῶν Ἑλλήνων κοινωνίαν 23
ἐπεπράκειν ἐγὼ Φιλίππῳ, σοὶ τὸ μὴ σιγῆσαι λοιπὸν

9. οὐδ' ἂν σὺ διαρραγῇς, not even
if you split: cf. the common imprecation διαρραγείης (Ar. Av. 2). See
note on § 17⁶.
10. ὅτου δήποτε ἕνεκα, for whatever reason (it may have been): δήποτε,
like οὖν, makes ὅστις indefinite. This
is as strong language as Demosthenes
wishes to use of Eubulus, after his
death. See Hist. § 14.
11. οὐδαμοῦ: cf. § 15⁷, and ἔστιν
ὅπου, § 22⁷. Demosth. is fully justified in this strong denial.
§ 22. 1, 2. ὄντων, δεικνυμένων:
adversative (M.T. 842).
4. γεγενῆσθαι, κεκωλυκὼς εἴην:
for the perfects see M.T. 103, 109.
The whole sentence (3—6) ὡς ἄρ'...
ποιήσασθαι refers to the elaborate
charge of Aeschines (58—64), that
Demosthenes pressed the negotiations
for peace with indecent haste and
thereby excluded other Greek states
from the benefits of the treaty. The

answer in § 23 is perfectly satisfactory.
(See Hist. §§ 15, 24.)
5. συνεδρίου: a special meeting of
delegates to be summoned by Athens
from various Greek states, which never
met; not the regular synod of the
allies of Athens, which was in session
when the peace was made (Aesch. III.
69, 70).
6. ὦ, τί ἂν...προσείποι; ἀποσιώπησις followed by a question: for the
regular position of ἂν before εἰπών,
see M.T. 224. Cf. ὦ τί σ' εἴπω; Ar.
Nub. 1378.
7. ἔστιν ὅπου: temporal, like
οὐδαμοῦ in § 21¹¹.—παρὼν belongs to
ὁρῶν...ἠγανάκτησας, ἢ...διεξῆλθες; (as
a whole): the meaning is, were you
ever present when you saw me, etc.?—
πρᾶξιν καὶ συμμαχίαν: the general
before the particular. In § 191⁹ the
order is reversed.
§ 23. 2, 3. ἐπεπράκειν: even the
best MSS. of Demosth. give this form

ἦν, ἀλλὰ βοᾶν καὶ διαμαρτύρεσθαι καὶ δηλοῦν του-
233 τοισί. οὐ τοίνυν ἐποίησας οὐδαμοῦ τοῦτο, οὐδ' ἤκουσέ
σου ταύτην τὴν φωνὴν οὐδείς· οὔτε γὰρ ἦν πρεσβεία 5
πρὸς οὐδέν· ἀπεσταλμένη τότε τῶν Ἑλλήνων, ἀλλὰ
πάλαι πάντες ἦσαν ἐξεληλεγμένοι, οὔθ' οὗτος ὑγιὲς
περὶ τούτων εἴρηκεν οὐδέν. χωρὶς δὲ τούτων καὶ δια- 24
βάλλει τὴν πόλιν τὰ μέγιστα ἐν οἷς ψεύδεται· εἰ γὰρ
ὑμεῖς ἅμα τοὺς μὲν Ἕλληνας εἰς πόλεμον παρεκα-
λεῖτε, αὐτοὶ δὲ πρὸς Φίλιππον περὶ τῆς εἰρήνης
πρέσβεις ἐπέμπετε, Εὐρυβάτου πρᾶγμα, οὐ πόλεως 5
ἔργον οὐδὲ χρηστῶν ἀνθρώπων διεπράττεσθε. ἀλλ'
οὐκ ἔστι ταῦτα, οὐκ ἔστι· τί γὰρ καὶ βουλόμενοι
μετεπέμπεσθ' ἂν αὐτοὺς ἐν τούτῳ τῷ καιρῷ ; ἐπὶ
τὴν εἰρήνην ; ἀλλ' ὑπῆρχεν ἅπασιν. ἀλλ' ἐπὶ τὸν
πόλεμον ; ἀλλ' αὐτοὶ περὶ εἰρήνης ἐβουλεύεσθε. 10

of the plupf., while those of Plato
generally have the older Attic form
in -η (for -εα), as ἑωράκη in Rep.
336 D. (G. 683.)—σοὶ λοιπὸν ἦν, *it
remained for you*, after εἰ ἐπεπράκειν,
supposing that I had sold (a simple
supposition).—βοᾶν might refer to
the loud voice of Aesch., like πεφωνασκηκώς, § 308¹⁰; but Demosth. uses
it also of himself (§ 143⁶), and it is
probably no more than our *cry out*.
   5. οὔτε ἦν...ἀπεσταλμένη τότε :
Holmes·calls this an "audacious assertion." It must be remembered
that ἦν ἀπεσταλμένη is not an ordinary
plupf. like ἀπέσταλτο (M. T. 45),
which would have meant *that no
embassy had ever been sent* : the compound form means that *there was no
embassy then out on its mission*. The
embassies were probably informal in
most cases, and no definite report
was expected from them in case of
failure. (See Hist. § 24.) The next
sentence tells the whole truth, πάλαι
...ἐξεληλεγμένοι, i.e. *all had long*

before this been thoroughly canvassed
(and found wanting). Cf. 207,⁸ οὔτε
...ὑμῖν. Even Aeschines (II. 79) took
the same view fourteen years earlier:
οὐδενὸς δ' ἀνθρώπων ἐπικουροῦντος τῇ
πόλει, ἀλλὰ τῶν μὲν περιορώντων ὅ τι
συμβήσεται, τῶν δὲ συνεπιστρατευ-
όντων.
   § 24.   2. ἐν οἷς ψεύδεται : cf. §
19³. The argument of 2—6 is that
the negotiations for peace show that
Athens could not have been expecting
such envoys at this time.
   5. Εὐρυβάτου πρᾶγμα : Eurybatus
was a proverbial scoundrel, said to
have been an Ephesian who was hired
by Croesus to raise an army and gave
the money to Cyrus.—πόλεως ἔργον,
an act fit for a state.
   7. οὐκ ἔστι...ἔστι : see the same
repetition before the oath in § 208¹.
—τί καὶ μετεπέμπεσθ' ἄν ; *with what
possible object (καὶ) would you have
been sending?*
   9. ὑπῆρχεν ἅπασιν, i.e. *peace was
open to them all* : see note on § 1³.

οὐκοῦν οὔτε τῆς ἐξ ἀρχῆς εἰρήνης ἡγεμὼν οὐδ' αἴτιος
ὢν ἐγὼ φαίνομαι, οὔτε τῶν ἄλλων ὧν κατεψεύσατό
μου οὐδὲν ἀληθὲς ὂν δείκνυται.

Ἐπειδὴ τοίνυν ἐποιήσατο τὴν εἰρήνην ἡ πόλις, 25
ἐνταῦθα πάλιν σκέψασθε τί ἡμῶν ἑκάτερος προείλετο
πράττειν· καὶ γὰρ ἐκ τούτων εἴσεσθε τίς ἦν ὁ Φιλίππῳ πάντα συναγωνιζόμενος, καὶ τίς ὁ πράττων
ὑπὲρ ὑμῶν καὶ τὸ τῇ πόλει συμφέρον ζητῶν. ἐγὼ 5
μὲν τοίνυν ἔγραψα βουλεύων ἀποπλεῖν τὴν ταχίστην
τοὺς πρέσβεις ἐπὶ τοὺς τόπους ἐν οἷς ἂν ὄντα Φίλιππον πυνθάνωνται, καὶ τοὺς ὅρκους ἀπολαμβάνειν·
οὗτοι δὲ οὐδὲ γράψαντος ἐμοῦ ταῦτα ποιεῖν ἠθέλησαν.
τί δὲ τοῦτ' ἠδύνατο, ὦ ἄνδρες Ἀθηναῖοι ; ἐγὼ διδάξω. 26
Φιλίππῳ μὲν ἦν συμφέρον ὡς πλεῖστον τὸν μεταξὺ
χρόνον γενέσθαι τῶν ὅρκων, ὑμῖν δ' ὡς ἐλάχιστον.
διὰ τί ; ὅτι ὑμεῖς μὲν οὐκ ἀφ' ἧς ὠμόσαθ' ἡμέρας
234 μόνον, ἀλλ' ἀφ' ἧς ἠλπίσατε τὴν εἰρήνην ἔσεσθαι, 5
πάσας ἐξελύσατε τὰς παρασκευὰς τὰς τοῦ πολέμου·

---

11. **τῆς ἐξ ἀρχῆς εἰρήνης**, i.e. *the
earlier stages of the peace.*

§ 25. 1. **ἐπειδὴ** : see note on §
42 ⁵.

2. **ἐνταῦθα**, *here* (temporal): cf.
οὐδαμοῦ, § 15 ⁷.—**τί προείλετο πράττειν**; *what was his* προαίρεσις (*purpose
or policy?*)

6. **βουλεύων** : Demosth. was one
of the Senate of 500 in 347—346 B.C.
—**ἀποπλεῖν**, with **ἔγραψα**, *proposed.*
The bill was passed on the third of
Munychion (April 29): see Aesch. II.
92, Hist. § 29.

7. **ἐν οἷς ἂν πυνθάνωνται** (M.T.
694¹): cf. §§ 26⁸, 27³.

8. **τοὺς ὅρκους ἀπολαμβάνειν**, *to
administer the oaths* (i.e. *to receive
them*) : ὅρκους ἀποδιδόναι is *to take
the oaths* (i.e. *to give them*). See
§ 26⁹.

9. **οὐδὲ γράψαντος**, *not even after*

I had proposed the bill (its passage is
implied).

§ 26. 1. **τί...ἠδύνατο**; *what did
this* (§ 25⁵⁻⁸) *signify?* Cf. VIII. 57,
XXI. 31.

2. **τὸν μεταξὺ χρόνον τῶν ὅρκων**,
the intervening time (after making
the peace) *before he* (Philip) *should
take the oath.* ὅρκων refers to Philip's
oath, not to the oaths of the two
parties. See Shilleto's note on XIX.
164: he quotes Ar. Av. 187 ἐν μέσῳ
ἀήρ ἐστι γῆς, *between earth* (and
heaven); Ach. 433, κεῖται δ' ἄνωθεν
τῶν Θυεστείων ῥακῶν, μεταξὺ τῶν
Ἰνοῦς, i.e. *between these rags and
those of Ino.*

6. **ἐξελύσατε**, *you broke off* (*stopped*):
the active, though somewhat less expressive than the middle, conveys the
whole idea, and has the best MSS.
authority.

ὁ δὲ τοῦτ' ἐκ παντὸς τοῦ χρόνου μάλιστ' ἐπραγμα-
τεύετο, νομίζων, ὅπερ ἦν ἀληθὲς, ὅσα τῆς πόλεως
προλάβοι πρὸ τοῦ τοὺς ὅρκους ἀποδοῦναι, πάντα
ταῦτα βεβαίως ἕξειν· οὐδένα γὰρ τὴν εἰρήνην λύ- 10
σειν τούτων ἕνεκα. ἀγὼ προορώμενος, ἄνδρες 'Αθη- 27
ναῖοι, καὶ λογιζόμενος τὸ ψήφισμα τοῦτο γράφω,
πλεῖν ἐπὶ τοὺς τόπους ἐν οἷς ἂν ᾖ Φίλιππος καὶ
τοὺς ὅρκους τὴν ταχίστην ἀπολαμβάνειν, ἵν' ἐχόντων τῶν Θρακῶν, τῶν ὑμετέρων συμμάχων, ταῦτα 5
τὰ χωρία ἃ νῦν οὗτος διέσυρε, τὸ Σέρριον καὶ τὸ
Μυρτηνὸν καὶ τὴν Ἐργίσκην, οὕτω γίγνοινθ' οἱ
ὅρκοι, καὶ μὴ προλαβὼν ἐκεῖνος τοὺς ἐπικαίρους τῶν
τόπων κύριος τῆς Θρᾴκης κατασταίη, μηδὲ πολλῶν
μὲν χρημάτων πολλῶν δὲ στρατιωτῶν εὐπορήσας ἐκ 10
τούτων ῥᾳδίως τοῖς λοιποῖς ἐπιχειροίη πράγμασιν.
εἶτα τοῦτο μὲν οὐχὶ λέγει τὸ ψήφισμα οὐδ' ἀναγι- 28

7. **τοῦτ'**, his own plan, to prolong the time when Athens must be quiet while he could act, referring to 4, 5.— **ἐκ παντὸς τοῦ χρόνου**, i.e. from Philip's first suggestions of peace.
8. **ὅσα προλάβοι**, all that he might secure from the city: we might have ὅσ' ἂν προλάβῃ in the same sense (cf. § 25⁷).
10. **οὐδένα...λύσειν** continues the or. obl. from ἕξειν. Even an optative may be thus continued, as in 1. 22.
§ **27**. 2. **ψήφισμα γράφω πλεῖν**: cf. ἔγραψα ἀποπλεῖν (§ 25⁸).—**τοῦτο**, i.e. the decree just mentioned.
6. **διέσυρε**, ridiculed (tore in pieces), refers to Aesch. III. 82, where he charges Demosth. with making trouble, after the peace was concluded, by mentioning all the insignificant places captured by Philip: οὗτός ἐστιν ὁ πρῶτος ἐξευρὼν Σέρριον τεῖχος καὶ Δορίσκον καὶ Ἐργίσκην καὶ Μυρτίσκην

καὶ Γάνος καὶ Γανιάδα, χωρία ὧν οὐδὲ τὰ ὀνόματα ᾔδεμεν πρότερον.
7. **οὕτω**, under these circumstances (hardly translatable), sums up the preceding ἐχόντων...Ἐργίσκην.—**γίγνοινθ'** with ἵνα depends on γράφω, historic present.
8. **ἐπικαίρους**, seasonable, here advantageous for attacking the Athenian possessions, especially the Chersonese.
9. **κατασταίη** and **ἐπιχειροίη** (11) continue the final clause with ἵνα (4). —**πολλῶν χρημάτων**: from the rich Thracian gold mines. Diod. XVI. 8 says that Philip had a revenue of a thousand talents (£200,000) from his mines at Philippi.
11. **τοῖς λοιποῖς** (cf. § 95¹¹), what remained to be done.
§ **28**. 1. **λέγει—ἀναγιγνώσκει**, recites—has it read (by the clerk). **λέγε**, properly recite, repeat, is the term most commonly used for read in addressing his clerk.

γνώσκει· εἰ δὲ βουλεύων ἐγὼ προσάγειν τοὺς πρέσβεις ᾤμην δεῖν, τοῦτό μου διαβάλλει. ἀλλὰ τί ἐχρῆν
με ποιεῖν ; μὴ προσάγειν γράψαι τοὺς ἐπὶ τοῦθ᾽
ἥκοντας, ἵν᾽ ὑμῖν διαλεχθῶσιν ; ἢ θέαν μὴ κατα- 5
νεῖμαι τὸν ἀρχιτέκτονα αὐτοῖς κελεῦσαι ; ἀλλ᾽ ἐν
τοῖν δυοῖν ὀβολοῖν ἐθεώρουν ἄν, εἰ μὴ τοῦτ᾽ ἐγράφη.
τὰ μικρὰ συμφέροντα τῆς πόλεως ἔδει με φυλάττειν, τὰ δ᾽ ὅλα, ὥσπερ οὗτοι, πεπρακέναι ; οὐ δήπου.
λέγε τοίνυν μοι τὸ ψήφισμα τουτὶ λαβών, ὃ σαφῶς 10
οὗτος εἰδὼς παρέβη.

2. **προσάγειν τοὺς πρέσβεις** (sc. εἰς
τὴν ἐκκλησίαν): these were the ambassadors sent by Philip to negotiate
the peace. Foreign embassies first
presented themselves to the Senate,
which by a decree provided for their
introduction to the Assembly : see
Aesch. II. 58, ταῖς δὲ ξενικαῖς πρεσβείαις ἡ βουλὴ τὰς εἰς τὸν δῆμον προσόδους προβουλεύει. Such a bill was
proposed by Demosth. in the Senate
before the arrival of the ambassadors,
appointing a special meeting of the
Assembly to receive them on the
eighth of Elaphebolion : afterwards
the discussion of the peace was postponed to the eighteenth and nineteenth.

5. **θέαν...κελεῦσαι** (sc. ἐχρῆν) :
*ought I not to have ordered the
architect* (of the theatre) *to assign
them seats* (as I did)? θέαν, *place to
see*; cf. ἐθεώρουν (7): this would be
the προεδρία (Aesch. III. 76). The
stone Dionysiac theatre was at this
time building under the direction of
Lycurgus ; and the lessee was called
ἀρχιτέκτων, as an important part of his
duties was the superintendence of
the work of building. See Dörpfeld
and Reisch, Griech. Theater, 36—40,
where the building of the theatre is
assigned to about 350—325 B.C.
Aeschines (61, 76) makes this official

politeness of Demosthenes one ground
of his grotesque charge of flattering
Philip! To this Demosth. alludes in
§ 294², ὃς γὰρ ἐμοὶ Φιλιππισμόν, κ.τ.λ.
Aesch., however, mentions only the introduction of the envoys to the theatre.

6. **ἐν τοῖν δυοῖν ὀβολοῖν**, *in the
two-obol seats*, the threepenny seats
of the ordinary citizens. The διωβελία,
which was then given from the theoric
fund as festival money to every citizen
who asked for it, paid the entrance
fee to the theatre. It is implied that
the distinguished strangers could have
been admitted, like other people, to
the common seats by merely paying
their two obols. With ἐν τοῖν δυοῖν
ὀβολοῖν cf. ἐν τοῖς ἰχθύσιν, Ar. Vesp.
789 (see Ran. 1068), *in the fish-
market*, ἐν τῷ μύρῳ, Eq. 1375.

7. **εἰ μὴ τοῦτ᾽ ἐγράφη**, i.e. *had
I not proposed my bill.*

8. **τὰ μικρὰ συμφέροντα**: it is jo-
cosely assumed that Aesch. objected to
the higher price which the state probably paid for the front seats, or
perhaps to the state paying for the
seats at all.--**φυλάττειν, πεπρακέναι**:
the change of tense may perhaps be
seen in a paraphrase ; *was it my duty
to watch the petty interests of the state,
after I had sold her highest interests
like these men?* With ὅλα, *whole*,
entire, cf. τῶν ὅλων τι, § 278⁹.

235   ΨΗΦΙΣΜΑ ΔΗΜΟΣΘΕΝΟΥΣ.   29

['Επὶ ἄρχοντος Μνησιφίλου, ἑκατομβαιῶνος ἔνῃ καὶ νέᾳ,
φυλῆς πρυτανευούσης Πανδιονίδος, Δημοσθένης Δημοσθένους Παιανιεὺς εἶπεν, ἐπειδὴ Φίλιππος ἀποστείλας πρέσβεις
περὶ τῆς εἰρήνης ὁμολογουμένας πεποίηται συνθήκας, δεδόχθαι 5
τῇ βουλῇ καὶ τῷ δήμῳ τῷ Ἀθηναίων, ὅπως ἂν ἡ εἰρήνη
ἐπιτελεσθῇ ἡ ἐπιχειροτονηθεῖσα ἐν τῇ πρώτῃ ἐκκλησίᾳ, πρέσβεις ἑλέσθαι ἐκ πάντων Ἀθηναίων ἤδη πέντε, τοὺς δὲ χει-
ροτονηθέντας ἀποδημεῖν, μηδεμίαν ὑπερβολὴν ποιουμένους,
ὅπου ἂν ὄντα πυνθάνωνται τὸν Φίλιππον, καὶ τοὺς ὅρκους 10
λαβεῖν τε παρ' αὐτοῦ καὶ δοῦναι τὴν ταχίστην ἐπὶ ταῖς ὡμο-
λογημέναις συνθήκαις αὐτῷ πρὸς τὸν Ἀθηναίων δῆμον, συμ-
περιλαμβάνοντας καὶ τοὺς ἑκατέρων συμμάχους. πρέσβεις
ᾑρέθησαν Εὔβουλος Ἀναφλύστιος, Αἰσχίνης Κοθωκίδης,
Κηφισοφῶν Ῥαμνούσιος, Δημοκράτης Φλυεύς, Κλέων Κο- 15
θωκίδης.]

Ταῦτα γράψαντος ἐμοῦ τότε καὶ τὸ τῇ πόλει 30
συμφέρον οὐ τὸ Φιλίππῳ ζητοῦντος, βραχὺ φροντί-
σαντες οἱ χρηστοὶ πρέσβεις οὗτοι καθῆντ' ἐν Μακεδονίᾳ τρεῖς ὅλους μῆνας, ἕως ἦλθε Φίλιππος ἐκ
Θρᾴκης πάντα καταστρεψάμενος, ἐξὸν ἡμερῶν δέκα, 5

§ 29. This decree is a good specimen of ignorant forgery. The Archon's
name and the date are both wrong;
it is called a decree of the Senate and
the People, when it was passed by
the Senate alone; it provides for the
appointment of five envoys when there
were ten, and these had been appointed long before; it provides for
the oaths to be taken by Athens and
her allies, when these had already
been taken; and most of the five
names of the envoys are wrong.

§ 30. 1. τὸ τῇ πόλει συμφέρον :
cf. 28⁸, where τὰ συμφέροντα (with
the gen.) is a pure substantive.

4. τρεῖς ὅλους μῆνας : "sat still in

Macedonia three whole months," is of
course a rhetorical exaggeration, which
is corrected by Demosth. himself. In
XIX. 57 he says ἀπεδημήσαμεν τρεῖς
μῆνας ὅλους (cf. 158), somewhat less
incorrectly ; but in 58—60 he gives
the exact dates, by which we see that
the embassy was absent from Athens
only about ten weeks. (See Hist.
§ 33.)

5. πάντα καταστρεψάμενος : see
§ 27.—ἐξὸν...ἀφῖχθαι...σῶσαι : ἐξόν
represents ἐξῆν, and ἀφῖχθαι is a proper
perfect (M.T. 109) ; lit. it was in our
power to have (already) arrived and
to save the towns, i.e. we might have
done both of these.

ὁμοίως δὲ τριῶν ἢ τεττάρων, εἰς τὸν Ἑλλήσποντον
ἀφῖχθαι καὶ τὰ χωρία σῶσαι, λαβόντας τοὺς ὅρκους
πρὶν ἐκεῖνον ἐξελεῖν αὐτά· οὐ γὰρ ἂν ἦψατ' αὐτῶν
παρόντων ἡμῶν, ἢ οὐκ ἂν ὡρκίζομεν αὐτὸν, ὥστε τῆς
236 εἰρήνης ἂν διημαρτήκει καὶ οὐκ ἂν ἀμφότερ' εἶχε, καὶ 10
τὴν εἰρήνην καὶ τὰ χωρία.

Τὸ μὲν τοίνυν ἐν τῇ πρεσβείᾳ πρῶτον κλέμμα 31
μὲν Φιλίππου δωροδόκημα δὲ τῶν ἀδίκων τούτων
ἀνθρώπων τοιοῦτον ἐγένετο· ὑπὲρ οὗ καὶ τότε καὶ
νῦν καὶ ἀεὶ ὁμολογῶ καὶ πολεμεῖν καὶ διαφέρεσθαι
τούτοις. ἕτερον δ' εὐθὺς ἐφεξῆς ἔτι τούτου μεῖζον 5
κακούργημα θεάσασθε. ἐπειδὴ γὰρ ὡμολόγησε τὴν 32
εἰρήνην ὁ Φίλιππος προλαβὼν τὴν Θράκην διὰ
τούτους οὐχὶ πεισθέντας τῷ ἐμῷ ψηφίσματι, πάλιν
ὠνεῖται παρ' αὐτῶν ὅπως μὴ ἄπιμεν ἐκ Μακεδονίας
ἕως τὰ τῆς στρατείας τῆς ἐπὶ τοὺς Φωκέας εὐτρεπῆ 5
ποιήσαιτο, ἵνα μὴ, δεῦρ' ἀπαγγειλάντων ἡμῶν ὅτι

6. **ὁμοίως,** *quite as well* (as in ten
days) : the common reading μᾶλλον
would mean *rather*.
9. **παρόντων** = εἰ παρῆμεν, *if we had
been there.* For the various past tenses
with ἄν, all of which are in 8—10, see
M.T. 413: thus τῆς εἰρ. ἂν διημαρτήκει is *he would have failed to secure
the peace* (which he had already secured
by our absence), and οὐκ ἂν ἀμφότερ'
εἶχε is *he would not have had both* (as
he did have).
§ **31.** 1. **κλέμμα μὲν** : cf. μὴ κλέπτε
νόῳ, Il. I. 132. The position of μὲν
shows that the seven words before
κλέμμα belong to both κλέμμα and
δωροδόκημα.
4. **πολεμεῖν καὶ διαφέρεσθαι** : these
represent (in *or. obl.*) the past, the present, and the emphatic future indicated
by τότε, νῦν, and ἀεί (M.T. 32, 119).
§ **32.** 2. **διὰ τούτους οὐχὶ πεισθέντας** (without τοὺς) is, *because of*

their *disobedience,* like μετὰ Συρακούσας
οἰκισθείσας, Thuc. VI. 3, and post
urbem conditam. This is rare in
Greek, where we should expect διὰ τὸ
μὴ πεισθῆναι (M.T. 829b). See § 42 B,
with τῶν...μισθωσάντων.
4. **ὠνεῖται...ὅπως μὴ ἄπιμεν,** *he
bribes them* (to effect) *that we shall
not depart* (M. T. 339): ἄπιμεν (as
fut., M. T. 29) is more regular after
ὠνεῖται than ἀπίωμεν, and has com-
mended itself to nearly all recent
editors, though it rests only on a
grammarian's authority. (Bekker's
Anecd. p. 129⁴.)
5. **ἕως...ποιήσαιτο,** after the historic present ὠνεῖται. The clause
with ἕως has a final force (M.T. 614),
the idea being that he bribed them to
wait *long enough for him to get his
army ready.*
6. **ἵνα μὴ...ποιῆσαι** (11): the
purpose of ὠνεῖται.

ΠΕΡΙ ΤΟΥ ΣΤΕΦΑΝΟΥ 23

μέλλει καὶ παρασκευάζεται πορεύεσθαι, ἐξέλθοιθ᾿
ὑμεῖς καὶ περιπλεύσαντες ταῖς τριήρεσιν εἰς Πύλας
ὥσπερ πρότερον κλείσαιτε τὸν τόπον, ἀλλ᾿ ἅμ᾿
ἀκούοιτε ταῦτ᾿ ἀπαγγελλόντων ἡμῶν κἀκεῖνος ἐντὸς 10
εἴη Πυλῶν καὶ μηδὲν ἔχοιθ᾿ ὑμεῖς ποιῆσαι. οὕτω δ᾿ 33
ἦν ὁ Φίλιππος ἐν φόβῳ καὶ πολλῇ ἀγωνίᾳ, μὴ καὶ
ταῦτα προειληφότος αὐτοῦ, εἰ πρὸ τοῦ τοὺς Φωκέας
ἀπολέσθαι ψηφίσαισθε βοηθεῖν, ἐκφύγοι τὰ πράγ-
ματ᾿ αὐτόν, ὥστε μισθοῦται τὸν κατάπτυστον 5
τουτονί, οὐκέτι κοινῇ μετὰ τῶν ἄλλων πρέσβεων,
ἀλλ᾿ ἰδίᾳ καθ᾿ αὑτόν, τοιαῦτα πρὸς ὑμᾶς εἰπεῖν καὶ
ἀπαγγεῖλαι δι᾿ ὧν ἅπαντ᾿ ἀπώλετο. ἀξιῶ δὲ, ὦ 34
ἄνδρες Ἀθηναῖοι, καὶ δέομαι τοῦτο μεμνῆσθαι παρ᾿
ὅλον τὸν ἀγῶνα, ὅτι μὴ κατηγορήσαντος Αἰσχίνου
237 μηδὲν ἔξω τῆς γραφῆς οὐδ᾿ ἂν ἐγὼ λόγον οὐδέν·
ἐποιούμην ἕτερον· πάσαις δ᾿ αἰτίαις καὶ βλασφη- 5
μίαις ἅμα τούτου κεχρημένου ἀνάγκη κἀμοὶ πρὸς
ἕκαστα τῶν κατηγορημένων μίκρ᾿ ἀποκρίνασθαι.

7, 8. ἐξέλθοιθ᾿ refers to the land
force.—περιπλεύσαντες ὥσπερ πρότερον refers to the famous expedition
in 352 B.C., when Athens stopped
Philip at Thermopylae. See IV. 17;
XIX. 84, 319; Grote XI. 403—405;
and Hist. § 6.
9. κλείσαιτε τὸν τόπον, i.e. make
Thermopylae impassable.
10. ἀπαγγελλόντων: present to
ἀκούοιτε, as ἀπαγγειλάντων in 6 is
past to ἐξέλθοιτε.
§ 33. 1. οὕτω: antecedent of ὥστε
(5).
2. ἀγωνίᾳ, conflict (of mind) :
Vömel refers Hesych. ἐν ἀγωνίᾳ, ἐν
μερίμνῃ, to this passage.
3. εἰ πρὸ τοῦ: the older editions
with nearly all MSS. omit εἰ and read
καὶ ἐκφύγοι in 4, making ψηφίσαισθε
depend on μή.—πρὸ τοῦ...ἀπολέσθαι,
i.e. before he could have time to lay

Phocis waste: cf. XIX. 123.
5. ὥστε μισθοῦται : a clear case
of ὥστε requiring the indicative (M.T.
582, 583).
6. οὐκέτι κοινῇ : Aeschines alone
was indicted for παραπρεσβεία. See
§ 41³.
8. δι᾿ ὧν here and δι᾿ οὓς in § 35²
approach each other very closely, both
referring to the same thing.
§ 34. 1, 2. ἀξιῶ, I ask of you (as
something ἄξιον); δέομαι, I entreat.
See § 6².
4. ἔξω τῆς γραφῆς: he has already
(§ 9) justified his discussion of the
peace ; and he repeats his apology
now, chiefly to call special attention
to what follows.
4, 5. ἐποιούμην ἂν refers to his
present argument (cf. § 9³).—ἕτερον,
foreign to the subject, like ἀλλότριον:
cf. ἕτερος λόγος οὗτος, § 44⁸.

τίνες οὖν ἦσαν οἱ παρὰ τούτου λόγοι τότε ῥηθέντες, 35
καὶ δι᾽ οὓς ἅπαντ᾽ ἀπώλετο; ὡς οὐ δεῖ θορυβεῖσθαι
τῷ παρεληλυθέναι Φίλιππον εἴσω Πυλῶν· ἔσται
γὰρ ἅπανθ᾽ ὅσα βούλεσθ᾽ ὑμεῖς, ἂν ἔχηθ᾽ ἡσυχίαν,
καὶ ἀκούσεσθε δυοῖν ἢ τριῶν ἡμερῶν, οἷς μὲν ἐχθρὸς 5
ἥκει, φίλον αὐτὸν γεγενημένον, οἷς δὲ φίλος, τοὐναντίον ἐχθρόν. οὐ γὰρ τὰ ῥήματα τὰς οἰκειότητας ἔφη
βεβαιοῦν, μάλα σεμνῶς ὀνομάζων, ἀλλὰ τὸ ταὐτὰ
συμφέρειν· συμφέρειν δὲ Φιλίππῳ καὶ Φωκεῦσι καὶ
ὑμῖν ὁμοίως ἅπασι τῆς ἀναλγησίας καὶ τῆς βαρύτη- 10
τος ἀπαλλαγῆναι τῆς τῶν Θηβαίων. ταῦτα δ᾽ 36
ἀσμένως τινὲς ἤκουον αὐτοῦ διὰ τὴν τόθ᾽ ὑποῦσαν
ἀπέχθειαν πρὸς τοὺς Θηβαίους. τί οὖν συνέβη μετὰ

§ 35. 1. οἱ...ῥηθέντες : see the fuller account of this speech in XIX. 20—22. Aeschines said that the Thebans had set a price on his head for his anti-Theban advice to Philip. See Hist. § 34.

3. τῷ παρεληλυθέναι : he begged the people not to be disturbed by news that Philip *had already passed* Thermopylae.

5, 6. οἷς μὲν, the Phocians ; οἷς δὲ, the Thebans.

7. ῥήματα : e.g. the Thebans' title of allies of Philip (cf. § 213²).

8. μάλα σεμνῶς ὀνομάζων, *using very solemn expressions*. He often jokes about the σεμνότης of Aesch. See §§ 130, 133, 258, and XIX. 23.

9. συμφέρειν· συμφέρειν : a striking ἀναστροφή.

10. ἀναλγησίας, *want of feeling*, explained by the Schol. as ἀναισθησίας. There can be little doubt that this word, like ἀναίσθητοι in § 43², refers to the dulness and lack of keen perception for which the Thebans were proverbial. See Nep. Epam. 5, 2, namque illi genti plus virium quam ingenii, and Alcib. 11, 3, omnes enim

Boeotii magis firmitati corporis quam ingenii acumini inserviunt ; Cic. de Fato IV. 7, Athenis tenue caelum, ex quo acutiores putantur Attici ; crassum Thebis, itaque pingues Thebani et valentes ; Hor. Epist. II. 1, 244, Boeotum in crasso aere natum. This dulness, and the consequent illiteracy of Thebes compared with Athens, gave rise to the proverb Βοιωτίαν ὗν, Pind. Ol. VI. 90: see the Schol., τὸ ἀρχαῖον ὄνειδος, τουτέστι τὴν παλαιὰν διαβολὴν τὴν ἐπὶ τῇ ἀμουσίᾳ. Aristotle, Eth. III. 7, 7, says of a man lacking in φόβος, εἴη δ᾽ ἄν τις μαινόμενος ἢ ἀνάλγητος, εἰ μηδὲν φοβοῖτο, μήτε σεισμὸν μήτε κύματα, and in III. 11, 7, of those insensible to pleasure, ἐλλείποντες δὲ τὰ περὶ τὰς ἡδονὰς καὶ ἧττον ἢ δεῖ χαίροντες οὐ πάνυ γίνονται· οὐ γὰρ ἀνθρωπική ἐστιν ἡ τοιαύτη ἀναισθησία. Aristotle here means stupidity and slowness, not moral obliquity, by both ἀνάληπτος and ἀναισθησία.—βαρύτητος : cf. § 19⁶.

§ 36. 2. τὴν τόθ᾽ ὑποῦσαν (cf. ὕπεστι, § 315²): a mild way of speaking of the enmity against Thebes in 346·B.C. See § 18³ with note.

ταῦτ' εὐθὺς, οὐκ εἰς μακράν ; τοὺς μὲν Φωκέας ἀπολέσθαι καὶ κατασκαφῆναι τὰς πόλεις αὐτῶν, ὑμᾶς δ' 5
ἡσυχίαν ἀγαγόντας καὶ τούτῳ πεισθέντας μικρὸν
ὕστερον σκευαγωγεῖν ἐκ τῶν ἀγρῶν, τοῦτον δὲ χρυσίον λαβεῖν, καὶ ἔτι πρὸς τούτοις τὴν μὲν ἀπέχθειαν
τὴν πρὸς Θηβαίους καὶ Θετταλοὺς τῇ πόλει γενέσθαι,
τὴν δὲ χάριν τὴν ὑπὲρ τῶν πεπραγμένων Φιλίππῳ. 10
ὅτι δ' οὕτω ταῦτ' ἔχει, λέγε μοι τό τε τοῦ Καλλισθέ- 37
νους ψήφισμα καὶ τὴν ἐπιστολὴν τοῦ Φιλίππου, ἐξ
ὧν ἀμφοτέρων ταῦθ' ἅπανθ' ὑμῖν ἔσται φανερά.
λέγε.

238   ΨΗΦΙΣΜΑ.   5

['Επὶ Μνησιφίλου ἄρχοντος, συγκλήτου ἐκκλησίας ὑπὸ
στρατηγῶν καὶ πρυτάνεων, [καὶ] βουλῆς γνώμῃ, μαιμακτη-
ριῶνος δεκάτῃ ἀπιόντος, Καλλισθένης 'Ετεονίκου Φαληρεὺς
εἶπε μηδένα 'Αθηναίων μηδεμιᾷ παρευρέσει ἐν τῇ χώρᾳ
κοιταῖον γίγνεσθαι, ἀλλ' ἐν ἄστει καὶ Πειραιεῖ, ὅσοι μὴ ἐν 10
τοῖς φρουρίοις εἰσὶν ἀποτεταγμένοι· τούτων δ' ἑκάστους ἣν
παρέλαβον τάξιν διατηρεῖν μήτε ἀφημερεύοντας μήτε ἀπο-
κοιτοῦντας. ὃς δ' ἂν ἀπειθήσῃ τῷδε τῷ ψηφίσματι, ἔνοχος 38
ἔστω τοῖς τῆς προδοσίας ἐπιτιμίοις, ἐὰν μή τι ἀδύνατον
ἐπιδεικνύῃ περὶ ἑαυτὸν ὄν· περὶ δὲ τοῦ ἀδυνάτου ἐπικρινέτω
ὁ ἐπὶ τῶν ὅπλων στρατηγὸς καὶ ὁ ἐπὶ τῆς διοικήσεως καὶ
ὁ γραμματεὺς τῆς βουλῆς. κατακομίζειν δὲ καὶ τὰ ἐκ τῶν 5

---

4. οὐκ εἰς μακράν (sc. ὁδόν), not
much later, not a long way off : εἰς
of looking forward to an end, as in
§ 151⁸, εἰς Πυλαίαν.—τοὺς μὲν...ἐκ τῶν
ἀγρῶν (7): eleven days after the report
of the second embassy to the Assembly,
the alarming news of the surrender of
the Phocians at Thermopylae arrived.
See Hist. § 36.
7. σκευαγωγεῖν, i.e. were bringing
your goods into the towns, as ordered
by the decree of Callisthenes (§ 37).—

χρυσίον λαβεῖν : in malicious contrast
to σκευαγωγεῖν.
8. τὴν μὲν ἀπέχθειαν...Φιλίππῳ :
i.e. Athens by her vacillating course
got nothing but the ill will of Philip's
Greek friends, who believed that she
would have protected the Phocians if
she had dared to; while Philip had
all the credit for ending the Sacred
War and punishing the sacrilegious
Phocians.

ἀγρῶν πάντα τὴν ταχίστην, τὰ μὲν ἐντὸς σταδίων ἑκατὸν
εἴκοσιν εἰς ἄστυ καὶ Πειραιᾶ, τὰ δὲ ἐκτὸς σταδίων ἑκατὸν
εἴκοσιν εἰς Ἐλευσῖνα καὶ Φυλὴν καὶ Ἀφιδναν καὶ Ῥαμνοῦντα
καὶ Σούνιον.]

Ἆρ’ ἐπὶ ταύταις ταῖς ἐλπίσι τὴν εἰρήνην ἐποι- 10
εῖσθε, ἢ ταῦτ’ ἐπηγγέλλεθ’ ὑμῖν οὗτος ὁ μισθωτός ;
Λέγε δὴ τὴν ἐπιστολὴν ἣν ἔπεμψε Φίλιππος 39
μετὰ ταῦτα.

ΕΠΙΣΤΟΛΗ.

[Βασιλεὺς Μακεδόνων Φίλιππος Ἀθηναίων τῇ βουλῇ
καὶ τῷ δήμῳ χαίρειν. ἴστε ἡμᾶς παρεληλυθότας εἴσω Πυλῶν 5
καὶ τὰ κατὰ τὴν Φωκίδα ὑφ’ ἑαυτοὺς πεποιημένους, καὶ ὅσα
μὲν ἑκουσίως προσετίθετο τῶν πολισμάτων, φρουρὰς εἰσαγηο-
239 χότας, τὰ δὲ μὴ ὑπακούοντα κατὰ κράτος λαβόντες καὶ ἐξαν-
δραποδισάμενοι κατεσκάψαμεν. ἀκούων δὲ καὶ ὑμᾶς παρα-
σκευάζεσθαι βοηθεῖν αὐτοῖς γέγραφα ὑμῖν, ἵνα μὴ ἐπὶ πλέον 10
ἐνοχλῆσθε περὶ τούτων· τοῖς μὲν γὰρ ὅλοις οὐδὲν μέτριόν μοι
δοκεῖτε ποιεῖν, τὴν εἰρήνην συνθέμενοι καὶ ὁμοίως ἀντιπαρεξά-
γοντες, καὶ ταῦτα οὐδὲ συμπεριειλημμένων τῶν Φωκέων ἐν
ταῖς κοιναῖς ἡμῶν συνθήκαις. ὥστε ἐὰν μὴ ἐμμένητε τοῖς
ὡμολογημένοις, οὐδὲν προτερήσετε ἔξω τοῦ ἐφθακέναι ἀδι- 15
κοῦντες.]

Ἀκούετε ὡς σαφῶς δηλοῖ καὶ διορίζεται ἐν τῇ 40
πρὸς ὑμᾶς ἐπιστολῇ πρὸς τοὺς ἑαυτοῦ συμμάχους,
ὅτι ἐγὼ πεποίηκα ταῦτ’ ἀκόντων Ἀθηναίων

§ 38. 11. ταῦτ’ ἐπηγγέλλεθ’; i.e. how does the decree just read to you agree with the report of Aeschines (§ 35)?
§ 39. This letter must be spurious. The genuine letter would have more definite allusions to the dissatisfaction of Athens, to justify what is said of it in § 40. Grote remarks that

Demosthenes would have spoken much more severely of a letter so insolent as this one.
§ 40. 2. πρὸς συμμάχους, with δηλοῖ καὶ διορίζεται. The letter, though addressed to the Athenians, was really written for Philip's allies.
3. ὅτι before the direct quotation (M.T. 711).

καὶ λυπουμένων, ὥστ', εἴπερ εὖ φρονεῖτε, ὦ
Θηβαῖοι καὶ Θετταλοί, τούτους μὲν ἐχθροὺς 5
ὑπολήψεσθε ἐμοὶ δὲ πιστεύσετε,—οὐ τούτοις
τοῖς ῥήμασι γράψας, ταῦτα δὲ βουλόμενος δεικνύναι.. τοιγαροῦν ἐκ τούτων ᾤχετ' ἐκείνους λαβὼν
εἰς τὸ μηδ' ὁτιοῦν προορᾶν τῶν μετὰ ταῦτα μηδ'
αἰσθάνεσθαι, ἀλλ' ἐᾶσαι πάντα τὰ πράγματα ἐκεῖ- 10
νον ὑφ' ἑαυτῷ ποιήσασθαι· ἐξ ὧν ταῖς παρούσαις
συμφοραῖς οἱ ταλαίπωροι κέχρηνται. ὁ δὲ ταύτης 41
τῆς πίστεως αὐτῷ συνεργὸς καὶ συναγωνιστής, καὶ
ὁ δεῦρ' ἀπαγγείλας τὰ ψευδῆ καὶ φενακίσας ὑμᾶς,
οὗτός ἐστιν ὁ τὰ Θηβαίων ὀδυρόμενος νῦν πάθη καὶ
διεξιὼν ὡς οἰκτρά, καὶ τούτων καὶ τῶν ἐν Φωκεῦσι 5
κακῶν καὶ ὅσ' ἄλλα πεπόνθασιν οἱ Ἕλληνες ἁπάντων αὐτὸς ὢν αἴτιος. δῆλον γὰρ ὅτι σὺ μὲν ἀλγεῖς
ἐπὶ τοῖς συμβεβηκόσιν, Αἰσχίνη, καὶ τοὺς Θηβαίους
ἐλεεῖς, κτῆμ' ἔχων ἐν τῇ Βοιωτίᾳ καὶ γεωργῶν τὰ
ἐκείνων, ἐγὼ δὲ χαίρω, ὃς εὐθὺς ἐξῃτούμην ὑπὸ τοῦ 10
240 ταῦτα πράξαντος.

8. ᾤχετ' ἐκείνους λαβών, *he carried
them* (his allies) *away* (M.T.
895); the figure is continued in εἰς τό with
the infinitives.

11. ἐξ ὧν, as a result of which.

12. οἱ ταλαίπωροι: Θηβαῖοι is
added in all MSS. except Σ. Of
course the destruction of Thebes by
Alexander is chiefly meant, and this
suggests the digression in § 41; but
the condition of Thessaly after the
peace, which had been in Philip's
power since 352 B.C., may well be
included. See IX. 26: Θετταλία πῶς
ἔχει; οὐχὶ τὰς πολιτείας καὶ τὰς πόλεις
αὐτῶν παρῄρηται καὶ τετραρχίας κατέ-
στησεν, ἵνα μὴ μόνον κατὰ πόλεις ἀλλὰ
καὶ κατ' ἔθνη δουλεύωσιν;

§ 41. 1. ὁ δὲ...συνεργός, i.e. *he who
helped him thus to persuade his allies*:
with πίστεως cf. πιστεύσετε, § 40⁶.

3. ἀπαγγείλας τὰ ψευδῆ: see § 35.
In XIX. 4, Demosth. puts ὧν ἀπήγγειλε,
his report, first among the things for
which an ambassador should render
an account.

4. ὀδυρόμενος: see the solemn
and eloquent invocation of Aesch.
in III. 133, Θῆβαι δὲ, Θῆβαι, πόλις
ἀστυγείτων, κ.τ.λ., with 156, 157.

9. κτῆμ' ἔχων: Aesch. is charged
with holding a confiscated Theban
estate (κτῆμα is in Σ alone) by the
gift of Alexander; as in XIX. 145
Philocrates and Aeschines are charged
with having κτήματα καὶ γεωργίαι
παμπληθεῖς in Phocis by gift of Philip.
We have no independent evidence on
either of these charges.

10. ἐξῃτούμην: Demosth. was
among the eight or ten Attic orators
who were *demanded* by Alexander

Ἀλλὰ γὰρ ἐμπέπτωκα εἰς λόγους οὓς αὐτίκα **42**
μᾶλλον ἴσως ἁρμόσει λέγειν. ἐπάνειμι δὴ πάλιν
ἐπὶ τὰς ἀποδείξεις ὡς τὰ τούτων ἀδικήματα τῶν
νυνὶ παρόντων πραγμάτων γέγονεν αἴτια.
Ἐπειδὴ γὰρ ἐξηπάτησθε μὲν ὑμεῖς ὑπὸ τοῦ 5
Φιλίππου διὰ τούτων τῶν ἐν ταῖς πρεσβείαις μισθω-
σάντων ἑαυτοὺς καὶ οὐδὲν ἀληθὲς ὑμῖν ἀπαγγειλάντων, ἐξηπάτηντο δὲ οἱ ταλαίπωροι Φωκεῖς καὶ
ἀνήρηντο αἱ πόλεις αὐτῶν, τί ἐγένετο ; οἱ μὲν κα- **43**
τάπτυστοι Θετταλοὶ καὶ ἀναίσθητοι Θηβαῖοι φίλον,
εὐεργέτην, σωτῆρα τὸν Φίλιππον ἡγοῦντο· πάντ᾽
ἐκεῖνος ἦν αὐτοῖς· οὐδὲ φωνὴν ἤκουον εἴ τις ἄλλο τι
βούλοιτο λέγειν. ὑμεῖς δ᾽ ὑφορώμενοι τὰ πεπραγ- 5
μένα καὶ δυσχεραίνοντες ἤγετε τὴν εἰρήνην ὅμως·
οὐ γὰρ ἦν ὅ τι ἂν ἐποιεῖτε. καὶ οἱ ἄλλοι δ᾽ Ἕλληνες,
ὁμοίως ὑμῖν πεφενακισμένοι καὶ διημαρτηκότες ὧν
ἤλπισαν, ἦγον τὴν εἰρήνην [ἄσμενοι, καὶ] αὐτοὶ τρό-

after his destruction of Thebes in
335 B.C.; Aeschines was not. See
Grote XII. 59—62.

§§ 42—49. After the digression
in § 41, the orator here speaks of the
disastrous consequences which have
come from the peace and from the
corruption by which it was made, and
of the miserable fate of most of the
traitors in Greece who aided Philip
in his schemes.

§ 42. 5. **ἐπειδὴ** here has three
pluperfects, while commonly it has
the less precise aorist, as in §§ 25¹, 32¹
(M.T. 59). So in Latin *postquam
venit* is more common than *postquam
venerat*. Both ἐπειδή and *postquam*
contain the idea of *after that*, which
the plpf. only emphasizes.

6. **διὰ τούτων τῶν......μισθωσάν-
των** (i.e. οἳ ἐμίσθωσαν): contrast διὰ
τούτους οὐχὶ πεισθέντας, § 32², and see
note.

§ 43. 2. **ἀναίσθητοι**: see note
on § 35¹⁰.

3. **πάντ᾽ ἐκεῖνος ἦν:** cf. πάντ᾽ ἦν
Ἀλέξανδρος, XXIII. 120; Εὔβοια αὐτοῖς
πάντα ἦν, Thuc. VIII. 95; Demetrius
iis unus omnia est, Liv. XL. 11.

4. **οὐδὲ...βούλοιτο** (M.T. 462):
ἤκουον is strongly frequentative, like
ἡγοῦντο (3), and ἄλλο τι is anything
opposed to φίλον, εὐεργέτην, σωτῆρα.

5. **ὑφορώμενοι**, *viewing with suspicion* (ὑπό like *sub* in *suspicio*).

7. **οὐ...ἐποιεῖτε**: not MSS. (but
not Σ) add μόνοι. This passage represents the state of mind in which
Demosthenes delivered his speech on
the Peace (V.) in 346 B.C. See Hist.
§ 40.

9. **[ἄσμενοι, καὶ]:** Σ and the newly
found Oxyrhynchus papyrus (2nd cent.
A.D.) omit these words.—**αὐτοὶ ...
πολεμούμενοι**, *though they themselves
in a certain way had been warred*

πον τιν' ἐκ πολλοῦ πολεμούμενοι. ὅτε γὰρ περιιὼν 44
Φίλιππος Ἰλλυριοὺς καὶ Τριβαλλοὺς, τινὰς δὲ καὶ
τῶν Ἑλλήνων κατεστρέφετο, καὶ δυνάμεις πολλὰς
καὶ μεγάλας ἐποιεῖθ' ὑφ' ἑαυτῷ, καί τινες τῶν ἐκ
τῶν πόλεων ἐπὶ τῇ τῆς εἰρήνης ἐξουσίᾳ βαδίζοντες 5
ἐκεῖσε διεφθείροντο, ὧν εἷς οὗτος ἦν, τότε πάντες
ἐφ' οὓς ταῦτα παρεσκευάζετ' ἐκεῖνος ἐπολεμοῦντο.
εἰ δὲ μὴ ᾐσθάνοντο, ἕτερος λόγος οὗτος, οὐ πρὸς ἐμέ.
ἐγὼ μὲν γὰρ προὔλεγον καὶ διεμαρτυρόμην καὶ παρ' 45
ὑμῖν ἀεὶ καὶ ὅποι πεμφθείην· αἱ δὲ πόλεις ἐνόσουν,
τῶν μὲν ἐν τῷ πολιτεύεσθαι καὶ πράττειν δωρο-
δοκούντων καὶ διαφθειρομένων ἐπὶ χρήμασι, τῶν δ'
241 ἰδιωτῶν καὶ πολλῶν τὰ μὲν οὐ προορωμένων, τὰ δὲ 5

against for a long time: πολεμούμενοι (impf.) is past to ἦγον, which covers the whole time of the peace to 340 B.C. See ἐπολεμοῦντο, § 44⁷.

§ 44. 2. Ἰλλυριοὺς καὶ Τριβαλλοὺς: Diodorus (XVI. 69) mentions a victorious inroad of Philip into Illyria in 344 B.C., and Porphyrius Tyr. (Müller, Hist. Gr. III. p. 691) says of Philip, οὗτος τοὺς περὶ τὴν χώραν ἅπαντας ἐδουλώσατο πολεμίους, μεγάλην κτησάμενος δύναμιν, καὶ Τριβαλλοὺς ὑποτάξας.

3. Ἑλλήνων: see Grote XI. 612—614, and Hist. §§ 41, 46—49.—δυνάμεις, like our forces, but including allies (even without troops): see § 234¹.

4. τῶν ἐκ τῶν πόλεων: he counts Aesch. as one of those who took advantage of the peace to visit Macedonia, implying that the process of corruption was still going on. In XIX. 13 he says he first discovered the corruption of Aesch. on the return of the first embassy in the spring of 346 B.C.

8. ἕτερος λόγος οὗτος, this is another matter: cf. ἄλλος ἂν εἴη λόγος οὗτος, IX. 16; ἄλλος ἂν ἦν λόγος, [XIII.] 7.

§ 45. 1. διεμαρτυρόμην, protested (called Gods and men to witness): cf. obtestor. See § 199⁶.—παρ' ὑμῖν probably refers to orations VI., VIII. and IX.

2. ὅποι πεμφθείην, whithersoever I was sent, referring to the embassies mentioned in § 244 (below) and probably to others. In § 244⁴ we have ὅποι ἐπέμφθην, referring to some of the same embassies as ὅποι πεμφθείην here. But there the leading clause, οὐδαμοῦ...ἀπῆλθον, is particular, and its verb is aorist, not imperfect (as here); the relative clause is therefore particular and has the indicative regularly (M. T. 536). If he had said I always came off superior in § 244⁴, we should have ὅποι πεμφθείην there: see ἐν οἷς κρατηθεῖεν...κατεστρέφετο, § 244⁹.—ἐνόσουν: Demosth. is especially fond of this figure of a diseased state: see II. 21; IX. 12, 39, 50; XIX. 259 (West.).

3. τῶν...πράττειν (one substantive): cf. § 11²,³ and note on § 4⁶.

4. ἐπὶ χρήμασι, for (with a view to) money; not by money, like ὑπὸ χρημάτων.

5. ἰδιωτῶν: here opposed to τῶν...

τῇ καθ' ἡμέραν ῥαστώνῃ καὶ σχολῇ δελεαζομένων,
καὶ τοιουτονί τι πάθος πεπονθότων ἀπάντων, πλὴν
οὐκ ἐφ' ἑαυτοὺς ἑκάστων οἰομένων τὸ δεινὸν ἥξειν
καὶ διὰ τῶν ἑτέρων κινδύνων τὰ ἑαυτῶν ἀσφαλῶς
σχήσειν ὅταν βούλωνται. εἶτ' οἶμαι συμβέβηκε 46
τοῖς μὲν πλήθεσιν ἀντὶ τῆς πολλῆς καὶ ἀκαίρου
ῥαθυμίας τὴν ἐλευθερίαν ἀπολωλεκέναι, τοῖς δὲ
προεστηκόσι καὶ τἄλλα πλὴν ἑαυτοὺς οἰομένοις
πωλεῖν πρώτους ἑαυτοὺς πεπρακόσιν αἰσθέσθαι· 5
ἀντὶ γὰρ φίλων καὶ ξένων, ἃ τότ' ὠνομάζοντο ἡνίκ'
ἐδωροδόκουν, νῦν κόλακες καὶ θεοῖς ἐχθροὶ καὶ τἄλλ'
ἃ προσήκει πάντ' ἀκούουσιν. οὐδεὶς γὰρ, ἄνδρες 47
Ἀθηναῖοι, τὸ τοῦ προδιδόντος συμφέρον ζητῶν
χρήματ' ἀναλίσκει, οὐδ' ἐπειδὰν ὧν ἂν πρίηται
κύριος γένηται τῷ προδότῃ συμβούλῳ περὶ τῶν
λοιπῶν ἔτι χρῆται· οὐδὲν γὰρ ἂν ἦν εὐδαιμονέστε- 5
ρον προδότου. ἀλλ' οὐκ ἔστι ταῦτα· πόθεν ; πολλοῦ
γε καὶ δεῖ. ἀλλ' ἐπειδὰν τῶν πραγμάτων ἐγκρατὴς
ὁ ζητῶν ἄρχειν καταστῇ, καὶ τῶν ταῦτα ἀποδομένων

πράττειν (3), private citizens; generally,
any men who are not of a given class,
as not senators, XIX. 18; cf. ἰατρὸς
καὶ ἰδιώτης, Thuc. II. 48.
6. δελεαζομένων, caught, as by a
bait (δέλεαρ).
7. τοιουτονί ... πεπονθότων is explained by ἑκάστων οἰομένων κ.τ.λ.—
πλὴν οὐκ ἐφ' ἑαυτοὺς, upon all but
themselves.
9. τῶν ἑτέρων κινδύνων, others'
(not other) dangers.
§ 46. 2. τοῖς μὲν πλήθεσιν, the
common people (cf. τῶν πολλῶν, § 45⁵)
in various states : cf. τῶν μὲν...τῶν δὲ
in § 45³,⁴.
3, 5. ἀπολωλεκέναι (M.T. 109):
i.e. the result has been that they have
lost their liberty; the idea of the perfect in the next clause appears more

naturally in πεπρακόσιν (5) than in
αἰσθέσθαι, to find out that they have
sold themselves first (M.T. 904). For
the case of πεπρακόσιν see G. 928¹.
8. ἀκούουσιν, audiunt, they hear
themselves called : cf. Hor. Ep. I. 16,
17, si curas esse quod audis.
§ 47. 3. ἐπειδὰν...γένηται, after
he has become master of what he has
bought (M.T. 90). For the assimila-
tion of ὧν ἂν πρίηται, which really
conditions κύριος γένηται, see M.T.
563.
5. οὐδὲν ... προδότου, for (otherwise) nothing would be happier than
a traitor.
6. πόθεν;...δεῖ : cf. §§ 52², 140⁹,
and πῶς γάρ; § 312⁷.
8. καὶ, also, with τῶν ἀποδομένων.

δεσπότης ἐστὶ, τὴν δὲ πονηρίαν εἰδὼς τότε δὴ, τότε
καὶ μισεῖ καὶ ἀπιστεῖ καὶ προπηλακίζει. σκοπεῖτε **48**
δέ· καὶ γὰρ εἰ παρελήλυθεν ὁ τῶν πραγμάτων
καιρὸς, ὁ τοῦ γ᾽ εἰδέναι τὰ τοιαῦτα καιρὸς ἀεὶ
πάρεστι τοῖς εὖ φρονοῦσι. μέχρι τούτου Λασθένης
φίλος ὠνομάζετο, ἕως προὔδωκεν Ὄλυνθον· μέχρι 5
τούτου Τιμόλας, ἕως ἀπώλεσε Θήβας· μέχρι τούτου
Εὔδικος καὶ Σῖμος ὁ Λαρισαῖος, ἕως Θετταλίαν ὑπὸ
Φιλίππῳ ἐποίησαν. εἶτ᾽ ἐλαυνομένων καὶ ὑβριζο-
242 μένων καὶ τί κακὸν οὐχὶ πασχόντων πᾶσ᾽ ἡ οἰκουμένη μεστὴ γέγονεν. τί δ᾽ Ἀρίστρατος ἐν Σικυῶνι, 10
καὶ τί Πέριλλος ἐν Μεγάροις ; οὐκ ἀπερριμμένοι ;
ἐξ ὧν καὶ σαφέστατ᾽ ἄν τις ἴδοι ὅτι ὁ μάλιστα **49**
φυλάττων τὴν ἑαυτοῦ πατρίδα καὶ πλεῖστ᾽ ἀντιλέ-
γων τούτοις, οὗτος ὑμῖν, Αἰσχίνη, τοῖς προδιδοῦσι
καὶ μισθαρνοῦσι τὸ ἔχειν ἐφ᾽ ὅτῳ δωροδοκήσετε

§ 48. 4. **μέχρι τούτου** with ἕως,
twice repeated. See πολλὰ in § 81^{2,3};
cf. οὐχ in § 250^{10,11} and 322^{1-3}. Expressions like this show the relative
character of ἕως and other particles
meaning *until*. (M.T. 611, 612.)—
Λασθένης: Lasthenes and Euthycrates
are often mentioned as traitors who
betrayed Olynthus to Philip: see Plut.
Mor. p. 178 B: τῶν δὲ περὶ Λασθένην
τὸν Ὀλύνθιον ἐγκαλούντων καὶ ἀγανακ-
τούντων ὅτι προδότας αὐτοὺς ἔνιοι τῶν
περὶ τὸν Φίλιππον ἀποκαλοῦσι, σκαιοὺς
ἔφη (sc. Φίλιππος) φύσει καὶ ἀγροί-
κους εἶναι Μακεδόνας καὶ τὴν σκαφὴν
σκαφὴν λέγοντας, i.e. *they called a
spade a spade.*
6. **Τιμόλας** : Timolaus was a
Theban, who was probably active in
causing the surrender of Thebes to
Philip after Chaeronea. Theopompus
calls him the greatest voluptuary who
was ever engaged in state affairs. See
§ 295^{15}.
7. **Σῖμος** : Simus belonged to the

Thessalian house of the Aleuadae at
Larissa, who called in Philip against
the tyrants of Pherae in 352 B.C. See
Hist. § 5. Eudicus is not otherwise
known.
9. **τί κακὸν οὐχὶ πασχόντων;** =
οὐδὲν κακὸν οὐχὶ (i.e. τὰ πάντα κακά)
πασχόντων.—**πᾶσ᾽ ἡ οἰκουμένη** is properly *the whole habitable world*, i.e.
the Greek world; as in Ev. Luc. ii. 1
it is *the whole Roman world*. But
here it is merely a loose expression
say, we should call this world full of these
with no special limit. We should
say, "all the world is full of these
wretches."
10. **Ἀρίστρατος**, a tyrant of Sicyon.
11. **Πέριλλος**, of Megara : see
XIX. 295. Perillus and Aristratus are
in the "black-list" of Cor. § 295.
For Philip's intrigues in Megara see
Grote XI. 613, 621.
§ 49. 4. **τὸ ἔχειν ... περιποιεῖ,**
*secures for you your opportunities for
being bribed* (the wherewithal to be
bribed).

περιποιεῖ, καὶ διὰ τοὺς πολλοὺς τουτωνὶ καὶ τοὺς 5
ἀνθισταμένους τοῖς ὑμετέροις βουλήμασιν ὑμεῖς ἐστε
σῷοι καὶ ἔμμισθοι, ἐπεὶ διά γε ὑμᾶς αὐτοὺς πάλαι ἂν
ἀπωλώλειτε.

Καὶ περὶ μὲν τῶν τότε πραχθέντων ἔχων ἔτι 50
πολλὰ λέγειν, καὶ ταῦτα ἡγοῦμαι πλείω τῶν ἱκανῶν
εἰρῆσθαι. αἴτιος δ' οὗτος, ὥσπερ ἑωλοκρασίαν τινά
μου τῆς πονηρίας τῆς ἑαυτοῦ [καὶ τῶν ἀδικημάτων]
κατασκεδάσας, ἣν ἀναγκαῖον ἦν πρὸς τοὺς νεωτέρους 5
τῶν πεπραγμένων ἀπολύσασθαι. παρηνώχλησθε δ'
ἴσως οἱ καὶ πρὶν ἐμὲ εἰπεῖν ὁτιοῦν εἰδότες τὴν τούτου
τότε μισθαρνίαν. καίτοι φιλίαν γε καὶ ξενίαν αὐτὴν 51
ὀνομάζει, καὶ νῦν εἶπέ που λέγων ὁ τὴν Ἀλεξάνδρου ξενίαν ὀνειδίζων ἐμοί. ἐγώ σοι ξενίαν

6. **ἐστε σῷοι καὶ ἔμμισθοι**, i.e. *you rvive to be venal.*

7. **διά...αὐτοὺς**, *if you were left to yourselves* (M.T. 472). The orator surprises his audience by this original reason why the Athenian traitors have been saved from the fate of traitors in other states, i.e. the honest citizens thwart their schemes and thus save them from the ruin of success. This brilliant attack is followed up sharply in what follows.

§§ **50—52** : the peroration to the argument on the Peace of Philocrates.

§ **50**. 1. **τῶν τότε πραχθέντων**, i.e. the transactions concerning the peace. This suggestion that he will drop the subject makes this sudden recurrence to the charge of venality all the more effective.

3. **αἴτιος**, i.e. of my speaking πλείω τῶν ἱκανῶν.—**ὥσπερ**, *as it were* (M. T. 867), with ἑωλοκρασίαν, not with κατασκεδάσας.—**ἑωλοκρασίαν**, a *mixture of stale dregs*, lit. *a mixture of the refuse* (esp. *heel-taps*) *of last night's feast* (ἕωλα, *hesterna*). This burst of indignation refers especially

to the audacity of Aeschines (III. 60) in charging Demosthenes with the same coöperation with Philocrates in making the peace which he had once claimed for himself as a merit (I. 174). See § 17⁶ (above). Demosthenes calls this treatment "deluging me with the stale refuse of his own villainy."

4. **[καὶ τῶν ἀδικημάτων]** is in all MSS., but is omitted in many ancient quotations of the passage.

5. **νεωτέρους** : the youngest judges present might have been only fourteen years old in 346 B.C.

6. **ἀπολύσασθαι**, *to clear myself of* : see Thuc. VIII. 87, ἀπολύεσθαι πρὸς αὐτοὺς τὰς διαβολάς.—**παρηνώχλησθε**: addressed to the older judges (cf. ἐνοχλεῖ, § 4³).

§ **51**. 1. **φιλίαν, ξενίαν**, properly *friendship* and *guest-friendship*, here seem to be used with little thought of the distinction. Cf. ξενίαν Ἀλεξάνδρου (3) and οὔτε Φιλ. ξένον οὔτε Ἀλεξ. φίλον (below).

2. **εἶπε λέγων**: cf. εἶπε φωνῶν, Aeschyl. Ag. 205, "spake, saying."

3. **ὀνειδίζων**: Aesch. had said (66),

Ἀλεξάνδρου ; πόθεν λαβόντι ἢ πῶς ἀξιωθέντι ; οὔτε
Φιλίππου ξένον οὔτ' Ἀλεξάνδρου φίλον εἴποιμ' ἂν 5
ἐγώ σε, οὐχ οὕτω μαίνομαι, εἰ μὴ καὶ τοὺς θεριστὰς
καὶ τοὺς ἄλλο τι μισθοῦ πράττοντας φίλους καὶ
ξένους δεῖ καλεῖν τῶν μισθωσαμένων. ἀλλ' οὐκ ἔστι 52
ταῦτα· πόθεν ; πολλοῦ γε καὶ δεῖ. ἀλλὰ μισθωτὸν
ἐγώ σε Φιλίππου πρότερον καὶ νῦν Ἀλεξάνδρου
καλῶ, καὶ οὗτοι πάντες. εἰ δ' ἀπιστεῖς, ἐρώτησον
αὐτούς· μᾶλλον δ' ἐγὼ τοῦθ' ὑπὲρ σοῦ ποιήσω. 5
243 πότερον ὑμῖν, ὦ ἄνδρες Ἀθηναῖοι, δοκεῖ μισθωτὸς
Αἰσχίνης ἢ ξένος εἶναι Ἀλεξάνδρου ; ἀκούεις ἃ
λέγουσιν.

Βούλομαι τοίνυν ἤδη καὶ περὶ τῆς γραφῆς αὐτῆς 53
ἀπολογήσασθαι καὶ διεξελθεῖν τὰ πεπραγμέν' ἐμαυτῷ,
ἵνα καίπερ εἰδὼς Αἰσχίνης ὅμως ἀκούσῃ δι' ἅ φημι

ὁ τὴν ξενίαν ἐμοὶ προφέρων τὴν
Ἀλεξάνδρου.
4. πόθεν … ἀξιωθέντι; with dramatic energy for πόθεν ἔλαβες ἢ πῶς ἠξιώθης; cf. § 128³.
6. θεριστὰς, *reapers*, properly *extra farm-hands*, called in at the harvest.
§ 52. 4. οὗτοι πάντες probably included both court and audience.
6. μισθωτὸς : most MSS. (Σ only by correction) read μίσθωτος. following the absurd story of Ulpian (see Schol.), that Demosth. pronounced this word μίσθωτος to make the judges correct his accent by shouting out the very word μισθωτός which he wanted

to hear. It is much more likely— indeed, it is certain—that he saw by the faces of his hearers that it was safe for him to put this question boldly; and he was probably greeted by an overwhelming shout of μισθωτός, μισθωτός, from both court and audience. The judges, more than four-fifths of whom voted in a few hours to acquit Ctesiphon and to condemn Aeschines to a fine and ἀτιμία, were by this time ready to respond to such a sudden appeal, after listening to this most conclusive argument with its brilliant close.

---

§§ 53—125. Having finished his reply to the charges foreign to the indictment, he now proceeds to the indictment itself. We have (1) an introduction (§§ 53–59), (2) a discussion of his public life (§§ 60—109), (3) a reply to the charge that the

orator was ἐπεύθυνος when it was proposed to crown him (§§ 110—119), (4) a defence of the proposal to crown him in the theatre (§§ 120, 121), and (5) a conclusion (§§ 122—125).
§§ 53—59. Introduction, including the reading of the indictment.

καὶ τούτων τῶν προβεβουλευμένων καὶ πολλῷ μει-
ζόνων ἔτι τούτων δωρεῶν δίκαιος εἶναι τυγχάνειν. 5
καί μοι λέγε τὴν γραφὴν αὐτὴν λαβών.

ΓΡΑΦΗ.   54

[Ἐπὶ Χαιρώνδου ἄρχοντος, ἐλαφηβολιῶνος ἕκτῃ ἱσταμένου, Αἰσχίνης Ἀτρομήτου Κοθωκίδης ἀπήνεγκε πρὸς τὸν
ἄρχοντα παρανόμων κατὰ Κτησιφῶντος τοῦ Λεωσθένους
Ἀναφλυστίου, ὅτι ἔγραψε παράνομον ψήφισμα, ὡς ἄρα δεῖ 5
στεφανῶσαι Δημοσθένην Δημοσθένους Παιανιέα χρυσῷ στεφάνῳ, καὶ ἀναγορεῦσαι ἐν τῷ θεάτρῳ Διονυσίοις τοῖς μεγάλοις,
τραγῳδοῖς καινοῖς, ὅτι στεφανοῖ ὁ δῆμος Δημοσθένην Δημοσθένους Παιανιέα χρυσῷ στεφάνῳ ἀρετῆς ἕνεκα, καὶ εὐνοίας ἧς
ἔχων διατελεῖ εἴς τε τοὺς Ἕλληνας ἅπαντας καὶ τὸν δῆμον 10
τὸν Ἀθηναίων, καὶ ἀνδραγαθίας, καὶ διότι διατελεῖ πράττων
καὶ λέγων τὰ βέλτιστα τῷ δήμῳ καὶ πρόθυμός ἐστι ποιεῖν
ὅ τι ἂν δύνηται ἀγαθόν, πάντα ταῦτα ψευδῆ γράψας καὶ 55
παράνομα, τῶν νόμων οὐκ ἐώντων πρῶτον μὲν ψευδεῖς γραφὰς
εἰς τὰ δημόσια γράμματα καταβάλλεσθαι, εἶτα τὸν ὑπεύθυνον
στεφανοῦν (ἔστι δὲ Δημοσθένης τειχοποιὸς καὶ ἐπὶ τῷ θεωρικῷ τεταγμένος), ἔτι δὲ μὴ ἀναγορεύειν τὸν στέφανον ἐν 5
244 τῷ θεάτρῳ Διονυσίοις τραγῳδῶν τῇ καινῇ, ἀλλ᾽ ἐὰν μὲν ἡ
βουλὴ στεφανοῖ, ἐν τῷ βουλευτηρίῳ ἀνειπεῖν, ἐὰν δὲ ἡ πόλις,
ἐν Πυκνὶ ἐν τῇ ἐκκλησίᾳ. τίμημα τάλαντα πεντήκοντα.

§ 53. 4. τῶν προβεβουλευμένων
(pass.), strictly accurate for *the pro-*
visions of the προβούλευμα of Ctesiphon, which had passed only the
Senate. The corresponding phrase
for the items of a ψήφισμα would be
τῶν ἐψηφισμένων. Cf. τῶν γεγραμμένων, § 56⁴.
5. δίκαιος εἶναι, *that I deserve*:
personal use of δίκαιος (M.T. 762).
§§ 54, 55. This spurious document once passed for the "single
undoubtedly genuine Athenian indictment." Chaerondas was archon in

338—337 B.C.; but the indictment
was brought in the spring of 336.
The γραφὴ παρανόμων came before
the θεσμοθέται, not before the Chief
Archon.
The expression τραγῳδοῖς καινοῖς,
§ 54⁸, *on the day of the new tragedians,*
i.e. when new tragedies were performed, is confirmed by τοῖς τραγῳδοῖς,
Aesch. III. 45. In § 55⁶ τραγῳδῶν τῇ
καινῇ is probably corrupt.
See note on the spurious προβούλευμα of Ctesiphon in § 118.

κλητῆρες Κηφισοφῶν Κηφισοφῶντος Ῥαμνούσιος, Κλέων
Κλέωνος Κοθωκίδης.] 10

Ἃ μὲν διώκει τοῦ ψηφίσματος, ὦ ἄνδρες Ἀθη- 56
ναῖοι, ταῦτ' ἐστιν. ἐγὼ δ' ἀπ' αὐτῶν τούτων πρῶτον
οἶμαι δῆλον ὑμῖν ποιήσειν ὅτι πάντα δικαίως ἀπολο-
γήσομαι· τὴν γὰρ αὐτὴν τούτῳ ποιησάμενος τῶν
γεγραμμένων τάξιν, περὶ πάντων ἐρῶ καθ' ἕκαστον 5
ἐφεξῆς καὶ οὐδὲν ἑκὼν παραλείψω. τοῦ μὲν οὖν 57
γράψαι πράττοντα καὶ λέγοντα τὰ βέλτιστά με τῷ
δήμῳ διατελεῖν καὶ πρόθυμον εἶναι ποιεῖν ὅ τι δύνα-
μαι ἀγαθόν, καὶ ἐπαινεῖν ἐπὶ τούτοις, ἐν τοῖς πεπολιτευμένοις τὴν κρίσιν εἶναι νομίζω· ἀπὸ γὰρ τούτων 5
ἐξεταζομένων εὑρεθήσεται εἴτ' ἀληθῆ περὶ ἐμοῦ
γέγραφε Κτησιφῶν ταῦτα καὶ προσήκοντα εἴτε καὶ

§ 56. 1. **Ἃ μὲν διώκει** : the
passages of the decree quoted in the
indictment are all that are accused of
illegality.
3. **πάντα δικαίως ἀπολογήσομαι** :
this is a sarcastic allusion to the demand of Aesch. (202) that the court
compel Demosth., if he is allowed to
speak at all, to follow his opponent's
order of argument : ἀξιώσατε τὸν
Δημοσθένην τὸν αὐτὸν τρόπον ἀπολο-
γεῖσθαι ὅνπερ κἀγὼ κατηγόρηκα. See
note on § 2⁶. It happens that Aesch.
states the charges in the indictment in
the order in which Demosth. wishes
to reply to them, just the order which
Aesch. is anxious to prevent him
from following : in his speech he has
followed an entirely different order.
See Essay I. § 4.
4. **τῶν γεγραμμένων** (pass.), *of the
items of the indictment*: see note on
§ 53⁴. γέγραμμαι and ἐγράφην may
be used as passives of both γράφω,
propose (a bill), and γράφομαι, *indict*:
see δικαίως γεγραμμένα, XXIII. 101,
ᾧ γέγραπται, *ibid.* 18; τὰ γραφέντα,
the proposed measures, Cor. § 86⁴; οὐδὲ

γραφέντα, *not even indicted*, § 222⁸.
But γέγραμμαι is generally middle
(seldom passive, as here) of γράφομαι,
indict : see § 59⁵, γεγραμμένος ταῦτα :
cf. γέγραψαι, § 119².
5. **καθ' ἕκαστον ἐφεξῆς** : by taking
up each point in the order of the indictment, he will ensure completeness
in his defence. The same sarcasm is
kept up.
§ 57. 1. **τοῦ γράψαι...καὶ ἐπαινεῖν**
(sc. Κτησιφῶντα) depends on τὴν
κρίσιν (5). πράττοντα...ἀγαθὸν (2—4)
is in substance quoted from the decree:
cf. § 59⁴. Aesch. (III. 49) professes
to quote the exact words, ὅτι διατελεῖ
καὶ λέγων καὶ πράττων τὰ ἄριστα τῷ
δήμῳ: cf. other references in Aesch.
101, 237.
4. **ἐπαινεῖν** : see § 113³ and note.
6—8. **ἀληθῆ, προσήκοντα**, and
ψευδῆ are predicates to ταῦτα (sc.
ὄντα).—**εἴτε καὶ ψευδῆ** : καὶ, *on the
other hand* (perhaps untranslatable),
expresses parallelism with ἀληθῆ : cf.
εἴτε καὶ μή, § 58⁵. See note on καί
before διεκωλύθη, § 60⁴.

ψευδῆ· τὸ δὲ μὴ προσγράψαντα ἐπειδὰν τὰς 58
εὐθύνας δῶ στεφανοῦν καὶ ἀνειπεῖν ἐν τῷ θεάτρῳ
τὸν στέφανον κελεῦσαι, κοινωνεῖν μὲν ἡγοῦμαι καὶ
τοῦτο τοῖς πεπολιτευμένοις, εἴτ' ἄξιός εἰμι τοῦ
στεφάνου καὶ τῆς ἀναρρήσεως τῆς ἐν τούτοις εἴτε 5
καὶ μή· ἔτι μέντοι καὶ τοὺς νόμους δεικτέον εἶναί
μοι δοκεῖ καθ' οὓς ταῦτα γράφειν ἐξῆν τούτῳ.
οὑτωσὶ μὲν, ὦ ἄνδρες Ἀθηναῖοι, δικαίως καὶ ἁπλῶς
τὴν ἀπολογίαν ἔγνωκα ποιεῖσθαι, βαδιοῦμαι δ' ἐπ'
αὐτὰ ἃ πέπρακταί μοι. καί με μηδεὶς ὑπολάβῃ 59
ἀπαρτᾶν τὸν λόγον τῆς γραφῆς, ἐὰν εἰς Ἑλληνικὰς
πράξεις καὶ λόγους ἐμπέσω· ὁ γὰρ διώκων τοῦ
245 ψηφίσματος τὸ λέγειν καὶ πράττειν τὰ ἄριστά με
καὶ γεγραμμένος ταῦθ' ὡς οὐκ ἀληθῆ, οὗτός ἐστιν 5
ὁ τοὺς περὶ ἁπάντων τῶν ἐμοὶ πεπολιτευμένων
λόγους οἰκείους καὶ ἀναγκαίους τῇ γραφῇ πεποιηκώς.
εἶτα καὶ πολλῶν προαιρέσεων οὐσῶν τῆς πολιτείας

§ 58. 1. τὸ...κελεῦσαι (3), the
bidding me (in his decree) to be
crowned...and the crown to be proclaimed in the theatre (στεφανοῦν and
ἀνειπεῖν in the usual active form):
this clause is repeated in τοῦτο (4)
as subject of κοινωνεῖν.—μὴ προσγράψαντα...δῶ : Aesch. makes it a
special act of shamelessness in Ctesiphon (see 11, 12) to omit this saving
clause. It was frequently added in
such decrees: see C. Att. II. no. 114
(343 B.C.), στεφανῶσαι χρυσῷ στεφάνῳ
ἐπειδὰν τὰς εὐθύνας δῷ. This proviso,
according to Aesch. (12), did not
make the decree legal, though it
showed a sense of shame in the
mover.
3. κοινωνεῖν ... πεπολιτευμένοις,
εἴτ'...καὶ μή (6), lit. I think this too
is concerned with my public acts,
(namely with the question) whether
I deserve the crown etc. or not. The
loose relation of εἴτ' ἄξιός εἰμι κ.τ.λ. to

τοῖς πεπολιτευμένοις, which it explains,
is permissible after the full form in
§ 57[1-5]; without this it would be
obscure.
5. ἐν τούτοις: i.e. before the people
(in the theatre).
6. τοὺς νόμους : the arguments are
given in §§ 110—121.—δεικτέον εἶναι
= δεικνύναι δεῖν.
9. βαδιοῦμαι, I will proceed (cf.
4[7]).
§ 59. 2. Ἑλληνικὰς...λόγους,
i.e. a discussion of our foreign policy,
i.e. our relations to other Greek states.
See note on οἰκείων, Ἑλληνικῶν, and
ξενικῶν, § 311[5]. Demosthenes selected
foreign affairs as his special department : see § 62[6].
3. τοῦ ψηφίσματος, depending on
ὁ λέγειν...με, i.e. the clause declaring
etc.
5. γεγραμμένος (middle): see note
on § 56[4].
8. προαιρέσεων τῆς πολιτείας,

τὴν περὶ τὰς Ἑλληνικὰς πράξεις εἱλόμην ἐγώ, ὥστε
καὶ τὰς ἀποδείξεις ἐκ τούτων δίκαιός εἰμι ποιεῖσθαι. 10
Ἃ μὲν οὖν πρὸ τοῦ πολιτεύεσθαι καὶ δημηγο- 60
ρεῖν ἐμὲ προὔλαβε καὶ κατέσχε Φίλιππος, ἐάσω·
οὐδὲν γὰρ ἡγοῦμαι τούτων εἶναι πρὸς ἐμέ· ἃ δ' ἀφ'
ἧς ἡμέρας ἐπὶ ταῦτ' ἐπέστην ἐγὼ καὶ διεκωλύθη,
ταῦτ' ἀναμνήσω καὶ τούτων ὑφέξω λόγον, τοσοῦτον 5
ὑπειπών. πλεονέκτημα, ἄνδρες Ἀθηναῖοι, μέγ' ὑπῆρξε Φιλίππῳ. παρὰ γὰρ τοῖς Ἕλλησιν, οὐ τισὶν, 61
ἀλλ' ἅπασιν ὁμοίως, φορὰν προδοτῶν καὶ δωροδό-
κων καὶ θεοῖς ἐχθρῶν ἀνθρώπων συνέβη γενέσθαι
τοσαύτην ὅσην οὐδείς πω πρότερον μέμνηται γε-
γονυῖαν· οὓς συναγωνιστὰς καὶ συνεργοὺς λαβὼν 5
καὶ πρότερον κακῶς τοὺς Ἕλληνας ἔχοντας πρὸς

departments of the government (open
to choice).

§§ 60—109. In this general defence of his public policy, (1) he defends his fixed principle of opposition
to Philip's aggressions (§§ 60—72);
(2) he speaks of the events which immediately preceded the outbreak of
war with Philip in 340 B.C. (§§ 73—
101), avoiding all mention of the later
Amphissian war and the other events
which led to the battle of Chaeronea;
(3) he defends his trierarchic law
(§§ 102—109).

§ **60.** 1. **πρὸ τοῦ πολιτεύεσθαι** :
the public life of Demosth. properly
began with his speech on the Symmories in 354 B.C. (Hist. § 8); but
his responsibility for the foreign policy
of Athens began after the peace of
346 (§ 18²). Still, his fixed policy of
opposing Philip, though unsuccessful
at first, goes back at least to the
First Philippic in 351; and he is here
(§§ 60—72) defending his public life
as a whole, seldom mentioning his
special acts. He reserves these for a

later part of his argument (§§ 79—94,
and after § 159).

2. **προὔλαβε** and **κατέσχε** combined have the idea of securing by
being beforehand.

4. **καὶ διεκωλύθη** : see note on
καὶ in § 57⁷. καὶ expresses parallelism with προὔλαβε καὶ κατέσχε, and
strengthens the antithesis between
what Philip did before Dem. appeared
and what he was prevented from doing
afterwards. ἃ διεκωλύθη represents
an active form ἃ αὐτὸν διεκώλυσα : no
infinitive is understood.

5. **τοσοῦτον ὑπειπών,** after pre-
mising the following. Demosth. has
no preference for the forms in -δε
(e.g. τοσόνδε) in referring to what is
to follow.

6. **ὑπῆρξε:** cf. ὑπάρξαι μοι, § 1³.

§ **61.** 2. **φορὰν,** a crop: see the
list of this crop of traitors in § 295.
For φορά, rush, see note on § 271⁶.

6. **καὶ πρότερον...ἔχοντας** = οἳ καὶ
πρότερον κακῶς εἶχον, impf. partic. Cf.
νοσοῦντας ἐν αὐτοῖς, IX. 50, and κακῶς
διεκείμεθα, IX. 28. See §§ 45—49.

ἑαυτοὺς καὶ στασιαστικῶς ἔτι χεῖρον διέθηκε, τοὺς
μὲν ἐξαπατῶν, τοῖς δὲ διδούς, τοὺς δὲ πάντα τρόπον
διαφθείρων, καὶ διέστησεν εἰς μέρη πολλά, ἑνὸς τοῦ
συμφέροντος ἅπασιν ὄντος, κωλύειν ἐκεῖνον μέγαν 10
γίγνεσθαι. ἐν τοιαύτῃ δὲ καταστάσει καὶ ἔτ᾽ ἀγνοίᾳ 62
τοῦ συνισταμένου καὶ φυομένου κακοῦ τῶν ἁπάντων
Ἑλλήνων ὄντων, δεῖ σκοπεῖν ὑμᾶς, ἄνδρες Ἀθηναῖοι,
τί προσῆκον ἦν ἑλέσθαι πράττειν καὶ ποιεῖν τὴν
πόλιν, καὶ τούτων λόγον παρ᾽ ἐμοῦ λαβεῖν· ὁ γὰρ 5
ἐνταῦθ᾽ ἑαυτὸν τάξας τῆς πολιτείας εἴμ᾽ ἐγώ. πότε- 63
246 ρον αὐτὴν ἐχρῆν, Αἰσχίνη, τὸ φρόνημ᾽ ἀφεῖσαν καὶ
τὴν ἀξίαν τὴν αὑτῆς ἐν τῇ Θετταλῶν καὶ Δολόπων
τάξει συγκατακτᾶσθαι Φιλίππῳ τὴν τῶν Ἑλλήνων
ἀρχὴν καὶ τὰ τῶν προγόνων καλὰ καὶ δίκαι᾽ ἀναι- 5

9. διέστησεν...πολλά: cf. [x.] 52,
γεγόνασι καθ᾽ αὑτοὺς ἕκαστοι, Ἀργεῖοι,
Θηβαῖοι, Λακεδαιμόνιοι, Κορίνθιοι, Ἀρ-
κάδες, ἡμεῖς. (Bl.)
10. κωλύειν : in apposition with
ἑνὸς τοῦ συμφέροντος. An appositive
infinitive generally has the article in
the fully developed language.
§ 62. 1. ἔτ᾽ ἀγνοίᾳ (sc. ἐν)...
ὄντων = ἔτ᾽ ἀγνοούντων, ἔτ᾽ belonging
in sense to ἀγνοίᾳ. Vömel : quum
adhuc ignorarent etc.
2. συνισταμένου: cf. VI. 35, ἕως...
συνίσταται τὰ πράγματα.
4. πράττειν καὶ ποιεῖν: see § 46.
When these words do not have their
proper distinction of do and make,
they sometimes have no apparent distinction: see 246⁵, ¹¹, and IV. 5, οὐδὲν
ἂν ὧν νυνὶ πεποίηκεν ἔπραξεν.
6. ἐνταῦθ᾽...τῆς πολιτείας : partitive. Cf. § 59⁸.
§ 63. 1. πότερον αὐτὴν ἐχρῆν...
ἀναιρεῖν; should she...have helped
Philip to gain his dominion over the
Greeks, and (so) have set at naught
the glorious and just deeds of our

ancestors? Here, and in μὴ ποιεῖν and
περιιδεῖν (also depending on ἐχρῆν),
in προσῆκε ποιεῖν and ἔδει λέγειν η
γράφειν in § 66², ⁴, in ἐχρῆν ποιεῖν in
§ 69⁶, and φανῆναι ἐχρῆν in § 71¹⁰ ⁻¹²,
we have simply the ordinary use of
the infinitive depending on a past
verb expressing duty or propriety, with
none of the idiomatic force by which
(for example) ἔδει σε ἐλθεῖν often
means you ought to have gone (but did
not go). These expressions are all
repetitions or enlargements of τί προσῆκον ἦν in § 62⁴, which obviously asks
only what was it right for Athens to
do? with no implied idea that she did
or did not do the right thing. So in
§ 63¹ the question is simply was it
her duty to help Philip etc.?
2. τὸ φρόνημα καὶ τὴν ἀξίαν, her
spirit and her dignity.
3. ἐν...τάξει implies a descent to
their level and serving in their ranks.
The Thessalians helped Philip in the
Amphissian war ; the Dolopians are
probably mentioned only to disparage
the Thessalians further.

ρεῖν ; ἢ τοῦτο μὲν μὴ ποιεῖν, δεινὸν γὰρ ὡς ἀληθῶς,
ἃ δ' ἑώρα συμβησόμενα εἰ μηδεὶς κωλύσει, καὶ προη-
σθάνεθ' ὡς ἔοικεν ἐκ πολλοῦ, ταῦτα περιιδεῖν γιγνόμενα ; ἀλλὰ νῦν ἔγωγε τὸν μάλιστ' ἐπιτιμῶντα τοῖς 64
πεπραγμένοις ἡδέως ἂν ἐροίμην, τῆς ποίας μερίδος
γενέσθαι τὴν πόλιν ἐβούλετ' ἄν, πότερον τῆς συναι-
τίας τῶν συμβεβηκότων τοῖς Ἕλλησι κακῶν καὶ
αἰσχρῶν, ἧς ἂν Θετταλοὺς καὶ τοὺς μετὰ τούτων 5
εἴποι τις, ἢ τῆς περιεορακυίας ταῦτα γιγνόμενα ἐπὶ
τῇ τῆς ἰδίας πλεονεξίας ἐλπίδι, ἧς ἂν Ἀρκάδας καὶ
Μεσσηνίους καὶ Ἀργείους θείημεν. ἀλλὰ καὶ τούτων 65
πολλοὶ, μᾶλλον δὲ πάντες, χεῖρον ἡμῶν ἀπηλλάχασιν.
καὶ γὰρ εἰ μὲν ὡς ἐκράτησε Φίλιππος ᾤχετ' εὐθέως
ἀπιὼν καὶ μετὰ ταῦτ' ἦγεν ἡσυχίαν, μήτε τῶν αὐτοῦ
συμμάχων μήτε τῶν ἄλλων Ἑλλήνων μηδένα μηδὲν 5
λυπήσας, ἦν ἄν τις κατὰ τῶν ἐναντιωθέντων οἷς
ἔπραττεν ἐκεῖνος μέμψις καὶ κατηγορία· εἰ δὲ ὁμοίως
ἁπάντων τὸ ἀξίωμα, τὴν ἡγεμονίαν, τὴν ἐλευθερίαν
περιείλετο, μᾶλλον δὲ καὶ τὰς πολιτείας, ὅσων

---

7. **συμβησόμενα εἰ μηδεὶς κωλύσει**:
cf. Aesch. III. 90, ὃ πρόδηλον ἦν ἐσό-
μενον εἰ μὴ κωλύσετε. In both we
might have the future optative.

8. **ταῦτα περιιδεῖν γιγνόμενα**, to
allow these acts to go on ; περιιδεῖν
γενόμενα would be to allow them to
happen (M. T. 148 and 903⁶).

§ 64. 1. **νῦν**, now, when the fight
for liberty is ended : τοῖς πεπραγμένοις
refers to the fight itself.—**τὸν μάλιστ'
ἐπιτιμῶντα**, i.e. the severest critic.

3. **γενέσθαι**, to join (not to belong
to): cf. Ar. Nub. 107, τούτων γενοῦ
μοι.

§ 65. 3. **ὡς ἐκράτησε**: i.e. at
Chaeronea. Philip treated Athens
with great consideration after the
battle, restoring her 2000 prisoners
without ransom ; but wreaked his

vengeance on Thebes (as a former
ally) and invaded Peloponnesus.
Hist. § 68. (Grote XI. 699—705.)—
ᾤχετ' ἀπιών, had taken himself off.

6. **ἦν ἄν τις...κατηγορία**, there
might perhaps be some ground for
blame and accusation etc. : the older
editions have ὅμως ἦν ἄν τις and
κατὰ τῶν οὐκ ἐναντιωθέντων, with an
entirely different meaning.

8. **ἀξίωμα...ἡγεμονίαν...ἐλευθερίαν**:
see XIX. 260, τοῦτο τὸ πρᾶγμα (the
corruption of leading men by Philip)
Θετταλῶν μὲν...τὴν ἡγεμονίαν καὶ τὸ
κοινὸν ἀξίωμα ἀπωλώλεκει, νῦν δ' ἤδη
καὶ τὴν ἐλευθερίαν παραιρεῖται· τὰς
γὰρ ἀκροπόλεις αὐτῶν ἐνίων Μακεδόνες
φρουροῦσιν. For Euboea see § 71
(below).

9. **πολιτείας**, free governments.

ἐδύνατο, πῶς οὐχ ἁπάντων ἐνδοξότατα ὑμεῖς ἐβου- 10
λεύσασθε ἐμοὶ πεισθέντες;
Ἀλλ' ἐκεῖσ' ἐπανέρχομαι. τί τὴν πόλιν, Αἰσχίνη, 66
προσῆκε ποιεῖν ἀρχὴν καὶ τυραννίδα τῶν Ἑλλήνων
ὁρῶσαν ἑαυτῷ κατασκευαζόμενον Φίλιππον; ἢ τί
247 τὸν σύμβουλον ἔδει λέγειν ἢ γράφειν τὸν Ἀθήνησιν
(καὶ γὰρ τοῦτο πλεῖστον διαφέρει), ὃς συνῄδειν μὲν 5
ἐκ παντὸς τοῦ χρόνου μέχρι τῆς ἡμέρας ἀφ' ἧς αὐτὸς
ἐπὶ τὸ βῆμα ἀνέβην, ἀεὶ περὶ πρωτείων καὶ τιμῆς
καὶ δόξης ἀγωνιζομένην τὴν πατρίδα, καὶ πλείω καὶ
χρήματα καὶ σώματα ἀνηλωκυῖαν ὑπὲρ φιλοτιμίας
καὶ τῶν πᾶσι συμφερόντων ἢ τῶν ἄλλων Ἑλλήνων 10
ὑπὲρ αὑτῶν ἀνηλώκασιν ἕκαστοι, ἑώρων δ' αὐτὸν 67
τὸν Φίλιππον, πρὸς ὃν ἦν ἡμῖν ὁ ἀγών, ὑπὲρ ἀρχῆς
καὶ δυναστείας τὸν ὀφθαλμὸν ἐκκεκομμένον, τὴν

See Arist. Pol. VI. (IV.) 8, 3, ἔστι
γὰρ ἡ πολιτεία ὡς ἁπλῶς εἰπεῖν μίξις
ὀλιγαρχίας καὶ δημοκρατίας, εἰώθασι δὲ
καλεῖν τὰς μὲν ἀποκλινούσας ὡς πρὸς
τὴν δημοκρατίαν πολιτείας, τὰς δὲ πρὸς
τὴν ὀλιγαρχίαν μᾶλλον ἀριστοκρατίας
διὰ τὸ μᾶλλον ἀκολουθεῖν παιδείαν καὶ
εὐγένειαν τοῖς εὐπορωτέροις.
10. ἁπάντων: partitive with ἐνδοξότατα, in the most glorious way
possible. So εὐφημότατ' ἀνθρώπων in
XIX. 50, ἀναισχυντότατ' ἀνθρώπων in
XXVII. 18, δικαιότατ' ἀνθρώπων in
XXIX. 28.
§ 66. 1. ἐκεῖσ' ἐπανέρχομαι, I return to my question, i.e. after the
digression in § 65.
2. προσῆκε ποιεῖν: see note on
§ 63¹.
5. ὃς συνῄδειν: the antecedent,
τὸν σύμβουλον, refers to the speaker,
and most MSS. (not Σ and L¹) insert
ἐμέ after Ἀθήνησιν.
6. ἐκ...χρόνου: see § 203³.—ἀφ'
ἧς, when (on which), strictly beginning
with which, counting from which (as
a date).

8. ἀγωνιζομένην: or. obl. after
συνῄδειν, like ἀνηλωκυῖαν (9); cf. four
participles after ἑώρων, § 67¹.
9. χρήματα καὶ σώματα, money
and lives. With the lordly boast of
this passage compare the allusion to
Salamis in § 238.—φιλοτιμίας, her
honour; properly love of honour, but
often used like τιμή.
§ 67. 1. ἑώρων continues the
construction of ὃς συνῄδειν (§ 66⁵).
2. ὑπὲρ...δυναστείας, contrasted
with ὑπὲρ...συμφερόντων in § 66⁹.
δυναστεία is properly a government
of force, not based on the popular
will; see § 270⁵. Cf. Arist. Pol. VI.
(IV.) 5, 2. But Demosth. uses δυναστείας in § 322⁷ of the power of
Athens. It is generally, however, an
odious term.
3. τὸν ὀφθαλμὸν ἐκκεκομμένον, had
had his eye knocked out, passive of
the active form ἐκκόπτει τις αὐτῷ τὸν
ὀφθαλμόν, retaining the accus. of the
thing. The following κατεαγότα is
passive in sense, and has the same
construction. Cf. ἀποτμηθέντες τὰς

κλεῖν κατεαγότα, τὴν χεῖρα, τὸ σκέλος πεπηρωμένον,
πᾶν ὅ τι βουληθείη μέρος ἡ τύχη τοῦ σώματος 5
παρελέσθαι, τοῦτο προϊέμενον, ὥστε τῷ λοιπῷ μετὰ
τιμῆς καὶ δόξης ζῆν; καὶ μὴν οὐδὲ τοῦτό γ' οὐδεὶς 68
ἂν εἰπεῖν τολμήσαι, ὡς τῷ μὲν ἐν Πέλλῃ τραφέντι,
χωρίῳ ἀδόξῳ τότε γ' ὄντι καὶ μικρῷ, τοσαύτην
μεγαλοψυχίαν προσῆκεν ἐγγενέσθαι ὥστε τῆς τῶν
Ἑλλήνων ἀρχῆς ἐπιθυμῆσαι καὶ τοῦτ' εἰς τὸν νοῦν 5
ἐμβαλέσθαι, ὑμῖν δ' οὖσιν Ἀθηναίοις καὶ κατὰ τὴν
ἡμέραν ἑκάστην ἐν πᾶσι καὶ λόγοις καὶ θεωρήμασι
τῆς τῶν προγόνων ἀρετῆς ὑπομνήμαθ' ὁρῶσι τοσαύτην κακίαν ὑπάρξαι ὥστε τῆς ἐλευθερίας αὐτεπαγγέλτους ἐθελοντὰς παραχωρῆσαι Φιλίππῳ. οὐδ' ἂν 10
εἰς ταῦτα φήσειεν. λοιπὸν τοίνυν ἦν καὶ ἀναγκαῖον 69
ἅμα πᾶσιν οἷς ἐκεῖνος ἔπραττεν ἀδικῶν ὑμᾶς ἐναντιοῦσθαι δικαίως. τοῦτ' ἐποιεῖτε μὲν ὑμεῖς ἐξ ἀρχῆς

κεφαλάς, Xen. An. II. 6, 1, representing ἀπέτεμον αὐτοῖς τὰς κεφαλάς (G. 1239, with examples).

6. προϊέμενον, i.e. always ready to sacrifice, followed by ὅ τι βουληθείη.

§ 68. 2. τολμήσαι (so Σ and L): the form in -ειε is far more common in Demosthenes and in other Attic prose.—ἐν Πέλλῃ τραφέντι: cf. Hegesippus [Dem. VII.] 7, πρὸς τὸν ἐκ Πέλλης ὁρμώμενον, with the same sarcasm. Pella was a small place until Philip enlarged and adorned it. See Strab. VII. fr. 23: τὴν Πέλλαν οὖσαν μικρὰν πρότερον Φίλιππος εἰς μῆκος ηὔξησε τραφεὶς ἐν αὐτῇ.

4. μεγαλοψυχίαν, lofty aspirations. Aristotle (Eth. IV. 3, 3) says of the μεγαλόψυχος, the great-souled or high-minded man, δοκεῖ εἶναι ὁ μεγάλων ἑαυτὸν ἀξιῶν ἄξιος ὤν. Cf. μικροψυχίας, § 279⁶.

5. εἰς τόν νοῦν ἐμβαλέσθαι: cf. our phrase take it into his head.

7. ἐν πᾶσι...θεωρήμασι, i.e. in all

that you hear and see: θεώρημα is very rare for θέαμα.

8. ὑπομνήμαθ' ὁρῶσι, beholding memorials; ὁρῶσι by a slight zeugma including λόγοις: cf. Aeschyl. Prom. 21 οὔτε φωνὴν οὔτε του μορφὴν βροτῶν ὄψει.

9. κακίαν: see note on § 20⁴.—ὑπάρξαι, like ἐγγενέσθαι (4), depends on προσῆκεν.—αὐτεπαγγέλτους ἐθελοντὰς, as self-offered volunteers: cf. § 99¹⁰.

10. οὐδ' ἂν εἰς: see M.T. 219: οὐδ' εἰς (separated) = ne unus quidem, not a man.

§ 69. 1. ἀναγκαῖον ἅμα: cf. ἀναγκαῖον καὶ δίκαιον ἅμα, § 9⁵.

2. ἔπραττεν ἀδικῶν, in strong antithesis to ἐναντιοῦσθαι δικαίως.

3. ἐξ ἀρχῆς: this refers strictly only to the time of his own leadership (καθ' οὓς ἐπολιτευόμην χρόνους). But he modestly and speciously appears to represent his own vigorous policy as a continuation of earlier energy. Yet

εἰκότως καὶ προσηκόντως, ἔγραφον δὲ καὶ συνεβού-
248 λευον καὶ ἐγὼ καθ' οὓς ἐπολιτευόμην χρόνους. ὁμο- 5
λογῶ. ἀλλὰ τί ἐχρῆν με ποιεῖν ; ἤδη γάρ σ' ἐρωτῶ,
πάντα τἄλλ' ἀφεὶς, Ἀμφίπολιν, Πύδναν, Ποτείδαιαν,
Ἁλόννησον· οὐδενὸς τούτων μέμνημαι· Σέρριον δὲ 70
καὶ Δορίσκον καὶ τὴν Πεπαρήθου πόρθησιν καὶ ὅσ'
ἄλλ' ἡ πόλις ἠδικεῖτο, οὐδ' εἰ γέγονεν οἶδα. καίτοι
σύ γ' ἔφησθά με ταῦτα λέγοντα εἰς ἔχθραν ἐμβαλεῖν
τουτουσὶ, Εὐβούλου καὶ Ἀριστοφῶντος καὶ Διοπεί- 5
θους τῶν περὶ τούτων ψηφισμάτων ὄντων, οὐκ ἐμῶν,
ὦ λέγων εὐχερῶς ὅ τι ἂν βουληθῇς. οὐδὲ νῦν περὶ
τούτων ἐρῶ. ἀλλ' ὁ τὴν Εὔβοιαν ἐκεῖνος σφετεριζό- 71

when Philip was capturing Amphipolis, Pydna, and Potidaea, Athens
was supinely inactive; but Demosthenes was not yet a responsible
adviser. In §§ 18 and 60 he expressly
disclaims all responsibility for these
earlier times.

6. τί ἐχρῆν με ποιεῖν; see § 63[1].
—ἤδη σ' ἐρωτῶ: the third time of
asking.

7. ἀφείς, leaving out of account :
for Amphipolis, Pydna, and Potidaea,
see Hist. § 3; for Halonnesus, Hist.
§§ 44, 45, 53.

§ 70. 1. For Serrhium and Doriscus see note on § 27[6]. For the
sacking of Peparethus (in 341—340
B.C.) see Hist. § 53. ταύτην ἐπόρ-
θησεν Ἄλκιμος ναύαρχος τοῦ Φιλίππου,
Schol. The people of Peparethus, an
ally of Athens, had taken Halonnesus
from Philip and captured his garrison.

3. οὐδ' εἰ γέγονεν οἶδα: cf. XXI.
78, τοῦτον οὐδ' εἰ γέγονεν εἰδώς, not being
aware even of his existence.

4. σύ γ' ἔφησθα: see Aesch. III.
82, ἀρχὰς αὐτοῖς ἐνεδίδου πολέμου καὶ
ταραχῆς.—ταῦτα λέγοντα, i.e. by ever-
lastingly talking about these.

5. Εὐβούλου καὶ Ἀριστοφῶντος:
in replying to Aeschines (as just

quoted) he is glad to be able to refer
to decrees of his political opponents
while there were none of his own.
Eubulus, though he was the leader
of the peace party and always friendly
to Philip, might have proposed decrees
directing negotiations with Philip
about the towns captured by Philip
or the later affair of Peparethus; and
he might have proposed one remon-
strating against the seizure of Athenian
ships (§ 73), like the spurious one in
§§ 73, 74.

7. οὐδὲ...ἐρῶ : the third παράλειψις
(cf. §§ 69[7], 70[3]), in which a fact is
impressively stated by declaring that it
shall not be mentioned.

§ 71. 1. ἐκεῖνος: this position is
allowed the demonstrative when another qualifying word follows the
article : cf. ἡ στενὴ αὕτη ὁδός, Xen.
An. IV. 2, 6. But even then, the
regular order may be kept.--σφετερι-
ζόμενος (from σφέτερος), appropriating,
making his own, of unlawful or unjust
appropriation : cf. XXXII. 2, σφετερί-
σασθαι, and Aeschyl. Suppl. 39,
λέκτρων σφετεριξάμενον ἐπιβῆναι. The
verb spheterize has been used in
English by Sir William Jones : see
larger edition.

μενος καὶ κατασκευάζων ἐπιτείχισμ᾽ ἐπὶ τὴν Ἀττικήν,
καὶ Μεγάροις ἐπιχειρῶν, καὶ καταλαμβάνων Ὠρεὸν,
καὶ κατασκάπτων Πορθμὸν, καὶ καθιστὰς ἐν μὲν
Ὠρεῷ Φιλιστίδην τύραννον ἐν δ᾽ Ἐρετρίᾳ Κλείταρ- 5
χον,. καὶ τὸν Ἑλλήσποντον ὑφ᾽ ἑαυτῷ ποιούμενος,
καὶ Βυζάντιον πολιορκῶν, καὶ πόλεις Ἑλληνίδας
ἃς μὲν ἀναιρῶν εἰς ἃς δὲ τοὺς φυγάδας κατάγων,
πότερον ταῦτα πάντα ποιῶν ἠδίκει καὶ παρεσπόνδει
καὶ ἔλυε τὴν εἰρήνην ἢ οὔ; καὶ πότερον φανῆναί 10
τινα τῶν Ἑλλήνων τὸν ταῦτα κωλύσοντα ποιεῖν
αὐτὸν ἐχρῆν ἢ μή; εἰ μὲν γὰρ μὴ ἐχρῆν, ἀλλὰ τὴν 72
Μυσῶν λείαν καλουμένην τὴν Ἑλλάδ᾽ οὖσαν ὀφθῆναι ζώντων καὶ ὄντων Ἀθηναίων, περιείργασμαι μὲν

2. **ἐπιτείχισμ᾽ ἐπὶ τὴν Ἀττικήν,**
as a *fortress commanding Attica*. An
ἐπιτείχισμα is properly a fortress in
an enemy's country, used as a military
basis, like the Spartan fort at Decelea
in the Peloponnesian War. Here
Euboea in Philip's hands is figura-
tively described as such a fortress
commanding Attica; and the sight of
its high mountains across the narrow
strait made the figure especially vivid
to dwellers in the east of Attica : see
§ 87⁴. This passage relates to Philip's
operations in Euboea in 343—342 B.C.
See § 79⁸ with note, and Hist. § 46.

3. **Μεγάροις ἐπιχειρῶν:** in 344—
343 B.C. Philip attempted to get
possession of Megara, with the help
of his friends in the city. See § 48¹¹
and note. Megara in Philip's hands
would have been another ἐπιτείχισμα
ἐπὶ τὴν Ἀττικήν.

6. **τὸν Ἑλλήσποντον:** for Philip's
operations in the Hellespont and at
Byzantium, see §§ 87—89 and 244.

8. **ἃς μὲν...εἰς ἃς δὲ:** very rare for
τὰς μὲν...εἰς τὰς δὲ: in XLI. 11 we have
ἃ μὲν (cod. A τὰ μὲν)...τῶν δὲ...τὰ δὲ.
See Philem. frag. 99 (Kock), ὧν μὲν
διὰ τύχην, ὧν δὲ δι᾽ ἑαυτούς.—**τοὺς**

φυγάδας κατάγων: i.e. *restoring* his
own exiled partizans.

10. **ἢ οὔ:** sc. ἠδίκει κ.τ.λ.; but (in
12) **ἢ μή** : sc. φανῆναι.

11. **τὸν ταῦτα κωλύσοντα** = ὃς τ.
κωλύσει (final) ; in § 72⁶ is the simple
κωλυτήν; both predicates with **φανῆ-**
ναι.

12. **ἐχρῆν ἢ μή:** the question is
here put for the fourth time; see note
on § 63¹.

§ 72. 1. **εἰ μὲν γὰρ μὴ ἐχρῆν :**
the alternative is εἰ δ᾽ ἔδει (6).—**τὴν
Μυσῶν λείαν,** *Mysian booty*, i.e. like
the Mysians, a prey to everybody.
παροιμία, ἥν φησι Δήμων τὴν ἀρχὴν
λαβεῖν ἀπὸ τῶν καταδραμόντων ἀστυγειτόνων τε καὶ λῃστῶν τὴν Μυσίαν
κατὰ τὴν Τηλέφου τοῦ βασιλέως ἀπο-
δημίαν, Harpocr. This refers to the
wanderings of Telephus, disguised as
a beggar, in quest of Achilles, who
had wounded him and alone could
cure his wound. This was the plot
of the much-ridiculed *Telephus* of
Euripides.

2. **ὀφθῆναι:** sc. ἐχρῆν (without
μή).

3. **ζώντων καὶ ὄντων:** see note on
§ 4⁶. See Plat. Rep. 369 D, τοῦ εἶναι

ἐγὼ περὶ τούτων εἰπὼν, περιείργασται δ' ἡ πόλις ἡ
πεισθεῖσ' ἐμοὶ, ἔστω δὲ ἀδικήματα πάνθ' ἃ πέπρακται 5
καὶ ἁμαρτήματ' ἐμά. εἰ δ' ἔδει τινὰ τούτων κωλυτὴν
249 φανῆναι, τίν' ἄλλον ἢ τὸν Ἀθηναίων δῆμον προσῆκεν
γενέσθαι ; ταῦτα τοίνυν ἐπολιτευόμην ἐγὼ, καὶ ὁρῶν
καταδουλούμενον πάντας ἀνθρώπους ἐκεῖνον ἠναντιούμην, καὶ προλέγων καὶ διδάσκων μὴ προῖεσθαι 10
διετέλουν.

Καὶ μὴν τὴν εἰρήνην γ' ἐκεῖνος ἔλυσε τὰ πλοῖα 73
λαβὼν, οὐχ ἡ πόλις, Αἰσχίνη.

Φέρε δ' αὐτὰ τὰ ψηφίσματα καὶ τὴν ἐπιστολὴν
τὴν τοῦ Φιλίππου, καὶ λέγε ἐφεξῆς· ἀπὸ γὰρ τούτων
τίς τίνος αἴτιός ἐστι γενήσεται φανερόν. 5

ΨΗΦΙΣΜΑ.

[Ἐπὶ ἄρχοντος Νεοκλέους, μηνὸς βοηδρομιῶνος, ἐκκλησίας συγκλήτου ὑπὸ στρατηγῶν, Εὔβουλος Μνησιθέου Κό-
πρειος εἶπεν, ἐπειδὴ προσήγγειλαν οἱ στρατηγοὶ ἐν τῇ
ἐκκλησίᾳ ὡς ἄρα Λεωδάμαντα τὸν ναύαρχον καὶ τὰ μετ' 10
αὐτοῦ ἀποσταλέντα σκάφη εἴκοσιν ἐπὶ τὴν τοῦ σίτου παρα-

τε καὶ ζῆν.—περιείργασμαι, *I have
done a useless* (superfluous) *work*:
περιττῶς καὶ οὐκ ἀναγκαίως παρηνεσά
τε ἐγὼ καὶ ἡ πόλις ἡ πεισθεῖσα μάτην
ἐπείσθη (Schol.).

5. ἔστω...ἐμά: ἀδικήματα καὶ ἁμαρτήματα ἐμά is predicate to ἔστω. See
ἀδίκημα, *crime*, and ἁμάρτημα, *blunder*,
distinguished in § 274.

10. μὴ προῖεσθαι, *not to make surrenders* (*not to give up your own*),
here absolute, as in Arist. Eth. III.
5, 14: τότε μὲν οὖν ἐξῆν αὐτῷ μὴ
νοσεῖν, προεμένῳ δ' οὐκέτι, i.e. *after he
has sacrificed his health*.

§ 73. 1. **καὶ μὴν...λαβών**: this
seizure of merchant ships, of which
we have no other knowledge, was
the overt act which Athens made the
occasion of her declaration of war. It

perhaps hastened this declaration by
a few weeks ; but after the letter of
Philip (§ 76), which was practically a
declaration of war on his part, only
one course was open to Athens.

3. τὴν ἐπιστολήν: this was a
detailed statement of Philip's grievances, with a defence of his own
conduct toward Athens, ending with
a formal declaration of war. The
document numbered XII. among the
orations of Demosthenes purports to
be this letter. See Hist. § 55.

5. τίς τίνος: such double inter-
rogatives are common in Greek, but
colloquial or comic in English, as
who's who? An increase of the number
becomes comic in Greek ; as in IV. 36,
τίς χορηγὸς...πότε καὶ παρὰ τοῦ καὶ τί
λαβόντα τί δεῖ ποιεῖν.

ΠΕΡΙ ΤΟΥ ΣΤΕΦΑΝΟΥ 45

πομπὴν εἰς Ἑλλήσποντον ὁ παρὰ Φιλίππου στρατηγὸς
Ἀμύντας καταγήγοχεν εἰς Μακεδονίαν καὶ ἐν φυλακῇ ἔχει,
ἐπιμεληθῆναι τοὺς πρυτάνεις καὶ τοὺς στρατηγοὺς ὅπως
ἡ βουλὴ συναχθῇ καὶ αἱρεθῶσι πρέσβεις πρὸς Φίλιππον, 15
οἵτινες παραγενόμενοι διαλέξονται πρὸς αὐτὸν περὶ τοῦ 74
ἀφεθῆναι τὸν ναύαρχον καὶ τὰ πλοῖα καὶ τοὺς στρατιώτας.
καὶ εἰ μὲν δι' ἄγνοιαν ταῦτα πεποίηκεν ὁ Ἀμύντας, ὅτι οὐ
μεμψιμοιρεῖ ὁ δῆμος οὐδὲν αὐτῷ· εἰ δέ τι πλημμελοῦντα
παρὰ τὰ ἐπεσταλμένα λαβὼν, ὅτι ἐπισκεψάμενοι Ἀθηναῖοι 5
ἐπιτιμήσουσι κατὰ τὴν τῆς ὀλιγωρίας ἀξίαν. εἰ δὲ μηδέ-
250 τερον τούτων ἐστὶν, ἀλλ' ἰδίᾳ ἀγνωμονοῦσιν ἢ ὁ ἀποστείλας
ἢ ὁ ἀπεσταλμένος, καὶ τοῦτο λέγειν, ἵνα αἰσθανόμενος ὁ
δῆμος βουλεύσηται τί δεῖ ποιεῖν.]

Τοῦτο μὲν τοίνυν τὸ ψήφισμα Εὔβουλος ἔγραψεν, 75
οὐκ ἐγώ, τὸ δ' ἐφεξῆς Ἀριστοφῶν, εἶθ' Ἡγήσιππος,
εἶτ' Ἀριστοφῶν πάλιν, εἶτα Φιλοκράτης, εἶτα Κηφισοφῶν, εἶτα πάντες· ἐγὼ δ' οὐδὲν περὶ τούτων.
λέγε. 5

ΨΗΦΙΣΜΑ.

[Ἐπὶ Νεοκλέους ἄρχοντος, βοηδρομιῶνος ἕνῃ καὶ νέᾳ,
βουλῆς γνώμῃ, πρυτάνεις καὶ στρατηγοὶ ἐχρημάτισαν τὰ
ἐκ τῆς ἐκκλησίας ἀνενεγκόντες, ὅτι ἔδοξε τῷ δήμῳ πρέσβεις
ἑλέσθαι πρὸς Φίλιππον περὶ τῆς τῶν πλοίων ἀνακομιδῆς 10
καὶ ἐντολὰς δοῦναι κατὰ τὰ ἐκ τῆς ἐκκλησίας ψηφίσματα.
καὶ εἵλοντο τούσδε, Κηφισοφῶντα Κλέωνος Ἀναφλύστιον,
Δημόκριτον Δημοφῶντος Ἀναγυράσιον, Πολύκριτον Ἀπη-
μάντου Κοθωκίδην. πρυτανείᾳ φυλῆς Ἱπποθωντίδος, Ἀριστοφῶν Κολλυτεὺς πρόεδρος εἶπεν.] 15

§ **75.** 4. ἐγὼ δ' οὐδὲν περὶ τούτων : this with § 76² is a positive
denial of the statement of Aeschines
(III. 55) that the decree declaring
war was proposed by Demosthenes :
Hist. § 55, notes 4, 5. Though Demos-

thenes was constantly proposing decrees at this time, he cannot have
proposed the one which formally
declared war or any on the matters
mentioned in § 70 or about the seizure
of ships (i.e. περὶ τούτων).

"Ωσπερ τοίνυν ἐγὼ ταῦτα δεικνύω τὰ ψηφίσματα. 76
οὕτω καὶ σὺ δεῖξον, Αἰσχίνη, ὁποῖον ἐγὼ γράψας
ψήφισμα αἴτιός εἰμι τοῦ πολέμου. ἀλλ᾽ οὐκ ἂν
ἔχοις· εἰ γὰρ εἶχες, οὐδὲν ἂν αὐτοῦ πρότερον νυνὶ
παρέσχου. καὶ μὴν οὐδ᾽ ὁ Φίλιππος οὐδὲν αἰτιᾶται 5
ἔμ᾽ ὑπὲρ τοῦ πολέμου, ἑτέροις ἐγκαλῶν. λέγε δ᾽
αὐτὴν τὴν ἐπιστολὴν τὴν τοῦ Φιλίππου.

ΕΠΙΣΤΟΛΗ.

[Βασιλεὺς Μακεδόνων Φίλιππος Ἀθηναίων τῇ βουλῇ καὶ 77
251 τῷ δήμῳ χαίρειν. παραγενόμενοι πρὸς ἐμὲ οἱ παρ᾽ ὑμῶν
πρεσβευταί, Κηφισοφῶν καὶ Δημόκριτος καὶ Πολύκριτος,
διελέγοντο περὶ τῆς τῶν πλοίων ἀφέσεως ὧν ἐναυάρχει
Λεωδάμας. καθ᾽ ὅλου μὲν οὖν ἔμοιγε φαίνεσθε ἐν μεγάλῃ 5
εὐηθείᾳ ἔσεσθαι, εἰ οἴεσθ᾽ ἐμὲ λανθάνειν ὅτι ἐξαπεστάλη
ταῦτα τὰ πλοῖα πρόφασιν μὲν ὡς τὸν σῖτον παραπέμψοντα
ἐκ τοῦ Ἑλλησπόντου εἰς Λῆμνον, βοηθήσοντα δὲ Σηλυβριανοῖς τοῖς ὑπ᾽ ἐμοῦ μὲν πολιορκουμένοις, οὐ συμπεριει-
λημμένοις δὲ ἐν ταῖς τῆς φιλίας κοινῇ κειμέναις ἡμῖν 10
συνθήκαις. καὶ ταῦτα συνετάχθη τῷ ναυάρχῳ ἄνευ μὲν 78
τοῦ δήμου τοῦ Ἀθηναίων, ὑπὸ δέ τινων ἀρχόντων καὶ ἑτέρων ἰδιωτῶν μὲν νῦν ὄντων, ἐκ παντὸς δὲ τρόπου βουλομένων
τὸν δῆμον ἀντὶ τῆς νῦν ὑπαρχούσης πρὸς ἐμὲ φιλίας τὸν
πόλεμον ἀναλαβεῖν, πολλῷ μᾶλλον φιλοτιμουμένων τοῦτο 5
συντετελέσθαι ἢ τοῖς Σηλυβριανοῖς βοηθῆσαι. καὶ ὑπολαμ-
βάνουσιν αὐτοῖς τὸ τοιοῦτο πρόσοδον ἔσεσθαι· οὐ μέντοι
μοι δοκεῖ τοῦτο χρήσιμον ὑπάρχειν οὔθ᾽ ὑμῖν οὔτ᾽ ἐμοί.
διόπερ τά τε νῦν καταχθέντα πλοῖα πρὸς ἡμᾶς ἀφίημι ὑμῖν,
καὶ τοῦ λοιποῦ, ἐὰν βούλησθε μὴ ἐπιτρέπειν τοῖς προεστη- 10
κόσιν ὑμῶν κακοήθως πολιτεύεσθαι, ἀλλ᾽ ἐπιτιμᾶτε, πειράσομαι κἀγὼ διαφυλάττειν τὴν εἰρήνην. εὐτυχεῖτε.]

Ἐνταῦθ᾽ οὐδαμοῦ Δημοσθένην γέγραφεν, οὐδ᾽ 79
αἰτίαν οὐδεμίαν κατ᾽ ἐμοῦ. τί ποτ᾽ οὖν τοῖς ἄλλοις

§ 76. 7. ἐπιστολήν: see note on § 73³. The following letter is spurious.

ἐγκαλῶν τῶν ἐμοὶ πεπραγμένων οὐχὶ μέμνηται; ὅτι
τῶν ἀδικημάτων ἂν ἐμέμνητο τῶν αὐτοῦ, εἴ τι περὶ
252 ἐμοῦ γ' ἔγραφεν· τούτων γὰρ εἰχόμην ἐγὼ καὶ τού- 5
τοις ἠναντιούμην. καὶ πρῶτον μὲν τὴν εἰς Πελοπόννησον πρεσβείαν ἔγραψα, ὅτε πρῶτον ἐκεῖνος
εἰς Πελοπόννησον παρεδύετο, εἶτα τὴν εἰς Εὔβοιαν,
ἡνίκ' Εὐβοίας ἥπτετο, εἶτα τὴν ἐπ' Ὠρεὸν ἔξοδον,
οὐκέτι πρεσβείαν, καὶ τὴν εἰς Ἐρέτριαν, ἐπειδὴ 10
τυράννους ἐκεῖνος ἐν ταύταις ταῖς πόλεσι κατέστη-
σεν. μετὰ ταῦτα δὲ τοὺς ἀποστόλους ἅπαντας 80
ἀπέστειλα, καθ' οὓς Χερρόνησος ἐσώθη καὶ τὸ Βυζάντιον καὶ πάντες οἱ σύμμαχοι. ἐξ ὧν ὑμῖν μὲν
τὰ κάλλιστα, ἔπαινοι, δόξαι, τιμαί, στέφανοι, χάριτες
παρὰ τῶν εὖ πεπονθότων ὑπῆρχον· τῶν δ' ἀδικου- 5
μένων τοῖς μὲν ὑμῖν τότε πεισθεῖσιν ἡ σωτηρία
περιεγένετο, τοῖς δ' ὀλιγωρήσασι τὸ πολλάκις ὧν
ὑμεῖς προείπατε μεμνῆσθαι καὶ νομίζειν ὑμᾶς μὴ

§ **79.** 3. **ὅτι...τῶν αὐτοῦ**: this
implies that Philip could not speak
of any recent case in which Demosthenes had opposed him, without
alluding to some disgraceful act of
his own.
4. **εἴ......γ' ἔγραφεν**: this absolutely certain but long neglected correction of Droysen (1839), hardly an
emendation, is now generally adopted
for the impossible γέγραφεν (Σ) or
γέγραφε of the MSS.
5. **εἰχόμην**, clung to, followed up
closely.
6. **εἰς Πελοπόννησον**: probably
the embassy of 344, on which Demosthenes made the speech quoted in the
Second Philippic, 20—25.
8. **παρεδύετο**, was working his
way, stealing in.—**τὴν εἰς Εὔβοιαν**
(sc. πρεσβείαν): in 343—342 B.C.
(§ 71).
9. **τὴν ἐπ' Ὠρεὸν...Ἐρέτριαν**: the
two military expeditions to Euboea

in 341 B.C., by which the tyrannies in
Oreus and Eretria were suppressed.
See Hist. § 52.
§ **80.** 1. **ἀποστόλους**: the orators
use ἀπόστολος, properly a messenger
(N. Test. apostle), and στόλος for a
naval armament: cf. οὔτε ναυσὶ κρα-
τήσας ἦλθεν ἄν ποτε στόλῳ, οὔτε πεζῇ
κ.τ.λ., VI. 36.
2. **ἀπέστειλα**: properly used with
ἀποστόλους, I sent out (by my decrees):
cf. πρεσβείαν ἔγραψα, § 79⁷.—**Χερρόνησος...σύμμαχοι**: see §§ 87—89,
240, 241.
4. **ἔπαινοι...χάριτες**: the decrees
conferring these grateful rewards on
Athens were read after § 89.
7. **τοῖς δ' ὀλιγωρήσασι**: this refers
to the Peloponnesians who neglected
the advice of Demosthenes in 344 B.C.
(§ 79⁸) and later (IX. 27, 34), and to
the early refusal of Oreus and Eretria
to listen to Athens (IX. 57, 66, 68).

μόνων εὔνους ἑαυτοῖς ἀλλὰ καὶ φρονίμους ἀνθρώπους καὶ μάντεις εἶναι· πάντα γὰρ ἐκβέβηκεν ἃ 10
προείπατε. καὶ μὴν ὅτι πολλὰ μὲν ἂν χρήματ᾽ ἔδωκε 81
Φιλιστίδης ὥστ᾽ ἔχειν Ὠρεὸν, πολλὰ δὲ Κλείταρχος
ὥστ᾽ ἔχειν Ἐρέτριαν, πολλὰ δ᾽ αὐτὸς ὁ Φίλιππος
ὥστε ταῦθ᾽ ὑπάρχειν ἐφ᾽ ὑμᾶς αὐτῷ καὶ περὶ τῶν
ἄλλων μηδὲν ἐξελέγχεσθαι μηδ᾽ ἃ ποιῶν ἠδίκει 5
μηδέν᾽ ἐξετάζειν πανταχοῦ, οὐδεὶς ἀγνοεῖ, καὶ πάντων
ἥκιστα σύ· οἱ γὰρ παρὰ τοῦ Κλειτάρχου καὶ τοῦ 82
Φιλιστίδου τότε πρέσβεις δεῦρ᾽ ἀφικνούμενοι παρὰ
σοὶ κατέλυον, Αἰσχίνη, καὶ σὺ προὐξένεις αὐτῶν·
οὓς ἡ μὲν πόλις ὡς ἐχθροὺς καὶ οὔτε δίκαια οὔτε
συμφέροντα λέγοντας ἀπήλασεν, σοὶ δ᾽ ἦσαν φίλοι. 5
οὐ τοίνυν ἐπράχθη τούτων οὐδέν, ὦ βλασφημῶν περὶ
253 ἐμοῦ καὶ λέγων ὡς σιωπῶ μὲν λαβὼν βοῶ δ᾽ ἀναλώσας. ἀλλ᾽ οὐ σὺ, ἀλλὰ βοᾷς μὲν ἔχων, παύσει δὲ
οὐδέποτ᾽ ἐὰν μή σε οὗτοι παύσωσιν ἀτιμώσαντες

§ **81.** 4. **ὥστε ταῦθ᾽ ὑπάρχειν,**
i.e. *that he might have these* (the two
towns under the two tyrants) *to depend
on*, i.e. as ἐπιτειχίσματα ἐπὶ τὴν
Ἀττικήν (§ 71).
5. **μηδὲν ἐξελέγχεσθαι** (sc. subj.
αὐτόν): cf. the active constr. in Plat.
Ap. 23 A, ἅ ἂν ἄλλον ἐξελέγξω.
6. **πανταχοῦ,** *anywhere* : cf. πάντων, § 5⁴.—**πάντων ἥκιστα σύ**: a
sudden outburst of personality.
§ **82.** 2. **ἀφικνούμενοι...κατέ-
λυον** : the tenses imply that such
envoys of the tyrants were regular
guests of Aeschines.
3. **κατέλυον** : *lodged* (as we say
put up), lit. *let down*, originally *un-
harnessed*; cf. Od. IV. 28, καταλύ-
σομεν ὠκέας ἵππους.—**προὐξένεις αὐτῶν,**
you were their πρόξενος : this might be
metaphorical; but there is good reason
for thinking that Aeschines was the
official representative at Athens of
Oreus, if not of Eretria.

5. **ἀπήλασεν,** *rejected* (i.e. their
proposals).
6. **οὐ τοίνυν...οὐδὲν** : i.e. *nothing
of the kind was ever successful with
me*, referring to πολλὰ μὲν ἂν χρήματ᾽
ἔδωκε κ.τ.λ. in § 81¹.
7. **ὡς σιωπῶ......ἀναλώσας** : quoted
from memory from the speech of
Aeschines. (218), σὺ δ᾽ οἶμαι λαβὼν μὲν
σεσίγηκας, ἀναλώσας δὲ κέκραγας.
8. **βοᾷς ἔχων,** *you keep on shouting* :
cf. Ar. Nub. 509, τί κυπτάζεις ἔχων;
(M. T. 837). The Scholia understand
χρήματα with ἔχων (as with λαβών);
there may be a double meaning in
ἔχων.—**παύσει...παύσωσιν,** *you will
not stop unless these judges stop you.*
9. **ἀτιμώσαντες,** i.e. by not giving
you a fifth of their votes, the result
of which would be the partial ἀτιμία
of losing the right to bring a similar
suit hereafter, with a fine of 1000
drachmas. This was actually the
result of this trial.

τήμερον. στεφανωσάντων τοίνυν ὑμῶν ἔμ᾽ ἐπὶ τού- 83
τοις τότε, καὶ γράψαντος 'Αριστονίκου τὰς αὐτὰς
συλλαβὰς ἅσπερ οὑτοσὶ Κτησιφῶν νῦν γέγραφεν,
καὶ ἀναρρηθέντος ἐν τῷ θεάτρῳ τοῦ στεφάνου,—καὶ
δευτέρου κηρύγματος ἤδη μοι τούτου γιγνομένου,— 5
οὔτ᾽ ἀντεῖπεν Αἰσχίνης παρὼν οὔτε τὸν εἰπόντ᾽ ἐγράψατο. καί μοι λέγε καὶ τοῦτο τὸ ψήφισμα λαβών.

ΨΗΦΙΣΜΑ.

['Επὶ Χαιρώνδου Ἡγήμονος ἄρχοντος, γαμηλιῶνος ἕκτῃ 84
ἀπιόντος, φυλῆς πρυτανευούσης Λεοντίδος, 'Αριστόνικος
Φρεάρριος εἶπεν, ἐπειδὴ Δημοσθένης Δημοσθένους Παιανιεὺς πολλὰς καὶ μεγάλας χρείας παρέσχηται τῷ δήμῳ τῷ
'Αθηναίων καὶ πολλοῖς τῶν συμμάχων καὶ πρότερον, καὶ 5
ἐν τῷ παρόντι καιρῷ βεβοήθηκε διὰ τῶν ψηφισμάτων, καί
τινας τῶν ἐν τῇ Εὐβοίᾳ πόλεων ἠλευθέρωκε, καὶ διατελεῖ
εὔνους ὢν τῷ δήμῳ τῷ 'Αθηναίων, καὶ λέγει καὶ πράττει ὅ
τι ἂν δύνηται ἀγαθὸν ὑπέρ τε αὐτῶν 'Αθηναίων καὶ τῶν
ἄλλων Ἑλλήνων, δεδόχθαι τῇ βουλῇ καὶ τῷ δήμῳ τῷ Ἀθη- 10
ναίων ἐπαινέσαι Δημοσθένην Δημοσθένους Παιανέα καὶ
στεφανῶσαι χρυσῷ στεφάνῳ, καὶ ἀναγορεῦσαι τὸν στέφανον
ἐν τῷ θεάτρῳ Διονυσίοις, τραγῳδοῖς καινοῖς, τῆς δὲ ἀναγορεύσεως τοῦ στεφάνου ἐπιμεληθῆναι τὴν πρυτανεύουσαν
254 φυλὴν καὶ τὸν ἀγωνοθέτην. εἶπεν 'Αριστόνικος ὁ Φρεάρριος.] 15

---

§ 83. 2. **γράψαντος...γέγραφεν:**
i.e. the two decrees were essentially
identical in form. In § 223¹ he says
of a later decree, τὰς αὐτὰς συλλαβὰς
καὶ ταὐτὰ ῥήματα ἔχει. Even this
does not include such details as dates,
names, etc.
4. **ἐν τῷ θεάτρῳ:** this anticipates
the argument on the place of proclamation (§§ 120, 121), and gives a
precedent for Ctesiphon's proposal.
5. **δευτέρου...τούτου γιγνομένου:**
τούτου is here ambiguous, but it pro-

bably refers to the crown proposed
by Aristonicus, the clause δευτέρου...
γιγνομένου meaning that one crown
had been given to Demosthenes in
the theatre before that of Aristonicus.
γιγνομένου is imperfect and we might
have had δεύτερον κήρυγμα ἤδη μοι
τοῦτο ἐγίγνετο, the imperf. implying
that he *was then receiving* the distinction for the second time.
6. **παρών,** *though present.*---**ἐγράψατο:** sc. παρανόμων.

Ἔστιν οὖν ὅστις ὑμῶν οἶδέ τινα αἰσχύνην τῇ 85
πόλει συμβᾶσαν διὰ τοῦτο τὸ ψήφισμα ἢ χλευα-
σμὸν ἢ γέλωτα, ἃ νῦν οὗτος ἔφη συμβήσεσθαι ἂν ἐγὼ
στεφανῶμαι ; καὶ μὴν ὅταν ᾖ νέα καὶ γνώριμα πᾶσι
τὰ πράγματα, ἐάν τε καλῶς ἔχῃ, χάριτος τυγχάνει, 5
ἐάν θ' ὡς ἑτέρως, τιμωρίας. φαίνομαι τοίνυν ἐγὼ
χάριτος τετυχηκὼς τότε, καὶ οὐ μέμψεως οὐδὲ τιμωρίας.

Οὐκοῦν μέχρι μὲν τῶν χρόνων ἐκείνων ἐν οἷς 86
ταῦτ' ἐπράχθη, πάντ' ἀνωμολόγημαι τὰ ἄριστα
πράττειν τῇ πόλει, τῷ νικᾶν ὅτ' ἐβουλεύεσθε λέγων
καὶ γράφων, τῷ καταπραχθῆναι τὰ γραφέντα καὶ
στεφάνους ἐξ αὐτῶν τῇ πόλει καὶ ἐμοὶ καὶ πᾶσιν 5
γενέσθαι, τῷ θυσίας τοῖς θεοῖς καὶ προσόδους ὡς
ἀγαθῶν τούτων ὄντων ὑμᾶς πεποιῆσθαι.

Ἐπειδὴ τοίνυν ἐκ τῆς Εὐβοίας ὁ Φίλιππος ὑφ' 87
ὑμῶν ἐξηλάθη,——τοῖς μὲν ὅπλοις, τῇ δὲ πολιτείᾳ καὶ
τοῖς ψηφίσμασι, κἂν διαρραγῶσί τινες τούτων, ὑπ'

§ 85. 2. **συμβᾶσαν**=ὅτι συνέβη :
cf. φαίνομαι τετυχηκὼς (6).
3. **ἔφη συμβήσεσθαι**: see Aesch.
231, ὅταν τὸν τοιοῦτον ἄνθρωπον στε-
φανῶτε, οὐκ οἴεσθε ἐν ταῖς τῶν Ἑλλήνων δόξαις συρίττεσθαι;
6. **ὡς ἑτέρως**, otherwise, in the
other way (opposed to καλῶς), used
to avoid κακῶς. This is the adverb
of τὸ ἕτερον, as ὡσαύτως (ὡς αὕτως)
of τὸ αὐτό, and ὡς ἀληθῶς of τὸ
ἀληθές. See XXII. 12, ἀγαθὰ ἢ θάτερα,
ἵνα μηδὲν εἴπω φλαῦρον, which shows
the euphemistic character of ὡς ἑτέρως
here.
§ 86. 2. **πάντ'**...**πράττειν**, that
I did everything that was best. It is
difficult to choose even the most
probable reading here. Both πάντας
(Σ) and πάντας τοὺς χρόνους (Vulg.)
are objectionable, and we seem com-

pelled to decide between the conjec-
tures πάντ' and πάντως. **πράττειν** is
imperfect (for ἔπραττον). On the
contrary, νικᾶν, καταπραχθῆναι, and
γενέσθαι are distinguished only like
ordinary present and aorist infinitives
(M.T. 87, 96).
4. **τὰ γραφέντα**=ἃ ἔγραψα : see
note on § 56⁴.
5. **καὶ ἐμοὶ καὶ πᾶσιν** repeats the
idea of τῇ πόλει.
6. **προσόδους**, processions : cf. §
216¹⁰.
§ 87. 2. **τοῖς μὲν ὅπλοις**, I mean,
by arms, added, as if by afterthought,
to limit ὑφ' ὑμῶν, as πολιτείᾳ and
ψηφίσμασι limit ὑπ' ἐμοῦ. The inter-
ruption is colloquial and designedly
spontaneous. See note on § 121⁷,
τῶν δ' ἀφαιρῶν μέρη.
3. **κἂν διαρραγῶσι**: see § 21⁹.

ἐμοῦ,—ἕτερον κατὰ τῆς πόλεως ἐπιτειχισμὸν ἐζήτει.
ὁρῶν δ᾽ ὅτι σίτῳ πάντων ἀνθρώπων πλείστῳ χρώ- 5
μεθ᾽ ἐπεισάκτῳ, βουλόμενος τῆς σιτοπομπίας κύριος
γενέσθαι, παρελθὼν ἐπὶ Θρᾴκης Βυζαντίους, συμμάχους ὄντας αὐτῷ, τὸ μὲν πρῶτον ἠξίου συμπολεμεῖν
τὸν πρὸς ὑμᾶς πόλεμον, ὡς δ᾽ οὐκ ἤθελον οὐδ᾽ ἐπὶ
τούτοις ἔφασαν τὴν συμμαχίαν πεποιῆσθαι, λέγον- 10
τες ἀληθῆ, χάρακα βαλόμενος πρὸς τῇ πόλει καὶ
μηχανήματ᾽ ἐπιστήσας ἐπολιόρκει. τούτων δὲ γιγ- 88
νομένων ὅ τι μὲν προσῆκε ποιεῖν ὑμᾶς, οὐκ ἐπερω-
255 τήσω· δῆλον γάρ ἐστιν ἅπασιν. ἀλλὰ τίς ἦν ὁ
βοηθήσας τοῖς Βυζαντίοις καὶ σώσας αὐτούς; τίς ὁ

4. **ἐπιτειχισμόν**, i.e. Byzantium, as a point from which to threaten Athens: see note on § 71 [2].

5. **σίτῳ ἐπεισάκτῳ**: the same words are found in XX. 31, where it is said that the grain from the Euxine was about half of the whole amount imported by Athens. See Sandys's notes on XX. 31—33. The thin soil of Attica (τὸ λεπτόγεων, Thuc. I. 2) could not supply grain enough for the population, even in the best seasons, and the fruitful shores of the Euxine were the most important sources of supply. Hence it would have been fatal to Athens to have the Hellespont and the Bosporus in hostile hands (cf. §§ 241, 301). Boeckh estimates the grain annually consumed in Attica at about 3,400,000 μέδιμνοι (5,100,000 bushels), of which only 2,400,000 μέδιμνοι could be raised at home. See the story of Xerxes in Hdt. VII. 147.

7. **παρελθὼν ἐπὶ Θρᾴκης**: this probably refers to the advance of Philip to the siege of Perinthus in 340, when he protected his fleet in its passage through the Hellespont by marching an army through the

Chersonese. The appeal to Byzantium, as an ally, to help him in his coming war with Athens was perhaps sent from Perinthus, which he besieged unsuccessfully before he attacked Byzantium. See Hist. §§ 54, 55.—**Βυζαντίους**: with both ἠξίου and ἐπολιόρκει (12).—**συμμάχους**: after Byzantium left the Athenian alliance in the Social war, she became an ally of Philip (XV. 3, IX. 35). But now she had been brought into friendship and alliance with Athens by the skilful diplomacy of Demosthenes before Philip's appeal to her for help (Hist. §§ 51, 53).

9. **οὐκ ἤθελον οὐδ᾽ ἔφασαν**, refused and denied.

11. **χάρακα**, here a palisade, generally a pale or pole: see Harpocr. χάρακα· Δημοσθένης τὸ χαράκωμα ὃ περιεβάλλοντό τινες στρατοπέδῳ ἐπὶ σωτηρίᾳ.

12. **μηχανήματ᾽ ἐπιστήσας**: cf. IX. 17, 50. The siege of Byzantium marks an epoch in engines of war.

§ **88**. 2. **οὐκ ἐπερωτήσω**, i.e. I will not repeat the question, already asked in §§ 63, 66, 69, 71.

κωλύσας τὸν Ἑλλήσποντον ἀλλοτριωθῆναι κατ᾽ 5
ἐκείνους τοὺς χρόνους ; ὑμεῖς, ἄνδρες Ἀθηναῖοι. τὸ
δ᾽ ὑμεῖς ὅταν λέγω, τὴν πόλιν λέγω. τίς δ᾽ ὁ τῇ
πόλει λέγων καὶ γράφων καὶ πράττων καὶ ἁπλῶς
ἑαυτὸν εἰς τὰ πράγματ᾽ ἀφειδῶς διδούς ; ἐγώ. ἀλλὰ 89
μὴν ἡλίκα ταῦτ᾽ ὠφέλησεν ἅπαντας, οὐκέτ᾽ ἐκ τοῦ
λόγου δεῖ μαθεῖν, ἀλλ᾽ ἔργῳ πεπείρασθε· ὁ γὰρ τότε
ἐνστὰς πόλεμος ἄνευ τοῦ καλὴν δόξαν ἐνεγκεῖν ἐν
πᾶσι τοῖς κατὰ τὸν βίον ἀφθονωτέροις καὶ εὐωνοτέ- 5
ροις διῆγεν ὑμᾶς τῆς νῦν εἰρήνης, ἣν οὗτοι κατὰ τῆς
πατρίδος τηροῦσιν οἱ χρηστοὶ ἐπὶ ταῖς μελλούσαις
ἐλπίσιν, ὧν διαμάρτοιεν, καὶ μετάσχοιεν ὧν ὑμεῖς οἱ
τὰ βέλτιστα βουλόμενοι τοὺς θεοὺς αἰτεῖτε, μὴ

8, 9. **λέγων...διδούς**: these participles are imperfect, and so contrasted
with the preceding βοηθήσας etc.
Few venture to accept δούς for διδούς,
though it is supported by Σ and L.
Vömel says : "Nec puto Demosthenis
aures tolerasse continuatas syllabas—
δῶς δούς. Sed in talibus nihil affir-
marim."

§ **89.** 2. **ἐκ τοῦ λόγου**, in the
familiar antithesis to ἔργῳ.

3. **ὁ ἐνστὰς**, *which broke out* (ὃς
ἐνέστη) : cf. ἐνειστήκει, *was upon us*,
§ 139[7].

4. **ἄνευ**, *besides* (*without reckoning*):
cf. [XIII.] 7, ἄνευ τοῦ συμφέρειν, and
XXIII. 112, ἄνευ τούτου.—**ἐν πᾶσι**...
διῆγεν ὑμᾶς, *saw you supplied* (*carried
you through*) *with all the necessaries
of life in greater abundance and
cheaper.*

6. **τῆς νῦν εἰρήνης**: τῆς ἐπὶ Ἀλεξάνδρου (Schol.), the peace of Demades,
under which Athens had been living
since Chaeronea.—**ἣν...τηροῦσιν**: the
Macedonian party had been strong
enough to prevent Athens from openly
helping Thebes in her revolt 335 B.C.,

or the Peloponnesians under Agis in
330. See Grote XII. 44, 59; 380—383.
7. **χρηστοὶ**: cf. the sarcastic
χρηστέ, § 318[4].—**ἐπὶ**...**ἐλπίσιν**, *in*
(with a view to) *their hopes of future
gain*: ἐλπίζουσι γὰρ ἐπανελθόντα τὸν
Ἀλέξανδρον ἀπὸ τῶν Περσῶν μεγάλα
αὑτοῖς χαρίζεσθαι ὡς προδόταις (Schol.).
8—10. **καὶ μετάσχοιεν...μὴ μεταδοῖεν**: this reading of Σ gives an
entirely different sense from that of
the common text, καὶ μὴ μετάσχοιεν...
μηδὲ μεταδοῖεν. The meaning is,
*May they fail in their hopes;
and may they rather be allowed to
share with you patriots in the blessings
for which you pray, that they may not
involve you in the calamities which
would result from their policy.* Μὴ
μεταδοῖεν cannot be a mere continuation of the wish of μετάσχοιεν: the
asyndeton would be too harsh. It
must be a final clause, assimilated to
the optative μετάσχοιεν (M.T. 182),
as in ἔλθοι ὅπως γένοιτο λυτήριος,
Aeschyl. Eum. 297, and γένοιτο...ἵν᾽
αἱ Μυκῆναι γνοῖεν, Soph. Phil. 324.
See M.T. 181. I know no other

μεταδοῖεν ὑμῖν ὧν αὐτοὶ προήρηνται. λέγε δ' αὐτοῖς 10
καὶ τοὺς τῶν Βυζαντίων στεφάνους καὶ τοὺς τῶν
Περινθίων, οἷς ἐστεφάνουν ἐκ τούτων τὴν πόλιν.

ΨΗΦΙΣΜΑ ΒΥΖΑΝΤΙΩΝ.

['Επὶ ἱερομνάμονος Βοσπορίχω Δαμάγητος ἐν τᾷ ἁλίᾳ 90
ἔλεξεν, ἐκ τᾶς βωλᾶς λαβὼν ῥάτραν, ἐπειδὴ ὁ δᾶμος ὁ
'Αθαναίων ἔν τε τοῖς προγεγεναμένοις καιροῖς εὐνοέων δια-
τελέει Βυζαντίοις καὶ τοῖς συμμάχοις καὶ συγγενέσι Περιν-
θίοις καὶ πολλὰς καὶ μεγάλας χρείας παρέσχηται, ἔν τε τῷ 5
παρεστακότι καιρῷ Φιλίππω τῶ Μακεδόνος ἐπιστρατεύσαντος
ἐπὶ τὰν χώραν καὶ τὰν πόλιν ἐπ' ἀναστάσει Βυζαντίων καὶ
256 Περινθίων καὶ τὰν χώραν δαίοντος καὶ δενδροκοπέοντος, βοηθήσας πλοίοις ἑκατὸν καὶ εἴκοσι καὶ σίτῳ καὶ βέλεσι καὶ
ὁπλίταις ἐξείλετο ἀμὲ ἐκ τῶν μεγάλων κινδύνων καὶ ἀποκατέ- 10
στασε τὰν πάτριον πολιτείαν καὶ τὼς νόμως καὶ τὼς τάφως,
δεδόχθαι τῷ δάμῳ τῷ Βυζαντίων καὶ Περινθίων 'Αθαναίοις 91
δόμεν ἐπιγαμίαν, πολιτείαν, ἔγκτασιν γᾶς καὶ οἰκιᾶν, προε-
δρίαν ἐν τοῖς ἀγῶσι, πόθοδον ποτὶ τὰν βωλὰν καὶ τὸν δᾶμον
πράτοις μετὰ τὰ ἱερά, καὶ τοῖς κατοικέειν ἐθέλουσι τὰν πόλιν
ἀλειτουργήτοις ἦμεν πασᾶν τᾶν λειτουργιᾶν· στᾶσαι δὲ καὶ 5
εἰκόνας τρεῖς ἑκκαιδεκαπάχεις ἐν τῷ Βοσπορείῳ, στεφανούμενον τὸν δᾶμον τὸν 'Αθαναίων ὑπὸ τῶ δάμω τῶ Βυζαντίων
καὶ Περινθίων· ἀποστεῖλαι δὲ καὶ θεωρίας ἐς τὰς ἐν τᾷ
Ἑλλάδι παναγύριας, Ἴσθμια καὶ Νέμεα καὶ Ὀλύμπια καὶ
Πύθια, καὶ ἀνακαρῦξαι τὼς στεφάνως οἷς ἐστεφάνωται ὁ 10
δᾶμος ὁ 'Αθαναίων ὑφ' ἡμῶν, ὅπως ἐπιστέωνται οἱ Ἕλλανες
τάν τε 'Αθαναίων ἀρετὰν καὶ τὰν Βυζαντίων καὶ Περινθίων
εὐχαριστίαν.]

Λέγε καὶ τοὺς παρὰ τῶν ἐν Χερρονήσῳ στε- 92
φάνους.

such final optative in prose; but I
know no other final clause (of any
kind) depending on a wishing optative
in prose, which is hardly strange.
  10. ὧν αὐτοὶ προήρηνται, i.e. their

προαίρεσις: τῆς δουλείας δηλονότι
(Schol.).
  11. τοὺς τῶν Περινθίων, i.e. the
crowns voted by these towns and
sent to Athens as marks of honour.

54 ΔΗΜΟΣΘΕΝΟΥΣ

ΨΗΦΙΣΜΑ ΧΕΡΡΟΝΗΣΙΤΩΝ.

[Χερρονησιτῶν οἱ κατοικοῦντες Σηστὸν, Ἐλεοῦντα, Μά-
δυτον, Ἀλωπεκόννησον, στεφανοῦσιν Ἀθηναίων τὴν βουλὴν 5
καὶ τὸν δῆμον χρυσῷ στεφάνῳ ἀπὸ ταλάντων ἑξήκοντα, καὶ
Χάριτος βωμὸν ἱδρύονται καὶ δήμου Ἀθηναίων, ὅτι πάντων
μεγίστου ἀγαθῶν παραίτιος γέγονε Χερρονησίταις, ἐξελόμε-
νος ἐκ τῆς Φιλίππου καὶ ἀποδοὺς τὰς πατρίδας, τοὺς νόμους,
257 τὴν ἐλευθερίαν, τὰ ἱερά. καὶ ἐν τῷ μετὰ ταῦτα αἰῶνι παντὶ 10
οὐκ ἐλλείψει εὐχαριστῶν καὶ ποιῶν ὅ τι ἂν δύνηται ἀγαθόν.
ταῦτα ἐψηφίσαντο ἐν τῷ κοινῷ βουλευτηρίῳ.]

Οὐκοῦν οὐ μόνον τὸ Χερρόνησον καὶ Βυζάντιον 93
σῶσαι, οὐδὲ τὸ κωλῦσαι τὸν Ἑλλήσποντον ὑπὸ
Φιλίππῳ γενέσθαι τότε, οὐδὲ τὸ τιμᾶσθαι τὴν πόλιν
ἐκ τούτων ἡ προαίρεσις ἡ ἐμὴ καὶ ἡ πολιτεία διε-
πράξατο, ἀλλὰ καὶ πᾶσιν ἔδειξεν ἀνθρώποις τήν τε 5
τῆς πόλεως καλοκαγαθίαν καὶ τὴν Φιλίππου κακίαν.
ὁ μὲν γὰρ σύμμαχος ὢν τοῖς Βυζαντίοις πολιορκῶν
αὐτοὺς ἑωρᾶτο ὑπὸ πάντων, οὗ τί γένοιτ' ἂν αἴσχιον
ἢ μιαρώτερον; ὑμεῖς δ', οἱ καὶ μεμψάμενοι πολλὰ 94
καὶ δίκαι' ἂν ἐκείνοις εἰκότως περὶ ὧν ἠγνωμονήκεσαν εἰς ὑμᾶς ἐν τοῖς ἔμπροσθεν χρόνοις, οὐ μόνον
οὐ μνησικακοῦντες οὐδὲ προϊέμενοι τοὺς ἀδικουμένους ἀλλὰ καὶ σῴζοντες ἐφαίνεσθε, ἐξ ὧν δόξαν, 5

§ 93. 1. οὐκοῦν introduces the
conclusion to which the decrees point.
2. οὐδὲ (sc. μόνον): cf. οὐδὲ, § 2⁴.
4. ἡ προαίρεσις καὶ ἡ πολιτεία:
cf. §§ 292⁴, ⁸, 317². In § 192⁵ we
have τὴν προαίρεσιν τῆς πολιτείας in
nearly the same sense. προαίρεσις is
deliberate choice.
7. σύμμαχος ὢν: cf. § 87⁷.
§ 94. 1. οἱ μεμψάμενοι ἄν = οἳ
ἐμέμψασθε ἄν.—πολλὰ καὶ δίκαι'
ἐκείνοις: cf. Αr. Plut. 8, Λοξίᾳ
μέμψιν δικαίαν μέμφομαι ταύτην.
2. ὧν ἠγνωμονήκεσαν εἰς ὑμᾶς:

cf. οἷς εὐτυχήκεσαν, § 18⁶. This
"want of feeling" (cf. 207⁷, 248⁷)
refers to the conduct of Byzantium in
the Social war: see note on § 87⁷,
and Hist. §§ 2, 51.
4. μνησικακοῦντες: remembering
old grudges (maliciously): cf. § 99⁵.
See μὴ μνησικακήσειν in the oath of
oblivion after the restoration in 403
B.C., Xen. Hell. II. 4, 43.
5. δόξαν, εὔνοιαν: the asyndeton
is more emphatic than δόξαν καὶ
εὔνοιαν: see §§ 96⁴,⁵, 234⁵, and XIX.
190 and 220.

εὔνοιαν παρὰ πάντων ἐκτᾶσθε. καὶ μὴν ὅτι μὲν
πολλοὺς ἐστεφανώκατ᾽ ἤδη τῶν πολιτευομένων ἅπαντες ἴσασι· δι᾽ ὅντινα δ᾽ ἄλλον ἡ πόλις ἐστεφάνωται,
σύμβουλον λέγω καὶ ῥήτορα, πλὴν δι᾽ ἐμέ, οὐδ᾽ ἂν εἰς
εἰπεῖν ἔχοι. 10

"Ινα τοίνυν καὶ τὰς βλασφημίας ἃς κατὰ τῶν 95
Εὐβοέων καὶ τῶν Βυζαντίων ἐποιήσατο, εἴ τι δυσχερὲς αὐτοῖς ἐπέπρακτο πρὸς ὑμᾶς ὑπομιμνῄσκων,
συκοφαντίας οὔσας ἐπιδείξω μὴ μόνον τῷ ψευδεῖς
εἶναι (τοῦτο μὲν γὰρ ὑπάρχειν ὑμᾶς εἰδότας ἡγοῦ- 5
μαι), ἀλλὰ καὶ τῷ, εἰ τὰ μάλιστ᾽ ἦσαν ἀληθεῖς,
οὕτως ὡς ἐγὼ κέχρημαι τοῖς πράγμασι συμφέρειν
χρήσασθαι, ἐν ᾗ δύο βούλομαι τῶν καθ᾽ ὑμᾶς πε-
258 πραγμένων καλῶν τῇ πόλει διεξελθεῖν, καὶ ταῦτ᾽ ἐν
βραχέσι· καὶ γὰρ ἄνδρα ἰδίᾳ καὶ πόλιν κοινῇ πρὸς 10

---

7. τῶν πολιτευομένων, *your public
men*.

9. σύμβουλον...ῥήτορα : Phocion
as general was probably one of the
exceptions here implied.

§§ 95—101. Historical parallels
are cited to show that the considerate
treatment of Euboea and Byzantium
was in accordance with the traditional
policy of Athens.

§ 95. 1. τὰς βλασφημίας refers
to the long tirade of Aeschines (III.
85—93) against the proceedings in
Euboea in 341—340. There is nothing in the speech of Aesch., as it
now stands, relating to the help sent
to Byzantium.

2. δυσχερές, *unpleasant*, is a
euphemism adapted to the changed
state of feeling towards Euboea and
Byzantium since 343.

5. ὑπάρχειν ὑμᾶς εἰδότας, *that
you may be presumed to know* : cf.
§ 228³. This is not a mere expanded
εἰδέναι (as if εἶναι were used), but we
have the fundamental idea of ὑπάρχω

(§ 1³) added. In line 11, τῶν ὑπαρχόντων applies to the glories of our
ancestors as material stored up for
us to emulate.

6. τῷ...συμφέρειν, like τῷ ψευδεῖς
εἶναι, expresses means.—εἰ...ἦσαν, *si
erant* (not *si essent*): cf. § 12⁷.—τὰ μά-
λιστ᾽ ἀληθεῖς, *never so true*: cf. § 21³.

8. χρήσασθαι, *deal with*, *manage*.
—τῶν καθ᾽ ὑμᾶς, *of the events of your
time*, beginning with the Corinthian
war of 395 B.C. This war was now
65 years old ; but there were probably
old men in the immense audience
who distinctly remembered it and
who would be pleased to have it
spoken of as *in their day*. Still, he
feels that these earlier events hardly
fall within his limit of καθ᾽ ὑμᾶς, for
he says τῶν τότε Ἀθηναίων in § 96⁸,
directly after ἐξήλθετε εἰς Ἁλίαρτον,
and οἱ ὑμέτεροι πρόγονοι, followed by
ὑμεῖς οἱ πρεσβύτεροι, in § 98¹.

10. πρός, *with reference* (or *regard*)
to : cf. τὸ πρός τι, Aristotle's category
of relation.

τὰ κάλλιστα τῶν ὑπαρχόντων ἀεὶ δεῖ πειρᾶσθαι τὰ
λοιπὰ πράττειν. ὑμεῖς τοίνυν, ἄνδρες Ἀθηναῖοι, 96
Λακεδαιμονίων γῆς καὶ θαλάττης ἀρχόντων καὶ τὰ
κύκλῳ τῆς Ἀττικῆς κατεχόντων ἁρμοσταῖς καὶ φρου-
ραῖς, Εὔβοιαν, Τάναγραν, τὴν Βοιωτίαν ἅπασαν,
Μέγαρα, Αἴγιναν, Κέων, τὰς ἄλλας νήσους, οὐ ναῦς 5
οὐ τείχη τῆς πόλεως τότε κτησαμένης, ἐξήλθετε εἰς

11. **τὰ λοιπά** (cf. § 27[11]), opposed
to τῶν ὑπαρχόντων.
§ 96. 2. **Λακεδαιμονίων...ἀρχόν-
των**: after the Peloponnesian war,
Lysander established in most of the
conquered towns, and even in some
which were previously friendly to
Sparta, a Spartan governor (ἁρμοστής)
with a military force (φρουρά), and a
board of ten citizens of the subject
state (δεκαδαρχία), who were partizans
of Sparta. See Plutarch, Lysand. 13,
and Grote IX. 255.—**τὰ κύκλῳ τῆς
Ἀττικῆς**: more rhetorical than τὰ
περὶ τὴν Ἀττικήν, κύκλῳ having the
adverbial sense of *around*. See IV.
4[5], εἴχομεν πάντα τὸν τόπον οἰκεῖον
κύκλῳ, and XIX. 155, ἐπορεύοντο
κύκλῳ, *they travelled round*.
4, 5. **Εὔβοιαν...Αἴγιναν**: Euboea
and Megara had been in the hands
of the Spartans before the end of the
Peloponnesian war. Aegina, which
Athens had settled with her own
people in 431, after expelling the
native population, was restored to its
former owners (so far as this was
possible) by Lysander in 405, as he
was on his way to attack Athens
(Thuc. II. 27 ; Xen. Hell. II. 2, 9).
Boeotia as a whole was nominally
allied with Sparta ; but Thebes and
other towns became disgusted with
Sparta's tyrannical conduct soon after
the end of the war, and though
Thebes had been the greatest enemy
of Athens when the peace was made,
she harboured Thrasybulus and his

fellow exiles before they attacked the
Thirty in 403. This disaffection
ended in the Boeotian war in 395,
in which Athens aided Thebes ; in
the battle of Haliartus the allies
gained a doubtful victory over Sparta,
which was made decisive by the death
of Lysander on the field. (See Grote
IX. 409.) The invasion of Boeotia
by Lysander and his Spartan army
justifies τὴν Βοιωτίαν ἅπασαν from
the Athenian point of view.
5. **Κέων, τὰς ἄλλας νήσους**, i.e.
Ceos and the adjacent islands, Tenos,
Andros, Cythnus, Melos, etc. Melos
is mentioned as restored to its old
inhabitants by Lysander (Plut. Lys.
14). The emendation **Κέων**, τὰς
ἄλλας νήσους for Κλεωνάς, ἄλλας
νήσους (Σ) removes the difficulty
caused by the mention (for no
apparent reason) of Cleonae, a town
between Corinth and Argos, under τὰ
κύκλῳ τῆς Ἀττικῆς.—**οὐ ναῦς οὐ τείχη
τότε κτησαμένης** : Athens was required by Sparta to demolish her
Long Walls and the walls of the
Piraeus, not those of the ἄστυ; and
she was allowed to keep twelve
war-ships: see Xen. Hell. II. 2,
20. Here τότε κτησαμένης (not
κεκτημένης) means that she had not
yet *acquired* any ships or walls
beyond what were left her at the
end of the war.
6. **εἰς Ἁλίαρτον** : see note on
ll. 4, 5.

ΠΕΡΙ ΤΟΥ ΣΤΕΦΑΝΟΥ 57

Ἁλίαρτον καὶ πάλιν οὐ πολλαῖς ἡμέραις ὕστερον εἰς
Κόρινθον, τῶν τότε Ἀθηναίων πόλλ᾽ ἂν ἐχόντων
μνησικακῆσαι καὶ Κορινθίοις καὶ Θηβαίοις τῶν περὶ
τὸν Δεκελεικὸν πόλεμον πραχθέντων· ἀλλ᾽ οὐκ 10
ἐποίουν τοῦτο, οὐδ᾽ ἐγγύς. καίτοι τότε ταῦτα ἀμ- 97
φότερα, Αἰσχίνη, οὔθ᾽ ὑπὲρ εὐεργετῶν ἐποίουν οὔτ᾽
ἀκίνδυν᾽ ἑώρων. ἀλλ᾽ οὐ διὰ ταῦτα προΐεντο τοὺς
καταφεύγοντας ἐφ᾽ ἑαυτοὺς, ἀλλ᾽ ὑπὲρ εὐδοξίας καὶ
τιμῆς ἤθελον τοῖς δεινοῖς αὐτοὺς διδόναι, ὀρθῶς καὶ 5
καλῶς βουλευόμενοι. πέρας μὲν γὰρ ἅπασιν ἀνθρώποις ἐστὶ τοῦ βίου θάνατος, κἂν ἐν οἰκίσκῳ τις
αὐτὸν καθείρξας τηρῇ· δεῖ δὲ τοὺς ἀγαθοὺς ἄνδρας
ἐγχειρεῖν μὲν ἅπασιν ἀεὶ τοῖς καλοῖς, τὴν ἀγαθὴν
προβαλλομένους ἐλπίδα, φέρειν δ᾽ ἂν ὁ θεὸς διδῷ 10
γενναίως. ταῦτ᾽ ἐποίουν οἱ ὑμέτεροι πρόγονοι, ταῦθ᾽ 98

7. **οὐ πολλαῖς ἡμέραις**: according
to the accepted chronology, the battle
of Haliartus was in the autumn of
395 B.C., and that of Corinth in
the summer of 394, in the year of
Eubulides. The Corinthian war was
the result of a combination of
Athenians, Corinthians, Boeotians,
Euboeans, Argives, and others against
Sparta. In the battle of Corinth,
the Spartans were victorious. See
Grote IX. 426—429. The beautiful
monument, representing a young
warrior on horseback, now standing
near the Dipylon gate of Athens,
was erected in honour of Dexileos,
one of the Athenian horsemen slain
in this battle. The inscription is:
Δεξίλεως Λυσανίου Θορίκιος.
ἐγένετο ἐπὶ Τεισάνδρου ἄρχοντος,
ἀπέθανε ἐπ᾽ Εὐβουλίδου
ἐγ Κορίνθῳ τῶν πέντε ἱππέων.
8. **πόλλ᾽ ἂν ἐχόντων** (πόλλ᾽ ἂν
εἶχον), i.e. they might have done so,
potuissent.
10. **Δεκελεικὸν πόλεμον**, a name

often given to the last years of the
Peloponnesian war (413—404 B.C.)
when the Spartans held a fort at
Decelea in Attica.
11. **οὐδ᾽ ἐγγύς**: cf. § 12⁸.
§ **97**. 6. **πέρας μὲν...τηρῇ**: this
was celebrated as a gnomic saying in
various forms. The meaning is not
the flat truism, "death is the end of
all men's lives," but *all men's lives
have a fixed limit in death*, and this
is made a ground for devoting our
lives to noble ends, for which it is
worthy to die.
7. **ἐν οἰκίσκῳ**. in a chamber: ἀντὶ
τοῦ μικρῷ τινι οἰκήματι, Harpocration.
10. **προβαλλομένους ἐλπίδα**, protecting themselves by hope (holding
it before them, as a shield). See
Menand. fr. 572 (Kock) :
ὅταν τι πράττῃς ὅσιον, ἀγαθὴν ἐλπίδα
πρόβαλλε σαυτῷ, τοῦτο γιγνώσκων ὅτι
τόλμῃ δικαίᾳ καὶ θεὸς συλλαμβάνει.
Cf. § 195¹³.
§ **98**. 1. **πρόγονοι** : see note on
§ 95⁸.

58 ΔΗΜΟΣΘΕΝΟΥΣ

ὑμεῖς οἱ πρεσβύτεροι, οἳ, Λακεδαιμονίους οὐ φίλους
ὄντας οὐδ᾽ εὐεργέτας, ἀλλὰ πολλὰ τὴν πόλιν ἡμῶν
ἠδικηκότας καὶ μεγάλα, ἐπειδὴ Θηβαῖοι κρατήσαντες
ἐν Λεύκτροις ἀνελεῖν ἐπεχείρουν, διεκωλύσατε, οὐ 5
259 φοβηθέντες τὴν τότε Θηβαίοις ῥώμην καὶ δόξαν
ὑπάρχουσαν, οὐδ᾽ ὑπὲρ οἷα πεποιηκότων ἀνθρώπων
κινδυνεύσετε διαλογισάμενοι· καὶ γάρ τοι πᾶσι τοῖς 99
"Ελλησιν ἐδείξατε ἐκ τούτων ὅτι, κἂν ὁτιοῦν τις εἰς
ὑμᾶς ἐξαμάρτῃ, τούτων τὴν ὀργὴν εἰς τἄλλ᾽ ἔχετε,
ἐὰν δ᾽ ὑπὲρ σωτηρίας ἢ ἐλευθερίας κίνδυνός τις
αὐτοὺς καταλαμβάνῃ, οὔτε μνησικακήσετε οὔθ᾽ ὑπο- 5
λογιεῖσθε. καὶ οὐκ ἐπὶ τούτων μόνον οὕτως ἐσχή-
κατε, ἀλλὰ πάλιν σφετεριζομένων Θηβαίων τὴν

---

2. **ὑμεῖς** : cf. παρ᾽ ὑμῶν τῶν πρεσ-
βυτέρων, XX. 52.—**Λακεδαιμονίους,**
obj. of ἀνελεῖν (5), διεκωλύσατε having
τοὺς Θηβαίους, or perhaps simply τὸ
πρᾶγμα, understood as its object.
From the position of Λακ. we should
expect it to belong to the leading
verb.

4. **κρατήσαντες ἐν Λεύκτροις** :
the "Leuctric insolence" of Thebes
(Diod. XVI. 58), which made her
rather than Sparta the natural enemy
of Athens from 371 to 339 B.C., was
notorious. See §§ 18⁶ and 36². In
370 Epaminondas with a Theban
army invaded Laconia and marched
up to the city of Sparta itself; but he
did not venture to enter the unwalled
town and withdrew into Arcadia. At
this time he established Messene and
Megalopolis, to hold Sparta in check.
In this trying emergency, Sparta
humiliated herself so far as to ask
help from her old enemy, Athens.
Her request was granted, and Iphicrates was sent into Peloponnesus
to the aid of Sparta with 12,000
Athenians in the spring of 369 B.C.
This saved Sparta from another invasion at this time. The alliance

then formed remained unbroken,
though sometimes strained, until after
the battle of Mantinea in 362 B.C.,
in which Athens fought on the side
of Sparta.

7. **ὑπὲρ οἷα πεπ. ἀνθρώπων,** i.e.
what the men had done for whom.
§ **99.** 3. **τούτων,** *for this,* referring to ὁτιοῦν, as ὅστις can always
have a plural antecedent.

4. **ὑπὲρ,** *concerning, involving.*

5. **μνησικακήσετε...ὑπολογιεῖσθε** :
μνησικακεῖν, though usually intran-
sitive (cf. § 101⁶), may have an
accusative, as μνησικακῆσαι τὴν
ἡλικίαν, Ar. Nub. 999. Thus both
verbs may here have the same object,
suggested by ὁτιοῦν.

6. **ἐπὶ τούτων μόνον:** cf. XV. 15,
τῷ Ῥοδίων δήμῳ μόνον, and IX. 57,
παρὰ τούτοις μόνον. In these cases
μόνον modifies the whole sentence
loosely as an adverb, where we
should expect the adjective μόνων
or μόνῳ with the noun. We are
often careless about the position of
only ; as "he only went to London
once."

7. **σφετεριζομένων τὴν Εὔβοιαν** :
cf. 71¹. Euboea had been under the

Εὔβοιαν οὐ περιείδετε, οὐδ' ὧν ὑπὸ Θεμίσωνος καὶ
Θεοδώρου περὶ Ὠρωπὸν ἠδίκησθε ἀνεμνήσθητε,
ἀλλ' ἐβοηθήσατε καὶ τούτοις, τῶν ἐθελοντῶν τότε 10
τριηράρχων πρῶτον γενομένων τῇ πόλει, ὧν εἰς ἦν
ἐγώ. ἀλλ' οὔπω περὶ τούτων. καὶ καλὸν μὲν ἐποιή- 100
σατε καὶ τὸ σῶσαι τὴν νῆσον, πολλῷ δ' ἔτι τούτου
κάλλιον τὸ καταστάντες κύριοι καὶ τῶν σωμάτων
καὶ τῶν πόλεων ἀποδοῦναι ταῦτα δικαίως αὐτοῖς
τοῖς ἐξημαρτηκόσιν εἰς ὑμᾶς, μηδὲν ὧν ἠδίκησθε 5
ἐν οἷς ἐπιστεύθητε ὑπολογισάμενοι. μυρία τοίνυν
ἕτερ' εἰπεῖν ἔχων παραλείπω, ναυμαχίας, ἐξόδους
πεζὰς, στρατείας καὶ πάλαι γεγονυίας καὶ νῦν ἐφ'

control of Thebes since Leuctra, but
in 357 B.C. a Theban army was sent
to quiet some disturbances in the
island. The Athenians with great
energy sent an army to Euboea, and
drove the whole Theban force from
the island in thirty days. This is
the famous expedition to which the
orators always referred with pride.
See Dem. VIII. 74, 75, IV. 17; Grote
XI. ch. 86, pp. 306—309; and Hist.
§ 2.
8. **οὐ περιείδετε** : cf. διεκωλύσατε,
§ 98⁵. — **Θεμίσωνος** : a tyrant of
Eretria, who in 366 B.C. took from
Athens the frontier town of Oropus
and gave it to Thebes. (Grote,
X. ch. 79, p. 392.) Oropus had
long been a bone of contention
between Athens and Thebes. It
was stipulated that Thebes should
now hold the town only until the
right to it could be settled by
arbitration (μέχρι δίκης, Xen. Hell.
VII. 4, 1). The "case of Oropus"
was a protracted one; and it is said
that Demosthenes as a boy was first
inspired with a passion for oratory
by hearing an eloquent plea of
Callistratus in defence of the rights
of Athens (Plut. Dem. 5).

10. **τούτοις** : the Euboeans.—**τῶν
ἐθελοντῶν...τῇ πόλει**, i.e. the state
then for the first time obtained the
services (γενομένων) of volunteer trierarchs (ἐθελονταί) : τῶν, because these
became an institution.
12. **ἀλλ' οὔπω περὶ τούτων** : this
may look forward to the orator's
account of his public services in
§ 267, or possibly to the discussion
of his trierarchic reform in §§ 102—
109. **οὔπω**: sc. λέξω, but in XIX.
200, μήπω ταῦτα : sc. εἴπωμεν.
§ **100**. 2. **καὶ τὸ σῶσαι τὴν
νῆσον**, even saving the island, i.e.
this by itself, opposed to πολλῷ δ'...
κάλλιον, sc. ἐποιήσατε.
5. **μηδὲν......ὑπολογισάμενοι** : μηδὲν shows that the participial clause
is closely connected with τὸ ἀποδοῦναι,
not with ἐποιήσατε (understood). G.
1611. The meaning is without taking
into account, rather than not taking
into account.
6. **ἐν οἷς ἐπιστεύθητε** (for ἐν ἐκείνοις ἅ), representing the active πισ-
τεύειν ταῦτα ὑμῖν, as ὧν ἠδίκησθε
represents ἀδικεῖν ταῦτα ὑμᾶς.
7. **ἐξόδους πεζὰς**, land expeditions
(after ναυμαχίας) ; **στρατείας**, cam-
paigns.

ἡμῶν αὐτῶν, ἃς ἁπάσας ἡ πόλις τῆς τῶν ἄλλων
Ἑλλήνων ἐλευθερίας καὶ σωτηρίας πεποίηται. εἶτ' 101
ἐγὼ τεθεωρηκὼς ἐν τοσούτοις καὶ τοιούτοις τὴν
πόλιν ὑπὲρ τῶν τοῖς ἄλλοις συμφερόντων ἐθέλου-
σαν ἀγωνίζεσθαι, ὑπὲρ αὐτῆς τρόπον τινὰ τῆς
βουλῆς οὔσης τί ἔμελλον κελεύσειν ἢ τί συμβου- 5
λεύσειν αὐτῇ ποιεῖν; μνησικακεῖν νὴ Δία πρὸς
τοὺς βουλομένους σῴζεσθαι, καὶ προφάσεις ζητεῖν
260 δι' ἃς ἅπαντα προησόμεθα. καὶ τίς οὐκ ἂν ἀπέ-
κτεινέ με δικαίως, εἴ τι τῶν ὑπαρχόντων τῇ πόλει
καλῶν λόγῳ μόνον καταισχύνειν ἐπεχείρησ' ἄν; ἐπεὶ 10
τό γε ἔργον οὐκ ἂν ἐποιήσαθ' ὑμεῖς, ἀκριβῶς οἶδ'
ἐγώ· εἰ γὰρ ἐβούλεσθε, τί ἦν ἐμποδών; οὐκ ἐξῆν;
οὐχ ὑπῆρχον οἱ ταῦτ' ἐροῦντες οὗτοι;

9, 10. τῆς...σωτηρίας, rare genitive
of purpose or motive, generally found
with ἕνεκα, which is added here in
most MSS. So XIX. 76, πᾶσ' ἀπάτη
καὶ τέχνη συνεσκευάσθη τοῦ περὶ Φωκέας
ὀλέθρου, with similar variety of reading. (See G. 1127.) The infinitive
with τοῦ is common in this construction, especially in Thucydides (M.T.
798): an example occurs in § 107²,
τοῦ μὴ ποιεῖν.

§ 101. 4. ὑπὲρ αὐτῆς...οὔσης,
when the question in a manner concerned herself.

6. νὴ Δία, in bitter irony: cf. XX.
161.

8. δι' ἃς προησόμεθα (excuses) for
sacrificing (final).

9. ὑπαρχόντων (cf. § 95⁵): the
glories (καλά) are viewed as a public
possession.

10. ἐπεχείρησ' ἄν (M.T. 506):
there is no objection here to εἰ
ἐπεχείρησ' ἄν, as to either grammar
or sense. It is amply justified by XIX.
172: εἰ μὴ διὰ τὸ τούτους βούλεσθαι
σῶσαι, ἐξώλης ἀπολοίμην καὶ προώλης

εἰ προσλαβὼν γ' ἂν ἀργύριον πάνυ πολὺ
μετὰ τούτων ἐπρέσβευσα. There εἰ
ἐπρέσβευσα ἄν is if I would have
gone on the embassy, as εἰ ἐπεχείρησα
ἄν here is if I would have undertaken
(for any consideration). There may
be a justification of ἐπεχείρησ' ἄν in
the following τό γ' ἔργον οὐκ ἂν
ἐποιήσαθ' ὑμεῖς, you would not have
done the thing in reality (ἔργῳ),
opposed to the preceding supposition,
if I had been capable of undertaking
it even in word (λόγῳ).

13. οὐχ ὑπῆρχον...οὗτοι; were
not these men here ready to tell you
this? ταῦτα refers to μνησικακεῖν...
προησόμεθα (6—8).

§§ 102—109. The orator defends his Trierarchic Law against
the attacks of Aeschines. This important measure was enacted in 340
B.C., at about the time of the outbreak of the war with Philip (see
§ 107⁶). For an account of the
trierarchy at Athens, see Boeckh's
Staatsh. d. Athener, I. Book 4, ch.
11—16.

Βούλομαι τοίνυν ἐπανελθεῖν ἐφ᾽ ἃ τούτων ἑξῆς 102
ἐπολιτευόμην· καὶ σκοπεῖτε ἐν τούτοις πάλιν αὖ τί
τὸ τῇ πόλει βέλτιστον ἦν. ὁρῶν γάρ, ὦ ἄνδρες
Ἀθηναῖοι, τὸ ναυτικὸν ὑμῶν καταλυόμενον, καὶ τοὺς
μὲν πλουσίους ἀτελεῖς ἀπὸ μικρῶν ἀναλωμάτων 5
γιγνομένους τοὺς δὲ μέτρι᾽ ἢ μικρὰ κεκτημένους τῶν
πολιτῶν τὰ ὄντ᾽ ἀπολλύοντας, ἔτι δ᾽ ὑστερίζουσαν
ἐκ τούτων τὴν πόλιν τῶν καιρῶν, ἔθηκα νόμον καθ᾽
ὃν τοὺς μὲν τὰ δίκαια ποιεῖν ἠνάγκασα, [τοὺς πλουσίους,] τοὺς δὲ πένητας ἔπαυσ᾽ ἀδικουμένους, τῇ 10
πόλει δ᾽ ὅπερ ἦν χρησιμώτατον, ἐν καιρῷ γίγνεσθαι
τὰς παρασκευὰς ἐποίησα. καὶ γραφεὶς τὸν ἀγῶνα 103
τοῦτον εἰς ὑμᾶς εἰσῆλθον καὶ ἀπέφυγον, καὶ τὸ
μέρος τῶν ψήφων ὁ διώκων οὐκ ἔλαβεν. καίτοι
πόσα χρήματα τοὺς ἡγεμόνας τῶν συμμοριῶν ἢ

§ 102. 4. καταλυόμενον, *break-ing up* : notice the following descriptive present participles.

5. ἀτελεῖς...γιγνομένους, *becoming exempt* (from all 'liturgies') *by small payments*. As all the members of a συντέλεια (under the former system) were assessed equally for the support of their ship, the richer συντελεῖς might satisfy the law (as in the case supposed in § 104) by paying $\frac{1}{16}$ of the expense of one ship ; and as no one could be required to take more than one 'liturgy' in the same year, they would thus be exempt from all other services. But the richest of all, the leaders of the symmories (§ 103[4]), sometimes ingeniously used their legal duty of advancing the money for the trierarchy in case of special necessity as a means of avoiding even their own legal share of the expense. They could bargain with a contractor to do all the work for a fixed sum (e.g. a talent), which they advanced, afterwards assessing this whole sum, or

an unfair part of it, on their poorer colleagues. See Dem. XXI. 155.

7. τὰ ὄντ᾽ ἀπολλύοντας, *losing what they had* : a strong expression of the injustice to which the poorer συντελεῖς were liable.—ὑστερίζουσαν ...τῶν καιρῶν, as we say, *behind time*.

9. [τοὺς πλουσίους] : these words probably crept into the text as an explanation of τοὺς μέν, which needs no such note. The text is very doubtful, though the sense is clear.

§ 103. 1. γραφεὶς : sc. παρανόμων. —τὸν ἀγῶνα τοῦτον...εἰσῆλθον, i.e. *I stood* (entered on) *my trial on this issue before you*, εἰς ὑμᾶς implying *coming into court*. τοῦτον refers to γραφεὶς, meaning the trial which followed his being indicted. Cf. εἰσῆλθον τὴν γραφήν, § 105[2].

2. τὸ μέρος (sc. πέμπτον) : cf. § 266[6]. See note on § 82[9].

4. ἡγεμόνας τῶν συμμοριῶν, *leaders of the symmories*, here probably the symmories of the trierarchy, though the term commonly refers to the 300

τοὺς δευτέρους καὶ τρίτους οἴεσθέ μοι διδόναι ὥστε 5
μάλιστα μὲν μὴ θεῖναι τὸν νόμον τοῦτον, εἰ δὲ μὴ,
καταβάλλοντ᾽ ἐᾶν ἐν ὑπωμοσίᾳ; τοσαῦτ᾽, ὦ ἄνδρες
Ἀθηναῖοι, ὅσα ὀκνήσαιμ᾽ ἂν πρὸς ὑμᾶς εἰπεῖν. καὶ
ταῦτ᾽ εἰκότως ἔπραττον ἐκεῖνοι. ἦν γὰρ αὐτοῖς ἐκ 104
μὲν τῶν προτέρων νόμων συνεκκαίδεκα λῃτουργεῖν,
αὐτοῖς μὲν μικρὰ καὶ οὐδὲν ἀναλίσκουσι, τοὺς δ᾽

richest citizens (οἱ τριακόσιοι, § 171⁵),
who were leaders of the symmories
of the property-tax (εἰσφορά). Under
the system which prevailed from 357
to 340 B.C., the 1200 richest citizens,
who alone were liable to the duty of
the trierarchy, were divided into 20
symmories, regularly of 60 men each.
But exemption or changes in property
might reduce the whole number of
1200 and the number in each symmory in any year. To each of these
symmories was assigned a number of
triremes to be fitted out in each year,
regulated by the needs of the state.
The symmory divided itself into
smaller bodies (συντέλειαι), each of
which equipped a single ship. The
expense was borne equally by all the
members, without regard to their
wealth. Each symmory probably
had a single leader, and the 20
leaders, with the two classes called
δεύτεροι and τρίτοι (who are not
mentioned elsewhere), evidently belonged to the τριακόσιοι, perhaps
including all of that class in the
symmories (15 in each). The new
law of Demosthenes imposed the
burden of the trierarchy on the members of each symmory according to
their taxable property, thus greatly
increasing the assessment of the
richer and diminishing that of the
poorer members. Of this a striking
case is given in § 104⁶,⁷.

5. διδόναι, offered, representing
ἐδίδοσαν, which appears in § 104¹⁰.
6. μάλιστα μέν, above all things,

opposed to εἰ δὲ μὴ, otherwise, if not
(M.T. 478).—μὴ θεῖναι, not to enact ;
see next note.
7. καταβάλλοντ᾽ ἐᾶν ἐν ὑπωμοσίᾳ,
to drop it and let it lie under notice of
indictment (lit. under the prosecutor's
oath to bring an indictment). Whenever anyone brought a γραφὴ παρανόμων against a law or decree, he
was required to bind himself by an
oath, called ὑπωμοσία, to prosecute
the case. This had the effect of
suspending the law or decree if it was
already finally passed, or of stopping
a decree which had passed only the
Senate (i.e. a προβούλευμα) from
being voted on by the Assembly,
until the γραφὴ παρανόμων could be
tried. (See Essay II.) The meaning
here is that Demosthenes was offered
large sums if he would either decline
to bring his new law before the νομοθέται (μὴ θεῖναι) or else quietly let it
drop (ἐᾶν) when a γραφὴ παρανόμων
was brought against it after it was
passed.

§ 104. 1. ἦν...λῃτουργεῖν, i.e.
they might perform the service (of the
trierarchy) in bodies of sixteen : this
is probably stated as an extreme case
under the old law, in contrast with
an equally extreme case of a man with
two whole triremes to support under
the new law. A συντέλεια of sixteen
implies a change from 60 in the size
of the symmory : see note on § 103⁵.
3. αὐτοῖς μέν, themselves (ipsis),
opposed to τοὺς δ᾽ ἀπόρους.—μικρὰ
καὶ οὐδέν: see note on § 102⁵.

261 ἀπόρους τῶν πολιτῶν ἐπιτρίβουσιν, ἐκ δὲ τοῦ ἐμοῦ
νόμου τὸ γιγνόμενον κατὰ τὴν οὐσίαν ἕκαστον τιθέ- 5
ναι, καὶ δυοῖν ἐφάνη τριήραρχος ὁ τῆς μιᾶς ἕκτος καὶ
δέκατος πρότερον συντελής· οὐδὲ γὰρ τριηράρχους
ἔτ᾽ ὠνόμαζον ἑαυτούς, ἀλλὰ συντελεῖς. ὥστε δὴ
ταῦτα λυθῆναι καὶ μὴ τὰ δίκαια ποιεῖν ἀναγκασθῆ-
ναι, οὐκ ἔσθ᾽ ὅ τι οὐκ ἐδίδοσαν. καί μοι λέγε πρῶτον 105
μὲν τὸ ψήφισμα καθ᾽ ὃ εἰσῆλθον τὴν γραφήν, εἶτα
τοὺς καταλόγους, τόν τ᾽ ἐκ τοῦ προτέρου νόμου καὶ
τὸν κατὰ τὸν ἐμόν. λέγε.

ΨΗΦΙΣΜΑ. 5

['Επὶ ἄρχοντος Πολυκλέους, μηνὸς βοηδρομιῶνος ἕκτῃ
ἐπὶ δέκα, φυλῆς πρυτανευούσης 'Ιπποθωντίδος, Δημοσθένης
Δημοσθένους Παιανιεὺς εἰσήνεγκε νόμον τριηραρχικὸν ἀντὶ
τοῦ προτέρου, καθ᾽ ὃν αἱ συντέλειαι ἦσαν τῶν τριηράρχων·
καὶ ἐπεχειροτόνησεν ἡ βουλὴ καὶ ὁ δῆμος· καὶ ἀπήνεγκε 10

4. ἐπιτρίβουσιν, *distressing (grinding).*
5. τὸ γιγνόμενον τιθέναι, *to pay their quota (what fell to each)*: cf. τιθέναι τὰς εἰσφοράς, XXII. 42.—κατὰ τὴν οὐσίαν, *according to his property*: κατὰ τὸ τίμημα, *according to his valuation*, would be more strictly accurate, as the τίμημα, or *taxable property*, in different classes bore a differing proportion to the οὐσία.
6. δυοῖν ... συντελής: it was a possible case that a man who had been assessed (as supposed above) for only one-sixteenth part of the expense of one ship might be compelled to pay for two whole ships under the new law. τριήραρχος suggests τριήροιν and τριήρους with δυοῖν and μιᾶς.
8. συντελεῖς, *partners* in a συντέλεια: sixteen trierarchs of a single ship, of whom perhaps no one even saw the ship, were absurd!
10. ἐδίδοσαν, *offered*: cf. διδόναι

as imperfect in § 103⁵.
§ 105. 2. ψήφισμα: this cannot be the trierarchic law itself, which was no ψήφισμα; but a decree passed after the ὑπωμοσία, which may have ordered the suspension of the law or have provided for the trial of the case.—καθ᾽ ὃ = *secundum quod, ex quo*, not *propter quod* (see West.).
3. τοὺς καταλόγους; the stupidity of the interpolator of the false documents never shows to greater advantage than in the two fragments of a pretended decree given as κατάλογοι in § 106. The real documents were two lists of citizens of various degrees of wealth, with statements of their assessments for the trierarchy under the old law and under the law of Demosthenes. The contrast between the two called forth the question with which § 107 begins. The document in § 105 is not a decree, but a memorandum.

παρανόμων Δημοσθένει Πατροκλῆς Φλυεύς, καὶ τὸ μέρος τῶν
ψήφων οὐ λαβὼν ἀπέτισε τὰς πεντακοσίας δραχμάς.]
Φέρε δὴ καὶ τὸν καλὸν κατάλογον.   106

ΚΑΤΑΛΟΓΟΣ.

[Τοὺς τριηράρχους καλεῖσθαι ἐπὶ τὴν τριήρη συνεκκαίδεκα
ἐκ τῶν ἐν τοῖς λόχοις συντελειῶν, ἀπὸ εἴκοσι καὶ πέντε ἐτῶν
εἰς τετταράκοντα, ἐπὶ ἴσον τῇ χορηγίᾳ χρωμένους.]   5
Φέρε δὴ παρὰ τοῦτον τὸν ἐκ τοῦ ἐμοῦ νόμου
κατάλογον.

262   ΚΑΤΑΛΟΓΟΣ.

[Τοὺς τριηράρχους αἱρεῖσθαι ἐπὶ τὴν τριήρη ἀπὸ τῆς
οὐσίας κατὰ τίμησιν, ἀπὸ ταλάντων δέκα· ἐὰν δὲ πλειόνων 10
ἡ οὐσία ἀποτετιμημένη ᾖ χρημάτων, κατὰ τὸν ἀναλογισμὸν
ἕως τριῶν πλοίων καὶ ὑπηρετικοῦ ἡ λειτουργία ἔστω. κατὰ
τὴν αὐτὴν δὲ ἀναλογίαν ἔστω καὶ οἷς ἐλάττων οὐσία ἐστὶ τῶν
δέκα ταλάντων, εἰς συντέλειαν συναγομένοις εἰς τὰ δέκα
τάλαντα.]   15

Ἆρα μικρὰ βοηθῆσαι τοῖς πένησιν ὑμῶν δοκῶ, ἢ 107
μίκρ' ἀναλῶσαι ἂν τοῦ μὴ τὰ δίκαια ποιεῖν ἐθέλειν
οἱ πλούσιοι; οὐ τοίνυν μόνον τῷ μὴ καθυφεῖναι
ταῦτα σεμνύνομαι, οὐδὲ τῷ γραφεὶς ἀποφυγεῖν, ἀλλὰ
καὶ τῷ συμφέροντα θεῖναι τὸν νόμον καὶ τῷ πεῖραν 5

§ 107. 2. μίκρ' ἀναλῶσαι ἄν...
ἐθέλειν, does it seem likely that the
rich would have been willing to spend
(only) a little to escape doing justice?
With οἱ πλούσιοι supply δοκοῦσιν from
δοκῶ in l. 1 (see M.T. 754). ἀναλῶσαι
depends on ἐθέλειν ἄν, which represents ἤθελον ἄν. τοῦ μὴ ποιεῖν is
genitive of purpose (cf. § 100⁹).
3. καθυφεῖναι, dropping: cf. κατα-
βάλλοντα, § 103⁷.
5. συμφέροντα θεῖναι τὸν νόμον :
cf. πτηνὰς διώκεις τὰς ἐλπίδας, Eur.

frag. 273.—τῷ πεῖραν δεδωκέναι, on
the law having given a test of itself
(sc. τὸν νόμον αὐτοῦ). See § 195¹²,
ἃ γε μηδὲ πεῖραν ἔδωκε, with note ;
XXIV. 24, πεῖραν αὐτῶν πολλάκις
δεδώκασιν (sc. οἱ νόμοι) (with αὐτῶν
expressed); Thuc. I. 138⁹ (of Themistocles), ἀπὸ τοῦ πεῖραν διδοὺς ξυν-
ετὸς φαίνεσθαι, i.e. on trial. Compare
the perfect δεδωκέναι with the timeless aorists which precede (M.T. 109,
96).

ἔργῳ δεδωκέναι. πάντα γὰρ τὸν πόλεμον τῶν ἀποστόλων γιγνομένων κατὰ τὸν νόμον τὸν ἐμὸν, οὐχ
ἱκετηρίαν ἔθηκε τριήραρχος οὐδεὶς πώποθ᾽ ὡς ἀδικού-
μενος παρ᾽ ὑμῖν, οὐκ ἐν Μουνιχίᾳ ἐκαθέζετο, οὐχ ὑπὸ
τῶν ἀποστολέων ἐδέθη, οὐ τριήρης οὔτ᾽ ἔξω κατα- 10
λειφθεῖσ᾽ ἀπώλετο τῇ πόλει, οὔτ᾽ αὐτοῦ ἀπελείφθη
οὐ δυναμένη ἀνάγεσθαι. καίτοι κατὰ τοὺς προτέρους 108
νόμους ἅπαντα ταῦτα ἐγίγνετο. τὸ δ᾽ αἴτιον, ἐν τοῖς
πένησιν ἦν τὸ λῃτουργεῖν· πολλὰ δὴ τἀδύνατα συνέ-
βαινεν. ἐγὼ δ᾽ ἐκ τῶν ἀπόρων εἰς τοὺς εὐπόρους
μετήνεγκα τὰς τριηραρχίας· πάντ᾽ οὖν τὰ δέοντ᾽ 5
ἐγίγνετο. καὶ μὴν καὶ κατ᾽ αὐτὸ τοῦτο ἄξιός εἰμι
ἐπαίνου τυχεῖν, ὅτι πάντα τὰ τοιαῦτα προῃρούμην
πολιτεύματα ἀφ᾽ ὧν ἅμα δόξαι καὶ τιμαὶ καὶ δυνάμεις συνέβαινον τῇ πόλει· βάσκανον δὲ καὶ πικρὸν
263 καὶ κακόηθες οὐδέν ἐστι πολίτευμ᾽ ἐμὸν, οὐδὲ ταπει- 10

6. **ἀποστόλων** : see § 80¹ ; and
cf. IV. 35, τοὺς δ᾽ ἀποστόλους πάντας
ὑμῖν ὑστερίζειν τῶν καιρῶν.
8. **ἱκετηρίαν** (sc. ῥάβδον), *suppliant's bough*, generally of olive,
bound with wool, which a suppliant
laid on the altar of a divinity whose
succour he invoked.
9. **ἐν Μουνιχίᾳ** : ἔνθα ἐστὶν ἱερὸν
Μουνυχίας Ἀρτέμιδος· κἀκεῖ ἔφευγον
οἵτινες τῶν τριηράρχων ἠδικοῦντο, ἢ
ναῦται ἤ τινες τῶν ἐξεταζομένων ἐν τῷ
Πειραιεῖ (Schol.). See Lys. XIII.
24, καθίζουσιν ἐπὶ τὸν βωμὸν Μουνι-
χίασιν. Munychia is the high hill of
the peninsula of Piraeus.
10. **ἀποστολέων** : see Bekk. Anecd.
435, 29 : ἀποστολεῖς : δέκα τὸν ἀριθμὸν ἄρχοντες ἦσαν, οἱ ἐπὶ τῆς ἐκπομπῆς
τῶν πλεουσῶν τριήρων καὶ τῶν ἀπαγο-
μένων στόλων ἀποδεδειγμένοι. They
were chosen for each occasion, and
had charge of supplying the trierarchs
with rigging and other material for
the triremes from the public stores,

and of seeing that these were properly
restored at the end of the voyage.
10, 11. **ἔξω καταλειφθεῖσ᾽**, *abandoned at sea* ; **αὐτοῦ ἀπελείφθη**, *was
left behind in port.*—**αὐτοῦ**, *on the
spot*, i.e. in port, where she was lying :
ἐν τῷ λιμένι ἀνεπισκεύαστος (Schol.).
See Plat. Rep. 371 C, αὐτοῦ μένοντας
περὶ τὴν ἀγοράν.
§ **108**. 2. **τὸ δ᾽ αἴτιον**, without
ὅτι, like σημεῖον δέ and τεκμήριον δέ :
cf. VIII. 32.
3. **λῃτουργεῖν**: the η here is settled
by inscriptions.—**ἀδύνατα**, *cases of im-
possibility.*
7. **προῃρούμην** : cf. προαιρεσις,
§ 93⁴.
8. **δυνάμεις**, *power* (of various
kinds) : cf. §§ 44³, 233², 237⁶.
9. **βάσκανον**, *malicious*: see Harpocr., ἀντὶ τοῦ φιλαίτιον καὶ συκοφαν-
τικόν.
10. **κακόηθες**, *low-principled* : see
ἦθος, § 109¹.

νὸν, οὐδὲ τῆς πόλεως ἀνάξιον. ταὐτὸ τοίνυν ἦθος 109
ἔχων ἔν τε τοῖς κατὰ τὴν πόλιν πολιτεύμασι καὶ ἐν
τοῖς Ἑλληνικοῖς φανήσομαι· οὔτε γὰρ ἐν τῇ πόλει
τὰς παρὰ τῶν πλουσίων χάριτας μᾶλλον ἢ τὰ τῶν
πολλῶν δίκαια εἱλόμην, οὔτ' ἐν τοῖς Ἑλληνικοῖς τὰ 5
Φιλίππου δῶρα καὶ τὴν ξενίαν ἠγάπησ' ἀντὶ τῶν
κοινῇ πᾶσι τοῖς Ἕλλησι συμφερόντων.

Ἡγοῦμαι τοίνυν λοιπὸν εἶναί μοι περὶ τοῦ κηρύγ- 110
ματος εἰπεῖν καὶ τῶν εὐθυνῶν· τὸ γὰρ ὡς τἄριστά τ'
ἔπραττον καὶ διὰ παντὸς εὔνους εἰμὶ καὶ πρόθυμος
εὖ ποιεῖν ὑμᾶς, ἱκανῶς ἐκ τῶν εἰρημένων δεδηλῶσθαί
μοι νομίζω. καίτοι τὰ μέγιστά γε τῶν πεπολιτευ- 5
μένων καὶ πεπραγμένων ἐμαυτῷ παραλείπω, ὑπολαμβάνων πρῶτον μὲν ἐφεξῆς τοὺς περὶ αὐτοῦ τοῦ παρα-

§ **109.** 1. **ἦθος**, *principles* (of action), *political character* : see note on § 114[2].

2. **ἐν τοῖς Ἑλληνικοῖς**, opposed to *ἐν τοῖς κατὰ τὴν πόλιν*: see 59[2].

6. **ἀντί**, *rather than*, like μᾶλλον ἤ (4).

§§ **110—121** contain the reply to the first two arguments of Aeschines, that on the responsibility of Demosthenes as an ἄρχων at the time when Ctesiphon proposed his decree (§§ 111—119), and that on the place of proclamation (§§ 120, 121). § 110 is introductory. §§ 122—125 are a peroration to the division of the argument beginning with § 53.

§ **110.** 1. **περὶ τοῦ κηρύγματος**, i.e. *about the place of proclamation*, this being the only point in dispute under this head.

2. **τῶν εὐθυνῶν**: this concerns only the question whether Demosthenes was a "responsible magistrate" when Ctesiphon proposed to crown him.— **τὸ γὰρ...ὑμᾶς**, i.e. the statement in Ctesiphon's decree *that I did etc.*, subj. of δεδηλῶσθαι (4) : with this

reference to the words of the decree cf. 57[1].

5. **τὰ μέγιστα** refers especially to his important public services in the year before Chaeronea (339—338), the account of which comes in later with far greater effect.

6. **παραλείπω**, *I leave aside* (not necessarily *I omit*). This whole passage is full of rhetorical art. He has no intention whatever of omitting these acts; but he skilfully implies that his earlier acts, already related, are ample for the legal justification of Ctesiphon, so that he could afford to leave his greatest achievements unmentioned. He also diverts attention from the weakness of his argument on the εὔθυναι by placing it between two most effective political harangues. See Essay I. § 5.

7. **ἐφεξῆς**, *in due order* : cf. § 56[6], οὐδὲν ἑκὼν παραλείψω, where he simply states his general purpose of giving a full account of his public life.—**αὐτοῦ τοῦ παρανόμου**, *the strict question of illegality*, with which alone the γραφὴ παρανόμων is properly concerned.

νόμου λόγους ἀποδοῦναί με δεῖν, εἶτα, κἂν μηδὲν
εἴπω περὶ τῶν λοιπῶν πολιτευμάτων, ὁμοίως παρ᾽
ὑμῶν ἑκάστῳ τὸ συνειδὸς ὑπάρχειν μοι. 10
Τῶν μὲν οὖν λόγων, οὓς οὗτος ἄνω καὶ κάτω 111
διακυκῶν ἔλεγε περὶ τῶν παραγεγραμμένων νόμων,
οὔτε μὰ τοὺς θεοὺς οἶμαι ὑμᾶς μανθάνειν οὔτ᾽ αὐτὸς
ἐδυνάμην συνεῖναι τοὺς πολλούς· ἁπλῶς δὲ τὴν
ὀρθὴν περὶ τῶν δικαίων διαλέξομαι. τοσούτῳ γὰρ 5
δέω λέγειν ὡς οὐκ εἰμὶ ὑπεύθυνος, ὃ νῦν οὗτος διέβαλλε καὶ διωρίζετο, ὥσθ᾽ ἅπαντα τὸν βίον ὑπεύθυνος εἶναι ὁμολογῶ ὧν ἢ διακεχείρικα ἢ πεπολίτευμαι παρ᾽ ὑμῖν. ὧν μέντοι γ᾽ ἐκ τῆς ἰδίας οὐσίας 112

9. **ὁμοίως**, all the same.—**παρ'
ὑμῶν**...**ὑπάρχειν μοι**, that I may rely
on a consciousness of them in each of
your minds: cf. § 95⁵ and note.
§ **111**. 1. **τῶν λόγων**, depending on τοὺς πολλούς.—**ἄνω καὶ κάτω
διακυκῶν**, mixing them in utter confusion. See IX. 36, **ἄνω καὶ κάτω
πεποίηκε**, and without καί IV. 41,
συμπαραθεῖτε **ἄνω κάτω**, up and down.
2. **παραγεγραμμένων** : the laws
which the indicted decree (τὸ φεῦγον
ψήφισμα) was charged with violating
were written on a tablet (σανίδιον) by
its side, and this was posted in the
court-room. See Aesch. III. 200 : ἐν
ταῖς γραφαῖς τῶν παρανόμων παράκειται
κανὼν τοῦ δικαίου τουτὶ τὸ σανίδιον καὶ
τὸ ψήφισμα καὶ οἱ παραγεγραμμένοι
νόμοι.
4. **τὴν ὀρθὴν** (sc. ὁδόν), as we
say, straightforward : see Ar. Av. 1,
ὀρθὴν κελεύεις;
5. **τῶν δικαίων**, the rights of the
case, opposed to τῶν λόγων (1).—
τοσούτῳ δέω λέγειν, I am so far from
saying: τοσούτῳ (Σ) with δέω as with
comparatives : so in IX. 17. Most
MSS. have τοσούτου in both passages.
6. **διέβαλλε καὶ διωρίζετο** : see
§ 4⁶.

8. **ὧν**...**πεπολίτευμαι**, i.e. either
for money that I have handled or for
public acts that I have done.
§ **112**. The sophistical character
of the argument of §§ 112—119 explains the anxiety of the orator to
cover its weakness by its position in
the oration. The reply of Aeschines
(III. 17 ff.) to this ἄφυκτον λόγον, ὅν
φησι Δημοσθένης, probably written or
greatly modified after hearing this
passage, is conclusive. The law
quoted by Aesch. (11), τοὺς ὑπευθύνους μὴ στεφανοῦν, certainly made
no exception for those who gave
money to the state while in office.
Indeed, this very claim is one which
needed to be established by the
εὔθυναι, in which it might be disputed : see Aesch. 23, ἔασον ἀμφισ-
βητῆσαί σοι τὸν βουλόμενον τῶν πολιτῶν ὡς οὐκ ἐπέδωκας. The claim of
Demosthenes at least amounts to
this, that any officer who asserts that
he has expended more in the service
of the state than he received should
be exempt from the law τοὺς ὑπευθύνους μὴ στεφανοῦν. The specious
argument that a man cannot fairly
be called to account for the ex-
penditure of his own money on public

ἐπαγγειλάμενος δέδωκα τῷ δήμῳ, οὐδεμίαν ἡμέραν
264 ὑπεύθυνος εἶναί φημι (ἀκούεις, Αἰσχίνη ;) οὐδ᾽ ἄλλον
οὐδένα, οὐδ᾽ ἂν τῶν ἐννέ᾽ ἀρχόντων τις ὢν τύχῃ. τίς
γάρ ἐστι νόμος τοσαύτης ἀδικίας καὶ μισανθρωπίας 5
μεστὸς ὥστε τὸν δόντα τι τῶν ἰδίων καὶ ποιήσαντα
πρᾶγμα φιλάνθρωπον καὶ φιλόδωρον τῆς χάριτος
μὲν ἀποστερεῖν, εἰς τοὺς συκοφάντας δ᾽ ἄγειν, καὶ
τούτους ἐπὶ τὰς εὐθύνας ὧν ἔδωκεν ἐφιστάναι ; οὐδὲ
εἷς. εἰ δέ φησιν οὗτος, δειξάτω, κἀγὼ στέρξω καὶ 10
σιωπήσομαι. ἀλλ᾽ οὐκ ἔστιν, ἄνδρες Ἀθηναῖοι, ἀλλ᾽ 113
οὗτος συκοφαντῶν, ὅτι ἐπὶ τῷ θεωρικῷ τότε ὢν ἐπέδωκα τὰ χρήματα, ἐπῄνεσεν αὐτὸν, φησὶν, ὑπεύθυνον ὄντα. οὐ περὶ τούτων γ᾽ οὐδενὸς ὧν ὑπεύ-

works could not release Demosthenes
from εὔθυναι when he had obviously
had public money in his hands.
  1. **ὢν μέντοι γ᾽** : γε emphasizes
the whole relative clause.
  2. **ἐπαγγειλάμενος δέδωκα**, *have
offered and given*, i.e. *have given by
my free act*, openly declared.
  4. **τῶν ἐννέ᾽ ἀρχόντων** : The Archons, as the chief magistrates and as
candidates for the Areopagus, would
be subject to special scrutiny at their
εὔθυναι.
  5. **μισανθρωπίας**, *misanthropy*, opposed to φιλάνθρωπον (7).
  8. **εἰς τοὺς συκοφάντας** : ironical
allusion to εἰς τοὺς λογιστάς, as if the
sycophants were a board of officers
(hence τούς).
  9. **τούτους...ἐφιστάναι**, *to set them
to audit the accounts etc.*
  § **113.** 1. **ἀλλ᾽ οὐκ ἔστιν** (sc.
νόμος τοιοῦτος).
  2. **ἐπὶ τῷ θεωρικῷ ὤν**, *being treas-
urer of the Theoric Fund*: for the
importance of this office see Aesch.
III. 25, 26, ending with Κτησιφῶν δὲ
Δημοσθένην τὸν συλλήβδην ἁπάσας τὰς
Ἀθήνησιν ἀρχὰς ἄρχοντα οὐκ ὤκνησε

γράψαι στεφανοῦν.—**ἐπέδωκα**, properly
gave in addition (to the public fund
in his charge). Gifts to the state
were often called ἐπιδόσεις : cf. note
on § 171[7].
  3. **ἐπῄνεσεν αὐτὸν** (sc. Κτησιφῶν)
=ἔγραψεν ἐπαινέσαι. All MSS. except Σ insert ἡ βουλή as subject of
ἐπῄνεσεν. The true subject appears
in l. 10, ταῦτ᾽ ἔγραψεν ὁ δεῖ περὶ ἐμοῦ.
ἐπαινεῖν, *compliment by a vote of
thanks*, and στεφανοῦν are both used
of the vote conferring the crown: see
§§ 57[4], 58[2], 117[5].
  4. **οὐ περὶ τούτων...ἐπέδωκα** : this
argument assumes that an ordinary
ὑπεύθυνος could be crowned, before
passing his εὔθυναι, for a gift to the
state which was not connected with
his office. But this was not the case
with the gifts of Demosthenes.
These were both closely connected
with the funds which he held as an
officer of state, and the argument of
Aeschines (23) applies to them in its
full force. Demosthenes says nothing
which shows that Ctesiphon did not
violate the letter and even the spirit

θυνος ἦν, ἀλλ᾽ ἐφ᾽ οἷς ἐπέδωκα, ὦ συκοφάντα. ἀλλὰ 5
καὶ τειχοποιὸς ἦσθα. καὶ διά γε τοῦτ᾽ ὀρθῶς
ἐπῃνούμην, ὅτι τἀνηλωμέν᾽ ἔδωκα καὶ οὐκ ἐλογι-
ζόμην. ὁ μὲν γὰρ λογισμὸς εὐθυνῶν καὶ τῶν ἐξετασόντων προσδεῖται, ἡ δὲ δωρεὰ χάριτος καὶ ἐπαίνου
δικαία ἐστὶ τυγχάνειν· διόπερ ταῦτ᾽ ἔγραψεν ὁδὶ 10
περὶ ἐμοῦ· ὅτι δ᾽ οὕτω ταῦτ᾽ οὐ μόνον ἐν τοῖς νό- 114
μοις ἀλλὰ καὶ ἐν τοῖς ὑμετέροις ἤθεσιν ὥρισται,
ἐγὼ ῥᾳδίως πολλαχόθεν δείξω. πρῶτον μὲν γὰρ
Ναυσικλῆς στρατηγῶν ἐφ᾽ οἷς ἀπὸ τῶν ἰδίων προεῖτο
πολλάκις ἐστεφάνωται ὑφ᾽ ὑμῶν· εἶθ᾽ ὅτε τὰς ἀσπί- 5
δας Διότιμος ἔδωκε καὶ πάλιν Χαρίδημος, ἐστεφα-
νοῦντο· εἶθ᾽ οὑτοσὶ Νεοπτόλεμος πολλῶν ἔργων ἐπιστάτης ὢν, ἐφ᾽ οἷς ἐπέδωκε τετίμηται. σχέτλιον γὰρ

of the law τοὺς ὑπευθύνους μὴ στεφανοῦν. And yet it is more than likely
that the friends of Demosthenes, in
their eagerness to crown him for his
noble services, overlooked the technical obstacle to their action ; and the
court appears to have decided to overlook their oversight.

6. τειχοποιὸς, one of a board of
commissioners appointed to super-
intend the repairs of the city walls.
The argument seems to have been
the same about both of the offices
which Demosthenes held in 337—
336 B.C. See Essay III. § 1.

8. τῶν ἐξετασόντων (= οἳ ἐξετά-
σουσι), *men to investigate*: the present
would be simply *investigators*, with
no temporal or final force.

§ 114. 2. **ἤθεσιν**, *your moral
feelings*, which impel you to act thus.
Cf. § 204². Cf. ἠθικά, mores, *morals.*
See note on § 275³.

3. **πολλαχόθεν δείξω** : Aeschines
anticipates or rather answers this
argument in 193 : λέγει δὲ ὁ φεύγων...
οὐχ ὡς ἔννομα γέγραφεν, ἀλλ᾽ ὡς ἤδη

ποτὲ καὶ πρότερον ἕτερος τοιαῦτα γράψας
ἀπέφυγεν.

4. **Ναυσικλῆς** : the general who
commanded the well-known expedition which stopped Philip at Thermopylae in 352 B.C.

6. **Διότιμος** : mentioned in XXI.
208 as a rich trierarch, included by
Arrian (I. 10, 4) among the generals
whom Alexander demanded after the
destruction of Thebes.—**Χαρίδημος** :
of Oreus, an adopted Athenian, the
object of severe invective in the oration
against Aristocrates (352 B.C.). He
was first a guerrilla leader in the service of Athens, later one of the patriotic
party, and was demanded by Alexander in 335.

7. **οὑτοσὶ** implies that Neoptolemus
was well known in Athens.—**πολλῶν
ἔργων ἐπιστάτης** : probably one of
those called δημοσίων ἔργων ἐπιστάται
by Aesch. (III. 29), specially appointed
to direct special works.

8. **σχέτλιον ἂν εἴη...ὑφέξει** : for
the peculiar form of conditional sentence see M.T. 503, 407.

ἂν εἴη τοῦτό γε, εἰ τῷ τιν' ἀρχὴν ἄρχοντι ἢ διδόναι
τῇ πόλει τὰ ἑαυτοῦ διὰ τὴν ἀρχὴν μὴ ἐξέσται, ἢ τῶν 10
265 δοθέντων ἀντὶ τοῦ κομίσασθαι χάριν εὐθύνας ὑφέξει.
ὅτι τοίνυν ταῦτ' ἀληθῆ λέγω, λέγε τὰ ψηφίσματά μοι 115
τὰ τούτοις γεγενημέν' αὐτὰ λαβών. λέγε.

ΨΗΦΙΣΜΑ.

['Άρχων Δημόνικος Φλυεύς, βοηδρομιῶνος ἕκτῃ μετ'
εἰκάδα, γνώμῃ βουλῆς καὶ δήμου, Καλλίας Φρεάρριος εἶπεν, 5
ὅτι δοκεῖ τῇ βουλῇ καὶ τῷ δήμῳ στεφανῶσαι Ναυσικλέα τὸν
ἐπὶ τῶν ὅπλων, ὅτι 'Αθηναίων ὁπλιτῶν δισχιλίων ὄντων ἐν
'Ίμβρῳ καὶ βοηθούντων τοῖς κατοικοῦσιν 'Αθηναίων τὴν
νῆσον, οὐ δυναμένου Φίλωνος τοῦ ἐπὶ τῆς διοικήσεως κεχει-
ροτονημένου διὰ τοὺς χειμῶνας πλεῦσαι καὶ μισθοδοτῆσαι 10
τοὺς ὁπλίτας, ἐκ τῆς ἰδίας οὐσίας ἔδωκε καὶ οὐκ εἰσέπραξε τὸν
δῆμον, καὶ ἀναγορεῦσαι τὸν στέφανον Διονυσίοις τραγῳδοῖς
καινοῖς.]

ΕΤΕΡΟΝ ΨΗΦΙΣΜΑ.

[Εἶπε Καλλίας Φρεάρριος, πρυτάνεων λεγόντων βουλῆς 116
γνώμῃ, ἐπειδὴ Χαρίδημος ὁ ἐπὶ τῶν ὁπλιτῶν, ἀποσταλεὶς
εἰς Σαλαμῖνα, καὶ Διότιμος ὁ ἐπὶ τῶν ἱππέων, ἐν τῇ ἐπὶ
τοῦ ποταμοῦ μάχῃ τῶν στρατιωτῶν τινων ὑπὸ τῶν πολεμίων
σκυλευθέντων, ἐκ τῶν ἰδίων ἀναλωμάτων καθώπλισαν τοὺς 5
νεανίσκους ἀσπίσιν ὀκτακοσίαις, δεδόχθαι τῇ βουλῇ καὶ τῷ
δήμῳ στεφανῶσαι Χαρίδημον καὶ Διότιμον χρυσῷ στεφάνῳ,
καὶ ἀναγορεῦσαι Παναθηναίοις τοῖς μεγάλοις ἐν τῷ γυμνικῷ
ἀγῶνι καὶ Διονυσίοις τραγῳδοῖς καινοῖς· τῆς δὲ ἀναγορεύσεως
266 ἐπιμεληθῆναι θεσμοθέτας, πρυτάνεις, ἀγωνοθέτας.]   10

Τούτων ἕκαστος, Αἰσχίνη, τῆς μὲν ἀρχῆς ἧς 117
ἦρχεν ὑπεύθυνος ἦν, ἐφ' οἷς δ' ἐστεφανοῦτο οὐχ

---

11. κομίσασθαι implies that the
receiver has a claim on the giver :
cf. ἀποδοῦναι, § 110[6], and Plat. Rep.
507 A, ἐμέ τε δύνασθαι αὐτὴν ἀποδοῦναι
καὶ ὑμᾶς κομίσασθαι.

§ 117. 2. ἐφ' οἷς ἐστεφανοῦτο :
we do not know whether there was
any distinction between these decrees
and that of Ctesiphon like that mentioned in § 113[4]. As Demosthenes

ὑπεύθυνος. οὐκοῦν οὐδ' ἐγώ· ταὐτὰ γὰρ δίκαι' ἐστί
μοι περὶ τῶν αὐτῶν τοῖς ἄλλοις δήπου. ἐπέδωκα·
ἐπαινοῦμαι διὰ ταῦτα, οὐκ ὧν ὧν ἔδωχ' ὑπεύθυνος. 5
ἦρχον· καὶ δεδωκά γ' εὐθύνας ἐκείνων, οὐχ ὧν ἐπέδωκα. νὴ Δί', ἀλλ' ἀδίκως ἦρξα· εἶτα παρὼν, ὅτε
μ' εἰσῆγον οἱ λογισταὶ, οὐ κατηγόρεις ;
῞Ινα τοίνυν ἴδηθ' ὅτι αὐτὸς οὗτός μοι μαρτυρεῖ 118
ἐφ' οἷς οὐχ ὑπεύθυνος ἦν ἐστεφανῶσθαι, λαβὼν
ἀνάγνωθι τὸ ψήφισμ' ὅλον τὸ γραφέν μοι. οἷς γὰρ
οὐκ ἐγράψατο τοῦ προβουλεύματος, τούτοις ἃ διώκει
συκοφαντῶν φανήσεται. λέγε. 5

identifies his own case absolutely with
these, the question is of little moment.
5. **ἐπαινοῦμαι**: cf. ἐπῄνεσεν, § 113³.
7. **νὴ Δί', ἀλλ'** : a more emphatic
form in stating an objection than the
common ἀλλά, νὴ Δία : cf. XIX. 272,
XX. 58.—**παρὼν** : i.e. *being present*
(as you were).
8. **μ' εἰσῆγον οἱ λογισταὶ** : see
Aristot. Pol. Ath. 54, καὶ (κληροῦσι
οἱ 'Αθ.) λογιστὰς δέκα καὶ συνηγόρους
τούτοις δέκα, πρὸς οὓς ἅπαντας ἀνάγκη
τοὺς τὰς ἀρχὰς ἄρξαντας λόγον ἀπενεγ-
κεῖν· οὗτοι γάρ εἰσι μόνοι τοῖς ὑπευθύνοις
λογιζόμενοι, καὶ τὰς εὐθύνας εἰς τὸ
δικαστήριον εἰσάγοντες. Before this
board of auditors every magistrate
had to appear for his εὔθυναι at the
end of his term of office ; and they
(generally as a matter of form)
brought him before a Heliastic court
of 501 judges, in which anyone might
appear and accuse him of any offence
connected with his office. His accounts of money expended were
audited at the same time. See
Aesch. III. 17—23. The question
τίς βούλεται κατηγορεῖν ; (Aesch. 23)
was probably asked in presence of
the court at the εὔθυναι of Demosthenes ; and to this Aeschines did

not respond. But these εὔθυναι must
have come several months after
Ctesiphon's bill had passed the
Senate and had been indicted by
Aeschines, so that accusation at the
εὔθυναι was superseded. See Essay
III. § 1.
§ **118.** 2. **ἐστεφανῶσθαι** (sc.
ἐμέ), that the proposal to crown me
has passed the Senate : cf. ἐπῄνεσεν
in § 113³.
3. **γραφέν μοι**, *proposed in my
honour* : see note on § 56⁴.
4. **τοῦ προβουλεύματος** : partitive
after οἷς. The meaning is, that he
will use the omissions from the decree
in the indictment to show the malice
of Aeschines in prosecuting the clauses
which he includes.
ἃ διώκει συκοφαντῶν : see XXIII.
61, συκοφαντοῦμεν τὸ πρᾶγμα.
The orator now calls for the reading
of the bill of Ctesiphon, ostensibly to
prove the point just made, but perhaps
chiefly to recall to the minds of the
judges Ctesiphon's enumeration of
his public services which the Senate
has approved. In the following
spurious decree the Archon's name
is wrong and different from that in
the indictment (which is also wrong).

ΨΗΦΙΣΜΑ.

['Επὶ ἄρχοντος Εὐθυκλέους, πυανεψιῶνος ἐνάτῃ ἀπιόντος,
φυλῆς πρυτανευούσης Οἰνηΐδος, Κτησιφῶν Λεωσθένους 'Ανα-
φλύστιος εἶπεν, ἐπειδὴ Δημοσθένης Δημοσθένους Παιανιεὺς
γενόμενος ἐπιμελητὴς τῆς τῶν τειχῶν ἐπισκευῆς καὶ προσανα- 10
λώσας εἰς τὰ ἔργα ἀπὸ τῆς ἰδίας οὐσίας τρία τάλαντα ἐπέδωκε
ταῦτα τῷ δήμῳ, καὶ ἐπὶ τοῦ θεωρικοῦ κατασταθεὶς ἐπέδωκε
τοῖς ἐκ πασῶν τῶν φυλῶν θεωροῖς ἑκατὸν μνᾶς εἰς θυσίας,
δεδόχθαι τῇ βουλῇ καὶ τῷ δήμῳ τῷ 'Αθηναίων ἐπαινέσαι
Δημοσθένην Δημοσθένους Παιανιέα ἀρετῆς ἕνεκα καὶ καλοκα- 15
γαθίας ἧς ἔχων διατελεῖ ἐν παντὶ καιρῷ εἰς τὸν δῆμον τὸν
'Αθηναίων, καὶ στεφανῶσαι χρυσῷ στεφάνῳ, καὶ ἀναγορεῦσαι
267 τὸν στέφανον ἐν τῷ θεάτρῳ Διονυσίοις τραγῳδοῖς καινοῖς τῆς
δὲ ἀναγορεύσεως ἐπιμεληθῆναι τὸν ἀγωνοθέτην.]

Οὐκοῦν ἃ μὲν ἐπέδωκα ταῦτ' ἐστὶν, ὧν οὐδὲν σὺ 119
γέγραψαι· ἃ δέ φησιν ἡ βουλὴ δεῖν ἀντὶ τούτων
γενέσθαι μοι, ταῦτ' ἔσθ' ἃ διώκεις. τὸ λαβεῖν οὖν
τὰ διδόμενα ὁμολογῶν ἔννομον εἶναι, τὸ χάριν τούτων ἀποδοῦναι παρανόμων γράφει. ὁ δὲ παμπόνηρος 5
ἄνθρωπος καὶ θεοῖς ἐχθρὸς καὶ βάσκανος ὄντως
ποῖός τις ἂν εἴη πρὸς θεῶν; οὐχ ὁ τοιοῦτος;
Καὶ μὴν περὶ τοῦ γ' ἐν τῷ θεάτρῳ κηρύττεσθαι, 120
τὸ μὲν μυριάκις μυρίους κεκηρῦχθαι παραλείπω καὶ

---

§ 119. Here the proof of the
malice of Aeschines, promised in
§ 118, is given on the authority of the
decree just read. It is argued that
Aeschines admits the gifts and their
legality by his silence concerning
them, while he brands as illegal the
proposal to return public thanks for
these gifts. As if the thanks for a
legal gift might not be given in an
illegal manner.

5. **παρανόμων γράφει**: cf. note
on § 13⁹.

§ 120. 2. **μυριάκις μυρίους**: this
means that 10,000 men had been
crowned on 10,000 occasions (not
10,000 times 10,000 men). This
was justified rhetorically by the
great frequency of decrees conferring
crowns to be proclaimed in the
theatre: the number of these on record
shows that any law which may
have forbidden the proclamation of
crowns in the theatre was a dead
letter.

τὸ πολλάκις αὐτὸς ἐστεφανῶσθαι πρότερον· ἀλλὰ
πρὸς θεῶν οὕτω σκαιὸς εἰ καὶ ἀναίσθητος, Αἰσχίνη,
ὥστ᾽ οὐ δύνασαι λογίσασθαι ὅτι τῷ μὲν στεφανου- 5
μένῳ τὸν αὐτὸν ἔχει ζῆλον ὁ στέφανος, ὅπου ἂν
ἀναρρηθῇ, τοῦ δὲ τῶν στεφανούντων εἵνεκα συμφέροντος ἐν τῷ θεάτρῳ γίγνεται τὸ κήρυγμα; οἱ γὰρ
ἀκούσαντες ἅπαντες εἰς τὸ ποιεῖν εὖ τὴν πόλιν προ-
τρέπονται, καὶ τοὺς ἀποδιδόντας τὴν χάριν μᾶλλον 10
ἐπαινοῦσι τοῦ στεφανουμένου· διόπερ τὸν νόμον
τοῦτον ἡ πόλις γέγραφεν. Λέγε δ᾽ αὐτόν μοι τὸν
νόμον λαβών.

ΝΟΜΟΣ.

[Ὅσους στεφανοῦσί τινες τῶν δήμων, τὰς ἀναγορεύσεις 15
τῶν στεφάνων ποιεῖσθαι ἐν αὐτοῖς ἑκάστους τοῖς ἰδίοις δήμοις,
ἐὰν μή τινας ὁ δῆμος ὁ τῶν Ἀθηναίων ἢ ἡ βουλὴ στεφανοῖ.
τούτους δ᾽ ἐξεῖναι ἐν τῷ θεάτρῳ Διονυσίοις ἀναγορεύεσθαι.]

Ἀκούεις, Αἰσχίνη, τοῦ νόμου λέγοντος σαφῶς, 121
268 πλὴν ἐάν τινας ὁ δῆμος ἢ ἡ βουλὴ ψηφίσηται·

---

3. **τὸ πολλάκις...πρότερον**: in the
note on § 83⁵ (δευτέρου...γιγνομένου)
I have given reasons for thinking that
the crown voted on the motion of
Aristonicus in 340 B.C., and proclaimed in the theatre, had been preceded by another, also proclaimed in
the theatre, of which we have no
other account than the allusion in
§ 83. These two, with the one voted
on the motion of Demomeles and
Hyperides in 338 B.C. (§§ 222, 223),
if the latter was actually proclaimed,
justify the use of πολλάκις, especially
after μυριάκις μυρίους.

5. **ὥστ᾽ οὐ δύνασαι** : see M.T.
601 and 584. The meaning is *are
you so stupid that you are not able?*
while with ὥστε μὴ δύνασθαι it would

be *are you stupid enough not to be
able?*

6. **τὸν αὐτὸν ἔχει ζῆλον**, i.e. *the
receiver of the crown feels the same
pride* : ζῆλος is emulation, *pride in
excelling*, hence *glorying* (see §§ 217³,
273⁵).

7. **εἵνεκα** : this Ionic and poetic
form is often found in the best MSS.
of Demosthenes.

9. **εἰς τὸ ποιεῖν εὖ** : this motive is
strongly urged in many decrees conferring crowns.

§ 121. This short but impassioned
outburst cannot be a reply to the long
and confused argument of Aeschines
(32—48). See Essay I., Remarks on
§§ 120, 121.

τούτους δ' ἀναγορευέτω; τί οὖν, ὦ ταλαίπωρε,
συκοφαντεῖς; τί λόγους πλάττεις; τί σαυτὸν οὐκ
ἐλλεβορίζεις ἐπὶ τούτοις; ἀλλ' οὐδ' αἰσχύνει φθόνου 5
δίκην εἰσάγων, οὐκ ἀδικήματος οὐδενός, καὶ νόμους
μεταποιῶν, τῶν δ' ἀφαιρῶν μέρη, οὓς ὅλους δίκαιον
ἦν ἀναγιγνώσκεσθαι τοῖς γ' ὀμωμοκόσι κατὰ τοὺς
νόμους ψηφιεῖσθαι. ἔπειτα τοιαῦτα ποιῶν λέγεις 122
πόσα δεῖ προσεῖναι τῷ δημοτικῷ, ὥσπερ ἀνδριάντα
ἐκδεδωκὼς κατὰ συγγραφὴν, εἶτ' οὐκ ἔχοντα ἃ προσ-

3. **τούτους δ' ἀναγορευέτω** (sc. ὁ κῆρυξ) : the quoted passage πλὴν ἐὰν …ἀναγορευέτω appears to be an addition to the law quoted by Aeschines in 32, ἐὰν μέν τινα ἡ βουλὴ στεφανοῖ, ἐν τῷ βουλευτηρίῳ ἀνακηρύττεσθαι, ἐὰν δὲ ὁ δῆμος, ἐν τῇ ἐκκλησίᾳ, ἄλλοθι δὲ μηδαμοῦ. This would mean that Aeschines read a mutilated law to the court, which in full would have told against him, and that Demosthenes simply supplied the omitted words and so ended the argument. This is more than we can believe either of Aeschines or of the court. Our trouble is, that we do not know what law the clerk read to the court at the end of § 120, and therefore do not know in what connection the words now quoted by Demosthenes stood.

5. **ἐλλεβορίζεις** : see Ar. Vesp. 1489, πῖθ' ἐλλέβορον, i.e. you are mad; Hor. Sat. II. 3, 166, naviget Anticyram; A. Poet. 300, tribus Anticyris caput insanabile. — **οὐδ' αἰσχύνει…εἰσάγων** : for the difference between αἰσχύνομαι εἰσάγειν and αἰσχύνομαι εἰσάγων, which in the negative form is not very important, see M.T. 881, 903[1]. This appears clearly in Xen. Cyr. I, 21 : τοῦτο μὲν οὐκ αἰσχύνομαι λέγων· τὸ δὲ… αἰσχυνοίμην ἂν λέγειν. —**φθόνου δίκην,** a suit based merely on φθόνος, opposed

to ἀδικήματος δίκην, a suit (to get redress) for an offence (cf. § 279[1]).

7. **τῶν δ' ἀφαιρῶν μέρη,** and cutting out parts of others, as if τοὺς μὲν μεταποιῶν had preceded, which is the reading of all MSS. except Σ. The use of τῶν δέ alone gives the clause the appearance of a sudden afterthought; and, so far from showing carelessness, it may be a rhetorical device to give emphasis. The same occurs in XIX. 180 : ὅσοι διὰ ταῦτ' ἀπολώλασι παρ' ὑμῖν, οἱ δὲ χρήματα πάμπολλ' ὠφλήκασιν, and XXVII. 9: κατέλιπε…μαχαιροποιοὺς μὲν τριάκοντα καὶ δύο ἢ τρεῖς, ἀνὰ πέντε μνᾶς καὶ ἕξ, τοὺς δ' οὐκ ἐλάσσονος ἢ τριῶν μνῶν ἀξίους.—**ὅλους δίκαιον ἦν ἀναγι·'** σκεσθαι, ought to be read entire.

8. **τοῖς γε ὀμωμοκόσι…ψηφιεῖσθαι** : see Aesch. III. 6, ὁ νομοθέτης τοῦτο πρῶτον ἔταξεν ἐν τῷ τῶν δικαστῶν ὅρκῳ, ψηφιοῦμαι κατὰ τοὺς νόμους.
§§ **122—125** are a peroration to the division §§ 53—125.
§ **122.** 2. **πόσα** : Blass for προσά (Σ). — **τῷ δημοτικῷ** : referring to Aesch. 168—170.—**ὥσπερ…συγγρ φὴν** : we find it convenient to translate, as if you had put out a statue be made by contract; but the participle with ὥσπερ (without ἄν or ἂν εἰ) is not conditional, as appears by its having οὐ (not μή) for its negative, as in § 323[7] (M.T. 867). ὥσπερ is simply as, or

ἧκεν ἐκ τῆς συγγραφῆς κομιζόμενος, ἢ λόγῳ τοὺς
δημοτικοὺς, ἀλλ᾽ οὐ τοῖς πράγμασι καὶ τοῖς πολιτεύ- 5
μασι γιγνωσκομένους. καὶ βοᾶς ῥητὰ καὶ ἄρρητα
ὀνομάζων, ὥσπερ ἐξ ἁμάξης, ἃ σοὶ καὶ τῷ σῷ γένει
πρόσεστιν, οὐκ ἐμοί. καίτοι καὶ τοῦτο, ὦ ἄνδρες 123
᾽Αθηναῖοι. ἐγὼ λοιδορίαν κατηγορίας τούτῳ δια-
φέρειν ἡγοῦμαι, τῷ τὴν μὲν κατηγορίαν ἀδικήματ᾽
ἔχειν, ὧν ἐν τοῖς νόμοις εἰσὶν αἱ τιμωρίαι, τὴν δὲ
λοιδορίαν βλασφημίας, ἃς κατὰ τὴν αὐτῶν φύσιν 5
τοῖς ἐχθροῖς περὶ ἀλλήλων συμβαίνει λέγειν. οἰ-
κοδομῆσαι δὲ τοὺς προγόνους ταυτὶ τὰ δικαστήρια
ὑπείληφα οὐχ ἵνα συλλέξαντες ὑμᾶς εἰς ταῦτα ἀπὸ
τῶν ἰδίων κακῶς τἀπόρρητα λέγωμεν ἀλλήλους,
ἀλλ᾽ ἵν᾽ ἐξελέγχωμεν ἐάν τις ἠδικηκώς τι τυγχάνῃ 10
τὴν πόλιν. ταῦτα τοίνυν εἰδὼς Αἰσχίνης οὐδὲν 124

---

as it were, but we can seldom translate it with a participle without an
if.
6. γιγνωσκομένους (with ὥσπερ):
accus. abs. (M.T. 853): cf. ὡς...
ἔχοντα, § 276⁵· ⁷.—ῥητὰ καὶ ἄρρητα,
dicenda, tacenda (sc. ὀνόματα), with
ὀνομάζων.
7. ὥσπερ ἐξ ἁμάξης : see note on
πομπείας, § 11⁷ ; and Suid. under τὰ
ἐκ τῶν ἁμαξῶν σκώμματα· ἐπὶ
τῆς ἁμάξης ὀχούμεναι αἱ γυναῖκες αἱ
τῶν ᾽Αθηναίων, ἐπὰν εἰς τὰ Ἐλευσίνια
ἐβάδιζον εἰς τὰ μεγάλα μυστήρια, ἐλοι-
δόρουν ἀλλήλας ἐν τῇ ὁδῷ· τοῦτο γὰρ
ἦν ἔθος αὐταῖς.
§ 123. 1. καίτοι καὶ τοῦτο : cf.
IV. 12.
2. λοιδορίαν κατηγορίας : see note
on § 10¹.
5. κατὰ τὴν αὐτῶν φύσιν, opposed
to ἐν τοῖς νόμοις (4) : the accident of
personal nature is expressed also in
συμβαίνει (6).
7. ταυτὶ τὰ δικαστήρια : most of

these were in the ἀγορά, as is implied
by Lysias, XIX. 55.
8. ἀπὸ τῶν ἰδίων, i.e. out of (our
stock of) private enmity. For the
use of ἀπό, cf. Thuc. I. 141, ἀπὸ τῶν
αὐτῶν δαπανῶντες.
9. κακῶς......ἀλλήλους, abuse one
another with lawless epithets : ἀπόρρητα were epithets which it was unlawful to apply to a citizen : cf. Lys.
X. 6, ἐρεῖ ὡς οὐκ ἔστι τῶν ἀπορρήτων
ἐάν τις εἴπῃ τὸν πατέρα ἀπεκτονέναι·
τὸν γὰρ νόμον οὐ ταῦτ᾽ ἀπαγορεύειν·
ἀλλ᾽ ἀνδροφόνον οὐκ ἐᾶν λέγειν.
This speech shows that ἀνδροφόνος,
ῥίψασπις, πατραλοίας, and μητραλοίας
were ἀπόρρητα, but the number must
have been much larger.
10. ἐὰν ... τυγχάνῃ, if it shall
happen that anyone has wronged :
the perfect participle is the common
form for expressing past time with
τυγχάνω etc. ; ἐὰν ἀδικήσας τύχῃ
would mean if he shall perchance
wrong (M.T. 144, 147¹).

76 ΔΗΜΟΣΘΕΝΟΥΣ

ἧττον ἐμοῦ, πομπεύειν ἀντὶ τοῦ κατηγορεῖν εἵλετο.
οὐ μὴν οὐδ' ἐνταῦθ' ἔλαττον ἔχων δίκαιός ἐστιν
ἀπελθεῖν. ἤδη δ' ἐπὶ ταῦτα πορεύσομαι, τοσοῦτον
αὐτὸν ἐρωτήσας. πότερόν σέ τις, Αἰσχίνη, τῆς πό- 5
λεως ἐχθρὸν ἢ ἐμὸν εἶναι φῇ ; ἐμὸν δῆλον ὅτι. εἶτα
269 οὗ μὲν ἦν παρ' ἐμοῦ δίκην κατὰ τοὺς νόμους ὑπὲρ
τούτων λαβεῖν, εἴπερ ἠδίκουν, ἐξέλειπες, ἐν ταῖς
εὐθύναις, ἐν ταῖς γραφαῖς, ἐν ταῖς ἄλλαις κρίσεσιν·
οὗ δ' ἐγὼ μὲν ἀθῷος ἅπασι, τοῖς νόμοις, τῷ χρόνῳ, 125
τῇ προθεσμίᾳ, τῷ κεκρίσθαι περὶ πάντων πολλάκις

§ 124. 2. **ἐμοῦ**: with οὐδὲν ἧττον.
—**πομπεύειν** (cf. πομπείας, § 11⁷ : referring to ἐξ ἀμάξης, § 122⁷, and λοιδορίαν, § 123².

3. **ἔλαττον ἔχων ἀπελθεῖν**, *to get off with any less* (than he has given): this fatal principle of paying off vituperation in the same base coin is the weak justification of the scurrility which follows (§§ 128—131) and elsewhere.

5. **πότερον...φῇ**; here φῇ τις ; hardly differs from φῶμεν ; the third person without τις in these questions is rare (M.T. 289).

7. **οὗ**, *where*, explained by ἐν...κρίσεσιν.—**ὑπὲρ τούτων** : the Athenians present, as representing the whole.

8. **ἐξέλειπες** expresses habitual neglect.

9. **εὐθύναις** : i.e. by bringing a suit in connection with my εὔθυναι (see note on § 117⁸), like the γραφὴ παραπρεσβείας against Aeschines (XIX.).

γραφαῖς: here ordinary *public suits*, not including εἰσαγγελία, εὔθυναι, etc., which come under γραφαί in its wider sense. See § 249³.

§ 125. 1. **οὗ δ'...ἀθῷος**, *but where I am scot-free*, opposed to οὗ μὲν ἦν, § 124⁷. — **τοῖς νόμοις** ... **πρότερον** : these four grounds of immunity (explaining ἅπασιν) do not all exclude each other, νόμοις in fact

including all the rest, with χρόνῳ being in great part identical with προθεσμίᾳ.

2. **τῇ προθεσμίᾳ**, the limitations of time set by law to bringing certain actions. Debts were outlawed in five years, and this limitation applied to many other cases. The mover of a law was personally liable to the γραφὴ παρανόμων only one year. Of course *in this suit* nothing could make Demosthenes personally amenable to any law, as he was only Ctesiphon's advocate ; but the meaning of ἀθῷος is that no suit could now legally be brought against him personally for any of the offences with which he is charged before the court. He bitterly complains of the power given to Aeschines by the form of this suit to accuse him of crimes for which he could not indict him : see §§ 9—16.— τῷ κεκρίσθαι πολλάκις πρότερον (sc. ἐμέ) : probably referring to the cases mentioned in §§ 83, 222—224, which covered important parts of the present case. He may also refer to actual indictments against himself: for the time since Chaeronea we have his statement in §§ 249, 250, e.g. κατὰ τὴν ἡμέραν ἑκάστην ἐκρινόμην. See note on § 224⁵. For the law forbidding new trials of cases already decided, see XXIV. 55, οὐκ ἐᾷ περὶ

πρότερον, τῷ μηδεπώποτε ἐξελεγχθῆναι μηδὲν ὑμᾶς
ἀδικῶν, τῇ πόλει δ᾽ ἢ πλέον ἢ ἔλαττον ἀνάγκη τῶν
γε δημοσίᾳ πεπραγμένων μετεῖναι τῆς δόξης, ἐνταῦθ᾽ 5
ἀπήντηκας ; ὅρα μὴ τούτων μὲν ἐχθρὸς ἦς, ἐμοὶ δὲ
προσποιῇ.

Ἐπειδὴ τοίνυν ἡ μὲν εὐσεβὴς καὶ δικαία ψῆφος 126
ἅπασι δέδεικται, δεῖ δέ με, ὡς ἔοικε, καίπερ οὐ φιλο-

ὦν ἂν ἅπαξ γνῷ δικαστήριον πάλιν
χρηματίζειν.

3. **ὑμᾶς ἀδικῶν** : ὑμᾶς shows that
the orator could address the audience
in the midst of a question addressed
to Aeschines personally.

5. **ἐνταῦθ᾽**, *there*, referring back
emphatically to οὗ (1).

6. **ἀπήντηκας** : cf. ἀπηντηκώς,

§ 15⁸.—**ὅρα μή...ῆς**, *see to it that
you do not prove to be their enemy* :
μή with the subjunctive always implies the future ; but φοβοῦμαι μὴ
ἀληθές ἐστιν is *I fear that it is true*
(M.T. 369).

6. **ἐμοί** : the MSS. are divided
between ἐμοί (Σ) and ἐμός.

§§ **126—226.** The next main
division of the argument is devoted
chiefly to the account of the means by
which Aeschines gained for Philip an
entrance into Greece with his army,
by getting up the Amphissian war
(§§ 139—159), and of the measures by
which Demosthenes opposed this
joint plot of Aeschines and Philip
(as he represents it), especially his
negotiations with Thebes in 339—338
B.C., which led to the alliance of
that city with Athens (§§ 160—226).
The orator introduces these accounts
by a general sketch of Aeschines'
life and that of his parents, full of
offensive scurrility (§§ 126—131),
followed by a brief account of some
of the lesser political offences of
Aeschines (§§ 132—138).

The orator's account of his own
political acts in the eventful year
before the battle of Chaeronea, connected with his vigorous defence of
the policy of Athens under his guid-
ance in her last resistance to the

power of Philip, is the most eloquent
passage in the oration (§§ 160—226).
This is a direct continuation of the
story of his political life which was
interrupted by his skilful design in § 110.

§ **126. 1. ἐπειδὴ τοίνυν κ.τ.λ.**
This is one of the few undoubted
cases of anacoluthon in Demosthenes.
The causal sentence introduced by
ἐπειδή goes on regularly through § 126,
when the sudden turn given by the
question **τίς οὐκ ἂν...φθέγξασθαι ;**
causes the orator to burst forth into
the fierce invective which follows,
forgetting his leading sentence, the
apodosis to ἐπειδή...φθέγξασθαι. This
exclamatory diversion carries him to
the end of § 128, where we find in a
changed form (in § 129) what would
be a natural apodosis to § 126. But
it is hardly possible that the orator
ever thought of the beginning of
§ 129 as a resumption of his broken
sentence.—**ἡ εὐσεβὴς...ψῆφος**, i.e.
*the vote which your oath and justice
both require of you.*

78 ΔΗΜΟΣΘΕΝΟΥΣ

λοίδορον ὄντα, διὰ τὰς ὑπὸ τούτου βλασφημίας εἰρη-
μένας ἀντὶ πολλῶν καὶ ψευδῶν αὐτὰ τἀναγκαιότατ'
εἰπεῖν περὶ αὐτοῦ, καὶ δεῖξαι τίς ὢν καὶ τίνων ῥαδίως 5
οὕτως ἄρχει τοῦ κακῶς λέγειν, καὶ λόγους τινὰς
διασύρει, αὐτὸς εἰρηκὼς ἃ τίς οὐκ ἂν ὤκνησε τῶν
μετρίων ἀνθρώπων φθέγξασθαι ;—εἰ γὰρ Αἰακὸς ἢ 127
Ῥαδάμανθυς ἢ Μίνως ἦν ὁ κατηγορῶν, ἀλλὰ μὴ
σπερμολόγος, περίτριμμ' ἀγορᾶς, ὄλεθρος γραμματεύς, οὐκ ἂν αὐτὸν οἶμαι ταῦτ' εἰπεῖν οὐδ' ἂν οὕτως
ἐπαχθεῖς λόγους πορίσασθαι, ὥσπερ ἐν τραγῳδίᾳ 5
βοῶντα ὦ γῆ καὶ ἥλιε καὶ ἀρετὴ καὶ τὰ τοιαῦτα,
καὶ πάλιν σύνεσιν καὶ παιδείαν ἐπικαλούμενον, ᾗ τὰ

4. αὐτὰ τἀναγκαιότατα, *what is barely necessary* (to satisfy the promise in § 124³, ⁴). Cf. ἀναγκαιό-τατα § 168⁷. See Thuc. I. 90 ὥστε ἀπομάχεσθαι ἐκ τοῦ ἀναγκαιοτάτου ὕψους, i.e. to have the wall just high enough to be defensible.

5. τίνων : sc. γενόμενος.

6. λόγους τινὰς διασύρει, *ridicules certain sayings of mine.* It is hard to decide between τινὰς and τίνας. With τίνας it is *what sayings of mine he ridicules,* i.e. *how he ridicules my sayings.* The reference is to Aesch. III. 167, ταῦτα τί ἐστιν, ὦ κίναιδος; ῥήματα ἢ θαύματα; also to 72 and 209.

7. ἃ τίς...φθέγξασθαι; this interrog. rel. sentence breaks the construction. For μετρίων see n. on § 108.

§ 127. I. Αἰακὸς...Μίνως : the three judges of the dead in Plat. Gorg. 523 E.

2. ὁ κατηγορῶν is subject : Vömel says, "Non dicit *si Aeacus accusaret,* sed *si accusator esset Aeacus.*"

3. σπερμολόγος : originally a little bird which *picked up seed* from newly sown fields (Ar. Av. 232, 579); then a man who lives by *picking up* what he can in the market and other places

of trade, *a vagabond,* and generally a worthless fellow; sometimes one who picks up and retails small scraps of gossip, *a babbler* or *prater,* as applied to St Paul in Acts xvii. 18. Either of the last two meanings, or perhaps a combination of both, suits the present passage.—περίτριμμ' ἀγορᾶς, *a hack of the market place*: see Arist. Nub. 447, περίτριμμα δικῶν, with the explanation in Bekk. Anecd. p. 59, οἷον τετριμμένον ἱκανῶς πράγμασιν.—ὄλεθρος γραμματεύς, *a curse of a scribe*: see IX. 31, ὀλέθρου Μακεδόνος (of Philip), and XXIII. 202, ἀνθρώπους οὐδ' ἐλευθέρους, ὀλέθρους.

4. οὐκ ἄν...εἰπεῖν (repr. εἶπεν ἄν): for the common position of ἄν before words like οἶμαι, see M.T. 220¹.

5. ἐπαχθεῖς, *ponderous, offensively pompous*: cf. ἐπαχθές, *offensive,* § 108. See Ar. Ran. 940, οἰδοῦσαν ὑπὸ κομπασμάτων καὶ ῥημάτων ἐπαχθῶν, of the style of Aeschylus. — πορίσασθαι, *provide one's self with, bring out*: cf. XIX. 186, XXXV. 41.—ὥσπερ ἐν τραγῳδίᾳ : see note on § 13⁶.

6. ὦ γῆ...ἀρετή: thus Aesch. begins his peroration (260), adding καὶ σύνεσις καὶ παιδεία, ᾗ διαγιγνώσκομεν τὰ καλὰ καὶ αἰσχρά.

καλὰ καὶ τὰ αἰσχρὰ διαγιγνώσκεται· ταῦτα γὰρ δή-
πουθεν ἠκούετ᾿ αὐτοῦ λέγοντος. σοὶ δὲ ἀρετῆς, ὦ 128
κάθαρμα, ἢ τοῖς σοῖς τίς μετουσία; ἢ καλῶν ἢ μὴ
τοιούτων τίς διάγνωσις; πόθεν ἢ πῶς ἀξιωθέντι;
ποῦ δὲ παιδείας σοι θέμις μνησθῆναι, ἧς τῶν μὲν ὡς
270 ἀληθῶς τετυχηκότων οὐδ᾿ ἂν εἷς εἴποι περὶ αὐτοῦ 5
τοιοῦτον οὐδέν, ἀλλὰ κἂν ἑτέρου λέγοντος ἐρυθριά-
σειε, τοῖς δ᾿ ἀπολειφθεῖσι μὲν, ὥσπερ σὺ, προσποιουμένοις δ᾿ ὑπ᾿ ἀναισθησίας τὸ τοὺς ἀκούοντας ἀλγεῖν
ποιεῖν ὅταν λέγωσιν, οὐ τὸ δοκεῖν τοιούτοις εἶναι,
περίεστιν.   10
Οὐκ ἀπορῶν δ᾿ ὅ τι χρὴ περὶ σοῦ καὶ τῶν σῶν 129
εἰπεῖν, ἀπορῶ τοῦ πρώτου μνησθῶ· πότερ᾿ ὡς ὁ
πατήρ σου Τρόμης ἐδούλευε παρ᾿ Ἐλπίᾳ τῷ πρὸς

§ 128. 1. **σοὶ ἀρετῆς...τίς**
μετουσία;=τί σοι ἀρετῆς μέτεστιν ;
2. **κάθαρμα**, properly *filth*, *off-*
scourings.
3. **πόθεν...ἀξιωθέντι**; see § 51⁴.
4. **ἧς** belongs to τετυχηκότων,
ἀπολειφθεῖσι, and προσποιουμένοις : it
has a partitive force with προσποιουμένοις (7), as in Ar. Eccl. 871,
προσποιῆ τῶν χρημάτων.
6. **κἂν...ἐρυθριάσειε** : M. T. 224.
7. **τοῖς ἀπολειφθεῖσι**, *those who*
have missed it (cf. § 257⁶).
8. **ἀναισθησίας** : see ἀναίσθητοι,
§ 43², and note on § 35¹⁰.
10. **περίεστιν**, *it remains for them* :
cf. περιεῖναι χρήματα, of a *balance of*
money due, § 227³. See II. 29, περίεστι
ἡμῖν ἐρίζειν.
§ 129. 2. **τοῦ** (=τίνος) **πρώτου**
μνησθῶ: indirect question (M.T.
677).—**ὁ πατήρ...ἐδούλευε** : it is a
hard problem for historical criticism
to evolve the real father of Aeschines
from this slave of a schoolmaster,
seen with his feet in the stocks or
wearing a wooden collar for punishment, and the patriotic citizen

described by his son (Aesch. II. 147,
III. 191), who had died about twelve
years before at the age of ninety-five,
who lived through the Peloponnesian
war, in which he lost his property,
was banished by the Thirty Tyrants,
served his country bravely in Asia,
was one of the restorers of the
democracy under Thrasybulus, and
in his old age discoursed learnedly
and wisely to his son on the early
history of the γραφὴ παρανόμων !
Fortunately Demosth. speaks of him
thirteen years before this, when he
was still living, in XIX. 281, where he
calls Aeschines *the son of Atrometus*
the schoolmaster. From this respectable station he has now descended to
be the son of Tromes, a schoolmaster's
slave (see § 130⁵).
3. **πρὸς τῷ Θησείῳ** : in XIX. 249,
Atrometus is said to have kept school
πρὸς τῷ τοῦ Ἥρω τοῦ ἰατροῦ, *near the*
shrine of the Hero Physician. For
this hero, the Scythian Toxaris, a
friend of Anacharsis and Solon, see
Essay VI. Cf. note on καλαμίτης
(line 6).

τῷ Θησείῳ διδάσκοντι γράμματα, χοίνικας παχείας
ἔχων καὶ ξύλον; ἢ ὡς ἡ μήτηρ, τοῖς μεθημερινοῖς 5
γάμοις ἐν τῷ κλεισίῳ τῷ πρὸς τῷ καλαμίτῃ ἥρῳ
χρωμένη, τὸν καλὸν ἀνδριάντα καὶ τριταγωνιστὴν
ἄκρον ἐξέθρεψέ σε; ἀλλ' ὡς ὁ τριηραύλης Φορμίων,
ὁ Δίωνος τοῦ Φρεαρρίου δοῦλος, ἀνέστησεν αὐτὴν
ἀπὸ ταύτης τῆς καλῆς ἐργασίας; ἀλλὰ νὴ τὸν Δία 10
καὶ θεοὺς ὀκνῶ μὴ περὶ σοῦ τὰ προσήκοντα λέγων
αὐτὸς οὐ προσήκοντας ἐμαυτῷ δόξω προῃρῆσθαι
λόγους. ταῦτα μὲν οὖν ἐάσω, ἀπ' αὐτῶν δ' ὧν αὐτὸς 130
βεβίωκεν ἄρξομαι· οὐδὲ γὰρ ὧν ἔτυχεν ἦν, ἀλλ' οἷς

4. διδάσκοντι γράμματα: the γραμματιστής was a teacher of γράμματα, *reading and writing*, the earlier γραμματική. —**χοίνικας παχείας**, crassas compedis (Plaut. Capt. III. 5, 64), *stocks* or *shackles* for the feet: see Ar. Plut. 275, αἱ κνῆμαι δέ σου βοῶσιν ἰοὺ ἰού, τὰς χοίνικας καὶ τὰς πέδας ποθοῦσαι.

5. ξύλον, a *wooden collar*, worn on the neck for punishment: see Ar. Nub. 592, ἢν φιμώσητε τούτου 'ν τῷ ξύλῳ τὸν αὐχένα, and Lys. 681. It meant also *stocks* for the feet, and the πεντεσύριγγον ξύλον was an instrument with five holes, for neck, arms, and legs. See Lexicon, ξύλον. —**τοῖς μεθημερινοῖς γάμοις**, a euphemism for *daylight prostitution*: the stories of the mother of Aeschines are as trustworthy as those of his father (see §§ 258, 259).

6. κλεισίῳ, a *hut*, opposed to a house, as in Lys. XII. 18, τριῶν ἡμῖν οἰκιῶν οὐσῶν,...κλείσιον μισθωσάμενοι. See Od. XXIV. 208.—**πρὸς τῷ καλαμίτῃ ἥρῳ**, *near the shrine* (or *statue*) *of the hero* καλαμίτης. Many identify this hero with the ἥρως ἰατρός of XIX. 249, notwithstanding strong objections. See Essay VI.

7. τὸν καλὸν ἀνδριάντα, *the pretty doll*: see Bekk. Anecd. 394,

29, ὡς ἐν τῇ συνηθείᾳ λέγουσιν αἱ μητέρες περὶ τῶν υἱῶν, "ὁ καλὸς ἀνδριάς μου."—**τριταγωνιστὴν ἄκρον**, a *tiptop third-part-actor*: see §§ 262, 265, and XIX. 246, 247, 337.

8. ἀλλ' ὡς: supply μνησθῶ from line 2, as a *direct* interrogative.—**τριηραύλης**, *galley-piper*, who gave the stroke to the rowers on a trireme.

9. ἀνέστησεν: "memineris *prostare in lupanari* Graece dici καθῆσθαι" (Dissen); there is also the idea of *raising* her from a low occupation. Cf. Aesch. I. 41.

§ 130. 1. ὧν αὐτὸς βεβίωκεν, *the life he has himself led,* = τῶν αὐτῷ βεβιωμένων: cf. § 265¹, XXII. 23 (τὰ τούτῳ βεβιωμένα), and XIX. 199, 200.

2. **οὐδὲ ὧν ἔτυχεν ἦν**, *he was not even of ordinary parents,* i.e. not of any of whom he merely *chanced* to be. ὧν ἔτυχεν is nearly equivalent to the common τῶν τυχόντων, *ordinary people* (οἱ ἔτυχον), such as might chance to fall in one's way: cf. Isocr. X. 21, εἰ εἰς ἦν τῶν τυχόντων ἀλλὰ μὴ τῶν πολὺ διενεγκόντων. After such a statement we should naturally expect to hear that he was of *higher than ordinary* parentage; but here (παρὰ προσδοκίαν) we have ἀλλ' οἷς ὁ δῆμος καταρᾶται added. In the religious ceremony before each meeting of the

ὁ δῆμος καταρᾶται. ὀψὲ γάρ ποτε—, ὀψὲ λέγω;
χθὲς μὲν οὖν καὶ πρώην ἅμ' Ἀθηναῖος καὶ ῥήτωρ
γέγονεν· καὶ δύο συλλαβὰς προσθεὶς τὸν μὲν πατέρα 5
ἀντὶ Τρόμητος ἐποίησεν Ἀτρόμητον, τὴν δὲ μητέρα
σεμνῶς πάνυ Γλαυκοθέαν, ἣν Ἔμπουσαν ἅπαντες
ἴσασι καλουμένην, ἐκ τοῦ πάντα ποιεῖν καὶ πάσχειν
καὶ γίγνεσθαι δηλονότι ταύτης τῆς ἐπωνυμίας τυ-
χοῦσαν· πόθεν γὰρ ἄλλοθεν; ἀλλ' ὅμως οὕτως 131
ἀχάριστος εἰ καὶ πονηρὸς φύσει ὥστ' ἐλεύθερος ἐκ
271 δούλου καὶ πλούσιος ἐκ πτωχοῦ διὰ τουτουσὶ γε-
γονὼς οὐχ ὅπως χάριν αὐτοῖς ἔχεις, ἀλλὰ μισθώσας
σαυτὸν κατὰ τουτωνὶ πολιτεύει. καὶ περὶ ὧν μὲν 5
ἔστι τις ἀμφισβήτησις ὡς ἄρα ὑπὲρ τῆς πόλεως

Senate and the Assembly, a curse
(ἀρά) was invoked against certain
classes of offensive people : see XXIII.
97, καταρᾶται καθ' ἑκάστην ἐκκλησίαν
ὁ κῆρυξ...εἴ τις ἐξαπατᾷ λέγων ἢ βουλὴν
ἢ δῆμον ἢ τὴν ἡλιαίαν, with XIX. 70.
Aeschines himself is elsewhere included among these " deceivers " :
see § 282⁶⁻⁸, καίτοι τίς...καταρᾶται
δικαίως ;

5. δύο συλλαβὰς προσθείς : on
the contrary, Demosth. probably
made Τρόμης (trembler) by cutting
off two syllables from Ἀτρόμητος
(dauntless).

7. Ἔμπουσαν, hobgoblin.

9. καὶ γίγνεσθαι : almost all
editors omit these words, which have
the best MS. authority and are
especially appropriate to the description of Empusa. See Ar. Ran.
289—293 : Xan. δεινόν· παντοδαπὸν
γοῦν γίγνεται· ποτὲ μέν γε βοῦς,
νυνὶ δ' ὀρεύς, ποτὲ δ' αὖ γυνὴ ὡραιοτάτη
τις. Dion. Ἔμπουσα τοίνυν ἐστί.

§ 131. 3. τουτουσὶ : i.e. the
Athenians, as represented by the
court.

4. οὐχ ὅπως...ἀλλά : οὐχ ὅπως

and οὐχ ὅτι came originally from
οὐ λέξω ὅπως (or ὅτι), I will not speak
of, I will not say that, etc., while the
nearly equivalent μὴ ὅπως (rare) or μὴ
ὅτι came from μὴ λέγε ὅπως (or ὅτι),
do not mention that, etc. Usually
not to speak of is a good English
equivalent ; but what is not to be
spoken of may be either affirmed or
denied. Thus here οὐχ ὅπως χάριν
ἔχεις, not to mention your being
grateful, means not only are you not
grateful ; but in Dem. XXIV. 7, οὐχ
ὅτι τῶν ὄντων ἂν ἀπεστερήμην means
not only should I have lost my property
(not to speak of losing my property).
These examples show that this construction is not related to that of non
modo for non modo non. (See M.T.
707, 708.)

6. ἔστι τις ἀμφισβήτησις ὡς
εἴρηκεν, i.e. it can be contended that
he has spoken, etc. ἀμφισβήτησις,
like ἀμφισβητῶ and Latin disputo,
refers to maintaining in a dispute.
See Plato Rep. 476 D, ἐὰν ἀμφισβητῇ
ὡς οὐκ ἀληθῆ λέγομεν, and Ter. Andr.
Prol. 15, in eo disputant contaminari
non decere fabulas.

εἴρηκεν, ἐάσω· ἃ δ' ὑπὲρ τῶν ἐχθρῶν φανερῶς
ἀπεδείχθη πράττων, ταῦτ' ἀναμνήσω.
Τίς γὰρ ὑμῶν οὐκ οἶδεν τὸν ἀποψηφισθέντ' 132
'Αντιφῶντα, ὃς ἐπαγγειλάμενος Φιλίππῳ τὰ νεώρι'
ἐμπρήσειν εἰς τὴν πόλιν ἦλθεν; ὃν λαβόντος ἐμοῦ
κεκρυμμένον ἐν Πειραιεῖ καὶ καταστήσαντος εἰς τὴν
ἐκκλησίαν, βοῶν ὁ βάσκανος οὗτος καὶ κεκραγὼς ὡς 5
ἐν δημοκρατίᾳ δεινὰ ποιῶ τοὺς ἠτυχηκότας τῶν πολιτῶν ὑβρίζων καὶ ἐπ' οἰκίας βαδίζων ἄνευ ψηφί-

7. **ἐάσω**: "Hier ist die τομπεία
aus, und der Redner wird ernst."
(Blass.)

§§ 132—138. Here the orator
alludes briefly to some lesser offences
of Aeschines, which preceded the
outbreak of the war with Philip. In
§ 139 these are called slight matters
compared with his conduct after the
war began.

§ 132. 1. **οἶδεν,** *know of.*—**ἀποψηφισθέντ'**, *rejected* from the list of
citizens. In 346—5 B.C. a general
revision of the lists of citizens was
ordered at Athens ; and the members
of each deme went through its own
list (the γραμματεῖον ληξιαρχικόν),
voting on each name which was
questioned. This process was called
διαψήφισις (διαψηφίζομαι), and the re-
jection of any person was called ἀποψή-
φισις (ἀποψηφίζομαι). Demosthenes
wrote his oration against Eubulides
(LVII.) for a client who had been thus
rejected and had appealed (as every
such person might) to a Heliastic
court. Antiphon was probably rejected at the same διαψήφισις (see
Dem. LVII. 2, πολλῶν ἐξεληλαμένων
δικαίως ἐκ πάντων τῶν δήμων), and
afterwards offered his services to
Philip.

4. **καταστήσαντος εἰς τὴν ἐκκλησίαν**: it is hardly probable that

Demosthenes brought Antiphon before
the Assembly without some official
authority. At the time of the passage
of his trierarchic law (340 B.C.) he
held the office of ἐπιστάτης τοῦ
ναυτικοῦ (Aesch. III. 222). Antiphon
was probably arrested by μήνυσις,
denunciation to the people, the process by which those charged with
mutilating the Hermae in 415 B.C.
were dealt with. Except in the rare
cases in which the Assembly itself
undertook the trial (as in the μήνυσις
against Phidias, Plut. Pericl. 31), the
people either sent the accused to a
Heliastic court for trial or discharged
him. The appeals of men like Aeschines moved the Assembly to dis-
charge Antiphon : but the Areopagus
interposed, and ordered (through the
Assembly) that Antiphon be tried
before a court, which condemned him
to the rack and to death. See Hist.
§ 43.

6. **ἠτυχηκότας**: referring to Antiphon's "bad luck" (as Aesch. called
it) in losing his citizenship.

7. **ἄνευ ψηφίσματος,** i.e. *without*
a vote of the Assembly or Senate.
An Athenian citizen, like an English-
man, looked upon his house as his
castle. But in extraordinary cases
officers of the state with proper
authority could search private houses
and arrest persons concealed therein.

σματος, ἀφεθῆναι ἐποίησεν. καὶ εἰ μὴ ἡ βουλὴ ἡ ἐξ 133
Ἀρείου πάγου, τὸ πρᾶγμα αἰσθομένη καὶ τὴν ὑμετέραν ἄγνοιαν ἐν οὐ δέοντι συμβεβηκυῖαν ἰδοῦσα, ἐπεζήτησε τὸν ἄνθρωπον καὶ συλλαβοῦσα ἐπανήγαγεν
ὡς ὑμᾶς, ἐξήρπαστ᾽ ἂν ὁ τοιοῦτος καὶ τὸ δίκην δοῦναι 5
διαδὺς ἐξεπέπεμπτ᾽ ἂν ὑπὸ τοῦ σεμνολόγου τουτουί.
νῦν δ᾽ ὑμεῖς στρεβλώσαντες αὐτὸν ἀπεκτείνατε, ὡς
ἔδει γε καὶ τοῦτον. τοιγαροῦν εἰδυῖα ταῦθ᾽ ἡ βουλὴ 134
ἡ ἐξ Ἀρείου πάγου τότε τούτῳ πεπραγμένα, χειροτονησάντων αὐτὸν ὑμῶν σύνδικον ὑπὲρ τοῦ ἱεροῦ τοῦ

8. **ἀφεθῆναι**: Antiphon was at first discharged by the Assembly without a trial. **§ 133.** 3. **ἐν οὐ δέοντι** (neut.), *unseasonably, just when it should not*: cf. ἀνηλώκαμεν εἰς οὐδὲν δέον, III. 28. —συμβεβηκυῖαν ἰδοῦσα, *seeing that it had occurred* (or. obl. M.T. 904).— **ἐπεζήτησε**, i.e. *ordered a new* (ἐπ-) *investigation of the man's case.* The Areopagus in these later times seems occasionally to have revived a part of its ancient power of directing the general welfare of the state.

4. **συλλαβοῦσα** shows that the Areopagus itself ordered Antiphon's arrest: Plutarch (Dem. 14) says that Demosth. arrested him and brought him before the Areopagus.

5. **ὡς ὑμᾶς**, i.e. before the court, which passed the sentence of death (7). But ἐπανήγαγεν implies that the Areopagus *brought him back* to some place, and this must be the Assembly, which had sent him to the court. See the Scholia: κυρίως εἶπε τὸ ἐπανή-γαγεν, εἰς τὸν αὐτὸν τόπον αὖθις κατέ-στησεν αὐτὸν ἡ βουλὴ ἐξ οὗ σέσωσται πρότερον.—**δίκην δοῦναι διαδὺς**: all notice the intentional alliteration.

6. **ἐξεπέπεμπτ᾽**: this slight change from ἐξεπέμπετ᾽ gives a form symmetrical with ἐξήρπαστ᾽: **ἂν** would

generally be omitted here (M.T. 226). —σεμνολόγου: see note on § 35[8].

7. **νῦν, as it was.**—στρεβλώσαντες: torture (βάσανος) could not legally be inflicted on an Athenian citizen; but Antiphon was now disfranchised. In Ar. Ran. 628, Dionysus, disguised as a slave, claims exemption from examination under torture as an immortal God: ἀγορεύω τινὶ ἐμὲ μὴ βασανίζειν ἀθάνατον ὄντ᾽.—**ὡς ἔδει γε καὶ τοῦτον** (sc. ἀποκτεῖναι) *as you ought to have dealt with this man* (Aesch.).

§ 134. 3. **σύνδικον...Δήλῳ**: about 343 B.C. the Delians contested the ancient right of Athens to administer the temple of Apollo on their island. The case came before the Amphictyonic Council, probably in the spring of 343, when Demosth. was one of the Athenian delegates to Delphi (XIX. 65). The Assembly chose Aeschines as their counsel; but the Areopagus, to which the people had given authority to revise the election, rejected him and sent Hyperides in his place. This showed that the tide had turned against Macedon. Hyperides then delivered his eloquent λόγος Δηλιακός at Delphi, and gained the case for Athens. See Hist. § 43.

ἐν Δήλῳ ἀπὸ τῆς αὐτῆς ἀγνοίας ἦσπερ πολλὰ προί-
εσθε τῶν κοινῶν, ὡς προείλεσθε κἀκείνην καὶ τοῦ 5
πράγματος κυρίαν ἐποιήσατε, τοῦτον μὲν εὐθὺς ἀπήλασεν ὡς προδότην, Ὑπερείδῃ δὲ λέγειν προσέταξε·
καὶ ταῦτ' ἀπὸ τοῦ βωμοῦ φέρουσα τὴν ψῆφον ἔπραξε,
272 καὶ οὐδεμία ψῆφος ἠνέχθη τῷ μιαρῷ τούτῳ. καὶ ὅτι 135
ταῦτ' ἀληθῆ λέγω, κάλει τούτων τοὺς μάρτυρας.

ΜΑΡΤΥΡΕΣ.

[Μαρτυροῦσι Δημοσθένει ὑπὲρ ἁπάντων οἵδε, Καλλίας
Σουνιεὺς, Ζήνων Φλυεὺς, Κλέων Φαληρεὺς, Δημόνικος Μαρα- 5
θώνιος, ὅτι τοῦ δήμου ποτὲ χειροτονήσαντος Αἰσχίνην σύνδικον ὑπὲρ τοῦ ἱεροῦ τοῦ ἐν Δήλῳ εἰς τοὺς Ἀμφικτύονας συνε-
δρεύσαντες ἡμεῖς ἐκρίναμεν Ὑπερείδην ἄξιον εἶναι μᾶλλον
ὑπὲρ τῆς πόλεως λέγειν, καὶ ἀπεστάλη Ὑπερείδης.]

Οὐκοῦν ὅτε τούτου μέλλοντος λέγειν ἀπήλασεν 10
ἡ βουλὴ καὶ προσέταξεν ἑτέρῳ, τότε καὶ προδότην
εἶναι καὶ κακόνουν ὑμῖν ἀπέφηνεν.

Ἐν μὲν τοίνυν τοῦτο τοιοῦτο πολίτευμα τοῦ 136
νεανίου τούτου, ὅμοιόν γε—οὐ γάρ ;—οἷς ἐμοῦ κατη-

---

4. ἀπὸ...ἦσπερ (see G. 1025) : cf.
XXI. 155, ὅτε κατὰ ταύτην τὴν ἡλικίαν
ἦν ἣν (for καθ' ἣν) ἐγὼ νῦν.

5. ὡς προείλεσθε κἀκείνην, i.e.
when you had previously associated it
(the Areopagus) *with yourselves in
the case*, i.e. giving it the right to
revise your choice (lit. *when you had
previously chosen it also, and given it
power*, etc.). καὶ in κἀκείνην, which
seems awkward, must refer to the
association of the two bodies in
power : in H. Wolf's emendation,
προσείλεσθε, προσ- would have the
same force as καί.

7. λέγειν προσέταξε: i.e. as the
σύνδικος of Athens.

8. ἀπὸ τοῦ βωμοῦ: the most
solemn form of voting, here on a

religious question. See XLIII. 14,
λαβόντες τὴν ψῆφον καιομένων τῶν
ἱερείων, ἀπὸ τοῦ βωμοῦ φέροντες τοῦ
Διὸς τοῦ φρατρίου. Cf. Hdt. VIII.
123; Plut. Them. 17; Cic. pro Balbo
V. 12.

9. ἠνέχθη: like φέρουσα (above).
—τούτῳ: cf. ἐμοὶ τὴν ψῆφον ἤνεγκαν,
Isae. XI. 18.

§ 135. 10. τούτου μέλλοντος
λέγειν, *when he was to be the speaker*,
i.e. after his election.

12. ἀπέφηνεν, *declared* him to be
so by its ἀπόφασις.

§ 136. 2. νεανίου : this sometimes (as here) expresses wantonness
or insolence, like νεανικός. See Eur.
Alc. 679, ἄγαν ὑβρίζεις, καὶ νεανίας
λόγους ῥίπτων ἐς ἡμᾶς, κ.τ.λ.—οὐ γάρ;

γορεῖ· ἕτερον δὲ ἀναμιμνήσκεσθε. ὅτε γὰρ Πύθωνα
Φίλιππος ἔπεμψε τὸν Βυζάντιον καὶ παρὰ τῶν αὑτοῦ
συμμάχων πάντων συνέπεμψε πρέσβεις, ὡς ἐν αἰ- 5
σχύνῃ ποιήσων τὴν πόλιν καὶ δείξων ἀδικοῦσαν, τότ'
ἐγὼ μὲν τῷ Πύθωνι θρασυνομένῳ καὶ πολλῷ ῥέοντι
καθ' ὑμῶν οὐχ ὑπεχώρησα, ἀλλ' ἀναστὰς ἀντεῖπον
καὶ τὰ τῆς πόλεως δίκαι' οὐχὶ προὔδωκα, ἀλλ' ἀδι-
κοῦντα Φίλιππον ἐξήλεγξα φανερῶς οὕτως ὥστε 10
τοὺς ἐκείνου συμμάχους αὐτοὺς ἀνιστ αμένους ὁμολο-
γεῖν· οὗτος δὲ συνηγωνίζετο καὶ τἀναντία ἐμαρτύρει
τῇ πατρίδι, καὶ ταῦτα ψευδῆ.
Καὶ οὐκ ἀπέχρη ταῦτα, ἀλλὰ πάλιν μετὰ ταῦθ' 137
ὕστερον Ἀναξίνῳ τῷ κατασκόπῳ συνιὼν εἰς τὴν
Θράσωνος οἰκίαν ἐλήφθη. καίτοι ὅστις τῷ ὑπὸ τῶν
273 πολεμίων πεμφθέντι μόνος μόνῳ συνῄει καὶ ἐκοινο-
λογεῖτο, οὗτος αὐτὸς ὑπῆρχε τῇ φύσει κατάσκοπος 5
καὶ πολέμιος τῇ πατρίδι. καὶ ὅτι ταῦτ' ἀληθῆ
λέγω, κάλει μοι τούτων τοὺς μάρτυρας.

ΜΑΡΤΥΡΕΣ.

[Τελέδημος Κλέωνος, Ὑπερείδης Καλλαίσχρου, Νικόμα-
χος Διοφάντου μαρτυροῦσι Δημοσθένει καὶ ἐπωμόσαντο ἐπὶ 10

this sarcastic question (after γε) implies a self-evident absurdity, which
is heightened by calling this affair
with Antiphon a πολίτευμα of Aesch.
and so comparing it with the πολιτεύματα of Demosth. (see next note).—
οἷς ἐμοῦ κατηγορεῖ: probably = τοῖς
ἐμοῦ πολιτεύμασιν οἷς κατηγορεῖ.
3. Πύθωνα: this eloquent orator
was sent to Athens by Philip in
343 B.C., to quiet apprehension and
to repeat assurances of the king's
friendly spirit. See Hist. §§ 44, 45.
7. θρασυνομένῳ, with his insolent
manner.—πολλῷ ῥέοντι καθ' ὑμῶν,
rushing upon you with a flood (of
eloquence). See Thuc. II. 5, ὁ Ἀσωπὸς

ποταμὸς ἐρρύη μέγας, and Ar. Eq. 526
(of Cratinus), ὃς πολλῷ ῥεύσας ποτ'
ἐπαίνῳ διὰ τῶν ἀφελῶν πεδίων ἔρρει.
All quote Hor. Sat. I. 7, 28, salso
multoque fluenti, with the preceding
ruebat flumen ut hibernum. See
§ 199¹, πολὺς ἔγκειται.
8. οὐχ ὑπεχώρησα, did not retreat
(before the flood).
11. συμμάχους: i.e. the παρὰ τῶν
συμμάχων πρέσβεις of l. 5.
§ 137. 2. Ἀναξίνῳ: see Aeschines (III. 223, 224).
5. αὐτὸς ὑπῆρχε...κατάσκοπος, he
was to be assumed to have the nature of
a spy himself. See § 95ᵇ.

τῶν στρατηγῶν εἰδέναι Αἰσχίνην Ἀτρομήτου Κοθωκίδην
συνερχόμενον νυκτὸς εἰς τὴν Θράσωνος οἰκίαν καὶ κοινολογού-
μενον Ἀναξίνῳ, ὃς ἐκρίθη εἶναι κατάσκοπος παρὰ Φιλίππου.
αὗται ἀπεδόθησαν αἱ μαρτυρίαι ἐπὶ Νικίου, ἑκατομβαιῶνος
τρίτῃ ἱσταμένου.] 15
Μυρία τοίνυν ἕτερ' εἰπεῖν ἔχων περὶ αὐτοῦ παρα- 138
λείπω. καὶ γὰρ οὕτω πως ἔχει. πόλλ' ἂν ἐγὼ ἔτι
τούτων ἔχοιμι δεῖξαι, ὧν οὗτος κατ' ἐκείνους τοὺς
χρόνους τοῖς μὲν ἐχθροῖς ὑπηρετῶν ἐμοὶ δ' ἐπηρεάζων
εὑρέθη. ἀλλ' οὐ τίθεται ταῦτα παρ' ὑμῖν εἰς ἀκριβῆ 5
μνήμην οὐδ' ἣν προσῆκεν ὀργήν, ἀλλὰ δεδώκατ' ἔθει
τινὶ φαύλῳ πολλὴν ἐξουσίαν τῷ βουλομένῳ τὸν λέ-
γοντά τι τῶν ὑμῖν συμφερόντων ὑποσκελίζειν καὶ
συκοφαντεῖν, τῆς ἐπὶ ταῖς λοιδορίαις ἡδονῆς καὶ
χάριτος τὸ τῆς πόλεως συμφέρον ἀνταλλαττόμενοι· 10
διόπερ ῥᾷόν ἐστι καὶ ἀσφαλέστερον ἀεὶ τοῖς ἐχθροῖς
ὑπηρετοῦντα μισθαρνεῖν ἢ τὴν ὑπὲρ ὑμῶν ἑλόμενον
τάξιν πολιτεύεσθαι.
Καὶ τὸ μὲν δὴ πρὸ τοῦ πολεμεῖν φανερῶς συνα- 139

§ **138**. **2**. **οὕτω πως**, *somewhat
as follows*, where earlier writers use ὧδε.
3. **ὧν**: assimilated to τούτων from
ἅ, cognate object of ὑπηρετῶν and
ἐπηρεάζων: for the latter see ἐπήρειαν,
§ 12⁴.
6. **ἣν προσῆκεν ὀργὴν** (with εἰς):
τίθεται εἰς ὀργήν naturally follows the
familiar τίθεται εἰς μνήμην.
8. **ὑποσκελίζειν**, *trip up* (cf.
σκέλη).
9. **τῆς... ἡδονῆς καὶ χάριτος**:
abusive language (λοιδορία) not only
pleased the populace, but also *gratified*
their whims and low tastes. A good
example of both ἡδονή and χάρις is
the scene in the Assembly when the
second embassy reported in July
346 B.C., described in XIX. 44—46.
Demosthenes was insulted and jeered
at by Aeschines and Philocrates, to

the delight of the people: notice the
single sarcastic remark of Demosthenes (46), καὶ ὑμεῖς ἐγελᾶτε. Hist.
§§ 34, 35.
12. **τὴν...πολιτεύεσθαι** is *to serve
the state as a patriot*, opposed to τοῖς
ἐχθροῖς ὑπηρετοῦντα μισθαρνεῖν.

§§ **139—159**. Next follows the
account of the conduct of Aeschines
in stirring up the Amphissian war in
339 B.C. (See note on §§ 126—226.)
§§ 139—144 are introductory, and
§§ 158, 159 are a peroration.
§ **139**. The first sentence depreciates the acts already mentioned,
done in time of nominal peace, to
heighten the enormity of helping
Philip in time of war: cf. δότε...αὐτῷ
τοῦτο (3).
1. **πρὸ τοῦ πολεμεῖν φανερῶς**:

γωνίζεσθαι Φιλίππῳ δεινὸν μὲν, ὦ γῆ καὶ θεοί,—πῶς
274 γὰρ οὔ ;—κατὰ τῆς πατρίδος· δότε δ᾽, εἰ βούλεσθε,
δότ᾽ αὐτῷ τοῦτο. ἀλλ᾽ ἐπειδὴ φανερῶς ἤδη τὰ πλοῖ᾽
ἐσεσύλητο, Χερρόνησος ἐπορθεῖτο, ἐπὶ τὴν Ἀττικὴν 5
ἐπορεύεθ᾽ ἄνθρωπος, οὐκέτ᾽ ἐν ἀμφισβητησίμῳ τὰ
πράγματ᾽ ἦν, ἀλλ᾽ ἐνειστήκει πόλεμος, ὅ τι μὲν
πώποτ᾽ ἔπραξεν ὑπὲρ ὑμῶν ὁ βάσκανος οὗτος ἰαμβειογράφος οὐκ ἂν ἔχοι δεῖξαι, οὐδ᾽ ἔστιν οὔτε μεῖζον
οὔτ᾽ ἔλαττον ψήφισμ᾽ οὐδὲν Αἰσχίνῃ ὑπὲρ τῶν 10
συμφερόντων τῇ πόλει. εἰ δέ φησι, νῦν δειξάτω ἐν

Demosth. often implies that the preceding peace was really a state of
war. See IX. 19, ἀφ᾽ ἧς ἡμέρας
ἀνεῖλε Φωκέας, ἀπὸ ταύτης ἔγωγ᾽
αὐτὸν πολεμεῖν ὁρίζομαι. φανερῶς
is repeated in l. 4.

3. κατὰ τῆς πατρίδος: not connected in construction with δεινὸν, but
an independent exclamation, justify-
ing the assertion in δεινὸν μὲν.

4. ἐπειδὴ…ἐπορθεῖτο, after your
ships had been openly seized (§ 73)
and the ravaging of the Chersonese
was going on. The ravaging of the
Chersonese was marching an army
through the Athenian territory there
to enable his fleet to pass the Hellespont for the siege of Perinthus
without molestation from the shore.
Hist. 53.

5. ἐπὶ τὴν Ἀττικὴν ἐπορεύεθ᾽ :
Philip's action at the Hellespont, if
it had not been checked, would have
opened the way for him into Attica
and the whole of Greece. Demosth.
had repeatedly warned the people of
this peril: even in the First Philippic
(351 B.C.) he had said (50), κἂν μὴ
νῦν ἐθέλωμεν ἐκεῖ πολεμεῖν αὐτῷ,
ἐνθάδ᾽ ἴσως ἀναγκασθησόμεθα τοῦτο
ποιεῖν. See especially VI. 35 (344 B.C.),
Πύλας…ὢν καταστὰς ἐκεῖνος κύριος τῆς
ἐπὶ τὴν Ἀττικὴν ὁδοῦ καὶ τῆς εἰς
Πελοπόννησον κύριος γέγονε, and fur-

ther τοῦ πρὸς τὴν Ἀττικὴν πολέμου,
ὃς λυπήσει μὲν ἕκαστον ἐπειδὰν παρῇ,
γέγονε δ᾽ ἐν ἐκείνῃ τῇ ἡμέρᾳ. See
§ 143⁷.

7. ἐνειστήκει πόλεμος: cf. ὁ ἐνστὰς
πόλεμος, § 89⁴. These words end the
clause with ἐπειδή.

8. ἰαμβειογράφος, writer of lam-
poons (ἰαμβεῖα), probably refers to
verses written by Aeschines in his
youth, to which he perhaps alludes in
I. 136, περὶ δὲ τῶν ποιημάτων ὧν φασιν
οὗτοί με πεποιηκέναι. This reading
has the best MS. authority; but ἰαμβειοφάγος, eater (or mouther) of
iambics, was and is the common
reading. If we read ἰαμβειοφάγος,
we must refer it to the career of
Aeschines as an actor, not to his
λοιδορία, to which the ancient inter-
preters generally referred it. See
Etym. Magn. Ἰαμβοφάγος.

10. Αἰσχίνῃ, dat. of possession :
has none to show.

11. ἐν τῷ ἐμῷ ὕδατι, in my time :
this general formula and ἐπὶ τοῦ ἐμοῦ
ὕδατος are often used when a speaker
offers part of his own time to his
opponent to prove something which
he believes cannot be proved. It is a
mere challenge, made with no idea of
its being accepted. For the genitive
with ἐπὶ see LVII. 61 (end). The
time allotted to each speaker in most

τῷ ἐμῷ ὕδατι. ἀλλ' οὐκ ἔστιν οὐδέν. καίτοι δυοῖν
αὐτὸν ἀνάγκη θάτερον, ἢ μηδὲν τοῖς πραττομένοις
ὑπ' ἐμοῦ τότ' ἔχοντ' ἐγκαλεῖν μὴ γράφειν παρὰ
ταῦθ' ἕτερα, ἢ τὸ τῶν ἐχθρῶν συμφέρον ζητοῦντα 15
μὴ φέρειν εἰς μέσον τὰ τούτων ἀμείνω.
'Αρ' οὖν οὐδ' ἔλεγεν, ὥσπερ οὐδ' ἔγραφεν, ἡνίκ' 140
ἐργάσασθαί τι δέοι κακόν; οὐ μὲν οὖν εἰπεῖν ἦν
ἑτέρῳ. καὶ τὰ μὲν ἄλλα καὶ φέρειν ἡδύναθ', ὡς
ἔοικεν, ἡ πόλις καὶ ποιῶν οὗτος λανθάνειν· ἐν δ'
ἐπεξειργάσατο, ἄνδρες 'Αθηναῖοι, τοιοῦτον ὃ πᾶσι 5
τοῖς προτέροις ἐπέθηκε τέλος· περὶ οὗ τοὺς πολ-

cases was measured by the clepsydra or water-clock (Dict. Antiq. under Horologium), a fixed number of ἀμφορεῖς of water being poured in according to the importance of the case. Thus Aeschines (II. 126) says, πρὸς ἕνδεκα γὰρ ἀμφορέας ἐν διαμεμετρημένῃ τῇ ἡμέρᾳ κρίνομαι, eleven ἀμφορεῖς (about 100 gallons), allowed each speaker in cases of παραπρεσβεία, being the largest amount mentioned. The term διαμεμετρημένη ἡμέρα is explained in Aesch. III. 197. In important public suits the day was divided into three parts, and the clepsydra was filled three times, the first measure of water being given to the accuser, the second (of equal amount) to the accused, and the third (in ἀγῶνες τιμητοί, if the accused was convicted), a smaller measure, to the τίμησις, the decision ὅ τι χρὴ παθεῖν ἢ ἀποτῖσαι.

12. δυοῖν...θάτερον : there is no infinitive or other verb to be supplied, and αὐτὸν is subject of γράφειν and φέρειν. δυοῖν θάτερον (or θάτερα), ἀμφότερον or ἀμφότερα, οὐδέτερον, and similar expressions, may stand emphatically, as adverbial phrases, before ἢ...ἢ, καὶ...καὶ, τε...τε, and in other cases where we simply say

either...or, both...and, etc. See Plat. Theaet. 187 B, ἐὰν οὕτω δρῶμεν, δυοῖν θάτερα, ἢ εὑρήσομεν ἐφ' ὃ ἐρχόμεθα, ἢ ἧττον οἰησόμεθα εἰδέναι ὃ μηδαμῇ ἴσμεν. So Il. III. 179, ἀμφότερον, βασιλεύς τ' ἀγαθὸς κρατερός τ' αἰχμητής.
13—15. μηδὲν...ἔχοντ' and ζητοῦντα are causal.—παρὰ ταῦθ', in opposition to these.

§ 140. 1. ἀρ' οὖν...ἔγραφεν; οὐδ'...οὐδ' correspond to καὶ...καὶ in positive expressions of this kind. We cannot express such negatives : the meaning is, as he proposed no measures, so did he also abstain from talking (so neither did he talk)? The sins of omission just described set these of commission in a stronger light.
2. οὐ μὲν...ἑτέρῳ, why, nobody else could get a chance to talk!
5. ἐπεξειργάσατο : the idea of addition, which ἐπί (like πρός) expresses, is further extended by ἐπέθηκε τέλος, capped the climax.
6. τοὺς πολλοὺς λόγους, his many words, referring to the long. and brilliant passage (III. 107—129) in which Aeschines describes his doings at Delphi when he stirred up the fatal Amphissian war. Cf. Aeschyl. Ag. 1456, μία τὰς πολλὰς, τὰς πάνυ πολλὰς ψυχὰς ὀλέσασ'.

λοὺς ἀνήλωσε λόγους, τὰ τῶν Ἀμφισσέων [τῶν
Λοκρῶν] διεξιὼν δόγματα, ὡς διαστρέψων τἀληθές.
τὸ δ' οὐ τοιοῦτόν ἐστι. πόθεν ; οὐδέποτ' ἐκνίψει σὺ
τἀκεῖ πεπραγμένα σαυτῷ· οὐχ οὕτω πόλλ' ἐρεῖς. 10
Καλῶ δ' ἐναντίον ὑμῶν, ἄνδρες Ἀθηναῖοι, τοὺς 141
θεοὺς ἅπαντας καὶ πάσας ὅσοι τὴν χώραν ἔχουσι
τὴν Ἀττικὴν, καὶ τὸν Ἀπόλλω τὸν Πύθιον, ὃς
πατρῷός ἐστι τῇ πόλει, καὶ ἐπεύχομαι πᾶσι τούτοις,
εἰ μὲν ἀληθῆ πρὸς ὑμᾶς εἴποιμι καὶ εἶπον καὶ τότ' 5
275 εὐθὺς ἐν τῷ δήμῳ, ὅτε πρῶτον εἶδον τουτονὶ τὸν
μιαρὸν τούτου τοῦ πράγματος ἁπτόμενον (ἔγνων
γὰρ, εὐθέως ἔγνων), εὐτυχίαν μοι δοῦναι καὶ σωτηρίαν, εἰ δὲ πρὸς ἔχθραν ἢ φιλονεικίας ἰδίας ἕνεκ'
αἰτίαν ἐπάγω τούτῳ ψευδῆ, πάντων τῶν ἀγαθῶν 10
ἀνόνητόν με ποιῆσαι.

7. **τὰ τῶν Ἀμφισσέων δόγματα**,
the decrees (of the Amphictyons) *about
the Amphissians*, like τὸ Μεγαρέων
ψήφισμα, *the Megarian decree*, Thuc. I.
140, called in I. 139 τὸ περὶ Μεγαρέων
ψήφισμα. So τούτων ψήφισμα, XX.
115. Two MSS. omit τῶν Λοκρῶν.

9. **τὸ δ'**, *but in fact* : this τὸ δέ,
with no correlative τὸ μέν, is common
in Plato, introducing an adversative
statement. See Apol. 23 A, οἴονταί
με...εἶναι σοφόν· τὸ δὲ κινδυνεύει. So
Rep. 340 D (end), 357 A.—**οὐ τοιοῦτόν ἐστι**, i.e. *this cannot be done
(the case is not of such a nature)*,
referring to ὡς διαστρέψων τἀληθές.—
πόθεν; cf. § 47⁶.—**ἐκνίψει**: cf. Act.
Apost. xxii. 16, ἀπόλουσαι τὰς ἁμαρτίας
σου, *wash away thy sins*.

§ **141.** The solemn invocation in
this chapter, resembling those which
begin and end the exordium (§§ 1, 8),
calls attention again to the gravity of
the charge about to be made, and to
the supreme importance of the events
which led to the fatal issue on the

field of Chaeronea. He defends his
invocation and his general earnestness
in §§ 142—144.

4. **πατρῷος**: Apollo was the *paternal* God of Athens, not only as the
great Ionic divinity, but as the father
of Ion (according to Athenian belief).
See Schol. on Ar. Av. 1527, πατρῷον
δὲ τιμῶσιν Ἀπόλλωνα Ἀθηναῖοι, ἐπεὶ
Ἴων, ὁ πολέμαρχος Ἀθηναίων, ἐξ Ἀπόλλωνος καὶ Κρεούσης τῆς Ξούθου ἐγένετο.
So in the Ion of Euripides.

5. **εἰ ἀληθῆ εἴποιμι καὶ εἶπον**, lit.
*if I should speak the truth to you now
and if I did speak it then on the spot* :
a double condition combining a future
and a past supposition (M.T. 509).
We should rather invert the order
and say, *if I then spoke the truth and
(shall) speak it again now*. Cf. § 190⁸.

9. **πρὸς ἔχθραν**, *with a view to
enmity*: cf. διὰ ..ἔχθραν in § 143¹⁰.—
φιλονεικίας, *contentiousness* (against
an enemy).

11. **ἀνόνητον**: so XIX. 315.

Τί οὖν ταῦτ᾽ ἐπήραμαι καὶ διετεινάμην οὑτωσὶ 142
σφοδρῶς; ὅτι γράμματ᾽ ἔχων ἐν τῷ δημοσίῳ κείμενα,
ἐξ ὧν ταῦτ᾽ ἐπιδείξω σαφῶς, καὶ ὑμᾶς εἰδὼς τὰ
πεπραγμένα μνημονεύσοντας, ἐκεῖνο φοβοῦμαι, μὴ
τῶν εἰργασμένων αὐτῷ κακῶν ὑποληφθῇ οὗτος 5
ἐλάττων· ὅπερ πρότερον συνέβη, ὅτε τοὺς ταλαιπώρους Φωκέας ἐποίησεν ἀπολέσθαι τὰ ψευδῆ δεῦρ᾽
ἀπαγγείλας. τὸν γὰρ ἐν Ἀμφίσσῃ πόλεμον, δι᾽ ὃν 143
εἰς Ἐλάτειαν ἦλθε Φίλιππος, καὶ δι᾽ ὃν ᾑρέθη τῶν
Ἀμφικτυόνων ἡγεμὼν ὃς ἅπαντ᾽ ἀνέτρεψε τὰ τῶν
Ἑλλήνων, οὗτός ἐστιν ὁ συγκατασκευάσας καὶ
πάντων εἰς ἀνὴρ μεγίστων αἴτιος κακῶν. καὶ τότ᾽ 5
εὐθὺς ἐμοῦ διαμαρτυρομένου καὶ βοῶντος ἐν τῇ ἐκκλησίᾳ πόλεμον εἰς τὴν Ἀττικὴν εἰσάγεις,
Αἰσχίνη, πόλεμον Ἀμφικτυονικὸν, οἱ μὲν ἐκ

§ 142. 1. ἐπήραμαι: referring
to the whole invocation of § 141, but
especially to the *imprecation* in the
last clause. τί ταῦτ᾽ ἐπήραμαι; is *why
have I made this imprecation?* while τί
διετεινάμην οὑτωσὶ σφοδρῶς; (aor.) is
*why did I express myself with all this
vehement earnestness?*
2. ἔχων and εἰδὼς (3) are con-
cessive.—ἐν τῷ δημοσίῳ, *in the public
record-office*: this was in the Μητρῷον
(see Aesch. III. 187, Paus. I. 3, 5).
4. μὴ...ἐλάττων, i.e. *lest Aeschines
may be thought too small a man to
work so great mischief.*
6. ὅπερ πρότερον συνέβη: this
allusion to a former time when Aesch.
*caused the ruin of the Phocians by
bringing home false reports*, can refer
only to the return of the second
embassy in 346 B.C. (see §§ 32--36).
This distinct statement that Aesch.
was then thought "too insignificant
to do so much harm," with the
apprehension that the court may
make the same mistake again in the

present case, is one of the strongest
proofs that the case against Aeschines
really came to trial, that the speeches
de Falsa Legatione were actually
spoken, and that Aeschines was acquitted by a small majority.
§ 143. 1. τὸν ἐν Ἀμφίσσῃ πόλεμον : for this and the seizure of
Elatea, see § 152⁸ and note.
2. ᾑρέθη ἡγεμὼν ὃς (sc. τις), *a
man was chosen leader, who* etc. (i.e.
Philip).
6. ἐν τῇ ἐκκλησίᾳ, i.e. in the
meeting in which Aesch. made his
report of his doings in the Amphictyonic Council (Hist. § 61).
7. εἰς τὴν Ἀττικὴν : Demosth.
saw at once the full meaning of the
Amphictyonic war, and knew that it
must end in bringing Philip into
Greece as the Amphictyonic general
(see note on § 139⁵).
8. οἱ...συγκαθήμενοι, *those who
sat together by his summons*, i.e. his
παράκλητοι, with whom he had
packed the meeting.

παρακλήσεως συγκαθήμενοι οὐκ εἴων με λέγειν, οἱ
δ' ἐθαύμαζον καὶ κενὴν αἰτίαν διὰ τὴν ἰδίαν ἔχθραν 10
ἐπάγειν μ' ὑπελάμβανον αὐτῷ. ἥτις δ' ἡ φύσις, 144
ἄνδρες Ἀθηναῖοι, γέγονεν τούτων τῶν πραγμάτων,
καὶ τίνος εἵνεκα ταῦτα συνεσκευάσθη καὶ πῶς
ἐπράχθη, νῦν ὑπακούσατε, ἐπειδὴ τότ' ἐκωλύθητε·
καὶ γὰρ εὖ πρᾶγμα συντεθὲν ὄψεσθε, καὶ μεγάλ' 5
ὠφελήσεσθε πρὸς ἱστορίαν τῶν κοινῶν, καὶ ὅση
δεινότης ἦν ἐν τῷ Φιλίππῳ θεάσεσθε.

Οὐκ ἦν τοῦ πρὸς ὑμᾶς πολέμου πέρας οὐδ' 145
276 ἀπαλλαγὴ Φιλίππῳ, εἰ μὴ Θηβαίους καὶ Θετταλοὺς ἐχθροὺς ποιήσειε τῇ πόλει· ἀλλὰ καίπερ
ἀθλίως καὶ κακῶς τῶν στρατηγῶν τῶν ὑμετέρων

9. **οὐκ εἴων με λέγειν**, i.e. *would
not let me go on speaking* (after my
warning).—**οἱ δ' ἐθαύμαζον**: the ordinary citizens were amazed at anyone
who dared to object to the pious
and (apparently) patriotic speech of
Aeschines. The decree of Demosthenes forbidding Athens to take
any part in the future action of the
Amphictyonic Council against Amphissa (Aesch. 125—127) was passed
at a later meeting, after the people
had opened their eyes.

§ **144.** 4. **ὑπακούσατε**: see Plat.
Theaet. 162 A, πάντως καὶ νῦν δὴ μάλ'
ἐμμελῶς σοι ἐφαίνετο ὑπακούειν, and
162 D, ταῖς οὖν δημηγορίαις ὀξέως
ὑπακούεις. The general meaning is,
*now take your opportunity to listen
to the story, since you were kept from
hearing it at the right time.*

5. **εὖ πρᾶγμα συντεθὲν**, *that the
plan was well concocted.*

6. **πρὸς ἱστορίαν**, *for gaining a
knowledge.* The real history of these
events must be disentangled from the
long story of Aeschines (106—131),
supplemented and often corrected by
the briefer account of Demosthenes

(145—159). See Hist. §§ 57—62.

§ **145.** 1. **οὐκ ἦν...εἰ μὴ ποιήσειε**:
see M.T. 696 and the examples. The
protasis depends on an apodosis implied in οὐκ ἦν...Φιλίππῳ, the real
meaning being *Philip felt that he
could not end or escape the war unless
he should make the Th. hostile to our
city.* This involves indirect discourse;
and we might therefore have had ἐὰν
μὴ ποιήσῃ here for εἰ μὴ ποιήσειε.
See Thuc. VII. 59, τἆλλα, ἦν ἔτι
ναυμαχεῖν οἱ Ἀθηναῖοι τολμήσωσι,
παρεσκευάζοντο, where the condition
really depends on the idea *to be ready*
implied in παρεσκευάζοντο, and εἰ...
τολμήσαιεν might have been used.
Cf. Thuc. VI. 100, πρὸς τὴν πόλιν, εἰ
ἐπιβοηθοῖεν, ἐχώρουν, they marched
towards the city, in case they (the
citizens) should rush out, i.e. to meet
them in that case ; the thought being
ἦν ἐπιβοηθῶσιν.

4. **ἀθλίως...πολεμούντων**: Chares
and Phocion were the Athenian commanders at the beginning of the war,
while Philip was besieging Byzantium.
Chares was much censured for in-
efficiency, but for Phocion's general-

πολεμούντων αὐτῷ, ὅμως ὑπ' αὐτοῦ τοῦ πολέμου 5
καὶ τῶν λῃστῶν μυρί' ἔπασχε κακά· οὔτε γὰρ
ἐξήγετο τῶν ἐκ τῆς χώρας γιγνομένων οὐδὲν οὔτ'
εἰσήγετο ὧν ἐδεῖτ' αὐτῷ· ἦν δ' οὔτ' ἐν τῇ θαλάττῃ 146
τότε κρείττων ὑμῶν, οὔτ' εἰς τὴν 'Αττικὴν ἐλθεῖν
δυνατὸς μήτε Θετταλῶν ἀκολουθούντων μήτε Θηβαίων διιέντων· συνέβαινε δ' αὐτῷ, τῷ πολέμῳ
κρατοῦντι τοὺς ὁποιουσδήποθ' ὑμεῖς ἐξεπέμπετε 5
στρατηγοὺς (ἐῶ γὰρ τοῦτό γε), αὐτῇ τῇ φύσει τοῦ
τόπου καὶ τῶν ὑπαρχόντων ἑκατέροις κακοπαθεῖν.
εἰ μὲν οὖν τῆς ἰδίας ἕνεκ' ἔχθρας ἢ τοὺς Θετταλοὺς 147
ἢ τοὺς Θηβαίους συμπείθοι βαδίζειν ἐφ' ὑμᾶς, οὐδέν'

ship there is only praise. These
operations are probably those of the
later part of 340—339, when Philip
was in Scythia (Hist. § 56).

5. **ὑπ' αὐτοῦ τοῦ πολέμου**, i.e. *by
the mere state of war.*

6. **λῃστῶν**: a state of war naturally encouraged pirates and plunderers.

7. **τῶν ἐκ τῆς χώρας γιγνομένων**:
see §§ 44[4], 213[12].

8. **ὧν ἐδεῖτ'** : sc. οὐδέν.—**αὐτῷ**,
with εἰσήγετο.

§ 146. 3. **μήτε…διιέντων**, i.e. εἰ
μήτε Θετταλοὶ ἀκολουθοῖεν μήτε Θηβαῖοι
διιεῖεν : Philip depended on Thessalian
troops to fill his army, but he would
have been satisfied with Thebes (under
the circumstances) if she had merely
made no objection to his marching
through Boeotia to attack Athens.
There was probably a coolness already
between Thebes and Philip, which
appears later when Thebes refused to
attend the Amphictyonic meeting in
the autumn of 339 B.C. (See Aesch.
III. 128.) See Hist. § 57, for these
relations.

5. **ὁποιουσδήποθ'** : here relative;
while generally relative forms with
οὖν and δήποτε are indefinite. See

τοὺς ὁποιουστινασοῦν in VIII. 20, and
ὅτου δήποτε ἕνεκα in § 21[10] (above).

7. **τῶν ὑπαρχόντων ἑκατέροις**, *of
the relative resources of each*, i.e. of
his own inferiority in resources,
especially in naval power. See
Thuc. I. 141[8], where Pericles speaks
of the comparative resources of Athens
and her enemies : τὰ δὲ τοῦ πολέμου
καὶ τῶν ἑκατέροις ὑπαρχόντων ὡς οὐκ
ἀσθενέστερα ἕξομεν.

§ 147. This is closely connected
in thought with the beginning of
§ 145. How, thought Philip, can I
induce the Thessalians and Thebans
to join me? He remembered their
zeal in the Phocian war : see XIX. 50,
τοῖς 'Αμφικτύοσι'…ποίοις ; οὐ γὰρ ἦσαν
αὐτόθι πλὴν Θηβαῖοι καὶ Θετταλοί. A
new Sacred war, or any war for the
rights of the Amphictyonic Council,
would be sure to rouse their interest
again.

1. **εἰ μὲν…συμπείθοι**, i.e. *if he
were to join in an attempt to persuade
them* etc. : συμ- implies that he would
depend greatly on the influence of
his friends in Thebes and Thessaly.—
ἕνεκ', *on the ground of.*

2. **οὐδέν' ἡγεῖτο προσέξειν** : I omit
ἂν before ἡγεῖτο, with L, A 1, and

ἡγεῖτο προσέξειν αὐτῷ τὸν νοῦν· ἐὰν δὲ τὰς ἐκείνων
κοινὰς προφάσεις λαβὼν ἡγεμὼν αἱρεθῇ, ῥᾷον ἤλπι-
ζεν τὰ μὲν παρακρούσεσθαι τὰ δὲ πείσειν. τί οὖν; 5
ἐπιχειρεῖ, θεάσασθ᾽ ὡς εὖ, πόλεμον ποιῆσαι τοῖς
Ἀμφικτύοσι καὶ περὶ τὴν Πυλαίαν ταραχήν· εἰς
γὰρ ταῦτ᾽ εὐθὺς αὐτοὺς ὑπελάμβανεν αὐτοῦ δεήσεσθαι. εἰ μὲν τοίνυν τοῦτο ἢ τῶν παρ᾽ ἑαυτοῦ πεμπο- 148
μένων ἱερομνημόνων ἢ τῶν ἐκείνου συμμάχων εἰση-
γοῖτό τις, ὑπόψεσθαι τὸ πρᾶγμ᾽ ἐνόμιζε καὶ τοὺς
Θηβαίους καὶ τοὺς Θετταλοὺς καὶ πάντας φυλάξε-

most recent editors, because its insertion is accounted for by the v. l.
προσέχειν, with which it would be
required. (See M. T. 208.) The
simple προσέξειν is also supported by
the following παρακρούσεσθαι and πείσειν and by the infinitives in § 148.
For the conditional forms in this
section and the following, see note
on § 148⁵.

3. **ἐὰν...αἱρεθῇ**, i.e. *if he should
adopt* (as his own) *some ground's
common to both Thebans and Thessalians, and so be chosen general.* See
τὰς ἰδίας προφάσεις, opposed to τὰς
Ἀμφικτυονικὰς (the real κοινάς), in
§ 158¹. The actual result of the
scheme is seen in §§ 151, 152.

5. **τὰ μὲν...πείσειν**, i.e. *to succeed
sometimes by deception, sometimes by
persuasion.* For the tense of the
infinitive with ἐλπίζω, see M. T. 136.

6. **θεάσασθ᾽ ὡς εὖ**, see how craftily :
cf. § 144⁵.—**πόλεμον ποιῆσαι** (not
ποιήσασθαι), *to get up a war*, i.e. to
get the Amphictyons into a war.

7. **τὴν Πυλαίαν** : the meeting of
the Amphictyonic Council was so
called, because twice in each year
(in the spring and the autumn) the
Council met first at Thermopylae in
the sanctuary of Demeter Amphic-
tyonis, and afterwards proceeded to
Delphi, where the regular sessions

were held. See Hyper. Epitaph.
§ 18, ἀφικνούμενοι γὰρ δὶς τοῦ
ἐνιαυτοῦ εἰς τὴν Πυλαίαν, θεωροὶ
γενήσονται τῶν ἔργων κ.τ.λ., with
Aesch. III. 126, πορεύεσθαι εἰς Πύλας
καὶ εἰς Δελφοὺς ἐν τοῖς τεταγμένοις
χρόνοις, and Strab. p. 429 (of Thermopylae) Δήμητρος ἱερὸν, ἐν ᾧ κατὰ
πᾶσαν Πυλαίαν θυσίαν ἐτέλουν οἱ
Ἀμφικτύονες. Records of Amphictyonic meetings at Delphi in the spring
as well as the autumn are found in
inscriptions. — **εἰς ταῦτ᾽...δεήσεσθαι**,
would need him for these, especially
for the war, as the only available
commander.

§ **148.** Having made up his mind
(1) that he must have the support of
Thebes and Thessaly (§§ 145, 146),
and (2) that he can secure this only by
an Amphictyonic war (§ 147), he now
(3) determines to find some Athenian
to instigate the war, to disarm all
suspicion in advance. For this important work he hires Aeschines
(§ 148).

2. **ἱερομνημόνων** : for the constitution of the Amphictyonic Council see
Essay V.—**ἐκείνου**, *his*, from the
orator's point of view, just after
ἑαυτοῦ, *his own*, from Philip's: cf.
Xen. Mem. IV. 7, 1, τὴν ἑαυτοῦ
γνώμην ἀπεφαίνετο πρὸς τοὺς ὁμι-
λοῦντας αὐτῷ.

σθαι, ἂν δ᾽ Ἀθηναῖος ᾖ καὶ παρ᾽ ὑμῶν τῶν ὑπεναντίων 5
ὁ τοῦτο ποιῶν, εὐπόρως λήσειν· ὅπερ συνέβη. πῶς
οὖν ταῦτ᾽ ἐποίησεν ; μισθοῦται τουτονί. οὐδενὸς δὲ 149
προειδότος, οἶμαι, τὸ πρᾶγμ᾽ οὐδὲ φυλάττοντος, ὥσπερ
277 εἴωθε τὰ τοιαῦτα παρ᾽ ὑμῖν γίγνεσθαι, προβληθεὶς
πυλάγορος οὗτος καὶ τριῶν ἢ τεττάρων χειροτονησάντων αὐτὸν ἀνερρήθη. ὡς δὲ τὸ τῆς πόλεως ἀξίωμα 5
λαβὼν ἀφίκετ᾽ εἰς τοὺς Ἀμφικτύονας, πάντα τἄλλ᾽
ἀφεὶς καὶ παριδὼν ἐπέραινεν ἐφ᾽ οἷς ἐμισθώθη, καὶ
λόγους εὐπροσώπους καὶ μύθους, ὅθεν ἡ Κιρραία

5. ἂν δ᾽ Ἀθηναῖος ᾖ : we have the same antithesis here between ἂν...ᾖ and the preceding εἰ...εἰσηγοῖτο which we had in § 147 between ἐὰν...αἱρεθῇ (3) and εἰ συμπείθοι (1). It is commonly assumed that ἐὰν with the subjunctive expresses greater probability or likelihood that the supposition may prove true than εἰ with the optative ; and this double antithesis is often cited as a strong confirmation of this view. It seems to be overlooked that all four suppositions are in *oratio obliqua* after past tenses, and would all be expressed in the *oratio recta* (i.e. as Philip conceived them) by subjunctives, ἐὰν συμπείθω, αἱρεθῶ, εἰσηγῆται, Ἀθηναῖος ᾖ, which would all be retained if the leading verb were present or future. If these forms now show any inherent distinction between subj. and opt. as regards probability, this has been introduced by the *oratio obliqua* after a past tense. The two subjunctives express the plans which Philip had most at heart, and the two optatives express the opposite alternatives. Cf. note on εἰ προαιρησόμεθ᾽ in § 176[1]. See Trans. of the Am. Philol. Assoc. for 1873, pp. 71, 72, and the Eng. Journ. of Philology vol. v. no. 10, p. 198.

§ 149. 3. προβληθεὶς, *nominated*:

the πυλάγοροι were chosen by hand vote (χειροτονησάντων), while the ἱερομνήμων, the higher officer, were chosen annually by lot (λαχών, Ar. Nub. 623).

4. τριῶν ἢ τεττάρων: this small vote shows how little the Assembly understood the importance of the election.

5. ἀξίωμα, *prestige, dignity* (of a delegate of Athens).

6. εἰς τοὺς Ἀμφικτύονας : this was the meeting in the spring of 339 B.C., described by Aeschines (III. 115—124).

8. εὐπροσώπους, *plausible (fairfaced ;* cf. *barefaced*).—**μύθους,** *tales,* referring to the eloquent account of the first Sacred war in the time of Solon (Aesch. III. 107—112).—**ὅθεν... καθιερώθη,** *from the time when the plain of Cirrha was consecrated:* cf. Aesch. III. 61, λέξω ὅθεν μάλιστα παρακολουθήσετε. We see by this that Aeschines repeated to the Amphictyons in 339 his story of the consecration of the plain of Cirrha, with all the terrible curses which were imprecated against those who should cultivate the devoted land, which he told in court in 330. The consecration was made at the end of the first Sacred war, about 586 B.C.

χώρα καθιερώθη, συνθεὶς καὶ διεξελθὼν, ἀνθρώπους
ἀπείρους λόγων καὶ τὸ μέλλον οὐ προορωμένους, 10
τοὺς ἱερομνήμονας, πείθει ψηφίσασθαι περιελθεῖν 150
τὴν χώραν ἣν οἱ μὲν Ἀμφισσεῖς σφῶν αὐτῶν οὖσαν
γεωργεῖν ἔφασαν, οὗτος δὲ τῆς ἱερᾶς χώρας ἠτιᾶτ'
εἶναι, οὐδεμίαν δίκην τῶν Λοκρῶν ἐπαγόντων ἡμῖν,
οὐδ' ἃ νῦν οὗτος προφασίζεται λέγων οὐκ ἀληθῆ. 5
γνώσεσθε δ' ἐκεῖθεν. οὐκ ἐνῆν ἄνευ τοῦ προσκαλέσασθαι δήπου τοῖς Λοκροῖς δίκην κατὰ τῆς πόλεως
τελέσασθαι. τίς οὖν ἐκλήτευσεν ἡμᾶς ; ἀπὸ ποίας

---

10. **ἀπείρους λόγων**: "to the comparatively rude men at Delphi, the
speech of a first-rate Athenian orator
was a rarity." (Grote.) The Amphictyonic Council was composed chiefly
of representatives of obscure and uncultivated states. It was, in fact, a
mere relic of antiquity, which had
outlived its right to exist ; and in
the time of Philip it was merely
galvanized into an unnatural vitality,
which proved fatal to Greece and
helpful only to the invader. See
Grote's remarks at the beginning of
chap. 87. Hist. §§ 59, 60.
§ 150. 1. **περιελθεῖν τὴν χώραν** :
*to make an inspection (περίοδος) of the
land.* An inscription of 380 B.C.
records an order of the Amphictyons
for official περίοδοι of the consecrated
land, and for imposing a fine on any
who should be found encroaching
on it.
3. **ἠτιᾶτ'**, *alleged* (in his accusation).
4. **οὐδεμίαν ἐπαγόντων** : Aesch.
(116) says the Amphissians *intended
to propose* a decree in the Council
(εἰσέφερον δόγμα) fining Athens fifty
talents for hanging up on the walls
of the new temple some old shields,
relics of Plataea, with the restored
inscription, Ἀθηναῖοι ἀπὸ Μήδων καὶ

Θηβαίων ὅτε τἀναντία τοῖς Ἕλλησιν
ἐμάχοντο. Demosthenes cannot understand by δίκην ἐπαγόντων what
Aeschines means by εἰσέφερον δόγμα.
An intention to introduce a decree
(εἰσέφερον) would not need a previous
summons, which δίκην ἐπάγειν, and
still more δίκην τελέσασθαι (7), *to
make a suit ready for trial*, would
require. And the further remark of
Demosthenes, οὐδ' ἃ νῦν οὗτος προφασίζεται (5), seems to imply that
Aeschines had told a different story
about the intentions of the Amphissians when he made his report of the
meeting at Delphi (III. 125) from
that which he told in court. It is
therefore difficult to judge the argument of Demosthenes about the want
of a legal summons.
8. **ἀπὸ ποίας ἀρχῆς** ; *from what
authority* did the summons come?
Witnesses to a summons were required at Athens when the defendant
was in Attica. These were called
κλητῆρες, which same name was given
to the officers of the law who served
a summons on persons outside of
Attica: see Ar. Av. 147, 1422. ἐκλή-
.τευσεν refers to the act of such an
Amphictyonic κλητήρ.
9. **δεῖξον**: cf. δεῖξον, XXIX. 41.—
ἀλλ' οὐκ ἂν ἔχοις : so § 76³.

96   ΔΗΜΟΣΘΕΝΟΥΣ

ἀρχῆς ; εἰπὲ τὸν εἰδότα, δεῖξον, ἀλλ᾽ οὐκ ἂν ἔχοις,
ἀλλὰ κενῇ προφάσει ταύτῃ κατεχρῶ καὶ ψευδεῖ. 10
περιιόντων τοίνυν τὴν χώραν τῶν Ἀμφικτυόνων 151
κατὰ τὴν ὑφήγησιν τὴν τούτου, προσπεσόντες οἱ
Λοκροὶ μικροῦ κατηκόντισαν ἅπαντας, τινὰς δὲ καὶ
συνήρπασαν τῶν ἱερομνημόνων. ὡς δ᾽ ἅπαξ ἐκ τούτων
ἐγκλήματα καὶ πόλεμος πρὸς τοὺς Ἀμφισσέας ἐτα- 5
ράχθη, τὸ μὲν πρῶτον ὁ Κόττυφος αὐτῶν τῶν
Ἀμφικτυόνων ἤγαγε στρατιάν· ὡς δ᾽ οἱ μὲν οὐκ
ἦλθον, οἱ δ᾽ ἐλθόντες οὐδὲν ἐποίουν, εἰς τὴν ἐπιοῦσαν
Πυλαίαν ἐπὶ τὸν Φίλιππον εὐθὺς ἡγεμόν᾽ ἦγον οἱ
κατεσκευασμένοι καὶ πάλαι πονηροὶ τῶν Θετταλῶν 10

10. Notice position of ταύτῃ.
§ 151. 1. περιιόντων : cf. περιελθεῖν, § 150¹. See Aesch. 122, 123.
3. μικροῦ (M.T. 779ᵇ), almost,
belongs to κατηκόντισαν : cf. Aesch.
123, εἰ μὴ ἐξεφύγομεν, ἐκινδυνεύσαμεν
ἀπολέσθαι. See § 269⁶.
5. ἐγκλήμ....ἐταράχθη : we have πόλεμον ταράσσειν, like proelia miscere or
confundere, Plat. Rep. 567 A, and ἐγκλήματα ταράξειν, Plut. Them. 5 (Bl.).
6. Κόττυφος : the president of the
Council, a Thessalian of Pharsalus.
7. οὐκ ἦλθον : e.g. Thebans and
Athenians, and doubtless others.
8. οὐδὲν ἐποίουν : see Aesch. 129.
—εἰς τὴν ἐπιοῦσαν...ἦγον (sc. τὰ
πράγματα), took measures at once,
against the coming meeting (autumn
of 339), to put things (i.e. the war)
into the hands of Philip as commander.
See IX. 57, οἱ μὲν ἐφ᾽ ἡμᾶς ἦγον τὰ
πράγματα, οἱ δ᾽ ἐπὶ Φίλιππον.
9. οἱ κατεσκευασμένοι (pass.), those
with whom arrangements had been
made.
10. πάλαι πονηροὶ : cf. § 158⁷,
ὑπὸ πολλῶν καὶ πονηρῶν.
Demosthenes distinctly implies that
Cottyphus was made general at the
spring meeting, but that, after a mere

pretence of war, intrigues at once
began for superseding him by Philip
at the autumnal meeting (εἰς τὴν
ἐπιοῦσαν Πυλαίαν). Aeschines, on
the contrary, whose whole object is
to show that a real Amphictyonic
war was intended, with no help or
thought of help from Philip, and to
represent Philip's final appointment
as commander as a remote afterthought, states that no action was
taken against the Amphissians in the
spring, but that a special meeting
was called before the regular autumnal
Πυλαία, to take such action (124).
At this special meeting, which Athens
and Thebes refused to attend (Aesch.
126—128), Cottyphus was chosen
general, (according to Aesch.) while
Philip was "away off in Scythia";
and after a successful campaign the
Amphissians were fined and their
offending citizens were banished. But
they refused to submit; and finally,
"a long time afterwards" (πολλῷ
χρόνῳ ὕστερον), a second expedition
became necessary "after Philip's
return from his Scythian expedition";
—he does not even then say that
Philip was actually made general !
See Hist. §§ 61—63.

καὶ τῶν ἐν ταῖς ἄλλαις πόλεσι. καὶ προφάσεις 152
εὐλόγους εἰλήφεσαν· ἢ γὰρ αὐτοὺς εἰσφέρειν καὶ
278 ξένους τρέφειν ἔφασαν δεῖν καὶ ζημιοῦν τοὺς μὴ
ταῦτα ποιοῦντας, ἢ 'κεῖνον αἱρεῖσθαι. τί δεῖ τὰ
πολλὰ λέγειν ; ἡρέθη γὰρ ἐκ τούτων ἡγεμών. καὶ 5
μετὰ ταῦτ' εὐθέως δύναμιν συλλέξας καὶ παρελθὼν
ὡς ἐπὶ τὴν Κιρραίαν, ἐρρῶσθαι φράσας πολλὰ
Κιρραίοις καὶ Λοκροῖς, τὴν Ἐλάτειαν καταλαμβάνει.
εἰ μὲν οὖν μὴ μετέγνωσαν εὐθέως, ὡς τοῦτ' εἶδον, οἱ 153
Θηβαῖοι καὶ μεθ' ἡμῶν ἐγένοντο, ὥσπερ χειμάρρους
ἂν ἅπαν τοῦτο τὸ πρᾶγμ' εἰς τὴν πόλιν εἰσέπεσε·
νῦν δὲ τό γ' ἐξαίφνης ἐπέσχον αὐτὸν ἐκεῖνοι, μάλιστα
μὲν, ὦ ἄνδρες Ἀθηναῖοι, θεῶν τινος εὐνοίᾳ πρὸς ὑμᾶς, 5

§ 152. 2. **αὐτοὺς εἰσφέρειν...
δεῖν,** they must themselves (ipsos) *pay
taxes.*

4. **ἢ 'κεῖνον αἱρεῖσθαι** : this alternative was one of the προφάσεις
εὔλογοι (§ 152¹) for choosing Philip.

6. **παρελθὼν** (sc. εἴσω Πυλῶν): cf.
§ 35³.

7. **ἐρρῶσθαι φράσας πολλά,** bidding
many farewells (a long adieu): so XIX.
248. Cf. ἔρρωσο, vale.

8. **Ἐλάτειαν** : when Philip had
passed Thermopylae, he hardly made
a pretence of entering into the war
with Amphissa, for which he was
chosen commander ; and he soon appeared at the Phocian town of Elatea,
which commanded the pass into
Boeotia and "the road to Athens."
This move left no further doubt as
to his real intentions. Aeschines says
(140) of Philip's sudden movement,
τὸν πόλεμον ὃν πρότερον ἐξήλασεν ἐκ
τῆς χώρας τῆς Βοιωτῶν (i.e. the Phocian
war), τοῦτον πάλιν τὸν αὐτὸν πόλεμον
(i.e. a similar sacred war) ἐπῆγε διὰ
τῆς Φωκίδος ἐπ' αὐτὰς τὰς Θήβας.
Philip must have been made general

in the early autumn of 339 B.C., and
probably seized Elatea in the late
autumn or early winter ; so that the
campaign lasted about eight or nine
months until the battle of Chaeronea
in August or September 338. A
"winter battle" is naturally mentioned in § 216⁶. The startling effect
at Athens of the news from Elatea
is described in §§ 169 ff.

§ 153. 2. **μεθ' ἡμῶν ἐγένοντο,**
joined us.—**ὥσπερ χειμάρρους,** *like a
winter torrent* : most of the rivers of
Greece are nearly or quite dry the
greater part of the year, and in the
winter and spring are often filled by
rushing torrents. Many of these,
when dry, still serve as paths over
the mountain passes. Similar simple
comparisons are ὥσπερ νέφος, § 188⁵
(cf. νυκτὶ ἐοικώς, Il. I. 47) ; ὥσπερ
πνεῦμα, § 308⁹.

3. **ἅπαν τοῦτο τὸ πρᾶγμ'** : we
might say *this whole thing*, but with
far less dignity.

4. **νῦν,** *as it was, in fact,* opposed
to εἰ μὴ μετέγνωσαν : cf. § 133⁷.—**τό
γ' ἐξαίφνης,** *for the moment.*

98 ΔΗΜΟΣΘΕΝΟΥΣ

εἶτα μέντοι, καὶ ὅσον καθ᾽ ἕν᾽ ἄνδρα, καὶ δι᾽ ἐμέ.
δὸς δέ μοι τὰ δόγματα ταῦτα καὶ τοὺς χρόνους ἐν οἷς
ἕκαστα πέπρακται, ἵν᾽ εἰδῆτε ἡλίκα πράγμαθ᾽ ἡ
μιαρὰ κεφαλὴ ταράξασ᾽ αὕτη δίκην οὐκ ἔδωκεν.
λέγε μοι τὰ δόγματα. 154

ΔΟΓΜΑ ΑΜΦΙΚΤΥΟΝΩΝ.

[Ἐπὶ ἱερέως Κλειναγόρου, ἐαρινῆς πυλαίας, ἔδοξε τοῖς
πυλαγόροις καὶ τοῖς συνέδροις τῶν Ἀμφικτυόνων καὶ τῷ
κοινῷ τῶν Ἀμφικτυόνων, ἐπειδὴ Ἀμφισσεῖς ἐπιβαίνουσιν
ἐπὶ τὴν ἱερὰν χώραν καὶ σπείρουσι καὶ βοσκήμασι κατανέ- 5
μουσιν, ἐπελθεῖν τοὺς πυλαγόρους καὶ τοὺς συνέδρους, καὶ
στήλαις διαλαβεῖν τοὺς ὅρους, καὶ ἀπειπεῖν τοῖς Ἀμφισ-
σεῦσι τοῦ λοιποῦ μὴ ἐπιβαίνειν.]

ΕΤΕΡΟΝ ΔΟΓΜΑ.

[Ἐπὶ ἱερέως Κλειναγόρου, ἐαρινῆς πυλαίας, ἔδοξε τοῖς 155
279 πυλαγόροις καὶ τοῖς συνέδροις τῶν Ἀμφικτυόνων καὶ τῷ
κοινῷ τῶν Ἀμφικτυόνων, ἐπειδὴ οἱ ἐξ Ἀμφίσσης τὴν ἱερὰν
χώραν κατανειμάμενοι γεωργοῦσι καὶ βοσκήματα νέμουσι, καὶ
κωλυόμενοι τοῦτο ποιεῖν, ἐν τοῖς ὅπλοις παραγενόμενοι, τὸ 5
κοινὸν τῶν Ἑλλήνων συνέδριον κεκωλύκασι μετὰ βίας,
τινὰς δὲ καὶ τετραυματίκασι, τὸν στρατηγὸν τὸν ᾑρημένον
τῶν Ἀμφικτυόνων Κόττυφον τὸν Ἀρκάδα πρεσβεῦσαι πρὸς
Φίλιππον τὸν Μακεδόνα, καὶ ἀξιοῦν ἵνα βοηθήσῃ τῷ τε
Ἀπόλλωνι καὶ τοῖς Ἀμφικτύοσιν, ὅπως μὴ περιίδῃ ὑπὸ τῶν 10

6. εἶτα...δι᾽ ἐμέ, lit. *but besides,
and so far as depended on any one
man, also through me*: the former
καὶ connects ὅσον...ἄνδρα to εἶτα.
7. δόγματα ταῦτα are Amphictyonic decrees about the Amphissian
affair.—τοὺς χρόνους: we see from
§ 155[14] that this was an official statement from the records, showing that
these decrees were passed when

Aeschines was πυλάγορος.
8. ἡ μιαρὰ κεφαλή: cf. XXI. 117,
καὶ ταῦτ᾽ ἔλεγεν ἡ μιαρὰ καὶ ἀναιδὴς
αὕτη κεφαλὴ ἐξεληλυθὼς κ.τ.λ., and
XIX. 313.
9. ταράξασ᾽: we should express
ταράξασα by the leading verb, and
δίκην οὐκ ἔδωκεν by *without being
punished*. With πράγματα ταράξασα
cf. § 151[5] and note.

ἀσεβῶν Ἀμφισσέων τὸν θεὸν πλημμελούμενον· καὶ διότι
αὐτὸν στρατηγὸν αὐτοκράτορα αἱροῦνται οἱ Ἕλληνες οἱ μετέ-
χοντες τοῦ συνεδρίου τῶν Ἀμφικτυόνων.]

Λέγε δὴ καὶ τοὺς χρόνους ἐν οἷς ταῦτ' ἐγίγνετο·
15 εἰσὶ γὰρ καθ' οὓς ἐπυλαγόρησεν οὗτος. λέγε.   15

ΧΡΟΝΟΙ.

[Ἄρχων Μνησιθείδης, μηνὸς ἀνθεστηριῶνος ἕκτῃ ἐπὶ
δέκα.]

Δὸς δὴ τὴν ἐπιστολὴν ἥν, ὡς οὐχ ὑπήκουον οἱ 156
Θηβαῖοι, πέμπει πρὸς τοὺς ἐν Πελοποννήσῳ συμμάχους ὁ Φίλιππος, ἵν' εἰδῆτε καὶ ἐκ ταύτης σαφῶς ὅτι
τὴν μὲν ἀληθῆ πρόφασιν τῶν πραγμάτων, τὸ ταῦτ'
ἐπὶ τὴν Ἑλλάδα καὶ τοὺς Θηβαίους καὶ ὑμᾶς πράτ- 5
τειν, ἀπεκρύπτετο, κοινὰ δὲ καὶ τοῖς Ἀμφικτύοσι
δόξαντα ποιεῖν προσεποιεῖτο· ὁ δὲ τὰς ἀφορμὰς
ταύτας καὶ τὰς προφάσεις αὐτῷ παρασχὼν οὗτος ἦν.
λέγε.
280   ΕΠΙΣΤΟΛΗ.

[Βασιλεὺς Μακεδόνων Φίλιππος Πελοποννησίων τῶν ἐν 157
τῇ συμμαχίᾳ τοῖς δημιουργοῖς καὶ τοῖς συνέδροις καὶ τοῖς
ἄλλοις συμμάχοις πᾶσι χαίρειν. ἐπειδὴ Λοκροὶ οἱ καλού-
μενοι Ὀζόλαι, κατοικοῦντες ἐν Ἀμφίσσῃ, πλημμελοῦσιν εἰς
τὸ ἱερὸν τοῦ Ἀπόλλωνος τοῦ ἐν Δελφοῖς καὶ τὴν ἱερὰν χώραν 5
ἐρχόμενοι μεθ' ὅπλων λεηλατοῦσι, βούλομαι τῷ θεῷ μεθ'

---

§ 156. 1. **οὐχ ὑπήκουον**: this
must refer to a refusal of the Thebans,
before the seizure of Elatea, to join
Philip in an expedition against the
Amphissians, against whom he professed to be marching: see § 152⁷,
ὡς ἐπὶ τὴν Κιρραίαν.
2. **συμμάχους**: i.e. the Arcadians,
Eleans, and Argives. See Isocr. v.
74, Ἀργεῖοι δὲ καὶ Μεσσήνιοι καὶ
Μεγαλοπολῖται καὶ τῶν ἄλλων πολλοὶ

συμπολεμεῖν (sc. ὑπάρχουσί σοι ἕτοιμοι),
and Dem. IX. 27. See Hist. §§ 41.
42.
6. **κοινὰ**: cf. κοινὰς προφάσεις, §§
147⁴, 158¹⁻³.—τοῖς Ἀμφικτύοσι δόξαντα, Amphictyonic decrees, ἃ τοῖς
Ἀμφ. ἔδοξεν. Cf. III. 14, τὸ ποιεῖν
ἐθέλειν τά γε δόξαντα. The older
Athenian decrees began with ἔδοξε τῇ
βουλῇ καὶ τῷ δήμῳ.

ὑμῶν βοηθεῖν καὶ ἀμύνασθαι τοὺς παραβαίνοντάς τι τῶν ἐν
ἀνθρώποις εὐσεβῶν· ὥστε συναντᾶτε μετὰ τῶν ὅπλων εἰς τὴν
Φωκίδα, ἔχοντες ἐπισιτισμὸν ἡμερῶν τετταράκοντα, τοῦ ἐνε-
στῶτος μηνὸς λῴου, ὡς ἡμεῖς ἄγομεν, ὡς δὲ Ἀθηναῖοι, βοη- 10
δρομιῶνος, ὡς δὲ Κορίνθιοι, πανήμου. τοῖς δὲ μὴ συναντήσασι
πανδημεὶ χρησόμεθα [τοῖς δὲ συμβούλοις ἡμῖν κειμένοις]
ἐπιζημίοις. εὐτυχεῖτε].

Ὁρᾶθ᾽ ὅτι φεύγει τὰς ἰδίας προφάσεις, εἰς δὲ τὰς 158
Ἀμφικτυονικὰς καταφεύγει. τίς οὖν ὁ ταῦτα συμ-
παρασκευάσας αὐτῷ ; τίς ὁ τὰς προφάσεις ταύτας
ἐνδούς ; τίς ὁ τῶν κακῶν τῶν γεγενημένων μάλιστ᾽
αἴτιος ; οὐχ οὗτος ; μὴ τοίνυν λέγετε, ὦ ἄνδρες 5
Ἀθηναῖοι, περιιόντες ὡς ὑφ᾽ ἑνὸς τοιαῦτα πέπονθεν
ἡ Ἑλλὰς ἀνθρώπου. οὐχ ὑφ᾽ ἑνὸς, ἀλλ᾽ ὑπὸ πολλῶν
καὶ πονηρῶν τῶν παρ᾽ ἑκάστοις, ὦ γῆ καὶ θεοί· ὧν 159
εἷς οὑτοσὶ, ὃν, εἰ μηδὲν εὐλαβηθέντα τἀληθὲς εἰπεῖν
δέοι, οὐκ ἂν ὀκνήσαιμ᾽ ἔγωγε κοινὸν ἀλιτήριον τῶν
μετὰ ταῦτ᾽ ἀπολωλότων ἁπάντων εἰπεῖν, ἀνθρώπων,
τόπων, πόλεων· ὁ γὰρ τὸ σπέρμα παρασχὼν, οὗτος 5
τῶν φύντων κακῶν αἴτιος. ὃν ὅπως ποτ᾽ οὐκ εὐθὺς

§ 158. 2. Ἀμφικτυονικὰς : see
§§ 147³, 156.—καταφεύγει, takes refuge,
opposed to φεύγει (1), shuns.
3. προφάσεις ἐνδούς: cf. Thuc. II.
87 (end), οὐκ ἐνδώσομεν πρόφασιν
οὐδενὶ κακῷ γενέσθαι.
5. μὴ λέγετε περιιόντες, do not go
about and tell.
6. ὑφ᾽ ἑνὸς ἀνθρώπου, i.e. by
Philip: cf. εἷς ἀνήρ (of Philip), XIX.
64. Philip (he says) could never have
accomplished his purpose, had he not
had such accomplices as Aeschines.
Notice the effective collocation in ἡ
Ἑλλὰς ἀνθρώπου.
§ 159. 2. μηδὲν εὐλαβηθέντα,
without reserve.
3. κοινὸν ἀλιτήριον, a common
curse and destroyer. An ἀλιτήριος is

a man who has sinned against the
Gods and is thereby under a curse,
which curse he transmits to others
with whom he has to do ; also an
avenging divinity : cf. Aen. II. 573,
Troiae et patriae communis Erinnys
(of Helen). See Andocides I. 130,
131. Ἀλάστωρ is similarly used in
both senses : see § 296⁵, XIX. 305;
see also Aeschyl. Eum. 236, δέχου
δὲ πρευμενῶς ἀλάστορα (one who has
already been purified); Pers. 354,
φανεὶς ἀλάστωρ ἢ κακὸς δαίμων ποθέν.
Aeschines twice (III. 131, 157) calls
Demosthenes τῆς Ἑλλάδος ἀλιτήριος
(see Blass).
6. τῶν φύντων κακῶν (so Σ), of
the harvest of woes : without κακῶν,
which many omit, we should have

281 ἰδόντες ἀπεστράφητε θαυμάζω. πλὴν πολύ τι σκότος,
ὡς ἔοικεν, ἐστὶν παρ' ὑμῖν πρὸ τῆς ἀληθείας.

Συμβέβηκε τοίνυν μοι τῶν κατὰ τῆς πατρίδος 160
τούτῳ πεπραγμένων ἀψαμένῳ εἰς ἃ τοί'τοις ἐναντιού-
μενος αὐτὸς πεπολίτευμαι ἀφῖχθαι· ἃ πολλῶν μὲν
ἕνεκ' ἂν εἰκότως ἀκούσαιτέ μου, μάλιστα δ' ὅτι
αἰσχρόν ἐστιν, ὦ ἄνδρες Ἀθηναῖοι, εἰ ἐγὼ μὲν τὰ 5
ἔργα τῶν ὑπὲρ ὑμῶν πόνων ὑπέμεινα, ὑμεῖς δὲ μηδὲ
τοὺς λόγους αὐτῶν ἀνέξεσθε ὁρῶν γὰρ ἐγὼ Θη- 161

the common saying about the harvest.
Cic. Phil. II. 22. 55 perhaps supports
κακῶν: ut igitur in seminibus est
causa arborum et stirpium, sic huius
luctuosissimi belli semen tu fuisti.—
δν: object of both ἰδόντες and ἀπεστράφητε: the latter becomes transitive
in the passive, like φοβέω, ἐκπλήσσω,
etc.

8. πρὸ τῆς ἀληθείας : i.e. so as to
conceal the truth from you.

§§ 160—226. The orator now
passes to his own agency in opposing
the joint plot of Aeschines and Philip.
See introductory note on §§ 126—226.
After speaking of the enmity between
Athens and Thebes, which men like
Aeschines had encouraged (§§ 160—
163), he gives a graphic account of
the panic excited at Athens by Philip's
seizure of Elatea, and of the manner
in which he took advantage of this
emergency to bring Athens and Thebes
to a better understanding and even to
an alliance against the common enemy
(§§ 168—226). Into this account he
introduces (§§ 189—210) a most eloquent and earnest defence of the whole
line of policy in opposition to Philip
which Athens had followed chiefly by
his advice. He pleads that Athens,
with her glorious traditions, could
have taken no other course, even if
she had seen the fatal defeat at Chae-

ronea in advance. This is the most
eloquent and impassioned passage in
the oration; and it is addressed not
merely to the court, but to the whole
people and to future ages.

§ 160. 4. ἀκούσαιτε: this reading, though it has slight MS. authority,
is necessary here, with ἕνεκ' ἂν in Σ
and L. Σ often has ε for αι or αι
for ε, from their identity in later pro-
nunciation.

5, 7. τὰ ἔργα...τοὺς λόγους : the
actual labours, contrasted with merely
listening to the account of them. Cf.
λόγῳ and τὰ ἔργα, Thuc. I. 22.

The orator introduces this continuation of his political history in an
apologetic way, as in § 110⁵ he professed to leave it doubtful whether he
should speak at all of these later acts,
τὰ μέγιστα......πεπραγμένων (see note).
This is a part of the skilful device by
which he divides the long account of
his public life, while at the same time
he reminds the court that the brilliant
passage which follows is over and
above what is needed to defend Ctesiphon (see § 126¹), and asks their
attention to it as a personal favour to
himself.

§ 161. The orator recurs to the
critical moment in the relations of
Athens and Thebes, when both were
astounded by the sudden seizure of
Elatea, and the great question was

βαίους σχεδὸν δὲ καὶ ὑμᾶς ὑπὸ τῶν τὰ Φιλίππου
φρονούντων καὶ διεφθαρμένων παρ' ἑκατέροις, ὃ μὲν
ἦν ἀμφοτέροις φοβερὸν καὶ φυλακῆς πολλῆς δεόμενον,
τὸ τὸν Φίλιππον ἐᾶν αὐξάνεσθαι, παρορῶντας καὶ 5
οὐδὲ καθ' ἓν φυλαττομένους, εἰς ἔχθραν δὲ καὶ τὸ
προσκρούειν ἀλλήλοις ἑτοίμως ἔχοντας, ὅπως τοῦτο
μὴ γένοιτο παρατηρῶν διετέλουν, οὐκ ἀπὸ τῆς ἐμαυτοῦ γνώμης μόνον ταῦτα συμφέρειν ὑπολαμβάνων,
ἀλλ' εἰδὼς Ἀριστοφῶντα καὶ πάλιν Εὔβουλον πάντα 162
τὸν χρόνον βουλομένους πρᾶξαι ταύτην τὴν φιλίαν,
καὶ περὶ τῶν ἄλλων πολλάκις ἀντιλέγοντας ἑαυτοῖς
τοῦθ' ὁμογνωμονοῦντας ἀεί. οὓς σὺ ζῶντας μὲν, ὦ
κίναδος, κολακεύων παρηκολούθεις, τεθνεώτων δ' οὐκ 5

whether Thebes would join Philip
against Athens, or Athens against the
invader.

1. ὁρῶν: with παρορῶντας (5), φυλαττομένους, and ἔχοντας (M.T. 904).

2. ὑπὸ τῶν...διεφθαρμένων: expressing the *agency* by which the
condition described in παρορῶντας etc.
was effected, as if the participles were
passive.

3. παρ' ἑκατέροις, i.e. in each
city. For Athens the great danger
was that her old enmity against Thebes
might prevent her from taking the
only safe course, union with Thebes.
For Philip's way of working in such
cases, see § 61. Dissen contrasts παρ'
ἑκατέροις, apud utrosque seorsim, *in
each city*, with ἀμφοτέροις (4), utrisque
simul, *both*.

5. τὸ...αὐξάνεσθαι: appositive to
the omitted antecedent of δ (3), which
is the object of παρορῶντας etc.

7. ὅπως τοῦτο (τὸ προσκρούειν) **μὴ
γένοιτο** (so Σ and L¹): most MSS.
have the more common γενήσεται
(M.T. 339, 340).

8. παρατηρῶν διετέλουν, *I kept
continual watch.*

9. ταῦτα: the policy of friendship

with Thebes (ταύτην τὴν φιλίαν, §
162²), implied in ὅπως τοῦτο μὴ γένοιτο.

§ 162. 1. Ἀριστοφῶντα (see §
70⁵), a leading statesman of the earlier
period and a strong friend of Thebes.
Aesch. says of him (III. 139), πλεῖστον
χρόνον τὴν τοῦ βοιωτιάζειν ὑπομείνας
αἰτίαν.—**Εὔβουλον** (cf. § 70⁵): see
Grote XI. 387.

2. βουλομένους and **ὁμογνωμονοῦντας** (4) are imperfect, past to
εἰδὼς and διετέλουν: but ἀντιλέγοντας
(3), *though they opposed one another*,
is present to ὁμογν., to which it is
subordinate. —**ταύτην τὴν φιλίαν**:
the friendship for Thebes during the
oppressive Spartan supremacy, which
appeared in the aid privately sent by
Athens to Thebes when she expelled
the Spartan garrison from the Cadmea
in 379 B.C. This friendship was
broken after Leuctra in 371. See §
98⁴ and note.

5. παρηκολούθεις is more than *you
were one of their followers*; it means
you followed them round or *hung on
to them* in a servile way. Eubulus
was one of the συνήγοροι who supported Aesch. at his trial for παραπρεσβεία (Aesch. II. 184). The anonymous

αἰσθάνει κατηγορῶν· ἃ γὰρ περὶ Θηβαίων ἐπιτιμᾷς
ἐμοί, ἐκείνων πολὺ μᾶλλον ἢ ἐμοῦ κατηγορεῖς, τῶν
πρότερον ἢ ἐγὼ ταύτην τὴν συμμαχίαν δοκιμασάν-
των. ἀλλ' ἐκεῖσ' ἐπάνειμι, ὅτι τὸν ἐν Ἀμφίσσῃ 163
πόλεμον τούτου μὲν ποιήσαντος, συμπερανα μένων δὲ
τῶν ἄλλων τῶν συνεργῶν αὐτῷ τὴν πρὸς Θηβαίους
282 ἔχθραν, συνέβη τὸν Φίλιππον ἐλθεῖν ἐφ' ἡμᾶς, οὗπερ
ἕνεκα τὰς πόλεις οὗτοι συνέκρουον, καὶ εἰ μὴ προεξ- 5
ανέστημεν μικρόν, οὐδ' ἀναλαβεῖν ἂν ἠδυνήθημεν·
οὕτω μέχρι πόρρω προήγαγον οὗτοι. ἐν οἷς δ' ἦτ'
ἤδη τὰ πρὸς ἀλλήλους, τουτωνὶ τῶν ψηφισμάτων
ἀκούσαντες καὶ τῶν ἀποκρίσεων εἴσεσθε. καί μοι
λέγε ταῦτα λαβών. 10

ΨΗΦΙΣΜΑ.

[Ἐπὶ ἄρχοντος Ἡροπύθου, μηνὸς ἐλαφηβολιῶνος ἕκτῃ 164
φθίνοντος, φυλῆς πρυτανευούσης Ἐρεχθῇδος, βουλῆς καὶ
στρατηγῶν γνώμῃ, ἐπειδὴ Φίλιππος ἃς μὲν κατείληφε πόλεις
τῶν ἀστυγειτόνων, τινὰς δὲ πορθεῖ, κεφαλαίῳ δὲ ἐπὶ τὴν

Life of Aeschines makes him a clerk
to both Eubulus and Aristophon.
6. ἁ...ἐπιτιμᾷς : the charge of
favouring Thebes in the terms of the
alliance in 339—338 B.C. (Aesch.
141—143).
§ 163. 1. ἐκεῖσ', i.e. *to the main
point.*
2. ποιήσαντος, συμπερανα μένων :
συμ- implies that, while Aesch. got
up the Amphissian war by himself,
he had active helpers in stirring up
enmity at Athens against Thebes.
When all was ready, Philip appeared
at Elatea (ἐλθεῖν ἐφ' ἡμᾶς, 4): cf.
§ 168[3].
5. εἰ μὴ...μικρόν, *if we had not
roused ourselves a little too soon* (for
the success of the plot): μικρόν chiefly
affects προ-.
6. ἀναλαβεῖν, *to recover* (intrans.):

cf. Plat. Rep. 467 B, ποιῆσαι καὶ τὴν
ἄλλην πόλιν ἀδύνατον ἀναλαβεῖν.
7. οὕτω with μέχρι πόρρω, *so far.*
—προήγαγον, *carried it,* i.e. the
quarrel with Thebes.
8, 9. ψηφισμάτων, ἀποκρίσεων :
as these documents were quoted to
show the enmity between Thebes and
Athens at the time of Philip's invasion,
the ψηφίσματα were probably Athenian decrees enacting measures hostile
to Thebes, and the replies were re-
monstrances or retaliatory measures
on the part of Thebes. Nothing could
be more absurd than the two decrees
against Philip and the two letters of
Philip which appear here in the text.
See § 168[2], where Philip is said to
have been *elated* (ἐπαρθείς) by the
decrees and the replies, i.e. by the evidence of hostility which they showed.

Ἀττικὴν παρασκευάζεται παραγίγνεσθαι, παρ' οὐδὲν ἡγού- 5
μενος τὰς ἡμετέρας συνθήκας, καὶ τοὺς ὅρκους λύειν ἐπιβάλλεται καὶ τὴν εἰρήνην, παραβαίνων τὰς κοινὰς πίστεις,
δεδόχθαι τῇ βουλῇ καὶ τῷ δήμῳ πέμπειν πρὸς αὐτὸν πρέσβεις,
οἵτινες αὐτῷ διαλέξονται καὶ παρακαλέσουσιν αὐτὸν μάλιστα
μὲν τὴν πρὸς ἡμᾶς ὁμόνοιαν διατηρεῖν καὶ τὰς συνθήκας, εἰ δὲ 10
μή, πρὸς τὸ βουλεύσασθαι δοῦναι χρόνον τῇ πόλει καὶ τὰς
ἀνοχὰς ποιήσασθαι μέχρι τοῦ θαργηλιῶνος μηνός. ᾑρέθησαν
ἐκ τῆς βουλῆς Σῖμος Ἀναγυράσιος, Εὐθύδημος Φυλάσιος,
Βουλαγόρας Ἀλωπεκῆθεν.]

ΕΤΕΡΟΝ ΨΗΦΙΣΜΑ.

[Ἐπὶ ἄρχοντος Ἡροπύθου, μηνὸς μουνυχιῶνος ἕνῃ καὶ 165
νέᾳ, πολεμάρχου γνώμῃ, ἐπειδὴ Φίλιππος εἰς ἀλλοτριότητα
Θηβαίους πρὸς ἡμᾶς ἐπιβάλλεται καταστῆσαι, παρεσκεύασται
δὲ καὶ παντὶ τῷ στρατεύματι πρὸς τοὺς ἔγγιστα τῆς Ἀττικῆς
283 παραγίγνεσθαι τόπους, παραβαίνων τὰς πρὸς ἡμᾶς ὑπαρ- 5
χούσας αὐτῷ συνθήκας, δεδόχθαι τῇ βουλῇ καὶ τῷ δήμῳ
πέμψαι πρὸς αὐτὸν κήρυκα καὶ πρέσβεις, οἵτινες ἀξιώσουσι
καὶ παρακαλέσουσιν αὐτὸν ποιήσασθαι τὰς ἀνοχὰς, ὅπως
ἐνδεχομένως ὁ δῆμος βουλεύσηται· καὶ γὰρ νῦν οὐ κέκρικε
βοηθεῖν ἐν οὐδενὶ τῶν μετρίων. ᾑρέθησαν ἐκ τῆς βουλῆς 10
Νέαρχος Σωσινόμου, Πολυκράτης Ἐπίφρονος, καὶ κῆρυξ
Εὔνομος Ἀναφλύστιος ἐκ τοῦ δήμου.]

Λέγε δὴ καὶ τὰς ἀποκρίσεις. 166

ΑΠΟΚΡΙΣΙΣ ΑΘΗΝΑΙΟΙΣ.

[Βασιλεὺς Μακεδόνων Φίλιππος Ἀθηναίων τῇ βουλῇ καὶ
τῷ δήμῳ χαίρειν. ἣν μὲν ἀπ' ἀρχῆς εἴχετε πρὸς ἡμᾶς αἵρεσιν,
οὐκ ἀγνοῶ, καὶ τίνα σπουδὴν ποιεῖσθε προσκαλέσασθαι βου- 5
λόμενοι Θετταλοὺς καὶ Θηβαίους, ἔτι δὲ καὶ Βοιωτούς· βέλτιον
δ' αὐτῶν φρονούντων καὶ μὴ βουλομένων ἐφ' ὑμῖν ποιήσασθαι
τὴν ἑαυτῶν αἵρεσιν, ἀλλὰ κατὰ τὸ συμφέρον ἱσταμένων, νῦν
ἐξ ὑποστροφῆς ἀποστείλαντες ὑμεῖς πρός με πρέσβεις καὶ

κήρυκα συνθηκῶν μνημονεύετε καὶ τὰς ἀνοχὰς αἰτεῖσθε, κατ' 10
οὐδὲν ὑφ' ἡμῶν πεπλημμελημένοι. ἐγὼ μέντοι ἀκούσας τῶν
πρεσβευτῶν συγκατατίθεμαι τοῖς παρακαλουμένοις καὶ ἕτοιμός
εἰμι ποιεῖσθαι τὰς ἀνοχάς, ἄν περ τοὺς οὐκ ὀρθῶς συμβου-
λεύοντας ὑμῖν παραπέμψαντες τῆς προσηκούσης ἀτιμίας ἀξιώ-
σητε. ἔρρωσθε.] 15

ΑΠΟΚΡΙΣΙΣ ΘΗΒΑΙΟΙΣ.

[Βασιλεὺς Μακεδόνων Φίλιππος Θηβαίων τῇ βουλῇ καὶ 167
τῷ δήμῳ χαίρειν. ἐκομισάμην τὴν παρ' ὑμῶν ἐπιστολὴν, δι'
284 ἧς μοι τὴν ὁμόνοιαν ἀνανεοῦσθε καὶ τὴν εἰρήνην ὄντως ἐμοὶ
ποιεῖτε. πυνθάνομαι μέντοι διότι πᾶσαν ὑμῖν 'Αθηναῖοι
προσφέρονται φιλοτιμίαν, βουλόμενοι ὑμᾶς συγκαταίνους 5
γενέσθαι τοῖς ὑπ' αὐτῶν παρακαλουμένοις. πρότερον μὲν οὖν
ὑμῶν κατεγίγνωσκον ἐπὶ τῷ μέλλειν πείθεσθαι ταῖς ἐκείνων
ἐλπίσι καὶ ἐπακολουθεῖν αὐτῶν τῇ προαιρέσει. νῦν δ' ἐπι-
γνοὺς ὑμᾶς τὰ πρὸς ἡμᾶς ἐζητηκότας ἔχειν εἰρήνην μᾶλλον ἢ
ταῖς ἑτέρων ἐπακολουθεῖν γνώμαις, ἥσθην καὶ μᾶλλον ὑμᾶς 10
ἐπαινῶ κατὰ πολλὰ, μάλιστα δ' ἐπὶ τῷ βουλεύσασθαι περὶ
τούτων ἀσφαλέστερον καὶ τὰ πρὸς ἡμᾶς ἔχειν ἐν εὐνοίᾳ· ὅπερ
οὐ μικρὰν ὑμῖν οἴσειν ἐλπίζω ῥοπὴν, ἐάν περ ἐπὶ ταύτης
μένητε τῆς προθέσεως. ἔρρωσθε.]

Οὕτω διαθεὶς ὁ Φίλιππος τὰς πόλεις πρὸς ἀλλή- 168
λας διὰ τούτων, καὶ τούτοις ἐπαρθεὶς τοῖς ψηφίσμασι
καὶ ταῖς ἀποκρίσεσιν, ἧκεν ἔχων τὴν δύναμιν καὶ τὴν
'Ελάτειαν κατέλαβεν, ὡς οὐδ' ἂν εἴ τι γένοιτ' ἔτι

---

§ 168. 1. **οὕτω** : as the documents showed.

4. **ὡς οὐδ' ἂν...συμπνευσάντων ἂν,** i.e. *feeling* (ὡς) *that under no possible circumstances would the Thebans and ourselves become harmonious* : συμπνευσάντων ἂν represents συμπνεύσαιμεν ἂν. The MSS. all have συμπνευσόντων ἂν, which Bekker retains. The future participle with ἂν is very rare and

generally doubtful: but here it would represent the future optative with ἂν, for which there is no recognized authority. Moreover, the future of πνέω is not πνεύσω, but πνεύσομαι or πνευσοῦμαι, and this should be decisive (see Veitch). See M. T. 216; and for the repetition of ἄν, 223.

συμπνευσάντων ἂν ἡμῶν καὶ τῶν Θηβαίων. ἀλλὰ 5
μὴν τὸν τότε συμβάντ᾽ ἐν τῇ πόλει θόρυβον ἴστε μὲν
ἅπαντες· μικρὰ δ᾽ ἀκούσαθ᾽ ὅμως [αὐτὰ τὰ] ἀναγκαιότατα.
Ἑσπέρα μὲν γὰρ ἦν, ἦκε δ᾽ ἀγγέλλων τις ὡς 169
τοὺς πρυτάνεις ὡς Ἐλάτεια κατείληπται. καὶ μετὰ
ταῦτα οἱ μὲν εὐθὺς ἐξαναστάντες μεταξὺ δειπνοῦντες
τούς τ᾽ ἐκ τῶν σκηνῶν τῶν κατὰ τὴν ἀγορὰν ἐξεῖργον
καὶ τὰ γέρρα ἐνεπίμπρασαν. οἱ δὲ τοὺς στρατηγοὺς 5

7. **μικρὰ ἀναγκαιότατα** (so Σ and
L¹): see § 126⁴ and note. Most MSS.
give αὐτὰ τὰ ἀναγκαιότατα here, perhaps correctly.

§§ 169—180. Here follows the
famous description of the panic in
Athens when the news of the seizure
of Elatea arrived, and of the meeting
of the Assembly which was suddenly
called to consider the alarming situation. This is a celebrated example
of διατύπωσις, *vivid delineation.*

§ 169. 1. The succession of tenses,
ἦν, ἦκε (*had come*), and κατείληπται (the
direct form for the indirect), makes
the narrative lively and picturesque
at the outset. Much would have been
lost if he had said ἦλθε δ᾽ ἀγγέλλων
τις ὡς κατειλημμένη εἴη.—ὡς τοὺς
πρυτάνεις: the message came to the
Prytanes, the fifty senators of one of
the ten tribes, who for their term of
one-tenth of the year represented the
authority of the state. Their office
was the θόλος or σκιάς, a round building
with a cupola in the ἀγορά, adjoining
the Senate-house and the μητρῷον with
its record-office. There the ἐπιστάτης
of the Prytanes was expected to spend
his whole day and night of office,
with a third of the Prytanes whom
he had selected (Arist. Pol. Ath. 44⁵),
so as to be accessible in emergencies
like the present; and there the state
provided meals for all the Prytanes.
The θόλος is distinct from the ancient

Prytaneum or City Hall, where certain
privileged persons (ἀείσιτοι) had their
meals at a public table, to which
ambassadors and other guests of the
state were sometimes invited.

4. **τοὺς...σκηνῶν:** cf. § 44⁴.

5. **τὰ γέρρα,** probably the wicker-
work with which the booths (σκῆναι)
in the market-place were covered.
The word can mean also anything
made of twigs, and is used of a wicker
fence which enclosed the ἐκκλησία
(see Harpocr. under γέρρα, and LIX.
90). But the close connection of the
two clauses, *drove out those in the
booths* and *burnt the γέρρα,* shows
that the γέρρα which were burnt were
taken from the booths. Otherwise
there is no reason for driving the
poor hucksters out at all. If it is said
that this was done to prepare for the
"monster meeting" the next morning,
we must remember, first, that the
Assembly was held in the Pnyx, not
in the ἀγορά; and, secondly, that
there was to be a meeting of the
Senate before that of the Assembly,
which would give time enough to
make all necessary preparations after
daybreak. To suppose, further, that
the booths were torn to pieces and
burnt on the spot after dark, merely
to clear the ἀγορά, when there was
no pressure of time, even if the place
needed clearing at all, is to impute to
the Prytanes conduct well worthy of

μετεπέμποντο καὶ τὸν σαλπικτὴν ἐκάλουν· καὶ θορύβου πλήρης ἦν ἡ πόλις. τῇ δ᾽ ὑστεραίᾳ ἅμα τῇ
ἡμέρᾳ οἱ μὲν πρυτάνεις τὴν βουλὴν ἐκάλουν εἰς τὸ
285 βουλευτήριον, ὑμεῖς δ᾽ εἰς τὴν ἐκκλησίαν ἐπορεύεσθε,
καὶ πρὶν ἐκείνην χρηματίσαι καὶ προβουλεῦσαι πᾶς 10
ὁ δῆμος ἄνω καθῆτο. καὶ μετὰ ταῦτα ὡς ἦλθεν ἡ 170
βουλὴ καὶ ἀπήγγειλαν οἱ πρυτάνεις τὰ προσηγγελ-

madmen. Such a panic as this sense-
less proceeding would have caused
was surely the last object which these
guardians of the state could have had,
when they left their supper unfinished
and hastened into the market-place.
Their first object certainly was to
secure a full meeting of the Assembly
the next morning. It will be noticed
that while some (οἱ μέν) of the Prytanes
were engaged in clearing the booths,
others (οἱ δέ) were summoning the ten
Generals. The Generals and the Prytanes had the duty of calling special
meetings of the Assembly (ἐκκλησίας
συγκλήτους) : see Thuc. IV. 118⁵²,
ἐκκλησίαν δὲ ποιήσαντας τοὺς στρατηγοὺς καὶ τοὺς πρυτάνεις, and II. 59¹¹
(of Pericles), σύλλογον ποιήσας (ἔτι δ᾽
ἐστρατήγει). There can, therefore,
be hardly a doubt that the two acts
were connected with summoning the
Assembly. To do this effectually it
was necessary to alarm the whole of
Attica immediately; and the natural
method for this was to light bonfires
on some of the hills near Athens,
which would be a signal to distant
demes to light fires on their own hills.
A fire on Lycabettus could thus give
signals directly and indirectly to the
whole of Attica, and probably this
was understood as a call of the citizens
to a special Assembly. As material
for lighting signal fires might not
always be on hand, it is likely that
the dry covering of the booths struck
the eyes of the Prytanes as they came
out of their office, and that they took

them in their haste for this purpose.
Their high authority was needed to
prevent resistance on the part of the
owners of the booths.

6. σαλπικτήν : to give signals with
his trumpet.

7. τὴν βουλὴν ἐκάλουν: see Arist.
Pol. Ath. 44⁷, ἐπειδὰν συναγάγωσιν οἱ
πρυτάνεις τὴν βουλὴν ἢ τὸν δῆμον.

10. χρηματίσαι καὶ προβουλεῦσαι,
proceed to business and pass a vote (προβούλευμα).

11. ἄνω καθῆτο, i.e. the people in
their impatience were already seated
in the Pnyx : ἄνω shows that the
Assembly sat on a hill, probably in
the place now known as the Pnyx.
See XXV. 9 and 20, τὸν δῆμον εἰς τὴν
ἐκκλησίαν ἀναβαίνειν. For the identity
of this famous place, see Crow in
Papers of the American School at
Athens, IV. pp. 205—260.

§ 170. 1. ὡς ἦλθεν ἡ βουλή, i.e.
when, after the adjournment of the
Senate, the senators entered the
Assembly.

2. ἀπήγγειλαν οἱ πρυτάνεις : the
fifty Prytanes were still the chief men
in both Senate and Assembly, though
at this time (certainly since 377 B.C.)
the duty of presiding in both bodies
was given to nine πρόεδροι, who were
chosen by lot each day from the senators
of the other nine tribes by the ἐπιστάτης of the Prytanes (Arist. Pol. Ath.
44⁷⁻⁹). The πρόεδροι had an ἐπιστάτης of their own, called ὁ ἐπιστάτης
τῶν προέδρων (Aesch. III. 39). This
is the office held by Demosthenes in

μέν' ἐαυτοῖς καὶ τὸν ἥκοντα παρήγαγον κἀκεῖνος
εἶπεν, ἠρώτα μὲν ὁ κῆρυξ τίς ἀγορεύειν βούλεται; παρήει δ' οὐδείς. πολλάκις δὲ τοῦ κήρυκος 5
ἐρωτῶντος οὐδὲν μᾶλλον ἀνίστατ' οὐδεὶς, ἀπάντων
μὲν τῶν στρατηγῶν παρόντων, ἀπάντων δὲ τῶν
ῥητόρων, καλούσης δὲ τῇ κοινῇ τῆς πατρίδος φωνῇ
τὸν ἐροῦνθ' ὑπὲρ σωτηρίας· ἣν γὰρ ὁ κῆρυξ κατὰ
τοὺς νόμους φωνὴν ἀφίησι, ταύτην κοινὴν τῆς πατρί- 10
δος δίκαιόν ἐστιν ἡγεῖσθαι. καίτοι εἰ μὲν τοὺς 171
σωθῆναι τὴν πόλιν βουλομένους παρελθεῖν ἔδει,
πάντες ἂν ὑμεῖς καὶ οἱ ἄλλοι Ἀθηναῖοι ἀναστάντες
ἐπὶ τὸ βῆμ' ἐβαδίζετε· πάντες γὰρ οἶδ' ὅτι σωθῆναι
αὐτὴν ἐβούλεσθε· εἰ δὲ τοὺς πλουσιωτάτους, οἱ 5
τριακόσιοι· εἰ δὲ τοὺς ἀμφότερα ταῦτα, καὶ εὔνους
τῇ πόλει καὶ πλουσίους, οἱ μετὰ ταῦτα τὰς μεγάλας
ἐπιδόσεις ἐπιδόντες· καὶ γὰρ εὐνοίᾳ καὶ πλούτῳ
τοῦτ' ἐποίησαν. ἀλλ' ὡς ἔοικεν, ἐκεῖνος ὁ καιρὸς 172
καὶ ἡ ἡμέρα 'κείνη οὐ μόνον εὔνουν καὶ πλούσιον
ἄνδρ' ἐκάλει, ἀλλὰ καὶ παρηκολουθηκότα τοῖς πράγμασιν ἐξ ἀρχῆς, καὶ συλλελογισμένον ὀρθῶς τίνος
ἕνεκα ταῦτ' ἔπραττεν ὁ Φίλιππος καὶ τί βουλόμενος· 5
ὁ γὰρ μὴ ταῦτ' εἰδὼς μηδ' ἐξητακὼς πόρρωθεν ἐπιμελῶς, οὔτ' εἰ εὔνους ἦν οὔτ' εἰ πλούσιος, οὐδὲν

---

the last meeting of the Assembly
before the departure of the second
embassy in 346: see Aesch. III. 74.
3. **τὸν ἥκοντα**, the messenger who
had brought the news about Elatea :
cf. § 28⁵.
4. **τίς ἀγορεύειν βούλεται**; the
regular formula for opening a debate:
cf. § 191². Aeschines (III. 2 and 4)
laments the omission of the additional
words, τῶν ὑπὲρ πεντήκοντα ἔτη γεγο-
νότων καὶ πάλιν ἐν μέρει τῶν ἄλλων
Ἀθηναίων, the Solonic form.

9. **τὸν ἐροῦνθ'** = ὃς ἐρεῖ, the man to
speak (M.T. 565) : cf. § 285³.
§ 171. 5. **οἱ τριακόσιοι**, the Three
Hundred: see note on § 103⁴.
6. **ἀμφότερα ταῦτα**: see note on
§ 139¹².
7. **τὰς μεγάλας ἐπιδόσεις**, the large
contributions, made after the battle of
Chaeronea (Hist. § 67): μετὰ ταῦτα
refers to the events which ended in
that battle.
§ 172. 3. **παρηκολουθηκότα**, one
who had followed the track of events.

μᾶλλον ἤμελλεν ὅ τι χρὴ ποιεῖν εἴσεσθαι οὐδ᾽ ὑμῖν
ἕξειν συμβουλεύειν. ἐφάνην τοίνυν οὗτος ἐν ἐκείνῃ 173
τῇ ἡμέρᾳ ἐγώ, καὶ παρελθὼν εἶπον εἰς ὑμᾶς, ἅ μου
286 δυοῖν ἕνεκ᾽ ἀκούσατε προσσχόντες τὸν νοῦν, ἑνὸς μὲν,
ἵν᾽ εἰδῆτε ὅτι μόνος τῶν λεγόντων καὶ πολιτευομένων
ἐγὼ τὴν τῆς εὐνοίας τάξιν ἐν τοῖς δεινοῖς οὐκ ἔλιπον, 5
ἀλλὰ καὶ λέγων καὶ γράφων ἐξηταζόμην τὰ δέονθ᾽
ὑπὲρ ὑμῶν ἐν αὐτοῖς τοῖς φοβεροῖς, ἑτέρου δέ, ὅτι
μικρὸν ἀναλώσαντες χρόνον πολλῷ πρὸς τὰ λοιπὰ
τῆς πάσης πολιτείας ἔσεσθ᾽ ἐμπειρότεροι.

Εἶπον τοίνυν ὅτι 174
"Τοὺς μὲν ὡς ὑπαρχόντων Θηβαίων Φιλίππῳ
λίαν θορυβουμένους ἀγνοεῖν τὰ παρόντα πράγμαθ᾽
ἡγοῦμαι· εὖ γὰρ οἶδ᾽ ὅτι, εἰ τοῦθ᾽ οὕτως ἐτύγχανεν
ἔχον, οὐκ ἂν αὐτὸν ἠκούομεν ἐν Ἐλατείᾳ ὄντα, ἀλλ᾽ 5
ἐπὶ τοῖς ἡμετέροις ὁρίοις. ὅτι μέντοι ἵν᾽ ἕτοιμα

See XIX. 257 (end), and Ev. Luc. i. 3
παρηκολουθηκότι ἄνωθεν πᾶσιν ἀκριβῶς.
8. οὐδὲν...εἴσεσθαι, i.e. *was none
the more likely to know*. The best
MSS. have ἤμελλεν here and in § 192⁴,
and ἔμελλον in § 101⁵.
§ 173. 1. οὗτος (pred.), *that man*,
whom ὁ καιρὸς...ἐκάλει (§ 172¹): cf. §
282¹⁰, οὗτος εὑρέθης.
2. ἅ...ἀκούσατε: relative as obj.
of imperative, as we say *which do at
your peril*. For this in οἶσθ᾽ ὃ δρᾶσον ;
and similar expressions, see M.T. 253.
3. προσσχόντες τὸν νοῦν, *atten-
tively*, cf. animum advertere.
5. τὴν...ἔλιπον, *I did not desert
my post of devotion to the state*, i.e.
I was never guilty of λιποταξία here.
This military figure was a favourite of
Demosthenes. See III. 36, μὴ παρα-
χωρεῖν τῆς τάξεως ἣν ὑμῖν οἱ πρόγονοι
τῆς ἀρετῆς...κατέλιπον ; XV. 32, 33
(with the figure often repeated) ; XIX.
9, 29; XXI. 120, λελοιπέναι τὴν τοῦ

δικαίου τάξιν. The same figure is seen
in ἐξηταζόμην (l. 6), in ἐξήτασαι (§
197¹⁰), ἐξητάζετο (§ 217⁷), ἐξεταζό-
μένων ὑπὲρ ὑμῶν (§ 277⁷), and in
ἐξέτασις, a *mustering* (as of troops),
a *call for* (§§ 310¹, 320¹⁰). Here there
is always an idea of being *counted in*
on one side or the other of some
contest.—εὐνοίας : see note on § 1².
6. λέγων...ἐξηταζόμην (see last
note), *I was found ready* (at my post),
when the test came, *speaking and
proposing measures*.
8. πολλῷ...ἐμπειρότεροι, *far more
experienced for the future in the whole
administration of the state* (πολιτείας).
§ 174. 1. εἶπον ὅτι: introducing
a direct quotation (M.T. 711).
2. ὡς...Φιλίππῳ, *in the belief* (ὡς)
that Philip can depend on the Thebans :
cf. §§ 95⁵, 228³.
3. θορυβουμένους, *disturbed*: cf.
θορύβου, § 169⁶.
6. ἵν᾽...ποιήσηται, i.e. to prepare
Thebes for his appearance there as a

ποιήσηται τὰ ἐν Θήβαις ἥκει, σαφῶς ἐπίσταμαι. ὡς
δ' ἔχει" ἔφην "ταῦτα, ἀκούσατέ μου. ἐκεῖνος ὅσους 175
ἢ πεῖσαι χρήμασι Θηβαίων ἢ ἐξαπατῆσαι ἐνῆν,
ἅπαντας εὐτρέπισται· τοὺς δ' ἀπ' ἀρχῆς ἀνθεστηκό-
τας αὐτῷ καὶ νῦν ἐναντιουμένους οὐδαμῶς πεῖσαι
δύναται. τί οὖν βούλεται, καὶ τίνος εἵνεκα τὴν 5
Ἐλάτειαν κατείληφεν ; πλησίον δύναμιν δείξας καὶ
παραστήσας τὰ ὅπλα τοὺς μὲν ἑαυτοῦ φίλους ἐπᾶραι
καὶ θρασεῖς ποιῆσαι, τοὺς δ' ἐναντιουμένους καταπλῆξαι, ἵν' ἢ συγχωρήσωσι φοβηθέντες ἃ νῦν οὐκ
ἐθέλουσιν, ἢ βιασθῶσιν. εἰ μὲν τοίνυν προαιρησόμεθ' 176
ἡμεῖς" ἔφην "ἐν τῷ παρόντι, εἴ τι δύσκολον πέπρακται Θηβαίοις πρὸς ἡμᾶς, τούτου μεμνῆσθαι καὶ
ἀπιστεῖν αὐτοῖς ὡς ἐν τῇ τῶν ἐχθρῶν οὖσι μερίδι,
πρῶτον μὲν ἂν εὔξαιτο Φίλιππος ποιήσομεν, εἶτα 5
φοβοῦμαι μὴ, προσδεξαμένων τῶν νῦν ἀνθεστηκότων
287 αὐτῷ καὶ μιᾷ γνώμῃ πάντων φιλιππισάντων, εἰς τὴν
Ἀττικὴν ἔλθωσιν ἀμφότεροι. ἂν μέντοι πεισθῆτ'
ἐμοὶ καὶ πρὸς τῷ σκοπεῖν ἀλλὰ μὴ φιλονεικεῖν περὶ

---

friend : cf. εὐτρέπισται (i.e. εὐτρεπεῖς
πεποίηται), § 175⁴.

§ 175. 6. πλησίον δύναμιν δείξας,
by making a display of force in their
neighbourhood, Elatea being near
enough to Thebes to make Philip's
presence there alarming.

7. ἐπᾶραι (cf. ἐπαρθεὶς, § 168²),
with ποιῆσαι and καταπλῆξαι, depends
on βούλεται understood, this answering
τί βούλεται; as the following ἵν'...
βιασθῶσιν answers τίνος ἕνεκα;

§ 176. 1. εἰ μὲν...προαιρησόμεθ':
this most vivid form of future supposition here expresses what the orator
wishes to make especially prominent
by way of warning and admonition,
though it happens that this is not
what he wishes or what actually occurs.
It is an excellent case of Gildersleeve's

"minatory and monitory conditions"
(see Trans. of Amer. Philol. Assoc.
for 1876, p. 13, and M.T. 447, with
footnote). On the other hand, ἂν
μέντοι πεισθῆτ' ἐμοί (8) happens to
express what he most desires and
what actually occurs. Compare the
antithesis of subjunctive and optative
in §§ 147, 148, with notes.

2. δύσκολον, unpleasant, euphemistic : cf. § 189⁶.

4. ὡς ἐν...μερίδι, looking at them
(ὡς) in the light of enemies (M.T.
864) : cf. § 292⁵ and III. 31, ἐν ὑπη-
ρέτου...μέρει.

7. μιᾷ γνώμῃ, uno consensu.

8. ἀμφότεροι, Thebans and Philip.

9. πρὸς τῷ σκοπεῖν...γένησθε,
devote yourselves to considering : cf.
VIII. 11, πρὸς τοῖς πράγμασι γίγνεσθαι.

ὧν ἂν λέγω γένησθε, οἶμαι καὶ τὰ δέοντα λέγειν 10
δόξειν καὶ τὸν ἐφεστηκότα κίνδυνον τῇ πόλει διαλύ-
σειν. τί οὖν φημὶ δεῖν; πρῶτον μὲν τὸν παρόντ' 177
ἐπανεῖναι φόβον, εἶτα μεταθέσθαι καὶ φοβεῖσθαι
πάντας ὑπὲρ Θηβαίων· πολὺ γὰρ τῶν δεινῶν εἰσιν
ἡμῶν ἐγγυτέρω, καὶ προτέροις αὐτοῖς ἐστιν ὁ κίνδυνος·
ἔπειτ' ἐξελθόντας Ἐλευσῖνάδε τοὺς ἐν ἡλικίᾳ καὶ 5
τοὺς ἱππέας δεῖξαι πᾶσιν ὑμᾶς αὐτοὺς ἐν τοῖς ὅπλοις
ὄντας, ἵνα τοῖς ἐν Θήβαις φρονοῦσι τὰ ὑμέτερ' ἐξ
ἴσου γένηται τὸ παρρησιάζεσθαι περὶ τῶν δικαίων,
ἰδοῦσιν ὅτι, ὥσπερ τοῖς πωλοῦσι Φιλίππῳ τὴν
πατρίδα πάρεσθ' ἡ βοηθήσουσα δύναμις ἐν Ἐλατείᾳ, 10
οὕτω τοῖς ὑπὲρ τῆς ἐλευθερίας ἀγωνίζεσθαι βουλο-
μένοις ὑπάρχεθ' ὑμεῖς ἕτοιμοι καὶ βοηθήσετ' ἐάν τις
ἐπ' αὐτοὺς ἴῃ. μετὰ ταῦτα χειροτονῆσαι κελεύω 178
δέκα πρέσβεις, καὶ ποιῆσαι τούτους κυρίους μετὰ
τῶν στρατηγῶν καὶ τοῦ πότε δεῖ βαδίζειν ἐκεῖσε καὶ

---

11. **δόξειν...διαλύσειν** : sc. ἐμέ.—
τὸν...τῇ πόλει : for this order of words
see §§ 190², 197⁸, 220³; and for the
common order §§ 179⁷, 188⁴.
§ 177. 2. **μεταθέσθαι**, *to turn
about*, explained by φοβεῖσθαι ὑπὲρ
Θηβαίων.
5. **Ἐλευσῖνάδε**, to the plain of
Eleusis, "but no further, lest a friendly
demonstration should pass for a menace
at Thebes" (Simcox). See note on
§ 178³. This was a convenient place
for the army to encamp, and they
would be within an easy march of
Thebes. The mountain road to
Thebes by Phyle was more direct,
but rougher and with no good camp-
ing place.—**τοὺς ἐν ἡλικίᾳ** : this term
properly included all citizens between
18 and 60 : see Arist. Pol. Ath. 42,
4—6 and 34—37. But those between
18 and 20 always remained at home
as φρουροί; while those between 50

and 60 were not regularly called into
service and served as διαιτηταί, or
public arbiters (Arist. Pol. Ath. 53,
20—37). Here the 1000 ἱππεῖς are
excluded from οἱ ἐν ἡλικίᾳ. See also
Lycurg. 39 : αἱ δ' ἐλπίδες τῆς σωτηρίας τῷ δήμῳ ἐν τοῖς ὑπὲρ πεντήκοντα
ἔτη γεγονόσι καθειστήκεσαν, i.e. when
the news of the defeat at Chaeronea
came, showing that those above fifty
were not in the battle.
7. **ἐξ ἴσου**, *on an equality* with
Philip's friends.
9. **τοῖς πωλοῦσι**, *to those who would
sell* (conative): M.T. 25.
12. **ὑπάρχεθ' ἕτοιμοι**, *you are ready
at hand*.
§ 178. 2. **ποιῆσαι...στρατηγῶν**,
i.e. to give the envoys (by decree)
concurrent authority with the board
of generals.
3. **πότε...ἐκεῖσε**; this question is
made a genitive with τοῦ. The sub-

τῆς ἐξόδου. ἐπειδὰν δ' ἔλθωσιν οἱ πρέσβεις εἰς
Θήβας, πῶς χρήσασθαι τῷ πράγματι παραινῶ; 5
τούτῳ πάνυ μοι προσέχετε τὸν νοῦν. μὴ δεῖσθαι
Θηβαίων μηδὲν (αἰσχρὸς γὰρ ὁ καιρός), ἀλλ' ἐπαγ-
γέλλεσθαι βοηθήσειν ἂν κελεύωσιν, ὡς ἐκείνων ὄντων
ἐν τοῖς ἐσχάτοις, ἡμῶν δ' ἄμεινον ἢ 'κεῖνοι προορω-
μένων· ἵν' ἐὰν μὲν δέξωνται ταῦτα καὶ πεισθῶσιν 10
288 ἡμῖν, καὶ ἃ βουλόμεθ' ὦμεν διῳκημένοι καὶ μετὰ
προσχήματος ἀξίου τῆς πόλεως ταῦτα πράξωμεν, ἂν
δ' ἄρα μὴ συμβῇ κατατυχεῖν, ἐκεῖνοι μὲν αὐτοῖς

ject of βαδίζειν is ὑμᾶς, the Athenian
army. The embassy probably departed
for Thebes at once, so as to lose no
time in securing the confidence of the
Thebans; but the army could not
march further than Eleusis until it
was invited by Thebes to cross her
frontier. This was done in due time
(§ 215[1]), after negotiations at Thebes
(§§ 211—214). To facilitate this
movement when the summons should
come, the people were asked to
empower the embassy at Thebes, in
concurrence with the generals at
Eleusis, to order a march to Thebes
at any moment, and to decide all
questions about *the march itself* (τῆς
ἐξόδου).

5. **χρήσασθαι τῷ πράγματι**, *to
manage the* (diplomatic) *business*.

6. **τούτῳ...νοῦν** : this special call
for close attention was made to excite
the audience with the expectation of
hearing just what the embassy was to
ask of the Thebans, and to impress
them the more by the unexpected
answer μὴ δεῖσθαι Θηβαίων μηδέν.
It was indeed an unheard of thing
for an embassy to be sent to a semi-
hostile state in such an emergency,
with no demands or even requests,
but with an unconditional offer of
military help whenever it might be

asked for. Aeschines does not fail to
misrepresent this noble act of Demosthenes, and to criticise the course
of the embassy : see III. 145, τὸ
βουλευτήριον τὸ τῆς πόλεως καὶ τὴν δημοκρατίαν ἄρδην ἔλαθεν ὑφελόμενος, καὶ
μετήνεγκεν εἰς Θήβας εἰς τὴν Καδμείαν.

9. **ἐν τοῖς ἐσχάτοις**, *in extremis*.
—**ἡμῶν...προορωμένων** (also with ὡς),
on the ground that we foresee (the
course of events) *better than they* (τὸ
μέλλον is omitted with Σ) : cf. τὸ μὴ
δύνασθαι προορᾶν, Plat. Theaet. 166 A.

10. **ἵν'...ὦμεν διῳκημένοι**, *that we
may* (*then*) *have accomplished what we
wish* : the perfect subjunctive here
and in l. 15 (ᾖ πεπραγμένον) is future-
perfect in time, in contrast to the
simple future of πράξωμεν and ἐγκαλῶσιν (M.T. 103).

12. **προσχήματος**, *ground of action* :
πρόσχημα is what appears on the outside, which may be either mere show
or (as here) an honest exhibition of
the truth. Cf. the double meaning of
πρόφασις, *ground of action* or *pretext*,
in § 225[5].—**ἂν δ' ἄρα**, *but if after all* :
cf. § 278[6].

13. **κατατυχεῖν**, *to succeed* (= ἐπιτυ-
χεῖν, Hesych.), acc. to Blass is not elsewhere found in classic writers.—**αὐτοῖς
ἐγκαλῶσιν**, *may have themselves to
blame.*

ἐγκαλῶσιν ἄν τι νῦν ἐξαμαρτάνωσιν, ἡμῖν δὲ μηδὲν
αἰσχρὸν μηδὲ ταπεινὸν ᾖ πεπραγμένον." 15
Ταῦτα καὶ παραπλήσια τούτοις εἰπὼν κατέβην. 179
συνεπαινεσάντων δὲ πάντων καὶ οὐδενὸς εἰπόντος
ἐναντίον οὐδέν, οὐκ εἶπον μὲν ταῦτα οὐκ ἔγραψα δὲ,
οὐδ' ἔγραψα μὲν οὐκ ἐπρέσβευσα δὲ, οὐδ' ἐπρέσβευσα
μὲν οὐκ ἔπεισα δὲ Θηβαίους, ἀλλ' ἀπὸ τῆς ἀρχῆς 5
ἄχρι τῆς τελευτῆς διεξῆλθον, καὶ ἔδωκ' ἐμαυτὸν ὑμῖν
ἁπλῶς εἰς τοὺς περιεστηκότας τῇ πόλει κινδύνους.
καί μοι φέρε τὸ ψήφισμα τὸ τότε γενόμενον.

Καίτοι τίνα βούλει σέ, Αἰσχίνη, καὶ τίνα ἐμαυτὸν 180
ἐκείνην τὴν ἡμέραν εἶναι θῶ; βούλει ἐμαυτὸν μὲν, ὃν
ἂν σὺ λοιδορούμενος καὶ διασύρων καλέσαις, Βάτ-

§ 179. 1. καὶ παραπλήσια : we have here only a single passage of what must have been one of the most eloquent speeches of Demosthenes.

3—5. οὐκ εἶπον μὲν...Θηβαίους : a most famous example of *climax* (κλῖμαξ, *ladder*), in which the antitheses of μέν and δέ give a wonderful effect. Each of the three leading negatives (οὐκ, οὐδ', οὐδ') introduces a pair of clauses of which the second is negative, and which *as a whole* it negatives. Thus the first οὐκ negatives the compound idea, *I spoke, but proposed no measures*; then the positive conclusion thus attained, *I did propose measures*, is taken as an assumption in the next step. Without the help of μέν and δέ the mixture of negatives would have made hopeless confusion. Quintilian (IX. 3, 55) thus translates the passage, skilfully using *quidem* for μέν and *sed* for δέ : *non enim dixi quidem sed non scripsi, nec scripsi quidem sed non obii legationem, nec obii quidem sed non persuasi Thebanis.*

7. ἁπλῶς, *without reserve, abso-*

lutely.—τοὺς...κινδύνους: for the order see note on § 176[11].
8. τὸ ψήφισμα...γενόμενον : cf. Aesch. III. 25, πρὶν ἢ τὸν Ἡγήμονος νόμον γενέσθαι, and II. 160, ποῖον (νόμον) γενέσθαι κωλύσας.

§ 180. While the clerk is preparing to read the decree, the orator amuses the audience by a few jokes at his opponent's expense.
1. καίτοι, *and now*: cf. § 123[1].— τίνα βούλει...εἶναι θῶ; *whom will you that I shall suppose you, and whom myself, to have been on that day?* εἶναι is imperfect infinitive (= ἦσθα) with θῶ, which in this sense takes the infinitive of indirect discourse: cf. Aesch. III. 163, βούλει σε θῶ φοβηθῆναι; See M.T. 287, 288, with the discussion of Plat. Rep. 372 E.
2. βούλει ἐμαυτὸν : sc. θῶ εἶναι ;— ὃν ἂν...καλέσαις, i.e. *as you would call me*, etc.
3. Βάτταλον : this nickname of Demosthenes, which the orator said was given him by his nurse (Aesch. I. 126), probably referred to his lean and sickly look in childhood and youth. See Plut. Dem. 4.

τάλον, σὲ δὲ μηδ' ἥρω τὸν τυχόντα, ἀλλὰ τούτων
τινὰ τῶν ἀπὸ τῆς σκηνῆς, Κρεσφόντην ἢ Κρέοντα ἢ 5
ὃν ἐν Κολλυτῷ ποτ' Οἰνόμαον κακῶς ἐπέτριψας;
τότε τοίνυν κατ' ἐκεῖνον τὸν καιρὸν ὁ Παιανιεὺς ἐγὼ
Βάτταλος Οἰνομάου τοῦ Κοθωκίδου σοῦ πλείονος
ἄξιος ὢν ἐφάνην τῇ πατρίδι. σὺ μέν γε οὐδὲν
οὐδαμοῦ χρήσιμος ἦσθα· ἐγὼ δὲ πάνθ' ὅσα προσῆκε 10
τὸν ἀγαθὸν πολίτην ἔπραττον. λέγε τὸ ψήφισμά
μοι.

ΨΗΦΙΣΜΑ ΔΗΜΟΣΘΕΝΟΥΣ.

[Ἐπὶ ἄρχοντος Ναυσικλέους, φυλῆς πρυτανευούσης Αἰαν- 181
τίδος, σκιροφοριῶνος ἕκτῃ ἐπὶ δέκα, Δημοσθένης Δημοσθένους

4. **μηδ' ἥρω τὸν τυχόντα,** *not even
a hero of the common kind* : see note
on ὧν ἔτυχεν, § 130². —**ἀλλά...σκηνῆς,**
but one of those (great) *heroes of the
stage*.

5. **Κρεσφόντην,** in the Cresphontes
of Euripides, in which Merope has
the chief part : cf. Arist. Eth. III. 1,
17. — **Κρέοντα** : Aeschines played
Creon in the Antigone of Sophocles
as τριταγωνιστής : see XIX. 247, ἐν
ἅπασι τοῖς δράμασι τοῖς τραγικοῖς
ἐξαίρετόν ἐστιν ὥσπερ γέρας τοῖς
τριταγωνισταῖς τὸ τοὺς τυράννους καὶ
τοὺς τὰ σκῆπτρα ἔχοντας εἰσιέναι.

6. **Οἰνόμαον** : i.e. this part in the
Oenomaus of Sophocles, which represented the chariot-race of Pelops
and Oenomaus, by which Pelops won
the hand of Hippodameia. This was
the subject of one of the pediment-
groups of the temple of Zeus at
Olympia. — **κακῶς ἐπέτριψας**, *you
wretchedly murdered* (as we say of a
bad actor). The anonymous Life of
Aeschines (7) gives a story that
Aeschines fell on the stage in acting
this part. As Oenomaus was finally
killed, there is probably a double
meaning in κακῶς ἐπέτριψας.—**ἐν
Κολλυτῷ** is an additional slur on the

tragic performance of Aeschines. See
Aesch. I. 157, πρώην ἐν τοῖς κατ'
ἀγροὺς Διονυσίοις κωμῳδῶν ὄντων ἐν
Κολλυτῷ. See ἀρουραῖος Οἰνόμαος,
§ 242⁵.

7. **τότε** refers to time generally :
κατ' ἐκεῖνον τὸν καιρὸν to a critical
moment.

8. **Οἰνομάου τοῦ Κοθωκίδου** : Aeschines was of the deme Κοθωκίδαι.

§§ **181—187** contain the spurious
"decree of Demosthenes." Its date,
the 16th of Scirophorion (June or
July), once brought hopeless confusion
into the chronology of the campaign
before Chaeronea. See Clinton, Fast.
Hellen. II. under 338 B.C. The real
decree was passed in the autumn or
early winter of 339—338 B.C., the
year of the Archon Lysimachides.
The style of the document is a
ridiculous parody of that of Demosthenes (see § 182). Lord Brougham's
remarks on this document, written of
course in full faith in its genuineness,
are now interesting. He says (p. 181):
"The style of this piece is full of
dignity, and the diction perfectly
simple as well as chaste, with the
solemnity of a state paper, but without the wordiness or technicality."

289 Παιανιεὺς εἶπεν, ἐπειδὴ Φίλιππος ὁ Μακεδόνων βασιλεὺς ἔν
τε τῷ παρεληλυθότι χρόνῳ παραβαίνων φαίνεται τὰς γεγενη-
μένας αὐτῷ συνθήκας πρὸς τὸν Ἀθηναίων δῆμον περὶ τῆς 5
εἰρήνης, ὑπεριδὼν τοὺς ὅρκους καὶ τὰ παρὰ πᾶσι τοῖς Ἕλλησι
νομιζόμενα εἶναι δίκαια, καὶ πόλεις παραιρεῖται οὐδὲν αὐτῷ
προσηκούσας, τινὰς δὲ καὶ Ἀθηναίων οὔσας δοριαλώτους
πεποίηκεν οὐδὲν προαδικηθεὶς ὑπὸ τοῦ δήμου τοῦ Ἀθηναίων,
ἔν τε τῷ παρόντι ἐπὶ πολὺ προάγει τῇ τε βίᾳ καὶ τῇ ὠμότητι· 10
καὶ γὰρ Ἑλληνίδας πόλεις ἃς μὲν ἐμφρούρους ποιεῖ καὶ τὰς 182
πολιτείας καταλύει, τινὰς δὲ καὶ ἐξανδραποδιζόμενος κατα-
σκάπτει, εἰς ἐνίας δὲ καὶ ἀντὶ Ἑλλήνων βαρβάρους κατοι-
κίζει ἐπὶ τὰ ἱερὰ καὶ τοὺς τάφους ἐπάγων, οὐδὲν ἀλλότριον
ποιῶν οὔτε τῆς ἑαυτοῦ πατρίδος οὔτε τοῦ τρόπου, καὶ τῇ 5
νῦν αὐτῷ παρούσῃ τύχῃ κατακόρως χρώμενος, ἐπιλελησμένος
ἑαυτοῦ ὅτι ἐκ μικροῦ καὶ τοῦ τυχόντος γέγονεν ἀνελπίστως
μέγας. καὶ ἕως μὲν πόλεις ἑώρα παραιρούμενον αὐτὸν βαρ- 183
βάρους καὶ ἰδίας, ὑπελάμβανεν ἔλαττον εἶναι ὁ δῆμος ὁ
Ἀθηναίων τὸ εἰς αὐτὸν πλημμελεῖσθαι· νῦν δὲ ὁρῶν Ἑλληνίδας πόλεις τὰς μὲν ὑβριζομένας, τὰς δὲ ἀναστάτους γιγνομένας,
δεινὸν ἡγεῖται εἶναι καὶ ἀνάξιον τῆς τῶν προγόνων δόξης τὸ 5
περιορᾶν τοὺς Ἕλληνας καταδουλουμένους. διὸ δεδόχθαι τῇ 184
βουλῇ καὶ τῷ δήμῳ τῷ Ἀθηναίων, εὐξαμένους καὶ θύσαντας
τοῖς θεοῖς καὶ ἥρωσι τοῖς κατέχουσι τὴν πόλιν καὶ τὴν χώραν
τὴν Ἀθηναίων, καὶ ἐνθυμηθέντας τῆς τῶν προγόνων ἀρετῆς,
290 διότι περὶ πλείονος ἐποιοῦντο τὴν τῶν Ἑλλήνων ἐλευθερίαν 5
διατηρεῖν ἢ τὴν ἰδίαν πατρίδα, διακοσίας ναῦς καθέλκειν εἰς
τὴν θάλατταν καὶ τὸν ναύαρχον ἀναπλεῖν ἐντὸς Πυλῶν, καὶ
τὸν στρατηγὸν καὶ τὸν ἵππαρχον τὰς πεζὰς καὶ τὰς ἱππικὰς
δυνάμεις Ἐλευσῖνάδε ἐξάγειν, πέμψαι δὲ καὶ πρέσβεις πρὸς
τοὺς ἄλλους Ἕλληνας, πρῶτον δὲ πάντων πρὸς Θηβαίους διὰ 10
τὸ ἐγγυτάτω εἶναι τὸν Φίλιππον τῆς ἐκείνων χώρας, παρακα- 185
λεῖν δὲ αὐτοὺς μηδὲν καταπλαγέντας τὸν Φίλιππον ἀντέχεσθαι
τῆς ἑαυτῶν καὶ τῆς τῶν ἄλλων Ἑλλήνων ἐλευθερίας, καὶ ὅτι ὁ
Ἀθηναίων δῆμος, οὐδὲν μνησικακῶν εἴ τι πρότερον γέγονεν
ἀλλότριον ταῖς πόλεσι πρὸς ἀλλήλας, βοηθήσει καὶ δυνάμεσι 5

καὶ χρήμασι καὶ βέλεσι καὶ ὅπλοις, εἰδὼς ὅτι αὐτοῖς μὲν πρὸς
ἀλλήλους διαμφισβητεῖν περὶ τῆς ἡγεμονίας οὖσιν Ἕλλησι
καλόν, ὑπὸ δὲ ἀλλοφύλου ἀνθρώπου ἄρχεσθαι καὶ τῆς ἡγεμονίας ἀποστερεῖσθαι ἀνάξιον εἶναι καὶ τῆς τῶν Ἑλλήνων
δόξης καὶ τῆς τῶν προγόνων ἀρετῆς. ἔτι δὲ οὐδὲ ἀλλότριον 186
ἡγεῖται εἶναι ὁ Ἀθηναίων δῆμος τὸν Θηβαίων δῆμον οὔτε τῇ
συγγενείᾳ οὔτε τῷ ὁμοφύλῳ. ἀναμιμνήσκεται δὲ καὶ τὰς
τῶν προγόνων τῶν ἑαυτοῦ εἰς τοὺς Θηβαίων προγόνους εὐερ-
γεσίας· καὶ γὰρ τοὺς Ἡρακλέους παῖδας ἀποστερουμένους 5
ὑπὸ Πελοποννησίων τῆς πατρῴας ἀρχῆς κατήγαγον, τοῖς
ὅπλοις κρατήσαντες τοὺς ἀντιβαίνειν πειρωμένους τοῖς Ἡρακλέους ἐκγόνοις, καὶ τὸν Οἰδίπουν καὶ τοὺς μετ᾽ ἐκείνου
ἐκπεσόντας ὑπεδεξάμεθα, καὶ ἕτερα πολλὰ ἡμῖν ὑπάρχει
291 φιλάνθρωπα καὶ ἔνδοξα πρὸς Θηβαίους· διόπερ οὐδὲ νῦν 187
ἀποστήσεται ὁ Ἀθηναίων δῆμος τῶν Θηβαίοις τε καὶ τοῖς
ἄλλοις Ἕλλησι συμφερόντων. συνθέσθαι δὲ πρὸς αὐτοὺς
συμμαχίαν καὶ ἐπιγαμίαν ποιήσασθαι καὶ ὅρκους δοῦναι καὶ
λαβεῖν. πρέσβεις Δημοσθένης Δημοσθένους Παιανιεύς, 5
Ὑπερείδης Κλεάνδρου Σφήττιος, Μνησιθείδης Ἀντιφάνους
Φρεάρριος, Δημοκράτης Σωφίλου Φλυεύς, Κάλλαισχρος
Διοτίμου Κοθωκίδης.]

Αὕτη τῶν περὶ Θήβας ἐγίγνετο πραγμάτων ἀρχὴ 188
καὶ κατάστασις πρώτη, τὰ πρὸ τούτων εἰς ἔχθραν
καὶ μῖσος καὶ ἀπιστίαν τῶν πόλεων ὑπηγμένων
ὑπὸ τούτων. τοῦτο τὸ ψήφισμα τὸν τότε τῇ πόλει
περιστάντα κίνδυνον παρελθεῖν ἐποίησεν ὥσπερ 5

§ **188.** 1. **αὕτη…πρώτη**, this
was the first step taken and the first
settlement effected in our relations with
Thebes: ἐγίγνετο refers to the progress
of the business in coming to a settlement. See Weil's note : "κατάστασις
est ici le contraire de ταραχή." Cf.
XX. 11, ἐπειδὴ δ᾽ ἡ πόλις εἰς ἐν ἦλθε
καὶ τὰ πράγματ᾽ ἐκεῖνα κατέστη (after
the rule of the Thirty), and Ar. Ran.

1003, ἡνίκ᾽ ἂν τὸ πνεῦμα λεῖον καὶ
καθεστηκὸς λάβῃς.
5. **παρελθεῖν ὥσπερ νέφος**, to pass
by like a cloud, or to vanish like a
passing cloud. The simplicity of this
simile was much admired by the Greek
rhetoricians, who quote it nine times
(see Spengel's index). See Longinus
on the Sublime, 39, 4 : ὑψηλόν γε
τοῦτο δοκεῖ νόημα, καὶ ἔστι τῷ ὄντι

νέφος. ἦν μὲν τοίνυν τοῦ δικαίου πολίτου τότε
δεῖξαι πᾶσιν, εἴ τι τούτων εἶχεν ἄμεινον, μὴ νῦν
ἐπιτιμᾶν· ὁ γὰρ σύμβουλος καὶ ὁ συκοφάντης, οὐδὲ 189
τῶν ἄλλων οὐδὲν ἐοικότες, ἐν τούτῳ πλεῖστον ἀλλήλων διαφέρουσιν· ὁ μέν γε πρὸ τῶν πραγμάτων
γνώμην ἀποφαίνεται, καὶ δίδωσιν ἑαυτὸν ὑπεύθυνον
τοῖς πεισθεῖσι, τῇ τύχῃ, τῷ καιρῷ, τῷ βουλομένῳ· ὁ 5
δὲ σιγήσας ἡνίκ᾽ ἔδει λέγειν, ἄν τι δύσκολον συμβῇ,
τοῦτο βασκαίνει. ἦν μὲν οὖν, ὅπερ εἶπον, ἐκεῖνος ὁ 190
καιρὸς τοῦ γε φροντίζοντος ἀνδρὸς τῆς πόλεως καὶ
τῶν δικαίων λόγων· ἐγὼ δὲ τοσαύτην ὑπερβολὴν
ποιοῦμαι ὥστε, ἂν νῦν ἔχῃ τις δεῖξαί τι βέλτιον, ἢ
ὅλως εἴ τι ἄλλ᾽ ἐνῆν πλὴν ὧν ἐγὼ προειλόμην, 5
ἀδικεῖν ὁμολογῶ. εἰ γὰρ ἔσθ᾽ ὅ τι τις νῦν ἑόρακεν,

θαυμάσιον, ὃ τῷ ψηφίσματι ὁ Δημοσθένης ἐπιφέρει...ἀλλ᾽ αὐτῆς τῆς διανοίας
οὐκ ἔλαττον τῇ ἁρμονίᾳ πεφώνηται.
He then discourses on the fatal effect
which would result from a change in
the order of the words, or from the
omission or addition of a single syl-
lable (as ὡς νέφος or ὥσπερ εἰ νέφος).
7. τούτων, i.e. *than my measures.*
In the last sentence of § 188, the
orator suddenly breaks off his narrative,
and digresses into a most eloquent
defence of the policy of Athens in
resisting Philip, and of his own conduct as her responsible leader. See
note before §§ 160—226.
§ 189. 1. σύμβουλος, *statesman.*
—συκοφάντης : no modern word,
least of all the English *sycophant,*
gives the full meaning of this expressive term, though the same combination of malicious informer, dirty
pettifogger, common slanderer and
backbiter, is unhappily still to be
seen. Cf. § 242². The word must
have referred originally to the petty
form of prosecution for violation of
the revenue laws known as φάσις, in

which half of the penalty went to the
informer. See Ar. Eq. 300 : καί σε
φαίνω τοῖς πρυτάνεσιν ἀδεκατεύτους
τῶν θεῶν ἱρὰς ἔχοντα κοιλίας.
4. ὑπεύθυνον, *responsible* in the
full Attic sense, e.g. liable to the
εὔθυναι and to the γραφὴ παρανόμων.
6. δύσκολον : see note on § 176².
7. βασκαίνει, *reviles* : Harpocr.
ἀντὶ τοῦ αἰτιᾶται καὶ μέμφεται καὶ
συκοφαντεῖ· Δημοσθ. ἐν τῷ ὑπὲρ Κτησιφῶντος.
§ 190. 1. ὅπερ εἶπον : see the
last sentence of § 188.
3. τῶν δικ. λόγων: with καιρὸς
(West., Bl.), or (better) with φροντίζοντος.—τοσαύτην ὑπερβολὴν ποιοῦμαι,
i.e. I go so far beyond what could be
asked of me.
5. ἐνῆν : used personally with τι
ἄλλο: cf. ὅσα ἐνῆν, § 193⁴. So
ἐνόντων (11) : such participles are
very often personal (M.T. 761).—
ὧν ἐγὼ προειλόμην: cf. § 192⁵, τὴν
προαίρεσίν μου τῆς πολιτείας.
6. ἀδικεῖν, in its so-called perfect
sense (M.T. 27).
7. τότε πραχθὲν = εἰ τότ᾽ ἐπράχθη.

ὃ συνήνεγκεν ἂν τότε πραχθὲν, τοῦτ' ἐγώ φημι δεῖν
ἐμὲ μὴ λαθεῖν. εἰ δὲ μήτ' ἔστι μήτ' ἦν μήτ' ἂν
292 εἰπεῖν ἔχοι μηδεὶς μηδέπω καὶ τήμερον, τί τὸν
σύμβουλον ἐχρῆν ποιεῖν; οὐ τῶν φαινομένων καὶ 10
ἐνόντων τὰ κράτιστα ἐλέσθαι; τοῦτο τοίνυν ἐποίησα, 191
τοῦ κήρυκος ἐρωτῶντος, Αἰσχίνη, τίς ἀγορεύειν
βούλεται; οὐ τίς αἰτιᾶσθαι περὶ τῶν παρεληλυθότων; οὐδὲ τίς ἐγγυᾶσθαι τὰ μέλλοντ'
ἔσεσθαι; σοῦ δ' ἀφώνου κατ' ἐκείνους τοὺς χρό- 5
νους ἐν ταῖς ἐκκλησίαις καθημένου, ἐγὼ παριὼν
ἔλεγον. ἐπειδὴ δ' οὐ τότε, ἀλλὰ νῦν δεῖξον· εἰπὲ
τίς ἡ λόγος, ὅντιν' ἐχρῆν εὐπορεῖν, ἢ καιρὸς συμφέρων ὑπ' ἐμοῦ παρελείφθη τῇ πόλει; τίς δὲ συμ-
μαχία, τίς πρᾶξις, ἐφ' ἣν μᾶλλον ἔδει μ' ἀγαγεῖν 10
τουτουσί;
Ἀλλὰ μὴν τὸ μὲν παρεληλυθὸς ἀεὶ παρὰ πᾶσιν 192
ἀφεῖται, καὶ οὐδεὶς περὶ τούτου προτίθησιν οὐδαμοῦ
βουλήν· τὸ δὲ μέλλον ἢ τὸ παρὸν τὴν τοῦ συμβούλου
τάξιν ἀπαιτεῖ. τότε τοίνυν τὰ μὲν ἤμελλεν, ὡς

—τοῦτ'...δεῖν ἐμὲ μὴ λαθεῖν, *I say
this ought not to have escaped me* (at
the time) : δεῖν...λαθεῖν represents ἔδει
ἐμὲ μὴ λαθεῖν.
8, 9. εἰ δὲ...τήμερον : for this compound protasis with a present, a past,
and a potential optative united in one
supposition, see M. T. 509 : notice
the three negatives and the emphatic
καὶ in μήτ' ἂν...τήμερον. See § 141⁵.—
μηδέπω καὶ τήμερον, *not yet, even at
this day*.
10. τῶν φαινομένων καὶ ἐνόντων,
*of the plans which offered themselves
to us and were feasible.*
§ 191. 3. τίς...παρεληλυθότων ;
a question to be addressed to a
συκοφάντης, not to a σύμβουλος.
7. οὐ τότε : sc. ἔδειξας.—**ἀλλὰ νῦν**
(M.T. 513).

8. εὐπορεῖν (Σ, εὑρεῖν vulg.), *to
have been provided with.*
9. τῇ πόλει : often taken with
συμφέρων ; better with παρελείφθη,
as in § 107¹¹, ἀπώλετο τῇ πόλει.
10. μᾶλλον, *rather* than to my
own.
§ 192. 2. ἀφεῖται (gnomic), *is
dismissed* from consideration.
3. τὴν...τάξιν, i.e. *the statesman
at his post* : τάξιν keeps up the
military figure of § 173⁵·⁶.
4. τότε...παρῆν : application of
the general principle to the case in
hand ; τὰ μὲν ἤμελλεν referring to
Chaeronea and its results, τὰ δ' ἤδη
παρῆν to Philip's presence at Elatea.
Though these are now past, they were
then future and present.

ἐδόκει, τῶν δεινῶν, τὰ δ' ἤδη παρῆν, ἐν οἷς τὴν 5
προαίρεσίν μου σκόπει τῆς πολιτείας, μὴ τὰ συμβάντα συκοφάντει. τὸ μὲν γὰρ πέρας ὡς ἂν ὁ
δαίμων βουληθῇ πάντων γίγνεται· ἡ δὲ προαίρεσις
αὐτὴ τὴν τοῦ συμβούλου διάνοιαν δηλοῖ. μὴ δὴ 193
τοῦθ' ὡς ἀδίκημ' ἐμὸν θῇς, εἰ κρατῆσαι συνέβη
Φιλίππῳ τῇ μάχῃ· ἐν γὰρ τῷ θεῷ τὸ τούτου τέλος
ἦν, οὐκ ἐμοί. ἀλλ' ὡς οὐχ ἅπαντα ὅσα ἐνῆν κατ'
ἀνθρώπινον λογισμὸν εἱλόμην, καὶ δικαίως ταῦτα 5
καὶ ἐπιμελῶς ἔπραξα καὶ φιλοπόνως ὑπὲρ δύναμιν,
ἢ ὡς οὐ καλὰ καὶ τῆς πόλεως ἄξια πράγματα
ἐνεστησάμην καὶ ἀναγκαῖα, ταῦτά μοι δεῖξον, καὶ
τότ' ἤδη κατηγόρει μου. εἰ δ' ὁ συμβὰς σκηπτὸς 194
[ἢ χειμὼν] μὴ μόνον ἡμῶν ἀλλὰ καὶ πάντων τῶν
293 ἄλλων Ἑλλήνων μείζων γέγονε, τί χρὴ ποιεῖν;

5. τὴν...πολιτείας : see note on
§ 190⁵. προαίρεσις implies the deliberate choice of a policy which a
statesman should make : here and in
τὰ συμβάντα συκοφάντει we have again
the σύμβουλος and the συκοφάντης contrasted. For the precise meaning of
προαίρεσις, see Arist. Eth. III. 2
(especially § 17) : ἀλλ' ἆρά γε τὸ
προβεβουλευμένρν (sc. τὸ προαιρετόν) ;
ἡ γὰρ προαίρεσις μετὰ λόγου καὶ
διανοίας. ὑποσημαίνειν δ' ἔοικε καὶ
τοὔνομα ὡς ὂν πρὸ ἑτέρου αἱρετόν.
9. αὐτὴ (emphatic) : the thought
is, purpose is the very thing which
shows etc.
§ 193. 3. τῇ μάχῃ : Chaeronea.
—ἐν τῷ θεῷ...τέλος : cf. πέρας and
δαίμων in § 192⁷·⁸. See Il. VII. 101,
αὐτὰρ ὕπερθεν νίκης πείρατ' ἔχονται ἐν
ἀθανάτοισι θεοῖσιν.
6. φιλοπόνως ὑπὲρ δύναμιν, i.e.
with greater labour than my strength
warranted : cf. §§ 160⁵, 218⁹.
8. ἐνεστησάμην, undertook (in-
stituted) : cf. § 4¹¹.—καὶ ἀναγκαῖα,
and necessary too, added after the

verb for emphasis. Blass remarks
that the orator has not yet attained
the height from which he speaks in
§§ 199 ff.
§ 194. 1. σκηπτὸς [ἢ χειμὼν]: most
recent editors omit ἢ χειμὼν on the
ground that the orator, after comparing
the sudden raid of Philip to a thunder-
bolt, would not weaken his figure by
adding a common storm. This holds
good even when we admit that χειμών
and σκηπτός are not the same thing.
Aristotle (de Mundo, 4, 19), after
describing κεραυνός, πρηστήρ, and
τυφῶν, adds ἕκαστον δὲ τούτων κατα-
σκήψαν εἰς τὴν γῆν σκηπτὸς ὀνομά-
ζεται. σκηπτός, therefore, is not only
a stroke of lightning, but also a
furious thunderstorm ; while χειμών
is winter, a winterstorm, or a storm
in general. Perhaps ἢ χειμὼν here
was originally a marginal reference to
χειμῶνι χρησάμενον (6).
3. τί χρὴ ποιεῖν (sc. ἡμᾶς), what
ought we to do? The answer is given
in the two following sentences. The
sense is : "What are we to do? We

ὥσπερ ἂν εἴ τις ναύκληρον πάντ᾽ ἐπὶ σωτηρίᾳ
πράξαντα, καὶ κατασκευάσαντα τὸ πλοῖον ἀφ᾽ ὧν 5
ὑπελάμβανε σωθήσεσθαι, εἶτα χειμῶνι χρησάμενον
καὶ πονησάντων αὐτῷ τῶν σκευῶν ἢ καὶ συντρι-
βέντων ὅλως, τῆς ναυαγίας αἰτιῷτο. ἀλλ᾽ οὔτ᾽
ἐκυβέρνων τὴν ναῦν, φήσειεν ἂν (ὥσπερ οὐδ᾽ ἐστρα-
τήγουν ἐγώ), οὔτε τῆς τύχης κύριος ἦν, ἀλλ᾽ ἐκείνη 10
τῶν πάντων. ἀλλ᾽ ἐκεῖνο λογίζου καὶ ὅρα· εἰ μετὰ 195
Θηβαίων ἡμῖν ἀγωνιζομένοις οὕτως εἵμαρτο πρᾶξαι,
τί χρῆν προσδοκᾶν εἰ μηδὲ τούτους ἔσχομεν συμμάχους ἀλλὰ Φιλίππῳ προσέθεντο, ὑπὲρ οὗ τότ᾽ ἐκεῖνος

are to do just what a ναύκληρος would
do if any one were to blame him, etc.
He would say ' I was not κυβερνήτης,'
just as I can say 'No more was I
στρατηγός.'" The apodosis to εἴ τις...
αἰτιῷτο being suppressed (except ἂν in
4), its subject ναύκληρος appears in
the protasis as ναύκληρον, and the
implied ὥσπερ ἂν ναύκληρος ποιήσειεν
appears in φήσειεν ἂν (9) with its
quotation, ἀλλ᾽ οὔτ᾽ ἐκυβέρνων...τῶν
πάντων. ἡμῶν (2) and ἐγὼ (10) show
that the orator identifies the people
with himself in the comparison with
ναύκληρος. Cf. § 243.

4. ναύκληρον, properly a *ship-
owner*, who sails in his own ship (as
ἔμπορος), but generally employs a
κυβερνήτης or *sailing-master* to navi-
gate the ship. In Plato's famous figure
of the ship of State (Rep. VI. p. 488),
the ναύκληρος is the honest old man
Δῆμος Πυκνίτης, who knows little of
navigation, and is not skilful enough
to keep a professional sailing-master
in authority, and soon lets the command of the ship fall into the hands
of the most artful and unscrupulous
landsmen on board.

6. χειμῶνι χρησάμενον: the ναύκληρος is said to have met with a storm.
—πονησάντων σκευῶν, *when his*

tackling laboured (as we speak of
a ship as *labouring* in a heavy
sea).

§ 195. 3. τί χρῆν προσδοκᾶν;
this apodosis (like the similar one in
lines 7—9) has two protases, one
simply past, the other past with the
condition unfulfilled. Each apodosis
conforms to the latter condition. But
we have in line 3 τί χρῆν προσδοκᾶν;
(without ἂν), but in 7—9 τί ἂν...προσ-
δοκῆσαι χρῆν; the two sentences being
otherwise similar. We certainly should
not notice the difference if the same
form (either with or without ἂν) were
used in both. And yet the distinction
is one of principle, and is generally
obvious and important. In the form
without ἂν the chief force falls on the
infinitive, while in the form with ἂν
it falls on ἔδει, ἐξῆν, χρῆν, etc., to
which the ἂν belongs. Thus ἐξῆν σοι
ἐλθεῖν (in this sense) is *you might have
gone* (but did not go), while ἐξῆν ἂν
σοι ἐλθεῖν is *it would have been possible
for you to go* in a certain case (but in
fact it was not possible). Here we
ma translate τί χρῆν προσδοκᾶν ;
what ought we to have expected (which
we did not find ourselves expecting)?
and τί ἂν προσδοκῆσαι χρῆν; *what
should we then have had to expect*

πάσας ἀφῆκε φωνάς; καὶ εἰ νῦν τριῶν ἡμερῶν ἀπὸ 5
τῆς Ἀττικῆς ὁδὸν τῆς μάχης γενομένης τοσοῦτος
κίνδυνος καὶ φόβος περιέστη τὴν πόλιν, τί ἂν, εἴ που
τῆς χώρας ταὐτὸ τοῦτο πάθος συνέβη, προσδοκῆσαι
χρῆν; ἀρ' οἶσθ' ὅτι νῦν μὲν στῆναι, · συνελθεῖν,
ἀναπνεῦσαι, πολλὰ μία ἡμέρα καὶ δύο καὶ τρεῖς 10
ἔδοσαν τῶν εἰς σωτηρίαν τῇ πόλει; τότε δὲ—οὐκ
ἄξιον εἰπεῖν ἅ γε μηδὲ πεῖραν ἔδωκε θεῶν τινὸς
εὐνοίᾳ καὶ τῷ προβάλλεσθαι τὴν πόλιν ταύτην τὴν
συμμαχίαν ἧς σὺ κατηγορεῖς.

Ἔστι δὲ ταυτὶ πάντα μοι τὰ πολλὰ πρὸς ὑμᾶς, 196
ἄνδρες δικασταὶ, καὶ τοὺς περιεστηκότας ἔξωθεν καὶ
ἀκροωμένους, ἐπεὶ πρός γε τοῦτον τὸν κατάπτυστον
βραχὺς καὶ σαφὴς ἐξήρκει λόγος. εἰ μὲν γὰρ ἦν σοὶ

(which in fact we did not have to
expect)? See M.T. App. v.
5. πάσας ἀφῆκε φωνάς, i.e. *used
all his eloquence* : cf. Plat. Rep. 475 A,
πάσας φωνὰς ἀφίετε. See § 218⁵.—
τριῶν ἡμερῶν ὁδόν, *three days' journey*,
i.e. from Chaeronea (via Thebes) to
the Attic frontier at Eleutherae, about
450 stadia. It was about 250 stadia
from Eleutherae to Athens; and the
whole distance from Chaeronea to
Athens is given (§ 230²) as 700 stadia,
about 80 miles. (See Blass.)
9. νῦν here and τότε in l. 11 refer
only to opposite alternatives (*as it
was*, and *in that case*), but to the
same time. See § 200¹. The ἀποσιώπησις after τότε δὲ is far more eloquent
than any description.
10. ἀναπνεῦσαι : cf. Il. XI. 801,
ὀλίγη δέ τ' ἀνάπνευσις πολέμοιο.
12. ἅ γε μηδὲ πεῖραν ἔδωκε, *which
never gave us even a trial* (of their
horrors) : ἑαυτῶν is omitted, leaving
πεῖραν ἔδωκε absolute. See note on
§ 107⁵. The negative is μηδὲ because the antecedent of ἅ is indefinite
(M.T. 518).

13. τῷ προβάλλεσθαι ... συμμαχίαν, *by the state having this alliance
to shield her* (lit. *holding it before
herself*). Cf. § 97¹⁰. The present
emphasizes the continued protection;
προβαλέσθαι would mean *putting it
before herself* : cf. § 300¹, ταῦτα προϋ-
βαλόμην πρὸ τῆς Ἀττικῆς.
§ 196. 1. ἔστι μοι πρὸς ὑμᾶς,
i.e. *I intend it for you.*—ταυτὶ πάντα
τὰ πολλὰ, *all this long argument* (so
West.) : τὰ πολλὰ may, however, be
adverbial, *for the most part, chiefly*,
the sense being *all this I intend chiefly
for you.*
2. τοὺς περιεστηκότας, the *spectators*, of whom great crowds were
present : see Aesch. III. 56, ἐναντίον...
τῶν ἄλλων πολιτῶν ὅσοι δὴ ἔξωθεν
περιεστᾶσι, καὶ τῶν Ἑλλήνων ὅσοις
ἐπιμελὲς γέγονεν ἐπακούειν τῆσδε τῆς
κρίσεως· ὁρῶ δὲ οὐκ ὀλίγους παρόντας,
ἀλλ' ὅσους οὐδεὶς πώποτε μέμνηται πρὸς
ἀγῶνα δημόσιον παραγενομένους.
4. βραχὺς καὶ σαφὴς λόγος : this
he now puts into a dilemma, εἰ μὲν
ἦν σοὶ πρόδηλα and εἰ δὲ μὴ προῄδεις.
ἐξήρκει, *was enough for him*; i.e.

πρόδηλα τὰ μέλλοντα, Αἰσχίνη, μόνῳ τῶν ἄλλων, 5
ὅτ' ἐβουλεύεθ' ἡ πόλις περὶ τούτων, τότ' ἔδει προλέ-
γειν· εἰ δὲ μὴ προῄδεις, τῆς αὐτῆς ἀγνοίας ὑπεύθυνος
εἰ τοῖς ἄλλοις, ὥστε τί μᾶλλον ἐμοῦ σὺ ταῦτα κατη-
294 γορεῖς ἢ ἐγὼ σοῦ ; τοσοῦτον γὰρ ἀμείνων ἐγὼ σοῦ 197
πολίτης γέγον' εἰς αὐτὰ ταῦθ' ἃ λέγω (καὶ οὔπω
περὶ τῶν ἄλλων διαλέγομαι), ὅσον ἐγὼ μὲν ἔδωκ'
ἐμαυτὸν εἰς τὰ πᾶσι δοκοῦντα συμφέρειν, οὐδένα
κίνδυνον ὀκνήσας ἴδιον οὐδ' ὑπολογισάμενος, σὺ δ' 5
οὔθ' ἕτερ' εἶπες βελτίω τούτων (οὐ γὰρ ἂν τούτοις
ἐχρῶντο), οὔτ' εἰς ταῦτα χρήσιμον οὐδὲν σαυτὸν
παρέσχες, ὅπερ δ' ἂν ὁ φαυλότατος καὶ δυσμενέστα-
τος ἄνθρωπος τῇ πόλει, τοῦτο πεποιηκὼς ἐπὶ τοῖς
συμβᾶσιν ἐξήτασαι, καὶ ἅμ' Ἀρίστρατος ἐν Νάξῳ 10
καὶ Ἀριστόλεως ἐν Θάσῳ, οἱ καθάπαξ ἐχθροὶ τῆς
πόλεως, τοὺς Ἀθηναίων κρίνουσι φίλους καὶ Ἀθήνη-

---

this would be a sufficient reply for
him. ἐξήρκει sometimes has a force
somewhat like that of δίκαιον ἦν, ἴσον
ἦν, καλὸν ἦν, etc., when they are
classed with ἔδει, χρῆν, etc. (M. T.
416). See Cic. Lael. XXVI. 96, satis
erat respondere *Magnas*: *Ingentes*
inquit, and Lane's Latin Grammar,
1496, 1497. Cf. θαυμαστὸν ἦν, § 248[7].
8. ταῦτα : the charge of ignorance
which you bring against me.
§ **197**. 2. ταῦθ' ἃ λέγω, i.e. the
events which preceded Chaeronea.
4. τὰ πᾶσι δοκοῦντα = ἃ πᾶσιν
ἐδόκει, with reference to votes of the
people : cf. 274[5].
5. ἴδιον, *personal*, e.g. the danger
of a γραφὴ παρανόμων: cf. §§ 235[11],
249.
6. οὐ...ἐχρῶντο: sc. εἰ ἕτερ' εἶπες
βελτίω.
7. εἰς ταῦτα, in support of my
measures.

8. ὅπερ δ' ἂν: sc. ποιήσειεν or
ἐποίησεν. See § 291[4].
9. τῇ πόλει: for the order see
§ 176[11].—πεποιηκὼς...ἐξήτασαι, *you
are shown to have done after the
events*: cf. Hdt. I. 170, ἐπὶ διε-
φθαρμένοισι Ἴωσι, and § 284[10].
10. Ἀρίστρατος, Ἀριστόλεως:
these men and the condition of Naxos
and Thasos at this time are known
only from this passage. It appears
that these islands were in the power
of Alexander, and that his great
successes in Asia were having the
same effect in them as in Athens,
encouraging the Macedonian party to
vex their opponents by prosecutions.
11. καθάπαξ ἐχθροί, *outright enemies*.
12. καὶ Ἀθήνησιν...κατηγορεῖ :
this brings out clearly the meaning of
τοῦτο πεποιηκὼς (9).

σιν Αἰσχίνης Δημοσθένους κατηγορεῖ. καίτοι ὅτῳ 198
τὰ τῶν Ἑλλήνων ἀτυχήματ᾽ ἐνευδοκιμεῖν ἀπέκειτο,
ἀπολωλέναι μᾶλλον οὗτός ἐστι δίκαιος ἢ κατηγορεῖν
ἑτέρου· καὶ ὅτῳ συνενηνόχασιν οἱ αὐτοὶ καιροὶ καὶ
τοῖς τῆς πόλεως ἐχθροῖς, οὐκ ἔνι τοῦτον εὔνουν εἶναι 5
τῇ πατρίδι. δηλοῖς δὲ καὶ ἐξ ὧν ζῇς καὶ ποιεῖς καὶ
πολιτεύει καὶ πάλιν οὐ πολιτεύει. πράττεταί τι
τῶν ὑμῖν δοκούντων συμφέρειν· ἄφωνος Αἰσχίνης.
ἀντέκρουσέ τι καὶ γέγονεν οἷον οὐκ ἔδει· πάρεστιν
Αἰσχίνης. ὥσπερ τὰ ῥήγματα καὶ τὰ σπάσματα, 10
ὅταν τι κακὸν τὸ σῶμα λάβῃ, τότε κινεῖται.
Ἐπειδὴ δὲ πολὺς τοῖς συμβεβηκόσιν ἔγκειται, 199
βούλομαί τι καὶ παράδοξον εἰπεῖν. καί μου πρὸς

---

§ 198. 1. **ὅτῳ...ἀπέκειτο,** who found matter for glorification in the calamities of the Greeks : ἀπέκειτο, were laid up (as material).

2. **ἐνευδοκιμεῖν** occurs only here in classic Greek, acc. to Blass, who remarks on the ease with which such compounds with εν are made, to be used thus in the infinitive : see Thuc. II. 44, ἐνευδαιμονῆσαι and ἐντελευτῆσαι ; II 20, ἐνστρατοπεδεῦσαι ; Hdt. II. 178, ἐνοικῆσαι ; VI. 102, ἐνιππεῦσαι ; Plat. Phaedr. 228 E, ἐμμελετᾶν.—Ἑλλήνων ...ἀπέκειτο is a dactylic hexameter.

4. **οἱ αὐτοὶ...ἐχθροῖς,** i.e. the same occasions in which also the enemies of the state have found their advantage.

5. **εὔνουν,** loyal: see note on § 1².

6. **ἐξ ὧν ζῇς,** by the life you live : cf. ἀπ᾽ αὐτῶν ὧν βεβίωκεν § 130¹. ζῆν is the regular present to βεβιωκέναι, βιῶ not being in common use.

7—10. **πράττεται...Αἰσχίνης** and **ἀντέκρουσε...Αἰσχίνης** : two paratactic conditional expressions,—suppose something is done, etc. See § 274. Dissen quotes Cicero's imitation (Phil. II. 22, 55): Doletis tres exercitus populi Romani interfectos:

interfecit Antonius. Desideratis clarissimos cives : eos quoque nobis eripuit Antonius. Auctoritas huius ordinis afflicta est : afflixit Antonius.

10. **ῥήγματα καὶ σπάσματα,** ruptures and strains : ῥῆγμα is a rupture, either of the flesh or of a vein ; σπάσμα is properly the state of tension which may lead to a rupture, though the two terms seem sometimes to be used in nearly or quite the same sense. See Hippocrates, de Flatibus 11 (Littré VI. p. 109), of ruptures of the flesh ; and de Morb. I. 20 (Litt. VI. p. 176), of the veins. See large edition.

§ 199. 1. **πολὺς ἔγκειται,** is severe (presses hard) upon : cf. Thuc. IV. 22, Hdt. VII. 158, and note on πολλῷ ῥέοντι in § 136⁷ (above).

2. **τι καὶ παράδοξον** : the orator now rises to a new height. Heretofore he has maintained vigorously (as in § 194) that the policy of Athens in opposing Philip under his lead was sound and hopeful, and that he cannot justly be censured now, even if events have shown the "mistake" of waging war against the Macedonian power. He now suddenly changes his ground.

Διὸς καὶ θεῶν μηδεὶς τὴν ὑπερβολὴν θαυμάσῃ, ἀλλὰ
μετ᾽ εὐνοίας ὃ λέγω θεωρησάτω. εἰ γὰρ ἦν ἅπασι
πρόδηλα τὰ μέλλοντα γενήσεσθαι, καὶ προῄδεσαν 5
πάντες, καὶ σὺ προύλεγες, Αἰσχίνη, καὶ διεμαρτύρου
βοῶν καὶ κεκραγὼς, ὃς οὐδ᾽ ἐφθέγξω, οὐδ᾽ οὕτως
295 ἀποστατέον τῇ πόλει τούτων ἦν, εἴπερ ἢ δόξης ἢ
προγόνων ἢ τοῦ μέλλοντος αἰῶνος εἶχε λόγον. νῦν 200
μέν γ᾽ ἀποτυχεῖν δοκεῖ τῶν πραγμάτων, ὃ πᾶσι
κοινόν ἐστιν ἀνθρώποις ὅταν τῷ θεῷ ταῦτα δοκῇ·
τότε δ᾽ ἀξιοῦσα προεστάναι τῶν ἄλλων, εἶτ᾽ ἀποστᾶσα τούτου, Φιλίππῳ προδεδωκέναι πάντας ἂν 5
ἔσχεν αἰτίαν. εἰ γὰρ ταῦτα προεῖτ᾽ ἀκονιτὶ, περὶ
ὧν οὐδένα κίνδυνον ὄντιν᾽ οὐχ ὑπέμειναν οἱ πρόγονοι,
τίς οὐχὶ κατέπτυσεν ἂν σοῦ ; μὴ γὰρ τῆς πόλεώς γε,
μηδ᾽ ἐμοῦ. τίσι δ᾽ ὀφθαλμοῖς πρὸς Διὸς ἑωρῶμεν ἂν 201
τοὺς εἰς τὴν πόλιν ἀνθρώπους ἀφικνουμένους, εἰ τὰ

He declares that there has been no "mistake," that no other policy was possible for Athens with her glorious antecedents, even if the whole future, with Chaeronea and its baneful consequences, had been foreseen from the beginning. This is the final answer to the petty criticisms of Aeschines "after the events" (ἐπὶ τοῖς συμβᾶσιν, § 197⁹).

6. καὶ σὺ προύλεγες : the figure of Aeschines himself joining in the general warning adds greatly to the picture.

7. ὃς οὐδ᾽ ἐφθέγξω, you who did not even open your mouth.—οὐδ᾽ οὕτως, not even then : οὕτως sums up in one word the whole of the preceding condition (4—7).

8. ἀποστατέον...ἦν = ἔδει τὴν πόλιν ἀποστῆναι.

9. τοῦ μέλλοντος αἰῶνος, future ages.

§ 200. 1, 4. νῦν μὲν...τότε δ᾽ : see note on § 195⁹.

2. ἀποτυχεῖν, to have failed (in securing). — τῶν πραγμάτων, mere material objects, opposed to the high principles which would have been sacrificed in the other case (τότε).

4. ἀξιοῦσα (imperf.), while she had claimed, followed by the aorist ἀποστᾶσα, and then withdrew, both past to ἔσχεν ἄν. We might have had ἠξίου and ἀπέστη : cf. XV. 27, ὧν ἀπέστη.

6. ἀκονιτὶ, without a struggle, sine pulvere; cf. XIX. 77.

7. οὐδένα ὄντιν᾽ οὐχ, emphatic equivalent of πάντα : the natural nominative οὐδεὶς ὅστις οὐ (= πᾶς) is illogically declined.

8. σοῦ (accented), with special emphasis.—μὴ γὰρ (sc. εἰπέ), don't say the state, or me : πόλεως and ἐμοῦ merely continue the case of σοῦ.

§ 201. 1. τίσι δ᾽...ἑωρῶμεν ἄν ; i.e. how should we now (dare to) look in the face, etc. ?

2—8. εἰ τὰ μὲν...ᾑρημένης : this elaborate protasis has three divisions;

μὲν πράγματ᾽ εἰς ὅπερ νυνὶ περιέστη ἡγεμὼν δὲ καὶ
κύριος ἡρέθη Φίλιππος ἁπάντων, τὸν δ᾽ ὑπὲρ τοῦ μὴ
γενέσθαι ταῦτ᾽ ἀγῶνα ἕτεροι χωρὶς ἡμῶν ἦσαν πε- 5
ποιημένοι, καὶ ταῦτα μηδεπώποτε τῆς πόλεως ἐν τοῖς
ἔμπροσθε χρόνοις ἀσφάλειαν ἄδοξον μᾶλλον ἢ τὸν
ὑπὲρ τῶν καλῶν κίνδυνον ᾑρημένης ; τίς γὰρ οὐκ 202
οἶδεν Ἑλλήνων, τίς δὲ βαρβάρων, ὅτι καὶ παρὰ
Θηβαίων καὶ παρὰ τῶν ἔτι τούτων πρότερον ἰσχυ-
ρῶν γενομένων Λακεδαιμονίων καὶ παρὰ τοῦ Περσῶν
βασιλέως μετὰ πολλῆς χάριτος τοῦτ᾽ ἂν ἀσμένως 5
ἐδόθη τῇ πόλει, ὅ τι βούλεται λαβούσῃ καὶ τὰ
ἑαυτῆς ἐχούσῃ τὸ κελευόμενον ποιεῖν καὶ ἐᾶν ἕτερον
τῶν Ἑλλήνων προεστάναι ; ἀλλ᾽ οὐκ ἦν ταῦθ᾽, ὡς 203
ἔοικε, τοῖς Ἀθηναίοις πάτρια οὐδ᾽ ἀνεκτὰ οὐδ᾽ ἔμφυτα, οὐδ᾽ ἐδυνήθη πώποτε τὴν πόλιν οὐδεὶς ἐκ

(1) εἰ τὰ μέν...ἁπάντων, (2) τὸν δὲ...
πεποιημένοι, (3) καὶ ταῦτα...ᾑρημένης.
The clause ἡγεμὼν δὲ...ἁπάντων belongs closely with the preceding εἰ
μὲν περιέστη, and τὸν δ᾽ (not ἡγεμὼν
δὲ) corresponds to τὰ μέν.
3. εἰς ὅπερ νυνὶ, to the present
state, explained by ἡγεμὼν δὲ...ἁπάν-
των.
4. τὸν...ἀγῶνα, the fight to prevent
this.
5. ἕτεροι χωρὶς ἡμῶν: this pathetic
picture of Athens sitting still and seeing others fight the battle for Grecian
liberty becomes more effective when
we remember (what Demosthenes
never forgot) that Greece at this crisis
had no state except Athens able or
willing to take the lead, or any important part, in such a struggle. See
§§ 304, 305.
6. καὶ ταῦτα, and this too, introducing the participial clause which
completes the supposition : hence
μηδεπώποτε.
§ 202. 1, 2. τίς...βαρβάρων :

cf. XIX. 312.—παρὰ Θηβαίων: in the
time of Epaminondas.
3. παρὰ... Λακεδαιμονίων : after
the Peloponnesian war, and before
Leuctra.
4. παρὰ..βασιλέως, from Xerxes :
see the order given to Mardonius
before the battle of Plataea, reported
to Athens by Alexander, king of
Macedonia (Hdt. VIII. 140): τοῦτο
μὲν τὴν γῆν σφι ἀπόδος, τοῦτο δὲ ἄλλην
πρὸς ταύτη ἑλέσθων αὐτοί, ἥντινα ἂν
ἐθέλωσι, ἐόντες αὐτόνομοι. See note
on 204ᵇ (end).
6. ὅ τι βούλεται...προεστάναι :
i.e. to keep her own and receive anything she wanted, on condition of being
subject to Persia.
§ 203. 1. ὡς ἔοικε, spoken with
sarcasm : cf. § 212ᵇ.
2. πάτρια, i.e. inherited from
their ancestors.—οὐδ᾽ ἀνεκτὰ implies
that they revolted morally against the
idea ; οὐδ᾽ ἔμφυτα that it was against
their nature as Athenians.
3. ἐκ παντὸς τοῦ χρόνου, from

παντὸς τοῦ χρόνου πεῖσαι τοῖς ἰσχύουσι μὲν μὴ
δίκαια δὲ πράττουσι προσθεμένην ἀσφαλῶς δου- 5
λεύειν, ἀλλ᾽ ἀγωνιζομένη περὶ πρωτείων καὶ τιμῆς
296 καὶ δόξης κινδυνεύουσα πάντα τὸν αἰῶνα διατετέλεκε.
καὶ ταῦθ᾽ οὕτω σεμνὰ καὶ προσήκοντα τοῖς ὑμετέροις 204
ἤθεσιν ὑμεῖς ὑπολαμβάνετ᾽ εἶναι ὥστε καὶ τῶν προγόνων τοὺς ταῦτα πράξαντας μάλιστ᾽ ἐπαινεῖτε.
εἰκότως· τίς γὰρ οὐκ ἂν ἀγάσαιτο τῶν ἀνδρῶν ἐκείνων τῆς ἀρετῆς, οἳ καὶ τὴν χώραν καὶ τὴν πόλιν 5
ἐκλιπεῖν ὑπέμειναν εἰς τὰς τριήρεις ἐμβάντες ὑπὲρ
τοῦ μὴ τὸ κελευόμενον ποιῆσαι, τὸν μὲν ταῦτα συμ-
βουλεύσαντα Θεμιστοκλέα στρατηγὸν ἑλόμενοι, τὸν
δ᾽ ὑπακούειν ἀποφηνάμενον τοῖς ἐπιταττομένοις
Κυρσίλον καταλιθώσαντες, οὐ μόνον αὐτὸν, ἀλλὰ καὶ 10
αἱ γυναῖκες αἱ ὑμέτεραι τὴν γυναῖκ᾽ αὐτοῦ; οὐ γὰρ 205

the beginning of time, a rhetorical
ὑπερβολή, as in § 66⁶; in § 26⁷ it
means from the beginning of the
transaction in question.
4. μὴ δίκαια: μὴ, not οὐ, as we
should say οἱ μὴ δίκαια πράττουσιν
(G. 1612).
5. προσθεμένην, taking the side
of, attaching herself to: cf. § 227⁵.—
ἀσφαλῶς δουλεύειν: the same idea of
security in slavery is found in the
speech of Pericles, Thuc. II. 63 (end).
6. ἀγωνιζομένη, as partic. of manner modifies κινδυνεύουσα διατετέλεκε.
—πρωτείων, τιμῆς, δόξης: cf. § 66⁷.
§ 204. **2.** ἤθεσιν, moral feelings: see note on § 114².
4. ἀγάσαιτο: an epic aorist (see
Blass).
5. πόλιν ἐκλιπεῖν refers to the
time before the battle of Salamis when,
by the advice of Themistocles, Athens
was abandoned to Xerxes, and all
was staked on a sea-fight: so VI. 11.
See Cicero, Offic. III. 11, 48: Cyrsilum
quendam, suadentem ut in urbe mane-
rent Xerxemque reciperent, lapidibus

obruerunt. Herodotus, IX. 5, tells a
similar story of the stoning of a senator
named Lycidas, with his wife and
children, before the battle of Plataea,
when Mardonius sent his second message to Athens (for the earlier message
see note on § 202⁴).
6. ὑπὲρ τοῦ μὴ...ποιῆσαι: ὑπὲρ
with the gen. of the infin. for a final
clause, as in § 205⁹, and in Aesch. III.
1, ὑπὲρ τοῦ...μὴ γίγνεσθαι.
8. τὸν ὑπακούειν ἀποφηνάμενον,
who declared himself for obedience:
cf. γνώμην ἀποφαίνεται, § 189⁴.
10. καταλιθώσαντες: acc. to Bl.,
the only Attic example of καταλιθόω
for καταλεύω.
11. αἱ γυναῖκες...αὐτοῦ: the vivid-
ness of the picture in the easy flowing
narrative is heightened by the irregular
insertion of a new subject, αἱ γυναῖκες,
as if without premeditation.
With this and § 205 compare the
speech of the Athenian envoy at
Sparta more than a century earlier,
Thuc. I. 73—75.

ἐζήτουν οἱ τότ᾽ Ἀθηναῖοι οὔτε ῥήτορα οὔτε στρατηγὸν δι᾽ ὅτου δουλεύσουσιν εὐτυχῶς, ἀλλ᾽ οὐδὲ
ζῆν ἠξίουν εἰ μὴ μετ᾽ ἐλευθερίας ἐξέσται τοῦτο
ποιεῖν. ἡγεῖτο γὰρ αὐτῶν ἕκαστος οὐχὶ τῷ πατρὶ 5
καὶ τῇ μητρὶ μόνον γεγενῆσθαι, ἀλλὰ καὶ τῇ πατρίδι.
διαφέρει δὲ τί; ὅτι ὁ μὲν τοῖς γονεῦσι μόνον γεγενῆσθαι νομίζων τὸν τῆς εἱμαρμένης καὶ τὸν αὐτόματον θάνατον περιμένει, ὁ δὲ καὶ τῇ πατρίδι ὑπὲρ τοῦ
μὴ ταύτην ἐπιδεῖν δουλεύουσαν ἀποθνήσκειν ἐθε- 10
λήσει, καὶ φοβερωτέρας ἡγήσεται τὰς ὕβρεις καὶ
τὰς ἀτιμίας, ἃς ἐν δουλευούσῃ τῇ πόλει φέρειν
ἀνάγκη, τοῦ θανάτου.
Εἰ μὲν τοίνυν τοῦτ᾽ ἐπεχείρουν λέγειν, ὡς ἐγὼ 206

§ 205. 3. **δι᾽ ὅτου δουλεύσουσιν** :
final relative (M.T. 565). With δουλεύσουσιν εὐτυχῶς (sarcastic) cf. ἀσφαλῶς δουλεύειν, § 203⁵.

4. **εἰ μὴ ἐξέσται**, if they could not
(were not to be able) : εἰ μὴ ἐξέσοιτο
might be used (M.T. 694, 695).

5. **οὐχὶ...γεγενῆσθαι** : cf. Plat.
Crit. 50 D—51 B; and Arist. Eth. I.
7, 6, τὸ δ᾽ αὔταρκες λέγομεν οὐκ αὐτῷ
μόνῳ τῷ ζῶντι βίον μονώτην, ἀλλὰ
(sc. τῷ ζῶντι) καὶ γονεῦσι καὶ τέκνοις
κ.τ.λ., where αὐτῷ μόνῳ and γονεῦσι
both depend on ζῶντι (living for
himself alone, and living also for
parents etc.), as πατρί, μητρί, and
γονεῦσι in Demosthenes depend on
γεγενῆσθαι. The passage of Aristotle
is sometimes called ungrammatical !

8. **τὸν τῆς εἱμαρμένης θάνατον**, the
death of Fate, i.e. death at an appointed time,—opposed to voluntary
death, as when one gives his life for
his country (cf. ἀποθνήσκειν ἐθελήσει,
10): **τὸν αὐτόματον θάν.** is natural
(opposed to violent) death. The two
are really the same, from different
points of view. See West., with
Aulus Gellius, XIII. 1, and Cicero,
Phil. I. 4, 10.

9. **καὶ τῇ πατρίδι** : sc. γεγενῆσθαι
νομίζων.—**ὑπὲρ τοῦ...ἐπιδεῖν** : cf. §
204⁶.

10. **δουλεύουσαν**, in a state of
slavery: see M. T. 885, 148. With
the pres. partic. cf. μή μ᾽ ἰδεῖν
θανόνθ᾽, not to see me killed, Eur.
Orest. 746.

§§ 206—310 conclude the digression which begins in § 188. The
orator here appeals to the judges not
to convict Ctesiphon, as this will be a
condemnation of the people of Athens
for maintaining the ancient glories of
the state, the glories of Marathon and
Salamis.

§ 206. 1—3. **εἰ...ἐπεχείρουν...
ἐπιτιμήσειέ μοι** : this combination of
a present unreal condition, if I were
undertaking, with a future conclusion,
everybody would justly censure me, is
rare, and perhaps strictly illogical
(M.T. 504). We should expect an
imperfect with ἄν in the apodosis ;
and this is implied in the condensed
form which we have. The real
meaning is, if I were (now) undertaking to tell you this, the result would
be (ἦν ἄν) that all would justly censure
me.

128 ΔΗΜΟΣΘΕΝΟΥΣ

προήγαγον ὑμᾶς ἄξια τῶν προγόνων φρονεῖν, οὐκ
ἔσθ' ὅστις οὐκ ἂν εἰκότως ἐπιτιμήσειέ μοι. νῦν δ'
ἐγὼ μὲν ὑμετέρας τὰς τοιαύτας προαιρέσεις ἀπο-
φαίνω, καὶ δείκνυμι ὅτι καὶ πρὸ ἐμοῦ τοῦτ' εἶχε τὸ 5
φρόνημ' ἡ πόλις, τῆς μέντοι διακονίας τῆς ἐφ' ἑκάστοις τῶν πεπραγμένων καὶ ἐμαυτῷ μετεῖναί φημι,
297 οὗτος δὲ τῶν ὅλων κατηγορῶν, καὶ κελεύων ὑμᾶς 207
ἐμοὶ πικρῶς ἔχειν ὡς φόβων καὶ κινδύνων αἰτίῳ
τῇ πόλει, τῆς μὲν εἰς τὸ παρὸν τιμῆς ἔμ' ἀποστερῆσαι γλίχεται, τὰ δ' εἰς ἅπαντα τὸν λοιπὸν χρόνον ἐγκώμι' ὑμῶν ἀφαιρεῖται. εἰ γὰρ ὡς οὐ τὰ 5
βέλτιστα ἐμοῦ πολιτευσαμένου τουδὶ καταψηφιεῖσθε,
ἡμαρτηκέναι δόξετε, οὐ τῇ τῆς τύχης ἀγνωμοσύνῃ τὰ
συμβάντα παθεῖν. ἀλλ' οὐκ ἔστιν, οὐκ ἔστιν ὅπως 208

---

4. ὑμετέρας: sc. οὔσας.
6. διακονίας, i.e. what he terms
the *menial service* is all that he claims
for himself. This is in striking contrast with his claim for full recognition
of his public services elsewhere: cf.
§§ 297—300. But in this grand glorification of Athens and her noble
services to freedom, the more he
depreciates himself and exalts the
state, the stronger does he make his
argument that the condemnation of
Ctesiphon now would be a condemnation of Athens herself and of all her
glorious history.
Notice the antitheses in this passage :—first, the main one, εἰ μὲν and
νῦν δὲ (§ 206¹·³); then, within the
latter, ἐγὼ μὲν and οὗτος δὲ (§ 207¹);
also ὑμετέρας and καὶ ἐμαυτῷ, προαιρέσεις and διακονίας.
§ 207. 1. τῶν ὅλων: opposed to
τῆς ἐφ' ἑκάστοις (διακονίας), § 206⁶.
3. τῆς εἰς τὸ παρὸν τιμῆς: the
crown.
4. τὰ...ἐγκώμι': i.e. your past
glories will be lost for all future time

if they are condemned by your vote
to-day.
5. ἀφαιρεῖται is conative: cf. § 13¹.
6. τουδὶ, Ctesiphon, like τουτονὶ
in § 15⁶.
7. ἀγνωμοσύνῃ, *harshness* (want
of feeling): cf. § 252¹. ἀγνωμονῶ may
mean *to be thoughtless* or *inconsiderate*:
cf. §§ 94², 248⁷. τα συμβάντα, *what
befell you*, including Chaeronea.
§ 208. The famous oath by the
heroes of Marathon, Plataea, Salamis,
and Artemisium here follows. The
grandeur of this solemn invocation of
the shades of the mighty dead, to
support the orator in his last and
noblest assertion of the true spirit of
Athenian liberty, will strike the most
indifferent reader. We do not envy
one who is strong enough to read
this passage without emotion. Lord
Brougham says: "The whole passage,
which ends here, and begins εἰ γὰρ
ταῦτα προεῖτο ἀκονιτί (§ 200), is de-
serving of close study, being one of
the greatest pieces of declamation on
record in any tongue." See Longinus

ἡμάρτετε, ἄνδρες Ἀθηναῖοι, τὸν ὑπὲρ τῆς ἁπάντων
ἐλευθερίας καὶ σωτηρίας κίνδυνον ἀράμενοι, μὰ τοὺς
Μαραθῶνι προκινδυνεύσαντας τῶν προγόνων καὶ
τοὺς ἐν Πλαταιαῖς παραταξαμένους καὶ τοὺς ἐν 5
Σαλαμῖνι ναυμαχήσαντας καὶ τοὺς ἐπ᾿ Ἀρτεμισίῳ
καὶ πολλοὺς ἑτέρους τοὺς ἐν τοῖς δημοσίοις μνήμασι
κειμένους, ἀγαθοὺς ἄνδρας, οὓς ἅπαντας ὁμοίως ἡ
πόλις τῆς αὐτῆς ἀξιώσασα τιμῆς ἔθαψεν, Αἰσχίνη,
οὐχὶ τοὺς κατορθώσαντας αὐτῶν οὐδὲ τοὺς κρατή- 10
σαντας μόνους. δικαίως· ὃ μὲν γὰρ ἦν ἀνδρῶν
ἀγαθῶν ἔργον, ἅπασι πέπρακται· τῇ τύχῃ δ᾿ ἦν ὁ
δαίμων ἔνειμεν ἑκάστοις, ταύτῃ κέχρηνται. ἔπειτ᾿, ὦ 209

on the Sublime 16: ἀπόδειξιν ὁ Δημοσθένης ὑπὲρ τῶν πεπολιτευμένων εἰσ-
φέρει·…"οὐχ ἡμάρτετε, ὦ τὸν ὑπὲρ
τῆς Ἑλλήνων ἐλευθερίας ἀγῶνα ἀρά-
μενοι· ἔχετε δὲ οἰκεῖα τούτου παρα-
δείγματα· οὐδὲ γὰρ οἱ ἐν Μαραθῶνι
ἥμαρτον οὐδ᾿ οἱ ἐν Σαλαμῖνι κ.τ.λ."

1, 2. οὐκ ἔστιν…ἡμάρτετε, *it cannot
be. that ye erred*: οὐκ ἔστιν ὅπως =
οὐδαμῶς.

3. ἀράμενοι: cf. πόλεμον ἄρασθαι,
v. 5.—μὰ τοὺς : most MSS. prefix οὐ,
which Σ omits, μά generally implying
a negation.—τοὺς…προγόνων (*those
of*) *our ancestors who bore the brunt
of battle at Marathon* : προκινδυνεύω
is here *stand forward* (as πρόμαχος)
to face the foe; from its idea of
contending it may take a dative like
μάχομαι, as in Thuc. I. 73, φαμὲν γὰρ
Μαραθῶνι μόνοι προκινδυνεῦσαι τῷ βαρ-
βάρῳ, a passage which may have
suggested προκινδυνεύσαντας to Demosthenes here.

4. Μαραθῶνι: as the name of an
Attic deme, this is usually a locative
dative : but here all MSS. except Σ,
and most quotations, prefix ἐν, which
is regular with Πλαταιαῖς and Σαλαμῖνι (G. 1197).

5. ἐν Σαλαμῖνι: this battle was
fought *at* Salamis ; the other sea-fight
was *off* (ἐπ᾿) Artemisium.

7. δημοσίοις μνήμασι : the *public
tombs* were in the outer Ceramicus,
on the road leading to the Academy :
see Paus. I. 29, Thuc. II. 34. Those
who fell at Marathon were buried
on the battlefield, as a special
honour.

8. ἀγαθοὺς ἄνδρας, in apposition
with the preceding accusatives: this
was by no means a weak term of
praise with Demosthenes: cf. l. 11.
—ὁμοίως and τῆς αὐτῆς mutually
strengthen each other.

10. αὐτῶν: I adopt this partitive
gen. rather than αὐτούς (found in Σ,
L¹), as I am not convinced that αὐτούς
can have the force of *especially* (*distinguished from others*), ipsos solos
(Rauchenstein). In defence of English, we may note that this renowned
passage has no less than fifty *sigmas*
in sixty-seven words.

§ 209. The descent from the impassioned patriotic eloquence of the
preceding passage to the personal
vituperation of this is depressing.

κατάρατε καὶ γραμματοκύφων, σὺ μὲν τῆς παρὰ
τουτωνὶ τιμῆς καὶ φιλανθρωπίας ἔμ' ἀποστερῆσαι
βουλόμενος τρόπαια καὶ μάχας καὶ παλαί' ἔργ'
ἔλεγες, ὧν τίνος προσεδεῖθ' ὁ παρὼν ἀγὼν οὑτοσί ; 5
ἐμὲ δὲ, ὦ τριταγωνιστὰ, τὸν περὶ τῶν πρωτείων σύμβουλον τῇ πόλει παριόντα, τὸ τίνος φρόνημα λαβόντ'
ἀναβαίνειν ἐπὶ τὸ βῆμ' ἔδει ; τὸ τοῦ τούτων ἀνάξι' 210
ἐροῦντος ; δικαίως μέντἂν ἀπέθανον. ἐπεὶ οὐδ' ὑμᾶς,
298 ἄνδρες Ἀθηναῖοι, ἀπὸ τῆς αὐτῆς διανοίας δεῖ τάς τ'
ἰδίας δίκας καὶ τὰς δημοσίας κρίνειν, ἀλλὰ τὰ μὲν
τοῦ καθ' ἡμέραν βίου συμβόλαια ἐπὶ τῶν ἰδίων 5
νόμων καὶ ἔργων σκοποῦντας, τὰς δὲ κοινὰς προαιρέσεις εἰς τὰ τῶν προγόνων ἀξιώματ' ἀποβλέποντας.

2. **γραμματοκύφων**: ἀντὶ τοῦ γραμ-
ματέως, ὅτι οἱ γραμματεῖς προκεκυφότες
γράφουσιν (Etym. Magn.).
4. **τρόπαια...ἔλεγες**: see Aesch.
181.
6. **τριταγωνιστά**: effectively chosen
with reference to **πρωτείων**, which
refers to Athens as competitor for the
first prize in the political **ἀγών**, in
which Demosthenes is her adviser.
7. **τὸ τίνος φρόνημα λαβόντ'**, *inspired by whose spirit?*
§ 210. 2. **δικαίως μέντἂν ἀπέθανον**, *but* (in that case) *I should have
deserved to die.* **μέντἂν** by crasis for
μέντοι ἄν.—**οὐδ' ὑμᾶς**...**δεῖ**, *neither
should you* (any more than I).
3. **διανοίας**, *spirit* (way of thinking).
4. **ἰδίας, δημοσίας**: this has no
reference to the ordinary distinction
of **γραφαί** and **δίκαι**, *public* and *private*
suits, which correspond generally to
our *criminal* and *civil* processes.
Here **δίκη** has its widest legal sense
of *lawsuit* in general, including both
γραφή and **δίκη** (in its narrower sense).
ἴδιαι δίκαι are suits which concern
individuals and their ordinary business
relations (**συμβόλαια**), which of course

must be judged *with reference to special
statutes* (**ἐπὶ ἰδίων νόμων**, cf. **ἐπ' ἀληθείας**, § 22¹), which may change from
year to year, and *to special facts* (**ἰδίων
ἔργων**), without regard to the general
policy or the traditions of the state :
even criminal suits (**γραφαί**) which
involve nothing more than the acts of
individuals would be included here.
But **δημόσιαι δίκαι** are suits like the
present one, which involve a judgment
on the general policy of statesmen
(**κοινὰς προαιρέσεις**), whose acts are
not prescribed by special statutes, but
must be governed to a great extent
by general principles and traditions
of state : these, the orator says, must
be judged by reference to the glorious
deeds of the past. Demosthenes
insists here, as elsewhere, that the
only real question involved in this
case is that of his own statesmanship
and his fidelity to the best traditions
of Athens, while Aeschines constantly
urges the court to treat it as a common
ἰδία δίκη and settle it by reference to
ordinary facts and petty details. (See
Aesch. 199, 200.) Aeschines saw
that here lay his only chance of
success in his suit.

καὶ παραλαμβάνειν γ' ἅμα τῇ βακτηρίᾳ καὶ τῷ
συμβόλῳ τὸ φρόνημα τὸ τῆς πόλεως νομίζειν ἕκαστον
ὑμῶν δεῖ, ὅταν τὰ δημόσι' εἰσίητε κρινοῦντες, εἴπερ 10
ἄξι' ἐκείνων πράττειν οἴεσθε χρῆναι.
Ἀλλὰ γὰρ ἐμπεσὼν εἰς τὰ πεπραγμένα τοῖς 211
προγόνοις ὑμῶν ἔστιν ἃ τῶν ψηφισμάτων παρέβην
καὶ τῶν πραχθέντων. ἐπανελθεῖν οὖν ὁπόθεν ἐνταῦθ'
ἐξέβην βούλομαι.
Ὡς γὰρ ἀφικόμεθ' εἰς τὰς Θήβας, κατελαμβάνομεν 5
Φιλίππου καὶ Θετταλῶν καὶ τῶν ἄλλων συμμάχων
παρόντας πρέσβεις, καὶ τοὺς μὲν ἡμετέρους φίλους ἐν
φόβῳ, τοὺς δ' ἐκείνου θρασεῖς. ὅτι δ' οὐ νῦν ταῦτα
λέγω τοῦ συμφέροντος ἕνεκ' ἐμαυτῷ, λέγε μοι τὴν
ἐπιστολὴν ἣν τότ' ἐπέμψαμεν εὐθὺς οἱ πρέσβεις. 10
καίτοι τοσαύτῃ γ' ὑπερβολῇ συκοφαντίας οὗτος 212
κέχρηται ὥστ', εἰ μέν τι τῶν δεόντων ἐπράχθη, τὸν
καιρὸν, οὐκ ἐμέ φησιν αἴτιον γεγενῆσθάι, τῶν δ' ὡς
ἑτέρως συμβάντων ἁπάντων ἐμὲ καὶ τὴν ἐμὴν τύχην
αἰτίαν εἶναι· καὶ, ὡς ἔοικεν, ὁ σύμβουλος καὶ ῥήτωρ 5

8. τῇ βακτηρίᾳ καὶ τῷ συμβόλῳ
his staff and his ticket: each judge
received in the morning a staff painted
with the same colour as the lintel
(σφηνίσκος) of the court house in
which he was to sit; after entering
the court, he gave up his staff to an
officer, and received a ticket (σύμ-
βολον), which entitled him to receive
his fee of three obols (δικαστικόν) after
his day's service.
§ 211. He now returns to the account of the embassy to Thebes, from
which he digressed in § 188.
5. ἀφικόμεθ': i.e. the ambassadors.
6. Φιλίππου...πρέσβεις: see Plut.
Dem. 18, and Philoch. frag. 135,
Φιλίππου δὲ καταλαβόντος Ἐλάτειαν
καὶ Κυτίνιον, καὶ πρέσβεις πέμψαντος
εἰς Θήβας Θετταλῶν, Αἰνιανῶν, Αἰ-

τωλῶν, Δολόπων, Φθιωτῶν· Ἀθηναίων
δὲ κατὰ τὸν αὐτὸν χρόνον πρέσβεις
ἀποστειλάντων τοὺς περὶ Δημοσθένη,
τούτοις συμμαχεῖν ἐψηφίσαντο.
8. ὅτι...λέγω is connected with
λέγε (9) by a suppressed phrase like
to show. See Krüger, Gr. Gr. 65, 1,
Anm. 6.
10. ἣν τότ' ἐπέμψαμεν: opposed
to νῦν λέγω (8).
§ 212. These words were spoken
while the clerk was preparing to read
the letter: cf. § 180.
2. τὸν καιρὸν: see Aesch. 137—
141 and 237—239; esp. ὁ δ' εἰσάγων
ἦν ὑμᾶς εἰς τὰς Θήβας καιρὸς καὶ
φόβος καὶ χρεία συμμαχίας, ἀλλ' οὐ
Δημοσθένης (141).
3. ὡς ἑτέρως: see note on § 85⁶.
4. τύχην: see Aesch. 157.

ἐγὼ τῶν μὲν ἐκ λόγου καὶ τοῦ βουλεύσασθαι πραχθέντων οὐδὲν αὐτῷ συναίτιος εἶναι δοκῶ, τῶν δ' ἐν
τοῖς ὅπλοις καὶ κατὰ τὴν στρατηγίαν ἀτυχηθέντων
μόνος αἴτιος εἶναι. πῶς ἂν ὠμότερος συκοφάντης
γένοιτ' ἢ καταρατότερος ; λέγε τὴν ἐπιστολήν. 10

299 ΕΠΙΣΤΟΛΗ.

Ἐπειδὴ τοίνυν ἐποιήσαντο τὴν ἐκκλησίαν, προσ- 213
ῆγον ἐκείνους προτέρους διὰ τὸ τὴν τῶν συμμάχων
τάξιν ἐκείνους ἔχειν. καὶ παρελθόντες ἐδημηγόρουν
πολλὰ μὲν Φίλιππον ἐγκωμιάζοντες, πολλὰ δ' ὑμῶν
κατηγοροῦντες, πάνθ' ὅσα πώποτ' ἐναντί' ἐπράξατε 5
Θηβαίοις ἀναμιμνήσκοντες. τὸ δ' οὖν κεφάλαιον,
ἠξίουν ὧν μὲν εὖ πεπόνθεσαν ὑπὸ Φιλίππου χάριν
αὐτοὺς ἀποδοῦναι, ὧν δ' ὑφ' ὑμῶν ἠδίκηντο δίκην
λαβεῖν, ὁποτέρως βούλονται, ἢ διέντας αὐτοὺς ἐφ'
ὑμᾶς ἢ συνεμβαλόντας εἰς τὴν Ἀττικήν· καὶ ἐδεί- 10
κνυσαν, ὡς ᾤοντο, ἐκ μὲν ὧν αὐτοὶ συνεβούλευον
τἀκ τῆς Ἀττικῆς βοσκήματα καὶ ἀνδράποδα καὶ
τἄλλ' ἀγαθὰ εἰς τὴν Βοιωτίαν ἥξοντα, ἐκ δ' ὧν ἡμᾶς

---

7. **συναίτιος**, *partner*, opposed to
μόνος αἴτιος (9).—**τῶν…ἀτυχηθέντων** =
ἃ ἠτυχήσαμεν.
.§ **213.** 1. **τὴν ἐκκλησίαν**: i.e.
at Thebes. The narrative is continued
from § 211⁸.
2. **τῶν συμμάχων**: i.e. of Thebes.
6. **τὸ κεφάλαιον**, adverbial, *in
short.*
7. **ὧν μὲν εὖ πεπόνθεσαν**, *for the
benefits they had received*, εὖ πάσχειν
as passive of εὖ ποιεῖν: this corresponds to ὧν δ' ἠδίκηντο (8).
8. **αὐτοὺς**: the Thebans, while
αὐτοὺς in 9 refers to the Macedonians.
9. **ὁποτέρως βούλονται**, *in whichever way they pleased*, in the mood
and tense of the direct form, the

exhortation being *take vengeance in
whichever way you please.* — **διέντας
αὐτοὺς**, i.e. *by letting them pass
through Boeotia into Attica* (cf. § 146⁴).
The aorists διέντας and συνεμβαλόντας
have the better authority here: when
an aor. partic. denotes that in which
the action of a verb (usually aorist)
consists, so that they really designate
one act, the two may coincide in
time, as in Plat. Phaed. 60 c, εὖ γ'
ἐποίησας ἀναμνήσας με, *you did well to
remind me.* (See M.T. 150, with the
examples.)
11. **ἐκ μὲν…συνεβούλευον**, *as a
consequence of following their advice*,
opposed to ἐκ δ' ὧν ἡμᾶς ἐρεῖν ἔφασαν
in l. 13.

ἐρεῖν ἔφασαν τὰν τῇ Βοιωτίᾳ διαρπασθησόμεν' ὑπὸ
τοῦ πολέμου. καὶ ἄλλα πολλὰ πρὸς τούτοις, εἰς 15
ταὐτὰ δὲ πάντα συντείνοντ', ἔλεγον. ἃ δ' ἡμεῖς πρὸς 214
ταῦτα, τὰ μὲν καθ' ἕκαστα ἐγὼ μὲν ἀντὶ παντὸς ἂν
τιμησαίμην εἰπεῖν τοῦ βίου, ὑμᾶς δὲ δέδοικα, μὴ
παρεληλυθότων τῶν καιρῶν, ὥσπερ ἂν εἰ καὶ κατακλυσμὸν γεγενῆσθαι τῶν πραγμάτων ἡγούμενοι, μάταιον 5
ὄχλον τοὺς περὶ τούτων λόγους νομίσητε· ὅ τι δ' οὖν
ἐπείσαμεν ἡμεῖς καὶ ἡμῖν ἀπεκρίναντο, ἀκούσατε.
λέγε ταυτὶ λαβών.

ΑΠΟΚΡΙΣΕΙΣ ΘΗΒΑΙΩΝ.

Μετὰ ταῦτα τοίνυν' ἐκάλουν ὑμᾶς καὶ μετεπέμ- 215
ποντο. ἐξῆτε, ἐβοηθεῖτε, ἵνα τὰν μέσῳ παραλείπω,

§ **214.** 1. **ἃ δ' ἡμεῖς**: sc. ἐλέγομεν.
2. **τὰ μὲν καθ' ἕκαστα**, the details,
with the subordinate ἐγὼ μὲν and ὑμᾶς
δὲ, is in antithesis to ὅ τι δ' οὖν ἐπείσαμεν (i.e. the sum of what we
accomplished) in l. 6.—**ἀντὶ ... τοῦ
βίου**, as we might say, I would give
my life: cf. τιμᾶν and τιμᾶσθαι used
of estimating the penalty in a lawsuit;
and I. 1, ἀντὶ πολλῶν ἂν χρημάτων
ἐλέσθαι. It is not hard to see why
Demosthenes should be unwilling to
repeat any part of this brilliant speech.
The hope of successes of the allies
against Philip, which he probably
held out, had been disappointed by
the crushing defeat at Chaeronea;
and the destruction of Thebes three
years later must have made the whole
tone of this speech now sadly untimely.
Plutarch (Dem. 18) gives a graphic
account of the Theban assembly and
of the address, which was probably
one of the orator's greatest efforts.
4. **ὥσπερ ἂν εἰ...ἡγούμενοι**, as (you
would think, ἐνομίζετε ἂν) if you
believed, etc. (M.T. 227, 868). Strictly
we should have either ὥσπερ ἂν εἰ

ἡγεῖσθε (impf.) or ὥσπερ ἂν ἡγούμενοι
(= εἰ ἡγεῖσθε), since a conditional
participle is not regularly preceded
by εἰ (M.T. 472). But it would seem
that the colloquial use of ὥσπερ ἂν
εἰ, quasi, sometimes caused the true
ellipsis to be overlooked and the εἰ
to be irregularly added.—**καὶ κατακλυσμὸν**; i.e. also a deluge, as well
as the lapse of opportunity (παρεληλυθότων τῶν καιρῶν).
5. **τῶν πραγμάτων**, objective genitive after κατακλυσμὸν.
6. **ὅ τι ἐπείσαμεν** and (ὅ τι)...ἀπε-
κρίναντο are the same thing.
§ **215.** 1. **ἐκάλουν ὑμᾶς**, i.e. called
your army to Thebes. This is what
Demosthenes provided for in § 178²⁻⁴
(see notes), when he proposed to give
the embassy concurrent power with
the generals over the movements of
the army. This march to Thebes,
after the answer of the Thebans had
been sent to Athens (μετὰ ταῦτα), is
commonly thought to be directly
opposed to the account of Aeschines
in III. 140: Dissen exclaims indig-
nantly, "Haeccine manifesta mendacia

οὕτως οἰκείως ὑμᾶς ἐδέχοντο, ὥστ' ἔξω τῶν ὁπλιτῶν
300 καὶ τῶν ἱππέων ὄντων εἰς τὰς οἰκίας καὶ τὸ ἄστυ
δέχεσθαι τὴν στρατιὰν ἐπὶ παῖδας καὶ γυναῖκας καὶ 5
τὰ τιμιώτατα. καίτοι τρί' ἐν ἐκείνῃ τῇ ἡμέρᾳ πᾶσιν
ἀνθρώποις ἔδειξαν ἐγκώμια Θηβαῖοι καθ' ὑμῶν τὰ
κάλλιστα, ἐν μὲν ἀνδρείας, ἕτερον δὲ δικαιοσύνης,
τρίτον δὲ σωφροσύνης. καὶ γὰρ τὸν ἀγῶνα μεθ'
ὑμῶν μᾶλλον ἢ πρὸς ὑμᾶς ἑλόμενοι ποιήσασθαι, καὶ 10
ἀμείνους εἶναι καὶ δικαιότερ' ἀξιοῦν ὑμᾶς ἔκριναν
Φιλίππου· καὶ τὰ παρ' αὐτοῖς καὶ παρὰ πᾶσι δ' ἐν

potuisse coram judicibus dici !" But
Aeschines says only that the march to
Thebes took place πρὶν περὶ συμμαχίας μίαν μόνην συλλαβὴν γράψαι
Δημοσθένην. Now that the "decree
of Demosthenes" (181—187) is known
to be a forgery, we have no reason
for thinking that any formal treaty of
alliance preceded the invitation of the
Athenian army to Thebes. Demosthenes could have proposed such a
treaty only after his return to Athens.
It appears from the criticisms of
Aeschines on the treaty (141—144)
that it was an elaborate document ;
and it is probable that it was not
made and ratified until some time
after the march to Thebes, which
required no further legislation than
the decree appointing the ambassadors. It must be remembered that
Demosthenes (§ 178) proposed that
the embassy should simply offer the
Athenian army to Thebes without
insisting on any formal terms, ἐπαγ-
γέλλεσθαι βοηθήσειν ἂν κελεύωσιν.

3. ἔξω...ὄντων : this is commonly
referred to the Athenian army, who
are supposed to have first encamped
outside the city and afterwards to
have been invited to enter Thebes
and occupy the houses. It is surely
far more natural and agrees better

with the context to understand that,
while the Theban infantry and cavalry
(i.e. the whole army) were encamped
outside the walls, the Athenian army
was quartered in the town. The lack
of a pronoun to designate which army
is meant is felt in both interpretations;
but as the subject is the Thebans, it
is more natural to refer the absolute
clause to them. Again, the emphasis
given twice to παῖδας καὶ γυναῖκας
(5 and 13) implies that the men were
absent; and ἐφ' ὑμῖν ποιήσαντες (13),
as a testimony to the σωφροσύνη of
the Athenians, implies this still more
strongly.

7. καθ' ὑμῶν, upon you, as in VI. 9,
καθ' ὑμῶν ἐγκώμιον, not in its common
hostile sense. See Arist. Pol. III. 13,
14, κατὰ δὲ τοιούτων οὐκ ἔστι νόμος,
αὐτοὶ γάρ εἰσι νόμος, in respect to such
men there is no law, for they are a
law unto themselves. In the parallel
passage of St Paul, Gal. v. 23, κατὰ
τῶν τοιούτων is translated against such.
See Rom. ii. 14, ἑαυτοῖς εἰσι νόμος,
where we have the rest of the passage
of Aristotle.

11. δικαιότερ' ἀξιοῦν, that you
made juster claims on them.

12. καὶ παρὰ πᾶσι δ', and indeed
(καὶ) with all mankind, parenthetically
after παρ' αὐτοῖς.

πλείστη φυλακῇ, παῖδας καὶ γυναῖκας, ἐφ᾽ ὑμῖν
ποιήσαντες, σωφροσύνης πίστιν περὶ ὑμῶν ἔχοντες
ἔδειξαν. ἐν οἷς πᾶσιν, ἄνδρες Ἀθηναῖοι, κατά γ᾽ 216
ὑμᾶς ὀρθῶς ἐφάνησαν ἐγνωκότες. οὔτε γὰρ εἰς τὴν
πόλιν εἰσελθόντος τοῦ στρατοπέδου οὐδεὶς οὐδὲν οὐδ᾽
ἀδίκως ὑμῖν ἐνεκάλεσεν· οὕτω σώφρονας παρέσχεθ᾽
ὑμᾶς αὐτούς· δίς τε συμπαραταξάμενοι τὰς πρώτας, 5
τήν τ᾽ ἐπὶ τοῦ ποταμοῦ καὶ τὴν χειμερινὴν, οὐκ
ἀμέμπτους μόνον ὑμᾶς αὐτοὺς ἀλλὰ καὶ θαυμαστοὺς
ἐδείξατε τῷ κόσμῳ, ταῖς παρασκευαῖς, τῇ προθυμίᾳ.
ἐφ᾽ οἷς παρὰ μὲν τῶν ἄλλων ὑμῖν ἐγίγνοντ᾽ ἔπαινοι,
παρὰ δ᾽ ὑμῶν θυσίαι καὶ πομπαὶ τοῖς θεοῖς. καὶ 217
ἔγωγ᾽ ἡδέως ἂν ἐροίμην Αἰσχίνην, ὅτε ταῦτ᾽ ἐπράττετο καὶ ζήλου καὶ χαρᾶς καὶ ἐπαίνων ἡ πόλις ἦν
μεστὴ, πότερον συνέθυε καὶ συνευφραίνετο τοῖς πολλοῖς, ἢ λυπούμενος καὶ στένων καὶ δυσμεναίνων τοῖς 5
κοινοῖς ἀγαθοῖς οἴκοι καθῆτο. εἰ μὲν γὰρ παρῆν καὶ
μετὰ τῶν ἄλλων ἐξητάζετο, πῶς οὐ δεινὰ ποιεῖ,

---

14. **ἔχοντες**: or. obl. with ἔδειξαν.
§ 216. 2. **ὀρθῶς ἐφάνησαν ἐγνω-**
κότες, it appeared (later) that they
had judged rightly (ἐγνώκασιν): cf.
§ 215¹⁴. —**οὔτε...οὐδὲν οὐδ᾽**: a remark-
able accumulation of emphatic negatives: οὔτε corresponds to τε (5).
3. **οὐδ᾽ ἀδίκως** (not) even unjustly.
5. **δίς τε...πρώτας** when you twice
stood in line with them in the earliest
encounters: some cognate object is
implied in συμπαραταξάμενοι. All
MSS. except Σ add μάχας, as if μαχε-
σάμενοι had preceded. The natural
accus. would be παρατάξεις, following
the meaning of συμπαραταξάμενοι and
so signifying battle array or battles.
See Aesch. III. 151, ἐπὶ τὴν παράταξιν
ὥρμησαν.
6. **τήν τ᾽ ἐπὶ τοῦ ποταμοῦ,** the
river battle, probably fought on the

upper Cephisus, which flows through
Phocis before it enters Boeotia near
Chaeronea. —**τὴν χειμερινὴν,** the
" winter battle," probably fought on
some wintry day in the hilly parts of
Phocis. Many still find chronological
difficulties in this winter campaign,
forgetting that the only trouble arose
from the spurious decree in §§ 181—
187, dated in midsummer. See notes
on §§ 152⁸ and 181—187, with Hist.
§ 65.
9. **παρὰ μὲν τῶν ἄλλων ὑμῖν** is in
strong (double) antithesis to **παρὰ δ᾽**
ὑμῶν τοῖς θεοῖς.
§ 217. 3. **ζήλου,** pride, glory: see
note on § 120⁶.
7. **μετὰ...ἐξητάζετο,** was counted
in with the rest, the same military
figure which is common in this speech:
see note on § 173⁵.

μᾶλλον δ' οὐδ' ὅσια, εἰ ὧν ὡς ἀρίστων αὐτὸς τοὺς
θεοὺς ἐποιήσατο μάρτυρας, ταῦθ' ὡς οὐκ ἄριστα νῦν
301 ὑμᾶς ἀξιοῖ ψηφίσασθαι τοὺς ὀμωμοκότας τοὺς θεούς; 10
εἰ δὲ μὴ παρῆν, πῶς οὐκ ἀπολωλέναι πολλάκις ἐστὶ
δίκαιος, εἰ ἐφ' οἷς ἔχαιρον οἱ ἄλλοι, ταῦτ' ἐλυπεῖθ'
ὁρῶν; λέγε δὴ καὶ ταῦτα τὰ ψηφίσματά μοι.

ΨΗΦΙΣΜΑΤΑ ΘΥΣΙΩΝ.

Οὐκοῦν ἡμεῖς μὲν ἐν θυσίαις ἦμεν τότε, Θηβαῖοι 218
δ' ἐν τῷ δι' ἡμᾶς σεσῶσθαι νομίζειν, καὶ περιειστήκει
τοῖς βοηθείας δεήσεσθαι δοκοῦσιν ἀφ' ὧν ἔπραττον
οὗτοι, αὐτοὺς βοηθεῖν ἑτέροις ἐξ ὧν ἐπείσθητ' ἐμοί.
ἀλλὰ μὴν οἵας τότ' ἠφίει φωνὰς ὁ Φίλιππος καὶ ἐν 5
οἵαις ἦν ταραχαῖς ἐπὶ τούτοις, ἐκ τῶν ἐπιστολῶν
τῶν ἐκείνου μαθήσεσθε ὧν εἰς Πελοπόννησον ἔπεμ-
πεν. καί μοι λέγε ταύτας λαβών, ἵν' εἰδῆτε ἡ ἐμὴ
συνέχεια καὶ πλάνοι καὶ ταλαιπωρίαι καὶ τὰ πολλὰ
ψηφίσματα, ἃ νῦν οὗτος διέσυρε, τί ἀπειργάσατο. 10

8. **οὐδ' ὅσια**, even impious: cf.
note on § 1⁶.
8, 9. **ὡς ἀρίστων...ὡς οὐκ ἄριστα**:
with reference to the words of Ctesiphon's decree, ὅτι διατελεῖ καὶ λέγων
καὶ πράττων τὰ ἄριστα τῷ δήμῳ
(Aesch. 49). If Aeschines joined in
the thanksgivings, he declared before
the Gods that the policy of Demosthenes was good: but he now asks
the court to declare this not good by
condemning Ctesiphon.
10. **ὀμωμοκότας**: of the Heliastic
oath.
11. **ἀπολωλέναι πολλάκις**: cf. XIX.
110, τρὶς οὐχ ἅπαξ ἀπολωλέναι δίκαιος.
§ 218. 2. **ἐν τῷ...νομίζειν**, in
the belief, corresponding to ἐν θυσίαις
(1), both denoting what occupied their
minds.
3. **τοῖς...δοκοῦσιν** (impf.), to those

who had seemed likely to need help, i.e.
ourselves.—**ἀφ' ὧν ἔπραττον**, in antithesis to ἐξ ὧν ἐπείσθητ' ἐμοί: cf.
§ 213¹¹⁻¹³.
4. **αὐτοὺς**, ipsos, i.e. ourselves: for
the accus. see Xen. Oec. 11, 23, συμφέρει αὐτοῖς φίλους εἶναι, where φίλοις
would be more common (G. 928¹).—
βοηθεῖν ἑτέροις: subj. of περιειστήκει,
it had come about.
5. **οἵας ἠφίει φωνὰς**: cf. § 195⁵.
6. **ἐπιστολῶν**: for an earlier letter
of Philip to Peloponnesus asking for
help, see § 156.
9. **πλάνοι** refers especially to his
frequent journeys to Thebes while the
negotiations were going on, and also
to his other embassies (cf. § 244).—
τὰ πολλὰ, the many.
10. **διέσυρε**: see the general ridi-
cule of his decrees in Aesch. III.

Καίτοι πολλοὶ παρ' ὑμῖν, ἄνδρες Ἀθηναῖοι, γεγό- **219**
νασι ῥήτορες ἔνδοξοι καὶ μεγάλοι πρὸ ἐμοῦ, Καλλίστρατος ἐκεῖνος, Ἀριστοφῶν, Κέφαλος, Θρασύβου-
λος, ἕτεροι μυρίοι· ἀλλ' ὅμως οὐδεὶς πώποτε τούτων
διὰ παντὸς ἔδωκεν ἑαυτὸν εἰς οὐδὲν τῇ πόλει, ἀλλ' ὁ **5**
μὲν γράφων οὐκ ἂν ἐπρέσβευσεν, ὁ δὲ πρεσβεύων οὐκ
ἂν ἔγραψεν. ὑπέλειπε γὰρ αὐτῶν ἕκαστος ἑαυτῷ
ἅμα μὲν ῥᾳστώνην, ἅμα δ' εἴ τι γένοιτ' ἀναφοράν.
τί οὖν ; εἴποι τις ἂν, σὺ τοσοῦτον ὑπερῆρας ῥώμῃ **220**
καὶ τόλμῃ ὥστε πάντα ποιεῖν αὐτός ; οὐ ταῦτα
λέγω, ἀλλ' οὕτως ἐπεπείσμην μέγαν εἶναι τὸν κατ-
ειληφότα κίνδυνον τὴν πόλιν ὥστ' οὐκ ἐδόκει μοι
χώραν οὐδὲ πρόνοιαν οὐδεμίαν τῆς ἰδίας ἀσφαλείας **5**

100¹⁻³. This remark may perhaps refer to the fierce criticism of the terms of the alliance with Thebes (III. 141—143).—**τί ἀπειργάσατο**: the position of τί is emphatic : cf. σκέψασθε πῶς, § 235⁴. We should expect συνέχεια etc. to be in the accus. by the usual attraction; but they are far more expressive as they stand.

§§ **219—221** were spoken while the clerk was preparing to read the letters of Philip.

§ **219.** 2. **Καλλίστρατος** : the famous orator whose eloquence is said to have inspired Demosthenes (as a boy) to devote himself to oratory : see note on § 99⁸.
3. **Ἀριστοφῶν**: mentioned in § 70⁵.
—**Κέφαλος**: see § 251.—**Θρασύβου-λος**, of Collytus, who served under his distinguished namesake in the Restoration of 403 B.C. (XXIV. 134). He was afterwards a warm friend of Thebes : see Aesch. III. 138, ἀνὴρ ἐν Θήβαις πιστευθεὶς ὡς οὐδεὶς ἕτερος.
5. **διὰ παντός**, *throughout*; like ἁπλῶς, §§ 88⁸, 179⁷.
6. **οὐκ ἂν ἐπρέσβευσεν...ἔγραψεν**: both iterative (M.T. 162): we often use *would* in such iterative expressions,

with no potential force ; as *he would often tell me stories* (see M.T. 249).
8. **ῥᾳστώνην**, *enjoyment of ease.*—**εἴ τι γένοιτ' ἀναφοράν**, i.e. *some retreat in case of accident* : εἴ τι γένοιτο depends on an apodosis implied in ἀναφοράν ; cf. Aeschyl. Sept. 1015, ὡς ὄντ' ἀναστατῆρα...εἰ μὴ θεῶν τις ἐμποδὼν ἔστη δορί (M.T. 480). The direct form, ἐάν τι γένηται, might have been used : see Aesch. II. 104, αὐτοῖς κατέλιπον τὴν εἰς τὸ ἀφανὲς ἀναφορὰν ἂν μὴ πείθωμεν. The meaning comes from the middle ἀναφέρεσθαι, *to carry oneself back.*
§ **220.** 1. **ὑπερῆρας**; *did you excel?* absolutely, or possibly sc. τούτους.—**ῥώμῃ** : i.e. so as to need no ἀναφορά (§ 219⁸).
3. **οὕτως ἐπεπείσμην**, *I had so thoroughly convinced myself.*
4. **ἐδόκει** is first personal (sc. ὁ κίνδυνος) ; then (without οὐκ) understood as impersonal with ἀγαπητὸν εἶναι.
5. **χώραν διδόναι** is *to allow room* for considerations of personal safety; πρόνοιαν διδόναι is *to allow thought* for this. We should say *to allow room for thought.*

302 διδόναι, ἀλλ' ἀγαπητὸν εἶναι εἰ μηδὲν παραλείπων
τις ἃ δεῖ πράξειεν. ἐπεπείσμην δ' ὑπὲρ ἐμαυτοῦ, 221
τυχὸν μὲν ἀναισθητῶν, ὅμως δ' ἐπεπείσμην, μήτε
γράφοντ' ἂν ἐμοῦ γράψαι βέλτιον μηδένα μήτε
πράττοντα πρᾶξαι, μήτε πρεσβεύοντα πρεσβεῦσαι
προθυμότερον μηδὲ δικαιότερον. διὰ ταῦτ' ἐν πᾶσιν 5
ἐμαυτὸν ἔταττον. λέγε τὰς ἐπιστολὰς τὰς τοῦ
Φιλίππου.

ΕΠΙΣΤΟΛΑΙ.

Εἰς ταῦτα κατέστησε Φίλιππον ἡ ἐμὴ πολιτεία, 222
Αἰσχίνη· ταύτην τὴν φωνὴν ἐκεῖνος ἀφῆκε, πολλοὺς
καὶ θρασεῖς τὰ πρὸ τούτων τῇ πόλει ἐπαιρόμενος
λόγους. ἀνθ' ὧν δικαίως ἐστεφανούμην ὑπὸ τουτωνί,
καὶ σὺ παρὼν οὐκ ἀντέλεγες, ὁ δὲ γραψάμενος 5
Διώνδας τὸ μέρος τῶν ψήφων οὐκ ἔλαβεν. Καί μοι
λαβὲ ταῦτα τὰ ψηφίσματα τὰ τότε μὲν ἀποπεφευγότα, ὑπὸ τούτου δ' οὐδὲ γραφέντα.

6. **ἀγαπητὸν...πράξειεν** : in the
direct form, ἀγαπητόν ἐστιν ἐάν τις...
ἃ δεῖ πράξῃ, *we must be content*
(impers.) *if we* (*shall*) *do our duty,*
omitting nothing.
7. **ἃ δεῖ** = τὰ δέοντα, *our duty* :
ἃ is here definite ; but with a slight
change in the view it might have been
ἃ ἂν δέῃ or ἃ δέοι (Dobree's conjecture),
with conditional force.
§ 221. 2. **τυχὸν**, *perhaps*, acc. abs.
(M.T. 851).—**ἀναισθητῶν**, *senseless-
ly*: I follow Vömel, Bekk., and West.
in this reading, though ἀναίσθητον
(adv.) has better MS. authority.—**ὅμως**,
nevertheless, with reference to ἀναισθητῶν.—**μήτε...γράψαι**: the direct
form would be οὔτ' ἂν ἐμοῦ γράψειε
βέλτιον οὐδείς : for μή thus used with
the infin. in *or. obl.*, see μή, B. 5, C.
ἂν belongs to γράψαι, πρᾶξαι, and
πρεσβεῦσαι, and βέλτιον to γράψαι and
πρᾶξαι.

§ 222. 3. **ἐπαιρόμενος**, of *raising*
(as a threat). Harpocr.: ἀντὶ τοῦ
ἐπανατεινόμενος, Δημοσθένης ἐν τῷ
ὑπὲρ Κτησιφῶντος. Cf. XIX. 153,
οὐδὲν ἂν ὑμῖν εἶχεν ἀνατείνασθαι φο-
βερόν (of threats of Philip) ; and Eur.
Iph. T. 1484, παύσω δὲ λόγχην ἣν
ἐπαίρομαι ξένοις (of a spear uplifted to
strike). (Bl.) ἐπαιρόμενος is imperfect, as is shown by τὰ πρὸ τούτων.
5. **παρὼν**, *though present* : see
§§ 83⁶ and 117⁷.
6. **Διώνδας** : mentioned with con-
tempt in § 249⁹.—**τὸ μέρος** (sc. πέμπτον), see notes on §§ 103², 266⁶.
7. **ψηφίσματα** : for the plural see
note on § 223⁵.—**ἀποπεφευγότα**, *acquitted* (on the γραφὴ παρανόμων) : τὸ
φεῦγον ψήφισμα, XXIII. 58, is *the
decree on trial*.
8. **γραφέντα**, *indicted* : cf. γραφέντα, *proposed*, § 86⁴. See note on
§ 56⁴.

ΨΗΦΙΣΜΑΤΑ.

Ταυτὶ τὰ ψηφίσματ', ἄνδρες Ἀθηναῖοι, τὰς αὐτὰς 223
συλλαβὰς καὶ ταὐτὰ ῥήματ' ἔχει ἅπερ πρότερον μὲν
Ἀριστόνικος νῦν δὲ Κτησιφῶν γέγραφεν οὑτοσί.
καὶ ταῦτ' Αἰσχίνης οὔτ' ἐδίωξεν αὐτὸς οὔτε τῷ
γραψαμένῳ συγκατηγόρησεν. καίτοι τότε τὸν Δη- 5
μομέλη τὸν ταῦτα γράφοντα καὶ τὸν Ὑπερείδην,
εἴπερ ἀληθῆ μου νῦν κατηγορεῖ, μᾶλλον ἀν εἰκότως ἢ
τόνδ' ἐδίωκεν. διὰ τί; ὅτι τῷδε μὲν ἔστ' ἀνενεγκεῖν 224
ἐπ' ἐκείνους καὶ τὰς τῶν δικαστηρίων γνώσεις καὶ
303 τὸ τοῦτον αὐτὸν ἐκείνων μὴ κατηγορηκέναι ταὐτὰ
γραψάντων ἅπερ οὗτος νῦν, καὶ τὸ τοὺς νόμους
μηκέτ' ἐᾶν περὶ τῶν οὕτω πραχθέντων κατηγορεῖν, 5
καὶ πόλλ' ἕτερα· τότε δ' αὐτὸ τὸ πρᾶγμ' ἀν ἐκρίνετ'

§ **223.** 1--3. For the questions
concerning the decree of Aristonicus
and δευτέρου κηρύγματος in § 83⁵, see
notes on that passage and on § 120⁴.
5. **συγκατηγόρησεν**, *aided in the
accusation* (as συνήγορος). —**Δημομέλη**
...' **Ὑπερείδην**: the two names probably
indicate a decree moved by Demomeles (cousin of Demosthenes) and
amended or enlarged by Hyperides.
Such double or treble bills were
common (see C. I. Att. II. no. 469;
whence τὰ ψηφίσματα in § 222⁷.
7. **εἴπερ—νῦν κατηγορεῖ**: the simple present condition is correct here,
and more effective than G. H. Schaefer's κατηγόρει. The meaning is, *if
he is now accusing me honestly, he
would have had more reason for
prosecuting* (i.e. if he had prosecuted)
*D. and H. then than he has for
prosecuting Ctes. now.*
§ **224.** 1. **τῷδε** (like τόνδε andτῷδε
in § 223⁸) is Ctesiphon, who is οὗτος
in 4; while Aeschines is τοῦτον αὐτὸν in 3.

5. **μηκέτ' ἐᾶν...κατηγορεῖν**: the
principle that "no man can be twice
put in jeopardy for the same offence"
is distinctly stated in the Attic law:
see XX. 147, οἱ νόμοι δ' οὐκ ἐῶσι δὶς
πρὸς τὸν αὐτὸν περὶ τῶν αὐτῶν οὔτε
δίκας οὔτ' εὐθύνας οὔτε διαδικασίαν οὔτ'
ἄλλο τοιοῦτον οὐδὲν εἶναι, and XXIV.
55. This could here be urged by
Ctesiphon as a moral, though not as
a legal, argument. Aeschines is prosecuting him now on the ground of
charges against Demosthenes which
were indirectly declared false by the
acquittal of Hyperides eight years
before,—charges for which he did not
similarly prosecute H. then and for
which he could not legally prosecute
Dem. now. This is all an answer to
διὰ τί; (which refers to § 223 (end)).
—**τῶν οὕτω πραχθέντων**, *matters so
settled* (as these charges against Dem.):
see XXXVI. 60, δικάζεσθαι τῶν οὕτω
πραχθέντων.

ἐφ᾽ αὑτοῦ, πρίν τι τούτων προλαβεῖν. ἀλλ᾽ οὐκ ἦν, 225
οἶμαι, τότε ὃ νυνὶ ποιεῖν, ἐκ παλαιῶν χρόνων καὶ
ψηφισμάτων πολλῶν ἐκλέξαντα ἃ μήτε προῄδει
μηδεὶς μήτ᾽ ἂν ᾠήθη τήμερον ῥηθῆναι, διαβάλλειν,
καὶ μετενεγκόντα τοὺς χρόνους καὶ προφάσεις ἀντὶ 5
τῶν ἀληθῶν ψευδεῖς μεταθέντα τοῖς πεπραγμένοις
δοκεῖν τι λέγειν. οὐκ ἦν τότε ταῦτα, ἀλλ᾽ ἐπὶ τῆς 226
ἀληθείας, ἐγγὺς τῶν ἔργων, ἔτι μεμνημένων ὑμῶν καὶ
μόνον οὐκ ἐν ταῖς χερσὶν ἕκαστ᾽ ἐχόντων, πάντες
ἐγίγνοντ᾽ ἂν οἱ λόγοι. διόπερ τοὺς παρ᾽ αὐτὰ τὰ
πράγματ᾽ ἐλέγχους φυγὼν νῦν ἥκει, ῥητόρων ἀγῶνα 5
νομίζων, ὥς γ᾽ ἐμοὶ δοκεῖ, καὶ οὐχὶ τῶν πεπολιτευμένων ἐξέτασιν ποιήσειν ὑμᾶς, καὶ λόγου κρίσιν οὐχὶ
τοῦ τῇ πόλει συμφέροντος ἔσεσθαι.
Εἶτα σοφίζεται, καὶ φησὶ προσήκειν ἧς μὲν οἰκο- 227

---

7. **ἐφ᾽ αὑτοῦ**, on its own merits:
i.e. before any judgment of the court
had been passed upon the case.
§ 225. 2. ὃ νυνὶ ποιεῖν : all MSS.
except Σ have ποιεῖ for ποιεῖν.—
παλαιῶν χρόνων : i.e. the time of the
peace of Philocrates, about which
Aeschines (III. 58—78) had cited
many decrees which had no real bearing on the argument.
4. **μήτ᾽ ἂν...ῥηθῆναι**, or thought
would be mentioned to-day (ῥηθῆναι
ἂν = ῥηθείη ἂν) : see M.T. 220¹. The
negatives μήτε etc. show that the
antecedent of ἃ is indefinite.—**διαβάλλειν**, to misrepresent (cast reproach
upon) the case.
5. **προφάσεις**, grounds for action,
whether true or false. See note on
§ 178¹².
Demosthenes still clings to his plea
that the story of the Peace of Philocrates is ancient history.
§ 226. 1. ἐπὶ τῆς ἀληθείας : cf.
§ 17².
3. **ἐν ταῖς χερσὶν** : for the figure

Westermann compares mani-festus.—
πάντες οἱ λόγοι, i.e. the whole discussion.
4. **τοὺς...φυγὼν** : cf. § 15².
5. **ῥητόρων ἀγῶνα** : cf. Thuc. III.
67²⁸, ποιήσατε δὲ τοῖς "Ελλησι παρά-
δειγμα οὐ λόγων τοὺς ἀγῶνας προθή-
σοντες ἀλλ᾽ ἔργων. Weil quotes XIX.
217 : οὐδὲ γὰρ ῥητόρων οὐδὲ λόγων
κρίσιν ὑμᾶς τήμερον...προσήκει ποιεῖν.
7. **λόγου ... συμφέροντος** : λόγου
κρίσιν is a trial of eloquence. Cf. the
verbal forms λόγον κρίνειν and τὸ τῇ
πόλει συμφέρον κρίνειν.
With § 226 the orator ends his
grand comparison (begun in § 139)
between the part played by Aeschines
in rousing the Amphissian war and
his own part in uniting Athens and
Thebes against Philip.
§§ 227—296. At § 226 the proper
defence ends, with the account of the
alliance with Thebes. The remainder
of the speech, before the epilogue, is
devoted to a reply to three arguments
of Aeschines, one comparing this trial

θεν ἥκετ' ἔχοντες δόξης περὶ ἡμῶν ἀμελῆσαι, ὥσπερ
δ', ὅταν οἰόμενοι περιεῖναι χρήματά τῳ λογίζησθε, ἂν
καθαιρῶσιν αἱ ψῆφοι καὶ μηδὲν περιῇ, συγχωρεῖτε,
οὕτω καὶ νῦν τοῖς ἐκ τοῦ λόγου φαινομένοις προσθέ- 5
σθαι. θεάσασθε τοίνυν ὡς σαθρὸν, ὡς ἔοικεν, ἐστὶ
φύσει πᾶν ὅ τι ἂν μὴ δικαίως ᾖ πεπραγμένον. ἐκ 228
γὰρ αὐτοῦ τοῦ σοφοῦ τούτου παραδείγματος ὡμο-
λόγηκε νῦν γ' ἡμᾶς ὑπάρχειν ἐγνωσμένους ἐμὲ μὲν
λέγειν ὑπὲρ τῆς πατρίδος, αὐτὸν δ' ὑπὲρ Φιλίπ-

to an investigation of an account
(§ 227–251), a second charging Demosthenes with being ill-starred (§§ 252
—275), and a third charging him
with being a crafty rhetorician (§§ 276
—296).

In §§ 227—251 the orator refers to
the exhortation of Aeschines to the
judges (59—61) to cast aside any
prejudices in favour of Demosthenes
which they may have, and to proceed
as they would if they were examining
a long account, prepared to accept
any result which the reckoning may
bring out. Aeschines refers here
only to the facts concerning the
peace of Philocrates; but Demosthenes chooses to apply the remarks
to his whole political life. While
Aeschines referred only to the debit
side of the account, Demosthenes
speaks of both sides, and especially
of what stands on the credit side of
his own account with the state,
including credit for preventing calamities by his judicious policy. He
ends (§ 251) by turning against
Aeschines the case of Cephalus,
which had been brought up against
himself.

§ **227.** 1. **εἶτα σοφίζεται,** *then
he puts on airs of wisdom,* or *becomes
very subtle,* with the same sarcasm as
in σοφοῦ παραδείγματος, § 228².

2. **ἀμελῆσαι,** *disregard*: Aeschines

(III. 60) says, μήτ' ἀπογνώτω μηδὲν
μήτε καταγνώτω πρὶν ἀκούσῃ.

3. **περιεῖναι χρήματά τῳ,** *that
one has a balance in his favour.*—
λογίζησθε: cf. Aesch. III. 59, καθεζώ-
μεθα ἐπὶ τοὺς λογισμούς.—**ἂν καθαιρῶσιν…περιῇ,** *if the counters are decisive
and there is no balance remaining.*
With most recent editors, I follow Σ¹
and read καθαιρῶσιν, the common text
having καθαραὶ ὦσιν, which was referred to the counters being *cleared
off* from the abacus (ἄβαξ or ἀβάκιον):
cf. § 231³. This was a reckoning-
board, on which counters (originally
ψῆφοι, *pebbles*) represented units,
tens, etc., according to their position.
See the article *Abacus* in Smith's
Dict. of Ant. Aeschines says (59),
ἐπινεύσας ἀληθὲς εἶναι ὅ τι ἂν αὐτὸς ὁ
λογισμὸς αἱρῇ, *whatever the account
proves* (cf. αἱρεῖν τινα κλέπτοντα), and
there is a strong presumption that
Demosthenes uses a similar expression in his reply. Köchly quotes
Dion. Hal. Ant. Rom. VII. 36, ὅ τι
δ' ἂν αἱ πλείους ψῆφοι καθαιρῶσι, τοῦτο
ποιεῖν (and again, slightly changed,
in 39): here the meaning *determine* is
beyond question.

5. **προσθέσθαι,** *acquiesce in*: cf.
προσθεμένην, § 203⁵.

7. **ᾖ πεπραγμένον**: see § 178¹⁵,
and note on § 178¹⁰.

§ **228.** 3. **ἡμᾶς** (so Σ)...**ἐγνω-**

304 πoυ· oὐ γὰρ ἂν μεταπείθειν ὑμᾶς ἐζήτει μὴ τοιαύτης 5
οὔσης τῆς ὑπαρχούσης ὑπολήψεως περὶ ἑκατέρου.

καὶ μὴν ὅτι γ' οὐ δίκαια λέγει μεταθέσθαι ταύτην 229
τὴν δόξαν ἀξιῶν, ἐγὼ διδάξω ῥαδίως, οὐ τιθεὶς
ψήφους (οὐ γάρ ἐστιν ὁ τῶν πραγμάτων οὗτος
λογισμός), ἀλλ' ἀναμιμνήσκων ἕκαστ' ἐν βραχέσι,
λογισταῖς ἅμα καὶ μάρτυσι τοῖς ἀκούουσιν ὑμῖν 5
χρώμενος. ἡ γὰρ ἐμὴ πολιτεία, ἧς οὗτος κατηγορεῖ,
ἀντὶ μὲν τοῦ Θηβαίους μετὰ Φιλίππου συνεμβαλεῖν
εἰς τὴν χώραν, ὃ πάντες ᾤοντο, μεθ' ἡμῶν παραταξαμένους ἐκεῖνον κωλύειν ἐποίησεν· ἀντὶ δὲ τοῦ ἐν τῇ 230
Ἀττικῇ τὸν πόλεμον εἶναι, ἑπτακόσια στάδια ἀπὸ
τῆς πόλεως ἐπὶ τοῖς Βοιωτῶν ὁρίοις γενέσθαι· ἀντὶ
δὲ τοῦ τοὺς λῃστὰς ἡμᾶς φέρειν καὶ ἄγειν ἐκ τῆς
Εὐβοίας, ἐν εἰρήνῃ τὴν Ἀττικὴν ἐκ θαλάττης εἶναι 5

σμένους, that it is assumed that we
(Aesch. and myself) have been thus
judged (have this reputation) : in the
direct form ὑπάρχομεν ἐγνωσμένοι.
It appears that ἔγνωσμαι is always
passive (see Veitch). The personal
construction is like that of Ar. Nub.
918, γνωσθήσει τοί ποτ' Ἀθηναίοις οἷα
διδάσκεις τοὺς ἀνοήτους, you shall be
shown (for it shall be shown).
5. μὴ τοιαύτης οὔσης = εἰ μὴ
τοιαύτη ἦν. The unique reading of
the Oxyrh. papyrus, μὴ τοιαύτης
ὑπαρχούσης, is suggestive.
§ 229. 2. οὐ τιθεὶς ψήφους (continuing the figure of § 227), i.e. not
by mere arithmetic or book-keep-
ing.
3. οὐ γάρ.. λογισμός, for that is
not the way to reckon affairs of state.
οὗτος is predicate.
4. ἀναμιμνήσκων ἕκαστ' : he
renders his account, not by setting
his services against his sins, but by
setting the positive gain from his
public policy against the calamities

which would have resulted from the
opposite policy.
5. λογισταῖς : in the double sense
of computers and comptrollers of
accounts : see note on § 117⁸.—τοῖς
ἀκούουσιν : addressed equally to the
court and the spectators.
7. μετὰ and συν- emphasize one
another.
9. κωλύειν : present, of the whole
business of checking Philip; the aor.
συνεμβαλεῖν (7) of an incursion.
§ 230. 2. ἑπτακόσια στάδια,
about 80 miles : see note on § 195⁵.
3. γενέσθαι : sc. ἐποίησε. By
ὁρίοις he means the further confines
of Boeotia.
4. λῃστὰς : see note on § 145⁶,
and for pirates in general [VII.] 3, 4,
14, 15. The rescue of Oreus and
Eretria from Philip (§§ 79, 87) prevented Euboea from being a nest for
plunderers.—φέρειν καὶ ἄγειν : the
common term for general plundering.
5. ἐκ θαλάττης, on the side of the
sea, with reference to ἐκ τῆς Εὐβοίας.

πάντα τὸν πόλεμον· ἀντὶ δὲ τοῦ τὸν Ἑλλήσποντον
ἔχειν Φίλιππον, λαβόντα Βυζάντιον, συμπολεμεῖν
τοὺς Βυζαντίους μεθ' ἡμῶν πρὸς ἐκεῖνον. ἀρά σοι 231
ψήφοις ὅμοιος ὁ τῶν ἔργων λογισμὸς φαίνεται; ἢ
δεῖν ἀντανελεῖν ταῦτα, ἀλλ' οὐχ ὅπως τὸν ἄπαντα
χρόνον μνημονευθήσεται σκέψασθαι; καὶ οὐκέτι
προστίθημι ὅτι τῆς μὲν ὠμότητος, ἢν ἐν οἷς καθάπαξ 5
τινῶν κύριος κατέστη Φίλιππος ἔστιν ἰδεῖν, ἑτέροις
πειραθῆναι συνέβη, τῆς δὲ φιλανθρωπίας, ἢν τὰ
λοιπὰ τῶν πραγμάτων ἐκεῖνος περιβαλλόμενος
ἐπλάττετο, ὑμεῖς καλῶς ποιοῦντες τοὺς καρποὺς
κεκόμισθε. ἀλλ' ἐῶ ταῦτα. 10
Καὶ μὴν οὐδὲ ταῦτ' εἰπεῖν ὀκνήσω, ὅτι ὁ τὸν 232
ῥήτορα βουλόμενος δικαίως ἐξετάζειν καὶ μὴ συκο-
305 φαντεῖν οὐκ ἂν οἷα σὺ νῦν ἔλεγες τοιαῦτα κατηγόρει,

---

6. τὸν Ἑλλήσποντον: for the
Hellespont and Byzantium in 340
B.C. see §§ 80, 87, 88, 93, 94, and
Hist. §§ 53—55.

§ 231. 2. ψήφοις ὅμοιος, cf.
κόμαι Χαρίτεσσιν ὁμοῖαι, Il. XVII. 51.

3. ἀντανελεῖν ταῦτα, to strike
these off (the services of § 230) in
balancing the account, as ψῆφοι would
be removed from the ἀβάκιον.

4. οὐκέτι προστίθημι, I do not go
on (ἔτι) to add, i.e. to the credit side
of the account.

5. ἐν οἷς...κατέστη: as in the
cases of Olynthus, Thessaly, and
Phocis.

7. φιλανθρωπίας: especially Philip's easy terms with Athens after
Chaeronea, which were the indirect
result of the firm and dignified
attitude of Demosthenes and his
friends. See Hist. § 68.

8. περιβαλλόμενος: the common
figure of investing oneself with anything (like a garment), hence ac-
quiring.

9. καλῶς ποιοῦντες, by the bless-
ing of Heaven: cf. I. 28, ὧν καλῶς
ποιοῦντες ἔχουσι, and καλῶς ποιοῦσι,
XXI. 212. This phrase sometimes
means fortunately (as here), approaching in sense the more common εὖ
πράσσειν, to be prosperous: sometimes
doing as one should, as in XXI. 2,
καλῶς καὶ τὰ δίκαια ποιῶν ὁ δῆμος
οὕτως ὠργίσθη, and LVII. 6, καλῶς
ποιοῦντες τοὺς ἠδικημένους σεσώκατε.
To show the distinction between
καλῶς ποιῶν and εὖ πράσσων, Dissen
quotes XX. 110, ὅτε δ' ὑμεῖς καλῶς
ποιοῦντες...ἄμεινον ἐκείνων πράττετε.
The active expressions εὖ ποιεῖν and
κακῶς ποιεῖν are entirely distinct from
καλῶς ποιεῖν.

§§ 232—241. We have here an
account of the power of Athens under
the leadership of Demosthenes, compared with her earlier resources.

§ 232. 3. τοιαῦτα: cognate (sc.
κατηγορήματα).

4. παραδείγματα, like the illustration just discussed (§ 227): cf. § 228².

παραδείγματα πλάττων καὶ ῥήματα καὶ σχήματα
μιμούμενος (πάνυ γὰρ παρὰ τοῦτο—οὐχ ὁρᾷς;— 5
γέγονε τὰ τῶν Ἑλλήνων, εἰ τουτὶ τὸ ῥῆμα ἀλλὰ μὴ
τουτὶ διελέχθην ἐγώ, ἢ δευρὶ τὴν χεῖρα ἀλλὰ μὴ
δευρὶ παρήνεγκα), ἀλλ᾽ ἐπ᾽ αὐτῶν τῶν ἔργων ἂν 233
ἐσκόπει τίνας εἶχεν ἀφορμὰς ἡ πόλις καὶ τίνας δυνάμεις, ὅτ᾽ εἰς τὰ πράγματ᾽ εἰσῄειν, καὶ τίνας συνήγαγον
αὐτῇ μετὰ ταῦτ᾽ ἐπιστὰς ἐγώ, καὶ πῶς εἶχε τὰ τῶν
ἐναντίων. εἶτ᾽ εἰ μὲν ἐλάττους ἐποίησα τὰς δυνάμεις, 5
παρ᾽ ἐμοὶ τἀδίκημ᾽ ἂν ἐδείκνυεν ὄν, εἰ δὲ πολλῷ
μείζους, οὐκ ἂν ἐσυκοφάντει. ἐπειδὴ δὲ σὺ τοῦτο
πέφευγας, ἐγὼ ποιήσω· καὶ σκοπεῖτε εἰ δικαίως
χρήσομαι τῷ λόγῳ.

Δύναμιν μὲν τοίνυν εἶχεν ἡ πόλις τοὺς νησιώτας, 234
οὐχ ἅπαντας, ἀλλὰ τοὺς ἀσθενεστάτους· οὔτε γὰρ

—ῥήματα...μιμούμενος : besides the *expressions* (ῥήματα) repeated by Aeschines (probably with no little exaggeration) in III. 166, of which he asks (167), ταῦτα δὲ τί ἐστιν, ὦ κίναδος; ῥήματα ἢ θαύματα; we have in 209, ποῖ φύγω, ἄνδρες Ἀθηναῖοι; περιγράψατέ με· οὐκ ἔστιν ὅποι ἀναπτήσομαι, quoted from Demosthenes. See other quotations in III. 71 and 72, especially ἀπορρῆξαι τῆς εἰρήνης τὴν συμμαχίαν. Imitations of *gestures* (σχήματα) are, of course, harder to detect; but there is a plain one in III. 167, κύκλῳ περιδινῶν σεαυτόν.
5. παρὰ τοῦτο γέγονε, depend on this. See Cic. Orat. 8, 27 : itaque se purgans iocatur Demosthenes : negat in eo positas esse fortunas Graeciae, hoc an illo verbo usus sit, et huc an illuc manum porrexerit.— οὐχ ὁρᾷς; cf. § 266⁷.
6. μὴ τουτὶ : in the second member of an alternative indirect question, μή can be used as well as οὐ. (G. 1609.)

§ 233. 1. ἐπ᾽...ἔργων : cf. ἐπὶ τῆς ἀληθείας, § 226¹.
2. ἀφορμάς, *means* (for war): ἀφορμή is properly *a starting-point*, or *something to set out from* (ἀφ᾽ ὧν τις ὁρμᾶται), as in Thuc. I. 90, τήν τε Πελοπόννησον πᾶσιν ἔφασαν ἱκανὴν εἶναι ἀναχώρησίν τε καὶ ἀφορμήν.— δυνάμεις : here in the same general sense as δύναμιν in § 234¹.
3. ὅτ᾽...εἰσῄειν : before the renewal of the war in 340 B.C. Cf. § 60⁴.
8. εἰ...λόγῳ : cf. § 252⁹, and XXIII. 24, ὡς ἁπλῶς καὶ δικαίως χρήσομαι τῷ λόγῳ.
§ 234. 1. δύναμιν here refers to sources of *military power*, like allies, even when no actual troops are included : see ὁπλίτην δ᾽, ἱππέα οὐδένα (5). Both δυνάμεις and δύναμις, however, may denote troops : cf. § 237⁶, τῶν πολιτικῶν δυνάμεων, and 247⁵ ; so Xen. An. I. 2, ἔχει δύναμιν καὶ πεζὴν καὶ ἱππικὴν καὶ ναυτικήν.
2. οὔτε...ἦν : this refers to the early part of 340 B.C., when Chios

Χίος οὔτε Ῥόδος οὔτε Κέρκυρα μεθ' ἡμῶν ἦν·
χρημάτων δὲ σύνταξιν εἰς πέντε καὶ τετταράκοντα
τάλαντα, καὶ ταῦτ' ἦν προεξειλεγμένα· ὁπλίτην δ', 5
ἱππέα πλὴν τῶν οἰκείων οὐδένα. ὁ δὲ πάντων καὶ
φοβερώτατον καὶ μάλισθ' ὑπὲρ τῶν ἐχθρῶν, οὗτοι
παρεσκευάκεσαν τοὺς περιχώρους πάντας ἔχθρας ἢ
φιλίας ἐγγυτέρω, Μεγαρέας, Θηβαίους, Εὐβοέας. τὰ 235
μὲν τῆς πόλεως οὕτως ὑπῆρχεν ἔχοντα, καὶ οὐδεὶς
ἂν ἔχοι παρὰ ταῦτ' εἰπεῖν ἀλλ' οὐδέν· τὰ δὲ τοῦ
Φιλίππου, πρὸς ὃν ἦν ἡμῖν ὁ ἀγών, σκέψασθε πῶς.
πρῶτον μὲν ἦρχε τῶν ἀκολουθούντων αὐτὸς αὐτο- 5
κράτωρ, ὃ τῶν εἰς τὸν πόλεμον μέγιστόν ἐστιν
ἁπάντων· εἶθ' οὗτοι τὰ ὅπλ' εἶχον ἐν ταῖς χερσὶν
ἀεί· ἔπειτα χρημάτων εὐπόρει, καὶ ἔπραττεν ἃ
306 δόξειεν αὐτῷ, οὐ προλέγων ἐν τοῖς ψηφίσμασιν,

and Rhodes were independent of
Athens as the result of the Social
War (357—355 B.C.), but Byzantium,
which then followed Chios and
Rhodes, had already renewed her
friendship (§ 230[7]): see Hist. §§ 2,
51. Corcyra, the old friend and ally
of Athens, had become hostile to her
before 353 B.C. (see XXIV. 202).

4. **χρημάτων σύνταξιν**: the payment of the original assessment made
on the Delian confederacy by Aristides
in 478—477 B.C. was first called
φόρος from φέρω, as Thucydides
explains it, οὕτω γὰρ ὠνομάσθη τῶν
χρημάτων ἡ φορά. The First Athenian
Empire made the name odious, so
that, when the new federation was
formed in 378, the term σύνταξις,
agreement, was adopted for the annual
payment.—**πέντε καὶ τετταράκοντα
τάλαντα**: this sorry amount of 45
talents shows the decline of the
power of Athens after the Social
War. The original tribute of 460
talents was raised to 600 under
Pericles (Thuc. II. 13[23]), and (if we

may trust Aesch. II. 175 and Plut.
Arist. 24) to 1200 or 1300 after the
Peace of Nicias, in large part by the
allies commuting personal service for
payments of money (Thuc. I. 99).

5. **προεξειλεγμένα**, *collected in advance*, probably by generals to pay
their mercenaries. Aeschines (II. 71)
speaks of τοὺς περὶ τὸ βῆμα καὶ τὴν
ἐκκλησίαν μισθοφόρους, οἵ τοὺς μὲν
ταλαιπώρους νησιώτας καθ' ἕκαστον
ἐνιαυτὸν ἑξήκοντα τάλαντα εἰσέπρατ-
τον σύνταξιν.—**ὁπλίτην δ', ἱππέα**:
so Σ and L; cf. § 94[b].
7. **οὗτοι**: Aeschines and his party.
8. **παρεσκευάκεσαν...ἐγγυτέρω**: cf.
τοὺς θεοὺς ἵλεως αὐτῷ παρασκευάζειν,
Plat. Leg. 803 E.

§ 235. 2. **οὕτως ὑπῆρχεν ἔχοντα**,
i.e. *this is what we had to depend on.*
9. **οὐ προλέγων ... βουλευόμενος**:
two important advantages of a despotism in war. Athens is not the last
free state which has suffered from the
opposite evils. With this whole
passage compare § 249 and I. 4.

οὐδ' ἐν τῷ φανερῷ βουλευόμενος, οὐδ' ὑπὸ τῶν 10
συκοφαντούντων κρινόμενος, οὐδὲ γραφὰς φεύγων
παρανόμων, οὐδ' ὑπεύθυνος ὢν οὐδενί, ἀλλ' ἁπλῶς
αὐτὸς δεσπότης, ἡγεμών, κύριος πάντων. ἐγὼ δ' ὁ 236
πρὸς τοῦτον ἀντιτεταγμένος (καὶ γὰρ τοῦτ' ἐξετάσαι
δίκαιον) τίνος κύριος ἦν; οὐδενός· αὐτὸ γὰρ τὸ δημηγορεῖν πρῶτον, οὗ μόνου μετεῖχον ἐγώ, ἐξ ἴσου
προὐτίθεθ' ὑμεῖς τοῖς παρ' ἐκείνου μισθαρνοῦσι καὶ 5
ἐμοί, καὶ ὅσ' οὗτοι περιγένοιντ' ἐμοῦ (πολλὰ δ'
ἐγίγνετο ταῦτα, δι' ἣν ἕκαστον τύχοι πρόφασιν),
ταῦθ' ὑπὲρ τῶν ἐχθρῶν ἀπῆτε βεβουλευμένοι. ἀλλ' 237
ὅμως ἐκ τοιούτων ἐλαττωμάτων ἐγὼ συμμάχους μὲν
ὑμῖν ἐποίησα Εὐβοέας, Ἀχαιούς, Κορινθίους, Θηβαίους, Μεγαρέας, Λευκαδίους, Κερκυραίους, ἀφ' ὧν
μύριοι μὲν καὶ πεντακισχίλιοι ξένοι, δισχίλιοι δ' 5
ἱππεῖς, ἄνευ τῶν πολιτικῶν δυνάμεων, συνήχθησαν·
χρημάτων δ' ὅσων ἐδυνήθην ἐγὼ πλείστην συντέλειαν ἐποίησα. εἰ δὲ λέγεις ἢ τὰ πρὸς Θηβαίους 238

§ 236. 4. **πρῶτον**, *to begin with*:
cf. XX. 54, ὁ λόγος πρῶτον αἰσχρός.—
μετ-εῖχον: μετ- implies the *sharing*
of the right which the preceding
clause states.
5. **προὐτίθεθ'**, *offered* (see § 273³):
cf. IV. 1, εἰ προὐτίθετο λέγειν.
6. **ὅσ'**...**περιγένοιντ' ἐμοῦ**, i.e. *as
often as they got the better of me.*
The omitted antecedent of ὅσ' appears
in ταῦθ' (8).
7. **τύχοι** (M.T. 532): sc. γενόμενον.
8. **ταῦθ'**—**βεβουλευμένοι**, i.e. *just
so often had you taken counsel in
the enemy's interest when you left
the Assembly*: ταῦθ' (cognate with
βεβουλευμένοι) are the βουλεύματα in
which περιγένοιντ' ἐμοῦ, and these
counsels you always took in the
enemy's interest. Cf. Thuc. II. 44¹⁵,
ἴσον τι ἢ δίκαιον (sc. βούλευμα) βουλεύ-
εσθαι.

§ 237. 2. **ἐκ τοιούτων ἐλαττωμάτων**, i.e. with such disadvantages at
the outset. —**συμμάχους...ἐποίησα**:
this refers to the grand league against
Philip, formed early in 340 B.C. by
Demosthenes and Callias of Chalcis.
See Hist. § 51 (end). For the
Euboeans see § 79 (above): for
the Euboeans, Peloponnesians, and
Acarnanians see Aesch. III. 95—97.
5. **μύριοι καὶ πεντακισχίλιοι**: this
includes the Theban forces, which
were added a year after the league
was formed.
6. **πολιτικῶν**, *citizen soldiers* (of
the various states).
7. **συντέλειαν**: this term was
applied to the contributions of the new
league, rather than σύνταξις (§ 234⁴):
Aesch. (III. 97) calls them σύνταγμα.
§ 238. The orator here exposes
with great effect one of the most

δίκαια, Αἰσχίνη, ἢ τὰ πρὸς Βυζαντίους ἢ τὰ πρὸς
Εὐβοέας, ἢ περὶ τῶν ἴσων νυνὶ διαλέγει, πρῶτον μὲν
ἀγνοεῖς ὅτι καὶ πρότερον τῶν ὑπὲρ τῶν Ἑλλήνων
ἐκείνων ἀγωνισαμένων τριήρων, τριακοσίων οὐσῶν 5
τῶν πασῶν, τὰς διακοσίας ἡ πόλις παρέσχετο, καὶ
οὐκ ἐλαττοῦσθαι νομίζουσα οὐδὲ κρίνουσα τοὺς ταῦτα
συμβουλεύσαντας οὐδ' ἀγανακτοῦσ' ἐπὶ τούτοις ἑωρᾶτο (αἰσχρὸν γάρ), ἀλλὰ τοῖς θεοῖς ἔχουσα χάριν,
εἰ κοινοῦ κινδύνου τοῖς Ἕλλησι περιστάντος αὐτὴ 10
διπλάσια τῶν ἄλλων εἰς τὴν ἁπάντων σωτηρίαν
παρέσχετο. εἶτα κενὰς χαρίζει χάριτας τουτοισὶ
307 συκοφαντῶν ἐμέ. τί γὰρ νῦν λέγεις οἳ ἐχρῆν πράτ- 239
τειν, ἀλλ' οὐ τότ' ὢν ἐν τῇ πόλει καὶ παρὼν ταῦτ'
ἔγραφες, εἴπερ ἐνεδέχετο παρὰ τοὺς παρόντας καιροὺς, ἐν οἷς οὐχ ὅσ' ἠβουλόμεθα ἀλλ' ὅσα δοίη τὰ
πράγματ' ἔδει δέχεσθαι· ὁ γὰρ ἀντωνούμενος καὶ 5

unlucky blunders of Aeschines (143),
that of charging him with imposing
two-thirds of the expense of the war
on Athens, and only one-third on
Thebes. Aeschines had forgotten
the fleet at Salamis, of which Athens
furnished *two-thirds*!

1, 2. **τὰ δίκαια**, *our rights.*

4. **καὶ πρότερον**, i.e. *once also in
former days.*

5, 6. **τριακοσίων, διακοσίας**: the
numbers of the ships at Salamis are
variously given; but nearly all agree
in making the Athenian fleet about
two-thirds of the whole. Aeschylus,
who was in the battle, is our best
authority when (Pers. 339) he gives
the total as 310, and Demosthenes
nearly agrees with him. Herodotus
(VIII. 1, 44, 48, 61) gives the total
as 378 (the items giving 366), the
Athenians having 200, of which they
lent 20 to the Chalcidians. The
Athenian orator in Thucydides (I.

74⁶) gives the total as 400 and the
Athenian ships as *nearly two-thirds.*

7. **ἐλαττοῦσθαι**, *that they had less
than their rights.*

9. **αἰσχρόν**: sc. **ἂν ἦν.—ἔχουσα**
goes with **ἑωρᾶτο** like the preceding
νομίζουσα, κρίνουσα, and **ἀγανακτοῦσ'**.

§ **239.** 2. **παρών**, i.e. in the Assembly, as Aesch. regularly was: see
§ 273¹.

3. **εἴπερ ἐνεδέχετο**: sc. ταῦτα
γράφειν. —**παρά...καιρούς**, *in the
crises through which we were then
living.*

4. **οὐχ ὅσ'...πράγματ'**, *not all
that we wanted* (continuously), *but
all that circumstances* (on each occasion) *allowed us* (M.T. 532). **οὐχ
ὅσα βουλόμεθα** would have meant
*not all that we wanted in each
case.*

5. **ἀντωνούμενος** (conative), *bidding
against us* (*trying to buy*). Cf. § 247⁸.

ταχὺ τοὺς παρ᾽ ἡμῶν ἀπελαυνομένους προσδεξόμενος καὶ χρήματα προσθήσων ὑπῆρχεν ἕτοιμος.

Ἀλλ᾽ εἰ νῦν ἐπὶ τοῖς πεπραγμένοις κατηγορίας 240
ἔχω, τί ἂν οἴεσθε, εἰ τότ᾽ ἐμοῦ περὶ τούτων ἀκριβολογουμένου ἀπῆλθον αἱ πόλεις καὶ προσέθεντο
Φιλίππῳ, καὶ ἅμ᾽ Εὐβοίας καὶ Θηβῶν καὶ Βυζαντίου κύριος κατέστη, τί ποιεῖν ἂν ἢ τί λέγειν τοὺς 5
ἀσεβεῖς ἀνθρώπους τουτουσί; οὐχ ὡς ἐξεδόθησαν; 241
οὐχ ὡς ἀπηλάθησαν βουλόμενοι μεθ᾽ ὑμῶν εἶναι;
εἶτα τοῦ μὲν Ἑλλησπόντου διὰ Βυζαντίων ἐγκρατὴς καθέστηκε, καὶ τῆς σιτοπομπίας τῆς τῶν Ἑλλήνων κύριος, πόλεμος δ᾽ ὅμορος καὶ βαρὺς εἰς τὴν 5
Ἀττικὴν διὰ Θηβαίων κεκόμισται, ἄπλους δ᾽ ἡ
θάλαττα ὑπὸ τῶν ἐκ τῆς Εὐβοίας ὁρμωμένων λῃστῶν
γέγονεν; οὐκ ἂν ταῦτ᾽ ἔλεγον, καὶ πολλά γε πρὸς
τούτοις ἕτερα; πονηρὸν, ἄνδρες Ἀθηναῖοι, πονηρὸν 242
ὁ συκοφάντης ἀεὶ καὶ πανταχόθεν βάσκανον καὶ
φιλαίτιον· τοῦτο δὲ καὶ φύσει κίναδος τἀνθρώπιόν
ἐστιν, οὐδὲν ἐξ ἀρχῆς ὑγιὲς πεποιηκὸς οὐδ᾽ ἐλεύ-

6. **προσδεξόμενος** ... **ἕτοιμος,** *was
ready at hand to receive them and to
pay them too* (**προσ-**) *for coming.*
§ **240.** 1. **νῦν**: opposed to εἰ
τότ᾽...ἀπῆλθον.—**ἐπὶ τοῖς πεπραγμένοις,** i.e. *for what I actually did.*
2. **τί ἂν οἴεσθε** : ποιεῖν would
naturally follow here, ἄν having its
common place before οἴεσθε (M.T.
220¹): cf. § 225⁴. But the long protasis εἰ τότ᾽...κατέστη causes τί and ἄν
to be repeated with ποιεῖν (5) ; cf.
IX. 35, τί οἴεσθε, ἐπειδὰν...γένηται,
τί ποιήσειν;—**ἀκριβολογουμένου,** *quib-
bling, splitting hairs,* part of the
unreal condition εἰ ἀπῆλθον : the
partic. is temporal.
5. **τί ποιεῖν ἂν ἢ τί λέγειν** represents τί ἐποίουν ἂν ἢ ἔλεγον; cf. § 241⁸.
§ **241.** 1. **οὐχ** : sc. ἔλεγον ἄν.
So in the next line.

3—8. **τοῦ μὲν...λῃστῶν γέγονεν;**
this seems to be a continuation of the
indirect quotation, with οὐκ ἂν ἔλεγον
ὡς understood. But there may be a
change to a direct quotation (not
interrogative) after **εἶτα**, without ὡς,
as Vömel and Westermann take it.
§ **242.** 2. **πανταχόθεν,** *in every
way (from every side).*
3. **φιλαίτιον,** *fond of (malicious)
accusation :* see LVII. 34, τοῦτο γάρ
ἐστιν ὁ συκοφάντης, αἰτιᾶσθαι μὲν
πάντα ἐξελέγξαι δὲ μηδέν. See
§ 189¹.—**καὶ φύσει κίναδος,** *a beast
by his very nature:* κίναδος nascitur,
συκοφάντης fit.—**τἀνθρώπιον,** *homun-
culus,* refers to *mental* not to *bodily*
stature.
4. **ἐλεύθερον,** i.e. *worthy of a free-
born Athenian :* cf. μηδὲν ἐλεύθερον
φρονῶν, Soph. Phil. 1006.

θερον, αὐτοτραγικὸς πίθηκος, ἀρουραῖος Οἰνόμαος, 5
παράσημος ῥήτωρ. τί γὰρ ἡ σὴ δεινότης εἰς ὄνησιν ἥκει τῇ πατρίδι; νῦν ἡμῖν λέγεις περὶ τῶν 243
παρεληλυθότων; ὥσπερ ἂν εἴ τις ἰατρὸς ἀσθενοῦσι
308 μὲν τοῖς κάμνουσιν εἰσιὼν μὴ λέγοι μηδὲ δεικνύοι δι'
ὧν ἀποφεύξονται τὴν νόσον, ἐπειδὴ δὲ τελευτήσειέ
τις αὐτῶν καὶ τὰ νομιζόμεν' αὐτῷ φέροιτο, ἀκολουθῶν 5
ἐπὶ τὸ μνῆμα διεξίοι εἰ τὸ καὶ τὸ ἐποίησεν ἄν-

5. **αὐτοτραγικὸς πίθηκος,** a natural tragic ape: Schol. οἴκοθεν καὶ ἀφ' ἑαυτοῦ ἔχει τὸ πιθηκίζεσθαι. αὐτο- seems to have the same force as φύσει in 3 (West.). Harpocr. under τρα- γικὸς πίθηκος has: ἔοικε λέγειν τοῦτο ὁ ῥήτωρ ὡς καὶ περὶ τὴν ὑπόκρισιν ἀτυχοῦντος τοῦ Αἰσχίνου, καὶ μιμουμέ- νου μᾶλλον τραγῳδοὺς ἢ τραγῳδεῖν δυναμένου. Paroem. Gr. I. p. 375: ἐπὶ τῶν παρ' ἀξίαν σεμνυνομένων. These describe both the imitative and the boastful ape. See Arist. Poet. 26. Cf. § 313[8], τραγικὸς Θεοκρίνης.

ἀρουραῖος Οἰνόμαος: see § 180[5,6] and note. Aeschines is called rustic, probably because he "murdered Oeno- maus" at the country Dionysia (τοῖς κατ' ἀγρούς).

6. **παράσημος,** counterfeit: Har- pocr. has ἐκ μεταφορᾶς εἴρηται ἀπὸ τῶν νομισμάτων.

§ 243. 1. **νῦν ἡμῖν λέγεις:** νῦν has great emphasis, and is repeated in 8: is this the time you take to talk to us of the past?

2. **ὥσπερ ἂν** (sc. ποιοίη) **εἰ:** i.e. in talking to us of the past now you act as a physician (would act) if he etc. If ποιοίη had been expressed with ἂν, ἰατρὸς would be its subject. Cf. § 194[4].

3. **τοῖς κάμνουσιν:** the general term for patients, not merely while they are ill (ἀσθενοῦσι) but even after they are dead (ἐπειδὴ τελευτήσειέ τις).

εἰσιών, i.e. in his visits.—**δι' ὧν ἀποφεύξονται:** final (M.T. 565).

4. **ἐπειδὴ...φέροιτο,** but when one of them had died and his relatives were carrying offerings to his tomb (all part of the supposition), depend- ing on εἰ...διεξίοι (M.T. 177, 558, 560). τὰ νομιζόμενα are the customary offerings to the dead (ἐναγίσματα), brought on the third and ninth days after death. Aeschines says, τελευτή- σαντος δὲ ἐλθὼν εἰς τὰ ἔνατα διεξίοι, and Demosthenes probably refers to these ninth-day offerings. For views of such offerings see Smith's Dict. Antiq. I. p. 888, and Gardner and Jevons's Greek Antiq. p. 367. Aes- chines (225) predicts that Demos- thenes will use this illustration, and (189) that he will allude to Philammon the boxer (which he does in § 319); both predictions were of course in- serted after the trial.

6. **τὸ μνῆμα,** the tomb, built above ground, which may at the same time be a monument; cf. μνήμασι, § 208[7]. In the same double sense we must take τάφος in the famous passage, Thuc. II. 43[18], ἀνδρῶν γὰρ ἐπιφανῶν πᾶσα γῆ τάφος.—**τὸ καὶ τὸ,** this and that, one of the few colloquial relics of the pronominal article: see IX. 68, ἔδει γὰρ τὸ καὶ τὸ ποιῆσαι καὶ τὸ μὴ ποιῆσαι.—**ἄνθρωπος οὑτοσί:** so all the MSS. The article may be omitted with demonstratives when the pro-

θρωπος ούτοσὶ, οὐκ ἂν ἀπέθανεν. ἐμβρόντητε,
εἶτα νῦν λέγεις ;
Οὐ τοίνυν οὐδὲ τὴν ἧτταν, εἰ ταύτῃ γαυριᾷς ἐφ᾽ ᾗ 244
στένειν σε, ὦ κατάρατε, προσῆκεν, ἐν οὐδενὶ τῶν
παρ᾽ ἐμοὶ γεγονυῖαν εὑρήσετε τῇ πόλει. οὑτωσὶ δὲ
λογίζεσθε. οὐδαμοῦ πώποθ᾽, ὅποι πρεσβευτὴς ἐπέμφθην ὑφ᾽ ὑμῶν ἐγώ, ἡττηθεὶς ἀπῆλθον τῶν παρὰ 5
Φιλίππου πρέσβεων, οὐκ ἐκ Θετταλίας οὐδ᾽ ἐξ
Ἀμβρακίας, οὐκ ἐξ Ἰλλυριῶν οὐδὲ παρὰ τῶν Θρᾳκῶν
βασιλέων, οὐκ ἐκ Βυζαντίου, οὐκ ἄλλοθεν οὐδαμόθεν,
οὐ τὰ τελευταῖ᾽ ἐκ Θηβῶν· ἀλλ᾽ ἐν οἷς κρατηθεῖεν οἱ
πρέσβεις αὐτοῦ τῷ λόγῳ, ταῦτα τοῖς ὅπλοις ἐπιὼν 10
κατεστρέφετο. ταῦτ᾽ οὖν ἀπαιτεῖς παρ᾽ ἐμοῦ, καὶ 245
οὐκ αἰσχύνει τὸν αὐτὸν εἴς τε μαλακίαν σκώπτων
καὶ τῆς Φιλίππου δυνάμεως ἀξιῶν ἕν᾽ ὄντα κρείττω
γενέσθαι ; καὶ ταῦτα τοῖς λόγοις ; τίνος γὰρ ἄλλου
κύριος ἦν ἐγώ ; οὐ γὰρ τῆς γ᾽ ἑκάστου ψυχῆς, οὐδὲ 5

noun emphatically points out a present
person or thing; as Plat. Gorg. 489 B,
οὑτοσὶ ἀνὴρ οὐ παύσεται φλυαρῶν, and
505 C, οὗτος ἀνὴρ οὐχ ὑπομένει ὠφελού-
μενος: see Thuc. I. 51⁶, νῆες ἐκεῖναι
ἐπιπλέουσι, yonder are ships sailing
up.
7. ἐμβρόντητε, thunderstruck, stupefied by βροντή: cf. ἐμβεβροντῆ-
σθαι, XIX. 231. For the relation of
these words to τετύφωμαι see note on
§ 11⁵.
8. εἶτα νῦν λέγεις; see note on 1.
§ 244. 1. τὴν ἧτταν : still having
in mind the figure of the reckoning
(§ 227), he now argues that the chief
item which his enemies place on the
debit side, the defeat of Chaeronea,
cannot justly be charged to him (cf.
λογίζεσθε in 4).
2. τῶν παρ᾽ ἐμοί, of what I was
responsible for.
4. ὅποι ἐπέμφθην : for the difference between this and ὅποι πεμφθείην

in § 45 (referring to the same thing),
and for ἐν οἷς κρατηθεῖεν (9), see note
on § 45². Little is known of any of
these embassies of Demosthenes except those to Byzantium (§§ 87—89)
and Thebes (§ 211 ff.).
10. ὅπλοις κατεστρέφετο, i.e. he
decided these cases by throwing his
sword into the scale.
§ 245. 1. ταῦτ᾽ ἀπαιτεῖς, you
call me to account for these (§ 244¹⁰).
2. εἰς μαλακίαν : West. cites
Aesch. III. 148, 152, 155, and 175.
In these Demosthenes is ridiculed
for having run away at Chaeronea,
when the whole allied army was put
to flight. Aeschines is never charged
with this; but he was probably not
in the battle at all, being over fifty
years old. Probably Demosthenes
refers also to the nickname Βάτταλος :
see note on § 180³.
5. τῆς ψυχῆς, the life.

τῆς τύχης τῶν παραταξαμένων, οὐδὲ τῆς στρατηγίας,
ἧς ἔμ' ἀπαιτεῖς εὐθύνας· οὕτω σκαιὸς εἶ. ἀλλὰ μὴν 246
ὧν γ' ἂν ὁ ῥήτωρ ὑπεύθυνος εἴη, πᾶσαν ἐξέτασιν
λαμβάνετε· οὐ παραιτοῦμαι. τίνα οὖν ἐστι ταῦτα ;
ἰδεῖν τὰ πράγματ' ἀρχόμενα καὶ προαισθέσθαι καὶ
προειπεῖν τοῖς ἄλλοις. ταῦτα πέπρακταί μοι. καὶ 5
ἔτι τὰς ἑκασταχοῦ βραδυτῆτας, ὄκνους, ἀγνοίας, φι-
309 λονεικίας, ἃ πολιτικὰ ταῖς πόλεσι πρόσεστιν ἁπάσαις καὶ ἀναγκαῖ' ἁμαρτήματα, ταῦθ' ὡς εἰς ἐλάχιστα
συστεῖλαι, καὶ τοὐναντίον εἰς ὁμόνοιαν καὶ φιλίαν
καὶ τοῦ τὰ δέοντα ποιεῖν ὁρμὴν προτρέψαι. καὶ 10
ταῦτά μοι πάντα πεποίηται, καὶ οὐδεὶς μήποθ' εὕρῃ
κατ' ἐμὲ οὐδὲν ἐλλειφθέν. εἰ τοίνυν τις ἔροιθ' ὁντιν- 247
οῦν τίσι τὰ πλεῖστα Φίλιππος ὧν κατέπραξε διῳ-
κήσατο, πάντες ἂν εἴποιεν τῷ στρατοπέδῳ καὶ τῷ

6. **τῶν παραταξαμένων,** the combatants: §§ 208⁵, 216⁵.
7. **εὐθύνας**: used metaphorically.
—**σκαιὸς,** awkward (mentally): cf.
§ 120⁴.
§ **246.** 3. **λαμβάνετε**: plural,
as he turns suddenly from Aeschines
to the whole assembly.
4. **ἰδεῖν...ἀρχόμενα κ.τ.λ.**: no one
can read the earlier orations of Demosthenes in the light of later events
without feeling the justice of this
claim to sagacity which he puts forward. He, indeed, of all the statesmen of Athens, saw things in their
beginnings, and steadily warned the
people of the coming danger.
7. **πολιτικὰ ταῖς πόλεσι,** inherent
in (free) governments: a striking case
of a favourite Greek form of emphasis,
which repeats the idea of a noun in
an adjective. Here the whole idea
could have been expressed either by
πολιτικά or by οἰκεῖα ταῖς πόλεσι ; but
it is made doubly strong by πολιτικὰ
ταῖς πόλεσι. The Greek constantly

emphasizes by what we should call
tautology, as in the repetition of
negatives. In Aeschyl. Ag. 56, οἰωνό-
θροον γόον ὀξυβόαν, the whole idea
could have been expressed by οἰωνῶν
γόον ὀξύν, shrill cry of birds, but the
idea of cry is added in both adjectives.
πόλεσι here has the same reference
to free governments which is usually
implied in πολιτεία (see note on
§ 65⁹) : cf. Soph. Ant. 737, πόλις γὰρ
οὐκ ἔσθ' ἥτις ἀνδρός ἐσθ' ἑνός. With
the whole passage cf. §§ 235, 236.
8. **ὡς** belongs to εἰς ἐλάχιστα,
into the smallest possible compass:
see § 288⁵.
9. **συστεῖλαι,** to contract : συστέλ-
λω sometimes means to shorten sail,
as in Ar. Ran. 999; cf. Eq. 432,
συστείλας τοὺς ἀλλᾶντας.
11. **πεποίηται**: in the same sense
as πέπρακται (5) : see note on § 4⁶.
12. **κατ' ἐμὲ**: most MSS. (not Σ
and L¹) have τὸ κατ' ἐμὲ, as in § 247¹¹.
§ **247.** 3, 4. **τῷ διδόναι,** by
making gifts.

152 ΔΗΜΟΣΘΕΝΟΥΣ

διδόναι καὶ διαφθείρειν τοὺς ἐπὶ τῶν πραγμάτων.
οὐκοῦν τῶν μὲν δυνάμεων οὔτε κύριος οὔθ' ἡγεμὼν ἦν 5
ἐγώ, ὥστε οὐδ' ὁ λόγος τῶν κατὰ ταῦτα πραχθέντων
πρὸς ἐμέ. καὶ μὴν τῷ διαφθαρῆναι χρήμασιν ἢ μὴ
κεκράτηκα Φίλιππον· ὥσπερ γὰρ ὁ ὠνούμενος νενίκηκε τὸν λαβόντα ἐὰν πρίηται, οὕτως ὁ μὴ λαβὼν
καὶ διαφθαρεὶς νενίκηκε τὸν ὠνούμενον. ὥστε ἀήτ- 10
τητος ἡ πόλις τὸ κατ' ἐμέ.

Ἃ μὲν τοίνυν ἐγὼ παρεσχόμην εἰς τὸ δικαίως 248
τοιαῦτα γράφειν τοῦτον περὶ ἐμοῦ, πρὸς πολλοῖς
ἑτέροις ταῦτα καὶ παραπλήσια τούτοις ἐστίν· ἃ δ' οἱ
πάντες ὑμεῖς, ταῦτ' ἤδη λέξω. μετὰ γὰρ τὴν μάχην
εὐθὺς ὁ δῆμος, εἰδὼς καὶ ἑορακὼς πάνθ' ὅσ' ἔπραττον 5
ἐγώ, ἐν αὐτοῖς τοῖς δεινοῖς καὶ φοβεροῖς ἐμβεβηκὼς,
ἡνίκ' οὐδ' ἀγνωμονῆσαί τι θαυμαστὸν ἦν τοὺς πολλοὺς πρὸς ἐμέ, πρῶτον μὲν περὶ σωτηρίας τῆς πόλεως

5. δυνάμεων, referring to στρατοπέδῳ (3) : see note on § 234¹.
6. ταῦτα (i.e. δυνάμεις): cf. κατὰ
τὴν στρατηγίαν (§ 212⁸).
7. τῷ διαφθαρῆναι ἢ μή, *in the
matter of being corrupted or not*, far
more expressive than τῷ μὴ διαφθαρῆναι. This corresponds to τῶν μὲν
δυνάμεων, in place of a clause with δέ.
Cf. XIX. 4, and 7, ὑπέρ γε τοῦ προῖκα
ἢ μή.
8. ὁ ὠνούμενος: conative, *he who
would buy.* Cf. § 239⁵.
9. ὁ μὴ λαβὼν καὶ διαφθαρεὶς
(Σ, L¹) = ὃς μὴ ἔλαβε καὶ διεφθάρη,
better than μηδὲ διαφθαρεὶς (vulg.),
as it more closely unites the corruption with the bribe, *he who refused to
take the bribe and he corrupted.*
§ 248. 1. εἰς τὸ...τοῦτον, i.e.
to justify Ctesiphon's language in his
decree: see § 57¹.
3. οἱ πάντες ὑμεῖς : sc. παρέ-
σχεσθε.

6. ἐμβεβηκὼς, *standing amid,*
surrounded by: βέβηκα, stand, is related to ἵσταμαι as γέγονα to εἰμί and
κέκτημαι to ἔχω.
7. ἡνίκ' οὐδ'...πρὸς ἐμέ, i.e. *when
most men might have shown some
want of feeling towards me without
surprising anyone* : this rather awkward translation shows the force of
the construction of θαυμαστὸν ἦν
(without ἄν) and the infinitive, where
the chief potential force falls on the
infinitive. (See M.T. 415, 416, and
Appendix V. p. 406.) We naturally
(but incorrectly) translate *when it
would have been no wonder,* throwing
the chief force on θαυμαστὸν ἦν, so
that ἄν seems necessary: Blass reads
οὐδ ἄν. For a similar case see Eur.
Med. 490, εἰ γὰρ ἦσθ' ἄπαις,
συγγνωστὸν ἦν σοι τοῦδ' ἐρασθῆναι
λέχους, i.e. *in that case you might
pardonably have been enamoured:* see
M.T. 422¹.

τὰς ἐμὰς γνώμας ἐχειροτόνει, καὶ πάνθ' ὅσα τῆς
φυλακῆς ἕνεκ' ἐπράττετο, ἡ διάταξις τῶν φυλάκων, 10
310 αἱ τάφροι, τὰ εἰς τὰ τείχη χρήματα, διὰ τῶν ἐμῶν
ψηφισμάτων ἐγίγνετο· ἔπειθ' αἱρούμενος σιτώνην ἐκ
πάντων ἔμ' ἐχειροτόνησεν ὁ δῆμος. καὶ μετὰ ταῦτα 249
συστάντων οἷς ἦν ἐπιμελὲς κακῶς ἐμὲ ποιεῖν, καὶ
γραφὰς, εὐθύνας, εἰσαγγελίας, πάντα ταῦτ' ἐπαγόντων μοι, οὐ δι' ἑαυτῶν τό γε πρῶτον, ἀλλὰ δι' ὧν
μάλισθ' ὑπελάμβανον ἀγνοήσεσθαι (ὥστε γὰρ δήπου 5
καὶ μέμνησθ' ὅτι τοὺς πρώτους χρόνους κατὰ τὴι
ἡμέραν ἑκάστην ἐκρινόμην ἐγὼ, καὶ οὔτ' ἀπόνοια
Σωσικλέους οὔτε συκοφαντία Φιλοκράτους οὔτε
Διώνδου καὶ Μελάντου μανία οὔτ' ἄλλ' οὐδὲν ἀπεί-

9. **τὰς ἐμὰς γνώμας,** *my proposals*
of public measures: this and the
following **πάνθ' ὅσα**...ἐπράττετο do
not include such general measures for
the public safety as the famous decree
of Hyperides for the enfranchisement
of slaves, the recall of exiles, and
similar extreme provisions (see Hist.
§ 67).

. 10. **ἡ διάταξις τῶν φυλάκων:** see
Thuc. II. 24, φυλακὰς κατεστήσαντο
κατὰ γῆν καὶ κατὰ θάλασσαν, ὥσπερ
δὴ ἔμελλον διὰ παντὸς τοῦ πολέμου
φυλάξειν.

11. **τάφροι**...**τείχη**: this has nothing to do with the more elaborate
work on the walls undertaken in the
following year, when Demosthenes
was τειχοποιός (§ 113⁶).

12. **σιτώνην,** an extraordinary
official appointed in special times of
distress to regulate the trade in grain
and to guard against scarcity. The
grain trade was ordinarily in the
charge of 35 σιτοφύλακες (20 in the
city, 15 in the Piraeus): see Arist.
Pol. Ath. 51⁸.

§ 249. 1. **μετὰ ταῦτα,** i.e. after
the first excitement, when Philip's
party gained courage at Athens.

2. **συστάντων**: gen. absol. with
the implied antecedent of οἷς.

3. **γραφὰς**: here in the most restricted sense of *ordinary public suits*,
excluding εἰσαγγελία, εὔθυναι, etc.
The chief form of γραφή here would
be the γραφὴ παρανόμων (§ 250⁵).—
πάντα ταῦτ': emphatic apposition,
all these, I say.

4. **οὐ δι' ἑαυτῶν,** *not in their own
names*: at first the leading philip-
pizers kept in the background, and
put forward such obscure men as
those mentioned below.

7—9. **ἀπόνοια, μανία**: "the first
is the deliberate desperation of a man
with nothing to lose, the last the
desperation of blind passion" (Simcox).—**Σωσικλέους**...**Μελάντου**: So-
sicles and Melantus are otherwise
unknown; for Diondas see § 222⁶;
Philocrates is not the one who gave
his name to the peace of 346 B.C.
(he disappears after he was condemned on the εἰσαγγελία brought
by Hyperides, XIX. 116), but an
Eleusinian (XXV. 44). The imitation
of this passage by Cicero (Cat. III. 7)
is familiar: hoc providebam animo,
...nec mihi P. Lentuli somnum, nec

ρατον ἦν τούτοις κατ' ἐμοῦ), ἐν τοίνυν τούτοις πᾶσι 10
μάλιστα μὲν διὰ τοὺς θεούς, δεύτερον δὲ δι' ὑμᾶς καὶ
τοὺς ἄλλους Ἀθηναίους ἐσῳζόμην. δικαίως· τοῦτο
γὰρ καὶ ἀληθές ἐστι καὶ ὑπὲρ τῶν ὀμωμοκότων καὶ
γνόντων τὰ εὔορκα δικαστῶν. οὐκοῦν ἐν μὲν οἷς 250
εἰσηγγελλόμην, ὅτ' ἀπεψηφίζεσθέ μου καὶ τὸ μέρος
τῶν ψήφων τοῖς διώκουσιν οὐ μετεδίδοτε, τότ' ἐψηφί-
ζεσθε τἄριστά με πράττειν· ἐν οἷς δὲ τὰς γραφὰς
ἀπέφευγον, ἔννομα καὶ γράφειν καὶ λέγειν ἀπεδεικνύ- 5
μην· ἐν οἷς δὲ τὰς εὐθύνας ἐπεσημαίνεσθε, δικαίως
καὶ ἀδωροδοκήτως πάντα πεπρᾶχθαί μοι προσωμο-
λογεῖτε. τούτων οὖν οὕτως ἐχόντων, τί προσῆκον ἢ
τί δίκαιον ἦν τοῖς ὑπ' ἐμοῦ πεπραγμένοις θέσθαι τὸν
Κτησιφῶντα ὄνομα; οὐχ ὃ τὸν δῆμον ἑώρα τιθέμενον, 10
οὐχ ὃ τοὺς ὀμωμοκότας δικαστάς, οὐχ ὃ τὴν ἀλήθειαν
παρὰ πᾶσι βεβαιοῦσαν;

L. Cassii adipes, nec Cethegi furiosam
temeritatem pertimescendam.
11. **δι' ὑμᾶς**, i.e. through the
courts.
13. **ἀληθές**, *in accordance with
truth.*—**ὑπὲρ…δικαστῶν**, *to the credit
of judges*, etc.
14. **γνόντων τὰ εὔορκα**, *who* (not
only had sworn, but) *gave judgment
in accordance with their oaths.*
§ **250.** 1. **ἐν οἷς εἰσηγγελλόμην**
(cf. *ἐν οἷς ἡμάρτανον*, § 19³). The
εἰσαγγελία was partly a state prosecution, which was first brought before
the Senate (rarely before the Assembly). If the Senate accepted the
εἰσαγγελία, it referred the case to the
Heliastic court for trial, unless it
settled it by inflicting a fine not ex-
ceeding 500 drachmas.
2. **τὸ μέρος τῶν ψήφων**: cf.
§§ 103², 266⁶. A comparison of
Hyperides (Lycoph. 8), διὰ τὸ ἀκίνδυνον
αὐτοῖς εἶναι τὸν ἀγῶνα, with Lycurgus
(Leocr. 3), τὸν ἰδίᾳ κινδυνεύοντα,

and Pollux (VIII. 52, 53), shows that
in earlier times no penalty was inflicted on the εἰσαγγέλλων who failed
to get one-fifth of the votes, but that
afterwards he was subject to the fine
without the ἀτιμία.
4. **τἄριστά με πράττειν**: i.e. the
judgment of the court justified this
expression in Ctesiphon's decree (§ 57¹).
5. **ἔννομα γράφειν**: opposed to
παράνομα γράφειν: see note on γρα-
φάς, § 249³.
6. **τὰς εὐθύνας ἐπεσημαίνεσθε**,
put your seal on my accounts: this
probably refers to the official seal of
the δικαστήριον before which Demosth.
appeared to render his accounts (εὔθυναι) at the end of each term of
office. See Aristotle, Pol. Ath.
48¹⁸, 54⁶.
10. **τὸν δῆμον τιθέμενον**: this repeated approval of the people refers
to the votes mentioned in § 248.
11. **δικαστάς**: sc. τιθεμένους.
The present judges are addressed

ΠΕΡΙ ΤΟΥ ΣΤΕΦΑΝΟΥ 155

Ναὶ, φησὶν, ἀλλὰ τὸ τοῦ Κεφάλου καλὸν, τὸ 251
μηδεμίαν γραφὴν φεύγειν. καὶ νὴ Δί᾽ εὔδαιμόν γε.
311 ἀλλὰ τί μᾶλλον ὁ πολλάκις μὲν φυγὼν μηδεπώποτε
δ᾽ ἐξελεγχθεὶς ἀδικῶν ἐν ἐγκλήματι γίγνοιτ᾽ ἂν διὰ
τοῦτο δικαίως ; καίτοι πρός γε τοῦτον, ἄνδρες Ἀθη- 5
ναῖοι, καὶ τὸ τοῦ Κεφάλου καλὸν εἰπεῖν ἔστι μοι.
οὐδεμίαν γὰρ πώποτ᾽ ἐγράψατό με οὐδ᾽ ἐδίωξε
γραφὴν, ὥστε ὑπὸ σοῦ γ᾽ ὡμολόγημαι μηδὲν εἶναι
τοῦ Κεφάλου χείρων πολίτης.
Πανταχόθεν μὲν τοίνυν ἄν τις ἴδοι τὴν ἀγνω- 252
μοσύνην αὐτοῦ καὶ τὴν βασκανίαν, οὐχ ἥκιστα δ᾽
ἀφ᾽ ὧν περὶ τῆς τύχης διελέχθη. ἐγὼ δ᾽ ὅλως μέν,

above (6) as if they had themselves judged the previous cases.—τὴν ἀλή-θειαν: with special emphasis, after τὸν δῆμον and τοὺς δικαστάς. This passage is a dignified and fitting conclusion to the line of argument beginning with § 227 concerning the orator's account (λογισμός) with the state. Now, after a brief allusion (§ 251) to the case of Cephalus, he passes to another matter.

§ 251. 1. τὸ τοῦ Κεφάλου καλὸν may be exclamatory, there is the glory of Cephalus; cf. l. 6. But καλόν is generally taken here as predicate to τὸ τοῦ Κεφάλου (sc. ἐστί). (See Aesch. III. 194.) This Cephalus (already mentioned in § 219³) is not the father of Lysias, who opens the dialogue of Plato's Republic with Socrates and was ἐπὶ γήραος οὐδῷ in the lifetime of Socrates; but a later statesman, who with Thrasybulus of Collytus was a leader of the Theban party in Athens, and highly respected.—τό...φεύγειν, the (glory of) never being under indictment. Aeschines (194), after mentioning the boast of Aristophon that he had been acquitted (ἀπέφυγεν) seventy-five times on the γραφὴ παρανόμων, compares this with

the higher boast of Cephalus, that he had proposed more decrees than any other man, and yet had never once been indicted by this process.
5. πρός γε τοῦτον, so far as this man is concerned; i.e. Aeschines has done nothing to prevent me from making the boast of Cephalus.
7. ἐδίωξε γραφὴν, prosecuted an indictment, cognate accusative, as in ἐγράψατο γραφήν. The English translation obscures the construction.
8. μηδὲν εἶναι: see M.T. 685.

§§ 252—275. Here Demosthenes replies at great length to scattered remarks of Aeschines about his "bad fortune," which involved in calamity every person, state, or thing which he touched. Though Aeschines refers only to his general fortune, Demosthenes chooses to speak chiefly of his fortunes in life, which he compares with those of his opponent. He concludes (§§ 270—275) with some forcible remarks on his fortune in the other sense.

§ 252. 1. ἀγνωμοσύνην (cf. §§ 94², 207⁷), want of feeling.
3. περὶ τῆς τύχης: see Aesch. III. 114, 157, 158, with 135, 136; cf. § 212

ὅστις ἄνθρωπος ὢν ἀνθρώπῳ τύχην προφέρει, ἀνόη-
τον ἡγοῦμαι· ἢν γὰρ ὁ βέλτιστα πράττειν νομίζων 5
καὶ ἀρίστην ἔχειν οἰόμενος οὐκ οἶδεν εἰ μενεῖ τοιαύτη
μέχρι τῆς ἑσπέρας, πῶς χρὴ περὶ ταύτης λέγειν ἢ
πῶς ὀνειδίζειν ἑτέρῳ; ἐπειδὴ δ' οὗτος πρὸς πολλοῖς
ἄλλοις καὶ περὶ τούτων ὑπερηφάνως χρῆται τῷ
λόγῳ, σκέψασθ', ὦ ἄνδρες Ἀθηναῖοι, καὶ θεωρήσαθ' 10
ὅσῳ καὶ ἀληθέστερον καὶ ἀνθρωπινώτερον ἐγὼ περὶ
τῆς τύχης τούτου διαλεχθήσομαι. ἐγὼ τὴν τῆς πό- 253
λεως τύχην ἀγαθὴν ἡγοῦμαι, καὶ ταῦθ' ὁρῶ καὶ τὸν
Δία τὸν Δωδωναῖον ὑμῖν μαντευόμενον, τὴν μέντοι
τῶν πάντων ἀνθρώπων, ἢ νῦν ἐπέχει, χαλεπὴν καὶ
δεινήν· τίς γὰρ Ἑλλήνων ἢ τίς βαρβάρων οὐ πολλῶν 5

(above).—**ὅλως μὲν** is opposed to the
special exception, **ἐπειδὴ δ' οὗτος** (8).
4. **προφέρει**, *taunts with*.
5. **ἢν**, after suggesting the object
of **ἔχειν**, is the object of **οἶδεν**.—
βέλτιστα πράττειν : superlative of **εὖ
πράττειν**. See Soph. O.C. 567: **ἔξοιδ'
ἀνὴρ ὢν χὤτι τῆς ἐς αὔριον οὐδὲν πλέον
μοι σοῦ μέτεστιν ἡμέρας** (Weil).
9. **ὑπερηφάνως**, *arrogantly* : opposed to **ἀνθρωπινώτερον**, *more hu-
manly*, i.e. more as one man should
speak of another: cf. **ὅστις...προφέρει**
(4).—**χρῆται τῷ λόγῳ**: cf. **εἰ δικαίως
χρήσομαι τῷ λόγῳ**, § 233[8].
§ **253**. 1. **τὴν...τύχην** : the
general good fortune of Athens, as
it is here understood, is not mere
chance or luck (as in §§ 207[7] and
306[6]), but the result of divine protection and the care of the Gods.
See the poem on Solon, quoted in
XIX. 255, which begins
Ἡμετέρα δὲ πόλις κατὰ μὲν Διὸς οὔποτ'
ὀλεῖται
αἶσαν καὶ μακάρων θεῶν φρένας ἀθα-
νάτων·
τοίη γὰρ μεγάθυμος ἐπίσκοπος ὀβριμο-
πάτρη
Παλλὰς Ἀθηναίη χεῖρας ὕπερθεν ἔχει·

with the orator's comment (256), **ἐγὼ
δ' ἀεὶ μὲν ἀληθῆ τὸν λόγον τοῦτον
ἡγοῦμαι καὶ βούλομαι, ὡς ἄρ' οἱ θεοὶ
σῴζουσιν ἡμῶν τὴν πόλιν**. So IV. 12:
(τῆς τύχης) **ἥπερ ἀεὶ βέλτιον ἢ ἡμεῖς
ἡμῶν αὐτῶν ἐπιμελούμεθα**.
3. **τὸν...Δωδωναῖον**: cf. Il. XVI.
233, **Ζεῦ ἄνα Δωδωναῖε, Πελασγικὲ,
τηλόθι ναίων**, in the prayer of Achilles.
Oracles sent from Dodona to Athens
are quoted by Demosthenes, XXI. 53;
cf. XIX. 299, ὁ Ζεὺς, ἡ Διώνη (the
Queen of Zeus at Dodona), πάντες οἱ
θεοί. At this time Dodona was probably more revered at Athens because
of the Macedonian influence at Delphi:
cf. Aesch. III. 130, **Δημοσθένης δὲ
ἀντέλεγε, φιλιππίζειν τὴν Πυθίαν φάσκων, ἀπαίδευτος ὢν κ.τ.λ.**
4. **τῶν πάντων ἀνθρώπων**, *mankind in general*, as opposed to Athens
alone.
5. **πολλῶν κακῶν** : witness the
destruction of Thebes by Alexander ;
and the overthrow of the Persian
Empire, which was then going on.
See Aesch. III. 132, 133; in 134 he
includes Athens in the general bad
fortune which she owes to the baneful
influence of Demosthenes.

κακῶν ἐν τῷ παρόντι πεπείραται; τὸ μὲν τοίνυν 254
προελέσθαι τὰ κάλλιστα, καὶ τὸ τῶν οἰηθέντων
Ἑλλήνων εἰ πρόοινθ' ἡμᾶς ἐν εὐδαιμονίᾳ διάξειν
αὐτῶν ἄμεινον πράττειν, τῆς ἀγαθῆς τύχης τῆς
πόλεως εἶναι τίθημι· τὸ δὲ προσκροῦσαι καὶ μὴ 5
312 πάνθ' ὡς ἠβουλόμεθ' ἡμῖν συμβῆναι τῆς τῶν ἄλλων
ἀνθρώπων τύχης τὸ ἐπιβάλλον ἐφ' ἡμᾶς μέρος
μετειληφέναι νομίζω τὴν πόλιν. τὴν δ' ἰδίαν τύχην 255
τὴν ἐμὴν καὶ τὴν ἑνὸς ἡμῶν ἑκάστου ἐν τοῖς ἰδίοις
ἐξετάζειν δίκαιον εἶναι νομίζω. ἐγὼ μὲν οὑτωσὶ περὶ
τῆς τύχης ἀξιῶ, ὀρθῶς καὶ δικαίως, ὡς ἐμαυτῷ δοκῶ,
νομίζω δὲ καὶ ὑμῖν· ὁ δὲ τὴν ἰδίαν τύχην τὴν ἐμὴν 5
τῆς κοινῆς τῆς πόλεως κυριωτέραν εἶναί φησι, τὴν
μικρὰν καὶ φαύλην τῆς ἀγαθῆς καὶ μεγάλης. καὶ
πῶς ἔνι τοῦτο γενέσθαι;
Καὶ μὴν εἴ γε τὴν ἐμὴν τύχην πάντως ἐξετάζειν, 256
Αἰσχίνη, προαιρεῖ, πρὸς τὴν σαυτοῦ σκόπει, κἂν
εὕρῃς τὴν ἐμὴν βελτίω τῆς σῆς, παῦσαι λοιδορούμενος αὐτῇ. σκόπει τοίνυν εὐθὺς ἐξ ἀρχῆς. καὶ

§ **254.** I. **τὸ προελέσθαι τὰ κάλλιστα,** *our choice of the most glorious
course*: the whole sentence through
ἄμεινον πράττειν is the subject of
εἶναι (5), i.e. he includes all this in
the special good fortune of Athens.
2. **τῶν οἰηθέντων** introduces εἰ
πρόοινθ'...διάξειν in *or. obl.*: the gen.
depends on ἄμεινον πράττειν (4).
4. **αὐτῶν**: intensive with τῶν Ἑλλήνων, *than those very Greeks*; almost
reiterative.—**ἄμεινον πράττειν**: cf.
βέλτιστα πράττειν, § 252⁵.—**τῆς τύχης**
with εἶναι τίθημι: see I. 10, τὸ μὲν
γὰρ πολλὰ ἀπολωλεκέναι...τῆς ἡμετέρας ἀμελείας ἄν τις θείη δικαίως.
τίθημι in this sense takes the infinitive
regularly in *or. obl.*: see Aesch. III.
163, βούλει σε θῶ φοβηθῆναι καὶ χρήσασθαι τῷ σαυτοῦ τρόπῳ;
5. **τὸ δὲ προσκροῦσαι καὶ μὴ...**

συμβῆναι, i.e. our disaster (euphe-
mistically called *collision*) *and our
not having everything done as we
wished*: this is the object of μετειληφέναι, with τὸ...μέρος as appositive,
*this I believe that our city has received
as the share of the general (bad) fortune
of the rest of mankind which falls to
our lot.*
7. **τὸ ἐπιβάλλον μέρος**: cf. τὸ
γιγνόμενον, *the quota*, § 104⁵. Cf.
ἐπιβάλλει, § 272³.
§ **255.** 2. **ἐν τοῖς ἰδίοις**: Aesch.
had sought for the fortune of Demosth.
ἐν τοῖς δημοσίοις, as in III. 114, συμβέβηκεν αὐτῷ ὅτου ἄν προσάψηται...
τούτων ἑκάστους ἀνιάτοις συμφοραῖς
περιβάλλειν.
4. **ἀξιῶ,** *judge*: οὑτωσὶ ἀξιῶ = τοῦτο
ἄξιον εἶναι νομίζω.
5. **νομίζω ὑμῖν**: sc. δοκεῖν.

μου πρὸς Διὸς μηδεμίαν ψυχρότητα καταγνῷ μηδείς. 5
ἐγὼ γὰρ οὔτ᾽ εἴ τις πενίαν προπηλακίζει, νοῦν ἔχειν
ἡγοῦμαι, οὔτ᾽ εἴ τις ἐν ἀφθόνοις τραφεὶς ἐπὶ τούτῳ
σεμνύνεται· ἀλλ᾽ ὑπὸ τῆς τουτουὶ τοῦ χαλεποῦ
βλασφημίας καὶ συκοφαντίας εἰς τοιούτους λόγους
ἐμπίπτειν ἀναγκάζομαι, οἷς ἐκ τῶν ἐνόντων ὡς ἂν 10
δύνωμαι μετριώτατα χρήσομαι.

Ἐμοὶ μὲν τοίνυν ὑπῆρξεν, Αἰσχίνη, παιδὶ τὰ 257
προσήκοντα διδασκαλεῖα, καὶ ἔχειν ὅσα χρὴ τὸν
μηδὲν αἰσχρὸν ποιήσοντα δι᾽ ἔνδειαν, ἐξελθόντι δ᾽
ἐκ παίδων ἀκόλουθα τούτοις πράττειν, χορηγεῖν,
τριηραρχεῖν, εἰσφέρειν, μηδεμιᾶς φιλοτιμίας μήτ᾽ 5
ἰδίας μήτε δημοσίας ἀπολείπεσθαι, ἀλλὰ καὶ τῇ
πόλει καὶ τοῖς φίλοις χρήσιμον εἶναι· ἐπειδὴ δὲ
πρὸς τὰ κοινὰ προσελθεῖν ἔδοξέ μοι, τοιαῦτα πολι-

---

§ 256. 5. ψυχρότητα, coldness, want of feeling.
7. ἐν ἀφθόνοις, in affluence.
8. χαλεποῦ, harsh, stronger than ψυχροῦ.
10. ἐκ τῶν...μετριώτατα, as moderately as the state of the case (τὰ ἐνόντα) will permit. We have again an apology, perhaps an honest one, for the personal vituperation which follows, §§ 257—262.
§ 257. 1. ὑπῆρξεν : the subjects are διδασκαλεῖα and the infinitives ἔχειν and πράττειν, with ἐλέσθαι (9). Most MSS. (not Σ and L¹) insert μὲν ὄντι φοιτᾶν εἰς after παιδί.
2, 3. προσήκοντα, i.e. such as children of the better classes attended : one of the charges against his guardian Aphobus (XXVII. 46) is τοὺς διδασκάλους τοὺς μισθοὺς ἀπεστέρηκε.—τὸν ...ποιήσοντα=ὃς ποιήσει, he who is to do etc. (M.T. 527, 530).—αἰσχρόν, i.e. ἀνελεύθερον : this idea of the ignobility of toil is a commonplace with the Greeks, as a slave-holding people.

Cf. Ar. Av. 1432, τί γὰρ πάθω ; σκάπτειν γὰρ οὐκ ἐπίσταμαι.
4. ἀκόλουθα πράττειν is explained by the rest of the clause, χορηγεῖν... χρήσιμον εἶναι.—χορηγεῖν, τριηραρχεῖν: testimony about all his λῃτουργίαι is given in § 267. He was χορηγός in 350 B.C., when he was assaulted by Midias (XXI. 13 ff.); for his numerous trierarchies see XXI. 78, 154, Aesch. III. 51, 52, and cf. § 99¹¹ (above).
5. εἰσφέρειν, to pay the εἰσφορά, or property-tax : this was assessed "progressively," the richer being taxed on a larger proportion (τίμημα) of their actual property than the poorer. (See Eisphora in Smith's Dict. Antiq.) The guardians of Demosthenes, to conceal their peculations, continued to enroll their ward in the highest class, so that he paid taxes on a τίμημα of one-fifth of his property (οὐσία), whereas he should have been placed in a much lower class after the inroads upon the estate. See XXVII. 7 and XXVIII. 4.

ΠΕΡΙ ΤΟΥ ΣΤΕΦΑΝΟΥ 159

313 τεύμαθ' ἐλέσθαι ὥστε καὶ ὑπὸ τῆς πατρίδος καὶ ὑπ'
ἄλλων Ἑλλήνων πολλῶν πολλάκις ἐστεφανῶσθαι, 10
καὶ μηδὲ τοὺς ἐχθροὺς ὑμᾶς ὡς οὐ καλά γ' ἦν ἃ
προειλόμην ἐπιχειρεῖν λέγειν. ἐγὼ μὲν δὴ τοιαύτη 258
συμβεβίωκα τύχῃ, καὶ πόλλ' ἂν ἔχων ἕτερ' εἰπεῖν
περὶ αὐτῆς παραλείπω, φυλαττόμενος τὸ λυπῆσαί
τιν' ἐν οἷς σεμνύνομαι. σὺ δ' ὁ σεμνὸς ἀνὴρ καὶ
διαπτύων τοὺς ἄλλους σκόπει πρὸς ταύτην ποία τινὶ 5
κέχρησαι τύχῃ, δι' ἣν παῖς μὲν ὢν μετὰ πολλῆς τῆς
ἐνδείας ἐτράφης, ἅμα τῷ πατρὶ πρὸς τῷ διδασκαλείῳ
προσεδρεύων, τὸ μέλαν τρίβων καὶ τὰ βάθρα σπογ-
γίζων καὶ τὸ παιδαγωγεῖον κορῶν, οἰκέτου τάξιν οὐκ
ἐλευθέρου παιδὸς ἔχων, ἀνὴρ δὲ γενόμενος τῇ μητρὶ 259
τελούσῃ τὰς βίβλους ἀνεγίγνωσκες καὶ τἆλλα συνε-

9. ὥστε, with perfect and present infinitive: M.T. 590, 109.
10. ἐστεφανῶσθαι: see §§ 83, 120, 222, 223.
11. ἃ προειλόμην, i.e. τὴν ἐμὴν προαίρεσιν: cf. § 190⁵.
§ 258. 2. συμβεβίωκα...εἰπεῖν: an accidental dactylic hexameter.—πόλλ' ἂν ἔχων = πόλλ' ἂν ἔχοιμι, though I might etc.: cf. § 138¹,².
3. φυλαττόμενος τὸ λυπῆσαι (M.T. 374): the object infinitive takes the place of μὴ λυπήσω, which in use had become an object clause (M.T. 303 c).
7. πρὸς τῷ διδασκαλείῳ: see notes on § 129²⁻⁴.
8. προσεδρεύων, attending (as a servant).—τὸ μέλαν τρίβων: the ink was probably rubbed from a cake (like India ink) and mixed with water.
9. παιδαγωγεῖον, probably a room in which the παιδαγωγοί, slaves who brought the boys to and from school, waited for these to be ready to go home: later it was used like διδασκαλεῖον for a schoolroom.—οἰκέτου... ἔχων: the mention of these menial

duties implies the same condition of father and son as appears in § 129.
§ 259. In this section and § 260 we have a lively comic description, highly caricatured, of some Asiatic ceremonies of initiation, in which the mother of Aeschines is said to have taken part. This was some form of Bacchic worship, with perhaps a mixture of Orphic mysteries. It seems there was a written service (τὰς βίβλους), which Aeschines read like a clerk while his mother officiated as priestess. The initiation of Strepsiades into the Socratic mysteries (Ar. Nub. 255—262) probably caricatures some similar worship.
1. τῇ μητρὶ τελούσῃ: see XIX. 281, Γλαυκοθέας τῆς τοὺς θιάσους συναγούσης, ἐφ' οἷς ἑτέρα τέθνηκεν ἱέρεια, and cf. 249. In XIX. 199 we have τὰς βίβλους ἀναγιγνώσκοντά σε τῇ μητρὶ τελούσῃ, καὶ παῖδ' ὄντ' ἐν θιάσοις καὶ μεθύουσιν ἀνθρώποις καλινδούμενον.
2. τἆλλα συνεσκευωροῦ, you helped to conduct the rest of the ceremony:

σκευωροῦ, τὴν μὲν νύκτα νεβρίζων καὶ κρατηρίζων
καὶ καθαίρων τοὺς τελουμένους καὶ ἀπομάττων τῷ
πηλῷ καὶ τοῖς πιτύροις, καὶ ἀνιστὰς ἀπὸ τοῦ καθαρ- 5
μοῦ κελεύων λέγειν ἔφυγον κακὸν, εὖρον ἄμεινον,
ἐπὶ τῷ μηδένα πώποτε τηλικοῦτ᾽ ὀλολύξαι σεμνυνό-
μενος (καὶ ἔγωγε νομίζω· μὴ γὰρ οἴεσθ᾽ αὐτὸν φθέγγεσθαι μὲν οὕτω μέγα, ὀλολύζειν δ᾽ οὐχ ὑπέρλαμ-
προν), ἐν δὲ ταῖς ἡμέραις τοὺς καλοὺς θιάσους ἄγων 260
διὰ τῶν ὁδῶν, τοὺς ἐστεφανωμένους τῷ μαράθῳ καὶ

σκευωροῦμαι is properly *look after*
σκεύη (of any kind), and generally
manage, direct, devise, concoct (often in
a bad sense): cf. IX. 17 τὰ ἐν Πελοποννήσῳ σκευωρούμενον (of Philip).

3. **νεβρίζων** and **κρατηρίζων** are
probably transitive and govern τοὺς
τελουμένους, like καθαίρων, ἀπομάττων,
and ἀνιστάς, i.e. *dressing them in
fawnskins and drenching them with
wine*. See Eur. Bacch. 24, νεβρίδ᾽
ἐξάψας χροός, and Sandys' note. They
are sometimes taken as neuter, meaning *dressing yourself in a fawnskin and
pouring out wine*.

4. **ἀπομάττων ... πιτύροις**, i.e.
*plastering them over with clay and
then rubbing them clean with bran*.

5. **ἀνιστάς**: the victim is supposed
to be sitting during the operation, like
Strepsiades (Nub. 256).—**καθαρμοῦ**:
the process was a purification and also
a charm.

6. **κελεύων**, subordinate to ἀνιστάς:
i.e. *making him get up as he bids him
say, etc.*—**ἔφυγον κακὸν, εὖρον ἄμεινον**:
this formula was borrowed from initia-
tions and other ceremonies of a higher
character, meaning that a new life was
opened as the result of the ceremony
just ended. Suidas gives (under ἔφυγον...ἄμεινον): τάττεται ἐπὶ τῶν ἀπὸ
κακοῦ εἰς κρεῖττον ἐλθόντων. The
saying originally referred to the change
from the acorns and thistles of primi-

tive life to the more civilized bread,
and was used at weddings and other
ceremonies. The words form a paroe-
miac, and probably belonged to some
metrical formula.

7. **ὀλολύξαι**, used especially of *cries*
or *shouts* in religious worship or
prayers: see Od. IV. 767, ὡς εἰποῦσ᾽
ὀλόλυξε (after a prayer): Aeschyl. Eum.
1043, ὀλολύξατε νῦν ἐπὶ μολπαῖς: Eur.
Bacch. 689, ὠλόλυξεν ἐν μέσαις στα-
θεῖσα Βάκχαις.

8. **φθέγγεσθαι μέγα** : the strong
voice of Aeschines is often mentioned
by Demosthenes; see below, §§ 280,
285[6], 291[8], 313[7], and especially XIX.
206—208, 216, 337—340; in XIX.
216 he says, μηδέ γε εἰ καλὸν καὶ
μέγα οὗτος φθέγξεται, μηδ᾽ εἰ φαῦλον
ἐγώ, alluding to his own weakness of
voice.

§ **260**. 1. **ἐν δὲ ταῖς ἡμέραις**
implies that the ceremonies just described were performed by night.—
θιάσους, used especially of Bacchanals;
see Eur. Bacch. 680, ὁρῶ δὲ θιάσους
τρεῖς γυναικείων χορῶν.

2. **τῷ μαράθῳ καὶ τῇ λεύκῃ** : from
μάραθον, *fennel*, Marathon is said to
have been named (cf. Strab. p. 160):
for the fondness of serpents for it,
see Ael. Hist. Animal. IX. 16. For
serpents in the Bacchic worship, see
Eur. Bacch. 102, 697. The white
poplar, λεύκη, *populus alba*, is men-

τῇ λεύκῃ, τοὺς ὄφεις τοὺς παρείας θλίβων καὶ ὑπὲρ
τῆς κεφαλῆς αἰωρῶν, καὶ βοῶν εὐοῖ σαβοῖ, καὶ
ἐπορχούμενος ὑῆς ἄττης ἄττης ὑῆς, ἔξαρχος καὶ 5
προηγεμὼν καὶ κιττοφόρος καὶ λικνοφόρος καὶ τοιαῦθ᾽
314 ὑπὸ τῶν γραδίων προσαγορευόμενος, μισθὸν λαμβάνων τούτων ἔνθρυπτα καὶ στρεπτοὺς καὶ νεήλατα,
ἐφ᾽ οἷς τίς οὐκ ἂν ὡς ἀληθῶς αὐτὸν εὐδαιμονίσειε
καὶ τὴν αὐτοῦ τύχην; ἐπειδὴ δ᾽ εἰς τοὺς δημότας 261
ἐνεγράφης ὁπωσδήποτε (ἐῶ γὰρ τοῦτο)—ἐπειδή γ᾽
ἐνεγράφης, εὐθέως τὸ κάλλιστον ἐξελέξω τῶν ἔργων,
γραμματεύειν καὶ ὑπηρετεῖν τοῖς ἀρχιδίοις. ὡς δ᾽

tioned in Ar. Nub. 1007. See Bekk.
Anecd. p. 279: ἡ δὲ λεύκη τὸ μὲν τῶν
φύλλων ἔχει λευκὸν τὸ δ᾽ ἕτερον μέλαν,
σύμβολόν τι τοῦ βίου καὶ τοῦ θανάτου.
3. **τοὺς παρείας**: see Harpocr.,
παρεῖαι ὀνομάζονταί τινες ὄφεις παρὰ
τὸ παρείας μείζους ἔχειν, and Ael.
Hist. An. VIII. 12, ὁ παρείας ἢ παρούας
πυρρὸς τὴν χρόαν, εὐωπὸς τὸ ὄμμα,
πλατὺς τὸ στόμα, δακεῖν οὐ σφαλερὸς
ἀλλὰ πρᾷος. These harmless snakes
were thus sacred to Aesculapius, and
were named παρεῖαι from their fat
cheeks. See Ar. Plut. 690.
4. **εὐοῖ σαβοῖ**: as εὐοῖ, evoe, was
the cry used in the regular Bacchic
worship, so σαβοῖ was used in invoking
Σαβάζιος, the Phrygian Bacchus. All
points to some Asiatic worship, more
or less caricatured.
5. **ὑῆς ἄττης ἄττης ὑῆς**: these
mystic words stand as a cognate accusative with ἐπορχούμενος; this is
what he danced.—**ἔξαρχος καὶ προηγεμὼν** designates Aeschines as *leader*
of the song or dance or both.
6. **κιττοφόρος**, *ivy-bearer*, the ivy
being sacred to Bacchus.—**λικνοφόρος**,
bearer of the winnowing-fan, λίκνον,
the *mystica vannus Iacchi*. See Verg.
Georg. I. 166.—**καὶ τοιαῦθ᾽**, i.e. *these*
(ἔξαρχος κ.τ.λ.) *and similar names*.

8. **ἔνθρυπτα, στρεπτοὺς**, *sops*,
twists: for ἔνθρυπτα see the Schol.,
ψωμοὶ οἴνῳ βεβρεγμένοι. στρεπτούς·
πλακοῦντος εἶδος (Harpocr.), evidently
from στρέφω.—**νεήλατα**: acc. to Harpocration, *barley buns*, made of newly-
ground (roasted) barley, soaked in
honey and covered with plums and
chick-peas.

§ **261.** 1. **εἰς τοὺς δημότας ἐνεγράφης**: each deme was responsible
for the correctness of its ληξιαρχικὸν
γραμματεῖον, or list of citizens. Aristotle's Constitution of Athens (42[2])
gives us clear information on the
whole subject of the enrolment of
new citizens.
2. **ὁπωσδήποτε**, *somehow*, with
ἐπειδή γ᾽ ἐνεγράφης, refers to the
story that his father was a slave, in
which case it would have been impossible for the son to be legally
enrolled as a citizen without an affir-
mative vote of 6000 in the Assembly;
while the safeguards against illegal
enrolment would have made this
almost impossible.
4. **γραμματεύειν**: see §§ 162[5], 209[2].
The occupation of a paid private clerk
(not that of a clerk of the Senate or
Assembly) was despised at Athens:
see § 127[3], ὄλεθρος γραμματεύς.—

ἀπηλλάγης ποτὲ καὶ τούτου, πάνθ' ἃ τῶν ἄλλων 5
κατηγορεῖς αὐτὸς ποιήσας, οὐ κατῄσχυνας μὰ Δί'
οὐδὲν τῶν προϋπηργμένων τῷ μετὰ ταῦτα βίῳ, ἀλλὰ 262
μισθώσας σαυτὸν τοῖς βαρυστόνοις ἐπικαλουμένοις
ἐκείνοις ὑποκριταῖς, Σιμύκκᾳ καὶ Σωκράτει, ἐτριταγωνίστεις, σῦκα καὶ βότρυς καὶ ἐλάας συλλέγων
ὥσπερ ὀπωρώνης ἐκ τῶν ἀλλοτρίων χωρίων, πλείω 5
λαμβάνων ἀπὸ τούτων ἢ τῶν ἀγώνων, οὓς ὑμεῖς
περὶ τῆς ψυχῆς ἠγωνίζεσθε· ἦν γὰρ ἄσπονδος καὶ
ἀκήρυκτος ὑμῖν πρὸς τοὺς θεατὰς πόλεμος, ὑφ' ὧν
πολλὰ τραύματ' εἰληφὼς εἰκότως τοὺς ἀπείρους τῶν

ἀρχιδίοις, *petty officers*: ἀρχίδιον is
here diminutive of ἀρχή in the sense
of ἀρχων. See Aesch. III. 21, ἀρχὴν
ὑπεύθυνον μὴ ἀποδημεῖν.
7. τῶν προϋπηργμένων, *of your
antecedents*.
§ 262. 2. τοῖς βαρυστόνοις, *the
heavy groaners*.
3. Σιμύκκᾳ (so Σ): Theophrastus
(Athen. VIII. 348 A) mentions Σιμ-
μύκαν τὸν ὑποκριτήν. —ἐτριταγωνίστεις : a company of strolling actors,
such as performed at the country
festivals, was probably composed of
two men, who played the first and
second parts and hired another to
play the third parts.
4. σῦκα...χωρίων: the meaning of
these much disputed words seems to
be, that the band of players subsisted
chiefly on the fruit which Aeschines,
as their hired servant, collected from
the neighbouring farms by begging,
stealing, or buying, as he found most
convenient. He is compared to a
small fruiterer (ὀπωρώνης), who each
morning collects his load of fruit from
farms which he has hired, or wherever
else he can get it cheapest. Pollux
(VI. 128) includes ὀπωρώνης (with
πορνοβοσκός and ἀλλαντοπώλης) in his
long list of βίοι ἐφ' οἶς ἄν τις ὀνει-
δισθείη.

5. πλείω..ἀγώνων, *getting more*
(profit) *from these than from your plays*
(*contests*).
6. οὓς (cogn. acc.)...ἠγωνίζεσθε,
*which you played at the risk of your
lives* (or *in which you fought for your
lives*), with a pun on the two meanings
of ἀγών and ἀγωνίζομαι, *fight* and *play*:
see IV. 47 τῶν στρατηγῶν ἕκαστος δὶς
καὶ τρὶς κρίνεται παρ' ὑμῖν περὶ θανάτου,
πρὸς δὲ τοὺς ἐχθροὺς οὐδεὶς οὐδὲ ἅπαξ
αὐτῶν ἀγωνίσασθαι περὶ θανάτου τολμᾷ,
where there is a similar pun on *being
tried* (ἀγωνίζεσθαι) *for their lives* in
court and in battle.
7. ἄσπονδος καὶ ἀκήρυκτος, *without truce or herald*, i.e. *implacable*,
without even the common decencies
of civilized warfare.
9. τραύματ' εἰληφὼς : see XIX.
337, ὅτε μὲν τὰ Θυέστου καὶ τῶν ἐπὶ
Τροίᾳ κακὰ ἠγωνίζετο, ἐξεβάλλετε αὐτὸν
καὶ ἐξεσυρίττετε ἐκ τῶν θεάτρων, καὶ
μόνον οὐ κατελεύετε οὕτως ὥστε
τελευτῶντα τοῦ τριταγωνιστεῖν ἀποστῆναι. This account of the πόλεμος
makes τραύματ' here perfectly intelligible ; but the reading τούτων τραύματα in 6 (which all MSS. except Σ
have) makes endless difficulty and
confusion. If τραύματα in 6 is referred
to wounds received in stealing fruit,
compared with those received on the

τοιούτων κινδύνων ὡς δειλοὺς σκώπτεις. ἀλλὰ γὰρ 263
παρεὶς ὧν τὴν πενίαν αἰτιάσαιτ' ἄν τις, πρὸς αὐτὰ
τὰ τοῦ τρόπου σου βαδιοῦμαι κατηγορήματα. τοι-
αύτην γὰρ εἵλου πολιτείαν, ἐπειδή ποτε καὶ τοῦτ'
ἐπῆλθέ σοι ποιῆσαι, δι' ἣν εὐτυχούσης μὲν τῆς 5
πατρίδος λαγὼ βίον ἔζης δεδιὼς καὶ τρέμων καὶ ἀεὶ
πληγήσεσθαι προσδοκῶν ἐφ' οἷς σαυτῷ συνῄδεις
ἀδικοῦντι, ἐν οἷς δ' ἠτύχησαν οἱ ἄλλοι, θρασὺς ὢν
ὑφ' ἁπάντων ὦψαι. καίτοι ὅστις χιλίων πολιτῶν 264
ἀποθανόντων ἐθάρρησε, τί οὗτος παθεῖν ὑπὸ τῶν
ζώντων δίκαιός ἐστιν; πολλὰ τοίνυν ἕτερ' εἰπεῖν
315 ἔχων περὶ αὐτοῦ παραλείψω· οὐ γὰρ ὅσ' ἂν δείξαιμι
προσόντ' αἰσχρὰ τούτῳ καὶ ὀνείδη, πάντ' οἶμαι δεῖν 5
εὐχερῶς λέγειν, ἀλλ' ὅσα μηδὲν αἰσχρόν ἐστιν εἰπεῖν
ἐμοί.

stage or after the play, there is a strange repetition of the latter ; if there is a reference (as Westermann suggests) to fruit used in pelting the actors, it is hard to see how figs, grapes, and olives could endanger the lives of the "heavy groaners."

10. **ὡς δειλοὺς σκώπτεις**: see § 245².

Demosthenes (XIX. 246, 247) says that Aeschines was a τριταγωνιστής also to actors of high repute, as Theodorus and Aristodemus; and he reminds him of the time when he used to play the part of Creon in the Antigone with these actors. He adds the following: ἐν ἅπασι τοῖς δράμασι τοῖς τραγικοῖς ἐξαίρετόν ἐστιν ὥσπερ γέρας τοῖς τριταγωνισταῖς τὸ τοὺς τυράννους καὶ τοὺς τὰ σκῆπτρ' ἔχοντας εἰσιέναι.

§ 263. 4. **πολιτείαν**, position in public life.—**καὶ** emphasizes the rest of the clause, τοῦτ'...ποιῆσαι, i.e. when at last you took it into your head to try this.

6. **λαγὼ βίον ἔζης**: Weil quotes

Trag. frag. incert. 373 (N.), λαγὼ βίον ζῆς, ὁ πρὶν ἄτρομος λέων. "Dicuntur leporis vitam vivere qui semper anxii trepidique vivunt; nam ut est apud Herod. III. 108, ὁ λαγὸς ὑπὸ παντὸς θηρεύεται θηρίου καὶ ὄρνιθος καὶ ἀνθρώπου, ac ne somnum quidem capit nisi oculis apertis" (Dissen).

8. **θρασὺς ὤν...ὦψαι** (M.T. 884): personal passive construction.

§ 264. 1. **χιλίων ἀποθανόντων**, at Chaeronea : see Diod. XVI. 86, τῶν δ' Ἀθηναίων ἔπεσον μὲν ἐν τῇ μάχῃ πλείους τῶν χιλίων, ἥλωσαν δὲ οὐκ ἐλάττους τῶν δισχιλίων. See Lycurg. Leocr. 142, χίλιοι τῶν ὑμετέρων πολιτῶν ἐν Χαιρωνείᾳ ἐτελεύτησαν, καὶ δημοσίᾳ αὐτοὺς ἡ πόλις ἔθαψεν. Diod. XVI. 88 quotes an eloquent passage of the speech of Lycurgus at the trial of Lysicles, one of the Athenian commanders at Chaeronea, who was condemned to death.

5. **προσόντ' αἰσχρὰ τούτῳ**: cf. § 276⁵.

6. **εὐχερῶς λέγειν**, to be ready to tell : cf. § 70⁷.

Ἐξέτασον τοίνυν παρ' ἄλληλα τὰ σοὶ κἀμοὶ 265
βεβιωμένα, πράως, μὴ πικρῶς, Αἰσχίνη· εἶτ' ἐρώτησον τουτουσὶ τὴν ποτέρου τύχην ἂν ἔλοιθ' ἕκαστος
αὐτῶν. ἐδίδασκες γράμματα, ἐγὼ δ' ἐφοίτων. ἐτέ-
λεις, ἐγὼ δ' ἐτελούμην. ἐγραμμάτευες, ἐγὼ δ' ἠκκλη- 5
σίαζον. ἐτριταγωνίστεις, ἐγὼ δ' ἐθεώρουν· ἐξέπιπτες,
ἐγὼ δ' ἐσύριττον. ὑπὲρ τῶν ἐχθρῶν πεπολίτευσαι
πάντα, ἐγὼ δ' ὑπὲρ τῆς πατρίδος. ἐῶ τἆλλα, ἀλλὰ 266
νυνὶ τήμερον ἐγὼ μὲν ὑπὲρ τοῦ στεφανωθῆναι δοκι-
μάζομαι, τὸ δὲ μηδ' ὁτιοῦν ἀδικεῖν ἀνωμολόγημαι,
σοὶ δὲ συκοφάντῃ μὲν εἶναι δοκεῖν ὑπάρχει, κινδυνεύεις δὲ εἴτε δεῖ σ' ἔτι τοῦτο ποιεῖν, εἴτ' ἤδη πεπαῦ- 5
σθαι μὴ μεταλαβόντα τὸ πέμπτον μέρος τῶν ψήφων.
ἀγαθῇ γ'—οὐχ ὁρᾷς ;—τύχῃ συμβεβιωκὼς τῆς ἐμῆς
κατηγορεῖς.

§ 265. In §§ 265, 266 the orator
sums up vigorously the substance of
§§ 257—264. Westermann points out
that each of the five stages of the life
of Aeschines is mentioned in order,
when he was (1) a schoolmaster's
assistant (§ 258), (2) initiator (§§ 259,
260), (3) scribe (§ 261), (4) actor (§
262), (5) politician (§§ 263, 264).
Many ancient rhetoricians quote these
famous antitheses with approval and
admiration. We are again shocked
by the open avowal of the disgrace
of earning an honest living ; the
ancients were certainly more honest
than many of our generation in *expressing* this.

1. **τὰ...βεβιωμένα** : passive of ἀ...
βεβιώκαμεν (cf. § 130¹).

4. **ἐφοίτων,** *went to school* : cf. Ar.
Nub. 916, διὰ σὲ δὲ φοιτᾶν οὐδεὶς
ἐθέλει τῶν μειρακίων.

5. **ἐτελούμην,** probably into the
Eleusinian mysteries.

6. **ἐξέπιπτες** : ἐκπίπτειν, *exigi*, is
used as a passive to ἐκβάλλειν ; cf.
XIX. 337, and Arist. Poet. 17², 18¹⁵.

§ 266. 2. **ὑπὲρ...δοκιμάζομαι** :
δοκιμασία is any investigation to test
the fitness or competency of a person
for anything, as for office (its ordinary
meaning) or for citizenship ; and δοκι-
μάζομαι here implies that this trial is
to test his fitness for the crown.

3. **τὸ...ἀδικεῖν ἀνωμολόγημαι** : cf.
§ 86², ἀνωμολόγημαι τὰ ἄριστα πράττειν. The articular infinitive in *or.
obl.* is rare (M.T. 794, 743).

4. **σοὶ ὑπάρχει,** *it is in store for
you.*—**κινδυνεύεις** corresponds to δοκι-
μάζομαι (2) : the meaning is, *the
question with you is.*

5. **τοῦτο ποιεῖν,** i.e. *to go on being
a συκοφάντης.*—**πεπαῦσθαι,** *to be stopped*
(once for all), i.e. by ἀτιμία (cf. § 82⁹).

6. **τὸ πέμπτον μέρος** : Dindorf
omits πέμπτον because it is omitted
in §§ 103, 222, 250, whereas it appears
in other speeches frequently (e.g.
XXII. 3). What modern orator or
writer would submit to such rules of
consistency as critics impose on the
ancients?

7. **οὐχ ὁρᾷς;** cf. 232⁵, 281⁶.

Φέρε δὴ καὶ τὰς τῶν λῃτουργιῶν μαρτυρίας ὧν 267
λελῃτούργηκα ὑμῖν ἀναγνῶ. παρ' ἃς παρανάγνωθι
καὶ σύ μοι τὰς ῥήσεις ἃς ἐλυμαίνου,

　　　ἥκω νεκρῶν κευθμῶνα καὶ σκότου πύλας,
καὶ　　　　　　　　　　　　　　　　　　　　　　　　　　5
　　　κακαγγελεῖν μὲν ἴσθι μὴ θέλοντά με,
καὶ κακὸν κακῶς σε μάλιστα μὲν οἱ θεοὶ ἔπειθ'
οὗτοι πάντες ἀπολέσειαν, πονηρὸν ὄντα καὶ πολίτην καὶ τριταγωνιστήν. λέγε τὰς μαρτυρίας.

ΜΑΡΤΥΡΙΑΙ.

'Εν μὲν τοίνυν τοῖς πρὸς τὴν πόλιν τοιοῦτος· ἐν 268
316 δὲ τοῖς ἰδίοις εἰ μὴ πάντες ἴσθ' ὅτι κοινὸς καὶ φιλάν-
θρωπος καὶ τοῖς δεομένοις ἐπαρκῶν, σιωπῶ καὶ οὐδὲν
ἂν εἴποιμι οὐδὲ παρασχοίμην περὶ τούτων οὐδεμίαν
μαρτυρίαν, οὔτ' εἴ τινας ἐκ τῶν πολεμίων ἐλυσάμην, 5

§ 267. 1. φέρε...ἀναγνῶ (M.T. 257): the orator does not read the testimony himself; cf. λέγε (9).—**λῃ-τουργιῶν**: this includes the public services mentioned in χορηγεῖν and τριηραρχεῖν in § 257⁴, ⁵, but not εἰσφέρειν, as the property tax was not a λῃτουργία. For the form λῃτουργία see note on § 108³.

3. **ἐλυμαίνου,** *used to outrage*: cf. ἐπέτριψας, § 180⁶.

4. **ἥκω...πύλας**: the *Hecuba* of Euripides begins

ἥκω νεκρῶν κευθμῶνα καὶ σκότου πύλας
λιπών, ἵν' ''Αιδης χωρὶς ᾤκισται θεῶν,
Πολύδωρος, 'Εκάβης παῖς.

All MSS. except Σ have λιπών for νεκρῶν, making the sense of the quotation complete. But such a change is unlikely in quoting so familiar a verse.

6. **κακαγγελεῖν...με**: this verse is otherwise unknown. κακαγγελεῖν must be pres. infin. of κακαγγελέω (otherwise unknown), depending on

θέλοντα. The readings of the best MSS., κακαγγέλλειν or κάκ' ἀγγέλλειν (Σ), are metrically impossible. The common reading is κάκ' ἀγγελεῖν, an irregular fut. infin. with θέλοντα (see M.T. 113).

7. The words **κακὸν κακῶς σε... ἀπολέσειαν** are probably an adaptation of a verse quoted from Lynceus by Athenaeus, IV. 150 c, κακὸς κακῶς σέ < γ' > ἀπολέσειαν οἱ θεοί, or both may go back to the source of Ar. Eq. 2, 3, κακῶς Παφλάγονα...ἀπολέσειαν οἱ θεοί. See Blass.

8. **πονηρὸν**: with both πολίτην and τριταγωνιστήν.

§ 268. 2. κοινός, in public relations, *public spirited*, in private matters (as here), *devoted, at the service of all*: cf. Isoc. I. 10, τοῖς φίλοις κοινός.

3. **ἐπαρκῶν**, i.e. *ready to help.*—**οὐδὲν ἂν εἴποιμι,** *I had rather not mention anything.*

5. **εἴ τινας ἐλυσάμην**: these were Athenians captured by Philip at Olynthus in 348 B.C., whom Demosthenes

οὔτ' εἴ τισι θυγατέρας συνεξέδωκα, οὔτε τῶν τοιούτων οὐδέν. καὶ γὰρ οὕτω πως ὑπείληφα. ἐγὼ 269
νομίζω τὸν μὲν εὖ παθόντα δεῖν μεμνῆσθαι πάντα
τὸν χρόνον, τὸν δὲ ποιήσαντ' εὐθὺς ἐπιλελῆσθαι, εἰ
δεῖ τὸν μὲν χρηστοῦ τὸν δὲ μὴ μικροψύχου ποιεῖν
ἔργον ἀνθρώπου. τὸ δὲ τὰς ἰδίας εὐεργεσίας ὑπομι- 5
μνήσκειν καὶ λέγειν μικροῦ δεῖν ὅμοιόν ἐστι τῷ
ὀνειδίζειν. οὐ δὴ ποιήσω τοιοῦτον οὐδέν, οὐδὲ
προαχθήσομαι, ἀλλ' ὅπως ποθ' ὑπείλημμαι περὶ
τούτων, ἀρκεῖ μοι.
Βούλομαι δὲ τῶν ἰδίων ἀπαλλαγεὶς ἔτι μικρὰ 270

ransomed at Pella in 346 (Hist. § 30).
See XIX. 166—170. Dem. lent various
sums to these prisoners, which they
paid for their ransoms ; when afterwards Philip set the other prisoners
free without ransom, Dem. forgave
the first their debts to him (ἔδωκα
δωρεὰν τὰ λύτρα), which otherwise
they would have been strictly required
by law to pay (XIX. 170).

6. **συνεξέδωκα,** i.e. *helped* poor
citizens *to endow their daughters* :
giving a dowry was an important
part of giving a daughter in marriage.
—**οὔτε**...**οὐδέν,** *nor anything else of
the kind.* These words are rather
loosely connected with the preceding
clauses with **οὔτε** : in all three **οὔτε**
repeats the negative of **οὐδὲν ἂν εἴποιμι**
κ.τ.λ., so that the construction here
is **οὔτε ἂν εἴποιμι τῶν τοιούτων οὐδέν.**

§ **269.** 1. **ὑπείληφα** : cf. pass.
ὑπείλημμαι (8).—**ἐγώ**...**δεῖν** : an iambic
trimeter.

3. **ποιήσαντ'** : sc. **εὖ.**—**ἐπιλελῆ-**
σθαι : cf. **πεπαῦσθαι,** § 266[5].

4. **μικροψύχου** : see note on § 279[6].

5. **ὑπομιμνήσκειν,** i.e. *to be always
calling to mind.*

6. **μικροῦ δεῖν,** the full form of
μικροῦ, *almost* (M.T. 779): cf. § 151[3].
West. quotes Cic. Lael. XX. 71,

odiosum sane genus hominum officia
exprobrantium ; quae meminisse debet
is in quem collata sunt, non com-
memorare qui contulit ; and Sen.
Benef. II. 10, haec enim beneficii
inter duos lex est: alter statim obli-
visci debet dati, alter accepti nunquam;
lacerat animum et premit frequens
meritorum commemoratio. Pericles
(Thuc. II. 40) looks at the matter
from a different point of view: οὐ γὰρ
πάσχοντες εὖ ἀλλὰ δρῶντες κτώμεθα
τοὺς φίλους· κ.τ.λ. There is a New
England saying, "If a man does you
a favour, he follows you with a toma-
hawk all your lifetime."

8. **προαχθήσομαι** : cf. προήχθην
(sc. τάξαι), VIII. 71.—**ὅπως ὑπείλημ-**
μαι, *as I have been understood,* i.e.
the general opinion which has been
formed of me.

9. **ἀρκεῖ μοι** : sc. οὕτως ὑπειλῆφθαι.

§§ **270—275.** We have here a
sort of peroration to the discourse on
Fortune (§§ 252—275), in which the
orator comes at last to the precise
point of his opponent's remark, that
Demosthenes has brought ill-luck
upon every person or state with which
he had to do (Aesch. III. 114).
Hitherto Demosthenes has spoken

πρὸς ὑμᾶς εἰπεῖν περὶ τῶν κοινῶν. εἰ μὲν γὰρ
ἔχεις, Αἰσχίνη, τῶν ὑπὸ τοῦτον τὸν ἥλιον εἰπεῖν
ἀνθρώπων ὅστις ἀθῷος τῆς Φιλίππου πρότερον καὶ
νῦν τῆς Ἀλεξάνδρου δυναστείας γέγονεν, ἢ τῶν 5
Ἑλλήνων ἢ τῶν βαρβάρων, ἔστω, συγχωρῶ τὴν
ἐμὴν—εἴτε τύχην εἴτε δυστυχίαν ὀνομάζειν βούλει—
πάντων γεγενῆσθαι. εἰ δὲ καὶ τῶν μηδεπώποτ᾽ ἰδόν- 271
των ἐμὲ μηδὲ φωνὴν ἀκηκοότων ἐμοῦ πολλοὶ πολλὰ
καὶ δεινὰ πεπόνθασι, μὴ μόνον κατ᾽ ἄνδρα, ἀλλὰ καὶ
πόλεις ὅλαι καὶ ἔθνη, πόσῳ δικαιότερον καὶ ἀληθέστερον τὴν ἁπάντων, ὡς ἔοικεν, ἀνθρώπων τύχην 5
κοινὴν καὶ φοράν τινα πραγμάτων χαλεπὴν καὶ οὐχ
οἵαν ἔδει τούτων αἰτίαν ἡγεῖσθαι. σὺ τοίνυν ταῦτ᾽ 272
ἀφεὶς ἐμὲ τὸν παρὰ τουτοισὶ πεπολιτευμένον αἰτιᾷ,
317 καὶ ταῦτ᾽ εἰδὼς ὅτι, καὶ εἰ μὴ τὸ ὅλον, μέρος γ᾽ ἐπιβάλλει τῆς βλασφημίας ἅπασι, καὶ μάλιστα σοί.
εἰ μὲν γὰρ ἐγὼ κατ᾽ ἐμαυτὸν αὐτοκράτωρ περὶ τῶν 5

far more of his "fortunes" than of
his "fortune." See remarks before
notes on § 252.

§ **270**. 3. ὑπὸ τοῦτον τὸν ἥλιον,
as we say, *under the Sun* (poetic).
See Il. v. 267, ὅσσοι ἔασιν ὑπ᾽ ἠῶ τ᾽
ἠέλιόν τε: Od. XV. 349, ζώουσιν ὑπ᾽
αὐγὰς ἠελίοιο.

4. ἀθῷος, *unharmed*: cf. § 125[1],
where we have the original meaning,
free from θωή, *penalty*, as in XXIII. 78,
ταύτης μὲν (δίκης) ἀθῷος ἀφίεται, *he is
acquitted*.

5. δυναστείας: see §§ 67[2, 3], 322[7],
with notes.

8. πάντων γεγενῆσθαι, *has fallen
to the lot of us all*: πάντων refers to
all the Athenians, opposed to τῶν
μηδεπώποτ᾽ ἰδόντων ἐμέ in § 271[1]. He
might admit (he implies) that his own
fortune had extended to Athens, were
it not that foreign states had suffered
the same ill fortune.

§ **271**. 3. κατ᾽ ἄνδρα, i.e. *individuals*, as opposed to πόλεις and
ἔθνη.

6. φοράν τινα πραγμάτων, *a rush
of events*: φορά in this sense (*impetus*)
belongs to φέρομαι, used as in βίᾳ
φέρεται, Plat. Phaedr. 254 A, and
φερόμενος, *with a rush* (M.T. 837):
φοράν, *crop*, in § 61[2], belongs to φέρω,
bear, produce.—οὐχ οἵαν ἔδει, *not what
it should be* (present in time, M.T.
417); ἔδει here is *ought to be* (but is
not).

§ **272**. 3. ἐπιβάλλει: see note on
τὸ ἐπιβάλλον μέρος, § 254[7].

4. ἅπασι: sc. τοῖς Ἀθηναίοις (cf.
πάντων, § 270[8]).

5. εἰ μὲν...ἐβουλευόμην is past,
while ἦν ἄν, its apodosis, is present.
—κατ᾽ ἐμαυτὸν αὐτοκράτωρ, *an absolute autocrat*: cf. αὐτὸς αὐτοκράτωρ,
§ 235[5].

πραγμάτων ἐβουλευόμην, ἦν ἂν τοῖς ἄλλοις ῥήτορσιν
ὑμῖν ἔμ' αἰτιᾶσθαι· εἰ δὲ παρῆτε μὲν ἐν ταῖς ἐκκλη- 273
σίαις ἁπάσαις, ἀεὶ δ' ἐν κοινῷ τὸ συμφέρον ἡ πόλις
προύτίθει σκοπεῖν, πᾶσι δὲ ταῦτ' ἐδόκει τότ' ἄριστ'
εἶναι, καὶ μάλιστα σοὶ (οὐ γὰρ ἐπ' εὐνοίᾳ γ' ἐμοὶ
παρεχώρεις ἐλπίδων καὶ ζήλου καὶ τιμῶν, ἃ πάντα 5
προσῆν τοῖς τότε πραττομένοις ὑπ' ἐμοῦ, ἀλλὰ τῆς
ἀληθείας ἡττώμενος δηλονότι καὶ τῷ μηδὲν ἔχειν
εἰπεῖν βέλτιον), πῶς οὐκ ἀδικεῖς καὶ δεινὰ ποιεῖς
τούτοις νῦν ἐγκαλῶν ὧν τότ' οὐκ εἶχες λέγειν βελτίω;
παρὰ μὲν τοίνυν τοῖς ἄλλοις ἔγωγ' ὁρῶ πᾶσιν ἀνθρώ- 274
ποις διωρισμένα καὶ τεταγμένα πως τὰ τοιαῦτα.
ἀδικεῖ τις ἑκών· ὀργὴν καὶ τιμωρίαν κατὰ τούτου.

§ **273.** 2. **ἐν κοινῷ.. προύτίθει
σκοπεῖν**, *put forward for public consideration*: cf. IV. 1, εἰ περὶ καινοῦ
τινος πράγματος προύτίθετο λέγειν.
See § 192², προτίθησι βουλήν, and
§ 236⁴, ἐξ ἴσου προύτίθετε. γνώμας
προτιθέναι often means *to open a debate*:
cf. Thuc. I. 139¹⁸, and III. 38², τῶν
προθέντων αὖθις λέγειν, where λέγειν
is like σκοπεῖν here.

4. **ἐπ' εὐνοίᾳ**, *out of devotion*, corresponds to ἀλλὰ ἡττώμενος (7). —**ἐμοὶ**
is dative of advantage with παρεχώρεις,
but is also felt with ἐπ' εὐνοίᾳ.

5. **ζήλου**, *pride*: see § 120⁶.

9. **ὧν**: with βελτίω.

Westermann thinks the argument of
this section not quite fair, as it is not
to be assumed that Aeschines assented
to all which he did not oppose. But,
apart from the obvious irony of parts
of the argument (as in οὐ γὰρ ἐπ'
εὐνοίᾳ κ.τ.λ.), it was surely not too
much to expect of the acknowledged
"leader of the opposition" in such a
desperate crisis, that he should at
least protest strongly against measures
of such vital importance as those which
he censures afterwards, even if he
could not propose any positive mea-

sures himself. Now it is an important
part of the argument of Demosthenes,
that Aeschines *said nothing whatever*
on such occasions as the sudden seizure
of Elatea by Philip. See § 191⁵, σοῦ
δ' ἀφώνου...καθημένου: see the whole
passage, §§ 188—191. The only ground
on which such neglect can be excused
is the one here assumed, that the
opposition had no better plan to
propose. The plain truth is, of course,
that Aeschines really wished to let
Philip have his own way at this time.

§ **274.** 1. **παρά...ἀνθρώποις** : see
two similar cases of παρά in § 297⁴,⁶.
—**τοῖς ἄλλοις πᾶσιν**, i.e. all except
Aesch.

2. **τὰ τοιαῦτα**, i.e. *such* (principles)
as the following, explained by the
statements in 3—8.

3. **ἀδικεῖ τις ἑκών**, a man (let us
suppose) *is guilty of voluntary injustice*. We have three such suppositions
in independent sentences, with paratactic replies or apodoses. For a
similar arrangement see § 117, ἐπέδωκα,
ἦρχον, ἀδίκως ἦρξα, with the replies.
See also § 198⁷⁻⁹.

ὀργὴν καὶ τιμωρίαν : sc. διωρισμέ-
νην ὁρῶ.

ἐξήμαρτέ τις ἄκων· συγγνώμην ἀντὶ τῆς τιμωρίας
τούτῳ. οὔτ' ἀδικῶν τις οὔτ' ἐξαμαρτάνων, εἰς τὰ 5
πᾶσι δοκοῦντα συμφέρειν ἑαυτὸν δοὺς οὐ κατώρθωσε
μεθ' ἁπάντων· οὐκ ὀνειδίζειν οὐδὲ λοιδορεῖσθαι τῷ
τοιούτῳ δίκαιον, ἀλλὰ συνάχθεσθαι. φανήσεται 275
ταῦτα πάνθ' οὕτως οὐ μόνον τοῖς νόμοις, ἀλλὰ καὶ
ἡ φύσις αὐτὴ τοῖς ἀγράφοις νομίμοις καὶ τοῖς ἀνθρωπίνοις ἤθεσι διώρικεν. Αἰσχίνης τοίνυν τοσοῦτον
ὑπερβέβληκεν ἅπαντας ἀνθρώπους ὠμότητι καὶ 5
συκοφαντίᾳ ὥστε καὶ ὧν αὐτὸς ὡς ἀτυχημάτων
ἐμέμνητο, καὶ ταῦτ' ἐμοῦ κατηγορεῖ.
Καὶ πρὸς τοῖς ἄλλοις, ὥσπερ αὐτὸς ἁπλῶς καὶ 276

5. **οὔτ' ἀδικῶν τις οὔτ' ἐξαμαρτά-**
νων, i.e. *one who neither is guilty of
injustice nor errs* (sc. ἀκών).
7. **μεθ' ἁπάντων,** i.e. *in common
with everybody.*
8. **συνάχθεσθαι,** *sympathize with
him.*
§ **275.** 2. **τοῖς νόμοις** (without
ἐν Σ, Α1), *by the laws*: cf. xx. 57,
ταῦτα καὶ νόμοις τισὶ καὶ δόξαις διώ-
ρισται.
3. **τοῖς ἀγράφοις νομίμοις,** *by the
principles of unwritten law,* further
explained by τοῖς ἀνθρωπίνοις ἤθεσι:
cf. § 114². The unwritten law is
known as the law of Nature, the
moral law, the divine law, or the
higher law, the law which is not alia
lex Romae, alia Athenis. Aristotle
distinguishes two kinds of unwritten
law, one the **κοινὸς νόμος, ὁ κατὰ**
φύσιν, the universal law of Nature,
the other a branch of the special law
of particular States, by which the
defects of the written law may be
remedied, that is, τὸ ἐπιεικές, *equity.*
See Rhet. I. 13. As an example of
the universal law he quotes Antig.
456, 457, οὐ γάρ τι...ἐξ ὅτου 'φάνη,
and the verses of Empedocles:
ἀλλὰ τὸ μὲν πάντων νόμιμον διά τ'
εὐρυμέδοντος

αἰθέρος ἠνεκέως τέταται διά τ' ἀπλέ-
του αὖ γῆς.
5. **ὠμότητι:** cf. ὠμότερος, § 212⁹.
6. **ὡς ἀτυχημάτων:** see Aesch.
III. 57, τῶν δὲ ἀτυχημάτων ἀπάντων
Δημοσθένην αἴτιον γεγενημένον.
§§ **276—296.** Here Demosthenes
begins by alluding to the attempt of
Aeschines to represent him as a skilful
sophist and rhetorician, who will impose on the judges by his wily arts.
He retorts by showing that his own
oratorical power has always been
exerted in behalf of Athens, while
that of Aeschines has been used to
help her enemies or to gratify personal
malice. He refers to the testimony
of the citizens in choosing him to
deliver the eulogy on those who fell
at Chaeronea, as a proof of his
patriotism. Finally, he declares that
the present calamities of Greece have
been caused by men of the stamp of
Aeschines in various Greek states;
and he gives a black list of these
traitors who have betrayed their
countries to the common enemy.
§ **276.** 1. **ὥσπερ...εἰρηκώς,** i.e.
*posing as one who had always spoken
his own thoughts honestly and loyally*:
we generally translate (for con-
venience) as *if he had spoken (quasi*

μετ' εὐνοίας πάντας εἰρηκὼς τοὺς λόγους, φυλάττειν
318 ἐμὲ καὶ τηρεῖν ἐκέλευεν, ὅπως μὴ παρακρούσομαι
μηδ' ἐξαπατήσω, δεινὸν καὶ γόητα καὶ σοφιστὴν καὶ
τὰ τοιαῦτ' ὀνομάζων, ὡς ἐὰν πρότερός τις εἴπῃ τὰ 5
προσόνθ' ἑαυτῷ περὶ ἄλλου, καὶ δὴ ταῦθ' οὕτως
ἔχοντα, καὶ οὐκέτι τοὺς ἀκούοντας σκεψομένους τίς
ποτ' αὐτός ἐστιν ὁ ταῦτα λέγων. ἐγὼ δ' οἶδ' ὅτι
γιγνώσκετε τοῦτον ἅπαντες, καὶ πολὺ τούτῳ μᾶλλον
ἢ ἐμοὶ νομίζετε ταῦτα προσεῖναι. κἀκεῖν' εὖ οἶδ' ὅτι 277
τὴν ἐμὴν δεινότητα—ἔστω γάρ. καίτοι ἔγωγ' ὁρῶ
τῆς τῶν λεγόντων δυνάμεως τοὺς ἀκούοντας τὸ πλεῖστον κυρίους· ὡς γὰρ ἂν ὑμεῖς ἀποδέξησθε καὶ πρὸς
ἕκαστον ἔχητ' εὐνοίας, οὕτως ὁ λέγων ἔδοξε φρονεῖν. 5
εἰ δ' οὖν ἐστι καὶ παρ' ἐμοί τις ἐμπειρία τοιαύτη,
ταύτην μὲν εὑρήσετε πάντες ἐν τοῖς κοινοῖς ἐξεταζομένην ὑπὲρ ὑμῶν ἀεὶ καὶ οὐδαμοῦ καθ' ὑμῶν οὐδ'

vero dixisset, West.), though there is
nothing conditional in the participle
with ὥσπερ, which merely expresses
comparison (M.T. 867): *having, as it
were, spoken*, would be more correct,
though less clear. See ὥσπερ οὐχ,
§ 323[7], and note on ὡς (5).
3. ἐκέλευεν: sc. ὑμᾶς.—ὅπως μὴ
παρακρούσομαι: the subject of the
object clause appears by attraction
(ἐμὲ) in the leading clause (M.T. 304[2]).
This is a reply to Aesch. 16, 174,
206, 207, and other passages.
5—7. ὡς...οὕτως ἔχοντα (accus.
abs., M.T. 853), i.e. *assuming that
this must needs be so.* ὡς has no more
conditional force than ὥσπερ (1),
though we often find it convenient
to use *as if* in translation (M.T. 864):
notice οὐκέτι with σκεψομένους, *will
not further consider*, showing that
there is nothing conditional in the
expression. τὰ προσόνθ' ἑαυτῷ, i.e.
things which are true of himself (cf.
προσεῖναι, l. 10).

§ 277. 2. ἔστω γάρ, *well! grant
that I have it.* Having broken his
sentence, he proceeds to say that
the hearers have it in their power
to neutralize the highest gifts of
eloquence by refusing to listen. See
XIX. 340, αἱ μὲν τοίνυν ἄλλαι δυνάμεις
ἐπιεικῶς εἰσιν αὐτάρκεις, ἡ δὲ τοῦ λέγειν,
ἂν τὰ παρ' ὑμῶν τῶν ἀκουόντων ἀντιστῇ,
διακόπτεται.
4. ὡς ἄν...πρὸς ἕκαστον ἔχητ'
εὐνοίας, i.e. *according to your goodwill towards each*, εὐνοίας being
partitive with ὡς, as in εἰς τοῦτο
εὐνοίας. (G. 1091.) Cf. Thuc. I. 22.
5. οὕτως φρονεῖν, i.e. εὖ or κακῶς
φρονεῖν.
6. ἐμπειρία, substituted modestly
for the stronger δεινότητα of l. 2, the
original construction being resumed
by ταύτην (7).
7. ἐξεταζομένην ὑπὲρ ὑμῶν, *mar-
shalled on your side*, the familiar
military figure: see notes on § 173[5]
and § 173[6].

ἰδίᾳ, τὴν δὲ τούτου τοὐναντίον οὐ μόνον τῷ λέγειν
ὑπὲρ τῶν ἐχθρῶν, ἀλλὰ καὶ εἴ τις ἐλύπησέ τι τοῦτον 10
ἢ προσέκρουσέ που, κατὰ τούτων. οὐ γὰρ αὐτῇ
δικαίως, οὐδ' ἐφ' ἃ συμφέρει τῇ πόλει, χρῆται. οὔτε 278
γὰρ τὴν ὀργὴν οὔτε τὴν ἔχθραν οὔτ' ἄλλ' οὐδὲν τῶν
τοιούτων τὸν καλὸν κἀγαθὸν πολίτην δεῖ τοὺς ὑπὲρ
τῶν κοινῶν εἰσεληλυθότας δικαστὰς ἀξιοῦν αὐτῷ
βεβαιοῦν, οὐδ' ὑπὲρ τούτων εἰς ὑμᾶς εἰσιέναι, ἀλλὰ 5
μάλιστα μὲν μὴ ἔχειν ταῦτ' ἐν τῇ φύσει, εἰ δ' ἄρ'
ἀνάγκη, πράως καὶ μετρίως διακείμεν' ἔχειν. ἐν
τίσιν οὖν σφοδρὸν εἶναι τὸν πολιτευόμενον καὶ τὸν
ῥήτορα δεῖ; ἐν οἷς τῶν ὅλων τι κινδυνεύεται τῇ
πόλει, καὶ ἐν οἷς πρὸς τοὺς ἐναντίους ἐστὶ τῷ δήμῳ, 10
ἐν τούτοις· ταῦτα γὰρ γενναίου καὶ ἀγαθοῦ πολίτου.
319 μηδενὸς δ' ἀδικήματος πώποτε δημοσίου—προσθήσω 279
δὲ μηδ' ἰδίου—δίκην ἀξιώσαντα λαβεῖν παρ' ἐμοῦ,
μήθ' ὑπὲρ τῆς πόλεως μήθ' ὑπὲρ αὐτοῦ, στεφάνου

---

9. τοὐναντίον (adv.): sc. ἐξεταζομένην εὑρήσετε.
11. κατὰ τούτων (sc. τῷ λέγειν),
opposed to ὑπὲρ τῶν ἐχθρῶν. τούτων
refers loosely to τις: see § 99³ and
II. 18, εἴ τις...τούτους. We are all
familiar with anybody becoming them
in conversation. The whole expression εἴ τις ἐλύπησέ τι...κατὰ τούτων
(gratifying private grudges) is opposed to οὐδ' ἰδίᾳ (8), as ὑπὲρ τῶν
ἐχθρῶν is opposed to ὑπὲρ ὑμῶν (8).
§ 278. 3. ὑπὲρ τῶν κοινῶν, with
εἰσεληλυθότας, i.e. who have come into
court to give judgment for the public
good, opposed to ὀργὴν...βεβαιοῦν.
4. ἀξιοῦν αὐτῷ βεβαιοῦν, to ask
(them) to confirm for him, i.e. by
condemning his opponent.
5. ὑπὲρ τούτων, for these ends,
i.e. to gratify his ὀργή or ἔχθρα.
6. μάλιστα μὲν, best of all.—εἰ δ'
ἄρ' ἀνάγκη, i.e. but if after all he
must have these feelings. Cf. § 178¹².

7. ἐν τίσιν...δεῖ; when should an
orator use all his vehemence?
9. τῶν ὅλων τι, any of the supreme
(entire) interests of the state: cf.
§§ 28⁹, 303⁹.
10. ἐστὶ τῷ δήμῳ, the people are
concerned, etc.
11. ἐν τούτοις: with strongest
emphasis, in reply to ἐν τίσιν;
§ 279. Still answering the question ἐν τίσιν...δεῖ; (§ 278⁷), he describes
the present suit as one which does not
justify vehemence in an orator.
2. μηδ' ἰδίου (sc. ἀδικήματος) continues the construction of δημοσίου:
cf. VIII. 39, 40, ἐχθρὸς ὅλῃ τῇ πόλει...
προσθήσω δὲ καὶ τοῖς ἐν τῇ πόλει πᾶσιν
ἀνθρώποις.
3. στεφάνου...κατηγορίαν, an accusation against a crown and a vote of
thanks (ἐπαίνου) (i.e. against a proposition to confer these): nearly all
decrees conferring a crown had the
words ἐπαινέσαι καὶ στεφανῶσαι.

172 ΔΗΜΟΣΘΕΝΟΥΣ

καὶ ἐπαίνου κατηγορίαν ἥκειν συνεσκευασμένον καὶ
τοσουτουσὶ λόγους ἀνηλωκέναι, ἰδίας ἔχθρας καὶ 5
φθόνου καὶ μικροψυχίας ἐστὶ σημεῖον, οὐδενὸς
χρηστοῦ. τὸ δὲ δὴ καὶ τοὺς πρὸς ἔμ' αὐτὸν ἀγῶνας
ἐάσαντα νῦν ἐπὶ τόνδ' ἥκειν καὶ πᾶσαν ἔχει κακίαν.
καί μοι δοκεῖς ἐκ τούτων, Αἰσχίνη, λόγων ἐπίδειξίν 280
τινα καὶ φωνασκίας βουλόμενος ποιήσασθαι τοῦτον
προελέσθαι τὸν ἀγῶνα, οὐκ ἀδικήματος οὐδενὸς
λαβεῖν τιμωρίαν. ἔστι δ' οὐχ ὁ λόγος τοῦ ῥήτορος,
Αἰσχίνη, τίμιον, οὐδ' ὁ τόνος τῆς φωνῆς, ἀλλὰ τὸ 5
ταὐτὰ προαιρεῖσθαι τοῖς πολλοῖς καὶ τὸ τοὺς αὐτοὺς
μισεῖν καὶ φιλεῖν οὕσπερ ἂν ἡ πατρίς. ὁ γὰρ οὕτως 281
ἔχων τὴν ψυχήν, οὗτος ἐπ' εὐνοίᾳ πάντ' ἐρεῖ· ὁ δ'
ἀφ' ὧν ἡ πόλις προορᾶται κίνδυνόν τιν' ἑαυτῇ,
τούτους θεραπεύων οὐκ ἐπὶ τῆς αὐτῆς ὁρμεῖ τοῖς
πολλοῖς, οὔκουν οὐδὲ τῆς ἀσφαλείας τὴν αὐτὴν ἔχει 5
προσδοκίαν. ἀλλ'—ὁρᾷς ;—ἐγώ· ταὐτὰ γὰρ συμφέ-

4. **συνεσκευασμ.**, *having trumped up.*
6. **μικροψυχίας**, *littleness of soul*, opposed to *μεγαλοψυχία*, § 68⁴: cf. § 269⁴.—**οὐδενὸς χρηστοῦ** : neuter, cf. **πάντα τὰ χρηστά**, XX. 165.
7. **τοὺς...ἀγῶνας ἐάσαντα** with **ἐπὶ τόνδ' ἥκειν** recurs to the idea of § 16.
8. **καὶ** strengthens **πᾶσαν**, *the very depth of baseness.*
§ **280.** 2. **φωνασκίας**, *declamation* (practice of voice): cf. § 308¹⁰, and **φωνασκήσας** and **πεφωνασκηκώς** in XIX. 255, 336.—**τοῦτον τὸν ἀγῶνα**, i.e. *this form of suit* (against Ctesiphon).
6. **ταὐτὰ προαιρεῖσθαι τοῖς πολλοῖς** : cf. §§ 281⁶, 292³.
§ **281.** 4. **τούτους** renews emphatically the antecedent implied in **ἀφ' ὧν**. —**οὐκ...ὁρμεῖ** (sc. **ἀγκύρας**), *does not ride at the same anchor*, an oft-quoted saying. See Harpocr. under **οὐκ ἐπὶ τῆς κ.τ.λ.**, and Apo-

stolius XIII. 55 (Paroem. Gr. II. p. 591): both note the ellipsis of **ἀγκύρας**. Another expression was **ἐπὶ δυοῖν ὁρμεῖ** (sc. **ἀγκύραιν**), **ἐπὶ τῶν ἀστεμφῶς ἐχόντων** (Apostol. VII. 61), to which Solon refers in his comparison of Athens with her two senates to a ship with two anchors : Plut. Sol. 19, **οἰόμενος ἐπὶ δυσὶ βουλαῖς ὥσπερ ἀγκύραις ὁρμοῦσαν ἧττον ἐν σάλῳ τὴν πόλιν ἔσεσθαι.** Cf. Soph. Ant. 188—190, quoted in XIX. 247.
5. **οὔκουν οὐδὲ** : the two negatives unite their force, and that of **οὖν**, *therefore*, remains : **οὐκοῦν οὐδὲ** would give essentially the same sense.
6. **ὁρᾷς** ; see **οὐχ ὁρᾷς** ; §§ 232⁵, 266⁷, and **οὐ γὰρ** ; § 136². —**ἐγώ** : the ellipsis may be supplied from **οὕτως ἔχων τὴν ψυχήν** (1), with the preceding **τὸ...μισεῖν καὶ φιλεῖν.**
7. **εἱλόμην**, in the sense of **προαιρεῖσθαι** (§ 280⁶).—**ἐξαίρετον**, *exclusive.*

ρονθ' εἰλόμην τουτοισὶ, καὶ οὐδὲν ἐξαίρετον οὐδ'
ἴδιον πεποίημαι. ἆρ' οὖν οὐδὲ σύ; καὶ πῶς; ὃς 282
εὐθέως μετὰ τὴν μάχην πρεσβευτὴς ἐπορεύου πρὸς
Φίλιππον, ὃς ἦν τῶν ἐκείνοις τοῖς χρόνοις συμφορῶν
αἴτιος τῇ πατρίδι, καὶ ταῦτ' ἀρνούμενος πάντα τὸν
ἔμπροσθε χρόνον ταύτην τὴν χρείαν, ὡς πάντες 5
ἴσασιν. καίτοι τίς ὁ τὴν πόλιν ἐξαπατῶν; οὐχ ὁ
μὴ λέγων ἃ φρονεῖ; τῷ δ' ὁ κῆρυξ καταρᾶται
δικαίως; οὐ τῷ τοιούτῳ; τί δὲ μεῖζον ἔχοι τις ἂν
320 εἰπεῖν ἀδίκημα κατ' ἀνδρὸς ῥήτορος ἢ εἰ μὴ ταὐτὰ
φρονεῖ καὶ λέγει; σὺ τοίνυν οὗτος εὑρέθης. εἶτα σὺ 283
φθέγγει καὶ βλέπειν εἰς τὰ τούτων πρόσωπα τολ-
μᾷς; πότερ' οὐχ ἡγεῖ γιγνώσκειν αὐτοὺς ὅστις εἶ; ἢ
τοσοῦτον ὕπνον καὶ λήθην ἅπαντας ἔχειν ὥστ' οὐ

§ **282.** 1. ἆρ' οὖν οὐδὲ σύ; can
the same be said also of you? i.e. οὐδὲν
...πεποίησαι.

2. πρεσβυτὴς πρὸς Φίλιππον :
Aeschines (III. 227) says of this, τῆς
μάχης ἐπιγενομένης...ὑπὲρ τῆς σωτηρίας
τῆς πόλεως ἐπρεσβεύομεν. Aeschines,
Demades (from whom the peace was
named, §285⁶), and probably Phocion,
went to Philip to negotiate a peace
after Chaeronea. See Hist. § 68.

5. ταύτην τὴν χρείαν : this, taken
with τὸν ἔμπροσθε χρόνον, refers to
earlier personal intercourse with
Philip. Aeschines is now less
anxious to repudiate this charge,
in the day of Alexander's great success in Asia : see III. 66, ὁ γὰρ μισα-
λέξανδρος νυνὶ φάσκων εἶναι καὶ τότε
μισοφίλιππος Δημοσθένης, ὁ τὴν ξενίαν
ἐμοὶ προφέρων τὴν Ἀλεξάνδρου, and cf.
§§ 51, 52 (above).

6. ὁ μὴ λέγων = ὃς μὴ λέγει.

7. καταρᾶται : a most compre-
hensive curse (ἀρά) was a part of the
religious ceremony at the opening
of each meeting of the Senate and

Assembly. See XXIII. 97 : διόπερ
καταρᾶται καθ' ἑκάστην ἐκκλησίαν ὁ
κῆρυξ...εἴ τις ἐξαπατᾷ λέγων ἢ βουλὴν
ἢ δῆμον ἢ τὴν ἡλιαίαν. Aeschines, as
ὑπογραμματεύων ὑμῖν καὶ ὑπηρετῶν τῇ
βουλῇ, had the duty of dictating this
curse to the herald. See Dinarch. I.
47 (of Demosth.), κατάρατος δὲ καθ'
ἑκάστην ἐκκλησίαν γινόμενος, ἐξεληλεγ-
μένος δῶρα κατὰ τῆς πόλεως εἰληφώς,
ἐξηπατηκὼς δὲ καὶ τὸν δῆμον καὶ τὴν
βουλὴν παρὰ τὴν ἀράν, καὶ ἕτερα μὲν
λέγων ἕτερα δὲ φρονῶν, which
shows that ὁ μὴ λέγων ἃ φρονεῖ (6)
was included in the same curse. See
note on § 130².

10. οὗτος : cf. ἐφάνην οὗτος ἐγώ,
§ 173¹.

§ **283.** 4. ὥστ' οὐ μεμνῆσθαι,
(so) that they do not remember, not
(so) as not to remember : this is a
regular case of ὥστε οὐ with the infinitive in indirect discourse, where
the direct form would have been τοσοῦτον ὕπνον...ἔχουσιν ὥστ' οὐ μέμνηνται
(M.T. 594).

μεμνῆσθαι τοὺς λόγους οὓς ἐδημηγόρεις ἐν τῷ πο- 5
λέμῳ, καταρώμενος καὶ διομνύμενος μηδὲν εἶναι σοὶ
καὶ Φιλίππῳ πρᾶγμα, ἀλλ' ἐμὲ τὴν αἰτίαν σοι
ταύτην ἐπάγειν τῆς ἰδίας ἕνεκ' ἔχθρας, οὐκ οὖσαν
ἀληθῆ. ὡς δ' ἀπηγγέλθη τάχισθ' ἡ μάχη, οὐδὲν 284
τούτων φροντίσας εὐθέως ὡμολόγεις καὶ προσεποιοῦ
φιλίαν καὶ ξενίαν εἶναί σοι πρὸς αὐτόν, τῇ μισθαρνίᾳ
ταῦτα μετατιθέμενος τὰ ὀνόματα· ἐκ ποίας γὰρ ἴσης
ἢ δικαίας προφάσεως Αἰσχίνῃ τῷ Γλαυκοθέας τῆς 5
τυμπανιστρίας ξένος ἢ φίλος ἢ γνώριμος ἦν Φίλιππος ; ἐγὼ μὲν οὐχ ὁρῶ, ἀλλ' ἐμισθώθης ἐπὶ τῷ τὰ
τουτωνὶ συμφέροντα διαφθείρειν. ἀλλ' ὅμως, οὕτω
φανερῶς αὐτὸς εἰλημμένος προδότης καὶ κατὰ σαυτοῦ
μηνυτὴς ἐπὶ τοῖς συμβᾶσι γεγονώς, ἐμοὶ λοιδορεῖ 10
καὶ ὀνειδίζεις ταῦτα, ὧν πάντας μᾶλλον αἰτίους
εὑρήσεις.

Πολλὰ καὶ καλὰ καὶ μεγάλα ἡ πόλις, Αἰσχίνη, 285

5. **ἐν τῷ πολέμῳ**: opposed to
μετὰ τὴν μάχην (§ 282²) when Aeschines went on his embassy to
Philip.
6. **καταρώμενος καὶ διομνύμενος**,
cursing (i.e. protesting, with curses
on himself if he was false) *and
swearing*; like Matth. Evang. xxvi.
74, τότε ἤρξατο (Πέτρος) καταθεματί-
ζειν καὶ ὀμνύειν, *then began he to curse
and to swear*.
7. **τὴν αἰτίαν ταύτην**: i.e. *the
charge* of intimate relations with
Philip.
§ **284**. 2. **ὡμολόγεις**: i.e. your
friendship with Philip.
3. **φιλίαν καὶ ξενίαν**: see §§ 51,
52.
4. **μετατιθέμενος**, *substituting (ap-
plying by exchange)*.
6. **τυμπανιστρίας**, *timbrel-beater* :
the τύμπανον, *kettle-drum*, was a
favourite instrument in the Asiatic
ceremonies described in §§ 259, 260.

—ἢ γνώριμος, or *even an acquaint-
ance.*
9. **κατὰ σαυτοῦ...συμβᾶσι**, *an informer against yourself after the facts*,
whereas παρὰ τὰ συμβάντα (cf. § 285⁴)
he had denied everything which told
against him (§ 283⁶). See § 197⁹ and
note.
11. **πάντας μᾶλλον**, i.e. *any rather
than myself* : most MSS. (not Σ and
L¹) add the implied ἢ ἐμέ.
§ **285**. 1. **πολλὰ καὶ καλὰ**
κ.τ.λ. : these accusatives are direct
objects of προείλετο, but cognate with
κατώρθωσε. Demosth. invariably uses
κατορθῶ in its neuter sense of *succeed*,
as in § 274⁸, οὐ κατώρθωσε. If an
object is added, as in XXI. 106, εἰ
γὰρ ἓν ὧν ἐπεβούλευσε κατώρθωσεν,
it is cognate: see XXIV. 7, XXXVII. 2.
So in Cor. § 290³ τοῦ κατορθοῦν τοὺς
ἀγωνιζομένους is not *causing* the combatants to succeed, but *the success of
the combatants*, as in πάντα κατορθοῦν,

καὶ προείλετο καὶ κατώρθωσε δι' ἐμοῦ, ὧν οὐκ ἠμνη-
μόνησεν. σημεῖον δέ· χειροτονῶν γὰρ ὁ δῆμος τὸν
ἐροῦντ' ἐπὶ τοῖς τετελευτηκόσι παρ' αὐτὰ τὰ συμβάντα οὐ σὲ ἐχειροτόνησεν προβληθέντα, καίπερ 5
εὔφωνον ὄντα, οὐδὲ Δημάδην, ἄρτι πεποιηκότα τὴν
εἰρήνην, οὐδ' Ἡγήμονα, οὐδ' ἄλλον ὑμῶν οὐδένα,
ἀλλ' ἐμέ. καὶ παρελθόντος σοῦ καὶ Πυθοκλέους
321 ὠμῶς καὶ ἀναιδῶς, ὦ Ζεῦ καὶ θεοί, καὶ κατηγορούντων ἐμοῦ ταῦθ' ἃ καὶ σὺ νυνὶ καὶ λοιδορουμένων, ἔτ' 10
ἄμεινον ἐχειροτόνησέν με. τὸ δ' αἴτιον οὐκ ἀγνοεῖς 286
μὲν, ὅμως δὲ φράσω σοι κἀγώ. ἀμφότερ' ᾔδεσαν
αὐτοί, τήν τ' ἐμὴν εὔνοιαν καὶ προθυμίαν μεθ' ἧς τὰ
πράγματ' ἔπραττον, καὶ τὴν ὑμετέραν ἀδικίαν· ἃ
γὰρ εὐθενούντων τῶν πραγμάτων ἠρνεῖσθε διομνύ- 5
μενοι, ταῦτ' ἐν οἷς ἔπταισεν ἡ πόλις ὡμολογήσατε.
τοὺς οὖν ἐπὶ τοῖς κοινοῖς ἀτυχήμασιν ὧν ἐφρόνουν
λαβόντας ἄδειαν ἐχθροὺς μὲν πάλαι, φανεροὺς δὲ

to succeed in all things, just preceding.
In other authors κατορθῶ is often
active, as in Soph. El. 416, κατώρθωσαν
βροτούς.

3. **τὸν ἐροῦντ'**, i.e. the orator for
the public funeral. The funeral
eulogy on those who fell in battle
was first introduced (acc. to Diod. XI.
33) in the Persian wars. We have
one genuine ἐπιτάφιος λόγος, that of
Hyperides in honour of those who fell
in the Lamian war (322 B.C.); the
famous eulogy of Pericles in 430 B.C.,
given in the words of Thucydides
(II. 35—46); with one in Plat. Menex.
(236—249), sportively ascribed to
Aspasia by Socrates. The one ascribed to Lysias (II.) is of doubtful
authenticity, and that found among
the speeches of Demosthenes (LX.)
is certainly spurious.

4. **παρ' αὐτὰ τὰ συμβάντα**: i.e.
when there might have been a
strong public prejudice against him,

as a leader who had failed (cf.
§ 248[7]).

5. **προβληθέντα**, *nominated*: cf.
§ 149[3].

7. **Ἡγήμονα**, mentioned by Ae-
schines (III. 25): he belonged to the
Macedonian party at Athens with
Demades and Pythocles.

8. **παρελθόντος** before **σοῦ καὶ**
Πυθοκλέους, but **κατηγορούντων** after
these words.

10. **ἃ καὶ σὺ νυνὶ**, i.e. *which you
again (καὶ) now charge me with*.—**ἔτ'**
ἄμεινον, *all the more eagerly*.

§ 286. 3. **αὐτοί**, *of themselves*
(without being told).

4—6. **ἃ γὰρ...ὡμολογήσατε** repeats for the whole Macedonian party
what was said of Aeschines in §§ 282,
283. For διομνύμενοι see § 283[6].

7. **τοὺς...λαβόντας ἄδειαν**, i.e.
*those who gained license to speak
their minds with impunity*, etc. See
§§ 198, 263[7].

τόθ' ἡγήσαντο αὐτοῖς γεγενῆσθαι· εἶτα καὶ προσή- 287
κειν [ὑπολαμβάνοντες] τὸν ἐροῦντ' ἐπὶ τοῖς τετελευτηκόσι καὶ τὴν ἐκείνων ἀρετὴν κοσμήσοντα μήθ'
ὁμωρόφιον μήθ' ὁμόσπονδον γεγενημένον εἶναι τοῖς
πρὸς ἐκείνους παραταξαμένοις, μηδ' ἐκεῖ μὲν κωμά- 5
ζειν καὶ παιωνίζειν ἐπὶ ταῖς τῶν Ἑλλήνων συμφοραῖς
μετὰ τῶν αὐτοχείρων τοῦ φόνου, δεῦρο δ' ἐλθόντα
τιμᾶσθαι, μηδὲ τῇ φωνῇ δακρύειν ὑποκρινόμενον τὴν
ἐκείνων τύχην, ἀλλὰ τῇ ψυχῇ συναλγεῖν. τοῦτο δ'
ἑώρων παρ' ἑαυτοῖς καὶ παρ' ἐμοί, παρὰ δ' ὑμῖν οὔ. 10
διὰ ταῦτ' ἔμ' ἐχειροτόνησαν καὶ οὐχ ὑμᾶς. καὶ οὐχ 288
ὁ μὲν δῆμος οὕτως, οἱ δὲ τῶν τετελευτηκότων πατέρες

§ **287.** 1. **εἶτα καὶ προσήκειν**:
sc. ἡγήσαντο (from § 286⁹).
I bracket ὑπολαμβάνοντες with Blass: a mere
carelessness in style, aiming at a
rhetorical effect, seems inadmissible
in *this* oration : see note on § 317⁶.

4. **ὁμωρόφιον**: to be *under the
same roof* with anyone had a peculiar
significance to the Greeks. Trials
for homicide were held in the open
air that neither the judges nor the
prosecutor (usually a relative) might
be under the same roof with the
accused.—**γεγενημένον εἶναι**, not a
mere pleonasm for γεγενῆσθαι, but
expressing more forcibly the combination of past and future which is
often seen in γεγενῆσθαι (M.T. 102,
109), i.e. they thought he *should not
be one who had been under the same
roof*, *etc.*

5. **παραταξαμένοις**: see § 208⁵,
and note on συμπαραταξάμενοι, § 216⁵.
—**ἐκεῖ κωμάζειν**: the *revelling* in
Philip's camp after the victory at
Chaeronea was notorious. See Plut.
Dem. 20, where the story is told of
the drunken Philip rushing out among
the slain and chanting the introductory
words of the decrees of Demosthenes,
which make an iambic tetrameter:

Δημοσθένης Δημοσθένους Παιανιεὺς τάδ' εἶπεν. See XIX. 128,
where Aeschines is charged with
joining familiarly in the festivities
held by Philip after the destruction
of the Phocians (see Hist. § 38).

7. **τῶν αὐτοχείρων**: αὐτόχειρ is
properly one who commits any deed
by his own hands or by his own act,
as in Soph. Ant. 306, τὸν αὐτόχειρα
τοῦδε τοῦ τάφου. It also, when
φόνου is easily understood, means a
murderer, as in Eur. H. F. 1359,
παίδων αὐθέντην ἐμῶν.

8. **τῇ φωνῇ δακρύειν**: a strong
metaphor, opposed to τῇ ψυχῇ
συναλγεῖν (9).—**ὑποκρινόμενον**, *like a
play-actor*.—**τὴν τύχην**: object of
δακρύειν. Blass takes it with ὑποκρινόμενον, as in XIX. 246, 'Ἀντιγόνην
ὑποκέκριται.

11. **ὑμᾶς**, i.e. *any one of you*. Cf.
ὑμῶν, § 285⁷.

§ **288.** 1. **οὐχ**, negativing the
two clauses with μὲν and δὲ: cf.
§ 13¹¹, and the grand climax in § 179,
with notes.

2. **πατέρες καὶ ἀδελφοί**: the public funeral was in charge of a com-
mittee of relatives of those who had
fallen.

καὶ ἀδελφοὶ οἱ ὑπὸ τοῦ δήμου τόθ᾽ αἱρεθέντες ἐπὶ
τὰς ταφὰς ἄλλως πως· ἀλλὰ δέον ποιεῖν αὐτοὺς τὸ
περίδειπνον ὡς παρ᾽ οἰκειοτάτῳ τῶν τετελευτηκότων, 5
ὥσπερ τἆλλ᾽ εἴωθε γίγνεσθαι, τοῦτ᾽ ἐποίησαν παρ᾽
ἐμοί. εἰκότως· γένει μὲν γὰρ ἕκαστος ἑκάστῳ μᾶλλον οἰκεῖος ἦν ἐμοῦ, κοινῇ δὲ πᾶσιν οὐδεὶς ἐγγυτέρω·
322 ᾧ γὰρ ἐκείνους σωθῆναι καὶ κατορθῶσαι μάλιστα
διέφερεν, οὗτος καὶ παθόντων ἃ μήποτ᾽ ὤφελον τῆς 10
ὑπὲρ ἁπάντων λύπης πλεῖστον μετεῖχεν.

Λέγε δ᾽ αὐτῷ τουτὶ τὸ ἐπίγραμμα, ὃ δημοσίᾳ 289
προείλεθ᾽ ἡ πόλις αὐτοῖς ἐπιγράψαι, ἵν᾽ εἰδῇς,
Αἰσχίνη, καὶ ἐν αὐτῷ τούτῳ σαυτὸν ἀγνώμονα καὶ
συκοφάντην ὄντα καὶ μιαρόν. λέγε.

ΕΠΙΓΡΑΜΜΑ.

[Οἵδε πάτρας ἕνεκα σφετέρας εἰς δῆριν ἔθεντο
ὅπλα, καὶ ἀντιπάλων ὕβριν ἀπεσκέδασαν.

4. τὸ περίδειπνον, the funeral
banquet: see Hermann (Blümner),
Gr. Priv. Ant. § 39 (p. 371); Smith,
Dict. Ant. under Funus.
5. ὡς παρ᾽ οἰκειοτάτῳ, at the
house of him who stood in the closest
possible relation to the deceased, as
at private funerals the nearest relative.
ὡς belongs to οἰκειοτάτῳ, in the usual
intensive sense: cf. § 246⁸, ὡς εἰς
ἐλάχιστα.
6. ὥσπερ...γίγνεσθαι, i.e. as is
the custom at private funerals.—
ἐποίησαν: like ποιεῖν in 4.
9. ᾧ...διέφερεν, i.e. who had most
at stake, i.e. in their success.
10. καί, likewise.—ἃ μήποτ᾽ ὤφελον (sc. παθεῖν), lit. which would they
had never suffered: this rather poetic
form of an unattained wish is used
here for animation, and again in
§ 320⁶. See M.T. 734, 736.

§ 289. 1. δημοσίᾳ, with ἐπιγράψαι.
2. προείλεθ᾽ ἡ πόλις, more formal
than ἔδοξε τῇ πόλει, perhaps implying
(as H. Jackson suggests) a choice from
epigrams sent in by competing poets.
—ἵν᾽ εἰδῇς...μιαρόν: explained in
§ 290.
EPIGRAM. This cannot be the
real epitaph inscribed on the public
monument of the heroes of Chaeronea. It has too little poetic
merit and too slovenly a style to be
accepted as genuine. It is not in the
older MSS., and it appears in the
Anthol. Graeca, IV. p. 249 (Jacobs).
We can be sure of one genuine verse
(9), which is quoted by Demosthenes
in § 290¹ (see note on this verse). A
small fragment of an inscription has
been found at Athens, cut (acc. to
Köhler) between 350 and 300 B.C.,

μαρνάμενοι δ' ἀρετῆς καὶ δείματος οὐκ ἐσάωσαν
ψυχὰς ἀλλ' Αΐδην κοινὸν ἔθεντο βραβῆ,
οὕνεκεν Ἑλλήνων, ὡς μὴ ζυγὸν αὐχένι θέντες   (5)
δουλοσύνης στυγερὰν ἀμφὶς ἔχωσιν ὕβριν.
γαῖα δὲ πατρὶς ἔχει κόλποις τῶν πλεῖστα καμόντων
σώματ', ἐπεὶ θνητοῖς ἐκ Διὸς ἥδε κρίσις·
μηδὲν ἁμαρτεῖν ἐστι θεῶν καὶ πάντα κατορθοῦν
ἐν βιοτῇ· μοῖραν δ' οὔ τι φυγεῖν ἔπορεν.]   (10)

which contains parts of six words of an epigram in the Anthol. Pal. VII. 245: this epigram was evidently inscribed to the heroes of Chaeronea. The full epigram is as follows, the letters found in the inscription being printed in heavy type:—

Ὦ Χρόνε, παντοίων θνητοῖς πανεπί-
σκοπε δαῖμον,
Ἄγγελος ἡμετέρων πᾶσι γενοῦ πά-
θεων
Ὡς ἱερὰν σῴζειν πειρώμενοι Ἑλλάδα
χώραν
Βοιωτῶν κλεινοῖς θνῄσκομεν ἐν δαπέ-
δοις.

This, though genuine, cannot be the inscription quoted by Demosthenes, as it does not have the verse μηδὲν... κατορθοῦν; but there were undoubtedly many epigrams commemorating the men of Chaeronea.

v. 1. **ἔθεντο ὅπλα**, arrayed themselves (lit. placed their arms): see Arist. Pol. Ath. 8²⁹, ὃς ἂν στασιαζούσης τῆς πόλεως μὴ θῆται τὰ ὅπλα μηδὲ μεθ' ἑτέρων, i.e. who takes sides with neither party. So Plat. Rep. 440 E. This is enough to show that the old interpretation of τίθεσθαι ὅπλα (as in Thuc. II. 2, twice), to pile and stack arms, is untenable, though it still lingers.

v. 2. **ἀπεσκέδασαν**, scattered, brought to nought: a patriotic exaggeration as applied to Chaeronea, perhaps referring to some special exploits of the Athenians. Diod. (XVI. 86) says, μέχρι μέν τινος ὁ ἀγὼν

ἀμφιδοξουμένας εἶχε τὰς ἐλπίδας τῆς νίκης. Cf. Lycurgus (Leoc. 49), εἰ δὲ δεῖ καὶ παραδοξότατον μὲν εἰπεῖν ἀληθὲς δέ, ἐκεῖνοι νικῶντες ἀπέθανον.

v. 3. **ἀρετῆς καὶ δείματος** must depend on βραβῆ, arbiter, by a hyperbaton which would be incredible in the genuine epitaph; οὐκ ἐσάωσαν ψυχὰς ἀλλ' being introduced in place of a participial clause like οὐ σώσαντες ψυχάς. The meaning evidently is, in the battle, while they sacrificed their lives, they left to the God of Death to judge whether they showed courage or fear. There is a similar hyperbaton in Xen. Hell. VII. 3, 7: ὑμεῖς τοὺς περὶ Ἀρχίαν καὶ Ὑπάτην,...οὐ ψῆφον ἀνεμείνατε, ἀλλ' ὁπότε πρῶτον ἐδυνάσθητε ἐτιμωρήσασθε (West.).

v. 5. **οὕνεκεν Ἑλλήνων** belongs to *vv.* 3, 4.—**ζυγὸν αὐχένι θέντες**, a strange expression for classical times, but common in later poetry, as in the Anthology (Blass).

v. 6. **ἀμφὶς ἔχωσιν** (with μὴ), have about them, wear, like a yoke: cf. Od. III. 486, σεῖον ζυγὸν ἀμφὶς ἔχοντες.

v. 7. **τῶν πλεῖστα καμόντων**, of men who most grievously laboured, referring to the defeat; to these words ἐπεί (*v.* 8) refers back.

vv. 9, 10. **μηδὲν...ἐν βιοτῇ**, it is the gift of the Gods (for men) never to fail and always to succeed in life, i.e. this is a miraculous exception in mortal life; opposed to which is the

Ἀκούεις, Αἰσχίνη, καὶ ἐν αὐτῷ τούτῳ μηδὲν ἁμαρ- 290
τεῖν ἐστι θεῶν καὶ πάντα κατορθοῦν; οὐ τῷ
συμβούλῳ τὴν τοῦ κατορθοῦν τοὺς ἀγωνιζομένους
ἀνέθηκε δύναμιν, ἀλλὰ τοῖς θεοῖς. τί οὖν, ὦ κατάρατ᾽,
ἐμοὶ περὶ τούτων λοιδορεῖ, καὶ λέγεις ἃ σοὶ καὶ τοῖς 5
σοῖς οἱ θεοὶ τρέψειαν εἰς κεφαλήν;
Πολλὰ τοίνυν, ὦ ἄνδρες Ἀθηναῖοι, καὶ ἄλλα 291
κατηγορηκότος αὐτοῦ καὶ κατεψευσμένου, μάλιστ᾽
ἐθαύμασα πάντων ὅτε τῶν συμβεβηκότων τότε τῇ
πόλει μνησθεὶς οὐχ ὡς ἂν εὔνους καὶ δίκαιος πολίτης ἔσχε τὴν γνώμην, οὐδ᾽ ἐδάκρυσεν, οὐδ᾽ ἔπαθε 5
τοιοῦτον οὐδὲν τῇ ψυχῇ, ἀλλ᾽ ἐπάρας τὴν φωνὴν καὶ

fixed rule that death is appointed for all, μοῖραν...ἔπορεν (sc. Ζεὺς βροτοῖς). The two verses contain the ἐκ Διὸς κρίσις; but the change of construction in μοῖραν...ἔπορεν is awkward, and ἐν βιοτῇ is an unnatural addition to *v.* 9. It is now known that μηδὲν ἁμαρτεῖν ἐστι θεοῦ (or θεῶν) καὶ πάντα κατορθοῦν is a verse of the epigram of Simonides on the heroes of Marathon, of which two other lines are preserved :

Ἑλλήνων προμαχοῦντες Ἀθηναῖοι
Μαραθῶνι
χρυσοφόρων Μήδων ἐστόρεσαν δύναμιν.

Kirchhoff (Hermes VI. pp. 487— 489) quotes from a MS. scholium : λέγει δὲ Σιμωνίδης ἐν ἐπιγράμματι ῥηθέντι αὐτῷ ἐπὶ τοῖς Μαραθῶνι πεσοῦσιν Ἀθηναίων τὸν στίχον τοῦτον, Μηδὲν ἁμαρτεῖν ἐστι θεοῦ καὶ πάντα κατορθοῦν. See Bergk, Poet. Lyr., Simon. fr. 82, with the note. See Themist. Or. XXII. p. 276 B, ἐπεὶ δὲ τὸ μηδὲν ἁμαρτάνειν ἔξω τῆς φύσεως κεῖται τῆς ἀνθρωπίνης,...τὸ ἐπίγραμμα ἀληθέστερον δ᾽ Ἀθήνησιν ἐπιγέγραπται ἐν τῷ τάφῳ τῷ δημοσίῳ· καὶ γὰρ τοῖς θεοῖς μόνοις τὸ πάντα κατορθοῦν

ἀπονέμει. These two quotations refer to a verse in which "never to fail and always to succeed" is called a divine prerogative ; while in the same words in the inscription quoted by Demosthenes these are called a privilege sometimes granted by the Gods to favoured mortals (see § 290). The original verse of Simonides, μηδὲν... κατορθοῦν (without ἐν βιοτῇ), was probably used, as a well-known verse, in the genuine epigram on those who fell at Chaeronea (still without ἐν βιοτῇ), but with a different meaning ; and in this new sense it was quoted by Demosthenes in § 290. The writer of our epigram probably borrowed the genuine line (perhaps from the text of Demosthenes), and added the whole of *v.* 10. See notes of West. and Bl.

§ **290.** **4.** ἀνέθηκε: the epigram or its composer, or perhaps ἡ πόλις, is the subject.

5. ἅ...εἰς κεφαλήν; cf. XIX. 130, ἃ νῦν εἰς κεφαλὴν ὑμᾶς αὐτῷ δεῖ τρέψαι, and § 294[8] (below).

§ **291.** **4.** ὡς ἄν: sc. ἔσχε or σχοίη: cf. § 197[8].

5. ἔσχε τὴν γνώμην, *was disposed.*

323 γεγηθὼς καὶ λαρυγγίζων ᾤετο μὲν ἐμοῦ κατηγορεῖν
δηλονότι, δεῖγμα δ' ἐξέφερε καθ' ἑαυτοῦ ὅτι τοῖς
γεγενημένοις ἀνιαροῖς οὐδὲν ὁμοίως ἔσχε τοῖς ἄλλοις.
καίτοι τὸν τῶν νόμων καὶ τῆς πολιτείας φάσκοντα 292
φροντίζειν, ὥσπερ οὗτος νυνί, καὶ εἰ μηδὲν ἄλλο,
τοῦτό γ' ἔχειν δεῖ, ταὐτὰ λυπεῖσθαι καὶ ταὐτὰ
χαίρειν τοῖς πολλοῖς, καὶ μὴ τῇ προαιρέσει τῶν
κοινῶν ἐν τῷ τῶν ἐναντίων μέρει τετάχθαι· ὃ σὺ 5
νυνὶ πεποιηκὼς εἶ φανερός, ἐμὲ πάντων αἴτιον καὶ
δι' ἐμὲ εἰς πράγματα φάσκων ἐμπεσεῖν τὴν πόλιν,
οὐκ ἀπὸ τῆς ἐμῆς πολιτείας οὐδὲ προαιρέσεως ἀρξαμένων ὑμῶν τοῖς Ἕλλησι βοηθεῖν· ἐπεὶ ἔμοιγ' εἰ 293
τοῦτο δοθείη παρ' ὑμῶν, δι' ἐμὲ ὑμᾶς ἠναντιῶσθαι
τῇ κατὰ τῶν Ἑλλήνων ἀρχῇ πραττομένῃ, μείζων ἂν
δοθείη δωρεὰ συμπασῶν ὧν τοῖς ἄλλοις δεδώκατε.
ἀλλ' οὔτ' ἂν ἐγὼ ταῦτα φήσαιμι (ἀδικοίην γὰρ ἂν 5
ὑμᾶς), οὔτ' ἂν ὑμεῖς εὖ οἶδ' ὅτι συγχωρήσαιτε·
οὗτός τ' εἰ δίκαια ἐποίει, οὐκ ἂν ἕνεκα τῆς πρὸς ἐμὲ

7. **λαρυγγίζων** : see Harpocr., τὸ
πλατύνειν τὴν φωνὴν καὶ μὴ κατὰ φύσιν
φθέγγεσθαι, ἀλλ' ἐπιτηδεύειν περιεργό-
τερον τῷ λάρυγγι χρῆσθαι οὕτως ἐλέ-
γετο. Cf. Ar. Eq. 358, λαρυγγιῶ
τοὺς ῥήτορας, *I will screech down the
orators.*
8. **δεῖγμα ἐξέφερε,** *he was making
an exhibition, giving a specimen* : cf.
XIX. 12.—**ὅτι...τοῖς ἄλλοις**: depending on the verbal force of δεῖγμα.—
τοῖς γεγεν. ἀνιαροῖς: causal dative
with ἔσχε, *was affected*; cf. ἔσχε τὴν
γνώμην (5).
9. **τοῖς ἄλλοις** : with ὁμοίως.
§ 292. 1. **τῶν νόμων**: Aeschines
began his speech (1—8) with a grand
glorification of the laws, and of the
γραφὴ παρανόμων as the great bulwark
of the constitution.
3. **ταὐτὰ ... τοῖς πολλοῖς** : cf.
§ 280⁶.

4. **τῇ προαιρέσει τῶν κοινῶν**: cf.
§ 192⁵ and l. 8 (below); see §§ 93⁴,
317².
5. **τετάχθαι**, *to be found (posted).*
6. **πεποιηκὼς**: in *or. obl.* with εἶ
φανερὸς (M.T. 907).
7. **πράγματα**, *troubles* : cf. Ar.
Ach. 310, ἁπάντων αἰτίους τῶν πραγμάτων. See Aesch. III. 57.
8. **οὐκ...βοηθεῖν**: i.e. the policy
of helping friendly states against
Philip has followed the true traditions
of Athens : see §§ 95—100. Demosth.
here only denies that he *began* this
policy (οὐκ ἀρξαμένων).
§ 293. 3. **τῇ...πραττομένῃ**, *the
dominion which was growing up*: cf.
§ 62².
6. **εὖ οἶδ' ὅτι**, as usual, parenthetic:
οἶδ' ὅτι can be thus used even with a
participle, as in IX. 1, XIX. 9.

ἔχθρας τὰ μέγιστα τῶν ὑμετέρων καλῶν ἔβλαπτε
καὶ διέβαλλεν.

Ἀλλὰ τί ταῦτ' ἐπιτιμῶ, πολλῷ σχετλιώτερ' 294
ἄλλα κατηγορηκότος αὐτοῦ καὶ κατεψευσμένου; ὃς
γὰρ ἐμοῦ φιλιππισμὸν, ὦ γῆ καὶ θεοὶ, κατηγορεῖ, τί
οὗτος οὐκ ἂν εἴποι; καίτοι νὴ τὸν Ἡρακλέα καὶ
πάντας θεοὺς, εἴ γ' ἐπ' ἀληθείας δέοι σκοπεῖσθαι, τὸ 5
καταψεύδεσθαι καὶ δι' ἔχθραν τι λέγειν ἀνελόντας
ἐκ μέσου, τίνες ὡς ἀληθῶς εἰσιν οἷς ἂν εἰκότως καὶ
δικαίως τὴν τῶν γεγενημένων αἰτίαν ἐπὶ τὴν κεφαλὴν
324 ἀναθεῖεν ἅπαντες, τοὺς ὁμοίους τούτῳ παρ' ἑκάστῃ
τῶν πόλεων εὕροιτ' ἂν, οὐ τοὺς ἐμοί· οἳ, ὅτ' ἦν 295
ἀσθενῆ τὰ Φιλίππου πράγματα καὶ κομιδῇ μικρὰ,
πολλάκις προλεγόντων ἡμῶν καὶ παρακαλούντων
καὶ διδασκόντων τὰ βέλτιστα, τῆς ἰδίας ἕνεκ'
αἰσχροκερδίας τὰ κοινῇ συμφέροντα προΐεντο, τοὺς 5

8. **ἔβλαπτε καὶ διέβαλλεν** (with
ἄν): conative.

In §§ **294—296** Demosthenes
gives a "black list" of the traitors
who have helped Philip or Alexander
in subjugating Greek states, and
declares that Aeschines is the representative of this pestilent class in
Athens. Saving his own country
from the disgrace of joining or abetting
this foul plot against liberty is the
great service for which he claims the
name of patriot.

§ **294.** 3. **ἐμοῦ φιλιππισμὸν**:
the pronoun is emphatic, *me, of all
men.* The word Philippic in all
languages is a standing answer to the
charge of Aeschines.

6. **ἀνελόντας ἐκ μέσου** (sc. ὑμᾶς),
discarding.

9. **ἀναθεῖεν**: cf. § 290⁶.

10. **εὕροιτ'** (εὕροιτε) **ἄν**, *you would
find,* appealing suddenly to the court
or the audience.

§ **295.** 1. **ὅτ' ἦν ἀσθενῆ**, i.e. in
the state described in II. 14—21.

2. **τὰ Φιλ. πράγματα**, i.e. *his
condition.*

3. **προλεγόντων...τὰ βέλτιστα**, as
Demosthenes in the Olynthiacs and
the First Philippic.

5. **τοὺς ὑπάρχοντας πολίτας**, *their
own fellow-citizens,* those with whom
each had to deal. Daochus and
Thrasydaus were the Thessalian
ambassadors sent by Philip to Thebes
in 339 B.C. (see note on § 211⁶).
Perillus, Timolaus, and Aristratus are
mentioned in § 48. Hipparchus and
Clitarchus were set up as tyrants in
Eretria by Philip about 343 B.C.:
see §§ 71, 80, and 81. Most of the
men in the list remain in deserved
obscurity.

With this whole passage compare
§§ 45—49, and Polyb. XVII. 14.
Polybius censures Demosthenes for
calling some of these men traitors,

ὑπάρχοντας ἕκαστοι πολίτας ἐξαπατῶντες καὶ δια-
φθείροντες, ἕως δούλους ἐποίησαν,—Θετταλοὺς Δάο-
χος, Κινέας, Θρασύδαος· Ἀρκάδας Κερκιδάς, Ἱερώ-
νυμος, Εὐκαμπίδας· Ἀργείους Μύρτις, Τελέδαμος,
Μνασέας· Ἠλείους Εὐξίθεος, Κλεότιμος, Ἀρίσταιχ- 10
μος· Μεσσηνίους οἱ Φιλιάδου τοῦ θεοῖς ἐχθροῦ
παῖδες Νέων καὶ Θρασύλοχος· Σικυωνίους Ἀρίστρατος, Ἐπιχάρης· Κορινθίους Δείναρχος, Δημάρετος·
Μεγαρέας Πτοιόδωρος, Ἕλιξος, Πέριλλος· Θηβαίους
Τιμόλας, Θεογείτων, Ἀνεμοίτας· Εὐβοέας Ἵππαρ- 15
χος, Κλείταρχος, Σωσίστρατος. ἐπιλείψει με λέ- 296
γονθ' ἡ ἡμέρα τὰ τῶν προδοτῶν ὀνόματα. οὗτοι
πάντες εἰσὶν, ἄνδρες Ἀθηναῖοι, τῶν αὐτῶν βουλευμάτων ἐν ταῖς αὐτῶν πατρίσιν ὧνπερ οὗτοι παρ'
ὑμῖν, ἄνθρωποι μιαροὶ καὶ κόλακες καὶ ἀλάστορες, 5
ἠκρωτηριασμένοι τὰς ἑαυτῶν ἕκαστοι πατρίδας, τὴν

maintaining that they did what they
believed to be for the best interest
of their own states. Demosthenes,
looking back on his long struggle
with Philip, felt that their selfish
regard for the temporary interests of
special cities, which always proved
fatal to Hellenic unity, and their
utter disregard of the good of Greece
as a whole, really amounted to
treachery.

§ 296. 1. ἐπιλείψει...ὀνόματα:
emphatic *asyndeton*. Cf. the Epistle
to the Hebrews, xi. 32, ἐπιλείψει με ὁ
χρόνος, and Cic. Nat. Deor. III. 32
(81), dies deficiat si velim numerare.

3. τῶν αὐτῶν βουλευμάτων, (men)
of the same purposes: this genitive of
quality is as rare in Greek as it is
common in Latin. See Aesch. III.
168, θεωρῆσαι' αὐτὸν, μὴ ὁποτέρου
τοῦ λόγου ἀλλ' ὁποτέρου τοῦ βίου ἐστίν,
and Thuc. III. 45²⁹, ἁπλῶς τε ἀδύνατον
καὶ πολλῆς εὐηθείας.

5. ἀλάστορες, *accursed wretches*

(applied to Philip in XIX. 305);
properly victims of divine vengeance,
as in Soph. Aj. 374, μεθῆκα τοὺς
ἀλάστορας. ἀλάστωρ also means *a
divine avenger*, as in Aeschyl. Pers.
354, φανεὶς ἀλάστωρ ἢ κακὸς δαίμων.
See note on ἀλιτήριος, § 159³.

6. ἠκρωτηριασμένοι, *who have
outraged* (lit. *mutilated*): see Harpocr.,
ἀντὶ τοῦ λελυμασμένοι· οἱ γὰρ λυμαινό-
μενοί τισιν εἰώθασι περικόπτειν αὐτῶν
τὰ ἄκρα. In Aeschyl. Cho. 439 and
Soph. El. 445 there is the same idea
in ἐμασχαλίσθη, μασχαλίζω being to
mutilate a dead body by cutting off
the extremities (τὰ ἄκρα) and putting
them under the armpits (μασχάλαι).
Perhaps such strong metaphors as
this suggested to Aeschines the absurd
expressions which he pretends to
quote from Demosthenes in III. 166,
ἀμπελουργοῦσί τινες τὴν πόλιν, ἀνα-
τετμήκασί τινες τὰ κλήματα τὰ τοῦ
δήμου, and others.—τὴν ἐλευθερίαν
προπεπωκότες: for the successive

έλευθερίαν προπεπωκότες πρότερον μὲν Φιλίππῳ
νῦν δ' Ἀλεξάνδρῳ, τῇ γαστρὶ μετροῦντες καὶ τοῖς
αἰσχίστοις τὴν εὐδαιμονίαν, τὴν δ' ἐλευθερίαν καὶ τὸ
μηδέν' ἔχειν δεσπότην αὐτῶν, ἃ τοῖς προτέροις 10
Ἕλλησιν ὅροι τῶν ἀγαθῶν ἦσαν καὶ κανόνες, ἀνατετροφότες.

Ταύτης τοίνυν τῆς οὕτως αἰσχρᾶς καὶ περι- 297
βοήτου συστάσεως καὶ κακίας, μᾶλλον δ', ὦ ἄνδρες
325 Ἀθηναῖοι, προδοσίας, εἰ δεῖ μὴ ληρεῖν, τῆς τῶν
Ἑλλήνων ἐλευθερίας, ἥ τε πόλις παρὰ πᾶσιν ἀν-

steps by which προπίνω comes to
mean *recklessly sacrifice*, see Liddell
and Scott. An intermediate mean-
ing, *present a cup* (or other gift) *after
drinking one's health*, is seen in XIX.
139, πίνων καὶ φιλανθρωπευόμενος
πρὸς αὐτοὺς ὁ Φίλιππος ἄλλα τε δὴ
πολλά,...καὶ τελευτῶν ἐκπώματ' ἀργυρᾶ
καὶ χρυσᾶ προὔπινεν αὐτοῖς, i.e. in
drinking their health, he gave them
these various gifts. See also Pind.
Ol. VII. 1—6, φιάλαν ὡς εἴ τις...
δωρήσεται νεανίᾳ γαμβρῷ προπί-
νων, οἴκοθεν οἴκαδε, and the Schol.
on v. 5, προπίνειν ἐστὶ κυρίως τὸ ἅμα

τῷ κράματι τὸ ἀγγεῖον χαρίζεσθαι...
καὶ Δημοσθένης τοὺς προδιδόντας τὰς
πατρίδας τοῖς ἐχθροῖς προπίνειν ἔφη.
8. τῇ γαστρὶ μετροῦντες: see note
on § 48⁶ (on Τιμόλας). See Cic. Nat.
Deor. I. 40 (113), quod dubitet omnia
quae ad beatam vitam pertinere
ventre metiri.
11. ὅροι καὶ κανόνες, *bounds and
rules*, i.e. they applied these as tests
to whatever was presented to them as
a public good.—ἀνατετροφότες, *having overturned* (i.e. reversed) these
tests.

THE EPILOGUE, §§ 297—323. In
these sections we have the four
characteristics of the ἐπίλογος, as
Aristotle gives them (Rhet. III. 19, 1):
arguments which will dispose the
hearers favourably to the speaker and
unfavourably to his opponent, amplification and depreciation, excitement of
emotions, and recapitulation. He begins by claiming the credit of keeping
Athens free from the notorious conspiracy against Grecian liberty just
mentioned ; and he charges Aeschines
with failing in all the characteristics
of a patriotic citizen which his own
course exemplifies (§§ 297—300).
He recapitulates some of his chief

services in providing Athens with
means of defence, and asks what
similar claims Aeschines has to the
public gratitude (§§ 301—313). He
objects to being compared with the
great men of former times, though he
declares that he can bear such a comparison far better than his opponent
(§§ 314—323).
§ 297. 1, 2. περιβοήτου, *notorious*.
3. εἰ δεῖ μὴ ληρεῖν, i.e. to call
it by its right name, προδοσίας.
4. παρὰ πᾶσιν ἀνθρώποις, i.e. *in
the minds of all men*; but παρὰ τοῖς
Ἕλλησι (8), *among the Greeks*: in
§ 274¹ both ideas are combined.

θρώποις ἀναίτιος γέγονεν ἐκ τῶν ἐμῶν πολιτευμάτων 5
καὶ ἐγὼ παρ' ὑμῖν. εἶτά μ' ἐρωτᾷς ἀντὶ ποίας ἀρετῆς
ἀξιῶ τιμᾶσθαι; ἐγὼ δέ σοι λέγω ὅτι, τῶν πολιτευομένων παρὰ τοῖς Ἕλλησι διαφθαρέντων ἁπάντων,
ἀρξαμένων ἀπὸ σοῦ, πρότερον μὲν ὑπὸ Φιλίππου
νῦν δ' ὑπ' Ἀλεξάνδρου, ἐμὲ οὔτε καιρὸς οὔτε φιλαν- 298
θρωπία λόγων οὔτ' ἐπαγγελιῶν μέγεθος οὔτ' ἐλπὶς
οὔτε φόβος οὔτ' ἄλλ' οὐδὲν ἐπῆρεν οὐδὲ προηγάγετο
ὧν ἔκρινα δικαίων καὶ συμφερόντων τῇ πατρίδι
οὐδὲν προδοῦναι, οὐδ', ὅσα συμβεβούλευκα πώποτε 5
τουτοισὶ, ὁμοίως ὑμῖν ὥσπερ ἂν τρυτάνη ῥέπων ἐπὶ
τὸ λῆμμα συμβεβούλευκα, ἀλλ' ἀπ' ὀρθῆς καὶ δικαίας
καὶ ἀδιαφθόρου τῆς ψυχῆς· καὶ μεγίστων δὴ πραγμάτων τῶν κατ' ἐμαυτὸν ἀνθρώπων προστὰς πάντα
ταῦθ' ὑγιῶς καὶ δικαίως πεπολίτευμαι. διὰ ταῦτ' 10
ἀξιῶ τιμᾶσθαι. τὸν δὲ τειχισμὸν τοῦτον, ὃν σύ μου 299
διέσυρες, καὶ τὴν ταφρείαν ἄξια μὲν χάριτος καὶ

6. **ἐρωτᾷς**; see Aesch. 236.
8. **ἁπάντων**: exaggeration; but
see § 304.
9. **ἀρξαμένων ἀπὸ σοῦ**, i.e. yourself first and foremost.
§ **298**. 3. **ἐπῆρεν**, induced
(roused): cf. §§ 168², 175⁸.
5—7. **οὐδ'...ὁμοίως ὑμῖν...συμ-
βεβούλευκα** (7), nor have I given my
advice, like you, inclining towards
gain like a balance, i.e. as a balance
would incline if a weight were put
into one of the scales: **ὥσπερ ἂν** (sc.
ῥέποι). The MSS. are corrupt: **ὥσπερ
ἂν τρυτάνη** is nearest to **ὥσπεράν-
τρυτανηι** of Σ. We have **ἐν τρυτ.** in
A, and **ἂν εἰ ἐν τρυτ.** vulg. This is
illustrated by a striking passage in
V. 12: **προῖκα τὰ πράγματα κρίνω καὶ
λογίζομαι, καὶ οὐδὲν λῆμμ' ἂν οὐδεὶς
ἔχοι πρὸς οἷς ἐγὼ πεπολίτευμαι καὶ
λέγω δεῖξαι προσηρτημένον. ὀρθὸν οὖν,**

ὅ τι ἂν ποτ' ἀπ' αὐτῶν ὑπάρχῃ τῶν
πραγμάτων, τὸ συμφέρον φαίνεταί μοι.
ὅταν δ' ἐπὶ θάτερα ὥσπερ εἰς τρυτάνην
ἀργύριον προσενέγκῃς, οἴχεται φέρον
καὶ καθείλκυκε τὸν λογισμὸν ἐφ' αὑτό,
καὶ οὐκ ἂν ἔτ' ὀρθῶς οὐδ' ὑγιῶς ὁ τοῦτο
ποιήσας περὶ οὐδενὸς λογίσαιτο.
7. **ὀρθῆς...ἀδιαφθόρου**: predicative
(cf. § 322⁶).
8. **μεγίστων...ἀνθρώπων**, lit. the
weightiest concerns of (any of) the men
of my time (partitive).
§ **299**. 1. **τειχισμὸν**, the repairing of the walls of Athens in 337—
336 B.C., for which Demosthenes was
τειχοποιός. See Aesch. III. 27.
Demosthenes was then appointed by
his tribe, the Πανδιονίς, and received
from the treasury (according to Aesch.
31) nearly ten talents for the expenses
(cf. § 113⁶,⁷).—**ὃν σύ μου διέσυρες**:
cf. τοῦτό μου διαβάλλει § 28³.

ἐπαίνου κρίνω, πῶς γὰρ οὔ ; πόρρω μέντοι που τῶν
ἐμαυτῷ πεπολιτευμένων τίθεμαι. οὐ λίθοις ἐτείχισα
τὴν πόλιν οὐδὲ πλίνθοις ἐγώ, οὐδ' ἐπὶ τούτοις μέγι- 5
στον τῶν ἐμαυτοῦ φρονῶ· ἀλλ' ἐὰν τὸν ἐμὸν τειχισμὸν
βούλῃ δικαίως σκοπεῖν, εὑρήσεις ὅπλα καὶ πόλεις
καὶ τόπους καὶ λιμένας καὶ ναῦς καὶ [πολλοὺς]
ἵππους καὶ τοὺς ὑπὲρ τούτων ἀμυνομένους. ταῦτα 300
προὐβαλόμην ἐγὼ πρὸ τῆς Ἀττικῆς, ὅσον ἦν ἀνθρωπίνῳ λογισμῷ δυνατόν, καὶ τούτοις ἐτείχισα τὴν
326 χώραν, οὐχὶ τὸν κύκλον τοῦ Πειραιῶς οὐδὲ τοῦ
ἄστεως. οὐδέ γ' ἡττήθην ἐγὼ τοῖς λογισμοῖς Φιλίπ- 5
που, πολλοῦ γε καὶ δεῖ, οὐδὲ ταῖς παρασκευαῖς, ἀλλ'
οἱ τῶν συμμάχων στρατηγοὶ καὶ αἱ δυνάμεις τῇ

3. πόρρω, i.e. *far below.*
4. οὐ λίθοις ἐτείχισα τὴν πόλιν: a famous passage, often quoted by the rhetoricians. See the beginning of the ὑπόθεσις of Libanius. Plutarch (Lycurg. 19) quotes a saying of Lycurgus the lawgiver, οὐκ ἂν εἴη ἀτείχιστος πόλις ἅτις ἀνδράσι καὶ οὐ πλίνθοις ἐστεφάνωται. Whiston refers to Sir Wm Jones's ode, "What constitutes a State?" The passage is a most effective answer to the taunts of Aeschines (236) about the walls and ditches.
5. πλίνθοις: *sun-dried bricks,* of which no small part of the walls of Athens and of the Long Walls to the Piraeus were built. The brick wall was built on a solid foundation of stone. See Thuc. I. 93, οἱ θεμέλιοι παντοίων λίθων ὑπόκεινται (of the walls of Athens). The stone walls of Mantinea, which are still standing almost complete, have at most only four courses of stone, which were once surmounted by a wall of brick: Pausanias (VIII. 8, 7) describes this wall as ὠμῆς ᾠκοδομημένον τῆς πλίνθου, *built of raw* (i.e. *unbaked*) *bricks.*

8. τόπους, *countries,* Euboea, Boeotia, the Chersonese, as opposed to cities.
9. τοὺς ὑπὲρ τούτων ἀμυνομένους, *the defenders of these* (our fellow-citizens).
§ 300. 2. προυβαλόμην: cf. §§ 97¹⁰ and 301⁴.—ἀνθρωπίνῳ λογισμῷ: cf. § 193⁵.
4. τὸν κύκλον τοῦ Πειραιῶς : *the circuit of the Piraeus* was assigned to the tribe Pandionis, to which Demosthenes belonged. See Essay III. § 1.
5. λογισμοῖς may refer to the encounter with Python (§ 136) and also to the embassies mentioned in § 244.—Φιλίππου: with ἡττήθην.
7. οἱ τῶν συμμάχων στρατηγοί : of these we hear only of two Thebans, Proxenus and Theagenes : of these Dinarchus (I. 74) says, ἐπὶ δὲ τοῖς ξένοις τοῖς εἰς Ἀμφισσαν συλλεγεῖσι Πρόξενος ὁ προδότης ἐγένετο· ἡγεμὼν δὲ τῆς φάλαγγος (at Chaeronea) κατέστη Θεαγένης, ἄνθρωπος ἀτυχὴς καὶ δωροδόκος ὥσπερ οὗτος (Demosthenes).

τύχῃ. τίνες αἱ τούτων ἀποδείξεις ; ἐναργεῖς καὶ
φανεραί. σκοπεῖτε δέ.

Τί χρῆν τὸν εὔνουν πολίτην ποιεῖν, τί τὸν μετὰ 301
πάσης προνοίας καὶ προθυμίας καὶ δικαιοσύνης ὑπὲρ
τῆς πατρίδος πολιτευόμενον ; οὐκ ἐκ μὲν θαλάττης
τὴν Εὔβοιαν προβαλέσθαι πρὸ τῆς Ἀττικῆς, ἐκ δὲ
τῆς μεσογείας τὴν Βοιωτίαν, ἐκ δὲ τῶν πρὸς Πελο- 5
πόννησον τόπων τοὺς ὁμόρους ταύτῃ ; οὐ τὴν
σιτοπομπίαν, ὅπως παρὰ πᾶσαν φιλίαν ἄχρι τοῦ
Πειραιῶς κομισθήσεται, προϊδέσθαι ; καὶ τὰ μὲν 302
σῶσαι τῶν ὑπαρχόντων ἐκπέμποντα βοηθείας καὶ
λέγοντα καὶ γράφοντα τοιαῦτα, τὴν Προκόννησον,
τὴν Χερρόνησον, τὴν Τένεδον, τὰ δ' ὅπως οἰκεῖα καὶ
σύμμαχ' ὑπάρξει πρᾶξαι, τὸ Βυζάντιον, τὴν Ἄβυδον, 5
τὴν Εὔβοιαν ; καὶ τῶν μὲν τοῖς ἐχθροῖς ὑπαρχουσῶν
δυνάμεων τὰς μεγίστας ἀφελεῖν, ὧν δ' ἐνέλειπε τῇ

In §§ **301—313** the orator recapitulates his own chief services,
with which he compares the public
career of Aeschines.

§ **301.** 1. **τί χρῆν** κ.τ.λ., i.e.
what was his duty?—**ποιεῖν**, of a
course of action, explained by several
aorists, each of a special act. In the
following series of questions, all introduced by **χρῆν**, the orator states
the various problems which faced the
Athenian statesman of that day and
the obvious solutions of them.
3. **ἐκ θαλάττης**: cf. § 230⁵.
4. **προβαλέσθαι**: cf. προὐβαλόμην,
§ 300². With this figure of *throwing
forward* Euboea *as a wall of defence*
to Attica, compare that in § 71² (see
note). See Aesch. III. 84, ναὶ, ἀλλὰ
χαλκοῖς καὶ ἀδαμαντίνοις τείχεσιν, ὥς
αὐτός φησι, τὴν χώραν ἡμῶν ἐτείχισε,
τῇ τῶν Εὐβοέων καὶ Θηβαίων συμμαχίᾳ.
6. **τοὺς ὁμόρους ταύτῃ**, our neigh-

bours on this side, as Megara and
Corinth (cf. § 237).
7. **παρὰ πᾶσαν φιλίαν** (sc. γῆν):
i.e. *that the corn-trade should pass
along an entirely friendly coast.* For
the subject of §§ 301, 302, see §§ 71,
79—82, 87—89, 240, 241, and Hist.
§§ 46, 51, 52, 54.
§ **302.** 1. The measures mentioned in **τὰ μὲν σῶσαι** and **τὰ δ'...
πρᾶξαι** (4) were designed to secure a
friendly coast for the corn-trade.
2. **βοηθείας**: cf. § 305⁸.
3. **γράφοντα τοιαῦτα**, *by proposing measures accordingly.*
4. **ὅπως ὑπάρξει πρᾶξαι**, i.e. *to
get possession of them* (cf. ὑπαρχόντων
in 2).
6. **Εὔβοιαν**: Euboea, with its
long coasts, was always essential to
the safety of the corn trade.
7. **τὰς μεγίστας**: especially Thebes
in 339 B.C.—**ὧν ἐνέλειπε τῇ πόλει**,
what the city lacked: ἐλλείπει is here

πόλει, ταῦτα προσθεῖναι; ταῦτα τοίνυν ἅπαντα
πέπρακται τοῖς ἐμοῖς ψηφίσμασι καὶ τοῖς ἐμοῖς
πολιτεύμασιν, ἃ καὶ βεβουλευμένα, ὦ ἄνδρες Ἀθη- 303
ναῖοι, ἐὰν ἄνευ φθόνου τις βούληται σκοπεῖν, ὀρθῶς
εὑρήσει καὶ πεπραγμένα πάσῃ δικαιοσύνῃ, καὶ τὸν
ἑκάστου καιρὸν οὐ παρεθέντα οὐδ᾽ ἀγνοηθέντα οὐδὲ
προεθέντα ὑπ᾽ ἐμοῦ, καὶ ὅσ᾽ εἰς ἑνὸς ἀνδρὸς δύναμιν 5
καὶ λογισμὸν ἧκεν, οὐδὲν ἐλλειφθέν. εἰ δὲ ἡ δαίμονός
τινος ἢ τύχης ἰσχὺς ἢ στρατηγῶν φαυλότης ἢ
τῶν προδιδόντων τὰς πόλεις ὑμῶν κακία ἢ πάντα
327 ταῦτ᾽ ἐλυμαίνετο τοῖς ὅλοις ἕως ἀνέτρεψεν, τί Δημοσθένης ἀδικεῖ; εἰ δ᾽ οἷος ἐγὼ παρ᾽ ὑμῖν κατὰ τὴν 304
ἐμαυτοῦ τάξιν, εἷς ἐν ἑκάστῃ τῶν Ἑλληνίδων πόλεων
ἀνὴρ ἐγένετο, μᾶλλον δ᾽ εἰ ἕν᾽ ἄνδρα μόνον Θετταλία
καὶ ἕν᾽ ἄνδρ᾽ Ἀρκαδία ταὐτὰ φρονοῦντ᾽ ἔσχεν ἐμοί,
οὐδεὶς οὔτε τῶν ἔξω Πυλῶν Ἑλλήνων οὔτε τῶν εἴσω 5
τοῖς παροῦσι κακοῖς ἐκέχρητ᾽ ἂν, ἀλλὰ πάντες ἂν 305
ὄντες ἐλεύθεροι καὶ αὐτόνομοι μετὰ πάσης ἀδείας
ἀσφαλῶς ἐν εὐδαιμονίᾳ τὰς ἑαυτῶν ᾤκουν πατρίδας,
τούτων τοσούτων καὶ τοιούτων ἀγαθῶν ὑμῖν καὶ τοῖς

---

impersonal, like ἐνδεῖ; so Plat. Leg.
844 B, εἴ τισι τόποις...ἐλλείπει τῶν
ἀναγκαίων σωμάτων, and 740 C.
§ 303. 1. βεβουλευμένα ὀρθῶς
εὑρήσει (or. obl.) refers chiefly to
πολιτεύματα.
4. οὐ παρεθέντα...προεθέντα, op-
portunitatem cuiusque rei non per
negligentiam praetermissam nec ignor-
atam nec proditam (Dissen). παρεθέντα implies carelessness (cf. VIII. 34),
προεθέντα wilfulness (cf. VIII. 56).
5. ὅσ᾽ implies τοσούτων, depending on οὐδέν.
6. δαίμονος ἢ τύχης: cf. τὸν
δαίμονα καὶ τὴν τύχην, Aesch. III.
115, 157. The strength (ἰσχύς) of
the superhuman powers is opposed
to the weakness and incapacity (φαυ-

λότης) or the treachery of men. See
notes on §§ 264¹ and 300⁷.
9. τοῖς ὅλοις: see note on § 278⁹.
—ἀνέτρεψεν, overset, the familiar
figure of the ship of state.
10. ἀδικεῖ, not is doing wrong,
but is to blame for a past wrong
(M.T. 27).
§ 304. 3. Θετταλία...Ἀρκαδία:
see §§ 63, 64. "Philip's party in
the one opened Northern Greece to
him, and in the other neutralized the
Peloponnesus" (Simcox).
6. ἐκέχρητ᾽ ἂν, would have experienced.
§ 305. 1. ἂν is repeated with
ᾤκουν (3), contrary to general usage,
because of the change of time from
ἐκέχρητ᾽ ἂν to ᾤκουν (present time).

ἄλλοις Ἀθηναίοις ἔχοντες χάριν δι' ἐμέ. ἵνα δ' 5
εἰδῆτε ὅτι πολλῷ τοῖς λόγοις ἐλάττοσι χρῶμαι τῶν
ἔργων, εὐλαβούμενος τὸν φθόνον, λέγε μοι ταυτὶ καὶ
ἀνάγνωθι λαβὼν τὸν ἀριθμὸν τῶν βοηθειῶν κατὰ τὰ
ἐμὰ ψηφίσματα.

ΑΡΙΘΜΟΣ ΒΟΗΘΕΙΩΝ.

Ταῦτα καὶ τοιαῦτα πράττειν, Αἰσχίνη, τὸν καλὸν 306
κἀγαθὸν πολίτην δεῖ, ὧν κατορθουμένων μὲν μεγίστοις ἀναμφισβητήτως ὑπῆρχεν εἶναι, καὶ τὸ
δικαίως προσῆν, ὡς ἑτέρως δὲ συμβάντων τὸ γοῦν
εὐδοκιμεῖν περίεστι καὶ τὸ μηδένα μέμφεσθαι τὴν 5
πόλιν μηδὲ τὴν προαίρεσιν αὐτῆς, ἀλλὰ τὴν τύχην
κακίζειν τὴν οὕτω τὰ πράγματα κρίνασαν· οὐ μὰ Δί' 307

---

7. **λέγε καὶ ἀνάγνωθι**: cf. § 28¹.

8. **βοηθειῶν**: forces sent out for special purposes, like those mentioned in § 302²: see IV. 32, μὴ βοηθείαις πολεμεῖν (ὑστεριοῦμεν γὰρ ἁπάντων) ἀλλὰ παρασκευῇ συνεχεῖ καὶ δυνάμει, and cf. IV. 41. The famous expedition which checked Philip at Thermopylae in 352 B.C. (IV. 17) is called a βοήθεια in XIX. 84. Often βοήθεια means a mere *raid*.

§ 306. 1. **ταῦτα...πράττειν...δεῖ** sums up the reply to the question τί χρῆν...ποιεῖν; in § 301¹, but with a change in tense. He asked *what was the duty*, with special reference to the case in hand; and he replies in general terms *this is the duty*. ποιεῖν (§ 301¹) and πράττειν here have the same sense, as have χρή (in χρῆν) and δεῖ.

2—4. **κατορθουμένων** = εἰ κατωρθοῦτο, *if they had been successful* (as they were not), to which the apodosis is ὑπῆρχεν εἶναι, *it belonged to us to be*, i.e. *we should properly have been* (M. T. 416).—**μεγίστοις** (sc. ἡμῖν)...

καὶ τὸ δικαίως προσῆν, i.e. *indisputably, and (I might add) justly, greatest*: δικαίως stands as a mere word with the article; and προσῆν is *belonged there*, i.e. *might properly be added*.

4. **ὡς ἑτέρως**, *otherwise*: see note on § 85⁶.—**συμβάντων**, simply temporal, *now, when they* (have) *resulted otherwise*.

5. **περίεστι**, *there is left to us*: the subject is τὸ εὐδοκιμεῖν καὶ τὸ μηδένα... κρίνασαν (7).

7. **κακίζειν**: the subject is πάντας, to be supplied from the preceding subject μηδένα. The same carelessness of expression is always common; a famous case is the clause of the United States Constitution concerning fugitive slaves: "No person held to service or labor in one state, escaping into another, shall...be discharged from said service or labor, but shall be delivered up etc."

§ 307. 1. **οὐ μὰ Δί' οὐκ**: emphatic repetition, not a double negative: δεῖ is understood here

οὐκ ἀποστάντα τῶν συμφερόντων τῇ πόλει μισθώ-
σαντα δ' αὑτὸν τοῖς ἐναντίοις, τοὺς ὑπὲρ τῶν ἐχθρῶν
καιροὺς ἀντὶ τῶν τῆς πατρίδος θεραπεύειν, οὐδὲ τὸν
μὲν πράγματ' ἄξια τῆς πόλεως ὑποστάντα λέγειν καὶ 5
γράφειν καὶ μένειν ἐπὶ τούτων βασκαίνειν, ἂν δέ τις
ἰδίᾳ τι λυπήσῃ, τοῦτο μεμνῆσθαι καὶ τηρεῖν, οὐδέ
328 γ' ἡσυχίαν ἄγειν ἄδικον καὶ ὕπουλον, ὃ σὺ ποιεῖς
πολλάκις. ἔστι γάρ, ἔστιν ἡσυχία δικαία καὶ συμ- 308
φέρουσα τῇ πόλει, ἣν οἱ πολλοὶ τῶν πολιτῶν ὑμεῖς
ἁπλῶς ἄγετε. ἀλλ' οὐ ταύτην οὗτος ἄγει τὴν ἡσυχίαν, πολλοῦ γε καὶ δεῖ, ἀλλ' ἀποστὰς ὅταν αὐτῷ
δόξῃ τῆς πολιτείας (πολλάκις δὲ δοκεῖ) φυλάττει 5
πηνίκ' ἔσεσθε μεστοὶ τοῦ συνεχῶς λέγοντος ἢ παρὰ
τῆς τύχης τι συμβέβηκεν ἐναντίωμα ἢ ἄλλο τι δύσκολον γέγονε (πολλὰ δὲ τἀνθρώπινα)· εἶτ' ἐπὶ τούτῳ
τῷ καιρῷ ῥήτωρ ἐξαίφνης ἐκ τῆς ἡσυχίας ὥσπερ
πνεῦμ' ἐφάνη, καὶ πεφωνασκηκὼς καὶ συνειλοχὼς 10
ῥήματα καὶ λόγους συνείρει τούτους σαφῶς καὶ

from § 306², and on it depend the
infinitives θεραπεύειν etc. through
ἄγειν (8).

1. ἀποστάντα: strongly opposed
to θεραπεύειν (4) and ὑποστάντα (5).

4. τῶν τῆς πατρίδος (sc. καιρῶν),
instead of the fuller form with ὑπέρ
(as in 3).—τὸν ὑποστάντα, the man
who has undertaken, object of βασκαίνειν.

8. ὕπουλον, lit. festering within,
of the quiet of Aesch., false,
treacherous; see Thuc. VIII. 64
(end), τὴν ἀπὸ τῶν Ἀθηναίων ὕπουλον
αὐτονομίαν (Bl.).

§ 308. 2. οἱ πολλοὶ here simply
the majority.

3. ἁπλῶς, in honest simplicity,
without pretence, opposed to ὕπουλος
ἡσυχία (307⁸).—οὐ ταύτην: cf. Aesch.
III. 216.

5. φυλάττει πηνίκ' (Σ, L) ἔσεσθε

μεστοί, he watches (to see) when you
will be sated, an indirect question
where we might expect a temporal
clause: ὁπηνίκα is the common
reading.

6. τοῦ συνεχῶς λέγοντος, with
your regular speaker, i.e. the one who
is continually advising you: see
Plut. Cim. 5, ὁ δῆμος...μεστὸς ὢν τοῦ
Θεμιστοκλέους.

8. τἀνθρώπινα: sc. ἐναντιώματα.

9. ῥήτωρ, as an orator, predicate
to ἐφάνη (gnomic).—ὥσπερ πνεῦμ',
with ἐξαίφνης.

10. πεφωνασκηκώς: cf. § 280².—
συνειλοχώς, the only proper perf.
act. of συλλέγω, though here Σ has
συνειλεχώς (but συνείλοχα in XXI. 23).
Cf. συμφυρήσας, § 15⁴.

11. ῥήματα: cf. § 232⁴.—συνείρει,
reels off (strings together).

ἀπνευστεὶ, ὄνησιν μὲν οὐδεμίαν φέροντας οὐδ' ἀγαθοῦ
κτῆσιν οὐδενός, συμφορὰν δὲ τῷ τυχόντι τῶν πολιτῶν καὶ κοινὴν αἰσχύνην. καίτοι ταύτης τῆς μελέτης 309
καὶ τῆς ἐπιμελείας, Αἰσχίνη, εἴπερ ἐκ ψυχῆς δικαίας
ἐγίγνετο καὶ τὰ τῆς πατρίδος συμφέροντα προῃρη-
μένης, τοὺς καρποὺς ἔδει γενναίους καὶ καλοὺς καὶ
πᾶσιν ὠφελίμους εἶναι, συμμαχίας πόλεων, πόρους 5
χρημάτων, ἐμπορίου κατασκευήν, νόμων συμφερόντων θέσεις, τοῖς ἀποδειχθεῖσιν ἐχθροῖς ἐναντιώματα.
τούτων γὰρ ἁπάντων ἦν ἐν τοῖς ἄνω χρόνοις ἐξέτα- 310
σις, καὶ ἔδωκεν ὁ παρελθὼν χρόνος πολλὰς ἀποδείξεις ἀνδρὶ καλῷ τε κἀγαθῷ, ἐν οἷς οὐδαμοῦ σὺ
φανήσει γεγονώς, οὐ πρῶτος, οὐ δεύτερος, οὐ τρίτος,
οὐ τέταρτος, οὐ πέμπτος, οὐχ ἕκτος, οὐχ ὁποστοσοῦν, 5

12. **ἀπνευστεὶ**, all in one breath
(without taking breath).
13. **τῷ τυχόντι**, cuivis, to any one
who happens to hear them.
14. **κοινὴν**, public, opposed to τῷ
τυχόντι.—**αἰσχύνην**: Blass refers this
to the speech described in § 35.
§ 309. 1, 2. μελέτης, ἐπιμελείας,
practice, study, referring to § 308¹⁰⁻¹².
3. **τά...προῃρημένης**, one wh'ch
had made the interests of the fatherland
its choice (προαίρεσιν), connected by
καὶ to δικαίας. Cf. § 315⁵.
4. **ἔδει εἶναι**, ought to have been,
implying that in the case of Aeschines
they were not so.—**γενναίους**: often
used literally of fruits, as in Plat. Leg.
844 E, τὴν γεννααίαν νῦν λεγομένην
σταφυλὴν ἢ τὰ γενναῖα σῦκα ἐπονο-
μαζόμενα (Bl.).
6. **ἐμπορίου κατασκευὴν**: (probably) securing new commercial
rights for Athens in some foreign
seaport: see XX. 33, κατασκευάσας
ἐμπόριον Θευδοσίαν, with Sandys's
note.
7. **ἀποδειχθεῖσιν**, declared, open.
Cf. ἀποδείξεις, 310².

§ 310. 1. τούτων ἦν ἐξέτασις:
ἐξέτασις is again a military term, as
in § 320¹⁰, where it means a mustering
or review of hirelings etc., in which
they were called forth to show themselves. Here, with a genitive denoting public services, it means likewise
calling out and arraying such services
to a man's credit. (See note on
§ 173⁵.)
2. **ἔδωκεν...ἀποδείξεις**, i.e. the past
gave many opportunities for showing
such services, as it were arraying
them for a review.
3. **ἐν οἷς**, in which class (the καλοί
τε κἀγαθοί), as if ἀνδράσι had preceded.—**οὐδαμοῦ**: cf. § 320⁵.
5. **οὐχ ὁποστοσοῦν** (cf. ὁστισοῦν),
not in any rank whatsoever. Dissen
thinks this alludes to a Delphic oracle
given to the Megarians, quoted in the
Scholia to Theoc. XIV. 48, 49, of
which the last two verses are:

ὑμεῖς δ' ὦ Μεγαρεῖς οὔτε τρίτοι οὔτε
τέταρτοι
οὔτε δυωδέκατοι, οὔτ' ἐν λόγῳ οὔτ' ἐν
ἀριθμῷ.

οὔκουν ἐπί γ' οἷς ἡ πατρὶς ηὐξάνετο. τίς γὰρ συμ- 311
μαχία σοῦ πράξαντος γέγονε τῇ πόλει; τίς δὲ
βοήθεια ἢ κτῆσις εὐνοίας ἢ δόξης; τίς δὲ πρεσβεία,
329 τίς διακονία δι' ἣν ἡ πόλις ἐντιμοτέρα; τί τῶν
οἰκείων ἢ τῶν Ἑλληνικῶν καὶ ξενικῶν οἷς ἐπέστης 5
ἐπηνώρθωται; ποῖαι τριήρεις; ποῖα βέλη; ποῖοι
νεώσοικοι; τίς ἐπισκευὴ τειχῶν; ποῖον ἱππικόν; τί
τῶν ἁπάντων σὺ χρήσιμος εἶ; τίς ἢ τοῖς εὐπόροις ἢ
τοῖς ἀπόροις πολιτικὴ καὶ κοινὴ βοήθεια χρημάτων;
οὐδεμία. ἀλλ', ὦ τᾶν, εἰ μηδὲν τούτων, εὔνοιά γε καὶ 312
προθυμία· ποῦ; πότε; ὅστις, ὦ πάντων ἀδικώτατε,
οὐδ' ὅθ' ἅπαντες ὅσοι πώποτ' ἐφθέγξαντ' ἐπὶ τοῦ
βήματος εἰς σωτηρίαν ἐπεδίδοσαν, καὶ τὸ τελευταῖον
Ἀριστόνικος τὸ συνειλεγμένον εἰς τὴν ἐπιτιμίαν, 5
οὐδὲ τότ' οὔτε παρῆλθες οὔτ' ἐπέδωκας οὐδέν, οὐκ

6. **οὔκουν ἐπί γ' οἷς**, at all events,
not in matters in which, etc.
§ **811.** These questions are arguments for the judgment just pronounced upon Aeschines. After the
third question, the conjunctions are
omitted in the speaker's vehemence.
With the whole passage compare
XIX. 282.
5. **τῶν Ἑλληνικῶν**, opposed to
τῶν οἰκείων, is the so-called *foreign
policy* of Athens, i.e. her policy with
other Greek states: see note on § 59².
Here **τῶν ξενικῶν** is added to include
her relations to other than Greek
states, both being opposed to **τῶν
οἰκείων**, *her domestic policy*.
6. **ποῖαι τριήρεις**; sc. γεγόνασι τῇ
πόλει.
7. **τί...χρήσιμος εἶ**; *what in the
world (τῶν ἁπάντων)* ARE *you good
for*?
8. **τίς ἢ χρημάτων**; *what public
financial help has ever come from you
to either rich or poor* (i.e. to anybody)?

9. **πολιτικὴ καὶ κοινή** is a rhetorical
amplification, like the cases in the
note to § 4⁶: in XXV. 22, **ἔρανος
πολιτικὸς καὶ κοινός** is a *public contribution for the general good.*
§ **812.** 1. **ὦ τᾶν**, a familiar form
of address, found in three other
passages of Demosthenes, I. 26,
III. 29, XXV. 78; in all introducing
an imaginary retort of an opponent.
3. **ἐφθέγξαντ'** : cf. § 199⁷.
4. **εἰς σωτηρίαν ἐπεδίδοσαν**, i.e.
made contributions (ἐπιδόσεις, § 171⁸)
for the safety of the state. Such were
made after Chaeronea, and again
before the destruction of Thebes by
Alexander: for the latter see XXXIV.
38, ὅτε μὲν Ἀλέξανδρος εἰς Θήβας
παρῄει, ἐπεδώκαμεν ὑμῖν τάλαντον
ἀργυρίου.
5. **τὸ συνειλεγμένον** (sc. ἀργύριον),
i.e. money *contributed* to pay some
debt to the state which made him
ἄτιμος, and thus to make him again
ἐπίτιμος. Every defaulting public
debtor was *ipso facto* ἄτιμος.

ἀπορῶν, πῶς γάρ; ὅς γε κεκληρονόμηκας μὲν τῶν
Φίλωνος τοῦ κηδεστοῦ χρημάτων πλειόνων ἢ πεντε-
ταλάντων, διτάλαντον δ' εἶχες ἔρανον δωρεὰν παρὰ
τῶν ἡγεμόνων τῶν συμμοριῶν ἐφ' οἷς ἐλυμήνω τὸν 10
τριηραρχικὸν νόμον. ἀλλ' ἵνα μὴ λόγον ἐκ λόγου 313
λέγων τοῦ παρόντος ἐμαυτὸν ἐκκρούσω, παραλείψω
ταῦτα. ἀλλ' ὅτι γ' οὐχὶ δι' ἔνδειαν οὐκ ἐπέδωκας, ἐκ
τούτων δῆλον, ἀλλὰ φυλάττων τὸ μηδὲν ἐναντίον
γενέσθαι παρὰ σοῦ τούτοις, οἷς ἅπαντα πολιτεύει. 5
ἐν τίσιν οὖν σὺ νεανίας καὶ πηνίκα λαμπρός; ἡνίκ'
ἂν κατὰ τούτων τι δέῃ, ἐν τούτοις λαμπροφωνότατος,
μνημονικώτατος, ὑποκριτὴς ἄριστος, τραγικὸς Θεοκρίνης.

7. **κεκληρονόμηκας ... πεντεταλάν-τῶν**, have inherited the estate of your brother-in-law Philo, which was (sc. ὄντων) more than five talents.

9. **διτάλαντον ἔρανον**, a contribution of two talents. There is probably a sarcastic reference to the common meaning of ἔρανος.

10. **ἡγεμόνων**: see note on § 103⁴.
—**ἐφ' οἷς ἐλυμήνω**, for the damage you did: οἷς for a cognate ἅ, as in § 18⁶. The attack of Aeschines on the trierarchic law was not made when it was enacted in 340 B.C., but probably after Chaeronea. Demosthenes says (§ 107⁶) that through the whole war (i.e. 340—338 B.C.) the naval armaments were fitted out under his law; and the statement of Aeschines (III. 222), ἐξηλέγχθης ὑπ' ἐμοῦ ἑξήκοντα καὶ πέντε νεῶν ταχυναυτουσῶν τριηράρχους ὑφῃρημένος, shows that evidence as to the working of the new law in details was derived from actual experience.

§ **313. 1. λόγον ἐκ λόγου λέγων**, by saying one thing after another.

2. **τοῦ παρόντος** (sc. λόγου) **ἐμαυ-τὸν ἐκκρούσω**, cut myself off from

(discussing properly) the subject immediately before us.

3. **ὅτι γ' οὐχὶ δι' ἔνδειαν οὐκ ἐπέδωκας**, that it was not through poverty that you did not contribute; each negative having its own force, as the second is not a compound (G. 1618).

4. **ἀλλὰ** connects φυλάττων to δι' ἔνδειαν, both being causal.—**φυλάττων τὸ...γενέσθαι**: see M. T. 374; and note on § 258³.

5. **τούτοις, οἷς**: not simply to those for whom (which would hardly be τούτοις), but to these persons (§ 312¹⁰), for whom (in whose interest) etc.

6. **νεανίας**, often used in the sense of vigorous, lively, like the adjective νεανικός: it occurs twice in Demosthenes, here and § 136².—**ἡνίκ' ἄν...τι δέῃ**: supply εἰπεῖν, which all MSS. except Σ¹ insert.

8. **τραγικὸς Θεοκρίνης**: see Harpocr., τὸν γοῦν πάλαι μὲν ὑποκριτὴν τραγικὸν ὕστερον δὲ συκοφάντην εἰκότως ὠνόμασε τραγικὸν Θεοκρίνην. Theocrines is the one accused in Or. I.VIII. Cf. § 242⁵.

Εἶτα τῶν πρότερον γεγενημένων ἀγαθῶν ἀνδρῶν 314
μέμνησαι. καὶ καλῶς ποιεῖς.

οὐ μέντοι δίκαιόν
ἐστιν, ἄνδρες Ἀθηναῖοι, τὴν πρὸς τοὺς τετελευτηκότας
330 εὔνοιαν ὑπάρχουσαν προλαβόντα παρ' ὑμῶν πρὸς
ἐκείνους ἐξετάζειν καὶ παραβάλλειν ἐμὲ τὸν νῦν 5
ζῶντα μεθ' ὑμῶν. τίς γὰρ οὐκ οἶδε τῶν πάντων ὅτι 315
τοῖς μὲν ζῶσι πᾶσιν ὕπεστί τις ἢ πλείων ἢ ἐλάττων
φθόνος, τοὺς τεθνεῶτας δ' οὐδὲ τῶν ἐχθρῶν οὐδεὶς
ἔτι μισεῖ; οὕτως οὖν ἐχόντων τούτων τῇ φύσει,
πρὸς τοὺς πρὸ ἐμαυτοῦ νῦν ἐγὼ κρίνωμαι καὶ θεωρῶ- 5
μαι; μηδαμῶς· οὔτε γὰρ δίκαιον οὔτ' ἴσον, Αἰσχίνη·
ἀλλὰ πρὸς σὲ καὶ ἄλλον εἴ τινα βούλει τῶν ταὐτά
σοι προῃρημένων καὶ ζώντων. κἀκεῖνο σκόπει. 316
πότερον κάλλιον καὶ ἄμεινον τῇ πόλει διὰ τὰς τῶν
πρότερον εὐεργεσίας, οὔσας ὑπερμεγέθεις,—οὐ μὲν
οὖν εἴποι τις ἂν ἡλίκας,—τὰς ἐπὶ τὸν παρόντα βίον

In §§ **814—828** the orator complains of the unfairness of judging
him, as Aeschines has done (178—
190), by comparison with the great
men of ancient times. But he shrinks
from no comparison with his con-
temporaries. In §§ 321—323 he
states two points, which he claims
for himself, in the character of the
μέτριος πολίτης.

§ **814.** 1. τῶν πρότερον γεγενημένων: in III. 181 Aeschines calls on
the court directly to compare Demosthenes with Themistocles, Miltiades,
the heroes of Phyle, and Aristides;
and he does this very effectively.

3. τὴν...ὑπάρχουσαν, *the devotion
which it is to be assumed you feel
towards the dead.*

4. προλαβόντα, *securing for himself in advance, taking advantage of.*
See Hor. Od. III. 24, 31, Virtutem
incolumem odimus, Sublatam ex

oculis quaerimus invidi.—πρὸς ἐκείνους: cf. πρὸς σὲ 315⁷.

§ **816.** 2. τοῖς μὲν ζῶσι...φθόνος,
κ.τ.λ.: cf. Thuc. II. 45, φθόνος γὰρ
τοῖς ζῶσι πρὸς τὸ ἀντίπαλον, τὸ δὲ
μὴ ἐμποδὼν ἀνανταγωνίστῳ εὐνοίᾳ
τετίμηται.—ὕπεστι, implying more or
less *concealment*: cf. § 36².

5. κρίνωμαι; *am I to be judged?*
With the answer, μηδαμῶς, we must
understand κρίνωμαι, in the sense *let
me not be judged*: cf. Plat. Rep.
527 C, τιθώμεν; with answer τιθῶμεν.

7, 8. Here πρὸς σὲ and ζώντων
were pronounced with special emphasis. Supply ἐμὲ κρίνεσθαι. With
προῃρημένων cf. § 309³.

§ **816.** 3. οὐ...ἡλίκας, *no man
can tell how great*: οὐ μὲν οὖν, as
usual, is emphatic and corrective.

4. ἐπὶ τὸν παρόντα βίον γιγνομένας (sc. εὐεργεσίας), *shown to the
present generation.*

γιγνομένας εἰς ἀχαριστίαν καὶ προπηλακισμὸν ἄγειν, 5
ἢ πᾶσιν ὅσοι τι μετ᾽ εὐνοίας πράττουσι τῆς τούτων
τιμῆς καὶ φιλανθρωπίας μετεῖναι; καὶ μὴν εἰ καὶ 317
τοῦτ᾽ ἄρα δεῖ μ᾽ εἰπεῖν, ἡ μὲν ἐμὴ πολιτεία καὶ
προαίρεσις, ἄν τις σκοπῇ, ταῖς τῶν τότ᾽ ἐπαινουμένων
ἀνδρῶν ὁμοία καὶ ταὐτὰ βουλομένη φανήσεται, ἡ δὲ
σὴ ταῖς τῶν τοὺς τοιούτους τότε συκοφαντούντων· 5
δῆλον γὰρ ὅτι καὶ κατ᾽ ἐκείνους ἦσάν τινες, οἳ διασύροντες τοὺς ὄντας τότε τοὺς πρότερον γεγενημέ-
νους ἐπῄνουν, βάσκανον πρᾶγμα καὶ ταὐτὸ ποιοῦντες
σοί. εἶτα λέγεις ὡς οὐδὲν ὅμοιός εἰμι ἐκείνοις ἐγώ; 318
σὺ δ᾽ ὅμοιος, Αἰσχίνη; ὁ δ᾽ ἀδελφὸς ὁ σός; ἄλλος
δέ τις τῶν νῦν ῥητόρων; ἐγὼ μὲν γὰρ οὐδένα φημί.
ἀλλὰ πρὸς τοὺς ζῶντας, ὦ χρηστέ, ἵνα μηδὲν ἄλλ᾽
εἴπω, τὸν ζῶντα ἐξέταζε καὶ τοὺς καθ᾽ αὑτόν, ὥσπερ 5
331 τἄλλα πάντα, τοὺς ποιητάς, τοὺς χορούς, τοὺς ἀγω-
νιστάς. ὁ Φιλάμμων οὐχ, ὅτι Γλαύκου τοῦ Καρυ- 319

5. **εἰς ἀχαριστίαν ἄγειν**: cf.
§ 112⁸.

7. **τιμῆς καὶ φιλανθρωπίας**: cf.
§ 209³.

§ 317. 1. **εἰ...εἰπεῖν**: he makes
this slight apology for asserting even
the following claim to be compared
with the great men of old.

3. **ἐπαινουμένων**: imperfect, like
συκοφαντούντων (5), as shown by τότε.

6. **διασύροντες...ἐπῄνουν**: I keep
διασύροντες, with Σ and L, but omit
δὲ before πρότερον (7). διασύρω, *ridi-
cule*, is a favourite word with Demosthenes: it occurs elsewhere in this
speech in §§ 27⁶, 126⁷, 180³, 218¹⁰,
299², 323⁷·⁸, always in the same
sense.

7. **τότε**: with ὄντας.

§ 318. 2. **ὁ δ᾽ ἀδελφὸς ὁ σός**:
Aeschines had two brothers, Philo-
chares, older, and Aphobetus, younger
than himself.

4. **ὦ χρηστέ**, *my good man*, ironical: cf. §§ 30³, 89⁷.—**ἵνα...εἴπω**:
this is generally understood to refer
to the gentle style of address in
χρηστέ, *to call you nothing more*:
see West. and Bl. But it may refer
to πρὸς τοὺς ζῶντας (4), and imply
that he will not press the slight claim
to a comparison with the men of old
made in § 317: it will then mean, *to
claim no more than this*.

5. **τοὺς καθ᾽ αὑτόν**: with πρὸς (4).
—**ὥσπερ τἄλλα πάντα**, i.e. *as in other
cases*, less exact than τοὺς ἄλλους
πάντας.

6. **τοὺς ποιητάς...ἀγωνιστάς**, i.e.
as in dramatic and other contests of
that nature, and in the public games.

§ 319. 1. **Φιλάμμων** is chosen as
an Athenian who had recently returned as an Olympic victor. Glaucus,
on the contrary, was one of the most
famous boxers of the time of the

στίου καί τινων ἑτέρων πρότερον γεγενημένων ἀθλητῶν
ἀσθενέστερος ἦν, ἀστεφάνωτος ἐκ τῆς Ὀλυμπίας
ἀπῄει, ἀλλ᾽ ὅτι τῶν εἰσελθόντων πρὸς αὐτὸν ἄριστ᾽
ἐμάχετο, ἐστεφανοῦτο καὶ νικῶν ἀνηγορεύετο. καὶ 5
σὺ πρὸς τοὺς νῦν ὅρα με ῥήτορας, πρὸς σαυτόν,
πρὸς ὅντινα βούλει τῶν ἁπάντων· οὐδέν᾽ ἐξίσταμαι.
ὧν, ὅτε μὲν τῇ πόλει τὰ βέλτισθ᾽ ἑλέσθαι παρῆν, 320
ἐφαμίλλου τῆς εἰς τὴν πατρίδ᾽ εὐνοίας ἐν κοινῷ πᾶσι
κειμένης, ἐγὼ κράτιστα λέγων ἐφαινόμην, καὶ τοῖς
ἐμοῖς καὶ ψηφίσμασι καὶ νόμοις καὶ πρεσβείαις
ἅπαντα διῳκεῖτο, ὑμῶν δ᾽ οὐδεὶς ἦν οὐδαμοῦ, πλὴν εἰ 5
τούτοις ἐπηρεάσαι τι δέοι· ἐπειδὴ δ᾽ ἃ μήποτ᾽ ὤφελεν
συνέβη, καὶ οὐκέτι συμβούλων, ἀλλὰ τῶν τοῖς ἐπιταττομένοις ὑπηρετούντων καὶ τῶν κατὰ τῆς πατρίδος μισθαρνεῖν ἑτοίμων καὶ τῶν κολακεύειν ἕτερον
βουλομένων ἐξέτασις, τηνικαῦτα σὺ καὶ τούτων 10

Persian wars, who, besides gaining
a victory at Olympia, gained two
Pythian, eight Nemean, and eight
Isthmian prizes. Pausanias (VI. 10,
1—3) saw his statue at Olympia.
See the fragment of the ode of
Simonides in his honour (fr. 8, Bergk):
οὐδὲ Πολυδεύκεος βία χεῖρας ἀντείναιτ᾽
ἂν ἐναντίον αὐτῷ, οὐδὲ σιδάρεον Ἀλκμά-
νας τέκος. Aeschines (III. 189) refers
to this comparison as one which he
"heard that Demosthenes would
make." This is evidently a bold
addition made to his speech after it
was spoken.
4. εἰσελθόντων: cf. Soph. El. 700;
Xen. An. VI. 1, 9.
6. ὅρα με: cf. θεωρῶμαι; (§ 315⁵)
and ἐξέταξε (§ 318⁵).
7. οὐδέν᾽ ἐξίσταμαι, I shrink from
no one: this reading of the best
MSS. agrees with Lobeck's rule (note
on Soph. Aj. 82), that ἐξίσταμαι,
declinare, takes the accusative, but in

the sense of cedere, the dative. For
the dative see Soph. Phil. 1053, νῦν
δὲ σοί γ᾽ ἑκὼν ἐκστήσομαι.
§ 320. 1. ὧν, partitive with
κράτιστα λέγων (3).
2. ἐφαμίλλου...κειμένης: the figure
of a public contest is kept up, the
privilege of showing devotion to the
state being a prize open to general
competition (ἐφαμίλλου). Cf. ἐνάμιλ-
λον, Plat. Rep. 433 D.
5. ἦν οὐδαμοῦ: cf. § 310³.—εἴ...
τι δέοι: the optative implies frequent
occasions for insulting the people.
6. ἃ μήποτ᾽ ὤφελεν (sc. συμβῆναι),
i.e. the defeat: see 288¹⁰, and note
οὐκέτι (7), opposed to ὅτε...παρῆν (1).
9. ἕτερον: this is the vague term
by which Demosthenes often alludes
to Alexander: see § 323¹, ¹⁰.
10. ἐξέτασις: the familiar military
figure recurs, i.e. a call for these, as
for a review; and this is carried out
in ἐν τάξει (11). Cf. note on § 173⁵.

ἕκαστος ἐν τάξει καὶ μέγας καὶ λαμπρὸς ἱπποτρόφος,
ἐγὼ δ᾽ ἀσθενής, ὁμολογῶ, ἀλλ᾽ εὔνους μᾶλλον ὑμῶν
τουτοισί. δύο δ᾽, ἄνδρες Ἀθηναῖοι, τὸν φύσει μέτριον 321
πολίτην ἔχειν δεῖ (οὕτω γάρ μοι περὶ ἐμαυτοῦ λέγοντι
ἀνεπίφθονώτατον εἰπεῖν), ἐν μὲν ταῖς ἐξουσίαις τὴν
τοῦ γενναίου καὶ τοῦ πρωτείου τῇ πόλει προαίρεσιν
διαφυλάττειν, ἐν παντὶ δὲ καιρῷ καὶ πράξει τὴν 5
εὔνοιαν· τούτου γὰρ ἡ φύσις κυρία, τοῦ δύνασθαι δὲ
καὶ ἰσχύειν ἕτερα. ταύτην τοίνυν παρ᾽ ἐμοὶ μεμενη-
κυῖαν εὑρήσεθ᾽ ἁπλῶς. ὁρᾶτε δέ. οὐκ ἐξαιτούμενος, 322
332 οὐκ εἰς Ἀμφικτύονας δίκας ἐπαγόντων, οὐκ ἀπειλούν-

11. **ἱπποτρόφος**: the keeping of
horses was a sign of wealth, and the
word implies that Aeschines had
become a richer and more powerful
man at Athens since the complete
establishment of Alexander's supremacy. Cf. Ar. Nub. 15.

12. **ἀσθενὴς**: Aeschines (159)
speaks of Dem. at this time as
ὑπότρομος, παριὼν ἡμιθνὴς ἐπὶ τὸ
βῆμα. Westermann refers this to the
time when Philip was made a citizen
of Athens and his statue was erected
in the city (Plut. Dem. 22 ; Paus. I.
9, 4). It more probably refers to the
recent honours paid to Alexander :
see C. I. Att. II. no. 741, dated by
Köhler in 331 B.C., στεφάνων δυοῖν,
οἷς ὁ δῆμος ὁ Ἀθηναίων ἐστεφάνωσε
Ἀλέξα[νδρον].

§ **321.** 1. **μέτριον**: see § 10[7, 8].
2. **οὕτω** (with εἰπεῖν): he uses
μέτριος here modestly, as he is speaking of himself ; but he means the
man called καλὸς κἀγαθὸς πολίτης
in § 278[3] and 306[1] (see Blass).

3, 4. **ἐν ταῖς ἐξουσίαις**, i.e. ὅτε...
ἐλέσθαι παρῆν, 320[1], *in time of power.*
—**τὴν...προαίρεσιν,** *the policy which
aims at nobility and pre-eminence ;*
and τῇ πόλει **διαφυλάττειν,** *to guard
this always for the state.* For **τοῦ
πρωτείου** see § 66[7].

5. **πράξει** (sc. ἐν πάσῃ) may mean
in every act (of the statesman). But
Blass is probably right in taking it in
the sense of *fortune,* like **εὖ** and
κακῶς πράττειν : see Aeschyl. Prom.
695, πρᾶξιν Ἰοῦς; Hdt. III. 65 (end),
ἀπέκλαιε πᾶσαν τὴν ἑωυτοῦ **πρᾶξιν:**
and Soph. Tr. 294, εὐτυχῆ κλύουσα
πρᾶξιν τήνδε.
6. **εὔνοιαν,** *loyal devotion* to the
state: so in § 322[5].—**τούτου,** i.e. τὴν
εὔνοιαν διαφυλάττειν.
7. **ἕτερα,** other things, as chance
or Fortune, which he cannot control.
—**ταύτην:** i.e. τὴν εὔνοιαν.
8. **ἁπλῶς,** *absolutely, without exception.*

§ **322.** 1. **ἐξαιτούμενος,** i.e. by
Alexander ; see the next note and
note on § 41[10].
2. **εἰς Ἀμφικτύονας,** *before the
Amphictyonic Council*: cf. ἐν Ἀμφικτύοσιν, XIX. 181 (also without the
article). When Alexander demanded
the orators of Athens in 335 B.C., he
doubtless intended to have them tried
by the Amphictyonic Council : see
Aesch. III. 161, καὶ τὸ πάντων δεινό-
τατον, ὑμεῖς μὲν τοῦτον οὐ προῦδοτε,
οὐδ᾽ εἰάσατε κριθῆναι ἐν τῷ τῶν Ἑλλήνων συνεδρίῳ. Notice the spirit of
this sentence. What a trial this
would have been for Demosthenes,

των, οὐκ ἐπαγγελλομένων, οὐχὶ τοὺς καταράτους
τούτους ὥσπερ θηρία μοι προσβαλλόντων, οὐδαμῶς
ἐγὼ προδέδωκα τὴν εἰς ὑμᾶς εὔνοιαν. τὸ γὰρ ἐξ 5
ἀρχῆς εὐθὺς ὀρθὴν καὶ δικαίαν τὴν ὁδὸν τῆς πολιτείας εἱλόμην, τὰς τιμὰς, τὰς δυναστείας, τὰς εὐδοξίας τὰς τῆς πατρίδος θεραπεύειν, ταύτας αὔξειν,
μετὰ τούτων εἶναι. οὐκ ἐπὶ μὲν τοῖς ἑτέρων εὐτυχή- 323
μασι φαιδρὸς ἐγὼ καὶ γεγηθὼς κατὰ τὴν ἀγορὰν
περιέρχομαι, τὴν δεξιὰν προτείνων καὶ εὐαγγελιζό-

Hyperides, and Lycurgus! Schaefer (III. 198) refers the passages of both Demosthenes and Aeschines to an attempt to bring Demosth. before the Amphictyonic Council in 330 B.C. on account of his complicity with the rebellion of Agis (see note on § 323⁴).
—δίκας ἐπαγόντων, bringing suits (against me): see § 249³.
3. ἐπαγγελλομένων: cf. ἐπαγγελιῶν μέγεθος, § 298².—τοὺς καταράτους τούτους, the whole pack of sycophants mentioned in § 249⁷⁻⁹.
4. προσβαλλόντων, setting them on (as θηρία); cf. προσβάλλεσθαι, to attack.
6. ὀρθὴν...εἱλόμην: cf. § 321³, τὴν...προαίρεσιν. For the predicate adjectives cf. § 298⁷.
7. δυναστείας: cf. §§ 67²,³, 170⁵. δυναστεία means lordly power; and when it refers to a ruler, it often means absolute power or despotism. But it can also mean (as here), in a good sense, the lordly power which Athens once exercised over her dependent states, and which she always aspired to exercise.
8. θεραπεύειν, αὔξειν, εἶναι explain ὀρθὴν...ὁδόν (6).
9. μετὰ τούτων εἶναι, to be faithful to these (τὰς τιμὰς...τὰς τῆς πατρίδος), lit. to be on their side: see Ar. Ach. 661, τὸ γὰρ εὖ μετ' ἐμοῦ καὶ τὸ δίκαιον ξύμμαχον ἔσται.

§ 323. 1. οὐκ belongs to both περιέρχομαι (3) and ἀκούω (5).—ἑτέρων, i.e. the Macedonians; as ἕτερος (10) and ἕτερον (§ 320⁹) refer to Alexander. — εὐτυχήμασι: the victories of Alexander at the Granicus (334 B.C.), at Issus (333 B.C.), and at Arbela (331 B.C.), were still fresh in recollection, the last not yet a year old.
3, 4. εὐαγγελιζόμενος, properly announcing good tidings (cf. εὐαγγέλιον, Gospel), but here congratulating on good news, e.g. saying "This is a great victory."—τούτοις οὓς ἄν... οἴωμαι: the apparently definite antecedent is peculiar before the conditional relative clause. He means any of those (a well-known class) who I ever think are likely to report thither (to Macedonia) such an event as my congratulating them on a victory of Alexander. It has, I believe, never been asked who these men may have been. There were, of course, many Macedonians in Athens at this time, and there were many Athenians who would welcome news of Macedonian victories. But the greatest Macedonian who ever lived, the philosopher Aristotle, was then a resident in Athens at the head of the Lyceum. His relations with the Court of Pella and with Alexander were most intimate. Who would be more

μένος τούτοις οὓς ἂν ἐκεῖσ' ἐπαγγέλλειν οἴωμαι, τῶν
δὲ τῆς πόλεως ἀγαθῶν πεφρικὼς ἀκούω καὶ στένων 5
καὶ κύπτων εἰς τὴν γῆν, ὥσπερ οἱ δυσσεβεῖς οὗτοι,
οἳ τὴν μὲν πόλιν διασύρουσιν, ὥσπερ οὐχ αὑτοὺς
διασύροντες ὅταν τοῦτο ποιῶσιν, ἔξω δὲ βλέπουσι,
καὶ ἐν οἷς ἀτυχησάντων τῶν Ἑλλήνων εὐτύχησεν
ἕτερος, ταῦτ' ἐπαινοῦσι καὶ ὅπως τὸν ἅπαντα χρόνον 10
μενεῖ φασὶ δεῖν τηρεῖν.

Μὴ δῆτ', ὦ πάντες θεοί, μηδεὶς ταῦθ' ὑμῶν ἐπινεύ- 324
σειεν, ἀλλὰ μάλιστα μὲν καὶ τούτοις βελτίω τινὰ
νοῦν καὶ φρένας ἐνθείητε, εἰ δ' ἄρ' ἔχουσιν ἀνιάτως,

likely to report to Pella, or even to Alexander himself, that Demosthenes had congratulated him on the victory at Arbela, if he had any such pleasant fact to report? It would be interesting, though not quite pleasant, to find an allusion to the great philosopher in this striking passage.

4. τῶν...ἀγαθῶν: these *advantages* may be the early successes of the Spartan king Agis in his revolt against Macedonia in the spring of 330 B.C. (Diod. XVII. 63). Aeschines (167) quotes Demosthenes as saying of this, ὡς ἀντιπράττων Ἀλεξάνδρῳ, "ὁμολογῶ τὰ Λακωνικὰ συστῆσαι· ὁμολογῶ Θετταλοὺς καὶ Περραιβοὺς ἀφιστάναι." See Grote XII., ch. 95. The words τῶν ...ἀγαθῶν more probably refer to the interest of Athens in the reverses of Alexander, which were occasionally reported from Asia. Aeschines (164) describes Demosthenes as once reporting that Alexander was shut up in Cilicia, and αὐτίκα μάλα ἔμελλε συμπατηθήσεσθαι ὑπὸ τῆς Περσικῆς ἵππου. This shows that the mere report of a disaster to Alexander roused the spirit of liberty at Athens, even in her deep humiliation.

6. κύπτων εἰς τὴν γῆν: cf. Caes.

B. G. I. 32, 2, tristes capite demisso terram intueri.

7. διασύρουσιν: see note on § 317⁶.—ὥσπερ οὐχ with the participle shows that there is nothing conditional in the expression: see note on § 276¹.

8. ἔξω βλέπουσι: cf. Plut. Arat. 15, ταῖς ἐλπίσιν ἔξω βλέπων.

9. ἐν οἷς (cf. § 19³) belongs equally to ἀτυχησάντων and εὐτύχησεν.

10. ταῦτ', *this state of things* (ἐν οἷς...ἕτερος), understood also as subject of μενεῖ.

§ 324. The Peroration is confined to this single impressive sentence. As he began his oration by beseeching the Gods to put it into the hearts of the judges to hear him impartially, so now he implores them to change the hearts of the traitors within the state, or, if it is too late for this, to annihilate them utterly as the only hope of safety to honest men.

2. μάλιστα μέν, *if possible, best of all.*

3. ἐνθείητε, *may you inspire even in them*: this combines the wish with an exhortation (M. T. 725). In the corresponding clause with δέ we have the imperatives ποιήσατε and δότε.—

εἰ δ' ἄρ', *but if after all.*

τούτους μὲν αὐτοὺς καθ᾽ ἑαυτοὺς ἐξώλεις καὶ προώλεις ἐν γῇ καὶ θαλάττῃ ποιήσατε, ἡμῖν δὲ τοῖς 5
λοιποῖς τὴν ταχίστην ἀπαλλαγὴν τῶν ἐπηρτημένων
φόβων δότε καὶ σωτηρίαν ἀσφαλῆ.

4. **αὐτοὺς καθ᾽ ἑαυτοὺς** : the
strongest expression for *by themselves.*
—**ἐξώλεις καὶ προώλεις ποιήσατε,**
*cause them to be destroyed utterly and
before their time*: see Shilleto's note
on XIX. 172, ἐξώλης ἀπολοίμην καὶ
προώλης. Westermann quotes an
inscription of Halicarnassus from
Keil, Sched. Epigr. p. 36: ἐξώλης
καὶ πανώλης ἔστω καὶ γένος ἐκ γένους,
καὶ μήτε γῆ βατὴ αὐτῷ μήτε θάλασσα
πλωτή.
5. **ἐν γῇ καὶ θαλάττῃ,** i.e. in all
their ways.
6. **ἐπηρτημένων,** *impending* : for
the passive of ἐπαρτῶ see XXIII.

140, τοσοῦτος ἐπήρτηται φόβος. Cf.
Aesch. I. 175, φόβους ἐπήρτησα τοῖς
ἀκρωμένοις, i.e. *I caused terrors to
hang over them* (impendere).
7. **σωτηρίαν ἀσφαλῆ,** *safety which
cannot be shaken.*

With these solemn but hopeful
words of good cheer, Demosthenes
leaves his case and his reputation
with perfect confidence in the hands
of the judges. Since the success of
his burst of eloquence in §§ 51, 52,
he has felt no anxiety about the
judgment, and his courage has increased steadily in every stage of his
argument.

HISTORICAL SKETCH

FROM THE ACCESSION OF PHILIP OF MACEDON TO THE BATTLE OF CHAERONEA.

I. FROM THE ACCESSION OF PHILIP IN 359 TO 352 B.C.

1. The battle of Mantinea and the death of Epaminondas in 362 B.C. mark the beginning of a new era in Greek history. The brilliant statesmanship and military genius of Epaminondas had raised Thebes to the highest position as a military power, and had reduced Sparta from her leadership of Greece to a condition of extreme danger. Sparta was held in check by the new hostile towns of Megalopolis and Messene, and she had for the first time seen an invading army within her streets. Athens now thought it expedient to forget her ancient enmity, and to make common cause with her old rival : at Mantinea Athens and Sparta fought side by side against Thebes. The death of Epaminondas at the moment of victory broke the spirit and the power of Thebes ; Athens was suddenly relieved of her great alarm, and now no longer feared the removal of her Propylaea to the Cadmea of Thebes. Greece was left without a head, and Athens was encouraged to hope for a recovery of the leadership which she had lost by the Peloponnesian War.

2. During the five succeeding years Athens devoted herself to establishing her power in the North, especially in her old dominion, the Thracian Chersonese, which came anew into her possession in 357 B.C. Earlier in the same year she had made her famous expedition

for the liberation of Euboea, of which Demosthenes often speaks with pride, when she cleared the whole island of Thebans in thirty days and wrested it permanently from Thebes, which had held it since the battle of Leuctra in 371 B.C. In 357 B.C. the new Athenian confederacy reached its greatest power and extent. It included a large part of the islands of the Aegean, Byzantium, the Chersonese and the south of Thrace, Potidaea, Methone, and Pydna, with much of the coast of the Thermaic Gulf. But in the autumn of that year the hopes of Athens were violently shattered by the outbreak of the Social War, in which Chios, Cos, Rhodes, and Byzantium, encouraged by Mausolus of Caria, suddenly revolted and weakened her power at its most vital points. This disastrous war ended in the spring of 355, when Athens was compelled to acknowledge the independence of the four seceding states. Thus crippled she found herself in the face of a new and more dangerous enemy.

3. In 359 B.C. Philip II. succeeded to the throne of Macedonia at the age of twenty-three. Macedonia had hitherto filled only a small place in Greek politics ; and it threatened no danger to Grecian liberty. Under Philip this was suddenly changed. This crafty king lost no time in laying his plans for his great object, the extension of his power and influence over Greece. His regular policy was to interfere in a friendly way in the quarrels of Greek states, in the hope of getting one or both of the parties into his own power. He began at once by offering help to Athens in her dispute about the possession of her old colony Amphipolis. He proposed a treaty of peace with Athens, with the understanding that he would secure Amphipolis for her and receive Pydna (on his own coast) in exchange. These negotiations, though known to the Senate, were kept secret from the people of Athens[1]; but great hopes were based on Philip's friendship, and Athens not only neglected to take Amphipolis when it was left ungarrisoned by Philip, but refused to help the town afterwards when Philip was besieging it[2]. But when Philip captured the place in 357 he refused to give it to her, though he had again promised to do so during the siege[3]. This soon led to a war between Philip and Athens, called the Amphipolitan War, which after eleven years was ended in

---

[1] This is the θρυλούμενον ἀπόρρητον of Dem. II. 6.   [2] Dem. I. 8.
[3] Dem. XXIII. 116.

346 by the Peace of Philocrates. One of Philip's first acts in this war was the seizure of Pydna, which was to have been the price of Amphipolis. He soon afterwards (356) captured Potidaea, then subject to Athens, and gave it to Olynthus, with which he was then forming an alliance. Soon after the capture of Potidaea three messages came to Philip at the same time, one announcing a victory of Parmenio over the Illyrians, another a victory of his horse in the Olympic races, and a third the birth of his son Alexander[1]. In the same year he founded Philippi, near Mt Pangaeus in Thrace, to enable him to work the goldmines of that region, from which he soon derived a revenue of over a thousand talents yearly. In 353 he besieged and captured the Athenian possession Methone.

4. He now entered upon a grander scheme of intervention, of which perhaps he hardly suspected the issue. This was to end in the bitter humiliation of Athens, the annihilation of an ancient Greek race, and his own instalment as the leading member of the venerable Amphictyonic Council. In 356—355 B.C. the disastrous Phocian War between the Amphictyonic Council and Phocis had begun. It resulted from a quarrel between Phocis and Thebes, in the course of which the Thebans and Thessalians induced the Council to fine the Phocians for some act of real or constructive sacrilege. They refused to pay the fine, and the Council voted to treat them as it had treated the sacrilegious Cirrhaeans in the time of Solon[2], by seizing their land and consecrating it to the Delphian Apollo, and putting the whole Phocian race under a terrible curse. The Phocians, under their leader Philomelus, decided to resist ; and they revived an old claim to the management of the temple of Delphi, which had caused a short Sacred War in 448 B.C.[3] Philomelus with a body of Phocians now seized the temple. The loyal Amphictyons, now chiefly Thebans, Thessalians, and Locrians, raised a large army to attack them ; and the Phocians in turn raised a large mercenary force to defend the temple. After many promises to respect the sacred treasures, Philomelus was soon reduced to the necessity of using these to pay his soldiers ; and in a few years the costly offerings of gold and silver, with which the

---

[1] Alexander was born (Plut. Alex. 3) on the 6th of Hecatombaeon (July 21), 356 B.C.

[2] See below, § 59 (end). [3] Thuc. I. 112.

religious pride of Greece and the munificence of strangers had stored
the temple, had been melted down to supply the needs of his
mercenaries. Philomelus was killed in a skirmish in 354 B.C.; his
successor Onomarchus continued the spoliation of the temple with still
greater energy. He and his successors gave the most precious relics,
as the necklaces of Helen and of Harmonia, to their wives or
mistresses to wear. This state of things caused a scandal throughout
Greece, which made it easy and attractive for an unscrupulous out-
sider like Philip to intervene on the side of piety, and thus to pose as
the champion of the God of Delphi. This Philip did at the earliest
opportunity.

5. He had already interfered in Thessaly by aiding the Aleuadae
of Larissa against Lycophron, despot of Pherae. In 353—352 B.C.
he attacked Lycophron with such vigour that the despot invoked the
aid of Onomarchus. The Phocians had now become so powerful that
they had marched forth from Delphi and were practically masters of
Boeotia and of the whole region south of Thermopylae. A force of
Phocians under Phayllus, the brother and afterwards the successor of
Onomarchus, which marched to the aid of Lycophron, was defeated by
Philip, and compelled to retreat beyond Thermopylae. Onomarchus
then entered Thessaly with his whole army, and defeated Philip in two
battles. But Philip soon returned with a new army, and defeated the
Phocians completely. Onomarchus, it was said, was slain in the
retreat by some of his own men. Lycophron abandoned Pherae,
which was taken by Philip, who also captured the seaport of Pagasae,
which gave him control of the Pagasaean Gulf. The Phocian army
was annihilated; but Phayllus took his brother's command, and easily
raised another mercenary force by offering double pay, which the sacred
treasures still provided[1].

6. While this new force was collecting, the road through Thermopylae lay open to Philip. Since his defeat of the Phocians he was
hailed as a protector by their enemies; and he was already recognized
as the avenger of Apollo, who was to restore the holy temple to its
rightful lord; and it was confidently expected that he would pass
Thermopylae with his army and become a power in Central Greece.
But at this momentous crisis Athens became fully alive to the danger

[1] Grote XI. 408—418.

which threatened Greece and especially herself. With an energy which was unusual at this period and recalled the most glorious of her older days, she sent a force by sea to Thermopylae, which prevented Philip from even attempting to force the pass, and which (strange to say) arrived in time. Demosthenes often alludes with pride to this exploit of Athens[1], which took place shortly before midsummer, 352 B.C. Though Philip received this temporary check, he was now recognized as a power to be reckoned with in the settlement of the Sacred War; and he used this position with great skill, until six years later he was enabled to end the war on his own terms, to humiliate Athens, and by a single blow to make himself a recognized partner in Greek affairs.

II. Early Life of Demosthenes.—Events from 352 to 348 B.C.

7. In 354 B.C., two years before Philip was repulsed at Thermopylae by Athens, a statesman appeared in the Athenian Assembly who was to be his most able and persistent opponent, and to whom it was chiefly due that his plans for the subjugation of Greece were delayed more than fifteen years. Demosthenes, son of Demosthenes, was born at Athens, according to the date now generally accepted, in 384–383 B.C., the year in which probably Aristotle was born at Stageiros[2]. The father of Demosthenes died in 376—375, leaving his son in his eighth year and a daughter in her fifth. He left an estate of about fifteen talents (£3000 or $15000)[3], to be managed during the son's minority by three guardians. These mismanaged the property ten years in the most dishonest manner, so that the estate had nearly vanished when their ward attained his majority in 366 at the age of

---

[1] Dem. Cor. 32, IV. 17, 35, XIX. 84.

[2] The lives of Demosthenes and Aristotle coincide almost exactly, as Aristotle died at Chalcis in the autumn of 322 B.C., a few weeks before the death of Demosthenes at Calauria.

[3] I give the modern value of the weight of silver in the Solonic talent (57¾ lbs. avoir.) at £200 or $1000, this being the average value for many years before the recent decline in silver (see Liddell and Scott under τάλαντον). In 1903 this weight of silver has sometimes been worth less than £100.

eighteen. Demosthenes immediately began legal proceedings against his chief guardian Aphobus. During two years he attempted to bring his guardians to terms by private negotiations; but all this time he was preparing for the great contest. He secured the services of Isaeus, a jurist of great experience in the courts, who was deeply learned in the Attic law relating to inheritance and the management of estates.

8. In 364 B.C. his suit came to trial, and he was awarded his full damages, ten talents. In this suit he delivered his two orations against Aphobus (XXVII. and XXVIII.). But he found it impossible to obtain either his estate or his damages from his wily opponent. The training in law and rhetoric which Demosthenes gained in preparing for this early contest, and his experience in the courts, were by no means lost. He found himself, at the age of twenty-three, mainly dependent on himself for support; and he adopted the profession of λογογράφος or legal adviser, the duties of which included writing speeches for clients to deliver in court. But he soon aimed at something much higher than writing speeches and giving advice in private lawsuits. Before he was thirty years old he had distinguished himself as an advocate in cases of important public interest, in which the constitutionality of laws or decrees was judicially tested. His arguments in such cases (355—351 B.C.) are those against Androtion (XXII.), Leptines (XX.), Timocrates (XXIV.), and Aristocrates (XXIII.). He had already twice appeared as a speaker in the Athenian Assembly, once in 354—353, when he delivered his speech on the Symmories (XIV.), proposing a reform in the system of assessing taxes and equipping the navy, and once again in 353—352, when he defended the rights of Megalopolis (XVI.) against Spartan aggression. In neither of these public speeches is there anything which shows that the orator was seriously anxious about the dangers which already threatened Athens from the north; but he probably thought that the moment for open and energetic speech and action on his part against Philip had not yet come.

9. Probably the sudden panic in 352, which roused Athens to her energetic movement to Thermopylae (§ 6), gave the question of checking Philip a more serious importance. A few months later (Nov. 352) the alarming news came that Philip was besieging Heraion Teichos, a fortified post near the Thracian Chersonese. Again Athens acted with energy, and voted to equip forty triremes and to levy a tax

of sixty talents. But a report that Philip was ill, followed by another that he was dead, stopped these preparations, and nothing was done[1]. Philip's cruisers committed some daring aggressions on the coasts of Euboea and even of Attica. In the spring of 351 the Athenian Assembly met to consider his hostile behaviour, which was now a familiar subject. Demosthenes was the first to speak, and he spoke with no uncertain sound. This earliest of his speeches against Philip, the First Philippic, is an earnest and solemn appeal to the people to take decisive steps against an enemy who is every day becoming more dangerous. Demosthenes is now thoroughly aroused, and henceforth the single object of his political life is to excite the Athenians to effective action against Philip. He now proposes a new plan for a permanent military and naval force, to supersede the spasmodic efforts of the past. In this speech he established his claim to statesmanship, on the ground of "seeing things in their beginning and proclaiming them to others"; and in his final review of his political life twenty-one years later he appeals to this with honest pride[2]. So far as we know, this great speech produced no effect.

A few months after the First Philippic, probably in the autumn of 351, Demosthenes made his speech in the Assembly for the Freedom of the Rhodians (XV.).

10. Philip's intrigues in Euboea soon made new troubles. Since the victorious expedition in 357 (§ 2) Euboea had been nominally in friendship with Athens. But after Philip gained control of southern Thessaly (§ 5), he constantly used his influence to alienate the island from Athens. In the First Philippic letters were read from Philip to Euboeans, showing hostility to Athens ; and we hear of his cruisers off Geraestus[3]. Early in 350 the Athenians were asked to help Plutarchus, a sort of despot in Eretria, who was hard pressed by his enemies and professed to be a friend of Athens. Against the strong opposition of Demosthenes, it was voted to send an army to help him, under the command of Phocion. This expedition had various fortunes in a few weeks. Plutarchus proved treacherous, and the Athenians were for a time in great danger ; but Phocion gained a

---

[1] Dem. III. 4, IV. 11.

[2] Cor. § 246: ἰδεῖν τὰ πράγματα ἀρχόμενα κ.τ.λ.

[3] IV. 34, 37.

decisive victory at Tamynae, and soon returned to Athens with most of his army. Affairs remained in this position two years, until a peace was made in 348, in which the independence of Euboea was recognized. Athens and Euboea remained unfriendly, until the intrigues of Philip in 343—342 again brought them into amicable relations[1].

11. The Great Dionysiac festival of 350 was important for the fortunes of Demosthenes. His tribe, the Pandionis, chose no choregus for this year, and he volunteered to take the duties and bear the expense of the χορηγία. While he was sitting in the orchestra of the theatre at the festival, amid all the pomp and state of the ceremony, being a sacred as well as a public official, wearing his crown of office, his old enemy, the wealthy Midias, came forward and struck him in the face with his clenched fist[2]. This was not merely a personal outrage, but an insult to the state and to a great religious festival; and it could be dealt with only by the most public legal process. This was the προβολή, in which the case first came before the Assembly for its preliminary judgment, and afterward, if the decision was adverse to the accused, could be tried before an ordinary popular court. The Assembly, at a special meeting in the Dionysiac Theatre, unanimously condemned Midias. After this decisive victory it is not surprising that the young orator yielded to the advice of judicious friends and avoided a further contest with a powerful man, who could always give him trouble in his public career. He compromised the case, and received a sum of money as damages. The existing oration against Midias (XXI.), which appears to have been composed for delivery in court about a year after the assault, was never spoken.

12. A year later (in 349) Philip took a most important step in his grand plan by attacking the Olynthiac confederacy of thirty-two free Greek towns in the Chalcidic peninsula. In less than a year he had captured and destroyed all these, and sold the inhabitants into slavery. Olynthus, the head of this confederacy, had long been an important and flourishing city, generally hostile to Athens, and before 352 friendly to Philip. He encouraged her in her enmity to Athens by

---

[1] See § 46 (below).

[2] For the affair of Midias and its consequences, see Dem. XXI., against Midias; Grote XI. 478, 479; Schaefer, Dem. II. 94—101. The date is much disputed: see large edition, p. 240.

giving her Potidaea, which he took from Athens in 356 (§ 3). But the rapid advance of Philip's power in 353—352 alarmed the enterprising city, and in the autumn of 352 she was in friendship, if not in alliance, with Athens[1]. In the autumn of 349 an embassy from Olynthus came to Athens, asking help against an attack from Philip, and proposing a formal alliance[2]. Athens accepted the alliance; but nothing was done with sufficient energy to save Olynthus or any of her confederate towns. Three embassies came from Olynthus to Athens, and three fleets were sent by Athens to Olynthus; the last fleet was still at sea when Olynthus fell. The city was captured, after a brave defence, by the help of traitors within the walls, probably in the early autumn of 348[3]. Many Athenian citizens were captured with the city. With Olynthus fell the other Chalcidic towns, and the destruction was complete and terrible. Seldom had anything shocked the feelings of the Grecian world like this. Travellers in Peloponnesus (Aeschines among others) saw on the roads troops of Olynthian captives driven off to slavery[4].

During the Olynthian war Demosthenes delivered his three Olynthiacs, masterpieces of eloquence, full of earnest appeals to the patriotism and public spirit of the Athenians and to their sense of duty and honour. The wise prediction of the First Philippic, "if we do not now fight Philip there (in the north), we shall perhaps be compelled to fight him here[5]," is now repeated in fresh words and with redoubled force. No more powerful arguments were ever addressed to any people; and yet the quieting influence of Eubulus and his party prevented all efficient and timely action. At the end of the Olynthian War (348) Demosthenes was probably in his thirty-sixth year. All the public speeches made by him before the events of 347—346 B.C. have already been mentioned.

---

[1] Dem. XXIII. 109, εἶτ' Ὀλύνθιοι μὲν ἴσασι τὸ μέλλον προορᾶν, κ.τ.λ.

[2] I. 2, 7.

[3] Diod. XVI. 53, φθείρας χρήμασι...Εὐθυκράτην τε καὶ Λασθένην, κ.τ.λ. See Dem. VIII. 40, IX. 56, 66, XIX. 265, and Grote XI. 454 ff.

[4] Dem. XIX. 305, 306, and Grote XI. 505, 510.   [5] IV. 50.

III. THE PEACE OF PHILOCRATES.
347—346 B.C.

13. When Philip had destroyed Olynthus and the thirty-two Greek towns of Chalcidice, he naturally turned his eyes to the land of his hopes beyond Thermopylae. He now saw that at least a temporary peace with Athens was absolutely necessary. Even before the capture of Olynthus envoys from Euboea had brought to Athens a pleasant message from Philip that he wished for peace. Soon after this Phrynon of Rhamnus was captured by one of Philip's cruisers. He was released on payment of a ransom, and he persuaded the Athenians to send a public envoy with him to ask Philip to restore his ransom money. Ctesiphon (not the defendant in the suit on the Crown) was sent with him on this mission. Philip received them with great kindness and granted their request. Ctesiphon reported that Philip wished to make peace as soon as possible[1]. The Athenians were delighted; and it was unanimously voted, on the motion of Philocrates, that Philip might send a herald and envoys to Athens to treat for peace.

At about this time Olynthus was captured (§ 12). The consternation caused by this event did much to excite the almost universal desire for peace at Athens. The relatives of two Athenians captured at Olynthus appeared in the Assembly with suppliant olive-branches and besought the people to rescue their kinsmen. The people were deeply moved, and voted to send the actor Aristodemus, who was professionally intimate at the Macedonian court, to intercede with Philip for the prisoners. This mission also was perfectly successful. Aristodemus reported that Philip was full of kindness and wished both peace and alliance with Athens. Aristodemus was complimented by a crown, on the motion of Demosthenes. His return to Athens took place after the beginning of 347—346, the archonship of Themistocles, in which Demosthenes was for the second time a senator, the year of the peace of Philocrates.

14. In the previous year, after the fall of Olynthus, a significant movement against Philip was made by Eubulus, with the active aid of Aeschines. Eubulus was the conservative statesman of the day, uni-

---

[1] For this and the following events of § 13, see Aesch. II. 12—19.

versally respected, incorruptibly honest, but a strong advocate of peace at any price[1]. Of Aeschines we then hear for the first time in political life. The famous rival of Demosthenes was the son of respectable parents, who had been reduced to poverty in the Peloponnesian War. We cannot accept as historical either of the two accounts of his parentage and his youth which are given by Demosthenes[2]. Neither orator is authority for the life or personal character of the other. Like Demosthenes, he was left to his own resources to earn his living ; but he was less favoured by genius and by fortune than his rival. As a young man he was a play-actor and took many important parts, as that of Creon in the *Antigone* and that of Oenomaus in the tragedy of Sophocles of that name[3]. He also did service as a clerk, publicly in the Senate and Assembly, and privately in the employ of Aristophon and Eubulus. His friendly relations with Eubulus were often of great service to him in his public life. He was strong and vigorous, had a powerful voice, and was a ready speaker[4]. In all these respects Nature had given him a great advantage over Demosthenes ; but he lacked the steady rhetorical training by which his rival, even as a young man, made himself an accomplished orator. Though he was about six years older than Demosthenes, he appeared in public life much later.

15. On the occasion referred to (§ 14), probably in the winter or spring of 348—347, Eubulus addressed the Assembly, calling Philip the common enemy of the Greeks and swearing by his children that he wished that Philip were dead. He proposed a decree for sending embassies to the Peloponnesus and all other parts of Greece— Demosthenes says, "all but to the Red Sea"—to summon an Hellenic synod at Athens and inaugurate a general Greek war against Philip[5]. This measure was eloquently supported by Aeschines and was adopted with enthusiasm. Demosthenes says that Aeschines then professed to be the first Athenian who had discovered that Philip was plotting against the Greeks. Aeschines was one of the envoys sent out ; and on his return he repeated the fine speeches which he had made in

---

[1] For Eubulus see Grote XI. 387, 388.

[2] Cf. Dem. XIX. 249, 250; Cor. 129, 130.   [3] XIX. 246, 247 ; Cor. 180.

[4] See Cic. de Orat. III. 28: suavitatem Isocrates, subtilitatem Lysias, acumen Hyperides, sonitum Aeschines, vim Demosthenes habuit.

[5] Dem. XIX. 292, 304.

behalf of Athens against Philip at Megalopolis[1]. Demosthenes appears to have taken no interest in these embassies, of which he speaks in a disparaging tone. He probably distrusted any movement in which men like Eubulus were leaders, and experience had shown him that their grand plan of uniting all Greece in a war against Philip would end in failure and give Philip fresh encouragement for conquest. The event proved Demosthenes right. No Hellenic synod met in Athens, and within a year Eubulus and Aeschines were both playing into Philip's hands. It must be remembered that the "still absent envoys," who play so important a part in the story of the peace (as told by Aeschines in 330 B.C.), for whose return Demosthenes is said to have refused to delay the negotiations *for peace*, are these very messengers of war[2].

16. A year later it is certain that the prospect of an honourable peace with Philip was extremely welcome to all sober-minded men at Athens. Her recent losses and disasters secured a favourable hearing for the friendly messages from Pella. There can be no doubt that Demosthenes then felt strongly inclined to peace, as a matter of policy; and it is hardly possible that he had yet begun to suspect the crafty scheme by which peace with Philip would be turned to the disgrace of Athens and the triumph of her bitterest foes. And yet it seems hardly possible that the terrible spectre of the Sacred War, just beyond their borders, should not have filled all sober Athenians with alarm, especially when they remembered Philip's march to Thermopylae five years before (§ 6). Philip himself, we may be sure, never lost sight of the prize which had once seemed within his grasp.

17. Since Philip's repulse from Thermopylae in 352, the Sacred War had been waged with increasing bitterness, but with no prospect of a conclusion. In 351 the death of Phayllus left the leadership to Phalaecus, son of Onomarchus (§ 5), a mere boy. The Thebans were now the chief opponents of the Phocians, and Boeotia became the chief seat of war. Neither side gained any decisive advantage, and the resources of both parties were now exhausted. The Phocians had come to the end of the Delphic treasures, after robbing the temple of gold and silver of the value of about 10,000 talents. They received help from various Greek states, including 1000 men from Sparta and

---

[1] Dem. XIX. 11.   [2] See § 24 (below).

2000 from Achaia. It is probable that their army never fell below 10,000[1]. (See § 36.)

18. The Phocians were now anxious lest a new invasion from Thessaly with help from Philip might suddenly end their power. Their army was mutinous from lack of pay, and the authority over it was divided. Envoys were sent to Athens asking help, and offering the Athenians the towns commanding the pass of Thermopylae. This offer pleased the Athenians greatly; and they ordered Proxenus to take possession of the three towns, and voted to call out the citizen soldiers up to the age of thirty and to man fifty triremes. But Proxenus now found men in authority at Thermopylae who repudiated the message sent to Athens; he was dismissed with insult, and the fleet and army were never sent. Still Athens felt that the fate of Greece depended on having Thermopylae held secure against any invasion from the North. Notwithstanding the sacrilegious plundering of Delphi, which no one ventured to approve openly, Athens had the strongest political reasons, which were easily reinforced by moral motives, for protecting the Phocians at Thermopylae, especially against Philip[2]. There was a formal alliance between Athens and Phocis, and it was naturally assumed at Athens (except by Philip's friends) that peace with Philip would protect the Phocians against all danger from him. It was probably in this spirit that Athens received the friendly propositions which Aristodemus brought from Philip. Soon after the cordial reception of Aristodemus (§ 13), Philocrates proposed a decree for sending ten ambassadors to Philip, to discuss terms of peace and to ask him to send ambassadors to Athens with full powers to negotiate[3]. The following were sent: Philocrates (the mover), Demosthenes, Aeschines, Ctesiphon (the former envoy to Philip), Phrynon, Iatrocles, Aristodemus, Nausicles, Cimon, Dercylus. To these Aglaocreon of Tenedos was afterwards added by the Assembly as a representative of the allies. The embassy was appointed and sent in February, 346 B.C.

19. We depend chiefly on Aeschines for the account of the first embassy[4]. The envoys went by land to Oreus, in the north of Euboea, and thence by sea to Halus, on the south side of the Gulf of Pagasae,

[1] Dem. XIX. 230.   [2] Dem. Cor. 18[2-4].

[3] Aesch. II. 18, III. 63.   [4] See Aesch. II. 20—43.

a town claimed by Athens as an ally. Parmenio, Philip's general, was then besieging Halus, which Philip wanted to give to his friends the Pharsalians. The embassy passed through the Macedonian camp to Pagasae, Larissa, and Pella. On arriving at Pella the envoys were courteously received by Philip at a formal interview, in which they addressed the king in the order of their ages, Demosthenes speaking last, directly after Aeschines. Aeschines devotes the greater part of his story to his own eloquent argument, in which (as he says) he made a powerful appeal to Philip in defence of the right of Athens to Amphipolis. He spoke of the appointment of Iphicrates as the Athenian commander there, and reminded Philip of the occasion when his mother, Eurydice, placed him with his brother Perdiccas (both children) on the knees of Iphicrates, and begged the general to treat her two boys with brotherly affection, as their father Amyntas had adopted him as a son.

20. Aeschines then describes the appearance of Demosthenes before Philip. He was (we are told) so embarrassed that he could hardly utter a word; and after a few vain attempts to speak he became silent. Philip encouraged him and tried to relieve his embarrassment, but all in vain. He remained speechless, and the herald conducted the embassy from the royal presence. This account is probably much exaggerated; but it is hardly possible that the whole story is an invention. Grote is probably right in thinking that Demosthenes was taken with a kind of "stage fright" when he suddenly found himself formally addressing the king whom he had so often denounced, and when he was probably insulted by the officers of Philip who were in attendance, so that he may well have been physically unable to speak[1]. Philip soon recalled the embassy, and replied to their arguments, ending his address with the usual assurances of friendship. Most of the envoys were struck by the dignity, wit, and gracious manners of Philip, and by his skill in replying to what had just been said to him[2].

21. The returning envoys arrived in Athens about the first of Elaphebolion (March 28) 346 B.C. They made their regular reports to the Senate and the Assembly; and they received the regular complimentary votes and the invitation to dinner in the Prytaneum.

---

[1] Grote XI. 530.   [2] Aesch. II. 41—43 : cf. 51, 52.

They brought home a letter from Philip, expressing great friendship and his hope of both peace and alliance. There can be no doubt that Demosthenes returned fully persuaded that *some* peace should be made as soon as possible, to settle the important questions which the war kept open. Down to this time—in fact, until the nineteenth of Elaphebolion—he had no suspicion of the loyalty and political honesty of Aeschines[1]. There can be little doubt that Philocrates was already secured for Philip's interest; and it was not long before Aeschines (perhaps honestly at first) was acting with him to gain Philip's ends.

22. Immediately after the return of the embassy Demosthenes proposed two decrees in the Senate to secure peace at the earliest moment. The Great Dionysiac festival was approaching, during which all public business would be suspended. These decrees enacted that safe-conduct should be granted to Philip's envoys and herald, who were now on their way to Athens, and that the Prytanes should call a special meeting of the Assembly, to be held on the eighth of Elaphebolion (April 5) if Philip's embassy should then have arrived, to discuss terms of peace. The envoys came too late for this day; but after their arrival Demosthenes proposed another decree appointing the eighteenth and nineteenth of Elaphebolion (April 15 and 16), after the Dionysia, for two meetings, in which both peace and alliance with Philip should be considered. The two meetings were held on the appointed days, and the Macedonian envoys, Antipater, Parmenio, and probably Eurylochus, were present during a part of the sessions. Demosthenes, as senator, showed the distinguished envoys all proper courtesies, and proposed decrees to admit them to the Assembly and to make them guests of honour at the Dionysia. He personally escorted them to the theatre, where curtains had been provided to shield them from the early morning air and cushions to cover the stone seats. And when they departed for home he hired three yoke of mules for them and escorted them to Thebes.

23. One of the strangest charges made by Aeschines against

---

[1] Dem. XIX. 13: καὶ μέχρι τοῦ δεῦρ' ἐπανελθεῖν ἀπὸ τῆς πρώτης πρεσβείας ἐμὲ...διεφθαρμένος καὶ πεπρακὼς ἑαυτὸν ἐλάνθανεν. The remainder of XIX. 12—16 shows his opinion after his eyes were opened.

Demosthenes is that of corrupt collusion with Philocrates in making the peace. Philocrates went into exile as a convicted criminal early in 343 B.C., fleeing from Athens to escape the sentence of death which was soon passed upon him for treachery and bribery in making the peace which is a reproach to his name. Aeschines can henceforth think of no graver charge than this, with which he introduces his accusation of Demosthenes with regard to the peace: "Now I return to the peace which you and Philocrates proposed." Can it be believed that this is the same Aeschines who fifteen years before had described this same peace as "the peace made by me and Philocrates"![1] His chief argument for the collusion is that Demosthenes caused the peace to be made in such unseemly haste that the Greek states which had been invited by Athens to an Hellenic council for mutual defence could not be represented in the negotiations. He constantly alludes to "the still absent embassies, which you sent to the Greeks."

24. These are the "roving envoys," which had been sent out on the motion of Eubulus, more than a year before, to unite the Greeks in a common cause against Philip. (See § 15.) Aeschines himself says that, when Philip's envoys came to Athens, the Athenian envoys were still absent, "summoning the Greeks against Philip[2]." On what possible ground now could Aeschines, who was one of the embassy which invited Philip's envoys to Athens to negotiate a peace, demand after their arrival that all negotiations should be suspended until the return of envoys who had been absent more than a year stirring up hostility against Philip, and had shown no signs of returning or reporting? These "absent envoys" were pure inventions. Aeschines declares positively that not one of them had returned when the peace was made, and Demosthenes that there was no embassy then out[3]. This contradiction can be reconciled only by the explanation given by Demosthenes, that all the Greeks had long ago been tried and found wanting—in fact, that Athens could find no states ready to join her in resisting Philip. Aeschines expressed the same opinion in

---

[1] Compare Aesch. III. 57 with I. 174. See the reply in Dem. Cor. 21.

[2] Aesch. III. 65, 68.

[3] Aesch. II. 58, 59; Dem. Cor. 23[6,7]. See note on the last passage, and the whole of Cor. 20 and 24.

343 B.C.[1] It is most probable that no reports had been made simply because there were no favourable responses to report, and that no delay of the peace would have changed the result.

25. We have the most contradictory accounts from the two orators of the proceedings in the two meetings of the Assembly. In the first, on the eighteenth of Elaphebolion, the Macedonian envoys appeared and stated plainly and firmly the terms on which Philip would make peace. These were, in general, ἑκατέρους ἃ ἔχουσιν ἔχειν, *uti possidetis*; that is, no questions were to be raised as to Philip's right to any of the places which he had taken from Athens and still held, of course including Amphipolis. It was also stated that Philip would not recognize as allies of Athens either the Halians or the Phocians. In conformity with these announcements, Philocrates proposed a formal decree, establishing peace and alliance between Philip and his allies and Athens and her allies, excepting the Halians and Phocians[2]. It is evident that the last clause was heard by most of the Athenians with surprise and alarm. It signified plainly that Philip would do, in spite of the peace, the very thing which it was supposed the peace would prevent, that is, pass Thermopylae and overwhelm the Phocians with the help of the Thebans, while Athens would have her hands tied by the peace. Demosthenes now had his eyes thoroughly opened. Though he had favoured and even urged peace, as preferable to disastrous war, he was no advocate of "peace at any price," and he now saw that the price was to be too high[3]. He strongly opposed the motion of Philocrates, and advocated "the resolution of the allies," which was, according to Aeschines, favoured by himself and all the other speakers in the first Assembly[4]. From Aeschines, who appears to be not yet in the complete confidence of Philocrates and the Macedonian envoys, we have a final burst of exalted patriotism. As Demosthenes reports him, he declared that, though he thought a peace should be made, he would never advise Athens to make the peace proposed by Philocrates so long as a single Athenian was left alive[5]. Finally, on the motion of Demosthenes, the

---

[1] Aesch. II. 79.
[2] Dem. XIX. 159 and 321 (quoted § 27, note 1), with 278.
[3] Ibid. 96. [4] Aesch. III. 71.
[5] Dem. XIX. 13—16.

Assembly rejected the proposition of Philocrates and adopted what was called the resolution of the allies, whose regular synod (συνέδριον) was then in session at Athens. The Macedonian envoys were then recalled and informed of this action[1].

26. It is somewhat uncertain what is here meant by "the resolution of the allies" (τὸ τῶν συμμάχων δόγμα). We have two accounts of this from Aeschines[2]. In one he mentions only a clause recommending a postponement of the discussion about peace until the return of the "absent envoys"; but the fact that the discussion was going on by general consent makes it impossible that this clause was advocated by "all the speakers in the former Assembly." In the other he mentions a recommendation that only peace, and not alliance, should be discussed; but this he deduces from the entire omission of the word "alliance" in the resolution, and it is obvious that neither Demosthenes nor all the other speakers could have opposed alliance[3]. He there mentions also the proposed provision that three months should be allowed after the making of the peace, in which any Greek state might claim its advantages and be recorded on the same column with Athens and her allies[4]. This is the only part of the resolution which had any significance whatever on that day; and it must be this, *and this alone*, which was adopted by the Assembly. This provision, if it were granted by Philip, would ensure the safety of the Phocians; for they could then have claimed the protection of the peace as Greeks, without being recognized by Philip as allies of Athens. This important provision, supported, as it appears, by the authority of the synod of allies, was advocated by Demosthenes, as the only substitute for the fatal proposition of Philocrates which was at all likely to be accepted by the Assembly. Aeschines says that the general opinion, when the first Assembly adjourned, was that there would be peace, but that alliance would be made (if at all) later, in conjunction with all the Greeks.

27. The following night brought about a great and sudden change in the whole situation. Philocrates had been too bold in pressing on

[1] Dem. XIX. 144.

[2] Aesch. II. 60 and III. 69, 70, 71.   [3] Aesch. III. 68, 71.

[4] Aesch. III. 70: ἐξεῖναι τῷ βουλομένῳ τῶν Ἑλλήνων ἐν τρισὶ μησὶν εἰς τὴν αὐτὴν στήλην ἀναγεγράφθαι μετ' Ἀθηναίων καὶ μετέχειν τῶν ὅρκων καὶ τῶν συνθηκῶν.

the Assembly the plan of the Macedonian envoys. The sudden disclosure of Philip's designs against the Phocians had caused so great excitement and opposition, that it was hopeless to attempt to pass the original excluding clause. At the same time it was seen to be fatal to all Philip's plans to allow the proposition of the allies to be finally adopted. Philocrates therefore amended his decree during the night, probably in consultation with Antipater and Parmenio. He brought it before the Assembly the next day without the excluding clause, reading simply "the Athenians and their allies." This change, which after the statements of the previous day meant nothing, appears to have allayed the excitement in great measure, and the decree in this form was finally passed without much opposition. This could not have been effected until the public apprehensions about the Phocians had been quieted by diplomatic promises, like those which were so effectual after the return of the second embassy a few months later[1]. Antipater and Parmenio simply maintained their ground, that Philip could not admit the Phocians as parties to the peace ; but their friends in the Assembly (Philocrates and perhaps Aeschines) assured the people "on authority" that, though Philip then could not offend the Thebans and Thessalians by publicly recognizing the Phocians, he would still, when the peace gave him greater freedom of action, do all that Athens could ask of him[1].

28. It is impossible to determine precisely what was said or done by Aeschines and Demosthenes in the second meeting of the Assembly, in which the peace was actually voted. Nowhere are our two witnesses more hopelessly at odds. Demosthenes says that Aeschines, after his eloquent speech the day before, protesting

---

[1] Dem. XIX. 159: τήν τε γὰρ εἰρήνην οὐχὶ δυνηθέντων ὡς ἐπεχείρησαν οὗτοι, πλὴν Ἀλέων καὶ Φωκέων, γράψαι, ἀλλ' ἀναγκασθέντος ὑφ' ὑμῶν τοῦ Φιλοκράτους ταῦτα μὲν ἀπαλεῖψαι, γράψαι δ' ἄντικρυς Ἀθηναίους καὶ τοὺς Ἀθηναίων συμμάχους. See also 321: ἐντεῦθεν οἱ μὲν παρ' ἐκείνου πρέσβεις προὔλεγον ὑμῖν ὅτι Φωκέας οὐ προσδέχεται Φίλιππος συμμάχους· οὗτοι δ' ἐκδεχόμενοι τοιαῦτ' ἐδημηγόρουν, ὡς φανερῶς μὲν οὐχὶ καλῶς ἔχει τῷ Φιλίππῳ προσδέξασθαι τοὺς Φωκέας συμμάχους διὰ τοὺς Θηβαίους καὶ τοὺς Θετταλούς, ἂν δὲ γένηται τῶν πραγμάτων κύριος καὶ τῆς εἰρήνης τύχῃ, ἅπερ ἂν συνθέσθαι νῦν ἀξιώσαιμεν αὐτόν, ταῦτα ποιήσει τότε. See further 220: μείζονα ἢ κατ' Ἀμφίπολιν εὖ ποιήσειν ὑμᾶς ἐὰν τύχῃ τῆς εἰρήνης, Εὔβοιαν Ὠρωπὸν ἀποδώσειν, κ.τ.λ.

vehemently against the motion of Philocrates, now told the people not to remember their ancestors nor to listen to stories of ancient sea-fights and trophies, but to enact that they would not help any who had not previously helped Athens (meaning the Phocians)[1]. Instead of simply denying that he had made such a speech and proving his denial by witnesses, Aeschines undertakes to show that he could not have spoken at all on the second day because by the decree of Demosthenes no speeches were to be made on that day[2]. But this argument (in 343 B.C.) is answered by his own account thirteen years later of a speech made by Demosthenes in that very meeting. He quotes what he calls a "disagreeable metaphor" then used by Demosthenes, that we must not *wrench off* (ἀπορρῆξαι) alliance from peace[3].

Though Aeschines denies so stoutly that no one could have spoken in the second meeting, he further recounts a speech of his own, which must have been the one to which Demosthenes alludes, in which he says he advised the people to remember the glorious deeds of their ancestors, but to forget their mistakes, like the Sicilian expedition and the delay in ending the Peloponnesian war[4]. But he maintains that this speech was made in the first meeting. When we consider that our testimony comes from the two opposing orators at the trial of Aeschines, and make all possible allowance for exaggeration and misrepresentation, we must admit that Aeschines reports his speech more fairly than Demosthenes, but we must decide that it was delivered on the second day, as Demosthenes declares. Eubulus finally told the people plainly that they must either accept the terms proposed by Philocrates, or man their fleet and levy a war tax[5]. We have the statement of Demosthenes that at the second meeting he opposed Philocrates (whom the people at first refused to hear) and tried to amend his proposition for the peace, still advocating the resolution of the allies[6]. He was probably made more hopeful by the

---

[1] Dem. XIX. 16.   [2] Aesch. II. 63—66.

[3] Aesch. III. 71, 72.

[4] See Aesch. II. 74—77, where the substance of this speech is given.

[5] Dem. XIX. 291.

[6] Ibid. 15: ἐμοῦ τῷ τῶν συμμάχων συνηγοροῦντος δόγματι καὶ τὴν εἰρήνην ὅπως ἴση καὶ δικαία γένηται πράττοντος. Cf. 291.

refusal of the people to exclude the Phocians by name, which left Athens free to act; and he perhaps trusted in the power of Athens to stop Philip again at Thermopylae if he should attempt to force the pass after the ratification of the peace[1]. There is no reason to doubt that he did his best, fighting almost single-handed in a desperate strait.

The Peace of Philocrates, thus voted by the Athenian Assembly on the nineteenth of Elaphebolion (April 16), 346 B.C., ended the Amphipolitan War, which was begun in 357. A few weeks later, the aged Isocrates sent to Philip his address called Φίλιππος, in which he expressed his joy at the peace and his hope of much good to result from Philip's leadership.

29. A few days after the peace was voted, the same ambassadors were appointed to return to Macedonia and receive the oaths of Philip and his allies to the peace and alliance. As Aeschines gives us our chief account of the first embassy, so Demosthenes tells the story of the second[2]. Demosthenes urged his colleagues to set out with all speed to administer the oaths to Philip, knowing well that every day might be of the greatest importance to Athens. Philip was all this time vigorously pressing his conquests in Thrace, after Athens had tied her hands by making the peace. As entreaties availed nothing, Demosthenes procured (3rd of Munychion, April 29) a decree of the Senate (which the people had empowered to act until the next Assembly), directing the embassy to depart at once, and ordering Proxenus, who still kept his fleet north of Euboea, to convey them to Philip, wherever he might be. In defiance of this vote, the embassy first waited a long time at Oreus; and then, instead of sailing with Proxenus, travelled by a circuitous land route to Pella, where they arrived twenty-three days after leaving Athens. There they waited

---

[1] The mixed feelings of Demosthenes appear in XIX. 150: μέχρι τούτου γε οὐδὲν ἀνήκεστον ἦν τῶν πεπραγμένων, ἀλλ' αἰσχρὰ μὲν ἡ εἰρήνη καὶ ἀναξία τῆς πόλεως, ἀντὶ δὲ τούτων δὴ τὰ θαυμάσια ἀγαθὰ ἡμῖν ἔμελλεν ἔσεσθαι.

[2] We have in Dem. XIX. a clear and full account of the second embassy and its results, generally in the following order: 150—173, 17—66; and in Cor. 25—27, 30—36, a brief but graphic résumé of the same events, somewhat modified by the lapse of thirteen years. Though Aeschines denies some of the details, he says nothing which breaks the force of the clear and straightforward statements of Demosthenes.

twenty-seven days for Philip's return from his conquests in Thrace[1]. In the time thus gained he had captured several Thracian towns.

30. The Athenians found at Pella envoys from Thebes, Thessaly, Sparta, and other Greek states, awaiting Philip's return. There were also envoys from Phocis, anxiously waiting to learn their fate. Philip received the Athenians in the presence of the other envoys, and surrounded by his army, which was ready for his march to Thermopylae. While the envoys were at Pella, Philip sent them large presents of gold, of which Demosthenes refused to accept his share[2]. He devoted much of his time to procuring the release of the Athenian captives who were still in Philip's hands. He lent several of these the money needed for their ransom, which he later refused to receive back when Philip released the other prisoners without ransom[3].

31. When Philip took his oath to the peace, the majority of the embassy allowed him formally to exclude the Phocians, the Halians, and Cersobleptes from the recognized allies of Athens[4]. Demosthenes was generally outvoted in the deliberations of the embassy. They refused by vote to send to Athens a letter written by him, and sent one of their own with a different account of their doings[5]. Demosthenes hired a vessel to take him home alone; but Philip forbade him to depart[6]. In this state of things we can easily believe what Aeschines says, that no one would willingly mess with Demosthenes or lodge at the same inn with him[7].

32. After Philip had sworn to the peace, the embassy had no further pretext for wasting time at Pella. Then followed a most disgraceful and humiliating spectacle. Philip marched forth from his capital with his army for the invasion of Greece, the result of which—whether he favoured the Thebans or the Phocians--must be the humiliation of a proud people; and in his train followed meekly (with one exception) an Athenian embassy which had basely betrayed the interests of Athens. There followed also a band of Phocian suppliants, who must now have known that their race was doomed. When they

---

[1] Dem. XIX. 154, 155: see note on Cor. § 30[4].
[2] Dem. XIX. 166—168.   [3] Ibid. 169, 170.
[4] Ibid. 44, 174, 278.   [5] Ibid. 174.
[6] Ibid. 51, 323.   [7] Aesch. II. 97.

arrived at Pherae, the long-neglected duty of administering the oath to Philip's allies—or rather to those whom Philip saw fit to summon as their representatives—was performed in a tavern, "in a manner which was disgraceful and unworthy of Athens," as Demosthenes adds[1].

33. The embassy now returned to Athens without more delay, arriving on the thirteenth of Scirophorion (July 7), after an absence of about ten weeks. When they arrived, Philip was already at Thermopylae, negotiating with the Phocians for a peaceable surrender of the pass[2]. This was just what Philip had planned. The Athenians had now little time to consider whether they should send a fleet to defend Thermopylae, and he trusted to the quieting reports of his friends on the embassy to prevent any hostile action. The scheme worked perfectly. A temporary obstruction was caused by the report of Demosthenes to the Senate. There he told the plain truth, that Philip was at the gates of Hellas, ready to attack the Phocians; and he urged that an expedition should even then be sent to Thermopylae with the fifty triremes which were kept ready for such an emergency. The Senate believed Demosthenes, and passed a vote expressing their approval of his conduct. They insulted the embassy in an unprecedented manner, by omitting the customary vote of thanks and the invitation to dine in the Prytaneum[3].

34. But Philocrates and Aeschines had planned their scheme too artfully to be thus thwarted; and in the Assembly of the sixteenth of Scirophorion, probably held the day after the meeting of the Senate, all was changed. Here Demosthenes found a body of his enemies, who would not permit him to be heard or the vote of the Senate to be read[4]. Aeschines at once took the platform, and easily carried the meeting with him by disclosing the private information about Philip's real plans which (he said) Philip had confided to him at Pella. He assured the people that, if they would stay at home quietly two or three days, they would hear that Philip was besieging Thebes, and compelling the Thebans (not the Phocians) to pay for the treasure

---

[1] Dem. XIX. 158.   [2] Ibid. 58.

[3] Ibid. 18, 31, 32; and 322, τὴν δὲ βοήθειαν ἔδει κωλῦσαι τὴν εἰς τὰς Πύλας, ἐφ' ἦν αἱ πεντήκοντα τριήρεις ὅμως ἐφώρμουν. See Cor. 32⁷⁻⁹.

[4] XIX. 23, 35.

stolen from Delphi. He repeated the advice to this effect which (he said) he had given to Philip, for which a price had been set on his head at Thebes. He also implied that Euboea was to be given to Athens as a recompense for Amphipolis, and hinted obscurely at a restitution of Oropus to Athens[1]. Then Philip's letter was read, full of general friendliness, but containing absolutely nothing about the Phocians and no promises of any kind.

35. In this temper the Assembly was ready to vote almost anything which would make it easy for Philip to carry out his beneficent plan. A decree was passed, on the motion of Philocrates, publicly thanking Philip for his friendly promises, extending the peace and alliance to posterity, and enacting that, if the Phocians still refused to surrender the temple "to the Amphictyons," the Athenians would compel them to do so by force[2]. They then appointed ten ambassadors, chiefly members of the previous embassies, to report these proceedings to Philip at Thermopylae. Demosthenes at once refused to go on this embassy. Aeschines made no objection at the time; but afterwards, when it was thought that his presence in Athens would be important at the coming crisis, he excused himself on the ground of illness, and his brother went in his place[3].

Soon afterwards came two letters from Philip, inviting the Athenians to send a force to join him at Thermopylae[4]. As Demosthenes shows, these were really sent to prevent them from marching out, as Philip thought this cordial invitation would quiet their alarm, and so be the surest means of keeping them at home. We hear of no appeals from Aeschines or his friends urging the acceptance of the invitation. Indeed, public opinion at Athens was changing, so that perhaps there was danger of the invitation being accepted in a different spirit.

---

[1] Dem. XIX. 19—22, 35, 74, 220, 324—327; Cor. 35; VI. 30; cf. Aesch. II. 136.

[2] Dem. XIX. 48—50: here it is said of the so-called Amphictyons, ποίοις; οὐ γὰρ ἦσαν αὐτόθι πλὴν Θηβαῖοι καὶ Θετταλοί.

[3] Ibid. 121—124.

[4] Ibid. 51, 52: ἐπιστολὰς δύο καλούσας ὑμᾶς, οὐχ ἵν' ἐξέλθοιτε. See Aesch. II. 137: ὑμῖν δὲ οὐκ ἔπεμψεν ἐπιστολὴν ὁ Φίλιππος ἐξιέναι πάσῃ τῇ δυνάμει βοηθήσοντας τοῖς δικαίοις; *to help the cause of justice!*

36. There were Phocian envoys at Athens on the return of the embassy, and they remained until after the meeting of the Assembly. The action then taken showed them that they had nothing to hope from Athens, and they returned home with this unwelcome news. With the help of Athens by land and sea, Phalaecus and his army of 10,000 infantry and 1000 cavalry might still have held Thermopylae against Philip. But without help this was impossible[1]. The Lacedaemonians had already deserted them, and now nothing was left but to surrender on the best terms which could be made. Demosthenes declares that the action of the Assembly on the 16th was the direct cause of the surrender of the Phocians on the 23rd[2].

37. The third Athenian embassy set out for Thermopylae about the 21st of Scirophorion (July 15). When they came to Chalcis, they heard that the Phocians had surrendered, while Philip had openly declared himself for the Thebans, and all the hopes of Athens were at an end. As the envoys had no instructions to meet this emergency, they returned to Athens at once. One of them, Dercylus, came directly into a meeting of the Assembly in the Piraeus (on the 27th) and reported his alarming news from Thermopylae[3]. The people were struck with panic at the tidings, and voted, on the motion of Callisthenes, to remove the women and children into protected places, to put the Piraeus and the forts in a state of defence, and to hold the coming Heraclea, usually held in the country, within the city walls[4]. Such a panic had not been known in Athens since the last days of the Peloponnesian War. They also voted to send to Philip the same embassy which had returned from Chalcis, with instructions to watch the proceedings of the Amphictyonic Council, which Philip was expected to summon at once[5]. The Athenians were not only in great alarm, but in absolute uncertainty about Philip's next step. He might even join the Thebans in a march upon Athens; and the road was

---

[1] Dem. XIX. 58, 123.

[2] See the calculation in Dem. XIX. 58, 59. Allowing four days for the news of the 16th to reach the Phocians and three days more for making terms, he puts the surrender on the 23rd (July 17). Four days later the news came to the Assembly in the Piraeus.

[3] Dem. XIX. 60, 125.   [4] Ibid. 86, Cor. 36; Aesch. III. 80.

[5] Aesch. II. 94, 95.

open. Even Aeschines admits the bitter disappointment at Athens and the bitter feeling against the ambassadors.

Soon after the surrender of the Phocians, Philip addressed a diplomatic letter to the Athenians, deprecating their indignation at his unexpected course, and trying to conciliate them by assurances of his continued friendship.

38. The embassy soon departed on its new mission by way of Thebes. Aeschines had now no fear of the Thebans or of the price they had set upon his head. They arrived at Philip's camp just in time for the festivities with which he and the Thebans were celebrating their triumph over the sacrilegious Phocians; and they appear to have had no scruples against joining in the celebration[1]. Philip had entered Phocis as the champion of Apollo, whose violated temple he was to restore to the Amphictyonic Council. He therefore lost no time in calling a meeting of this venerable body, or rather what he chose to call by this distinguished name[2]. The Council voted to expel the Phocians, and to give their two votes to Philip[3]. The Phocian towns, except Abae with its ancient temple of Apollo, twenty in number, were to be destroyed, and the people to be divided into villages of not more than fifty houses; their horses were to be sold for the benefit of the temple, and their arms thrown down precipices; and they were to pay sixty talents yearly to the temple until the stolen treasure should be made good[4]. We have records of large payments made by the Phocians on this account from 344 to 337 B.C.[5] Any

---

[1] Dem. XIX. 128, 130, Cor. 287. See the lame defence of Aeschines, II. 162, 163.

[2] Demosthenes (V. 14) calls this assembly τοὺς συνεληλυθότας τούτους καὶ φάσκοντας Ἀμφικτύονας νῦν εἶναι. See XIX. 50: οὐδενὸς δ' ἄλλου παρόντος τῶν Ἀμφικτυόνων πλὴν Θετταλῶν καὶ Θηβαίων. Cf. XIX. 327.

[3] A newly found inscription at Delphi records a meeting of the board of ναοποιοί, Temple-builders, in 346—345, ἐπεὶ ἁ εἰρήνα ἐγένετο, at which Thessalians, Thebans, Athenians, Spartans, and a Delphian were present, but no Phocians. In their place stands the ominous entry, Φίλιππος Μακεδών, Τιμανορίδας Μακεδών.

[4] Diod. XVI. 60; Paus. X. 3, 3; Dem. XIX. 81, 141, Cor. 36, 42, IK. 19, 26. Cf. Aesch. II. 9, III. 80.

[5] The French have found an interesting inscription at Delphi recording several of these payments made by the Phocians, published by Bourguet in

Phocian who was personally guilty of plundering the temple was declared accursed and outlawed. This terrible sentence was executed with more than strict exactness, with the Thebans for executioners. When Demosthenes went to Delphi more than two years later, he witnessed the pitiable condition of Phocis and its wretched people, with walls and houses destroyed, and nobody to be seen except old women and little children and miserable old men[1]. A harder fate still befell Orchomenus and Coronea for their adherence to the Phocians. Their walls were razed and the inhabitants sold into slavery. Boeotia, with a substantial piece of Phocis[2], was then brought under the dominion of Thebes. Sparta, for assisting the Phocians, was excluded from the Delphic temple. The προμαντεία, precedence in consulting the oracle, which the Phocians had granted to Athens in the time of Pericles for her help in the short Sacred War of 448 B.C., was taken from her and given to Philip[3]. Still, it was the decided policy of Philip to have no open breach with Athens at this time.

39. The Pythian games were celebrated by Philip at Delphi at their regular time, in September 346 B.C., with unusual splendour[4]. No delegates were present from either Athens or Sparta. For 240 years Athens had sent her deputation to these games with great pomp and ceremony over the Sacred Way, which Apollo had once trodden on his progress from Delos to Delphi; and her absence now was an historic event. Thus was Philip formally installed in his long-coveted position as a power in Greece.

So ended the disastrous Sacred War, after a duration of more than ten years, with the exaltation of Philip and the humiliation of Athens, though neither was a party to the war or was even interested in it when it began.

40. Philip now determined to secure from Athens a formal recognition of his new position as an Amphictyonic power. He therefore sent thither a deputation to ask for a confirmation of his election to the Council[5]. The conspicuous absence of Athens from both Council

---

the Bull. de Corresp. Hellén. (Athens), 1897, pp. 321—344. (See American Journal of Archaeology, 1899, p. 306.)

[1] Dem. XIX. 64, 66, 325.   [2] Ibid. 112, 127.
[3] Plut. Per. 21; Dem. IX. 32.
[4] Diod. XVI. 60.   [5] Dem. XIX. 111—113.

and games embarrassed and annoyed Philip greatly. Athens was in a delicate position. It would have been simple madness, in her isolation and humiliation, to defy him by a downright refusal. But the people were in no mood to assent to what they deemed a disgrace to Greece and an insult to themselves. When Aeschines came forward alone to urge compliance, he was hooted and could get no hearing. Demosthenes was perhaps the only man in Athens who could persuade the Assembly to take the humiliating course which prudence now made necessary. This he did in his speech On the Peace (v.), in which, while he makes no attempt to conceal the false position in which Athens had ignorantly allowed herself to be placed, he yet advises her not to court further calamity by a vain resistance to an accomplished fact[1].

IV. Six Years of nominal Peace.
346—340 B.C.

41. The peace of Philocrates lasted, at least in name, until the formal renewal of the war with Philip in 340 B.C. But all this time Philip was busy in extending his power, especially to the detriment of Athens. He interfered in the disputes of Sparta with Argos, Messene, and Megalopolis, sending help to the latter. Athens, on the motion of Demosthenes, voted to send envoys to Peloponnesus to counteract this dangerous influence, and of these Demosthenes was chief. In the Second Philippic he repeats parts of his speech to the Messenians, in which he warned them of the fate of Olynthus and exhorted them to repel Philip's friendly advances[2]. But Philip's promises were more powerful than the eloquence of Demosthenes, and we soon find Argos and Messene (instigated by Philip) sending envoys to Athens, complaining that she supported Sparta in preventing them from gaining their freedom. With these came envoys from Philip, complaining that Athens had charged their master with breaking his promises.

42. In the Assembly which discussed the reply to be given to these embassies (late in 344 B.C.), Demosthenes delivered his Second Philippic. This gives a statesmanlike review of Philip's conduct towards Athens since the peace, showing that he had been constantly aggressive

---

[1] See the speech On the Peace.   [2] VI. 9, 13, 15, 20—25.

and deceitful, while Athens had been kept quiet by his partisans, who assured her of his friendly intentions. He proposed a definite answer to the embassies, of which we can judge only by the firm character of the speech itself. We hear of no positive results of this mission, but we hear no more of the disputes in Peloponnesus which caused it. Still, Philip continued to acquire influence there, and the governments leaned on him for support and became more and more subservient to his wishes.

43. In the same year there occurred the summary arrest and condemnation of Antiphon, a disfranchised citizen, who offered his services to Philip to burn the dockyards at the Piraeus. He was arrested by the authority of Demosthenes, and brought before the Assembly ; but was released on the protest of Aeschines. He was again arrested by the intervention of the Areopagus, brought to trial and condemned to the rack and to death[1].

Not much later occurred an important trial before the Amphic-tyonic Council, in which the ancient right of Athens to control the temple of Delos was contested by the Delians. The Athenians chose Aeschines as their counsel in this case ; but the Areopagus, to which the people had by special vote given the right to revise the election, rejected him and chose Hyperides in his place. The election was made in the most formal and solemn manner, each senator taking his ballot from the altar[2]. At the trial Hyperides delivered his famous Delian oration, in which he defended the cause of Athens so eloquently that her rights in the Delian temple remained undisturbed.

44. A little later (probably before midsummer in 343 B.C.), Philip sent Python of Byzantium to Athens, to tell the old story of his un-alterable friendship and of his grief on hearing the calumnies which his enemies reported in the Assembly and the Athenians believed. He assured the people that he was ready to revise the peace if there was anything amiss in it, and begged them not to believe the orators who misrepresented him and his intentions. Python was an eloquent orator, a pupil of Isocrates, and his statement of Philip's grievances moved the Assembly greatly. He was accompanied by envoys from all Philip's allies, and he was supported by Aeschines. But his "tide of eloquence" was stemmed by Demosthenes, who replied to Philip's

---

[1] Cor. 132, 133, with notes. [2] Ibid. 134, 135.

complaints so effectively that the feeling of the Assembly was soon turned against Python[1]. He was followed by Hegesippus, another patriotic Athenian, who made two propositions for revising the peace. He proposed (1) that the clause which provided that *each should keep what they had*, ἑκατέρους ἔχειν ἃ ἔχουσιν, *uti possidetis*, should be changed to *each should have their own* (ἑκατέρους ἔχειν τὰ ἑαυτῶν); (2) that the freedom of all Greek states not included in the treaty should be recognized by both parties to the peace, who should agree to defend them if they were attacked. A decree was passed with these two provisions; and Hegesippus was sent with other envoys to Philip to ask his approval of these terms, and further to ask for the return to Athens of the island Halonnesus, which Philip then held, and for the surrender of the towns in Thrace (Serrhium, Doriscus, etc.) which he had taken after the peace was made. This embassy was rudely received by Philip, who ignored all his promises about a revision of the peace, and it returned to Athens with nothing accomplished.

45. Eight or nine months later (early in 342 B.C.) Philip sent a letter to the Athenians, in which he once more deplored the mis-representations of hostile orators and replied to some of the demands of Athens. We have the speech of Hegesippus in the Assembly, in which Philip's letter is discussed[2]. Philip (1) offered to *give* Halonnesus to Athens if she would accept it as a gift from him. He (2) proposed a treaty (σύμβολα) with Athens to provide for the trial of lawsuits between Macedonians and Athenians, reserving to himself the final ratification of the treaty. He (3) agreed to recognize and defend the freedom of Greeks who were not parties to the peace. He (4) offered to submit to arbitration all questions about the captured towns, with that about Halonnesus. He further denied that he had broken any promises.

Hegesippus in reply objects to receiving Halonnesus as a gift, while the right of Athens to the island is denied. He treats the proposed σύμβολα as a mere trick of Philip, and spurns his offer of arbitration.

---

[1] Aesch. II. 125; Dem. Cor. 136.

[2] This (VII. in editions of Demosthenes) is now universally recognized as a speech of Hegesippus. It professes to be made by the mover of the two proposals sent to Philip, who was also one of the embassy. This speech is the authority for many of the details of §§ 44 and 45.

Demosthenes also discussed Philip's letter in the same spirit[1]. So far as we know, no result followed these negotiations.

In the late summer or autumn of 343 B.C. Aeschines was brought to trial on the charge of παραπρεσβεία for his misconduct on the second embassy to Philip in 346. The speech of Demosthenes as accuser (XIX.) and that of Aeschines as defendant (II.) were delivered at the trial; and Aeschines, who was defended by Eubulus, was acquitted by a small vote. (See large edition, Essay IV.)

46. At about this time Philip renewed his intrigues in Euboea. The formal peace which Athens had made with the towns of Euboea in 348 B.C. recognized the independence of the island[2]. Philip saw more and more plainly the importance of Euboea as a basis of operations against Athens, and he never lost an opportunity of establishing his influence there. In 343—342 he supported Clitarchus, who had made himself tyrant of Eretria, and he sent troops to expel the popular party. An embassy sent by Athens on the motion of Demosthenes to counteract the intrigues of Philip was refused a hearing at Eretria, and the town fell into Philip's power. The banished democracy took possession of Porthmus, a harbour of Eretria, and Philip sent against them 1000 soldiers and destroyed the walls of Porthmus. He also sent troops to Oreus, to establish there the tyrant Philistides; and under the Macedonian influence the popular leader, Euphraeus, was sent to prison, where he slew himself to escape the vengeance of his enemies[3]. Athens, by the help of Demosthenes, was more fortunate in establishing her influence at Chalcis, where two brothers, Callias and Taurosthenes, who had once acted in Philip's interest, were now firm friends of the Athenians. Callias sent an embassy to Athens, and a treaty for mutual defence was made[4]. Aeschines violently attacks Callias as a friend of Demosthenes and an enemy of Athens.

47. In the winter of 343—342 Philip marched into Epirus, and placed Alexander, brother of his queen Olympias, on the throne[5].

---

[1] The speech of Demosthenes is lost ; but Aeschines probably alludes to it when he ridicules Demosthenes for "quarrelling about syllables." See Aesch. III. 83 : Ἀλόννησον ἐδίδου· κ.τ.λ.

[2] See § 10 (above).

[3] Dem. IX. 57—62, 66: Cor. 71, 79, 81.

[4] Aesch. III. 91—93.

[5] See Paus. I. 11³⁻⁵; Just. VII. 6, VIII. 6. 1.

He also threatened to attack Leucadia and Ambracia (colonies of Corinth) and to cross into Peloponnesus. He made a treaty with the Aetolians, in which he agreed to restore to them Naupactus, which the Achaeans then held. He was foiled by Athens, which sent Demosthenes and other envoys to urge Corinth and Achaea to defend their rights[1].

48. On his return from Epirus, Philip entered Thessaly, where he appointed tetrarchs, one for each of the original districts of Thessaly, —Thessaliotis, Phthiotis, Pelasgiotis, Hestiaeotis[2]. This completed the subjugation of Thessaly, which had been one of his main objects since his attack on the despots of Pherae in 353—352[3]. At about this time (342) Philip sent for Aristotle and made him the tutor of his son Alexander, who was now fourteen years old. In this year he gave great offence to Greece by sending a deputy to hold the Pythian games in his name[4].

49. Early in 342 B.C. Philip undertook to complete his conquest of Thrace, and especially to wrest the Thracian Chersonese from Athens. This ancient possession of Athens was equally important to her as a protection to her trade with the Euxine, and to Philip as a point of departure for invading Asia. Soon after the peace of 346, Athens had sent settlers to the Chersonese under Diopithes[5], an able and enterprising general, who was determined to defend the rights of Athens to the last extremity and to brook no interference from Philip. The Cardians, who had been admitted to the peace in 346 as Philip's allies, annoyed the Athenian settlers in every way. Philip sent troops to aid the Cardians, and Diopithes raised an army in Thrace to attack them, with which he invaded Philip's territory beyond Cardia. Against this Philip protested vehemently in a letter to the Athenians, and a meeting of the Assembly was held to consider the question. In this Demosthenes delivered his eloquent oration on the Affairs of the Chersonese. He admits that the action of Diopithes has not been precisely peaceful, but maintains that Philip has broken all the terms of the peace and that Athens is really at war with him by his own act.

---

[1] Dem. IX. 27, 34, 72.   See § 65 (below).
[2] Dem. IX. 26.   [3] See § 5 (above).
[4] See Dem. IX. 32, τοὺς δούλους ἀγωνοθετήσοντας πέμπει.
[5] Dem. VIII. 6, IX. 15.

He stoutly objects to making any concessions to Philip at this crisis, and above all he protests against recalling Diopithes or passing any vote which might discredit him or his conduct in Thrace[1].

50. Soon after this speech, before midsummer 341, Demosthenes delivered his Third Philippic. This powerful argument deals with the whole history of Philip's aggressions since the peace was made. He declares that Athens has been actually at war with Philip for a long time, indeed ever since the destruction of the Phocians[2]. He earnestly beseeches the people to recognize this fact and to prepare for active warfare. He justifies the recent proceedings of Athens in the Chersonese only as measures of defensive war, to which Philip's offensive acts have driven her. It would be madness, he urges, for the Athenians to allow Philip to wage war on them and not to defend themselves by arms.

The whole tone of the Third Philippic and the speech on the Chersonese shows that Demosthenes had no longer the least expectation of maintaining even a nominal peace ; while the increasing boldness of Philip's aggressions shows that he merely aimed at securing all possible advantages before the inevitable declaration of war.

51. We have only meagre and scattered accounts of the events of the year 341—340, before the outbreak of the war. One important result of the powerful arguments of Demosthenes was that Athens now universally recognized his leadership and gave him almost complete control of her foreign affairs. For this department, from this time until the battle of Chaeronea, he declares himself responsible in the fullest sense[3]. One of his wisest strokes of policy was his forestalling of Philip's designs on Byzantium by his embassy thither, probably in the early summer of 341. He thus secured for Athens the friendship and alliance of Byzantium, the control of the Hellespont,

---

[1] For a full discussion of these important events, which led directly to the renewal of the war with Philip, see the two orations of Demosthenes On the Chersonese (VIII.) and the Third Philippic (IX.). See Grote XI. 623—625.

[2] Dem. IX. 19: ἀφ᾽ ἧς ἡμέρας ἀνεῖλε Φωκέας, ἀπὸ ταύτης ἔγωγ᾽ αὐτὸν πολεμεῖν ὁρίζομαι. See also IX. 9, 15—18, and many similar passages in this speech.

[3] Cor. 59, 88, 218, 298 (μεγίστων...προστάς): cf. Cor. 320. Aeschines (III. 130) alludes to Demosthenes before the battle of Chaeronea as ἐμπιμπλάμενος τῆς δεδομένης ὑφ᾽ ὑμῶν αὐτῷ ἐξουσίας.

and the protection of her trade with the Euxine. Athens and Byzantium had had so many grounds of enmity, especially since the Social War, that it now required no ordinary diplomatic skill to bring them into friendship. Later in 341—340 an embassy was sent to the King of Persia, perhaps on the suggestion of Demosthenes, asking for help against Philip; but the King sent back a very insulting letter, refusing his assistance[1].

Even more important were the embassies to Peloponnesus which were undertaken by Demosthenes with Callias of Chalcis. These resulted in the formation of a powerful league against Philip, which, according to Aeschines, proposed to raise 100 talents, and to equip 100 ships of war, 10,000 foot soldiers, and 1000 horsemen, besides 2000 militia from Peloponnesus and 2000 from Acarnania. The leadership of the league was given to Athens, and a formal meeting of the allies at Athens was appointed, which probably was never held[2]. But the proposed forces appear to have been actually raised, as Demosthenes gives the number of the allies in the field as 15,000 mercenaries and 2000 cavalry, besides the militia[3].

52. These vigorous preparations, which preceded the open outbreak of the war, amply justify the boasts of Demosthenes about the allies and the revenues which were raised for Athens by his influence[4]. One of the most important results of the close union between Demosthenes and Callias was the formal alliance of Athens and the cities of Euboea, which grew out of the treaty made two years before[5]. This alliance was closely connected with the expulsion of Philip's tyrants at Oreus and Eretria. In the summer of 341, on the motion of Demosthenes, an expedition was sent, which freed Oreus from the tyrant Philistides, who was put to death[6]. Several months later a more decisive expedition was sent under Phocion, on the motion of

---

[1] Aeschines (III. 238) probably refers to the King's reply: ἐγὼ ὑμῖν χρυσίον οὐ δώσω· μή με αἰτεῖτε· οὐ γὰρ λήψεσθε.

[2] Aesch. III. 94—98.

[3] Cor. 237, where he includes the later Theban allies. The Ἀριθμὸς βοηθειῶν (Cor. 305) probably contained all the forces raised directly or indirectly by Demosthenes. See Cor. 301, 302.

[4] Cor. 234—237.   [5] See § 46 (above).

[6] Cor. 79[8], τὴν ἐπ' Ὠρεὸν ἔξοδον: cf. 87.

Demosthenes, which liberated Eretria from the tyrant Clitarchus, who was put to death[1]. This completed the liberation of Euboea from Philip's influence, and made the island a firm friend of Athens. The Athenians expressed their gratitude to Demosthenes for these successful labours by the gift of a crown of gold, which was conferred in the theatre, at the Great Dionysia of 340, in the very terms which were subsequently used by Ctesiphon in his own decree[2].

53. The dispute between Athens and Philip about Halonnesus in 343—342 left the island in Philip's hands, as Athens refused to take it as a gift from him, while he refused to "restore" it. At last, probably in 341—340, the people of Peparethus seized Halonnesus and made the Macedonian garrison prisoners. Philip soon avenged this act by sending a fleet to ravage Peparethus[3]. Athens then directed her commanders to make reprisals upon Philip. This shortly preceded the outbreak of the war.

Before midsummer 340 it was generally recognized throughout Greece that war was inevitable. Philip was then engaged in the conquest of Thrace, and had come to the point where the possession of Byzantium was indispensable to him. It was also of the utmost importance for him to become master of the grain traffic of the Euxine. He now called on the Byzantines, as his friends and former allies, to promise him their aid in his pending war with Athens. But here his way was blocked by the alliance already made by Demosthenes with Byzantium, and she refused to join him[4]. Upon this he resolved to secure her by force; and he began by attacking the neighbouring city of Perinthus. To this end he sent his fleet through the Hellespont, and he guarded it against attack during its passage by marching an army through the Chersonese to keep the Athenians well employed on shore[5].

54. Perinthus was attacked vigorously (probably late in the summer of 340) by land and by sea, but it was also vigorously defended. Though Philip brought to the siege an army of 30,000

---

[1] Diod. XVI. 74: Φωκίων μὲν κατεπολέμησε Κλείταρχον τὸν Ἐρετρίας τύραννον καθεσταμένον ὑπὸ Φιλίππου.

[2] See Cor. 83[2-4], with note. See large edition, p. 280, note 3.

[3] Cor. 70[1].   [4] See § 51 (above); Cor. 87.

[5] Cor. 139[5] (see note).

men, besides his large fleet, and employed the most improved engines
of war and towers two hundred feet high, the defenders were finally
successful. They were constantly aided by their neighbours of
Byzantium, and at last by a force sent by the King of Persia ; though
no help came from Athens or any other Greek city. Philip at length
decided to abandon the siege; but he still hoped to surprise
Byzantium, which was his real object, by a sudden attack. The
better and larger part of the Byzantine army was at Perinthus. He
therefore left about half his army at Perinthus, under his best
commander, to make a show of continuing the siege, while he
hastened with the rest to Byzantium and besieged it with all his skill.
The Byzantines were at first greatly alarmed; but timely help came
to them from a powerful friend. Athens was now openly at war with
Philip, and her naval power soon came to the help of her new ally.
A fleet under Chares, which was previously cruising in the northern
Aegean, was sent to Byzantium, and was followed by another under
Phocion, which was more powerful and more efficient. Chios, Cos,
and Rhodes also sent their help. Byzantium was rescued, and Philip
wisely abandoned this second siege. By some skilful device his fleet
eluded the Athenian ships in the Bosporus and escaped into the
Aegean.

55. In the late summer or early autumn of 340, probably after
the siege of Perinthus was begun, Philip sent to the Athenians a long
letter, full of complaints of their aggressions and justifications of his
own [1]. To this communication, which ended in a declaration of war,
Athens replied only by her own declaration of war and a vote to
remove the column on which the treaty of 346 B.C. was inscribed.
The special occasion alleged by Demosthenes for the declaration of
war was the capture of some Athenian merchant ships by Philip's
cruisers in the Hellespont [2]; but war had been an avowed fact on both
sides many weeks before it was declared.

When the Byzantine war was ended by the help of Athens and the
wise counsels of Demosthenes, the gratitude of Perinthus, Byzantium,

---

[1] A document purporting to be this letter appears as no. XII. in the editions
of Demosthenes. This is accepted as genuine, at least in substance, by Grote,
Weil, and Blass. The document in Cor. 77, 78 is spurious.

[2] Cor. 73.

and the towns in the Chersonese was expressed to Athens as their deliverer by votes of thanks and crowns[1].

56. We have very scanty accounts of Philip's movements from this time (probably early in 339 B.C.) until we find him the next summer fighting with the Scythians and the Triballi. An unimportant quarrel with Ateas, a Scythian king, gave him a ground for invading his dominions; and the aged king himself was defeated on the Danube and killed. Philip carried off as booty 20,000 boys and women, much cattle, and 20,000 breeding mares. On his return from Scythia, he passed through the country of the Triballi, with whom he had previously been in conflict[2]. These warlike mountaineers attacked him furiously; and in the battle he was severely wounded, his horse was killed under him, and he was thought to be dead. In the panic which followed, the Triballi took possession of the Scythian booty. Thus again humiliated, Philip returned to Macedonia[3].

About the time of the renewal of war with Philip, Demosthenes proposed and carried his important trierarchic reform, by which the navy of Athens was put on a new footing and many old abuses were corrected. It was under this new system of trierarchy that all the fleets were fitted out during the war, and its success in removing grievances is described by Demosthenes with glowing pride and satisfaction[4].

V. THE WAR WITH PHILIP, FROM 340 B.C. TO THE BATTLE OF CHAERONEA IN 338 B.C.

57. When Philip returned from Scythia in the summer of 339 B.C., he found that his war with Athens had been waged on both sides during his absence without decisive results. Though the Athenians had generally been defeated by land, yet the Macedonians felt

---

[1] Cor. 89—93. [2] Cor. 44[1] with note.

[3] See Justin IX. 2, and Lucian, Macrob. 11. Aeschines alludes briefly to the Scythian expedition, when he says of Philip in the summer of 339, οὐκ ἐπιδημοῦντος ἐν Μακεδονίᾳ Φιλίππου, ἀλλ' οὐδ' ἐν τῇ Ἑλλάδι παρόντος, ἀλλ' ἐν Σκύθαις οὕτω μακρὰν ἀπόντος. At the time of the regular meeting of the Amphictyonic Council (Aug. or Sept.), he had already returned, and he was then made general of the Amphictyons (Cor. 152; cf. Aesch. III. 129).

[4] Cor. 102—108: see note on 103[4].

severely their naval weakness, by which they suffered a constant blockade of their coast without being able to retaliate by sea[1]. It was obviously impossible for Philip to invade Attica by land without the coöperation of both Thessaly and Thebes, and his relations with them did not warrant even a proposal to this end. Thessaly had been alienated by the abolition of her free governments; and Thebes, though she had gained the lion's share of the spoils at the end of the Sacred War, was deeply offended by the loss of Nicaea in the pass of Thermopylae, which Philip had given to Thessaly, and of her own colony Echinus, which Philip had taken for himself[2]. Without the consent of Thessaly he could not command the pass of Thermopylae; and without Thebes he could not use the fertile plain of Boeotia for military operations. Some undertaking which would unite the two in a common interest with himself seemed indispensable[3]. Such was Philip's perplexity when he found himself again at war with Athens after six years of nominal peace. When he departed for Scythia this problem was still unsolved, though possibly he may already have confided to Aeschines directly or indirectly some practical hints for its solution. However this may have been, it so happened that before Philip's return Aeschines had suddenly stirred up an Amphictyonic war, which delivered him from all his difficulties and opened the way for himself and his army into the very heart of Greece[4]. He had passed Thermopylae in triumph in 346 as the champion of the God of Delphi; he was now to enter Greece a second time clothed with the same sacred authority, to aid the Amphictyonic Council in punishing new offenders who were openly defying their commands.

58. We are here reduced to the alternative of believing either that Aeschines deliberately devised this Amphictyonic war to give Philip a free passage into Greece (or at least took advantage of a slight incident at Delphi to excite a general conflict), or else that he ignorantly and recklessly roused a war which could have no other end than bringing Philip into Greece at the head of an army. The latter alternative attributes to Aeschines a reckless ignorance of Greek politics with which we have no right to charge him. We are almost wholly dependent on his own graphic narrative for the facts as to the

---

[1] Cor. 145, 146.   [2] Dem. IX. 34 (with Schol.); Aesch. III. 140.
[3] Cor. 147.   [4] Cor. 149.

origin of this baneful war, and he must be condemned, if at all, on his own testimony[1]. And this evidence, in my opinion, strongly confirms the view of Demosthenes, that Philip saw that his appointment as commander in an Amphictyonic war was the surest way in which he could march an army into Greece without the opposition of Thessaly or Thebes; that such a war would be useless to him if it were stirred up by any of his own delegates or friends; and that he must employ an Athenian to devise a scheme which should secure this end without exciting suspicion in the Amphictyonic Council. At all events, Aeschines was ready at Delphi to do him this very service.

59. In the archonship of Theophrastus (340—339), the Athenian delegation to the spring meeting of the Amphictyonic Council consisted of Diognetus, the Hieromnemon of the year, and three Pylagori, Midias, the old enemy of Demosthenes, Thrasycles, and Aeschines[2]. These four were present at the meeting in Delphi, when Diognetus and Midias were attacked by fever and Aeschines suddenly found himself in a position of great importance. The Athenian delegates had been privately informed that the Locrians of Amphissa intended to propose a vote in the Council to fine Athens fifty talents because she had re-gilded and affixed to the newly-built temple of Delphi[3] some shields, probably relics of the battle of Plataea, and had renewed the old inscription, Ἀθηναῖοι ἀπὸ Μήδων καὶ Θηβαίων, ὅτε

---

[1] Aeschines tells how he stirred up the Amphictyons to war in III. 107—124; and he slurs over the highly important matter of the appointment of Philip as commander in 128, 129, without expressly mentioning the appointment. Demosthenes, Cor. 149—152, alludes briefly to the Amphictyonic meeting at Delphi, being in essential agreement with Aeschines as to the main facts, and to Philip's appointment: in 163—179 and 211—218 he gives the subsequent events which led to the alliance of Athens and Thebes and those which followed that alliance.

[2] For the constitution of the Amphictyonic Council and the distinction of the two classes of delegates, Hieromnemons and Pylagori, see Essay V.

[3] See Aesch. III. 116, ὅτι χρυσᾶς ἀσπίδας ἀνέθεμεν πρὸς τὸν καινὸν νεὼν πρὶν ἐξαρέσασθαι. This "new temple" was not the temple built by the Alcmaeonidae two centuries before, nor any addition to that building. The temple built by the Alcmaeonidae was destroyed early in the fourth century B.C. See Homolle, Bulletin de Corresp. Hellén. for 1896, pp. 667—701. The disputed word ἐξαρέσασθαι probably refers to some ceremony of dedication.

τἀναντία τοῖς Ἕλλησιν ἐμάχοντο. This renewal of the ancient disgrace of Thebes in fighting on the side of the Persians at Plataea was, it must be confessed, neither a friendly nor a politic act; it shows the abiding exasperation between Thebes and Athens which followed the victory of Leuctra. But this was of little consequence now. The Hieromnemon sent for Aeschines, and asked him to attend the Amphictyonic meeting on that day in his place, as if he were a delegate with full powers, and defend Athens against the Locrian accusation. Aeschines was therefore present at the meeting by special authority. As he began to speak, apparently referring in some excitement to the threatened charge against Athens, he was rudely interrupted by an Amphissian, who protested against the very mention of the Athenians, declaring that they should be shut out of the temple as accursed because of their alliance with the Phocians. Aeschines replied in great anger; and among other retorts "it occurred to him" to mention the impiety of the Amphissians in encroaching on the accursed plain of Cirrha, which had been solemnly devoted to everlasting sterility and desolation by the Amphictyonic Council about 250 years before, on the motion of Solon[1], at the end of the first Sacred War.

60. Cirrha was the ancient seaport of Delphi on the Gulf of Corinth, while Crissa (often confounded with it) was a town on the height above the river Pleistus, on the road to Delphi (near the modern Χρυσό)[2]. The broad plain of Cirrha, one of the most fertile in Greece, lay between the foot of Parnassus and the coast, and was called by both names Cirrhaean and Crissaean. In obedience to the Amphictyonic curse, Cirrha with its harbour was destroyed, and the plain had remained uncultivated until recently, when the Amphissians had re-established the ancient port as a convenient landing-place for visitors to Delphi, and levied tolls on those who used it. They had also cultivated a part of the accursed plain and erected buildings upon it. The Amphictyons seem to have quietly acquiesced in this violation

---

[1] Aesch. III. 115—118. The destruction of Cirrha and the consecration of its plain took place in 586 B.C., at the end of the ten years' Sacred War.

[2] The ancient walls of Crissa, enclosing a large space on the brink of the cliff, are still to be seen, though buried and overgrown so as often to escape observation.

of the sacred edict, doubtless seeing the advantages of the newly opened port to themselves, and thinking little of the almost forgotten curse. But they were not proof against the arts and eloquence of an accomplished Athenian orator, who ingeniously presented the case in impassioned language and with powerful appeals to the prejudices and the bigotry of an antiquated religious assembly, with which a venerable curse had greater weight than the strongest political motives or the abstract idea of Hellenic unity. From the hill near Delphi where the Amphictyonic Council sat under the open sky, there is a magnificent view of the sacred plain, extending to the gulf of Corinth. Here Aeschines stood in the excited assembly, and showed them the plantations and buildings of the Amphissians on the forbidden land; and he caused the terrific imprecations of the ancient curse to be repeated, which declared any man, city, or state, which should cultivate or occupy the plain of Cirrha, accursed of Apollo, Artemis, Leto, and Athena, and devoted to utter destruction with their houses and their race. He reminded them that the same curse was invoked on all who should permit others to violate the sacred edict. We cannot wonder that the whole assemblage was fired with fierce enthusiasm to avenge the wrongs of Apollo upon the sacrilegious Amphissians. When Aeschines had finished his speech, as he tells the court, the question of the Athenian shields was wholly forgotten, and the only thought was of the punishment of the Amphissians. The flame had now been kindled, which was to end in the conflagration that Philip was eager to see. An Amphictyonic war was begun, which could be ended only by the intervention of Philip and his army. Thebes and Thessaly could now be united in a common cause with Philip[1].

61. Late in the day the meeting adjourned; and a herald was ordered to proclaim that all Delphians, freemen and slaves, above the age of eighteen, and all the Amphictyonic delegates, should meet the next morning at daybreak with spades and picks, ready "to aid the God and the sacred land"; and that any state which failed to obey should be accursed and excluded from the temple. This Amphictyonic mob assembled and descended to the plain, where they burned the houses and destroyed the moles which enclosed the harbour. On

<hr>

[1] Aesch. III. 119—122.

their way back to Delphi, they were attacked by a crowd from Amphissa, and barely escaped with their lives: some of the Council were captured. The next day an Amphictyonic Assembly (ἐκκλησία) was summoned, consisting of the delegates and all other citizens of Amphictyonic states who happened to be at Delphi. This body voted that the Hieromnemons, after consulting their respective states, should meet at Thermopylae at some time before the regular autumnal meeting of the Council, prepared to take some definite action concerning the Amphissians[1]. When this vote was first reported at Athens by her delegates, the people "took the pious side" (as Aeschines calls it); but a few days later, after a little consideration and when the influence of Demosthenes had prevailed, it was voted that the Athenian delegates "should proceed to Thermopylae and Delphi at the times appointed by our ancestors," and further that no Athenian representatives should take any part in the irregular meeting at Thermopylae, "either in speech or in action." This wise step precluded Athens in the most public manner from taking any part in the mad Sacred War which Aeschines had stirred up: in his own words, "it forbids you to remember the oaths which your ancestors swore, or the curse, or the oracle of the God[2]."

62. The appointed meeting was held at Thermopylae, with no representatives from Athens, and (what was more ominous for Philip's designs) with none from Thebes. It was voted to make war upon the Amphissians, and Cottyphus, the president of the Council, was made commander. The Amphissians at first yielded, and were fined and ordered to banish the leading rebels. But they paid no fine, and soon restored their exiles, and banished again "the pious" whom the Amphictyons had restored. The autumnal meeting of the Council (339 B.C.) found things in this condition; and it is hard to believe that the leaders in this miserable business expected any other issue. The Council was told plainly and with truth, that they must either raise a mercenary army and tax their states to pay for it, fining all who refused to do their part, or else make Philip the Amphictyonic general. It is not surprising that Philip was at once elected[3]. We are now

---

[1] This seems to be the meaning of the obscure words (Aesch. III. 124), ἔχοντας δόγμα (?) καθ᾽ ὅ τι δίκας δώσουσιν οἱ Ἀμφισσεῖς.

[2] Aesch. III. 122—127.

[3] Dem. Cor. 152: see the whole description 149—153.

just beyond the point at which Aeschines thought it wise to stop in his exciting narrative. When he told of the first expedition against Amphissa under the command of Cottyphus, he added that Philip was then "away off in Scythia," so that of course *he* was in nobody's mind. After this, he could not tell of Philip's election a few weeks later without an absurd anti-climax, which would be all the more ridiculous when he was compelled to add that the first act of the new Amphictyonic general in this pious war was one of open hostility to Athens and Thebes. Accordingly he does not mention in this narrative either the appointment of Philip or the seizure of Elatea which immediately followed his appointment. Instead of stating these important facts, the direct results of his own deliberate action, he bursts forth with a new flood of eloquence, and dilates on the terrible omens and the more terrible calamities which followed the refusal of Athens to take the leadership in the holy war against Amphissa, to which she was called by the voice of Heaven; and he once alludes to Elatea in the vaguest manner, without hinting that its seizure by Philip was an event for which he was himself even in the slightest degree responsible[1].

63. Demosthenes describes the action of Aeschines in stirring up the new Sacred War very briefly, but very plainly, representing it as a deliberate plot, devised by Philip and executed by Aeschines, for securing Philip and his army free admission into Greece to attack Athens. He mentions the choice of Philip as general, and adds that Philip immediately collected an army and entered Greece, professedly bound for the plain of Cirrha; but that he suddenly bade the Cirrhaeans and Locrians "a long farewell," and seized and fortified Elatea. This old Phocian town, which had been dismantled in 346 B.C., held a military position of the greatest importance for Philip's plans. It stood at the outlet of one of the chief passes leading from Thermopylae, and it commanded the broad plain through which the Cephisus flows on its way to Boeotia. It was also the key to the rough roads leading westward to Doris and Amphissa. From this point Philip threatened both Athens and Thebes so directly as to leave no doubt of his purpose in entering Greece. He hoped that

---

[1] See the end of III. 129, with its mysterious and obscure language, and the preceding narrative. For the tardy allusion to Elatea see 140.

the traditional feud between Athens and Thebes would bring Thebes into his alliance; but he trusted to his commanding position on the frontier of Boeotia to convince her that her only hope of safety lay in his friendship. The prospect of Boeotia being the seat of war was an alarming one, from which a united invasion of Attica by Thebes and Philip was the only sure escape[1]. Demosthenes states that the Macedonian party in both Athens and Thebes had long been fomenting discord between the two cities, which were now so estranged that Philip felt that there was no possibility of their uniting against him.

64. We are almost wholly dependent on Demosthenes for what we know of the skilful diplomacy by which Thebes was secured as an ally of Athens against Philip[2]. This was the crowning achievement of the political life of Demosthenes, and he always alludes to it with honest pride. We have his own graphic story of the wild excitement at Athens when a messenger at evening brought the news from Elatea, and of the solemn meeting of the people the next morning when he made his eloquent speech, by which he laid the foundation for a right understanding with Thebes and secured the appointment of a friendly embassy, of which he was himself the leader. He then describes briefly but clearly the critical negotiations with Thebes, which ended in a treaty of alliance. We are not informed of the details of this treaty; but the carping criticisms of Aeschines indicate that the liberal spirit towards Thebes which inspired Demosthenes in his first proposals was felt in all the negotiations. Aeschines gives one important item, designed to protect the alliance against the defection of any Boeotian cities to Philip. This provided that in case of any such defection Athens would stand by "the Boeotians at Thebes[3]." Demosthenes brings forward a letter addressed by Philip to his former friends in Peloponnesus when the Thebans deserted him, in which he solicits their help on the ground that he is waging an Amphictyonic war in a holy cause[4]. During the campaign which followed, Demosthenes appears to have had equal influence at Athens and at Thebes. Theopompus says that the generals at Athens and the Boeotarchs at Thebes were equally obedient to his commands, and that the public

---

[1] Dem. Cor. 213.   [2] Ibid. 169—188, 211—216.
[3] Aesch. III. 142.   [4] Dem. Cor. 156, 158.

assembly of Thebes was ruled by him as absolutely as that of Athens[1].

65. Of the campaign itself very little is known. We hear of one "winter battle" and one "battle by the river," in which the allies were victorious[2]. These victories were celebrated by festivals and thanksgivings ; and they caused Philip to renew his solicitations for help in letters to the Peloponnesians. The alliance with Thebes was so popular in Athens, that Demosthenes, as its author, was publicly crowned at the Great Dionysia in the spring of 338[3]. The allies suffered one serious defeat near Amphissa, which Philip—perhaps for the sake of appearances—finally attacked and destroyed[4]. He also captured Naupactus, put to death the Achaean garrison with its commander Pausanias, and gave the town to the Aetolians, thus fulfilling his promise of four years before[5]. At some time during this campaign, he sent a herald with proposals of peace to Thebes and Athens, which, it appears, the Boeotarchs were at first inclined to entertain. Even at Athens a peace-party appeared, with Phocion as its advocate. Aeschines relates that Demosthenes was so disturbed by the peace-movement at Thebes, that he threatened to propose to send an embassy to Thebes to ask for the Athenian army a free passage through Boeotia to attack Philip[6]. We hear no more of this movement, and a visit of Demosthenes to Thebes probably brought it to a speedy end.

66. Our accounts of the battle of Chaeronea are as meagre as those of the preceding campaign[7]. This decisive battle was fought on the seventh of Metageitnion (either August second or September first), 338 B.C. At first the battle was rather favourable to the allies ; but soon the superior discipline of the Macedonians prevailed, and the

---

[1] Theopompus, fr. 239 : see Plut. Dem. 18: ὑπηρετεῖν δὲ μὴ μόνον τοὺς στρατηγοὺς τῷ Δημοσθένει ποιοῦντας τὸ προσταττόμενον ἀλλὰ καὶ τοὺς βοιωτάρχας, διοικεῖσθαι δὲ τὰς ἐκκλησίας ἁπάσας οὐδὲν ἧττον ὑπ' ἐκείνου τότε τὰς Θηβαίων ἢ τὰς Ἀθηναίων.

[2] Dem. Cor. 216, 217.

[3] Ibid. 218, 222, 223.

[4] Polyaen. IV. 2, 8; Strab. 427; Aesch. III. 147.

[5] See § 47 (above).   [6] Aesch. III. 148—151.

[7] See Diod. XVI. 86.

Greeks were driven back on both wings. A general flight ensued, after which the Greeks were scattered, so that there was no longer any military force between Philip's camp and Thebes or Athens. These cities lay at his mercy; their armies were disbanded, and neither could help the other. A thousand Athenians were killed, and about two thousand were taken prisoners. The Boeotian loss was also great, and the famous Sacred Band of three hundred Thebans perished to a man.

67. The panic and despair in Athens when the first tidings of the defeat arrived were most pitiable. No one knew how soon the victorious army might follow in the steps of the messengers who brought the terrible news[1]. But the leaders of the people who were at home, especially Lycurgus and Hyperides, and Demosthenes after his return from the battlefield, did all that was possible to restore courage, and the panic soon changed to a resolute determination to save the city from destruction or capture. Hyperides, who was one of the Senate of Five Hundred (regularly exempt from military service), immediately proposed a bill ordering the Senate to go to the Piraeus under arms and there to hold a meeting to provide for the safety of the port; and further providing that all slaves in the mines and the country districts who would enlist should be free, and that exiles should be recalled, public debtors and other ἄτιμοι should be restored to their rights, and metics should be made citizens, on the same condition. It was hoped that these last measures might furnish a force of 150,000 men for immediate defence[2]. It was also voted to bring the women and children and such sacred property as was movable from unprotected places into the Piraeus. Lycurgus, who had charge of the finances, did wonders in replenishing the empty treasury, and in providing arms and ships for the emergency. Large sums of money were raised by private contributions, the μεγάλαι ἐπιδόσεις of Cor. § 171, Demosthenes giving one talent. Demosthenes devoted himself especially to preparing the city for immediate defence, especially by repairing the dilapidated

---

[1] See Lycurg. Leoc. 39, 40.

[2] Lycurg. Leoc. 37, 41; Hyper. fr. 29 (Blass). When Hyperides was indicted by γραφὴ παρανόμων for the illegality of some of these measures, he replied: ἐπεσκότει μοι τὰ Μακεδόνων ὅπλα· οὐκ ἐγὼ τὸ ψήφισμα ἔγραψα, ἡ δ' ἐν Χαιρωνείᾳ μάχη.

walls and other defences and by raising money for this object[1]. In adopting all these energetic measures the people showed that the spirit of Marathon and Salamis was not wholly extinct at Athens.

68. When Philip heard of these preparations for receiving him, he naturally thought seriously of his next steps. As a former ally, who had deliberately turned against him at a critical moment, Thebes could expect only severe punishment. Accordingly, he compelled her to ransom her prisoners and even to pay for the right to bury her dead at Chaeronea[2]; he broke up the Boeotian confederacy and made all the other towns independent of Thebes; he placed a Macedonian garrison in the Cadmea; and he recalled the exiles who were opposed to the Athenian alliance, and established from these a judicial council of three hundred. Some of the old leaders were exiled, and others put to death; and their estates were confiscated[3]. Philip's knowledge of the position of Athens in Greece probably convinced him that it would be the worst possible policy for him to treat her in this way. Athens could not be taken without a siege, which might be protracted into the winter; and such treatment would unite Athens against him in hopeless enmity. He fortunately had a good, though unprincipled, adviser at hand, the Athenian Demades. He was taken prisoner at Chaeronea; but had ingratiated himself with Philip, so that he was released and remained as a friend in the king's camp. Philip accordingly sent him as his messenger to Athens. The Athenians replied by sending Demades, Aeschines, and probably Phocion as envoys to Philip, to ask for a release of the Athenian captives. Philip received this embassy with great cordiality and immediately invited them to his table[4]. He released all the prisoners without ransom, and promised to return the ashes of those who had fallen. He sent these remains to Athens in charge of no less a person than Antipater, with whom

---

[1] See Cor. 248[10] and note; Lycurg. Leoc. 44. Aeschines, III. 236, ridicules the patriotic fervour with which this work was done : οὐ γὰρ περιχαρακώσαντα χρὴ τὰ τείχη οὐδὲ τάφους δημοσίους ἀνελόντα τὸν ὀρθῶς πεπολιτευμένον δωρεὰς αἰτεῖν.

[2] Justin IX. 4[6]: Thebanorum porro non modo captivos verum etiam interfectorum sepulturam vendidit.

[3] Diod. XVI. 87; Paus. IX. 1, 8; Justin IX. 4.

[4] See note on Cor. 287[4], with the references.

Alexander himself went as a special messenger with offers of peace and friendship[1]. The result was the treaty of peace, known as the Peace of Demades, by which both peace and alliance were again established between Philip and Athens. The Athenians were to remain free and independent, and Philip probably agreed never to send ships of war into the Piraeus. Oropus, which had been taken from Thebes, was now at length restored to Athens. Athens was to hold certain islands, among which were Salamis, Samos, and Delos; but all trace of her recent alliance and all thought of maritime empire had disappeared for ever[2]. Philip left it open to her to join the general Greek League which he proposed to form, and of which he was to be the head. This step would sacrifice the independence of Athens in many important points; but in the absence of Demosthenes, and in spite of the scruples of Phocion, who asked for more time to consider the question, the Assembly adopted the proposals of Demades in full, and these made Athens a member of the League[3]. By this step, which was probably a necessary one under the circumstances, Athens ceased to have any independent political existence; and the peace of Demades ends her history as a free state and as a power in the Hellenic world.

69. The feeling of Demosthenes about this peace after eight years' experience is seen in Cor. § 89. While he doubtless acquiesced quietly in it at the beginning, he never forgot the bitter humiliation. Under the influence of this quiet submission to Philip's authority, cloaked under the name of independence, the Macedonian party, with Aeschines at its head, again became powerful at Athens[4]. It was then that it was safe for the whole herd of the enemies of Demosthenes to persecute him with every form of process which was known to the Attic law, when (as he says) he was "brought to trial every day." But he mentions this only to testify to the affection of his fellow citizens, who always acquitted him in the popular courts, and thus justified his conduct in the most effective manner[5]. Indeed, though the party of Aeschines then had the courage to speak its sentiments more freely than ever before[6],

---

[1] See Polyb. v. 10; Justin IX. 4[5]; Diod. XVI. 87.
[2] See Paus. I. 25. 3.   [3] Plut. Phoc. 16.
[4] Dem. Cor. 320.   [5] Ibid. 248—250.
[6] Ibid. 286[6].

and in so doing gained the favour of Philip and his partizans, the sober sense of the people always recognized the services of men like Demosthenes in better times and expressed itself whenever an occasion offered. There was no testimony of the public esteem and affection which Demosthenes valued more highly than the choice of the people in making him their orator to deliver the eulogy on the heroes of Chaeronea[1]. Here the genuine feeling of patriotic gratitude to the man who had fought the battle of Grecian liberty almost single-handed impelled the citizens to reject all candidates who were in sympathy with Philip or his cause, including Aeschines and even Demades, and to choose the man who was most heartily identified with the lost cause for which these heroes had died. And the same public respect for Demosthenes and for his honest and unswerving devotion to what was now seen more clearly than ever to have been the cause of Grecian liberty, the cause which had made their ancestors glorious, was shown in the overwhelming vote by which the popular court acquitted Ctesiphon and condemned Aeschines, at the very moment when such a judgment might have been deemed a public defiance of Alexander's authority, while the whole Greek world was ringing with the news of the victory of Arbela.

[1] Dem. Cor. 285.

TABLE OF DATES.

B.C.

384—383. Birth of Demosthenes. (§ 7.)[1]
382—381. Birth of Philip of Macedon. (§ 3.)
378—377. New Athenian Confederacy formed. Financial reforms of Nausinicus. Introduction of Symmories for property tax.
376—375. Death of Demosthenes, father of the orator. Guardians appointed for the son. (§ 7.)
371—370. Battle of Leuctra (July 371).
366—365. Demosthenes comes of age at 18; devotes two years to preparation for the lawsuit against his guardians. (§ 7.)
364—363. Trial of suit against Aphobus. (§ 8.)
362—361. Battle of Mantinea and death of Epaminondas. (§ 1.)
359—358. Accession of Philip of Macedon. (§ 3.)
          Artaxerxes III. (Ochus) becomes king of Persia.
358—357. Symmories for the Trierarchy established.
357—356. Athenian expedition to Euboea frees the island from the Thebans. (§ 2.) Outbreak of Social War. (§ 2.) Philip captures Amphipolis, which leads to war with Athens, and takes Pydna and Potidaea from Athens. (§ 3.)
356—355. Birth of Alexander the Great, July 21, 356 B.C. (§ 3.)
          Beginning of Sacred (Phocian) War: seizure of temple of Delphi by Philomelus. (§ 4.)
          End of Social War, spring of 355. (§ 2.)
355—354. Speeches of Demosthenes against Androtion and Leptines.
354—353. First public speech of Demosthenes, on the Symmories. (§ 8.) Eubulus takes charge of the finances of Athens.
          Philomelus killed. Sacred War continued by Onomarchus. Spoliation of temple of Delphi. (§ 4.)
353—352. Philip takes Methone from Athens. (§ 3.)
          He attacks and defeats Lycophron of Pherae ; has battles

---

[1] The references in ( ) are made to sections of the Historical Sketch.

with Phocians, and finally defeats Onomarchus, who is slain. He secures control of Gulf of Pagasae. (§ 5.)

353—352. Speech of Demosthenes for the Megalopolitans. (§ 8.)
Athens sends force to Thermopylae and closes the pass to Philip, before midsummer 352. (§ 6.)

352—351. Philip besieges Heraion Teichos in Thrace, Nov. 352. (§ 9.)
First Philippic of Demosthenes, spring of 351. (§ 9.)

351—350. Speech of Demosthenes for the Rhodians. (§ 9.)
Athens sends Phocion with an army to help Plutarchus in Euboea (Feb. 350). Battle of Tamynae. (§ 10.)
Midias assaults Demosthenes at the Great Dionysia (March 350), and is condemned by vote of the Assembly. (§ 11.)

349—348. Demosthenes Senator: writes speech against Midias. (§ 11.)
Philip attacks the Olynthian confederation and besieges Olynthus. Alliance of Olynthus with Athens. Demosthenes delivers his Olynthiacs. (§ 12.) Philip sends peaceful messages to Athens and releases Phrynon. (§ 13.)

348—347. Olynthus captured by Philip, with all its confederate towns (early autumn of 348): consternation in Greece. (§§ 12, 13.)
Philocrates first proposes negotiations for peace with Philip. (§ 13.)
Mission of Aristodemus to Philip. (§ 13.)
Movement of Eubulus and Aeschines against Philip, and embassies to Greek states. (§§ 14, 15.)

347—346. Themistocles Archon. Demosthenes again Senator. Aristodemus brings friendly messages from Philip. (§ 13.)
Thebans and Phocians both exhausted by Sacred War. Phocians ask aid from Athens (early in 346), but reject it when sent. (§§ 17, 18.)
On motion of Philocrates (Feb. 346), ten envoys are sent to Philip to propose negotiations for peace (First Embassy). Envoys return end of March. (§§ 18—21.)
Two meetings of Assembly, to discuss terms of peace with Philip's envoys, 18th and 19th of Elaphebolion (April 15, 16), 346: peace voted on second day. (§§ 22—28.)

347—346. Same envoys sent again to Philip, to ratify the peace (Second Embassy). (§ 29.)

Assembly 25th of Elaphebolion, Demosthenes presiding : see note on Cor. § 170². Φίλιππος of Isocrates. (§ 28.) Decree of Senate ordering the departure of the Embassy (April 29). Further delays. (§§ 29—31.)

Return of Embassy to Athens, 13th of Scirophorion (July 7). Reports to Senate and Assembly. Philip already at Thermopylae. Assembly votes 16th of Scir. (July 10) to compel the Phocians to deliver the temple of Delphi to "the Amphictyons." Philip's letters. (§§ 33—35.)

Ten envoys (Third Embassy) sent to Thermopylae, to report action of the Assembly to Philip : they depart about 21st of Scirophorion (July 15). (§§ 35—37.)

Phalaecus surrenders Thermopylae to Philip 23rd of Sciroph. (July 17). Athenian envoys hear this news at Chalcis and return. Meeting of Assembly in Piraeus 27th of Scir. (July 21). Embassy ordered to proceed to Thermopylae, and departs at once. (§§ 36—38.)

End of Sacred War. (§ 39.)

346—345. Demosthenes and Timarchus begin proceedings against Aeschines for παραπρεσβεία (autumn of 346). See Essay IV. 1, 2.

Archias Archon. Philip summons Amphictyonic Council, which expels the Phocians and gives their two votes to Philip. Terrible punishment of the Phocians. (§ 38.)

Philip celebrates the Pythian games (Sept. 346). (§ 39.)

Philip demands recognition of his position in Amphictyonic Council. Speech of Demosthenes on the Peace. (§ 40.)

Prosecution of Timarchus by Aeschines (winter). See Essay IV. 1.

345—344. Philip interferes in disputes in Peloponnesus. Demosthenes sent as envoy to counteract his influence. (§ 41.)

344—343. Second Philippic of Demosthenes (late in 344). Philip's influence in Peloponnesus. (§ 42.)

Trial and condemnation of Antiphon. (§ 43.)

Prosecution of Philocrates on εἰσαγγελία by Hyperides, and his exile (before midsummer 343). See Essay IV. 2.

339—338. Amphictyonic Council (early autumn of 339) chooses Philip general. (§ 62.) Shortly afterwards Philip passes Thermopylae and seizes Elatea. (§ 63.)
Negotiations between Athens and Thebes, ending in alliance against Philip. (§§ 63, 64.)
Campaign (winter and spring) : allies victorious in "winter battle" and "river battle." Capture of mercenaries and destruction of Amphissa by Philip. (§§ 64, 65.)

338—337. Battle of Chaeronea, 7th Metageitnion 338 (August 2 or September 1) : utter defeat of the allies. (§ 66.) Active measures at Athens. (§ 67.)
Action of Philip. Peace of Demades. (§ 68.)
Position of Demosthenes after the peace. He delivers the eulogy on those who fell at Chaeronea. (§ 69.)

337—336. Demosthenes director of the Theoric Fund and τειχοποιός.
Ctesiphon proposes to crown Demosthenes at the Great Dionysia (spring of 336). Aeschines brings γραφὴ παρανόμων against Ctesiphon. (See 330—329.)

337—336. Philip assassinated, summer of 336. Alexander succeeds him.

335—334. Rebellion of Thebes. Alexander captures and destroys the city (autumn of 335).
Alexander demands the delivery of Demosthenes, Lycurgus, Hyperides, and other Athenian orators.
Aristotle returns to Athens and teaches in the Lyceum.

331—330. Alexander's victory at Arbela (Oct. 1, 331).
Rebellion of Spartan King Agis (early in 330), crushed by Antipater.

330—329. Aristophon Archon. Trial of suit of Aeschines against Ctesiphon (August, 330). Ctesiphon acquitted by more than four-fifths of the votes. See Essay III.

324—323. Demosthenes condemned to a fine of 50 talents in the affair of Harpalus. Unable to pay, he went into exile.
Death of Alexander the Great (May, 323) at Babylon.

323—322. Triumphant recall of Demosthenes from exile.

322. Death of Aristotle at Chalcis, autumn of 322.
Death of Hyperides October 5, and of Demosthenes October 12, 322.

The Attic Year.

The Athenians had a lunar year of 354 days, consisting of twelve months, alternately of 30 and 29 days, equivalent to 12 lunar months of 29½ days each. The longer months were called πλήρεις, the shorter κοῖλοι. This fell short of the solar year by 11¼ days, the difference in eight years amounting to 90 days. This was regulated by making the third, fifth, and eighth year in each cycle of eight years (ὀκταετηρίς) a leap year with 384 days, thus making the number of days in each cycle correct. (Thus $(354 \times 5) + (384 \times 3) = 2922 = 365\frac{1}{4} \times 8$.) The slight errors which remained were equated in various ways. The natural beginning of the Attic year was the summer solstice; but the great difference in the length of the years allowed the beginning to vary from about June 16 to August 7.

The twelve months in the ordinary year were as follows; 1 Hecatombaeon, 2 Metageitnion, 3 Boedromion, 4 Pyanepsion, 5 Maemacterion, 6 Posideon, 7 Gamelion, 8 Anthesterion, 9 Elaphebolion, 10 Munychion, 11 Thargelion, 12 Scirophorion. In the leap years a month of thirty days, Posideon II., was intercalated after Posideon. The same months appear to have been πλήρεις and κοῖλοι in different years. The first day of every month was generally called νουμηνία, and the last day ἕνη καὶ νέα, *old and new*; the latter name, which probably was first applied to the full months, showing that the thirtieth day in these months was supposed to belong equally to the old and the new month. The days from the 2nd to the 9th were called δευτέρα, τρίτη, etc., sometimes with ἱσταμένου or ἀρχομένου (sc. μηνός) added; the 10th was the δεκάς; those from the 11th to the 19th were called πρώτη, δευτέρα, etc., with ἐπὶ δέκα or μεσοῦντος added, though this could be omitted when it was obvious that the middle of the month was meant. The 20th was the εἰκάς; and the days from the 21st to the 29th in the full months were generally counted backwards, δεκάτη φθίνοντος (21st), ἐνάτη, ὀγδόη, etc. to δευτέρα φθίνοντος (22nd, 23rd, etc. to 29th). It is generally thought that the δευτέρα φθίνοντος was omitted in the "hollow" months.

The following is a possible statement of the arrangement of the thirteen months in 347—346 B.C., the year of the peace of Philocrates.

This was a leap year of 384 days, beginning July 6 and ending July 24. Other arrangements are possible ; but these would not affect any of the dates by more than a single day.

1.	Hecatombaeon	(30 days)	begins	July	6,	347	B.C.
2.	Metageitnion	(29 ,,)	,,	August	5		,,
3.	Boedromion	(30 ,,)	,,	Sept.	3		,,
4.	Pyanepsion	(29 ,,)	,,	Oct.	3		,,
5.	Maemacterion	(30 ,,)	,,	Nov.	1		,,
6.	Posideon	(29 ,,)	,,	Dec.	1		,,
7.	[Posideon II.]	(30 ,,)	,,	,,	30		,,
8.	Gamelion	(29 ,,)	,,	Jan.	29,	346	B.C.
9.	Anthesterion	(30 ,,)	,,	Feb.	27		,,
10.	Elaphebolion	(29 ,,)	,,	March	29		,,
11.	Munychion	(30 ,,)	,,	April	27		,,
12.	Thargelion	(29 ,,)	,,	May	27		,,
13.	Scirophorion	(30 ,,)	,,	June	25		,,

Thus Elaphebolion 18, 19 = April 15, 16 ;
    Munychion   3   = April 29 ;
    Thargelion   22   = June 17 ;
    Scirophorion 13   = July   7 ;
         ,,   23   = ,,   17 ;
         ,,   27   = ,,   21.

Hecatombaeon 346—345 begins July 25.

ESSAYS.

I.

The Argument of the Oration, with Remarks on §§ 120, 121.

1. THE argument of this Oration follows no recognized model, and it cannot be brought under any rhetorical system of rules. The occasion was unique ; and the orator treated it uniquely, and with a masterly skill which is far beyond the art of a mere rhetorician. Demosthenes is technically defending a client on a question of constitutional law ; he is really defending his own public life and his reputation as a patriot and a statesman against the unscrupulous charges of a personal enemy. He feels sure that the large body of his fellow-citizens who form the court will listen chiefly to his defence of himself and of his public policy and will overlook the technical questions of law ; and he judges rightly. The skill, however, with which he keeps these technical questions in the background, so that the judges shall never lose sight of the higher questions of state policy, and the art by which he conceals this art, are worthy of careful study.

2. The indictment (γραφὴ παρανόμων) brings three charges of illegality (παράνομα) against Ctesiphon's bill for conferring a crown on Demosthenes : (1) the bill proposes to crown Demosthenes while he is a responsible magistrate (ἄρχων ὑπεύθυνος), which is forbidden by law ; (2) it proposes to proclaim the crown in the theatre at the Great Dionysiac festival, whereas the law requires such a crown to be proclaimed elsewhere ; (3) it violates the law forbidding the insertion of false statements into the public records, such false statements being found in the clauses of the bill which praise Demosthenes, especially

in the words ἀρετῆς ἕνεκα καὶ ἀνδραγαθίας,—ὅτι διατελεῖ καὶ λέγων καὶ πράττων τὰ ἄριστα τῷ δήμῳ,—and πρόθυμός ἐστι ποιεῖν ὅ τι δύναται ἀγαθόν[1]. Aeschines, who must have felt the weakness of the vague charge of illegality in the last count, dwells with great energy and with his most powerful arguments on the first count, on which (so far as we can see) his position was legally unassailable. He shows beyond question that Demosthenes held two important offices at the time of Ctesiphon's proposal, for which he would still be responsible (ὑπεύθυνος) when the crown was proclaimed ; and this would be illegal. He naturally puts this strong argument in the front of his attack. On his second point, the illegality of the proposed place of proclamation, the actual state of the law is uncertain, and we cannot judge of the strength of the argument. He then discusses the life and character of Demosthenes, to show that the statements on which Ctesiphon justifies his proposal to crown him are false and therefore illegal. After a few words of introduction, followed by a short account of the private life of Demosthenes, he treats of his public life at great length, under four heads (see 3). He occupies the remainder of his time in the discussion of various matters, aiming in all to show the falseness of the terms used by Ctesiphon. He urges the judges not to allow Ctesiphon to call on Demosthenes to plead his cause ; or, if they permit Demosthenes to speak at all, to compel him to follow the same order of argument in the defence which he has himself adopted in the attack. This last would have compelled Demosthenes to reply in the beginning to the strong argument of Aeschines on the illegality of crowning a responsible magistrate ; this Demosthenes has no idea of doing, as it would weaken his whole position before the court.

3. The argument of Aeschines, briefly stated, is as follows:

I. Prooemium: §§ 1—8.

II. Argument on the responsibility of magistrates: §§ 9—31.

III. Argument on the place of proclamation: §§ 32—48.

IV. Review of the Life of Demosthenes (§§ 49—167):—

   1. Introduction: §§ 49, 50.

   2. Private Life of Demosthenes: §§ 51—53.

[1] See Aesch. III. 49, 237, Dem. Cor. 57, where the genuine decree professes to be quoted.

3. Four divisions of the Public Life of Demosthenes, §§ 54—
57, discussed as follows :—

(*a*) The Peace of Philocrates (346 B.C.): §§ 58—78.

(*b*) The time of peace until the renewal of war with Philip
in 340 B.C. : §§ 79—105.

(*c*) The Amphissian War, and other events ending with the
Battle of Chaeronea in 338 B.C. : §§ 106—158.

(*d*) The time from 338 to 330 B.C. (the year of the trial):
§§ 159—167.

V. Discussion of various points in the life and character of
Demosthenes, and general arguments: §§ 168—259.

VI. Peroration : § 260.

4. It might seem natural for Demosthenes to reply to the three
charges of the indictment in regular succession. But this would have
sacrificed the argumentative power of his speech to mere simplicity of
arrangement. If he had followed the order of Aeschines, and dealt
first with the question of his responsibility as a magistrate, he would
have begun his argument at its weakest point, on which he had nothing
to say which really answered the cogent legal argument of Aeschines.
Nothing could have been worse for his case than this. If, on the
other hand, he had introduced this matter after the discussion of his
public life, the weakness of his conclusion would have injured (perhaps
fatally) the effect of his previous argument. It was important, therefore, to bring in this weaker argument between two divisions of his
historical statement, and thus conceal its defects[1]. He could not
make a *single* break in his narrative and there introduce this foreign
subject without making his design too obvious. But he artfully
divides his account of his public life into *three* parts, for plausible
reasons, which do not suggest his real object. In § 9 he complains of

---

[1] Libanius saw this artful device : see his *Hypothesis*, § 6 : ὁ δὲ ῥήτωρ καὶ
ἀπὸ τῆς πολιτείας τὴν ἀρχὴν ἐποιήσατο καὶ πάλιν εἰς ταύτην τὸν λόγον κατέ-
στρεψε, τεχνικῶς ποιῶν· δεῖ γὰρ ἄρχεσθαί τε ἀπὸ τῶν ἰσχυροτέρων καὶ λήγειν
εἰς ταῦτα· μέσα δὲ τέθεικε τὰ περὶ τῶν νόμων. See also the second *Hypothesis*, § 5 : τοὺς μὲν γὰρ ἄλλους δύο νόμους, τόν τε τῶν ὑπευθύνων καὶ τὸν
τοῦ κηρύγματος, εἰς τὸ μέσον τοῦ λόγου ἀπέρριψε, στρατηγικῶς "κακοὺς ἐς
μέσσον ἐλάσσας" (see *Il.* IV. 299), τῷ δὲ ἰσχυροτάτῳ εἰς τὰ ἄκρα προσκέ-
χρηται, τὸ σαθρὸν τῶν ἄλλων ἐξ ἑκατέρου ῥωννύς.

the charges "foreign to the indictment" (ἔξω τῆς γραφῆς, § 34) which Aeschines has brought against him; and to these he proposes to reply before he comes to the charges which properly belong to the case. Under this head he puts the charges relating to the Peace of Philocrates (346 B.C.), and he proceeds at once to deal with the negotiations which led to this event. He would never have thought of omitting this important matter, in which later events had triumphantly vindicated his own course of action; and his indignation at Aeschines for bringing it into the case is all feigned. He is thus able to tell the story of this important period of his public life before he begins the real argument (as he represents it), even before the reading of the indictment. This has the effect of securing the goodwill of the court for himself and damaging the case of Aeschines in advance, by an eloquent harangue on a subject which (he claims) has been unfairly brought into the case (§§ 17—52).

5. After the reading of the indictment and a few general remarks upon this document, he proceeds (§§ 60—101) to a general defence of his policy of opposition to Philip, and of the course taken by Athens under his leadership before the renewal of the war with Philip in 340. He then speaks of his own trierarchic reform (§§ 102—109), and now (§ 110) declares that he has brought forward sufficient evidence to justify the language of Ctesiphon's decree in his praise. He states that he is here omitting the most important of his public acts (those concerning the alliance with Thebes and the other events which preceded the battle of Chaeronea), and he leaves it doubtful whether he will speak of these hereafter. He really has not the slightest intention of omitting these most important events, in which he gained the greatest diplomatic triumph of his life; but he postpones them until he can introduce them later as an offset to the acts of Aeschines done in Philip's interest, where the account of them forms the most eloquent passage in the oration (§§ 160—226). By this skilful plan he gains two important objects. First, he divides the account of his political life into three parts, and avoids wearying the judges by telling the whole story (covering eight most eventful years) in one continuous narrative, in which it would have been far less effective. Secondly, he succeeds in introducing his replies to the arguments περὶ τοῦ παρανόμου (§ 110) just after one exciting historic narrative and just before another, where they are least conspicuous, and where the weak-

ness of the reply on the εὔθυναι is soon forgotten amid the exciting events which led to Chaeronea. The three courses of events thus divided are so naturally distinct, that nothing is lost by their division to be compared with the double gain.

6. The following is the course of the argument in the oration on the Crown[1].

I. Prooemium : §§ **1—8.**

II. Reply to charges foreign to the indictment (§§ 9—52):—

  1. Introduction : § **9.**
  2. Charges against private life : §§ **10, 11.**
  3. Public policy (§§ 12—52):—
     A. Introductory : §§ **12—16.**
     B. Peace of Philocrates (§§ 17—52):—
        (a) Introductory : § **17.**
        (b) Narrative : §§ **18—49.**
        (c) Conclusion : §§ **50—52.**

III. Reply to the charges of the indictment (§§ 53—125):—

  1. Introductory : §§ **53—59.**
  2. Defence of his public policy (confined chiefly to the period from 346 to 340 B.C.) and of his trierarchic law : §§ **60—109.**
  3. Reply to charge of responsibility as a magistrate : §§ **110—119.**
  4. Reply to argument about the place of proclamation : §§ **120, 121.**
  5. Conclusion : §§ **122—125.**

IV. Life and character of Aeschines : and his public policy in the interest of Philip, compared with his own agency in negotiating an alliance with Thebes against Philip (§§ 126—226):

  1. Parentage and life of Aeschines : §§ **126—131.**
  2. Lesser political offences of Aeschines : §§ **132—138.**

---

[1] The subject of each of the seven main divisions is stated with greater detail in the notes where the division begins. See the remarks which precede the notes on §§ 1, 9, 53, 126, 227, 297, 324.

3. The Amphissian War, stirred up by the speech of Aeschines at Delphi (339 B.C.): §§ **139—159.**

4. Negotiation of Theban alliance by Demosthenes (339—338 B.C.),—continuation of narrative interrupted at § 110. Into this account is introduced (§§ 189—210) a defence of the whole policy of Athens, under his leadership, in opposition to Philip: §§ **160—226.**

With § 226 the defence of Ctesiphon, properly so called, is finished. The orator has reviewed his whole political life and has justified the language of Ctesiphon's decree; and he has replied briefly to the other charges of illegality. In the time which remains he discusses other matters suggested by the speech of Aeschines.

V. Replies to three arguments of Aeschines (§§ 227—296):—

1. Discussion of the comparison (Aeschines 59—61) of the case against Demosthenes to an account of money expended: §§ **227—251.**

2. Reply to the remarks of Aeschines upon his "bad fortune," and comparison of his own fortune with that of Aeschines: §§ **252—275.**

3. Reply to the charge of being a crafty rhetorician: §§ **276—296.**

VI. The Epilogue follows, in which he compares himself with Aeschines, protesting against the comparison of himself with the heroes of the past. There is also a recapitulation of some matters already discussed: §§ **297—323.**

VII. The Peroration, in a single earnest sentence, is an appeal to the Gods for help to Athens in her humiliation: § **324.**

Remarks on the Argument of §§ 120, 121.

(1) In these sections Demosthenes replies briefly, but with wrathful indignation, to the elaborate argument of Aeschines (32—48) about the place of proclamation. He simply quotes a few words from a law, which was read entire to the court, and then bursts out in triumphant invective against Aeschines for his audacity in suppressing the one important clause *in this law* in presenting it before the court. Unfortunately we have only a fragment of the law presented by Demosthenes; but this must be authentic: πλὴν ἐάν τινας ὁ δῆμος ἢ ἡ βουλὴ ψηφίσηται· τούτους δ' ἀναγορευέτω. It

must have been a clause which did not make the passionate outbreak which followed appear ridiculous to the court. On the other hand, we cannot for a moment believe that Aeschines (32) produced a law requiring those who were crowned by the Senate or by the Assembly to be crowned before those bodies and nowhere else, and actually suppressed a clause of *that very law*, which allowed either Senate or Assembly to make an exception to the law at its pleasure. When we remember that this mutilated law must have been quoted in the indictment, read to the court by its clerk after being submitted to the scrutiny of the presiding Thesmothetae at the anacrisis, and also posted in the court-room (see note on § 111²), we cannot ascribe such audacity even to Aeschines, or such careless indifference at once to six archons, the court, and its officers.

(2) I think we must assume (a) that Aeschines quoted a law forbidding the proclamation in the theatre, and that *this law* had no such addition as Demosthenes appears to make to it, and (b) that Demosthenes quoted another law, which (as he claimed) applied to the same cases but had the proviso ἐὰν μή (or πλὴν ἐάν) τινας ὁ δῆμος ἢ ἡ βουλὴ ψηφίσηται, etc. This supposes a conflict of laws, or at least two laws which could be harmonized only by a forced interpretation. The elaborate argument of Aeschines (37—39), to prove that no such conflict could occur in the Athenian laws, at once makes us suspect that this is the real solution. Even he admits that such conflicts *might* sometimes occur, κἄν τι τοιοῦτον εὑρίσκωσιν (39). What now was the law which Demosthenes brought before the court? It must have been the Dionysiac law, which Aeschines *predicts* (35) that Demosthenes will bring into the case.

(3) Aeschines thus describes this law in 44: διαρρήδην ἀπαγορεύει μήτ' οἰκέτην ἀπελευθεροῦν ἐν τῷ θεάτρῳ, μήθ' ὑπὸ τῶν φυλετῶν ἢ δημοτῶν ἀναγορεύεσθαι στεφανούμενον μήθ' ὑπ' ἄλλου (φησὶ) μηδενός, ἢ ἄτιμον εἶναι τὸν κήρυκα. He argues that the words μήθ' ὑπ' ἄλλου μηδενός cannot apply to any except foreign crowns, and then (47) adds : καὶ διὰ τοῦτο προσέθηκεν ὁ νομοθέτης μὴ κηρύττεσθαι τὸν ἀλλότριον στέφανον ἐν τῷ θεάτρῳ ἐὰν μὴ ψηφίσηται ὁ δῆμος. It will be noticed that he does not quote the last clause (ἐὰν...δῆμος) in connection with the law itself in 44, but only after *his own* interpretation of the law in 47. This is of itself suspicious, as it conceals the only important point, the exact relation of this clause to the rest of the law. Now the clause in 47, μὴ κηρύττεσθαι τὸν ἀλλότριον στέφανον ἐν τῷ θεάτρῳ, is certainly no part of the law, for with this the law could need no interpretation. Further, the authentic words following πλὴν ἐάν...ψηφίσηται in Demosthenes (121), τούτους δ' ἀναγορευέτω, have no sense if added to these words in Aeschines (47). They have, however, a very significant meaning if added to ἢ ἄτιμον εἶναι τὸν κήρυκα in Aeschines (44), supplying

ὁ κῆρυξ as the subject of the imperative. Now the last part of Aeschines 44 and ἐὰν μὴ ψηφίσηται ὁ δῆμος in 47 are the only real quotations from the Dionysiac law in Aeschines, and πλὴν ἐάν τινας...ἀγορευέτω is evidently a quotation from the law read by Demosthenes (121). If we fit these together, we have the most probable reconstruction of the Dionysiac law as it was presented by Demosthenes, as follows :—μήτ' οἰκέτην ἀπελευθεροῦν ἐν τῷ θεάτρῳ, μήθ' ὑπὸ τῶν φυλετῶν ἢ δημοτῶν ἀναγορεύεσθαι στεφανούμενον μήθ' ὑπ' ἄλλου μηδενὸς, ἢ ἄτιμον εἶναι τὸν κήρυκα, πλὴν ἐάν τινας ὁ δῆμος ἢ ἡ βουλὴ ψηφίσηται, τούτους δ' ἀναγορευέτω. This might easily have been read to the court in opposition to the other law read by order of Aeschines; and, so far as we can see, Demosthenes was justified in assuming that μήθ' ὑπ' ἄλλου μηδενός referred to all who had crowns to confer, not excluding the Senate and the Assembly.

(4) This explanation becomes much simpler if we suppose that all the confused talk about the Dionysiac law in Aeschines is an addition to his speech made after hearing the reply of Demosthenes. It seems incredible that Demosthenes could ignore so elaborate an argument as that of Aeschines (35—48) in his reply and merely quote "the law" as if there were but one. The court would never have been satisfied with so contemptuous an answer, which took no notice of the account of the Dionysiac law which they had just heard.

One fact is now made certain by inscriptions : whatever may have been the letter of the law against proclamation in the theatre, such proclamations were very frequent at Athens in the fourth century B.C., and earlier and later. The law was a dead letter, and Demosthenes was justified in making light of this part of the accusation. See note on Cor. § 120².

II.

The γραφὴ παρανόμων.

1. The Athenian γραφὴ παρανόμων, or *indictment for proposing illegal measures*, could be brought by any citizen against one who was charged with proposing a decree (ψήφισμα) which violated a law (νόμος), or with causing the enactment of a law which was opposed to an existing law without expressly providing for the repeal of the latter. The laws (νόμοι) of Athens were a comparatively fixed code, ascribed generally to Solon, but consisting of the original Solonic laws, enlarged and otherwise modified by succeeding enactments. These were

superior to the enactments of the Senate and the Assembly and were not subject to repeal or modification by these bodies. An enactment of the Senate and Assembly, the ordinary legislative bodies (in the modern sense of the term), was called a *decree* or ψήφισμα. This could legally contain no provisions which were opposed to a νόμος, and any such provision made it void. The γραφὴ παρανόμων was the simple but efficient process provided by the Attic law for causing an "illegal" decree or law to be annulled, and also for punishing the proposer. The mover, however, could be held personally responsible only for one year from the time of the proposal of a decree or the enactment of a law; after a year the decree or law could be attacked and annulled by the same process, while the mover was exposed to no risk. Whoever brought a γραφὴ παρανόμων was required to bind himself publicly by an oath (called ὑπωμοσία) to prosecute the case; after this oath was taken, a decree or law was suspended if it had already been enacted, and a decree which had passed only the Senate (a προβούλευμα) could not be brought before the Assembly for action until the suit had been tried and settled in favour of the defendant. (See note on Cor. § 103⁷.) It is probable that the γραφὴ παρανόμων could be brought against a νόμος only after its actual enactment, while it could be brought against a ψήφισμα at any one of three stages: (1) after its acceptance by the Senate, (2) after passing the Assembly, (3) after the lapse of a year from its proposal.

2. The distinction between a νόμος and a ψήφισμα at Athens was most important. A ψήφισμα was an enactment of the Senate and Assembly, which, if it was not in conflict with a νόμος, had the full force of a law. A νόμος could be changed only by an elaborate process, which was chiefly under the control of a court of law. In the first Assembly in each year a general question was put to the people, whether they would permit propositions to be made for changes in the laws. If the people voted to permit these, all who had such proposals to make were required to post them in the market-place, and the clerk of the Assembly read the proposals to the people in each of the two following meetings. In the last of these meetings (the third of the year), the people, if they saw fit, voted to refer the proposed changes to a special commission, called νομοθέται, chosen like an ordinary court (δικαστήριον) from those who were qualified to sit as judges for that year and had taken the Heliastic oath. The whole

proceeding before this board was conducted according to the forms of law. The proposer of the new law appeared as plaintiff and argued his case against the old law and for his own proposal, while advocates appointed by the state defended the existing law. The question of enacting the new law or retaining the existing one was decided by a vote of the νομοθέται, which, if favourable to the new law, made that one of the fixed code of νόμοι. It was strictly commanded by the Solonic law, that no new law should be enacted unless all laws opposed to it were expressly repealed; and, further, that no law should be repealed unless a new law were proposed, and accepted by the νομοθέται as suitable and fitting (ἐπιτήδειος) to take its place.

3. It was natural, as the democracy increased in power, that the distinction between decrees and laws should be neglected, and that the sovereign people should pass decrees which usurped the functions of laws and violated the spirit, if not the letter, of existing laws. Against this dangerous tendency the γραφὴ παρανόμων was the only legal security. We cannot wonder, therefore, that this is extolled as the great stronghold of constitutional liberty, the chief protection of free government against lawless demagogues. Even Aeschines, who was doing as much as any man to degrade the process, speaks of it as we speak of the *habeas corpus*[1]. It is significant that one of the first steps taken by the oligarchs who established the government of Four Hundred in 411 B.C. was the suspension of the γραφὴ παρανόμων[2].

4. The principle upon which the γραφὴ παρανόμων is based must always be recognized wherever the legislative power is limited by a superior code of laws or a written constitution to which all its enactments must conform. In such a case the allegiance of every citizen is due, first and foremost, to the superior law, as the supreme law of the land, and he cannot legally be compelled to obey the lower enactment. But as each citizen cannot be allowed to decide for himself whether an act of the legislature is or is not in harmony with the superior law,

---

[1] See Aesch. III. 3—8: ἐν ὑπολείπεται μέρος τῆς πολιτείας, αἱ τῶν παρανόμων γραφαί. εἰ δὲ ταύτας καταλύσετε,...προλέγω ὑμῖν ὅτι λήσετε κατὰ μικρὸν τῆς πολιτείας τισὶ παραχωρήσαντες (5). See the whole passage.

[2] Thuc. VIII. 67: ἐσήνεγκαν ἄλλο μὲν οὐδέν, αὐτὸ δὲ τοῦτο, ἐξεῖναι μὲν ἀζήμιον εἰπεῖν γνώμην ἣν ἄν τις βούληται· ἢν δέ τις τὸν εἰπόντα ἢ γράψηται παρανόμων ἢ ἄλλῳ τῳ τρόπῳ βλάψῃ, μεγάλας ζημίας ἐπέθεσαν. So Aristot. Pol. Ath. 29²³.

the decision must be entrusted to some tribunal which has authority to prevent a citizen from suffering unjustly if he disobeys an illegal enactment, and also to prevent the law from being disobeyed at the caprice of individuals.

5. This principle was first recognized, so far as we know, in the Athenian γραφὴ παρανόμων. Precisely the same principle is at the basis of what is now known as "the American doctrine of Constitutional Law," under which the Supreme Court of the United States has the power to declare acts of Congress or of the state legislatures unconstitutional and to treat them as without authority[1]. The Constitution of the United States is declared in one of its own articles to be "the supreme law of the land," to which all legislation of Congress and of the several states must conform. To enable the Supreme Court to act on a constitutional question, a case must come before it in the ordinary course of litigation, generally when a person who feels aggrieved by the operation of a law which he believes to be unconstitutional appeals from the decision of a lower court on this point and thus brings the constitutional question directly before the Supreme Court.

6. In the comparison which we are making, the decrees of the Athenian Senate and Assembly correspond to the laws of the U.S. Congress or of the state legislatures, and the Solonic laws of Athens to the U.S. Constitution. But this comparison regards only the relation of authority between the two codes in either case. The Solonic code dealt with all manner of details, while the U.S. Constitution is chiefly confined to broad statements of general principles. Further, it may seem strange to compare the solemn action of the U.S. Supreme Court in deciding a question of constitutional law with the trial of a citizen at Athens, before a court consisting of 501, 1001, or 1501 ordinary men, chosen by lot from the great body of citizens, for proposing an unconstitutional decree or law. But the fundamental principle is the same in both. Both courts have the same duty to perform, that of deciding whether a given enactment is or is not in conflict with a superior code. Athens, like the United States, assigned

---

[1] The Supreme Courts of the several states have the same right of declaring unconstitutional and null acts of their own state legislatures, as conflicting with either the state constitution or the U.S. constitution.

this duty to the highest court in her judicial system. When we come
to the details, the differences are more striking. The most serious
fault in the Athenian process was its personal character as a criminal
suit, which any citizen could bring directly before the court, and the
liability of the defendant to be punished at the discretion of the court
by a fine or even by death. This of course embittered the whole
process, which tended to degenerate into a vituperative quarrel of rival
litigants. This evil was to a great extent removed after the expiration
of a year, when the process became a sober and dignified trial of
a legal question, the nominal defendant being now exposed to no
personal risk. We may fairly compare the arguments addressed to
the judges in such cases (as in that of Leptines), after making due
allowance for the composition of the court, with those addressed to
modern judges in similar cases.

7. Even in the ordinary criminal process we notice a marked
difference between the older cases of γραφὴ παρανόμων in which
Demosthenes appears as counsel for the plaintiff and the process
against Ctesiphon as it is managed by Aeschines. The speeches of
Demosthenes against Androtion (355 B.C.), Timocrates (353—352),
Aristocrates (352), like that against Leptines (355), are in great part
legal arguments of high character, showing great legal knowledge, and
delivered with dignity and authority. This is especially true of the
discussion of the Draconic law of homicide in the oration against
Aristocrates (§§ 18—94), which is our chief authority for this important
department of Attic law. But when we come from these legal arguments to the speech of Aeschines against Ctesiphon, we are struck at
once, in the greater part of it, by the almost total absence of all that
makes the γραφὴ παρανόμων worthy of its name. Aeschines devotes
less than a tenth of his speech to a strictly legal argument, that on the
responsibility of Demosthenes as a magistrate; this is the strongest
point in his argument, and he elaborates it with great skill and cogent
reasoning. He also speaks more briefly of another legal point, the
question of the place of proclamation; but this concerns a law of
which we have very little knowledge. The greater part of the speech
is taken up with a most absurd attempt to connect his general account
of the public life and the character of Demosthenes with his legal
argument. He charges the references to Demosthenes in Ctesiphon's
decree, in which he is said to seek the best interests of Athens in all

that he says and does, with violating the law *forbidding the falsification of the public records*! It is absurd to suppose that the law in question had any reference to a case like this: for this would have exposed every personal compliment in a laudatory decree to public prosecution at any one's will. It clearly related to malicious and fraudulent falsification of the public records in the Metroum by adding, erasing, or changing. And yet this is brought forward soberly and earnestly by Aeschines as a legal argument in support of his indictment. Of course Demosthenes, as the defendant's advocate, was bound to reply to the plaintiff's argument, so that we cannot fairly compare this later with his earlier treatment of the γραφὴ παρανόμων. But the case against Ctesiphon, as Aeschines presents it, is in striking contrast to the cases against Leptines, Aristocrates, and others as Demosthenes presents them.

III.

The Suit against Ctesiphon.

1. Late in the year of Chaerondas (June 337 B.C.) Demosthenes proposed and carried a measure for permanent repairs of the walls of Athens. The hasty work done under the excitement of the defeat at Chaeronea had been only temporary. A commission of ten τειχοποιοί, one to be appointed by each tribe, was now established, to hold office during the following year, that of Phrynichus, 337—336 B.C.[1] Demosthenes was chosen by his own tribe, the Pandionis, to be one of this commission. The fortifications of the Piraeus were assigned him as his special charge, and he is said to have received ten talents from the state to be used in the work, to which he added a substantial amount on his own account, usually stated as a hundred minas

---

[1] Aesch. III. 27. As Ctesiphon's bill proposed to crown Demosthenes during his year of office, and as the bill was indicted shortly after it passed the Senate, the bill and the indictment belong to the year of Phrynichus (337—336). This agrees with the statement of Aeschines (219) that he brought the indictment before Philip's death (summer of 336), and with other data. This chronology was once hopelessly confused by the date in the spurious indictment in Cor. § 54.

(1⅔ talents). He also held the important office of superintendent of the Theoric Fund, which Aeschines says at that time included "nearly the whole administration of the state[1]." It was gratitude for his great public services in these offices and for his generous gift, together with the increasing confidence in his statesmanship and patriotism, which had recently been expressed in his appointment to deliver the funeral oration on those who fell at Chaeronea, that caused his political friends to propose to crown him in the theatre at the Great Dionysia in the spring of 336, as a mark of the public approbation of his whole political life.

2. Ctesiphon accordingly proposed a bill in the Senate to crown Demosthenes with a golden crown for his services and generosity in his two offices and for his life devoted to the interests of Athens. The bill passed the Senate at once, and it would doubtless have passed the Assembly with equal alacrity if it could have been brought to a vote there. Before it could be presented to the people, Aeschines brought a γραφὴ παρανόμων against Ctesiphon, charging his bill with illegality. This made it impossible to carry the measure further until the lawsuit was settled. For reasons of which we are not informed, but in which both Aeschines and Ctesiphon as well as Demosthenes must have acquiesced, the trial was postponed more than six years, until August 330. The destruction of the Persian Empire after the battle of Arbela (Oct. 1, 331 B.C.), when Darius was a fugitive and Alexander was at the summit of his glory, probably seemed to Aeschines a good occasion to revive his suit. He must have felt that no time could be more favourable for a judgment against Demosthenes; while Demosthenes naturally felt that shrinking from the trial would imply want of confidence in the goodwill of his fellow citizens, of which he was constantly receiving most flattering tokens. For these or other reasons, this famous case came before the Heliastic court, under the presidency of the six Thesmothetae, in the late summer, probably in August, 330 B.C.[2] We do not know the number

[1] Aesch. III. 25, 26.

[2] We have several independent data which fix this time. (1) See Dion. Hal. ad Amm. I. 12 (p. 746): οὗτος (the speech on the Crown) γὰρ μόνος εἰς δικαστήριον εἰσελήλυθεν μετὰ τὸν πόλεμον (the campaign of Chaeronea), ἐπ' Ἀριστοφῶντος ἄρχοντος (330—329), ὀγδόῳ μὲν ἐνιαυτῷ μετὰ τὴν ἐν Χαιρωνείᾳ μάχην (338), ἕκτῳ δὲ μετὰ τὴν Φιλίππου τελευτὴν (336), καθ' ὃν χρόνον

of the judges. A δικαστήριον commonly consisted of 501 ; but we hear of 1001, 1501, and 2001, and in so important a case one of the larger courts was likely to be impanelled. The long-delayed trial brought to Athens great numbers of visitors from all parts of Greece, who were eager to witness this final contest between the rival orators. It can hardly be doubted that the crowd of listeners were as deeply moved by the earnest eloquence of Demosthenes as the judges, and that they would gladly have followed the court in giving him more than four-fifths of their votes.

3. The day was divided into three parts for the trial of a γραφὴ παρανόμων, an equal amount of water being poured into the clepsydra for the plaintiff and the defendant, and a third (a smaller amount), in case of the conviction of the defendant, for the assessment of the penalty (τίμησις)[1]. The largest amount of water which is mentioned is that assigned to each plea in the γραφὴ παραπρεσβείας (11 ἀμφορείς, about 100 gallons), and this is probably the maximum[2]. The speech of Demosthenes against Aeschines in this suit (XIX.) is the longest that we have. That on the Crown is shorter, but much longer than any of the others delivered in a γραφὴ παρανόμων ; and we may presume that the orator here used all of his time. Aeschines, as plaintiff, spoke first ; after his argument, the court called on Ctesiphon, as defendant, to reply. He probably repeated a short speech composed for him by Demosthenes, and then asked leave of the court to call on Demosthenes, as his advocate, to finish his defence[3]. Strictly, each

'Αλέξανδρος τὴν ἐν 'Αρβήλοις ἐνίκα μάχην. This places the date after midsummer 330 B.C. (2) The year 330—329 began June 28 (Boeckh, Mondcyclen, p. 43). The death of Darius occurred in Hecatombaeon (i.e. July) of this year: Arrian III. 22[2]. The news of this had not come to Athens before the trial, as Aeschines (132) speaks of him as a fugitive. This would not allow the trial to be later than August. (3) Again, Aeschines (254) says, ἡμερῶν μὲν ὀλίγων μέλλει τὰ Πύθια γίγνεσθαι. The Pythian games came in the third year of each Olympiad, near the end of the Delphic month Βουκάτιος, which corresponds to the second month of the Attic year (Metageitnion). This would place the trial after the middle of August.

[1] Aesch. III. 197; Harpocration under διαμεμετρημένη ἡμέρα.

[2] Id. II. 126: πρὸς ἕνδεκα γὰρ ἀμφορέας ἐν διαμεμετρημένη τῇ ἡμέρᾳ κρίνομαι.

[3] Id. III. 201: ἐπειδὰν προελθὼν ἐνταυθοῖ Κτησιφῶν διεξέλθῃ πρὸς ὑμᾶς τοῦτο δὴ τὸ συντεταγμένον αὐτῷ προοίμιον.

party to the suit was required to plead his own cause ; or, if he called
in advocates, as Aeschines summoned Eubulus, Phocion, and others
to support him in the suit for false legation, to do this at the end of an
elaborate argument of his own. But here, as Demosthenes was the
real defendant, it would have been absurd to object to his arguing
the case in full. That the procedure was unusual is shown by the
audacious attempt of Aeschines to induce the court to refuse Demosthenes a hearing[1]; and his argument shows that the court had a
legal right to refuse to hear any except the parties to the suit. But
the great audience had not come to hear Ctesiphon, and we hear of no
further attempt to interfere with the argument of Demosthenes. The
orator probably delivered his famous speech substantially in the form
in which it has come down to us.

4. When the arguments were finished, the judges voted on the
question of convicting Ctesiphon ; and the result was his triumphant
acquittal by more than four-fifths of the votes[2]. This subjected
Aeschines to the two penalties of malicious prosecution, a fine of a
thousand drachmas, and partial ἀτιμία, which deprived him of the right
to bring a similar suit hereafter[3]. This result mortified him so deeply
that he withdrew from Athens and spent the rest of his life chiefly in
Rhodes, where he is said to have been a teacher of rhetoric in his later

---

[1] Aesch. III. 202—205.

[2] Plut. Dem. 24: οὕτω λαμπρῶς ἀπέλυσαν ὥστε τὸ πέμπτον μέρος τῶν ψήφων
Αἰσχίνην μὴ μεταλαβεῖν. Cf. Dem. Cor. 82, 266.

[3] Harpocr. under ἐάν τις : ἐάν τις γραψάμενος μὴ μεταλάβῃ τὸ πέμπτον
μέρος τῶν ψήφων, ὀφλισκάνει χιλίας καὶ πρόσεστιν ἀτιμία τις. Theophrastus (in
Schol. to Dem. p. 593, 24 R.) adds to this (explaining ἀτιμία) οἷον τὸ ἐξεῖναι
μήτε γράψασθαι παρανόμων μήτε φαίνειν μήτε ἐφηγεῖσθαι. But see Andoc. I. 76,
ἑτέροις οὐκ ἦν γράψασθαι, τοῖς δὲ ἐνδεῖξαι, where γράψασθαι seems to include all
γραφαί. See also [Dem.] XXVI. 9, ὅταν τις ἐπεξιὼν μὴ μεταλάβῃ τὸ πέμπτον
μέρος τῶν ψήφων, ἐφ᾽ οἷς οἱ νόμοι κελεύουσι τὸ λοιπὸν μὴ γράφεσθαι μηδ᾽ ἀπάγειν
μηδ᾽ ἐφηγεῖσθαι. These quotations leave the precise nature of the partial ἀτιμία
somewhat uncertain. But Theophrastus seems to mean that the ἄτιμος lost
his right to bring the same form of ordinary γραφή in which he had been
defeated (of which he gives the γραφὴ παρανόμων as an example), or any one
of the special forms of γραφή (in the wider sense), like εἰσαγγελία, φάσις,
ἐφήγησις, etc. See the full enumeration of γραφαί in Pollux, 40, 41.

years[1]. After such a decisive vindication of Demosthenes, there can be no doubt that his friends renewed in the Senate the bill for crowning him, and that this was promptly passed in both Senate and Assembly in time for the orator to receive his golden crown with enthusiastic applause at the Great Dionysia of 329.

IV.

The trials of Aeschines and Philocrates for misconduct in making the Peace of 346 B.C.

1. The trial of Aeschines in 343 B.C.[2] for his conduct on the Second Embassy, which negotiated the peace with Philip in 346, and the speech of Demosthenes as his accuser, have an important bearing on the discussions of the peace in the orations of Aeschines and Demosthenes thirteen years later. The suit against Aeschines was technically called εὔθυναι, i.e. a process arising from the εὔθυναι or

[1] Plut. Dem. 24: εὐθὺς ἐκ τῆς πόλεως ᾤχετ᾽ ἀπιών, καὶ περὶ ᾽Ρόδον καὶ Ἰωνίαν σοφιστεύων κατεβίωσε. Vit. X. Orat. 840 D: ἀπάρας εἰς τὴν ᾽Ρόδον, ἐνταῦθα σχολὴν καταστησάμενος ἐδίδασκεν. While teaching at Rhodes, Aeschines is said to have read his speech against Ctesiphon to a Rhodian audience; and when all were astonished that he was defeated after so eloquent a plea, he replied, οὐκ ἂν ἐθαυμάζετε, ᾽Ρόδιοι, εἰ πρὸς ταῦτα Δημοσθένους λέγοντος ἠκούσατε. Vit. X. Orat. ibid. Other versions of the story give his answer, εἰ ἠκούσατε τοῦ θηρίου ἐκείνου, οὐκ ἂν ὑμῖν τοῦτο ἠπόρητο. See Phot. Bibl. No. 61.

[2] Dionys. ad Amm. 1. 10 (p. 737), under the archonship of Pythodotus (343—342): καὶ τὸν κατ᾽ Αἰσχίνου συνετάξατο λόγον, ὅτε τὰς εὐθύνας ἐδίδου τῆς δευτέρας πρεσβείας τῆς ἐπὶ τοὺς ὅρκους. Hypoth. 2, § 11, to Dem. XIX.: μαθόντες οἱ ᾽Αθηναῖοι τὴν τῶν Φωκέων ἀπώλειαν,...μετὰ τρία ἔτη εἰσῆλθεν ὁ Δημοσθένης κατηγορήσων Αἰσχίνου. It has often been doubted whether the case ever came to trial, chiefly because of a doubt of Plutarch (Dem. 15), ὁ δὲ κατ᾽ Αἰσχίνου τῆς παραπρεσβείας ἄδηλον εἰ λέλεκται· καίτοι φησὶν Ἰδομενεὺς παρὰ τριάκοντα μόνας τὸν Αἰσχίνην ἀποφυγεῖν. For Plutarch's objection, that neither orator mentions the trial in the speeches on the Crown, see note on Cor. 142⁶. See also note 3, p. 277.

scrutiny which Aeschines, as an officer of state, was required to pass before he could be relieved of his responsibility as an ambassador¹. Within thirty days after the return of the second embassy to Athens (13 Scirophorion, 7 July, 346), Aeschines must have presented himself for his εὔθυναι. Demosthenes and Timarchus, with perhaps others, there appeared against him with a γραφὴ παραπρεσβείας, an *indictment for misconduct on an embassy*². The presiding Logistae, who had the presidency also in this suit, would naturally have brought the case at once before a Heliastic court. But before this could be done, Aeschines challenged the right of Timarchus to appear as an accuser in the courts, on the ground that he had once led a shameless life (αἰσχρῶς βεβιωκέναι). He served upon him publicly an ἐπαγγελία δοκιμασίας, i.e. a summons to appear at a δοκιμασία ῥητόρων, an investigation of his right to appear as a ῥήτωρ³. He charged him with ἑταίρησις and also with squandering his paternal estate, both of which disqualified a man from appearing as a speaker in either the Assembly or the courts of law. This case came to trial early in 345 B.C., and Timarchus was easily convicted. Aeschines then delivered the first of his three orations. This result suspended the case against himself for a time; and by disgracefully disqualifying one of his accusers, discredited the case in the eyes of the people. It is strange that such a man as Timarchus was allowed to be associated with Demosthenes in so important a political suit, and it soon appeared that this was a most fatal mistake.

2. This mortifying rebuff put off the trial more than two years. In the meantime the friends of Demosthenes prepared the way for a renewal of his suit against Aeschines, by a state prosecution of Philocrates for treasonable conduct in negotiating the peace which bore his name. Early in 343 B.C. Hyperides brought before the Senate of Five Hundred an εἰσαγγελία against Philocrates, charging him with

¹ See Dem. XIX. 17, ἐκ τῆς πρεσβείας ταύτης, ἦσπερ εἰσὶν αἱ νῦν εὔθυναι, and 82, 133, 256.

² Hypoth. 2, § 10, to Dem. XIX.: ἐπέστη Τίμαρχος καὶ Δημοσθένης κατηγορήσοντες τούτου.

³ Aesch. I. 19, 20, 28—32: τίνας δ' οὐκ ᾤετο δεῖν λέγειν; τοὺς αἰσχρῶς βεβιωκότας· τούτους οὐκ ἐᾷ δημηγορεῖν.—δοκιμασία ῥητόρων, ἐάν τις λέγῃ ἐν τῷ δήμῳ τὸν πατέρα τύπτων ἢ τὴν μητέρα.. ἢ πεπορνευμένος ἢ ἡταιρηκώς,...ἢ τὰ πατρῷα κατεδηδοκώς. Cf. I. 154.

serving Philip for bribes to the detriment of Athens. The Senate accepted the εἰσαγγελία, thus making the suit a public one[1]. It went for trial to a Heliastic court, and the state appointed advocates, among them Demosthenes, to assist Hyperides in managing the case. In his indictment (called εἰσαγγελία) Hyperides quoted verbatim five or six decrees of Philocrates in support of his charge[2]. There was no lack of decisive evidence. Philocrates had made an open show of his newly acquired wealth after the peace, by building houses, selling wheat, transporting timber, changing foreign gold openly at the bankers' counters in Athens; and (according to Demosthenes) he had even confessed that he received money from Philip[3]. He gave up his defence, and left the court and Athens before the judgment was declared; and in his absence he was condemned to death, the penalty which Hyperides proposed in his εἰσαγγελία. He passed the rest of his life in exile[4]. This result shows how public opinion about the peace had changed in three years, so that Philocrates, whose word was law when the peace was made, was now left to his fate, friendless and helpless. No man of influence, like Eubulus, attempted to save him; and we hear of no anxiety lest his condemnation should cause enmity with Philip. Demosthenes, as prosecuting attorney for the state, complained that Philocrates alone was selected for prosecution while others equally guilty were left untouched[5].

[1] See note on Cor. § 250². The state process called εἰσαγγελία was provided for the special trial of (1) those charged with conspiracy against the democracy of Athens, (2) those charged with betraying towns or military or naval forces to public enemies, or with holding treasonable communication with these, (3) orators (ῥήτορας) charged with being bribed by public enemies to give evil advice to the people. See Hyper. Eux. §§ 7, 8. It will be seen that εἰσαγγελία, so far from being applicable chiefly (or only) to crimes which were not provided for in the laws (as was once believed), is definitely restricted to certain high offences, all of which, moreover, might be dealt with by other processes, as is seen in the different treatment of the similar cases of Philocrates and Aeschines.

[2] Hyper. Eux. §§ 29, 30.

[3] Dem. XIX. 114: εἰ μὴ μόνον ὡμολόγει παρ' ὑμῖν ἐν τῷ δήμῳ πολλάκις, ἀλλὰ καὶ ἐδείκνυεν ὑμῖν, πυροπωλῶν, οἰκοδομῶν,...ξυληγῶν, τὸ χρυσίον καταλλαττόμενος φανερῶς ἐπὶ ταῖς τραπέζαις. Gold coins in Athens were generally foreign.

[4] Aesch. II. 6, III. 79, 81; Dinarch. I. 28. [5] Dem. XIX. 116—118.

3. This triumphant success inspired Demosthenes with new hopes for his own suit against Aeschines. This came to trial after midsummer in 343 B.C. when Demosthenes and Aeschines delivered their speeches περὶ τῆς παραπρεσβείας. The court probably consisted of 1501 judges ; and the Logistae presided, as the case still belonged to the εὔθυναι of the second embassy, for which Aeschines was still ὑπεύθυνος. Demosthenes brings his accusation under five heads, covering the five points on which an ambassador should be called to account at his εὔθυναι. These are (1) ὧν ἀπήγγειλε, (2) ὧν ἔπεισε, (3) ὧν προσετάξετε αὐτῷ, (4) τῶν χρόνων, (5) εἰ ἀδωροδοκήτως ἢ μή (or τοῦ προῖκα ἢ μή). In his elaborate argument he strives to prove that Aeschines (1) made a false report, (2) advocated pernicious measures on the ground of his report, (3) disobeyed his instructions, (4) wasted his time, (5) acted corruptly, being bribed by Philip[1]. The argument on these five heads occupies §§ 17—178, the remainder of the oration being chiefly given to general arguments tending to show the corruption of Aeschines and his collusion with Philip[2].

4. The reply of Aeschines, though eloquent and effective in certain passages, is weak and trifling as an answer to the powerful argument of Demosthenes. Though he denies some special statements, perhaps successfully, he says nothing which breaks the force of the main argument against himself. In cases in which we have other evidence, we sometimes find his most solemn assertions false or misleading[3]. He answers the grave charge of falsely reporting Philip's intentions by saying that he "only made a report and promised nothing[4]." He replies to the charge of joining Philip in the paeans and other rejoicings over the destruction of the Phocians by saying that, though he was present, he was only one of two hundred, and that Demosthenes (who was not present) has no evidence whether he sang with the chorus or not[5]!

---

[1] Dem. XIX. 4—8, 177—179.

[2] See, for example, the argument in 106—110.

[3] See Hist. § 28.

[4] Aesch. II. 119. The best that Aeschines could say on this subject thirteen years later is seen in III. 79—83.

[5] II. 162, 163: e.g. καὶ τῷ γε δῆλος ἦν, εἰ μή γε ὥσπερ ἐν τοῖς χοροῖς προῇδον ;

5. He brought before the court his aged father, his two little children, and his two brothers, to excite pity[1] ; and he finally called on Eubulus, Phocion, and other influential men to come forward as his supporters[2]. Eubulus addressed the court in his behalf, and probably urged prudential reasons for acquitting Aeschines. It might easily be thought by cautious men that the recent sacrifice of Philocrates was as much as it was safe to demand under the circumstances ; and this, added to the influence of men like Eubulus and Phocion, probably saved Aeschines from conviction. We are told merely that he was acquitted by only thirty votes[3] ; and this was no triumph—indeed, no justification—for a man in his position.

V.

The Constitution of the Amphictyonic Council.

1. Aeschines (II. 116) gives eleven of the twelve tribes which formed the Amphictyonic Council, as follows : Thessalians, Boeotians ("not merely Thebans"), Dorians, Ionians, Perrhaebians, Magnesians, Locrians, Oetaeans, Phthiotians (i.e. the Achaeans of Phthiotis), Malians, Phocians. He professes to give twelve names, and it is generally assumed that the Dolopians are accidentally omitted. An important inscription recently discovered at Delphi seems to me to show clearly that the Delphians are the omitted people. Bourguet, in the Bulletin de Correspondance Hellénique, 1896, p. 241, gives from this inscription a list of the Council at the time of Alexander. This has the Thessalians, "King Alexander," Delphians, Dorians, Ionians, Perrhaebians (with Dolopians), Boeotians, Locrians, Achaeans (i.e. of Phthiotis), Magnesians, Aenianians, and Malians, each with two delegates. King Alexander now holds the two Phocian votes; the Aenianians represent the Oetaeans, of whom they were an important tribe ; the Dolopians are included with the Perrhaebians ; and the Delphians, who are constantly mentioned in the Delphic

---

[1] Aesch. II. 179, 180.   [2] Ibid. 184.

[3] Vit. x. Orat. 840 c : ἐφ' ᾗ (πρεσβείᾳ) κατηγορηθεὶς ὑπὸ Δημοσθένους,... συνειπόντος αὐτῷ Εὐβούλου,...τριάκοντα ψήφοις ἀπέφυγεν.

inscriptions relating to the Council, are added. If we add the Delphians to the list of Aeschines, the two lists substantially agree.

2. Each of the twelve tribes had two votes in the Council, given by delegates called ἱερομνήμονες, two of whom were sent by each Amphictyonic tribe. But the Dorians, Ionians, and Locrians were geographically divided, so that each of two divisions had a single Hieromnemon with a single vote. Thus the two Dorian votes might be divided between the Spartans (with other Dorians of Peloponnesus) and the ancient Dorian Tetrapolis, near Parnassus ; the Ionian votes between the Athenians and the other Ionians (in Euboea and Asia Minor) ; the Locrian votes between the Eastern and Western Locrians. Aeschines explains that each tribe had the same representation with two equal votes. The Hieromnemon of Athens was chosen each year by lot : see Arist. Nub. 623, λαχὼν Ὑπέρβολος τῆτες ἱερομνημονεῖν.

3. Besides the twenty-four Hieromnemons, certain towns sent another class of delegates, called πυλάγοροι, who appear to have had the right to speak, but not to vote, in certain meetings of the Council. They represented the towns which sent them, not the tribe as a whole. Athens sent three, chosen by the people apparently for each Amphictyonic meeting. The meeting at which Aeschines made his inflammatory harangue, which stirred up the Amphissian War, appears to have been one of the ἱερομνήμονες exclusively, which Aeschines, as a πυλάγορος, attended by special invitation of the Hieromnemon and only as his representative, but with all his rights. See Hist. § 59.

VI.

The Hero Physician and the Hero Καλαμίτης.

1. In Demosthenes XIX. 249 the father of Aeschines is said to have kept a school near the shrine of the Hero Physician (πρὸς τῷ τοῦ Ἥρω τοῦ ἰατροῦ) ; and in Cor. 129 his mother is said to have lived a shameful life near the shrine of the Hero Καλαμίτης (πρὸς τῷ Καλαμίτῃ ἥρωι), while his father is said to have been the slave of a schoolmaster near the Theseum (πρὸς τῷ Θησείῳ διδάσκοντι γράμματα). Many scholars identify the two heroes, though on slight evidence. If the Hero

Physician was called Καλαμίτης, this name might mean *bowman* (or *arrow-man*) from κάλαμος, in the sense of *arrow*, like ὁπλίτης from ὅπλον.

2. Reiske recognized in the Hero Physician the Scythian Toxaris, of whom Lucian gives a pleasant account in his Σκύθης ἢ Πρόξενος. Toxaris, according to Lucian, came to Athens in the time of Solon, by whom he was kindly received. He was a physician and a man of general cultivation, though not of high rank at home. When his countryman, Anacharsis, came to Athens, he was recognized and welcomed by Toxaris, who introduced him to Solon. Toxaris died and was buried in Athens. When the plague was raging in the Peloponnesian War, the wife of an Areopagite reported that Toxaris came forth from his tomb and told her that the plague would cease if the narrow streets of the city were freely sprinkled with wine. This was done, and the plague disappeared. The tomb was examined, and the remains of Toxaris were found within, which were identified by a mutilated inscription, and also by the figure of a Scythian sculptured on the gravestone, having in his left hand a strung bow and in his right what *appeared to be a book* (βιβλίον, ὡς ἐδόκει). Lucian says that more than half of the figure was to be seen in his time, with the bow and the book entire. The upper part of the stone with the face was gone. The monument, he says, was not far from the gate Dipylum, on the left of the road leading to the Academy: the stone was lying flat on the ground. On account of his wonderful skill in stopping the horrors of the plague, Toxaris was made a hero and worshipped as the "Hero Physician." He had a shrine within the city walls ; and his tomb was always decked with wreaths, and miraculous cures were wrought there.

3. It happens that in the excavations outside the Dipylum gate at Athens a figure was found (now in the Museum at Athens) which in many respects agrees wonderfully with Lucian's description. It represents a headless crouching Scythian, in his native dress, who had once held a bow in his left hand (the opening through which the bow passed still remains); while under the left arm and held by the right hand is what, when viewed in front, appears to be a writing tablet but from the side is seen to be a pointed quiver. The chief point in which this figure fails to agree with Lucian's description is that Lucian calls the monument a στήλη, while this is a statue. This

might be explained by the figure lying flat on the ground, as Lucian describes it ; and it must have been flat on its back, or the pointed quiver could never have been mistaken for a book. If it was so covered by earth that only the front and the two hands, with the bow and the apparent book, were visible, it would have been a natural mistake to call it a στήλη. Indeed, any further exposure of the figure would at once have made the quiver visible. I therefore think there is sufficient evidence to identify this figure with the one seen by Lucian or his informant. See note on Cor. § 129[6].

Figure of Scythian Bowman.

VII.

The Manuscripts of the Oration on the Crown.

1. The chief of all the MSS. of Demosthenes, the basis of the present text, is Σ or S, of the tenth century, written on parchment, no. 2934 of the Greek MSS. of the National Library of Paris. On its last leaf is written, in a hand of a later period, Βιβλίον μονῆς τῶν Σωσάνδρων, showing that it once belonged to a society of monks named after Sosander, who is not otherwise known. The manuscript first appears in Europe in the possession of Janos Lascaris, a learned Greek, who left Constantinople after the Turkish capture and was in high favour with Lorenzo de' Medici at Florence. Lascaris was twice sent by Lorenzo to Greece and the neighbouring lands in search of manuscripts for the Medicean library. How rich a store he brought back to Florence may be seen from the curious manuscript now in the Vatican library, which was published by K. K. Müller in the Centralblatt für Bibliothekswesen for 1884. This contains a wonderful list of 300 or 400 books which were "bought" for Lorenzo by Lascaris, and also a πίναξ τῶν βιβλίων τοῦ Λασκάρεως, ἅπερ ἔχει παρ' ἑαυτοῦ. Among the latter we find Δημοσθένης, περγαμηνόν. The same volume probably appears in a list of the books of Lascaris made after his death at Rome in 1535. Here we find Δημοσθένης, παλαιός, no. 34 (corrected to 35). In the catalogue of the books of Cardinal Ridolfi, who is said to have acquired the books of Lascaris after his death, we find "35. Δημοσθένους λόγοι ξβ'," evidently the same book.

Ridolfi's manuscripts after his death came into the possession of Queen Catherine de' Medici. The title "Demosthenis Orationes" appears in a catalogue of the Queen's library, in the inventory of her goods after her death in 1589, and again in 1597 in the list of her books which had passed into the Royal library. The Codex Σ still has a splendid binding of red leather, bearing the united arms of France and Navarre and monograms of Henry IV., with the date 1602. From this time it appears in the various catalogues of the Royal library, until it was entered in the catalogue of 1740 with its present number 2934. We are therefore safe in assuming that Σ is one of the manuscripts which Lascaris, as the envoy of the Medici, brought to Florence from Greek lands at about the time of Lorenzo's death in 1492 ; and it may have come from Mount Athos, as Dindorf asserted.

The manuscript is written with great care, in large square upright minuscules, which mark the transition from the uncial to the cursive text. It is unquestionably by far the best manuscript of Demosthenes, and with its recently discovered companion L it forms a distinct class, which preserves a purer and older text than any others. The passages are few in which Σ and L¹ are not decisive against all other MSS.

The photographic facsimile of Σ has brought this precious document within the reach of scholars in all parts of the world. This, with the reproductions of the Medicean Aeschylus, the Laurentian Sophocles, and the Bodleian Plato, is a special boon to American scholars.

2. L (Vömel's Laur. S), the new companion of Σ, is in the Laurentian Library at Florence (LVI. 9, no. 136). It is written by various hands. It contains orations VI., VII., VIII., IX., X., XI., XXII., XXIV., all written in the 13th century (with some parts of IX. and X. wanting), followed by XX., XVIII., XIX., in another hand of the same century, and further by XXIII in another of the same age, and by XII. in a later hand. Orations I, II., and III., and the missing parts of IX. and X., are added by a much later hand. The older parts, as originally written (L¹), generally have the same purer form of the text which is in Σ ; but, though the two MSS. have a common archetype, L was not copied from Σ or descended from it. The second hand of L (L²) generally agrees with the class represented by F and B. One interesting bond of union between the first hands of Σ and L is that both omit the same disputed passages in the Third Philippic.

3. A 1, Augustanus primus, formerly at Augsburg (whence its name), now no. 485 in the Royal Library at Munich, on parchment, of the 11th century, is generally reckoned as next in rank to Σ and L¹. It is the chief basis of the text current before Bekker's study of Σ, the text as established by Reiske. It represents a text far below that of Σ and L in purity, and much corrected by grammarians.

4. A 2, Augustanus secundus, formerly at Augsburg, now in the Munich Library, is a paper manuscript of the 15th century. It has little distinctive character of its own.

5. F (or M) and Φ (or Q) of the 11th century, in St Mark's library in Venice, and B (or Bav.), Bavaricus, in Munich, of the 13th century,

represent the Vulgate text emended by the help of MSS. of the better class. B closely follows F, and is either copied from it or of a common origin with it.

Other MSS. are now of less account, since the supremacy of Σ has been established[1].

[1] A more detailed account of the important MSS. containing the Oration on the Crown will be found in the larger edition.

GREEK INDEX.

The references are made to pages, and relate especially to the notes.

ENGLISH INDEX.

The references are made to pages.